SCOTLAND *the* BEST!
THE ONE TRUE GUIDE

Peter Irvine

with additional research and words by
Keith Davidson (Edinburgh section)
Graeme Kelling (Glasgow section)
and **Emma Protopapadakis**

HarperCollins*Publishers*

To everyone who wrote, and everyone along the way.

Thanks. And Georgia.

Copyright © Peter Irvine, 1993, 1994, 1996, 1997
The moral right of the author has been asserted

First published in Great Britain in 1993 by
Mainstream Publishing Company (Edinburgh) Ltd

This edition published in 1997 by HarperCollins*Publishers*
PO Box, Glasgow G4 0NB

Hardback Edition 0 00 472150-0
Paperback Edition 0 00 472151-9

A catalogue record for this book is available from the British Library

Typeset in Garamond and Gill Sans
Printed and bound in Great Britain by the Bath Press

CONTENTS

A DECLARATION OF FALLIBILITY

This guide is 'true', but it may not always be absolutely accurate. Since this may seem like a contradiction in terms, I should explain. *Scotland the Best!*, is a handbook of information about all the 'best' places in Scotland. 'Best' you will understand is a subjective term; it means 'best' according to what I think. Needless to say there seem to be a lot of readers who agree with my judgement and even if you don't you may see that I and my associates have gone to some efforts to reach our assertions. It's intended to be obvious that I am conveying opinions and impressions. They're true because the motives are true; we believe in what we are saying. We take no bribes and and have no vested interest in any of the places recommended, other than that we do talk things up and shamelessly proclaim the places we like or admire.

Along with observations every 'item' conveys factual information; I hope it's plain where the facts end and the opinions begin. In guide books this is not always the case. However it's with 'the facts' that inconsistencies may appear. We try to give accurate and clear directions explaining how to find a place and basic details that might be useful. This information is gleaned from a variety of sources and may be supplied by the establishment concerned. We do try to verify everything usually by visiting, but the process of acquiring and transcribing information is tricky when there's so much of it. Things change and because nowhere we mention has solicited their inclusion (or if they have, it has made little difference), nor been invited to check what we say . . . well mistakes can be made. With this density of information it's impossible to run it past proprietors, and they might not like what we say because it's our opinion, not theirs. So I'm sorry if we get a number wrong. We hope there aren't any mistakes, but we may not find out until you let us know. Please do so we can fix it.

This admission is therefore made in advance. I hope you haven't gone up the glen with no cash to find that after all they don't accept credit cards, or arrive at the golf club to find that you've booked into a sauna parlour. My cringing excuse is that we are merely human. This guide is made by fallible humans like me for fallible humans, of which I hope you are one. However, be clear of one thing, this book is about searching for something better, it is actually about striving for perfection.

INTRODUCTION

Another edition, a new publisher. Even in old Scotland it feels like a new world. Welcome then to the best of it. To old readers who know how this guide is differs from others and new ones who hopefully will find that there's a lot to discover. Since the last book, which was compiled in 1995, there have been huge changes: a new government with the old Tories virtually expelled from Scotland, a booming economy with (currently) a strong pound and a new millennium fast approaching. Thankfully some things don't change and while every place in this book has been checked and probably visited again, some of the 'items' remain the same. If a description still holds good and the factual details are still correct, I haven't changed it. Prehistoric ruins and walks along the cliff tops aren't much affected by the times.

Scotland the Best! is now in its fourth edition. I know many people have followed it from the beginning. I'm deeply chuffed and touched by the letters and feedback I get, all of which help to make the book better and more complete. Readers seem to agree with me that some places are better than others and deserve recognition. While most of us are aware of environmental sensitivities, it's good to share a good place with others even if it means as I find, that you can't get a hotel room or a table at a restaurant as easily once you've given it the big plug. Since this is an inside track guide, it depends on news from the track itself, so please keep on writing. See details of our bribery scheme on p.12.

A note for new readers: this guide book is not like others. It is highly selective and nobody pays to be included. And it covers everything from where to eat to where to swim in the river. Basically it lists all the most recommendable aspects of Scotland across the spectrum from the very expensive to the outdoors and the free. Every item listed has been selected simply because it is better than the ordinary. Whether indoors or out, it has an atmosphere, a sense of history, individuality, class. If it's a business, the owners or management have an attitude to quality which sets it apart and deserves your attention.

All descriptions are avowedly subjective, complete with prejudice and personal observation. I and my small team admit to our preferences but we maintain that everywhere mentioned is superlative in some way and worth going to (assuming it's your sort of thing). This is not a 'list all options' kind of guide, and there *are* omissions; the obvious has not been omitted, only the mediocre.

For the first time I've been assisted by three researchers. I do have another life and it's just physically impossible to get round the whole of Scotland in one summer and keep down a real job. Emma and Keith and Graeme (picked from a huge number of applicants) have delivered the goods (meticulously separated from the bads). In case anyone should imagine that the task of visiting all the likely places in a town or area from museums to nightclubs, is a dream job ask any of them how they found it. Exhaustion and overload, frustration and confusion were symptoms oft cited. Four restaurants in a day, ten pubs and a hundred places between cannot be deeply enjoyed. Nevertheless they were a huge help. We nearly always agreed because in selecting the best from the rest, comprehensive criteria are employed for each category; factors like attitude and service, ambience and comfort, accessibility and (for walks or climbs) reward for effort. Many other people are also consulted – experts, connoisseurs, the locals.

All the places that anyone suggests are visited, and everywhere listed, including all the new entries, has been at least sampled; tried out not by a team of inspectors or evaluated using a rigid template of standards, but experienced in a personal way, one which tolerates error and idiosyncrasy, the odd bad night. The final selection has been made by me, a committee of one. This is a one lens perspective. Funny that so many of you seem to see it the same way. However your disagreements are welcome too (p.12 again). I hope you do find much in this book to agree with. Primarily it's supposed to be useful. It's written from a consumer's point of view. I don't pretend to be a golfer or a parent for example, but I try to imagine myself as one for those pages.

Increasingly Scotland has to compete in the worldwide destination marketplace. I happen to think that we will hold our own: the Scots always have, and I hope this book shows the incredible range of what we can offer. Scotland is not a holiday fantasy land, it's real. I reckon the Scots generally have the world's best bullshit detectors. If they use and like this book, I know it's ok.

A GUIDE TO THE OTHER GUIDES

I've got to have a go at the other 'guides'. When you schlepp up and down the land like I do, you see so many: in hotel rooms, in visitor information centres, in use. Sometimes I want to stop people and say 'dump that, don't believe it, it's not a guide, it's a business scheme'.

But, I don't say anything , I button the lip. If people are daft enough to think that a Les Routiers decal is an indicator of quality, well let them eat cake . . . But here at the front of my guide, where nobody pays to be included and I try damned hard to find excellence and be fair about the rest (probably visiting more hotels and restaurants in Scotland than any other single person or 'inspector'), I think I've earned the right to make a point. I'm personally concerned about the places I recommend, certainly enough to defend my choices without vested interest. I probably feel the same about my book as they feel about their restaurant.

I'm not saying they don't have to use many means to get noticed, but if you have read this far you're probably one of those folk who like clear indicators of contents and intents. Some 'promotional' guides can be spotted easily, made by marketing people with ad space to sell, who've not the faintest interest in what a place is like. Some are harder to spot.

The Taste of Scotland Guide is a good example, though I'd say right off that I support it's aims. In Scotland it's ubiquitous and it conveys the impression that it's discriminating, offering an official seal of approval. Well, up to a point. It's easy to use and they do include most of Scotland's best restaurants, while excluding others. They also actively encourage good practice and 'reward' excellence. But it's hard to tell e.g. in a particular town whether one place is merely ok and the other excellent. Every entry is written at the same pitch; restaurants can check their entry or even write their own. Fair enough they've paid to be there. But despite their best efforts the loyalty of TOS must be for 'them' and not for us; some of its loftier members will always feel uncomfortable in the wider grouping necessary to make it stack up. Like Tourist Board publications it can only include information from, and on behalf of, 'members'.

But Taste of Scotland is more reliable than most. Even the big time schemes where members pay big time fees to go in a heavy catalogue like *Ashley Courtney and Johansens*, can let you down (big time). And brand leaders like Egon Ronay and the *Rough Guide* are in my experience, often way off the mark. I gripe, because I do believe in guides - but like everything else, some are better than others. When I go to a new country I want one that plugs me in (immediately). Here's the ones that I think are among . . . the best (all used by *STB!*).

Big time : *Relais & Chateau*, It's a consortium of hotels, but you've got to be very good to get in. In Scotland there are only a handful of members.

News from elsewhere: *Frommers*. An American thing with not many (hotel/restaurant) choices in any given place, but they are meticulous and look after their own i.e. you the user. Nobody pays. There is one for Scotland.

The *Charming Hotels* series (for Europe) is a reliable source of exactly that - charming hotels. Try any one of them and you get the picture. I don't know how updated they are, but these guides are invariably reliable on ambience. Nobody pays. There isn't one for the UK yet.

Food: the *AA Guide*. Increasingly good and with serious 'inspections'. If a restaurant has been awarded 3 'rossettes', they're rarely wrong, 2 can be flakier, 1 is about 50% reliable. Sounds arrogant I know to be so assertive, but unlike most of their inspectors I eat in a lot of 1s and zeros. Nobody pays.

General guide: well you still can't beat *Michelin*. It's dry as old rubber tyres, but factually it's sound (probably sounder than *Scotland the Best!*, but then I'm a human program not a computer program). Its awards for food are still the most sought after. Nobody pays.

Having said all that, you're all right anyway, you've got this one. This guide also does fish 'n' chips. We do whisky, we do walks , we do . . . now read on.

HOW TO USE THIS BOOK

There are three ways to find things in this book:

1. There's an index at the back. Towns are in bold type and may have a number of entries. A number in bold type means there is a whole page or section devoted to the town (the numbers listed are page numbers).

2. The book can be used by category, e.g. you can look up the best restaurants in the Borders or the best scenic routes in the whole of Scotland. Each entry has an item number in the outside margin. These are in numerical order and allow easy cross-referencing.

3. You can start with the maps and see how individual items are located, how they are grouped together and how much there is that's worth seeing or doing in any particular area. Then just look up the item numbers. If you are travelling round Scotland I would urge you to use the maps and this method of finding the best of what an area or town has to offer.

The maps correspond to the recognisable regions of Scotland. There's also an overall map to show how the regions fit together. The list of maps is on p.281 and the map section is at the back of the book.

All items have a code which gives (1) the specific item number; (2) the map on which it can be found; and (3) the co-ordinate. For space reasons, items in Glasgow and Edinburgh are not marked on Maps A and B, although they do have co-ordinates in the margin to give you a rough idea of the location. City maps are readily available from any tourist office or newsagent.

THE CELTIC CROSSES

Although everything listed in the book is notable and remarkable in some way, there are places that are outstanding even in this superlative company. Instead of marking them with a rosette or a star, they have been 'awarded' a Celtic cross symbol, the traditional Scottish version of the cross.

☩　　Amongst the very best in Scotland

☩ ☩　　Amongst the best (of its type) in the UK

☩ ☩ ☩　　Amongst the best (of its type) in the world, or simply unique

Listings generally are not in an order of merit although if there is one outstanding item it will always be at the top of the page and this obviously includes anything which has been given a cross.

Hotels and restaurants are also grouped according to price and this is why a cross-marked place may appear further down the page (crosses also indicate exceptional value for money).

A NOTE ON CATEGORIES

Edinburgh and Glasgow, the destinations of most visitors and the nearest cities to more than half of the population, are covered in the substantial Sections 1 and 2. Both have been extended from the last edition mainly to cover the proliferation and diversification of restaurants. You will probably need a city map to get around, although Maps A and B should give you the rough layout.

For the purposes of maps, and particularly in Section 3 (Regional Hotels and Restaurants), I have used a combination of the subdivision of Scotland based on the current standard political regions along with the historical ones, e.g. Argyll, Clyde Valley. From Sections 4 to 11, categories are based on activities, interests and geography and refer to the whole of Scotland. Section 12 covers the islands, with a page-by-page guide to the larger ones.

Section 13 is intended to give a comprehensive and concise guide to the best of the major Scottish towns in each area. Some of the recommended hotels and restaurants will be amongst the best in the region and will have been referred to in Section 3, or even amongst the best in Scotland and referred to in Sections 4 to 12, but otherwise they have been selected because they are the best there is in the town or the immediate area.

There are some categories like Bed and Breakfasts, Fishing Beats, Antique Shops that haven't been included because they are impracticable to assess (there are too many of them, they are too small, or they change hands too often). Fishing places would be spoiled if too many people knew about them, and for similar reasons I've declined to draw attention to (for example) Places to see Birds of Prey. In this edition there are several new categories that might be useful like diving sites and annual events.

If there are other categories that you would like to see in future editions, please let us know (*see p. 12*).

The codes

1.   The Item Code

At the outside margin of every item is a code which will enable you to find it on a map. Thus **917** should be read as follows: MAP 2 *B3*. **917** is the item number, listed in simple consecutive order; MAP 2 refers to the Highlands – the map section is at the back of the book; *B2* is the map co-ordinate, to help pinpoint the item's location on the map grid. A co-ordinate such as *xC1* indicates that the item can be reached by leaving the map at grid reference *C1*.

2.   The Hotel Code

Below each hotel recommended is a band of codes as follows:

20RMS   JAN-DEC   T/T   PETS   CC   KIDS   TOS   LOTS

20RMS means the hotel has 20 bedrooms in total. No differentiation is made as to the type of room. Most hotels will offer twin rooms as singles or put extra beds in doubles if required. This code merely gives an impression of size.

JAN-DEC means the hotel is open all year round. APR-OCT means approximately from the beginning of April to the end of October.

T/T refers to the facilities: T/ means there are direct-dial phones in the bedrooms while /T means there are TVs in the bedrooms.

PETS means the hotel accepts dogs and other pets, probably under certain conditions (e.g. pets should be kept in the bedroom). It's usually best to check first.

XPETS indicates that the hotel does not generally accept pets.

CC means the hotel accepts major credit cards (e.g. Access and Visa).

XCC means the hotel does not accept credit cards.

KIDS indicates children are welcome and special provisions/rates may be available.

XKIDS does not necessarily mean that children are not able to accompany their parents, only that special provisions/rates are not usually made. Check by phone.

TOS means the hotel is part of the Taste of Scotland scheme and has been selected for having a menu which features imaginative cooking using Scottish ingredients. The Taste of Scotland produces an annual guide of members.

LOTS Rooms which cost more than £60 per night per person. The theory is that if you can afford over £120 a room, it doesn't matter too much if it's £125 or £150. Other price bands are:

EXP Expensive: £50-60 per person.

MED.EX Medium (expensive): £38-50.

MED.INX Medium (inexpensive): £28-38.

INX Inexpensive: £20-28.

CHP Cheap: less than £20.

Rates are per person per night. They are worked out by halving the published average rate for a twin room in high season and should be used only to give an impression of cost. They are based on 1995 prices. Add between £2 to £5 per year, though the band should stay the same unless the hotel undergoes improvements.

3.   The Restaurant Code

Found at the bottom right of all restaurant entries. It refers to the price of an average dinner per person with a starter, a main course and dessert. It doesn't include wine, coffee or extras.

EXP Expensive: more than £30

MED Medium: £20-30.

INX Inexpensive: £12-20.

CHP Cheap: under £12.

These are based on 1997 rates. With inflation, the relative price bands should stay about the same. Where a hotel is notable also for its restaurant, there is a restaurant line below the hotel entry and a separate code in the corner.

4.   The Walk Code

A great number of walks are described in the book, especially in section 8.

2-10km   CIRC   BIKE   1-A-1

2-10km means the walk(s) described may vary in length from 2km to 10km.

CIRC means the walk can be circular, while xCIRC shows the walk is not circular and you must return more or less the way you came.

BIKE indicates the walk has a path which is suitable for ordinary bikes.
xBIKE means the walk is not suitable for, or does not permit, cycling.
mtBIKE means the track is suitable for mountain or all-terrain bikes.

The 1-A-1 Code

First number (1, 2 or 3) indicates how easy the walk is.
1 the walk is easy.
2 medium difficulty, e.g. standard hillwalking, not dangerous nor requiring special knowledge or equipment.
3 difficult: care and preparation and a map are needed.

The letters (A, B or C) indicate how easy it is to find the path.
a the route is easy to find. The way is either marked or otherwise obvious.
b the route is not very obvious, but you'll get there.
c you will need a map and preparation or a guide.

The last number (1, 2 or 3) indicates what to wear on your feet.
1 ordinary outdoor shoes, including trainers, are probably okay unless the ground is very wet.
2 you will need walking boots.
3 you will need serious walking or hiking boots.

Apart from designated walks, the 1-A-1 code is employed wherever there is more than a short stroll required to get to somewhere, e.g. a waterfall or a monument. Found at bottom-right corner of item.

LIST OF ABBREVIATIONS

As well as codes and because of obvious space limitations, a personal shorthand and ad hoc abbreviation system has had to be created. I'm the first to admit some may be annoying, especially 'restau' for restaurant, but it's a long word and it comes up often. The others which are used are . . .

Aber	Aberdeen	accom	accomodation
admn	admission	adj	adjacent
app	approach	approx	approximately
atmos	atmosphere	av	average
AYR	all year round	bedrms	bedrooms
betw	between	br	bridge
BYOB	bring your own bottle	cl	closes/closed
		dining-rm	dining room
E	east	Edin	Edinburgh
esp	especially	excl	excluding
exhib(s)	exhibition(s)	exp	expensive
facs	facilities	ft	fort
Glas	Glasgow	gr	great
grd(s)	garden(s)	HS	Historic Scotland
hr(s)	hour(s)	incl	including
inexp	inexpensive	info	information
j/tie	jacket and tie	jnct	junction
L	loch	LO	last orders
min(s)	minute(s)	mt(s)	mountain(s)
N	north	NTS	National Trust Scotland
no smk	no smoking		
nr	near	o/look	overlook(s)/ing
opp	opposite	o/side	outside
pl	place	poss	possible
pt	point/port	R	river
r/bout	roundabout	rd	road
refurb	refurbished/ment	restau	restaurant
rm(s)	room(s)	RSPB	Royal Society for the Protection of Birds
rt	right		
S	south	sq	square
stn	station	st	street
TO	tourist office	SYHA	Scottish Youth Hostels Association
t/off	turn off		
tratt	trattoria	trad	traditional
v	very	univ	university
vegn	vegetarian	vac	vacation
w/end(s)	weekend(s)	W	west
		yr(s)	years

YOUR HELP NEEDED
(AND WIN GOOD WHISKY!)

Scotland the Best! wouldn't be the best if I didn't receive feedback and helpful suggestions from so many people. It really has become an interactive book because so many of you seem to know what sort of places are likely to fit. With each new edition I believe I get closer to the definitive best guide including everywhere in Scotland that's any good. It bothers me if I miss something - a new restaurant might be forgiveable, but there may be an established one that I've omitted from this edition. There are pubs for example that have been doing great food for years and as each edition passes I get closer to knowing all of them. This completeness is because people write to tell me. And I hope very much that they will continue to do so. *Scotland the Best!* is supposed to follow the inside track to Scotland and you who live here, or are experiencing it as a visitor, are on it. Send me the word!

Write and let me know whether you have found the information helpful and accurate and whether you agree or disagree with my selections. Have places lived up to your expectations and, in particular, are there any superlative places that ought to have been mentioned? Even if it's your own place and you think it deserves wider attention, let me know. Everywhere you recommend will be checked out for the next edition 1999/2000. Please send your comments or suggestions to:

Peter Irvine/*Scotland the Best!*, General Reference Department, HarperCollins*Publishers*, PO Box, Glasgow G4 0NB.

For sharing this information, HarperCollins will be happy to share out some good whisky and cheese. A bottle of malt (any from the list of my suggestions on p.152) together with a drum of Tobermory cheddar will be presented at the launch of the next edition, to the best three suggestions received by 30 September 1999. Recommendations can be for any category or for any number of categories, and anywhere that you recommend will be included next time, if it checks out. Please give reasons for your recommendation and specific directions if it is difficult to find.

You can also contact me on the Internet through the *Scotland the Best!* web site which is sponsored by Famous Grouse (they've got prizes too). The address is www.famousgrouse.com.

SECTION 1

Edinburgh

The telephone code for Edinburgh is 0131
Refer to MAP A, unless otherwise stated

THE BEST HOTELS

1
D2
✚ ✚ **THE BALMORAL:** 556 2414. Princes St at E end above Waverley Stn. Capital landmark with its clock always 2mins fast (except at Hogmanay) so you don't miss your train. The old pile changed hands again in spring 1997 and Sir Rocco Forte brought in the new broom esp in the restau dept. Expensive for a mere tourist but if you can't afford to stay there's always afternoon tea in the Palm Court. Few hotels anywhere are so much in the heart of things. Good business centre, fine sports facs; luxurious and distinctive rms with some ethereal views of the city. Main restau, The Grill (56/BEST RESTAUS) and new brasserie, Hadrians both excellent.

189RMS JAN-DEC T/T PETS CC KIDS LOTS

2
C3
✚ ✚ **THE CALEDONIAN:** 459 9988. Princes St, W End. Edin institution – former stn hotel built in 1903. Owners have spent £8 million recently upgrading it from merely grand to Grand and Businesslike. Brand-new sports club opened in late summer 1997 (open to public), endearing lack of uniformity about the rms, executive rms on fifth floor have gr views as well as facs. Capital kind of place in every respect. Main restau, The Pompadour (57/BEST RESTAUS), is an experience.

246RMS JAN-DEC T/T XPETS CC KIDS TOS LOTS

3
xE4
✚ ✚ **PRESTONFIELD HOUSE:** 668 3346. Off Priestfield Rd, 3km S of city centre. The Heilan' coos in the 14-acre grounds tell you this isn't your average urban bed for the night. 17th-century building with period features still intact. Architect Sir William Adam, responsible for the ceiling in the Tapestry Room, also 'did' the ornamental ceilings in Holyrood Palace. Bulk of rms – 26 – added in a sympathetic 1997 refurb, though older ones possibly have more character. Enjoy the history wherever you sleep.

31RMS JAN-DEC T/T PETS CC XKIDS LOTS

4
B2
✚ **CHANNINGS:** 315 2226. South Learmonth Gdns, parallel to Queensferry Rd after Dean Br. Diary of an Edwardian Urban Lady territory with five period town houses joined to form a v tasteful and discreet hotel. Impeccable decor with efficient and individual service. Gr views from top-floor rms, incl the Prime Minister's alma mater – Fettes College. A chic retreat from downtown throngs. Brasserie has sound reputation.

48RMS JAN-DEC T/T XPETS CC KIDS LOTS

5
C2
✚ **THE HOWARD:** 557 3500. 36 Gt King St. Elegant establishment in the heart of the New Town – gr individual rms with cupboards big enough for a horse and some baths ditto. Basement restau, 36, is one of the city's finest (54/BEST RESTAUS) and a marked design contrast to what's upstairs. Same owners as Channings (*see above*).

15RMS JAN-DEC T/T XPETS CC XKIDS TOS LOTS

6
E2
ROYAL TERRACE: 557 3222. 18 Royal Terr. Romanesque plunge pool, other sports facs, multi-level terraced grd out back, deceptively large number of rms and town house decor a tad on the Baroque side. In other words, fabulous. Bar/restau not so notable among the natives, so good place for discreet meets.

94RMS JAN-DEC T/T XPETS CC KIDS LOTS

7
D3
HOLIDAY INN CROWN PLAZA: 557 9797. 80 High St. (Formerly the Scandic Crown.) Modern but sympathetic building on the Royal Mile, handy for everything. Good facs but some say service lacking. Thin wallls, not gr views. Piano bar can be fun if taken in the right spirit. Gym and small pool. Unlike others, has parking.

238RMS JAN-DEC T/T PETS CC KIDS TOS LOTS

8
C3
THE SHERATON: 229 9131. Festival Sq on Lothian Rd and nr Conference Centre, this city-centre business hotel won no prizes for architecture when it opened late 1980s, but further refurb have tartaned it up and brought some cosiness to the concrete. A reliable stopover with excellent service. Larger rms and castle views carry premiums, but make big difference. Terrace restau adequate, but The Grill menu under Nicolas Laurent is elegant, Scottish and innovative.

261RMS JAN-DEC T/T PETS CC KIDS LOTS

9
C2
THE GEORGE: 225 1251. George St (betw Hanover St & St Andrew Sq). An Inter-Continental Hotel but Robert Adam-designed and dating back to late 18th century. Good views to Fife from the top two floors. Pricey, but you pay for the location and the Georgian niceties. Busy and grandiose carvery plus good Gallic restau, the Chambertin (80/FRENCH RESTAUS).

195RMS JAN-DEC T/T PETS CC KIDS LOTS

THE MORE INDIVIDUAL HOTELS

✝ ✝ **THE MALMAISON:** 555 6868. Tower Pl, Leith, at the dock gates. Award-winning, praise-laden designer hotel with individual and rather natty rms. *Wired* magazine called it 'rock 'n' roll'. Raging success; more than doubled it's accom in autumn 1997. CD players in each chambre (borrow CDs from reception). Brasserie and café bar have stylish ambience too (68/BISROS) and there are many others nearby in this waterfront quarter. Also in Glas (358/HOTELS) and spreading S as we speak.

10
xE1

60RMS JAN-DEC T/T PETS CC KIDS EXP

✝ **THE POINT:** 221 9919. 34 Bread St. You'd never guess this used to be a Co-operative department store. Space and colour combinations manage to look simultaneously rich and minimal, some castle views. Suites (LOTS) come with side-lit jacuzzis. You'll feel more like a film extra than a hotel guest in this rather handsome bed boutique. Bar and restau have a spacious, mid-Euro feel.

11
C3

95RMS JAN-DEC T/T PETS CC KIDS EXP

26 NORTHUMBERLAND ST: 556 1078. Jim and Aurore Sibbet have retired and are now in partnership with Jens and Anita Steffen so under new management, but not new ownership. Still the same remarkable Georgian town house that has been wowing guests for yrs. Timeless.

12
C2

5RMS JAN-DEC T/T XPETS CC KIDS MED.EX

17 ABERCROMBY PLACE: 557 8036. Another plush and private Georgian town house; discreet lack of signage. Once abode of the New Town's architect, Playfair, now belongs to advocate Eirlys Lloyd. No smk, 2 rms in a self-contained mews; main house for breakfast.

13
C2

8RMS JAN-DEC T/T XPETS CC KIDS MED.EX

THE ALBANY: 556 0397. 39 Albany St. Completely changed hotel due to new owners and total refurb spring 1997. Not cheap, but now featuring that New Town splendour and politesse – only a few mins walk uphill to Princes St. Basement restau Haldane's (120/SCOTTISH RESTAUS) is pretty good.

14
D2

21RMS JAN-DEC T/T PETS CC KIDS LOTS

BANK HOTEL: 556 9043. Corner of South Br and Royal Mile. Former bank converted into fashionable café bar with bedrms above, most with urban views. Same central location but more atmos than major hotels close by, and cheaper. Rm service minimal. Bar with v European city centre ambience a gr place to meet.

15
D3

9RMS JAN-DEC XPETS CC KIDS MED.EX

SIX ST MARY'S PLACE: 332 8965. On main st of Stockbridge (St Mary's Pl part of Raeburn Pl) and busy main rd out of town for Forth Rd Br and N, this is a tastefully converted Georgian town house. Informal, friendly, well-cared-for accom popular with academics and people we like. No smk. Vegn. Breakfast in conservatory. Jolly nice people.

16
B1

8RMS JAN-DEC X/X XPETS CC KIDS MED.INX

STUART HOUSE: 557 9030. 12 E Claremont St. Nr the corner of main rd and pleasant walk up to Princes St (1.5km). Residential New Town st and family house decorated with taste and attention to detail - bonny flower grd out front. Book well in advance. No smk.

17
D1

7RMS JAN-DEC T/T XPETS CC KIDS MED.EX

2 BONNINGTON TERRACE: 554 9007. Just by jnct of Ferry Rd and Newhaven Rd. Gillie McCowan Hill's tastefully furnished and welcoming house is the sort of place *StheB!* researchers would stay. No B&B sign at gate and do not confuse with guesthouse next door. Understated interior design qualities so good they make you want to spit.

18
xE1

3RMS JAN-DEC X/T PETS CC KIDS MED.INX

TEVIOTDALE HOUSE: 667 4376. 53 Grange Loan, towards E end. Fabulous fecund flower grd out front and bargain accom within. Ground-floor rm (popular with honeymooners) has a 4-poster with adj chaise longue and the whole effect is undeniably, unexpectedly sexy – although v respectable you understand. Healthy breakfasts.

19
xD4

7RMS JAN-DEC T/T XPETS CC KIDS MED.INX

HOTEL JAVA: 467 7527. Constitution St, Leith next to the estimable Port 'O' Leith (220/PUBS). Friendly, contemporary bar with basic but inexpensive rms in Leith nr docks and with many of the city's best bars and restaus nearby. Phillipa and Sue run a laid-back and happy house. Rms at back and round courtyard.

20
xE1

10RMS JAN-DEC X/X PETS CC KIDS CHP

WEST END HOTEL: 225 3656. 35 Palmerston Pl. Capital haunt for Highlanders and Islanders who feel like a blether in Gaelic or a good folk music session in the bar (decent measures). Popular with folkie non-guests too. Spacious rms with oddly familiar furniture.

21
B3

8RMS JAN-DEC T/T XPETS CC KIDS INX

BEST 'ECONOMY' HOTELS AND TRAVEL-LODGES

Hotels/B&Bs below are included on grounds of price, convenience or just because we like them for some idiosyncratic reason.

22 **THE APEX:** 300 3456. 31-35 Grassmarket. Once part of Heriot-Watt Univ, a
C3 determined conversion resulted in a central hotel with contemporary Euro-bland façade. Civilised although a tad characterless, main market is business but flat rate charge per rm attracts families and the occasional hen night (four lassies in a rm equals (CHP). Extra charge for rms with castle view, fifth floor restau (INX) also has nice outlook. Another Apex opened nr Haymarket Stn late 1997 with rather a good restau too late for us to check properly.

99RMS JAN-DEC T/T XPETS CC KIDS MED.EX

23 **PARLIAMENT HOUSE:** 478 4000. 15 Calton Hill. Good central location, only 200m
E2 from E end of Princes St and adj to Calton Hill (329/BEST VIEWS). New on the scene, opened autum 1996. Decidedly minimalist in terms of service – no restau or bar and Continental breakfast taken in your rm – but smart town house-style décor.

54RMS JAN-DEC T/T XPETS CC KIDS MED.EX

24 **STATION HOTEL:** 226 1446. 9-13 Market St, behind Waverley Stn. Some good views
D3 from upper floors to Princes St. Couldn't be handier for the stn or city centre. Rms feel a bit 'holiday package deal', basic but acceptable. No smk. Its restau is Italian-ish and curiously always empty.

30RMS JAN-DEC T/T XPETS CC KIDS MED.EX

25 **STAKIS EDINBURGH AIRPORT:** 519 4400. At the airport, 10km W of city centre. No
xA3 way 'economy', but a reliable travellers tryst. An L-shaped box with the buzz of a high-class transit camp; charming staff. You can virtually roll out of bed and check in.

134RMS JAN-DEC T/T XPETS CC KIDS LOTS

26 **TRAVEL INN:** 228 9819. 1 Morrison Link, nr Haymarket Stn. Likeable for the fact
B3 it makes no pretence to be anything other than a bed factory. Big, orthogonal and dull but v cheap - flat charge of under £40 applies per rm which can take 2 adults or a family of 4. 7 rms specially adapted for wheelchair users. Expanding to truly monster size in 1998.

128RMS JAN-DEC X/T XPETS CC KIDS CHP

27 **FORTE POSTHOUSE:** 334 0390. Corstorphine Rd next to Zoo. Entrance feels like
xA3 an underground car park, but there's a gr view across to the Pentlands. Bit of a featureless bed box all told, but has all the facs expected of a big chain hotel and you get to listen to Cheetah and his chums at night.

204RMS JAN-DEC T/T PETS CC KIDS MED.EX

28 **THISTLE INN:** 220 2299. 94-96 Grassmarket. Taken over in summer 1997 by a
C3 major brewery so changes poss. Otherwise, basic and boisterously located accom joined to Biddy Mulligan's next door which is open to 1am, 7 days. So don't bring grandma, do come on a stag/hen night.

29RMS JAN-DEC X/T PETS CC KIDS MED.INX

THE BEST HOSTELS

Edin has some YHA hostels (nae drinking) and independents (young and Hoochy, open 24 hrs), also some handy univ halls of residence to let o/side term time. With all the independent hostels, it's best to turn up around 11/11.30am if you haven't booked. The SYH(A) is the Scottish Youth Hostels Association. 01786 891400 for details, or contact any YHA hostel. Bus information: (0131) 225 3858.

✝ ✝ **THE HIGH STREET HOSTEL** : 557 3984. 8 Blackfriars St. Out the door, turn **29** left and you're on the Royal Mile, turn rt for the Cowgate with its late **D3** night bars. Ideal central cheap 24-hr crash-out dormitory accom with all the facs for itinerant youth seeking a capital experience. Two sister hostels: **ROYAL MILE BACKPACKERS**, 105 High St (557 6120); **CASTLE ROCK**, 15 Johnston Terr (225 9666) are both in the same area. Castle Rock, in the old Council Environmental Health HQ, is huge (150 beds in various dorms, but no singles/doubles) and has some gr views across the Grassmarket or to the castle which is just over there. Same folk (Mr Backpacker himself, Peter Macmillan) also have places in Ft William, Inverness, Oban and Skye. CHP

✝ ✝ **S.Y. HOSTEL, EGLINTON:** 337 1120. 18 Eglinton Cres. From the stained **30** glass over the main door to the tartan and wood entrance foyer, you **A3** know you're not in a typical hostel. Grand late-Victorian pile in a quiet W End street with 144 beds – majority in dorms but some rms for 4. Members only but you can join at reception. Booking recommended. Closes for a month in winter. Doors locked at 2am. CHP

✝ **BELFORD HOSTEL:** 225 6209. Douglas Gardens, nr Gallery of Modern Art **31** (excellent café, 164/COFFEE SHOPS) and quaint Dean Village, but still fairly **A2** central. Bizarre concept – 110 beds in partitioned-off 'rms' of 6-10 in a converted church. Top-bunk berth gets you a view of the vaulted wooden ceiling way above. Games rm, bar, MTV. Sister establishment is **EDINBURGH BACKPACKERS HOSTEL**, 65 Cockburn St (220 1717). CHP

PRINCES ST HOSTEL: 556 6894. 5 W Register St. Behind Burger King at E end of **32** Princes St. Incredibly central for cheap accom. Basic and attracts the usual **D2** international crowd. Same people now have **PRINCES ST WEST**, 3 Queensferry St (226 2939) with bar. CHP

S.Y. HOSTEL, BRUNTSFIELD: 447 2994. 7 Bruntsfield Cres. S of Tollcross about **33** 10mins walk from W End. Buses from Princes St (grd side), nos 11, 15, 16. **xD4** Reliable and secure hostel accom in a verdant corner of Bruntsfield. 158 beds but booking 2-3 months in advance is essential at peak times. Again, members only, join at reception and doors locked at 2am. CHP

From July-Sep, SYHA also opens a temp hostel in **ROBERTSON'S CLOSE** off Cowgate. Phone Edin district office for info 229 8660.

POLLOCK HALLS: 667 0662. Off Dalkeith Rd. The main accom for Edin Univ – a **34** village of modern low-rise blocks, situated 3km S of centre next to the **xE4** Commonwealth Swimming Pool and in the shadow of Arthur's Seat, on which to gaze or jog. Refectory, bar, shared kitchens and showers. Huge number of rms – 800 basic singles and more than 400 others, some doubles. Vacs only. MED.INX

NAPIER UNIVERSITY: 455 4291. Craiglockhart campus off Colinton Rd. College **35** halls in high-rise blocks about 10km SW of centre. In grounds of imposing **xC4** Craiglockhart Hospital where Siegfried Sassoon met Wilfred Owen. Too far out for some, but buses nos 23 and 27 from the Mound (Princes St). V good sports facs incl pool. Full meal service sometimes poss. Vacs only, availability may depend on conferences. B&B. Good value. CHP

Higher ed expansion means Napier now has fair number of student flats to let during vacs for 4, 5 or 6 people – weekly rate (CHP). 455 4211 for info.

QUEEN MARGARET COLLEGE: 317 3310. Clerwood Terr. Way out, midway betw **36** main rds W to Glas and N to Forth Br; about 10km, so transport probably **xA2** essential (or bus). Campus facs, e.g. refectory, laundry, bank, good sports. Shared bathrms, etc. and a bit dreary, so not exceptional value, but a private and well-equipped refuge from uptown hassles. Phone first. Also self-catering flats. Vacs only. CHP

THE BEST CAMPING AND CARAVAN PARKS

Refer to Map 7.

37
xC4
MORTONHALL PARK: 664 1533. Off Frogston Rd E, a kind of inner-city ring rd. About 12km SW of centre. From S and city bypass: take Lothianburn jnct into town and rt at first lights for 4km. From centre: take A702 via Morningside to last left turn before bypass. Mortonhall marked, but enter via (and pass) Klondyke Grd Centre. No. 7 or 11 bus from town. Well-equipped park with 4 toilet/shower-blocks, shop, laundry, lounge, play area and fully serviced pitches. Also bar/restau in converted stables/courtyard serving food until 9pm. Coffee shop with decent home-baking at grd centre. Mar-Oct. 268 places.

38
B1
THE EDINBURGH CARAVAN CLUB SITE: 312 6874. Marine Dr, Silverknowes. 8km E of centre via Ferry Rd then rt on Pennywell Rd, continue over r/bout to Marine Dv. Former local authority site, taken over and substantially refurb by the Caravan Club of GB – reopened Aug 1997. Accepts nonmembers. 200 pitches for caravans, tents and motor homes – all with electricity. Two heated toilet blocks, laundry, disabled facs and babies/toddlers washrm. Open AYR.

39
C2
FORDEL, DALKEITH: 660 3921. Lauder Rd. On A68, 4km S of Dalkeith; 18km SE of centre. V well-equipped and serviced site secluded from the busy rd. Behind a 24hr garage and pub/café (Fordel Inn). Some work done recently so improved pitches and more landscaping. Best to have a car; reasonable bus service to Dalkeith, but fewer go past gate. 110 pitches.

40
C1
DRUM MOHR, MUSSELBURGH: 665 6867. Levenhall. 4km out of Musselburgh on the coast rd to Prestonpans. 22km E of centre. Go through Musselburgh, signed off bypass and take rd rt at Mining Museum. Award-winning site is 400m up a country lane, within sight of the sea, quiet (apart from some traffic noise) and well maintained. You will be rather removed from Edin, but within easy reach of the golf/beaches/walks and ice cream of East Lothian. Disabled facs. Mar-Oct. 120 pitches.

41
D1
GOSFORD GARDENS, ABERLADY: 01875 870487. Just off the A198, the coast rd off the A1 and about 35km E of Edin. Caravan Club of GB site in former walled grd 1km from the neat little E Lothian village of Aberlady. Attractive, secluded but perhaps too intimate for some. Perfect for golf/pony-trekking/ beachcombing but no good for nightclubbing in Edin. 120 pitches. No tents, no yoof, no rock 'n' roll.

THE BEST HOTELS OUTSIDE TOWN

See also BEST HOTELS AND RESTAUS IN LOTHIAN, *p.100. Refer to Map 7.*

42
C2
✚ **BORTHWICK CASTLE, NORTH MIDDLETON:** 01875 820514. On B6367, 3km off the A7, 18km bypass, 26km S of centre. Accept no substitute - if you want to stay in a real Border castle go for the big red one. Walls 100ft high, this magnificent tower house knocks you off your horse with its authenticity - Mary Queen of Scots was blockaded here once and at night you expect to see her swishing up the spiral stairs. 8 rms in castle, 2 in gatehouse, the (v) grand banqueting hall is impressive, dinner (EXP) is not.

10RMS   MAR-DEC   T/X   PETS   CC   KIDS   TOS   LOTS

43
C2
✚ **JOHNSTOUNBURN HOUSE, HUMBIE:** 01875 833696. On B6457 2km fr A68 and 25km S of centre. Bypass 22km. Country class in this 17th-century manor with relaxed and friendly service. Some rms in its coach house, all have that upbeat frilliness. Public areas v cool, especially the panelled 18th-century dining-rm. Feels like a true escape. Mavis Hall park adj offers clay pigeon shooting, fishing, off-road etc, so it's an excellent all-round centre v close to the city. Cream of the county.

19RMS   JAN-DEC   T/T   PETS   CC   KIDS   TOS   LOTS

44
xA3
✚ **NORTON HOUSE, INGLESTON:** 333 1275. Off A8 nr airport, 10km W of city centre. Virgin hotel in extensive grounds (hence quiet) with those Bransonesque touches you'll love or loathe – teddy bear on the bed, ducks in the bath. But high standard of service and accom with country house feel and handy for the expanding business theme parks nearby. Conservatory Restau is easily worth its two AA rosettes.

47RMS   JAN-DEC   T/T   XPETS   CC   KIDS   TOS   LOTS

DALHOUSIE CASTLE, BONNYRIGG: 01875 820153. Just off A704 2km from the A7, 15km from bypass and 23km S of centre. The castle that tries too hard? It looks fantastic in its setting and dates way back to the 13th century but the facs are everything you would expect from a contemporary city hotel which is perversely disappointing. (Previous guests incl Edward I, Cromwell, Queen Victoria and assorted rock stars.) Our Braveheart researcher was quite fond of the William Wallace rm; dinner is taken in the dungeon. Another 6 rms planned for adj Victorian lodge in late 1997.   **45 C2**

29RMS JAN-DEC T/T PETS CC KIDS TOS LOTS

HOUSTON HOUSE, UPHALL: 01506 853831. On A899 at end of Broxburn/Uphall Main St, 8km from r/bout at the start of the M8 Edin-Glas motorway. Airport 10km, 18km W of centre. Bits of this tower house date to the 16th century, others far more recent (extension with 46 rms completed summer 1997). Yet more 4-posters, nice open fire in the bar, restau is rated and the place is stuffed with farmers during Royal Highland Show week. Set on 20 acres of greenery, atypical Uphall. Serious sports facs opening late 1997.   **46 B1**

72RMS JAN-DEC T/T XPETS CC KIDS TOS LOTS

DALMAHOY, KIRKNEWTON: 333 1845. On A71 (Kilmarnock rd) on edge of town – ring rd 5km, 15km W of centre, airport 6km. In the beginning was the word, and the word was golf. Two good courses, European Tour venue and that's what the groups of chaps (and occasionally ladies) come for. Hotel itself is Georgian with 7 distinctive rms, rest in new annexe where the extensive sports facs reside. Part of the Marriot chain.   **47 B1**

151RMS JAN-DEC T/T XPETS CC KIDS TOS LOTS

HAWES INN,1 SOUTH QUEENSFERRY: 331 1990. From city take rd N via Queensferry Rd heading for Forth Rd Br. On front at Hawes Pier and literally under the famous rail br (311/MAIN ATTRACTIONS). Pick the rt rm and lie back in the 4-poster to soak up an atmos that made RLS escape into the fantasy world of *Kidnapped*. Facs far from fab, but genuine 16th century with unique situation.   **48 B1**

8RMS (NONE *EN SUITE*) JAN-DEC T/T PETS CC KIDS MED.INX

QUEENSFERRY LODGE HOTEL, NR N QUEENSFERRY: 01383 410000. At Fife end of rd br (so Edin is a toll away), but a good stopping-off place for all points N. Dramatic setting with estuarine views. Restaus/bars/shop – a modern purpose-built roadhouse. N Queensferry less crowded than S (except for Deep Sea World); nice bistro the Channel (01383 412567).   **49 B5**

32RMS JAN-DEC T/T PETS CC KIDS MED.INX

GREYWALLS HOTEL: 01620 842114. 32km E of centre (707/LOTHIAN HOTELS).   **D1**

OPEN ARMS HOTEL, DIRLETON: 01620 850241. 35 km E centre (710/LOTHIAN HOTELS).   **D1**

OLD ABERLADY INN, ABERLADY: 01875 870503. 27km E centre (711/LOTHIAN HOTELS).   **D1**

THE BEST RESTAURANTS

✠ ✠ **THE ATRIUM:** 228 8882. Foyer of the Traverse Theatre, Cambridge St off Lothian Rd. Naked flames, strangely-lit chefs visible in the open kitchen, intelligent service, striking design and that wonderful 'wine reduction' smell. Add some quite remarkable food that's both modish and subtle and you have the capital's best all-rounder – courtesy of Andrew Radford. Even beats some restaus below on price too. The newer **BLUE** is upstairs (60/CAFÉ BARS). Lunch Mon-Fri, dinner Mon-Sat LO 10pm. Cl Sun.   **50 C3**

EXP

✠ ✠ **LA POTINIERE:** Main St, Gullane. 01620 843214. 36km W of city in delightful (and notable golfing) village on A198 coast rd off A1. David and Hilary Brown's intimate, much celebrated caff, the first truly gr restau in SE Scotland and still up there though facing stiffer competition in town. Nevertheless, worth the 45min drive for the elegant simplicity of their set menu of French classic and contemporary gastronomie. Outstanding wine list. Set menu. Dinner: Fri/Sat only (or groups by arrangement). Lunch: (Tue-Sun). Famously booked in advance, but lunch and Fri easier and often cancellations. No smk.   **51 xE2**

MED

✠ **THE WITCHERY:** 225 5613. Castlehill. At the top of the Royal Mile where the tourists throng, but many will be unaware that this is one of the city's best restaus and certainly its most stylishly atmospheric. 2 salons, the upper more witchery; in the 'secret grd' downstairs, a converted school playground, James   **52 C3**

Thompson has created a more spacious ambience for the (same) elegant Scottish menu. The after-theatre menu is an excellent prospect with LO at a v civilised 11.30pm. 7 days. Lunch and dinner.　EXP

53
xE1
✛ (fitz)**HENRY**: 555 6625. 19 Shore Pl. The inimitable Dave Ramsden has worked hard to turn his warehouse brasserie in an off-the-waterfront st in Leith into one of Edinburgh's top spots, the only one (1997) apart from the Atrium to get a Michelin red M. Chef Herve Veraille is the other reason. Fastidious, but non-intrusive service in a stylish setting. 6 days lunch and dinner. Cl Sun.　MED

54
C2
✛ **NUMBER 36**: 668 3636. Basement restau of the Howard Hotel (5/BEST HOTELS) in the New Town and in design contrast to the Georgian opulence upstairs. 36 is bold and clean-cut verging on minimalist. The food also is contemporary in every respect and when it opened in 1997, 36 quickly become one of *the* places to eat. Malcolm Warham is the chef heading, I suspect, for accolades other than this. 7 days lunch and dinner (cl Sat lunch). No smk.　MED

55
xE1
✛ **THE VINTNER'S ROOM**: 554 6767. 87 Giles St, Leith. Entering from a cobbled courtyard to the wine bar, the long rm with its woody ambience and open fire, these vaults, formerly used to store claret (Leith was an important wine pt), also incl a restaurant lit by candlelight. Both bar and restau have same menu in evening (French tone using fresh Scottish produce), but there are cheaper options at lunch in the bar and it's less formal. Excellent cheeseboard and wine list. Mon-Sat lunch and 6.30-10pm. Malt Whisky Society upstairs.　MED

56
D2
✛ **ONE PRINCES STREET, BALMORAL HOTEL**: 556 2414. Address with a certain ring for the principal restau of the Balmoral (1/BEST HOTELS) entered through lobby or off st. Based apparently on the Mandarin Grill, Hong Kong, these opulent subterranean salons have ample space around the tables, but the lighting and lacquering do little to cosify the ritziness. New chef Jeff Bland however is expected to reposition this place on the gastronomic st map of the city, with emphasis on the ONE. The revamped **HADRIEN'S BRASSERIE** at st level complements well. Cl Sat/Sun lunch. LO 10.30pm.　EXP

57
C3
✛ **POMPADOUR, CALEDONIAN HOTEL**: 225 2433. Princes St. One of the most expensive meals in town but actually worth it. A sensual assault on several levels: a pianist plays, waiters glide, the salon is ornate and the food – French style by Jerome Barbancon – careers between hauntingly simple (best asparagus Hollandaise in the universe) to pure mental intricate – chocolate pud in the shape of a grand piano. It could intimidate the socks off some of us, but no worries – manager Jordi Figuerola will see you rt. Dinner only, Tues-Sat LO 10pm.　EXP

58
C2
✛ **MARTIN'S**: 225 3106. 70 Rose St North Lane. Shabby lane behind busy shopping precinct nr Princes St – odd place to find a top restau but Martin probably likes it that way. Good service, v high standard of contemporary cooking, delicate desserts and an unsurpassed, unpasteurised Celtic cheeseboard. He knows his wines. Lunch Tues-Fri, dinner Tues-Sat LO 10pm.　EXP

59
xE1
THE ROCK: 555 2225. Commercial St and Commercial Quay, Leith. In a row of 'waterfront' restaus lured into converted warehouses opp the new Scottish Office, this is the one that stands out for excellent food (though others are notable). Modern set up with good sightlines to other diners and open kitchen. Grill menu of burgers and steaks (and salmon) is simple and sound; changing à la carte menu widens choice for non red-meaters. Gr chips. Easy place to drop in but you do dine. 7 days lunch and dinner, Cl Sat lunch, Sun even.　MED

WINTER GLEN: 477 7060. 3A1 Dundas St. Report : 116/SCOTTISH RESTAUS.

THE BEST BISTROS AND CAFÉ BARS

All open for lunch unless otherwise stated.

✚ ✚ **BLUE:** 221 1222. Cambridge St. Upstairs in the Traverse Theatre building. **60** From the makers of The Atrium (50/BEST RESTAUS) comes the latest Edin *C3* thing that might even have them dribbling into their Powerbooks in Soho. Furniture by Alasdair Gall and Tangram, design by Andrea Faed, best café-bar cooking in the city by a country mile. Blue is a light wood/metal/spacious establishment with a full menu from 12noon-3pm and 6pm-12midnight daily. Set snacks only in the afternoon, bar open to 1am daily. Minimal chic, maximal buzz.

CHP/INX

✚ ✚ **SKIPPERS:** 554 1018. 1A Dock Pl. In a corner of Leith off Commercial Rd **61** by the docks. Look for Waterfront (*see below*) and bear left into adj cul- *xE1* de-sac. The pioneer restaurant in the pre-yuppie Leith, it's still after all these yrs quite the best real bistro in town. V fishy, v quay side intimate and friendly. Look no further out to sea. Dinner: Tue-Sat, LO 10pm.

MED

✚ **HOWIE'S:** 668 2917. 75 St Leonard's St. Up on the S side, this extended set of **62** rms is always busy. Unfussy, extensive and eclectic menu the epitome of *E4* good Edin bistro food that's affordable. Totally reliable and inexp eating out. Though this is the original Howies, 2 others hit the same spot S and W of the city. 63 Dalry Rd. 313 3334. The best place to eat in the neighbourhood 100m up from Haymarket Stn. 208 Bruntsfield Pl. 221 1777 in a converted church. All 7 days lunch and dinner. LO 10/10.30pm. St Leonard's and Dalry. Cl Mon lunch. BYOB (with corkage) or unpretentious wine list.

INX

✚ **INDIGO YARD:** 220 5603. 7 Charlotte Lane. Food in bar area and in restau **63** upstairs in converted and glazed over yard behind the W End. Enormously *B3* popular and always buzzing so you may not hear your wine pop or your cookie crumble. Earlier therefore better for conservational meals, but snackier supper menu from 10pm-1am is worth remembering. Food modern Med/Mex-Scottish and far better than café bar standard. 7 days, lunch and evening menu LO 10pm, then supper.

INX

✚ **THE WATERFRONT:** 554 7427. 1C Dock Pl. In this foody corner of the **64** waterfront, The Waterfront conservatory o/looks the backwater dock. It's *xE1* *the* place to head in summer, but the warren of rms is cosy in winter. Food has wavered a bit over the yrs and new ownership imminent, but site and setting are mostly what you come for. Food update next time. 7 days, LO 10pm.

MED

✚ **THE SHORE:** 553 5080. 3 The Shore, Leith. Bar (often with live light jazz) **65** where you can eat from the same menu as the dining-rm/restaurant. Real fire *xE1* and large windows looking out to the Water of Leith. Food, listed on a blackboard, changes daily but is consistently good. Lots of fish, some meat, some vegn. No smk in restau/OK in bar. 7 days, LO 10pm.

MED

DANIEL'S: 553 5933. 88 Commercial Quay, off Dock Pl. Versatile with small deli, **66** takeaway and bistro. Main eaterie is housed in new conservatory at back of old *xE1* bonded warehouse. Clean lines, modern look and v popular. Offers contemporary French menu with Alsace and external influences that has been packing us in. Daniel himself is a gent and deserves to succeed. Daily 9am-10pm.

INX

NICOLSON'S: 57 4567. 6a Nicolson St opp Festival Theatre. An airy, blue-and- **67** yellow first floor eaterie – same owners as the Grain Store (119/SCOTTISH *D3* RESTAUS). Flexible menu offers everything from breakfast to post-theatre dinner. The cooking's competent, or you could always just waste a couple of hrs with a bottle of wine and a chum. 9am-midnight daily (late opening worth noting). INX

✚ **MALMAISON BRASSERIE AND CAFÉ MAL:** 555 6969. Tower Pl at Leith Dock **68** gates. Restau and café bar of Malmaison (10/BEST HOTELS). Authentic *xE1* brasserie atmos and menu with linen cloths, big windows, steak frites. Café has lighter more Mediterranean and vegn food. 7 days lunch and dinner. MED/INX

THE DORIC: 225 1084. 15 Market St. Opp the Fruitmarket Gallery and the back **69** entrance to Waverley Stn. Upstairs bistro with chequered cloths, awful paintings, *D3* eclectic menu. Famous for their unaccommodating attitude to late-comers and the rude expulsion you get when they want to close the bar; and it ain't cheap any longer. All this aside it's still a gr bistro; we always go back. 7 days, LO 10.30pm.

MED

70 **PIGS:** 667 6676. 41 W Nicolson St. Edin does have a fair complement of bistros
D4 and although the important ones are mentioned above there are others worthy of
note - like Pigs. Small, neat and sweet, the cooking dares to be different (Botswana
meat stew) and you can BYOB. Won't win awards; has won fans. Lunch Mon-Sat,
LO 10pm daily.   INX

71 **LE SEPT:** 225 5428. 7 Old Fishmarket Close. The cobbled close winds steeply off
D3 the High St below St Giles. Wee o/side terrace in summer and narrow woody
room inside for nonsmokers (but smokey rm too). Crêpes, omelettes, plats du
jour and Franco-bistro food. Cheerful, busy rendezvous with well-regarded staff.
Mon-Thurs lunch and LO 10.30pm; Fri 12noon-11.30pm; Sat 12noon-11pm; Sun
12.30pm-10.30pm.   INX

72 **THE DIAL:** 225 7179. 44-46 George IV Br. Modern Scottish with an international
D3 spin in this subterranean designer eaterie. Drawbacks: curious Edin basement
smell and question marks over the service. But then it looks cool, does a bargain
pre-theatre menu and much effort has gone into the aesthetics, edible or
otherwise. On balance: dial 225 7179.   MED

73 **MAISON HECTOR:** 332 5328. 47 Deanhaugh St, Stockbridge. Designer revelation
B1 when it opened, getting shabbified, but still going strong. Coffee and muffins all
day (nice cappuccino with Flake), lunch Mon-Fri, gr Sat/Sun brunch
(205/SUNDAY BREAKFAST) and decent dinner from 6pm-10.30pm daily. Or just go
for a drink. Mirrored pissoir in the gents for the inquisitive or narcissistic. Bar
Sun-Thurs 10.30am-12midnight, Fri-Sat until 1am.

CHAINS-U-LIKE

*None of the groups below will be too happy being described as a 'chain' but the bar/bistros have
common owners and Pierre Victoire is everywhere these days, so . . .*

74 **MONTPELIERS:** 229 3115. 159-161 Bruntsfield Pl. Food available at flexible times
C4 with that now ubiquitous Med-Mex menu to the fore. Busy with better-heeled
students, occasional footballers and the local, young bourgeoisie - so sometimes
loud. *Sympathy for the Devil* was playing when our researcher visited and he liked
that. 9am-1am, daily, LO dinner 10pm, supper menu until close. Same people
have **INDIGO YARD** (63/BISTROS) and **THE IGUANA** (274/HIP).

75 **THE CALEDONIAN ALEHOUSE/BISTRO:** 337 1006. 1 Haymarket Terr, adj Haymarket
A3 Stn. Green leather and wood in the downstairs bar, well thought-out candlelit
bistro upstairs where veggies needn't feel left out. A successful formula so the
C3 owners have also opened **THE CALEY BISTRO**, 622 7170. 30 Leven St, Tollcross.
Good robust modern Scottish nr the King's Theatre (352/NIGHTLIFE). Lunch and
LO 10.30pm daily. Meanwhile **EH1**: 197 High St, 220 5277, is perhaps the most
stylish of the lot. Another breakfast/lunch/dinner cafe/eaterie. V blue and yellow
- sit through the back and it feels like a balcony o/look Cockburn St. Until 1am
daily. Finally **THE QUADRANT** in North Berwick is a nineties thing (716/BEST
LOTHIANS) on an unfashionable coast.

76 **PIERRE VICTOIRE:** Apologies to Monsieur Levicky (proprietor) but the word that
keeps coming up in conversations about his restaus these days is 'McDonald's'.
With half a dozen PVs in Edin, another in South Queensferry and ten elsewhere
in Scotland, this is no longer a happily unique wee Franco-bistro selling a bargain
lunch. (And we're not counting other French, Italian and veggie spin-offs.)
Foodies swap stories about how 'their' PV just isn't as good as it was, although
this might be an example of that Scottish tendency to cry 'ah kent yer faither'. In
D3 the capital, the original restau (10 Victoria St, 225 1721) has a fine buzz and no
elbow rm in the evenings, so still a fave and perhaps we're havering. The Leith
outlet (5 Dock Pl, 555 6178) is v pop at lunch times - looking babelicious helps
get you served. Also at 8 Union St (557 8451), 38-40 Grassmarket (226 2442), 17
Queensferry St (226 1890) and 8 Gloucester St, Stockbridge (225 1037).

Elsewhere: **Aberdeen, Ayr, Dundee, Dumfries, Dunfermline, Falkirk, Glasgow (two),
Perth, South Queensferry, Stirling, Venus** and probably more coming.

THE BEST FRENCH RESTAURANTS

✚ **DUCK'S AT LE MARCHE NOIR:** 558 1608. 2/4 Eyre Pl. The Duck in question is 77
not the edible sort, but proprietor Malcolm Duck who presides with C2
meticulous attention to detail in his bistro/restau at the lower end of the New
Town. In a residential neighbourhood, an easy-going, but still business-like
atmos. It may remind you of somewhere in France. Various *menus complets* to
choose from with some imaginative regional variations and regular gourmet
evenings. Good-value wine list. Dinner 7 days, lunch Mon-Fri. LO 10.30pm
(earlier Sun).
MED

✚ **CAFÉ SAINT-HONORE:** 226 2211. 34 Thistle St Lane betw Frederick St and 78
Hanover St. Fund managers, business dudes, New Town regulars and C2
occasional lunching ladies all to be found in this grand, shining eaterie that
smacks of *fin de siècle* Paris. If the Impressionists were alive, they'd be cadging
desserts. International menu with v French flavour – veggies should phone ahead.
EXP

✚ **L'AUBERGE:** 556 5888. 58 St Mary's St. Proprietor Daniel Wencker pitched his 79
auberge on St Mary's *rue* 20yrs ago when French cuisine ruled the world and C2
places like this were culinary outposts. Now anywhere with a croissant on the
menu can call itself a brasserie, but few real French restaus remain; this is one of
them. The atmos is a tad formal but they know good service and they know good
wine. *Quel dommage* that the food and presentation is so uncompromisingly
bourgeois. Sun lunch is popular. 7 days, LO 9.30 pm.
EXP

✚ **CHAMBERTIN:** 225 1251. 21 George St. Discreet, v professionally run main 80
restau of George Hotel (9/BEST HOTELS) in opulent salon where suits dine at C2
lunch time and retired members of the Edin establishment whinge about their
grandkids. More relaxed in the evenings. Food has a welcome zing these days and
there are unexpected *au courant* flourishes like translucent blue croquery that
make for a pleasant clash with the décor. Lunch Mon-Fri, LO 10pm Mon-Sat. Cl
Sun.
EXP

LA BONNE VIE: 667 1110. 49 Causewayside. Popular bistro in Edinburgh's S side. 81
V agreeable. Sitting among the garlands, stone walls, shining glassware and xD4
candles for a few mins, there's a growing sense of personality, then it hits you.
This is the Felicity Kendall of capital restaus – and that's a compliment. Scottish
produce, French outlook. Lunch and LO 10.30pm daily.
MED

JACQUES: 229 6080. 8 Gillespie Pl, Bruntsfield. Endearing French staff and 82
endearing French typos – 'goast' cheese [sic] – make this a bistro to tug at your C4
heartstrings. A hard-working wee rustic eaterie close to the King's Theatre so
well placed for pre-/post-show meals. Has all those French dishes – mussels,
roulade – and throws in left-fielders like ostrich, yes, ostrich! Also Sun brunch.
Good work you Gauls! Lunch and LO 11pm Mon-Sat, 10am-10pm Sun.
INX

CHEZ JULES: 225 7007. 1 Craig's Close, off Cockburn St. Another chapter in the 83
Pierre Victoire histoire with CJ bistros following PVs in every big town. Fairly D3
similar – v French and pretty cheap. The restau feels subterranean, dishes on offer
include pigeon, moules, onion soup, etc. Mon-Sat 6pm-11pm. Cl Sun. Also at 61
Frederick St for brighter surroundings, 225 7983. Mon-Sat 12noon-3pm then
6pm.
INX

CAFÉ D'ODILE: 225 5366. 13 Randolph Cres. A secret grd and small cafeteria 84
downstairs at the French Institute. Lunch only but can be booked for parties at B2
night. Gr views over the New Town, simple French home-cooking, patronised by
ladies who lunch. Terribly genteel, but occasional studenty BYOB types. Tues-
Sat. Not licensed.
CHP

LA POTINIÈRE: 01620 843214. Main St, Gullane (51/BEST RESTAUS).

MARINETTE: 555 0922. 52 Coburg St (99/SEAFOOD RESTAUS).

POMPADOUR: 225 2433. Caledonian Hotel, Princes St (57/BEST RESTAUS).

THE BEST ITALIAN RESTAURANTS

85
xE1

✚ **SILVIO'S:** 553 3557. 54 The Shore. On the waterfront in Leith. Discreet frontage, deceptively low-key ristorante. This is excellent stuff. Classically simple, contemporary Italian/Mediterranean cuisine. Perfectly judged *antipasti* and invariably good fish and seafood of the day. Let them advise you. Some decent wines. Mon-Sat lunch and LO 10.30pm. No smk.   MED

86
B2

✚ **RAFFAELLI'S:** 225 6060. 10 Randolph Pl, W End. Capital's worst-kept secret Italian? Hidden away in a lane behind W Register House at the back of Charlotte Sq this excellent restau is the kind of place where unit trust bods tell pals about villas nr Lucca. V high standard of cooking indeed, attentive service, strong Italian wine list, fairly formal. Not simply interesting or remarkable – actually one of the best. Lunch Mon-Fri, LO 10.30pm Mon-Sat. Cl Sun.   MED

87
E1

✚ **VALVONA & CROLLA:** 556 6066. 19 Elm Row. The legendary deli (1160/DELIS) now with café (rather than restau), but given manageress Carina Contini's care and attention, produce shipped in from Italy (fresh veg from Milan markets) and gr Italian domestic cooking on offer, this has been a big hit since it opened in spring 1996. Everything from vegn breakfast to fab lemon polenta cake and coffee for afternoon nibblers via a damned fine lunch. May be queues. No smk. Mon-Sat 8am-5pm. Not cheap, but clearly worth every penny.   INX

88
C2

✚ **COSMO:** 226 6743. 58 N Castle St (a no through rd). V much in the old, discreet style for those with some time and cash on their hands. In Edin terms, has been the up-market Italian restau for yrs and it is often fully booked. Famous people like Sean do get brought here. The lighting and the music are soft, the service impeccable and the (Italian) wine list exemplary. Menu pragmatically brief; allow time to enjoy it. 6 days. Cl Sun and Sat lunch.   EXP

89
D2

✚ **LIBRIZZI'S:** 668 1997. 22A Nicolson St. Small basement ristorante opp Festival Theatre. The chef from Vito's and Cosmo (*above*) started up on his own, and this intimate and personal place is the result. Underrated, but one of the best in town, esp for fish. Good service, well-selected wines. Cl Sun, LO 11pm.   MED

90
E1

✚ **TINELLI:** 652 1932. 139 Easter Rd. Small and neat restau with unassuming frontage on unfashionable st that was serving air-dried beef long before anyone else. Not a pizza/pasta joint - grilled liver with balsamic vinegar more their style. One of the city's best Italians. Lunch and LO 10.30pm Mon-Sat.   MED

91
C2

✚ **VITO'S:** 225 5052. 55A Frederick St. Vito's has been in Edin for nigh on 20yrs, but this place seems as fresh and the menu as contemporary and Mediterranean as any. Basement rms are light but intimate and service is v good. They can always fit you in and get you sorted if you're in a hurry.   MED

92
C1

✚ **TONY'S:** 226 5877. 42 St Stephen St. Identifiable by the floral window box, this small tratt features a high standard of Italian cooking, comparable with the standard of patter from Tony himself. V popular so book. Daily, evenings only, LO 11pm. (Also now has another, larger restau at 19 Colinton Rd, 447 8781.)   INX

93
A4

PEPE'S TAVERNA: 337 9774. 96 Dalry Rd. Taverna's just the word - checked tablecloths, dark wooden fixtures and hanging pots and pans. Food is standard Italian but when virtually everywhere else has packed up for the night, Pepe's keeps on keeping on. A Dalry haven 6pm-2.30am. Cl Tues. (200/LATE-NIGHT RESTAUS).   INX

94
D2

GIULIANO'S: 556 6590. 18 Union Pl, top of Leith Walk nr the main r/bout, opp Playhouse Theatre. No change at Giuli's but something sets it apart as it's often heaving with happy punters. It's just pasta and pizza but in a no-nonsense manner that appeals. Lunch and LO 2am daily. Also another 'on the shore' in Leith (554 5272) which is esp good for kids (158/KID-FRIENDLY).   INX

95
D3

BEPPE VITTORIO: 226 7267. 7 Victoria St. Italian peasant kitchen kindathing from the makers of Pierre Victoire (76/CHAINS) with reliable bistro-ish nosh. Informal and rustic feel which is gr if you're in the mood for excellent linguine al pesto. From 10am for coffee, lunch daily, LO Mon-Sat 11pm, Sun 10pm.   INX

DAL MARE: 555 0122. 76 Commercial St, Leith. (101/SEAFOOD RESTUAS).

GORDON'S TRATTORIA: 225 7992. 231 High St (198/LATE-NIGHT RESTAUS).

BAR ROMA: 226 2977. 39A Queensferry St (199/LATE-NIGHT RESTAUS).

THE BEST RESTAURANTS FOR MEDITERRANEAN FOOD

IGG'S: 557 8184. 15 Jeffrey St nr Royal Mile. Maybe misleading to include Igg's here because although it serves the best tapas in town, they're only available at lunch. Overall, it's a v smart eaterie serving some of the best victuals in Edin – Spanish/Scots crossover. Excellent sauces and riojas. Other restau owners and notable Edinburgers eat here. Lunch; LO 10.30pm. Cl Sun. 96 D3 MED

TAPAS TREE: 556 7118. 1 Forth St. Bustling wee restau with upbeat Spanish staff and gypsy/Cajun soundtrack. Starter/main/pud is the heavier option but three well-chosen tapas (veg, fish and something else) with some robust bread and a bottle of house red makes for a v decent meal. Snappy service. Tapas in the £2 to £5 range, so not a pocket buster. 11am-10.30pm daily. 97 D2 INX

PHENECIA: 662 4493. 55-57 W Nicolson St, on corner nr Edin Univ. Unfussy yellow N African/Spanish eaterie with couscous, lots of grilled meats and wide vegn choice. Poss to eat v cheaply at lunch time – some people just pop in from that univ for hummus and salad. Lunch Mon-Sat, LO 11pm daily (10pm Sun). They have the Chateau Musar. 98 D4 INX

SILVIO'S: 553 3557. 54 The Shore (85/ITALIAN RESTAUS).

THE BEST SEAFOOD RESTAURANTS

MARINETTE: 555 0922. 52 Coburg St. My favourite seafood dining-rm on the other rd that leads to Leith. More *épatant* than anywhere else in the pt; you do find sailors and working girls, but not Simone Signoret sitting alone at the corner table with a fag. Straightforward ideal menu: mainly whatever fish is best of the day (breem, halibut and always monkfish) with a choice of sauces like ginger and coriander, served with *the* best bowl of chips in town. There are other options which the irrepressible Francis will advise; he will certainly be on your case (unobtrusive he ain't). Tue-Sat lunch, dinner. LO 10pm. 99 xD1 MED

FISHERS: 554 5666. Corner of The Shore and Tower St, Leith. At the foot of an 18th-century tower opp Malmaison Hotel and rt on the quay (though no boats come by). Seafood cooking with flair and commitment in boat-like surroundings where trad Scots dishes get an imaginative twist. V good indeed. Cheeseboard has some gr Brits if you have rm for a third course. Clientele can tend towards self-consciously chic types; impeccable staff working from galley kitchen deserve big tips. 7 days. 12noon-10.30pm. 100 xE1 MED

DAL MARE: 555 0722. Commercial St, Leith. On the 'quay' in restau row, an authentic Italian job specialising in fish and seafood. Antonio Iannozzi arrived with his team from Southern Italy, bedecked in the prestigious Green Ribbon (for light cuisine) in late 1997. Décor is sand 'n' surf; food is surf 'n' token turf incl veal, as the Italians do. Excellent vinos. Lunch and LO 11pm. Cl Sun. 101 xE1

CREELERS: 220 4447. 3 Hunter Sq. Tim and Fran James still have their excellent seafood restau and smokehouse in Arran, also called Creelers, (1933/ARRAN) and Tim somehow still manages to go fishing. But mainly they work damned hard in their corner of the revamped Hunter Sq behind the Tron Church, just a short cast from the Royal Mile (tables alfresco in summer) to make this one of the best seafood spots in town. Nice paintings, good atmos, not exp. Bar meals at front, restau at back. Lunch and LO 10.30/11pm (Cl Sun in winter). 102 D3 INX/MED

CAFÉ ROYAL OYSTER BAR: 556 4124. W Register St. A place for a flourish of insanity or sheer exhibitionism. Beluga Caviar followed by Homard Newburg with a bottle of Bolly came to £154 for two at last count. But you can also snack. Higher celeb quotient than most Edin restaus (Souness and Connolly when they're in town) there for the classy surroundings with spillover atmos from adj bar. Tiles, linen, dark wood, v Victorian. Visitors usually find it all v groovy; some locals lament that it ain't what it was. Lunch and LO 10.15pm daily. 103 D2 EXP

SKIPPERS: 554 1018. 1A Dock Pl, Leith. Bistro with truly maritime atmosphere; mainly seafood. Best to book. Footnore here, but many would argue Skippers *is* the best place to eat seafood in town. Full report: 61/BISTROS. 104 xE1

THE BEST VEGETARIAN RESTAURANTS

105 ✠ **BLACK BO'S:** 557 6136. 57 Blackfriars St. Unlike other eateries below, this is a
D3 ♦ restau not a way of life that just so happens to be meatless, so none of your
worthy veg crumble here – almond and potato terrine more their thing.
Adventurous use of fruit in main dishes, although proprietors fed up being
described as "fruity". Adj bar (760/BEST FOOD) now offers similar standard of
cooking during the day, restau open evenings only, LO 10.30pm daily.

106 ✠ **KALPNA:** 667 9890. 2-3 St Patrick Sq. Long-established vegn restau which is
D4 ♦ also something else – a good Indian one – so more interesting than many.
Thali gives a good overview while bargain Wed buffet features regional cuisine.
No Smk. Lunch Mon-Fri, dinner 7 days, LO 10.30pm.   INX

107 ✠ **ANN PURNA:** 662 1807. 45 St Patrick Sq. Excellent vegn restau nr Edin Univ
D4 ♦ with genuine Gujerati/S Indian cuisine. Good atmos – old customers are
greeted like friends. Indian beer, some suitable wines. Lunch Mon-Fri, dinner 7
days LO 11pm.

108 ✠ **BANNS:** 226 1112. 5 Hunter Sq just off Royal Mile at the Tron Church. Veggie
D3 ♦ burgers, Mexicana and many less predictable things in this informal eaterie on
a redeveloped corner of the Old Town which has a performance space making it a
good place to eat alfresco in summer. Snacks and full meals all day, some vegan.
Organic wines and beers, decent coffee from Gaggia machine and Pâtisserie
Florentin desserts. Daily 10am-11pm.   INX

109 **HENDERSON'S:** 225 2131. 94 Hanover St. Edinburgh's original and trail-blazing
C2 basement vegn self-serve café-cum-wine bar. Canteen seating to the left (avoid),
candles and live piano or guitar downstairs to the rt (better). Happy wee wine list
and bottles of some excellent organic real ales. Good cheese. Cl Sun. LO 10pm.
Also has the Farm Shop upstairs with a deli and takeaway and the more bar-like
Henderson's Thistle Bistro round the corner in Thistle St.

110 **SUSIE'S DINER:** 667 8729. 51-53 W Nicolson St. Formerly Seeds, this vegn/vegan
D4 diner now boasts a more varied menu with Mexican and Middle Eastern dishes,
occasional live music and belly dancing nights so less po-faced than its
predecessor (hurrah). But could they please abandon tofu 'cheesecake'?
Licenced, also BYOB. Mon 9am-9pm, Tues-Sat 9am-10pm, Cl Sun.   CHP

111 **PIERRE LAPIN:** 662 1849. 113 Buccleuch St. A vegetable rather than vegn restau and
D4 part of the pan-galactic Pierre Victoire empire (76/CHAINS-U-LIKE). This means
there's fish in them there menus, but no meat. Small whitewashed bistro affair with
too much duplication of ingredients between starters and mains so choose
carefully – and it's a long way from *cordon vert* at these prices. Lunch and LO
10pm (11pm Fr-Sat). Cl Sun.   CHP

112 **ENGINE SHED CAFÉ:** 662 0040. 19 St Leonard's Lane. Hidden away off St Leonard's
E4 St, this is a lunch-oriented vegn café where much of the work is done by adults
with learning difficulties on training placements, so worth supporting. Simple,
decent food and gr bread – baked on premises, for sale separately. Nice stopping-
off point after a tramp over Arthur's Seat. (Also has a shop at 123 Bruntsfield Pl.)
Mon-Thurs 10.30am-3.30pm, Fri 10.30am-2.30pm, Sat 10.30am-4pm, Sun
11.30am-4pm.   CHP

113 **HELIOS FOUNTAIN:** 229 7884. 7 Grassmarket. Old hippies eat sugar-free cake, their
C3 kids play with building blocks and browsers check out the tenets of Steinerism
(Rudolf, not George). Reliable self-service vegn caff, anthroposophical bookshop
and gewgaw emporium. No smk. Mon-Sat 10am-6pm, Sun 12noon-4pm.

114 **CORNERSTONE CAFÉ:** 229 0212. Underneath St John's Church at the corner of
C3 Princes St and Lothian Rd. V central and PC self-service coffee shop in church
vaults. Home-baking and hot dishes at lunchtime. Some seats outside in summer
(in graveyard!) and market stalls during the Festival. One World shop adj is full
of Third World-type crafts and v good for presents. A respite from the fast-food
frenzy of Princes St. Open 9.30am-4pm (later in Festival). Cl Sun.   CHP

115 **ISABEL'S:** 662 4014. 83 Clerk St (in basement of Nature's Gate wholefood shop).
E4 V small cafe selling vegn standards. Pop in some time. Mon-Sat 11.30am-6.30pm.
                                                                                    CHP

THE BEST SCOTTISH RESTAURANTS

✠ ✠ **WINTER GLEN:** 477 7060. 3A1 Dundas St which is on the rt going downhill opp the Scottish Gallery. Comfortable, intimate basement restau and above, a private dining-rm. Pleasing name comes not from sentiment, but from the surnames of the owners. Nevertheless this mainly Scottish menu originates from, glen and loch and bay; Scotland's first-class ingredients featured and presented to exemplary effect. Smart service, urbane atmos without the ennui. The sort of restau you'd hope to find in the capital of a European country (quietly confident of its own cuisine). 6 days. Cl Sun and Sat lunch. — MED

116 C2

✠ **DUBH PRAIS:** 557 5732. 123B High St. Slap bang (but downstairs) on the Royal Mile opp the Holiday Inn. Only 9 tables and a minature galley kitchen from which proprietor/chef James McWilliams and his team produce a remarkably reliable à la carte menu from sound and sometimes surprising Scottish ingredients. Remarkable and surprising because you might not expect the largely suburban clientele to feast so enthusiastically on ostrich or rabbit, but they do. Testimony to the chef; there are many more conventional options. An outpost of culinary integrity on the Royal Mile. Cl Sun/ Mon and Sat lunch. LO 10.30pm. — MED

117 D3

STAC POLLY: 229 5405. 8A Grindlay St. Opp Lyceum Theatre and not far from Usher Hall, Traverse and cinemas. Those haggis filo parcels that divide opinion are still on the menu which is largely local produce cooked up a storm (Scottish beef, salmon, game). The restau – dark wood and tartan curtains – is quietly smart. Cheeses come from Iain Mellis (1178/CHEESE). There's another basement **STAC POLLY** at 29-33 Dublin St in the New Town (556 2231). Similar menu but it feels clubbier. V fine. Both: lunch Mon-Fri and LO 11pm Mon-Sat. Dublin St also open Sun evening to 11pm. — MED

118 D2/C3

THE GRAINSTORE: 225 7635. 30 Victoria St. Regulars come for the pigeon, salmon or guinea fowl – perhaps the vegn alternative – then hang around this laid-back first-floor eaterie drinking wine or coffee. Informal and welcoming, there are few better places for a relaxed Sunday lunch extending far into the afternoon. More 'mod Brit' than simply 'Scottish' but this fine restau just has to fit in the book somewhere. Lunch and dinner daily, LO 11pm (10pm Sun). — MED

119 D3

HALDANE'S: 556 8407. 39 Albany St. New venture for the Kelsos from award-winning Ardsheal House at Kentallan. Restau is Scottish by nature rather than hype. Everything done in a country house style, down to the bar snacks. Best salmon starter in the capital? Lunch Mon-Fri, LO 9.30pm daily. — MED

120 D2

CIROS: 668 4207. 93 St Leonard's St. Small restau; small mention. Big secret.

121 E4

THE BEST MEXICAN RESTAURANTS

✠ **VIVA MEXICO:** 226 5145. Anchor Close, Cockburn St. Has it really been here 13yrs? That says something about its position among the come-and-go Mexicans. Still throws in something innovative now and again, although all the expected dishes are here. Reliable venue for those times when nothing else fits the mood but sour cream, tacos and limey lager; nice atmos downstairs. Another branch nr Tollcross at 50 E Fountainbridge. Lunch (not Sun) and LO 10.30pm. — INX

122 D3

TEX MEX: 225 1796. 47 Hanover St. Young, dumb and full of, er, tequila. A primal scream of a place in the city centre with all the usual Mexican faves, Jose Cuervo experiments and jolly soundtrack. Probably the best appointed of its ilk in Edin; infinitely preferable to others nearby. Slammersville. 12noon-1am Mon-Sat, until 12midnight Sun. — INX

123 C2

MOTHER'S: 662 0772. 107-109 St Leonard's St. Gr wee neighbourhood restau that manages to do the basics well (unlike many other Tex/Mexicans in town). Burgers, beef, burritos and one or two departures like Cajun veggie kebabs. Simple decor, good staff, proper coffee, home-made desserts. A hit, a palpable hit. Dinner 6pm-10pm Tues-Thurs and Sun, 6pm-10.30pm Fri-Sat. Cl Mon. — INX

124 E4

PANCHO VILLA'S: 557 4416. 240 Canongate. This spartan cantina remains a reliable exponent of what we've come to regard as Mexican cooking with nosh of the 'chilada, 'ajita, 'ichanga school. Plain décor, decent edibles, happy place. Lunch 12noon-2.30pm Mon-Sat, dinner 6pm-10.30pm daily. — INX

125 E3

THE BEST INDIAN RESTAURANTS

126 **SURUCHI:** 556 6583. 14a Nicolson St. Upstairs opp Festival Theatre. Owner
D3 from Jaipur called Mr Rodriguez plus chefs from Bengal, Delhi and S India
equals eclectic Indian menu. Unfussy decor and food with light touch (good
coconut rice) attracts students/academics from nearby univ as well as
theatregoers. This place is routinely praised to the skies; we agree. Live music
some nights. Lunch and LO 11.30pm daily. INX

127 **THE RAJ:** 553 3980. 89 Henderson St on S corner of The Shore, Leith. Take a
xE1 certain amount of care with the food, add Tommy Miah's marketing nous and
wadda-you-get? The most successful Indian/Bangladeshi restau in town. Regular
events (Bangladeshi New Year and Food/Culture Fest) add to the jollity; jars of
things available to buy and take home, also recipe books. Sun-Thurs still does
food 'at 1983 prices'. Try to sit up on the raised front area – better than the back.
Totally raj, in the non-Irvine Welsh sense. Lunch and LO 11.30pm 7 days. INX

128 **KALPNA:** 667 9890. 2-3 St Patrick Sq. The original Edin Indian veggie restau and
B1 still ragingly popular. Lighter, fluffier and not as attritional as so many tandooris.
Wed buffet quite a bargain. Report: 106/VEGN RESTAUS. Lunch Mon-Fri, dinner 7
days LO 10.30pm (10pm Sun). INX

129 **ANN PURNA:** 662 1807. 45 St Patrick Sq. Friendly and family-run Gujerati/S
B1 Indian veggie restau with seriously value-for-money business lunch Report:
107/VEGN RESTAUS. Lunch Mon-Fri, dinner 7 days LO 11pm. INX

130 **LANCERS:** 332 3444. 5 Hamilton Pl. Bengali/N Indian, off busy Hamilton Pl in
B1 Stockbridge/New Town area. A 'Brits in India, those were the days' type restau
(please may this go out of style soon) which can mean service on the precious
side, but the food speaks for itself. Dining area not so comfortable, but New
Townies with lovely kitchens do phone for a kerry-oot. 7 days. LO 11pm. INX

131 **INDIAN CAVALRY CLUB:** 228 3282. Athol Pl, W End, just off the main Glas rd,
B3 about 250m from Princes St. Bargain business lunch attracts the suits and another
restau you'll like if you go for the retro colonial style. We don't especially - but
no quibbles about the food. This seems an unlikely carry-out place, but they do
and it's one of *the* best in town. Lunch and LO 11.30pm daily. INX

132 **MOTHER INDIA:** 662 9020. 10 Newington Rd. Capital invaded by Weegie pakora
xE4 merchants shock! MI has branched out from its native Glas to offer
Edinbourgeois fresh-made pakora/snacks in the bar as well as a full monty restau
space (adj and upstairs). Food good in that Indo-wegian style; pakora fab. Odd
collision of student diner intent in premises that used to house one of the city's
swankiest Indians (the late Jaipur Manison). Opening TBC but 7 days. CHP/INX

133 **SHAMIANA:** 228 2265. 14 Brougham St, Tollcross. Recommended by everyone from
C4 Egon Ronay (not a recommendation we'd rely on) to Gordon Brown, a prominent
sign outside proclaims, 'Voted Best Restau in Scotland'. Well, up to a point Lord
Copper. Small eatery with quiet decor and v popular after rough patch. The food's
good again, the kulcha is fine; the staff could lighten up a bit. MED

134 **KEBAB MAHAL:** 667 5214. 7 Nicolson Sq. Nr Edin Univ and Festival Theatre. Gr
D4 vegetable biryani and delicious lassi for under a fiver? Hence high cult status.
Late-night Indo-Pakistani halal caff that attracts Asian families as well as students
and others who know. Kebabs, curries and sweets. Sun-Thurs 12noon-
12midnight, Fri-Sat 12noon-2am. No alco. CHP

135 **KUSHI'S:** 556 8996. 16 Drummond St. Long regarded as another cult classic, this
D3 basic Punjabi café (no restau twiddly bits) has been drawing in students and
others for cheap eats since Nehru was in nappies, or at least in the news. It's just
round the corner from Edin Univ's Old College. Short no-nonsense menu, cheap
no-nonsense prices. Unique, this is the stripped-down curry. Lunch Mon-Sat,
Dinner Mon-Thurs 5pm-9pm, Fri-Sat 5pm-9.30pm. Cl Sun. CHP

THE BEST FAR EASTERN RESTAURANTS

✝ **AYUTTHAYA:** 556 9351. 14B Nicolson St opp Festival Theatre. Good prospect pre- or post-show. Not large, not atmos restau, but attentive service, good vegn selection and a steady hand in the kitchen. We say the best Thai in town. Under the same ownership, is **SUKHOTHAI:** 229 1537. 23 Brougham Pl, Tollcross. Funkier eaterie where the waitresses do their best to look delicate but would perhaps feel more at home in baseball caps; all the more endearing. Sip your Singha Gold, don't think of Phuket. LO 10.20pm. **136 D3** INX

SIAM ERAWAN: 226 3675. 48 Howe St. On corner of Stockbridge area, the first proper Thai in town and still much enjoyed – manages that quiet eastern elegance v well. Same people also have **ERAWAN EXPRESS,** 220 0059, 176 Rose St, a kind of Thai canteen but not quite as inspired as its big sis although it's early days yet. Both establishments lunch Mon-Sat, dinner daily, LO 11pm. **137 C2**

DARUMA-YA: 554 7660. 82 Commercial St (entry via Dock Pl). Japanese dining in the capital has a history of high prices and high snob value but - but this restau is affordable and staff are happy to explain the unfamiliar dishes on offer. Bargain set meals. Frequented by visiting executives from W Lothian firms like Mitsubishi and NEC which says it all really. Lunch Tues-Sat, LO 10.30pm Mon-Sat. Cl Sun. **138 xE1** MED

YUMI: 337 2173. 2 W Coates (continues from Haymarket Terr, W End). The classier and more polite of the capital's Japanese restaus. Our intrepid researcher said it should go in the book over his dead body. Perhaps he will be appeased if we convey his opinion that this is the politest rip in town – sensationally expensive set meal based round tempura with Abigail's Party clientele. He thinks it sucks. If you're flush or an Abigail you may disagree. Let us know. **139 xA3** EXP

SINGAPURA: 538 7878. 69 North Castle St, corner of Queen St. Mainly Malaysian and Singaporean cuisine, which seems to mean from anywhere E of Suez. So there's a bit of Thai, some Indonesian and even things that look v Chinese. Some fish and tempe for vegetarians. Lunch Mon-Sat, dinner daily LO 10.30pm (11pm Fri-Sat). **140 C2** INX

THE KRIS: 556 6758. 20a Leopold Pl, London Rd. Odd setup. Malaysian restau in basement of unrelated and unremarkable hotel. At breakfast (8am-10am daily) it serves trad Brit-grub and early-morning body fiends from Edinburgh Club gym next door pop in for a bacon roll. Later the assorted gorengs come out to play. Genuinely different. Pop in on Tues night for the veggie buffet, or Wed when they do the full Malaysian one. Lunch Sun-Fri, LO 10pm daily. **141 E2** INX

TAMPOPO: 220 5254. 25a Thistle St. Not a restau at all but a gr wee Japanese noodle bar where you can pick up a ramen to go or one of those meal on a tray things. Open lunch Mon-Sat, also 6pm-9pm Tues-Sat. Cl Sun. **142 C2**

THE BEST CHINESE RESTAURANTS

KWEILIN: 557 1875. 19 Dundas St. Large New Town place with imaginative Cantonese cooking (real chefs); v good seafood and genuine dim sum in pleasant but somewhat uninspired setting. No kids allowed in the evening - somewhere for grown-ups to eat their quail in peace. Book. 7 days; LO 10.45pm. **143 C2** MED

DRAGON WAY: 668 1328. 74 South Clerk St. First thing that hits you as you go in - a big lacquer dragon wrapped around a pillar. Decor gloriously OTT and often described as 'Hollywood film set'. Good food mind you, and service, so one of the more interesting Chinese nights out. Lunch Mon-Fri and LO 10.30pm. **144 E4** INX

LOON FUNG: 556 1781. 2 Warriston Pl, Canonmills. Upstairs (and down when it's crowded), the famous lemon chicken and crispy duck go round for ever. And damned fine seaweed. LO 11.30pm (Sun-Thurs), 12.30am (Fri-Sat). **LOON FUNG:** 229 5757. 32 Grindlay St, opp Lyceum Theatre. A sister restau where seafood takes pride of place. **145 C1** INX

ORIENTAL DINING CENTRE: 221 1288. 8 Morrison St opposite cinema complex. It's a restau (Rainbow Arch) a dim sum basement bar and a late-night noodle shack (Ho Ho Mei - cash only, eat in or takeaway) so the choice is yours. Noodles 5.30pm-2.30am Mon-Sat. The restau is best option and best of the bunch by far in this neck of the W End; separate veggie menu. 12noon-11.30pm daily. **146 C3** INX

147 LUNE TOWN: 220 1688. 38 William St. The wee one hidden away behind the W End
B3 with porcelain figurines in the window - seems to have been there forever. Often busy, predominantly Cantonese nosh. Lunch and LO 11.30pm Mon-Fri. Open 3pm-12midnight Sat-Sun. MED

148 NEW EDINBURGH RENDEZVOUS: 225 2023. 10A Queensferry St. Hardly new and
B3 easy to miss (upstairs, next door to travel agents). Functional decor, short wine list to be taken seriously and dishes you won't find in any other Scottish Chinese restaus like shredded sea blubber or boneless ducks feet. (how do they breed the boneless ducks?) Lunch and LO 11pm Mon-Sat, 1pm-11pm Sun.

149 LEE ON: 229 7732. 3-5 Bruntsfield Pl. Through the big purple porthole-effect
C4 windows you'll find a restau popular with the city's Chinese community. Feels a bit *Man From UNCLE,* but the food's fine although veggies won't have that much to choose from. Lunch Mon-Sat 12noon-2pm, LO 12midnight Sun-Thurs, 1amFri-Sat. INX

150 GOOD YEAR: 229 4404. 21 Argyle Pl. Homely wee Chinese with a lighter than
xD4 usual touch on the cooking and good veggie choice. Location means it's v popular with students; you can BYOB (no licence). Dinner until 11pm, Cl Mon. Also has a takeaway nearby at 27 Roseneath Pl and another restau branch at 62 Ratcliffe Terr (667 7532) that does lunch as well as dinner 7 days. INX

151 YEE KIANG: 554 5833. 42 Dalmeny St. Peking home cooking courtesy of Johnny
E1 Wong deep in the heart of Hibbie land - feels like someone's living rm (probably because it was once). Halfway along a street of residential tenements, small, democratic and no half bad (local compliment). Does a mean fried crispy greens. An inside track choice. Tues-Sun 5pm-11.30pm. Cl Mon. INX

THE BEST RESTAURANTS FOR BURGERS AND STEAKS

152 ✚ ✚ **CHAMPANY'S:** 01506 834532. On A904, Linlithgow to S Queensferry rd
xA2 (3km Linlithgow), but nr M9 at jnct 3. Accolade-laden restau (and 'Chop and Ale House') different from others below because it's out of town (and out of most pockets). Both surf 'n' turf with live lobsters on premises. Good service, huge helpings (Americans may feel at home). Chop House 7 days, lunch and LO 10pm; restau lunch (not Sat) and LO 10pm, Cl Sun. INX/EXP

153 ✚ **BELL'S DINER:** 225 8116. 7 St Stephen St, Stockbridge. Bill Allan's almost-
C1 legendary small American diner actually predates the New Town (only kidding Bill). But it's been there a long time; an Edin reference pt. Successful formula with gr burgers and steaks to the fore, but veggies need not avoid - the best nutburger in town with mustard, roquefort etc. Staff are pretty cool too. Mon-Fri 6pm-10.30pm, Sat-Sun 12noon-10.30pm. INX

154 SMOKE STACK: 556 6032. 53-55 Broughton St. From the makers of The Basement
D2 (226/GREAT PUBS) comes something across the rd – a burgundy and blue diner rather than an orange and blue café/bar. Modish décor has a soothing effect. Loads of burgers (Scottish beef or vegn), seared salmon, etc. jollied along by a gr staff. (Santana at lunch time, just like old times). Proper menu available lunch and dinner, but food of some sort all day. Also does a good Sunday brunch (206/SUNDAY BREAKFAST). Open 12noon-10.30pm daily. INX

155 WIGWAM: 225 6127. 64 Thistle St. Bright colours in this central, but backstreet
C2 Native Americana diner. Mainly meat – a buffalo wings kinda joint – but vegn burgers too, with a good guacamole. Tex-Mex obviously, handy business lunch venue. Lunch and LO 11pm daily. INX

156 BUFFALO GRILL: 667 7427.12-14 Chapel St. Burn that beef! Although this diner
E4 trades on its reputation for steaks and suchlike, there are some Mexican concessions to veggies. Not big, so book and BYOB if you want. Lunch Mon-Fri, LO 10.15pm (Sun 10pm). INX

THE ROCK: 555 2225. Commercial St, Leith. Report: 59/BEST RESTAUS.

KID-FRIENDLY PLACES

✠ **UMBERTO'S:** 554 1314. Bonnington Rd Lane off Bonnington Rd to E of **157**
Newhaven Rd jnct. Whitewashed coach house hidden away in a v unlikely *xE1*
part of Leith. In contrast to some other 'kiddie' places, grown-ups would actually
want to eat here too. Downstairs is a civilised restau, upstairs a theme area for
kids where some booths form part of a big toy train and mobile youngsters can
run in and out of the Wendy house. Upstairs open Mon-Fri 12noon-2pm then
5pm-7.30pm; Sat 12noon-7.30pm; Sun 12noon-5.30pm. Downstairs lunch and
LO 10pm Mon-Sat.
INX

✠ **GIULIANO'S ON THE SHORE:** 554 5272. 1 Commercial St by the br. With its **158**
checked tablecloths, accented waiters and cheerful pizza/pasta menu, this is *xE1*
almost a cartoon version of an Italian restau – no slight intended – and kids love
it. Always a birthday party happening at w/ends. Lunch and LO 10.30/11pm.

YE OLDE PEACOCK INN: 552 8707. Newhaven Rd nr Newhaven Harbour and opp **159**
Harry Ramsden's (a more obvious place to take kids perhaps), but this is one of *xC1*
Edinburgh's unsung all-round family eateries for yrs, deserves wider recognition.
The fish here really is fresh, the menu is more adventurous than you'd think with
lots that wee kids and we kids like. High tea is a treat. Lunch and LO 9.30pm
Mon-Thurs, 12noon-9.30pm Fri-Sun.

FAT SAM'S: 228 3305. 56 Fountainbridge. Cavernous gr Italian-style barn with a **160**
couple of enormous television screens, fish tank and animatronic cartoon-like Fat *B3*
Sam to scare the unwary. The scale and sheer chutzpah appeal to children of all
ages (i.e. students' night out). Kids' menu has usual burgers, pizzas and all that
jazz. Main menu has all that's jazzier (swordfish, gnocchi) but really a place for
the young at heart and brain.
INX

BRIDGE INN, RATHO: 333 1320. Canal Centre, Ratho, W Lothian. 14km W of **161**
centre via A71, turning rt opp Dalmahoy Golf Club. Well worth the drive for an *xA4*
afternoon on, or by, the Union Canal. The Pop Inn Restau has special menus for
kids, play areas and numerous distractions. Sailings and walks. (270/BEST FOOD).
LO food 9pm, bar open 12noon-11pm (12midnight Fri-Sat).

CRAMOND INN: 336 2035. 30 Cramond Glebe Rd. At the R Almond as you hit **162**
Edin on the dual carriageway from the Forth Rd Br. This inn has put a lot of *xA2*
effort into attracting families with its indoor/outdoor play areas (Funky Forest).
If you've driven for hrs with a whingeing child and want steak and chips while
wee Daniel or Amy play themselves into a stupor then it's v convenient.
Otherwise a bit characterless. Lunch and LO 9.30pm 7 days. Open from lunch
straight through to close on Sat-Sun.

HUNTER'S TRYST: 445 3132. 97 Oxgangs Rd. Adj to Safeway, corner of Oxgangs **163**
Rd N. Big steaks in the boonies. If this place was another half mile S it would be *xC4*
up the Pentlands so a long schlep from town - but nr Fairmilehead exit from
bypass so happy for travellers. Alloa's bid for kid-friendliness sees a bright
Wacky Warehouse play area (it is a warehouse and it's v wacky) connected to
pub/inn selling pub/inn food. WW closes 7pm Mon-Wed, 9pm Sun-Thurs. Inn
until 11pm daily, LO food 9pm (snacks until close).

THE BEST TEAROOMS AND
COFFEE SHOPS

✠ ✠ **NATIONAL GALLERY OF MODERN ART CAFÉ:** Belford Rd (314/OTHER **164**
ATTRACTIONS). Utterly unbeatable on a fine day when you sit out on the *xA2*
patio by the grass, with sculptures around, have some wine and a plate of
excellent Scottish cheese and oatcakes. The hot dishes are excellent. Coffee and
cake whenever. Eventually it's back upstairs for the art. Oh well! Mon-Sat 10am-
4.30pm; Sun 2pm-4.30pm.

✠ ✠ **FRUITMARKET CAFÉ:** 226 1843. 29 Market St. Attached to the Fruitmarket **165**
Gallery, a cool spacious place for coffee, cake or a light lunch massively *D3*
improved under James Robb. Big windows to look out; good mix of tourists,
Edin faithfuls and art seekers – the latter go upstairs. Mon-Sat 10.30am-5.30pm,
Sun 12noon-5pm.

166 ☘ **QUEEN ST CAFÉ:** National Portrait Gallery, Queen St betw Hanover and St
D2 ☙ Andrew's Sq (313/OTHER ATTRACTIONS). And through the arched window . . . a civil slice of old Edin gentility. Serving seriously good light meals, tasteful sandwiches, coffee and cake – best scones in town, among other things. Mon-Sat 10am-4.30pm, Sun 2pm-4.30pm.

167 ☘ **CAFÉ FLORENTIN:** 225 6267. 8 St Giles St. Perhaps guilty of turning an entire
D3 ☙ generation of Edimbourgeois on to almond croissants and wicked tartelettes aux cassis. Uptown café with downtown décor, this establishment is the capital in a nutshell (or shortcrust pastry case). Advocates rub shoulders with student grunge queens over a blast of caffeine and Emmental baguette. Open 7am-11pm daily (2am Fri-Sat), really late during the Festival. Also at 5 N W Circus Pl, Stockbridge – with shop, 7am-7pm daily. And next to the Lyceum Theatre, Grindlay St (352/NIGHTLIFE), though we think this one has been a *pont* too far.

168 ☘ **LAIGH KITCHEN:** 225 1552. 117A Hanover St. You could only find somewhere
C2 ☙ like this in Scotland. Fundamental, friendly and 40-something; a basement coffee howf (Neil Grant the hairdresser is upstairs) with unimpeachable cakes, wooden seats and tables on a stone floor. Gr salads. Some folk live in the city for yrs and hardly notice it – others wouldn't go anywhere else. A true gem. Mon-Sat 8.30am-4pm.

169 **KAFFE POLITIK:** 446 9873. 146/148 Marchmont Rd. All black and white and wood
C4 and middle-Euro chic at another converted bank in the heart of student flat land. Rear wall speckled with quotes from assorted celebs - Indirha Gandhi to Woodrow Wilson. Damn fine cup of coffee, sodas, juice, soup 'n' sandwiches. Small choice of v good breakfasts (204/SUN BREAKFAST). 10am-10pm daily.

170 **KINNELLS:** 220 1150. 36 Victoria St. Stone and distressed tartan and aged - in an
D3 elegant way. A characteristic capital hideaway for wet and dry days. Some tables downstairs in the shop where they sell a big range of teas and coffees - but best to go up. Light meals, cake and good cheese. 10am-6pm daily (later during the Festival). Takeaway next door open Mon-Sat 10am-4pm.

171 **SEATTLE COFFEE COMPANY:** 226 3610. 128 Princes St, 2nd floor of Waterstone's
C3 bookshop. Dare we say better than the cramped original at London's Covent Garden? Easily. In among the books, a young and friendly staff dispense everything from caffè latte to iced Americano. Savouries and pâtisserie courtesy of Pâtisserie Florentin (see above). Nice view of the Castle. Open 9.30am-8pm Mon-Sat, 11am-5pm Sun. You'll find another more business-like branch in the basement of the Edin Solicitors Property Centre at 85 George St – also one more stand-alone branch to open winter 1997/98; they wouldn't say where.

172 **BROUGHTON STREET BRASSERIE:** 558 8868. 2 Broughton Pl. A high-ceilinged,
D2 chirpy kind of café where the coffee is resolute, the food is ok and the venue is airy with big windows quite excellent for whiling away a hazy afternoon. Has all that cakey, Italianate snack nacho stuff. And nice waitresses in a gay zone. Daily 8am-11pm.

173 **THE ELEPHANT HOUSE:** 220 5355. 21 George IV Bridge. Nr libraries and
D3 Edinburgh Univ, a rather self-conscious but big-time and well-run coffee shop with light snacks and multifarious choice of caffeines and tannins to speed your research. Cakes/pastries are bought in but can be taken out. Mon-Fri 8am-11pm, Sat-Sun 10am-11pm.

174 **COMMON GROUNDS:** 226 1416. 2/3 N Bank St, top of The Mound. We are family!
D3 The kind of coffee emporium where tourists wander in by accident and women can breast feed with impunity. Cake, light meals, insane range of espressos incl the 'Keith Richards' (a quadruple). Live music downstairs some nights, eclectic app - folk, cello, pop. 9am-10pm, Sat/Sun from 10am.

175 **G&T (GLASS & THOMPSON):** 557 0909. 2 Dundas St. Patrician New Town coffee
C2 shop and deli with contemporary good food attitude. Staff Like Us serve portions of spinach and nutmeg pâté discussing the holiday in Portugal you're going next week. Gr *antipasti*, salads and sandwiches to go. House copy of *Hello!* more thumbed than the *FT*. 8.30am-6.30pm, Sat till 5.30pm, Sun 11am-4.30pm.

176 **BOTANIC GARDENS CAFETERIA:** By 'the House' (where there are regular exhibs),
B1 within the grds (312/OTHER ATTRACTIONS). For café only, best to enter by Arboretum Pl. Catering-style food with light meals at lunch time, all self-service and distinctly lack-lustre. O/side, the view back N to the city skyscape is . . .

everything. There are also squirrels. 10am-5pm.

METROPOLE: 668 4999. 33 Newington Rd. Once a bank, now a civilised coffee house - the premises lend an air of art deco something. On a quiet afternoon it's where a Newington mum might mull over her life, the children at the nursery. Accompanied by a cappuccino with cinnamon . . . at least. 9am-10pm daily.
177
xE4

THE LOWER AISLE: Underneath St Giles Cathedral (316/OTHER ATTRACTIONS), enter round back via Parliament Sq, or through the body o' the kirk. Proximity of courts sees many legal eagles swooping in, tourists who have this book and regulars for coffee, tea, light meals. Mon-Fri 9am-4.30pm, Sun 10am-2pm. Cl Sat.
178
D3

CAFFE SARDI: 220 5553.18-20 Forrest Rd. More a restau perhaps with all the expected dishes but also serves a mean Danish pastry and espresso. Coffee machine is a Big Gold Dream and with waitresses from the old country and Italian television on cable; a hint of Soho's Bar Italia. Mon-Sat 9.30am-11pm, Sun 3pm-11pm.
179
D3
INX

ROUND THE WORLD: 15 N WCircus Pl, Stockbridge. Exceptional gift shop and kitchenware vendor with startling coffee bar in converted bank (once mine). Tea, cake and one of the v best espressos. Open 10am-6pm Mon-Sat.
180
B2

LA GRANDE CAFETIERE: 228 1188. 182/184 Brunstfield Pl. Coffee shop during the day, popular wee bistro at night INX. In among the assorted coffees and herbal teas, Bovril can be had. Nice restful alternative to the brashness of Montpeliers opp (74/CHAINS-U-LIKE). Something v attractive about their Venetian blinds. 9am-11pm, till midnight Thurs-Sat. 10am-6pm Sun.
181
C4

CALIFORNIA COFFEE CO: 228 5001. Once Edin had functional blue police boxes, just like the Tardis, which fell into disuse. Then an ex-solicitor and his pal decided to turn them into coffee booths. Similar range to the Seattle mob (above) - and unblended Java - so pretty good, also cakes and pastries. California booths can be found by the Odeon cinema (Clerk St) and top of Middle Meadow Walk (opp Forrest Rd). 7.45am-9pm Mon-Fri, 10am-9pm w/ends. Also Hope Park Cresc (E end of Meadows), 8.30am-7pm Mon-Fri, 10am-7pm Sat-Sun. Plans are afoot for as many as another 21 by summer 1999. Good news for those addicted.
182
E4/
D3

GREAT CAFÉS AND GREASY SPOONS

✝ **BLUE MOON CAFÉ:** 557 0911. 36 Broughton St. Longest-established gay café in the capital and still evolving (1860/GAY SCOTLAND). Now houses an espresso bar as well as the main bit with breakfast, snacks, meals or a drink. Female staff efficient, boys more spacey. Free condoms in the gents for the impecunious or impatient. Open 7am-12midnight Sun-Thurs, 7am-1am Fri-Sat. LO 40mins before close.
183
D2

NDEBELE: 221 1141. 59 Home St, Tollcross. The Ndebele are a southern African people, but this café has dishes from all over the continent so get your ostrich, mielie bread and biltong shavings here – or just have a coffee. Does loads of sandwiches, light meals and has a good groovalong soundtrack. Africa distant and usually hot, this delightfully chilled. Daily 10am-10pm.
184
C4

CENTRAL CAFÉ: 228 8550. 42 Home St, next to the Cameo Cinema. Graham Main's downtown deli/takeaway with urban cool and gr snacks and coffee (no cooking). Best music and crack in the area esp Faye on Sats. 8am-6pm. Cl Sun.
185
C4

LE MENU: 467 7847. 248 Dalry Rd. An oasis in the Gorgie lands - a small but superior café by day selling snacks and meals, then transforms into a down-home French bistro at night (BYOB). Dead cheap and pretty good fun. Mon-Sat 8.30am-9.30pm, shuts for an hour at tea time to effect its transformation.
186
A4
INX

CAFFE EUROPA: 667 6116. 53 Clerk St. Formerly Wayfarers, now a much more Italian-style establishment but still quite cheap. If you don't want the *pesce al forno*, there's always the Europa Mixed Grill – absolutely everything your medical adviser told you never to eat on one plate for a few quid. 10am-8pm daily.
187
E4

CANASTA: 554 5190. 10 Bonnington Rd, nr corner with Gr Jnct St, Leith. Adj small industrial estate this is a café for locals, not one of your downtown cappuccino numbers. Best omelettes in the burg, and usual café grub (haddock and chips, grills) and cakes home-made before you (I) get up. Di Rollo ice cream. Tea in a
188
xD1

mug. Takeaway. These people should win something. 8am-5pm. Cl Sun.

189 KUDOS: 558 1270. 2 Greenside Pl, next to Playhouse. Gay café/bar with light
D2 meal/snack menu, primitivist décor and a fair cup of tea or coffee. Nice place to dawdle over a cafetiere at an o/side table on a sunny afternoon. Open 12noon-1am daily, LO food 8pm.

KEBAB MAHAL: 667 5214. Nicolson Sq. Cult classic I (134/INDIAN RESTAUS).

KUSHI'S: 556 8996. 16 Drummond St. Cult Classic II (135/INDIAN RESTAUS).

INTERNET CAFÉS

190 CYBERIA: 220 4403. 88 Hanover St. If we can split hairs and say there's a
C2 distinction between cool and hip, then Cyberia takes the silicon wafer for coolest capital Internet cafe. Good coffee, fine sandwiches and cakes - you'd come for an espresso even if you had no interest in cyberspace. E-mail drop box facility, surfing sessions by the half hour etc. V chic, understated decor with sculpturey bits. E-mail: edinburgh@cybersurf.co.uk. Mon-Sat 10am-10pm, Sun 12noon-7pm. Staff most likely to say: 'Hi! And what can I getcha?' in fetching Antipodean accent.

191 ELECTRIC FROG: 226 1505. 42-44 Cockburn St. And this is the hippest Internet
D3 cafe in Edin. It has all the usual things - web access, IRC, coffee, snacks and cakes - but also regular exhibs of paintings and photography. On Sat from 4pm-7pm, DJs even pop in to do some pre-club choons of an eclectic stylee. E-mail: admin@electricfrog.co.uk. Staff most likely to say: 'Take it easy man.'

192 WEB 13: 229 8883. 13 Bread St. The city's most homely Internet boutique. At
C3 quieter times, bloke who looks much more attuned to messing around with motherboards will muck in to make you a sandwich. Again, all the usual facs for web, e-mail etc. Quarter and half-hour rates, dozen PCs, colour scanning, printing and all that jazz. E-mail: queries@web13.co.uk. Has a place in our researcher's heart as virtual home of the Aber FC e-mail list. Open Mon-Fri 9am-8pm, Sat 9am-6pm, Sun 11am-5pm. Staff most likely to say: 'Guy here wants to know about a Shockwave plug-in for Netscape 3.0 beta.'

THE BEST LATE-NIGHT RESTAURANTS

193 ✚ ✚ **BLUE:** 221 1222. Cambridge St. Upstairs in the Traverse Theatre
C3 building. The café bar associated with the Atrium (50/BEST RESTAUS), so the food's pretty good and you can graze and snack until midnight (same menu all day) in the place to be seen (60/BISTROS). INX

194 ✚ **WITCHERY:** 225 5613. Castlehill, top of Royal Mile nr the castle. Not open v
C3 late, but does take bookings up till 11.30pm, that crucial half hr beyond 11 that allows you to eat after the movies. Special after-theatre menu from 10.30pm has 2 courses for under £10, a v good deal from one of the best restaus in town. 7 days, lunch and LO 11.30pm (52/BEST RESTAUS).

195 ✚ **INDIGO YARD:** 220 5603. 7 Charlotte Lane. Late supper menu till 1am by
B3 fashionable, throbbing set of rms (with similar clientele). Seductive menu and situation. Report 63/BISTROS.

196 ✚ **NICOLSON'S:** 557 4567. 6A Nicolson St upstairs and opp Festival Theatre.
D3 Convenient and v Edin kind of bistro where you can eat lots or light (or just drink) till midnight every night (food LO 11.30pm). Diverse menu, diverse late-night people (67/BISTROS).

197 THE BLUE MOON CAFÉ: 556 2788. 36 Broughton St. Gay café bar in the quarter.
D2 Burgers to bagels into the night. Go on, they won't bite you (or maybe they will). LO 11.20pm (12.20am Fri-Sat) (183/BISTROS).

198 GORDON'S TRATTORIA: 225 7992. 231 High St. Although some tired and emotional
D3 late night visitors mistake this for a kebab house, it's v definitely Italian. Pasta 'n' pizza 'n' fish 'n' meat until the wee sma' hrs and ice cream to go. Sun-Thurs 12noon-12midnight. Fri-Sat 12noon-3am.

199 BAR ROMA: 226 2977. 39A Queensferry St. 2mins from the Caledonian Hotel at
B3 the W End of Princes St; busy day and night. Big rm with a real buzz attracts all sorts from late owls to families for Sun lunch. Basic pizza, pasta but smarter than

your av wine list. 12noon-12midnight Sun-Thurs; until 3am Fri-Sat.

PEPE'S: 337 9774. 96 Dalry Rd. Here's one to know about because it's good and friendly and open till 2.30am every night (though closed Tue). May be a schlepp to Dalry Rd on a cold night, but this pasta/pizza taverna is an oasis in the wee small hrs. Ask for the big glasses for the Amarone (93/ITALIAN RESTAUS). **200 A4 CHP**

ESSO SERVICE STATION: Canonmills. Bottom of Dundas St, then rt. 24hr petrol stn with shop that's like a mini-supermarket. Taxi drivers, clubbers and insomniacs drift down for magazines, coffee, pastries or anti-freeze in the middle of the night. Where to go for early editions of newspapers or to see desperate press researchers eat Pot Noodle while buying those early editions. Some people even come for petrol. **201 C1**

SAINBURY'S, BLACKHALL: Friday night 24hr shopping, snacking and going round and round. Convenient also for sleepwalkers. You never know who you'll find. **202 xA2**

GOOD PLACES FOR SUNDAY BREAKFAST

✚ **CAFÉ FLORENTIN:** St Giles St off Royal Mile opp Cathedral. The first to open for a civilised start (or finish). The authentically French coffee shop with croissants/pain au chocolat and the best whirly pastries in town. May be too early to eat cake. From 7am (167/TEAROOMS). **203 D3**

✚ **KAFFE POLITIK:** 446 9873. 146/148 Marchmont Rd (169/TEAROOMS). Quite possibly the best scrambled eggs with Emmental and chives on toast in town. And good coffee in serenely cerebral surroundings. From 10am. **204 C4**

MAISON HECTOR: Raeburn Pl. Brunch from 11am-4pm. Eggs Benedict, Finnan Haddies, Toulouse sausage, smoked salmon omelette or yer full-on fry-up in designery surroundings courtesy of Alloa Breweries. Sun papers provided (73/BISTROS). 11am-4pm. **205 B1**

SMOKE STACK: 556 6032. 53-55 Broughton St. In Maison Hector's league as far as Sun brunch is concerned – Arbroath smokies, Eggs Florentine or Benedict, all-out brekkers, vegn or carnivore style in burgundy and blue diner (154/BURGERS). 12noon-4pm. **206 D2**

IGUANA: 220 4288. 41 Lothian St. Even the appearance of a bizarre lentil croquette thing in the middle of the all-day vegn breakfast wasn't enough to stir the cynicism of our researcher. Service uploaded by blue-bloused femmes wearing Destiny Angel headsets in this café/bar with self-proclaimed cool (274/HIP). From 9am daily. **207 C3**

NEGOCIANTS: 45-47 Lothian St. Nr univ. Gr all-round pub (275/HIP), open v late and v early on Sun for breakfast. From 9am (brunch till 6pm). May be tables o/side. **208 C3**

BANNERMAN'S: Cowgate. Edin stalwart with gr atmos that serves a civilised Sun breakfast. Esp good in winter and univ term time. 11am onwards (248/REAL ALE). **209 D3**

THE BEST TAKEAWAY PLACES

210 ✤ **ROWLAND'S:** 225 3711. 42 Howe St. Top-notch New Town takeaway with
C2 ♈ hot dishes that really do change daily (never predictable – Sri Lankan chicken
curry for example). Interesting sandwich rolls, excellent cheeses, bread, cakes and
other carefully selected fare. Also does outside catering (mmm . . . those Thai
prawns) and you can phone your order. Open 6.30am-5pm Mon-Fri. Who comes
at half six? 'No-one,' says Rowland, 'but at least I'm here.' Cl w/ends.

211 ✤ **GLASS & THOMPSON:** 557 0909. 2 Dundas St. A deli and coffee shop on main
C2 ♈ st in New Town, but also takeaway sandwiches/rolls in infinite formats using
their drool-making selection of quality ingredients (breads, cheeses, salamis, etc.).
Ready-made Mediterranean snacks like wood-cooked aubergines, pâtés, tortes.
Take away to office, grds or dinner party. Excellent sit-in area and small terrace
for whiling away Edin days. Mon-Fri 8.30am-6.30pm, Sat 8.30am-5.30pm, Sun
11am-4.30pm.

212 ✤ **BUTLER'S:** 8 360. Lady Lawson St. Our office often make the detour over to
C3 ♈ Butler's at the top of the Grassmarket. Imaginative sandwiches and gr hot
dishes not lost by microwaving. Good vegn burger, cakes and pies. Cl Sat/Sun.

213 **THE GLOBE:** 558 3837. 42 Broughton St. A bright spot on the corner in the middle
D2 of Edinburgh's coolest st; this place is one of the reasons why. Open all day till
4/5pm for sandwiches/rolls and their toasted focaccia made as you wait. Big
window for people watching. Cl Sun.

214 **EASTERN SPICES:** 558 3609. 2 Canonmills Bri by the clock. Walk 100m in parts of
C1 the city and you'll trip over an Indian/Chinese takeaway. Choosing is a
nightmare, but according to the grapevine, and the taste test, his place is simply
better than most – phone in your order or just turn up wait. Also home delivery.
Full Indian menu from pakora to pasanda and vegn meals for one – if you're
down at the end of lonely st.

215 **CAPPUCCINO EXPRESS:** 622 7447. 62 Cockburn St. Some tables outside in summer
D3 and a few stools inside, but really an Italian takeaway par excellence. Soup, pasta
and fab ciabatta/focaccia sandwiches with some excellent deli-style fillings like
roast peppers in olive oil with mozzarella. Open 8am-6pm Mon-Sat. Cl Sun.

216 **CHARLIE McNAIR'S:** 226 6434. 30 Forrest Rd. Best takeaway on the S side. Fab
D3 sandwiches, Greek and Italian snacky things, some wine and bottles of v good
beer (Samuel Smith's for example). Mon-Fri 9am-5.45pm, Sat 9.30am-4pm. Cl
Sun.

217 **THE FORREST:** 225 4560. 52 George IV Br. Nr libraries and Edin Univ. Yer typical
D3 city sandwich howf, opening early to service workmen, office staff who skipped
breakfast and Japanese tourists up with the lark. My fave is sliced egg and tomato,
pepper and mayo roll. Mon-Fri 6.30am-3pm. Cl w/ends.

218 **SALVATORE'S:** 228 2334. 6 Gillespie Pl, Bruntsfield. Stonking Italian takeaway with
C4 all kinds of pizza, pasta and things. If you want to embark on a carbo-loading
sesh, this is a good place. 10am-11pm daily.

219 Last but far from least, **THE CLOCK** at the corner of The Shore and Bernard St in
xE1 Leith is a fine deli/takeaway with soup, sandwiches, quiche and chat.

SOME GREAT 'EDINBURGH' PUBS

✝ ✝ **PORT O'LEITH:** 58 Constitution St. You could walk into this bar once **220** every 5yrs and be hard pushed to see any changes. Occasionally wild, *xE1* usually interesting, always a gr leveller. The distilled spirit of auld Leith untouched by business/service developments in the last decade; no place for snobs. Good soundtrack both verbal and musical. Until 12.45am daily.

✝ **CAFÉ ROYAL:** Behind Burger King at the E end of Princes St, one of **221** Edinburgh's longest celebrated pubs. Unrelated to the London version, *D2* though there is a similar Victorian/Baroque elegance. Through the partition is the Oyster Bar (103/SEAFOOD RESTAUS). Central counter and often standing rm only. If you're going out on the tiles, the tiles here are a good place to start. Mon-Wed 11am-11pm, Thurs to 12midnight, Fri-Sat to 1am, Sun 12.30pm-11pm.

✝ **BENNET'S:** Leven St, by King's Theatre. Just stand at the back and watch light **222** stream through the stained glass on a sunny day. Same era as Café Royal and *C4* similar ambience, mirrors and tiles. Decent food at lunch (266/BEST FOOD). Till 11.30pm Mon-Wed, 12.30am Thurs-Sat, 11pm Sun.

BARONY BAR: 81 Broughton St. Real-ale venue with a young profile and **223** occasional live music, also some Belgian and wheat beers. Newspapers on hand to *D1* browse over a Sun afternoon breakfast or a (big) lunch time pie. Until 12 midnight Mon-Thurs, 12.30am Fri-Sat, 11pm Sun.

THE OYSTER BARS: Calton Rd (St James), 16A Queen St (Queen St); 28 W **224** Maitland St (W End); 10 Burgess St, The Shore (Leith). All mentioned elsewhere *D2/* but also here because, though the Brothers Donkin (whose empire they comprise) *C2* are Geordies, the Oyster Bars are a pure Edin creation. First two are most typical for ambience and good music (282/LIVE MUSIC).

EL BAR: 558 9139.15 Blackfriars St. It looks like a rm that used to be something **225** else with a few second-hand tables scattered around. It's small and it sells tapas, *D3* bocatas, Cruzcampo and plato del dia. Really scruffy, really Spanish and really good; we love it even when they run out of wine. Until 1am daily.

THE BASEMENT: 109 Broughton St. Now much-imitated which must count as **226** flattery, this is a chunky, happening sort of, er, basement where you can have *D2* Mex-style food during the day served by laaarvely staff in Hawaiian shirts. At night, the punters are well up for it – late, loud and lively. Daily until 1am.

BAR KOHL: 54 George IV Br. Nr libraries and univ. A dedicated vodka bar – first **227** in Europe – ideal if you want to get off your face drinking rare Siberian spirit with *D3* all the young dudes, but good anyway. Avoid sillier flavours like bubble gum. Cool Keith Haringesque toilets. Until 1am daily.

THE BANK BAR: The ground floor of the Bank Hotel on the corner of the Royal **228** Mile and South Br. V central wine bar/café in former banking hall, sym- *D3* pathetically redesigned to give it a relaxed, urbane, almost timeless atmos. Sometimes has jazz (15/INDIVIDUAL HOTELS). Till midnight; 1am Fri-Sat.

THE GREEN TREE: 180-184 Cowgate. Cement gdn in the Cowgate jungle. Lots of **229** people only ever go in summer when the weather's fine to have their 80/- alfresco. *D4* Until 12.30am.

Finally, 3 bars that say 'Edinburgh' (in various accents) as soon as you walk **230** through the door; all mentioned elsewhere, but worth another namecheck:

KAY'S BAR: 39 Jamaica St (250/REAL ALES).

MATHER'S: 1 Queensferry St (238/'UNSPOILT' PUBS).

ROBBIE'S: half-way down Leith Walk (235/'UNSPOILT' PUBS).

THE BEST OLD 'UNSPOILT' PUBS

Of course it's not necessarily the case that when a pub's done up, it's spoiled, or that all old pubs are worth preserving, but some have resisted change and that's part of their appeal. Money and effort are often spent to 'oldify' bars and contrive an atmos. The following places don't have to try. We are losing some from this list with every edition.

231 ⚓ **THE DIGGERS:** 1 Angle Park Terr. (Officially the Athletic Arms.) Jambo pub
A4 par excellence, stowed with the Tynecastle faithful before and after games. Still keeps a gr pint of McEwan's 80/-, allegedly the best in Edin. The food is basic pies and stovies. Until 12midnight Mon-Sat, 6pm Sun.

232 ⚓ **ROSEBURN BAR:** 1 Roseburn Terr on main Glas rd out W from Haymarket
xA3 and one of the nearest pubs to Murrayfield Stadium. Wood and grandeur and red leather, bonny wee snug, fine pint of McEwan's and wall-to-wall rugby of course. Heaving before internationals. Until 11pm Sun-Wed, 12midnight Thurs-Sat.

233 ⚓ **CLARK'S:** 142 Dundas St. A couple of snug snugs, red leather, brewery
C1 mirrors and decidedly no frills. Good McEwan's – just the place to pop in if you're tooling downhill from town to Canonmills. A local you would learn to love. Until 11pm (11.30pm Thurs-Sat).

234 ⚓ **BLUE BLAZER:** 2 Spittal St. No frills, no pretensions just wooden fixtures and
C3 fittings, pies and toasties in this fine S&N-owned howf that usually carries half a dozen real ales. More soul than any of its competitors nearby. Mon-Thurs 11am-12midnight, Fri-Sat 11am-12.30am, Sun 12.30pm-11pm.

235 ⚓ **ROBBIE'S:** Leith Walk on corner with Iona St. Real ales a-go-go in a smoky
xE1 old neighbourhood howf that tolerates everyone from the wifie in her raincoat to multi-pierced yoof of indeterminate gender. More rough than smooth of course, but with the footy on the box, pint of Bass, packet of Hula Hoops – this bar can save your life. Irvine wuz here, and me. Until 12midnight Mon-Sat, 11pm Sun.

236 **OXFORD BAR:** 8 Young St, one of the lanes behind W end of George St. No time
C2 machine needed – just step in the door to see an Edin that hasn't changed since nineteen-oatcake when real men drank heavy and the joke was on us. Some real ales but they're beside the point. Until 1am (12 midnight Sun).

237 **FIDDLER'S ARMS:** 9 Grassmarket. On a corner at the W end of the Grassmarket
C3 and about the only pub in the area that hasn't been interfered with, except for a relatively new carpet. McEwans 80/-, real fiddlers Mon nights. A pre-theme bar. Till midnight (1am Fri-Sat).

238 **MATHER'S:** 1 Queensferry St. Not only a reasonable real ale pub but almost worth
B2 visiting just to look at the ornate fixtures and fittings – frieze and bar esp. The latter looks as if it was carefully hewn from a single lump of wood by a Stakhanovite Victorian – they don't make 'em like that these days. Unreconstructed in every sense. Until 12midnight Mon-Thurs, 1am Fri-Sat, 11pm Sun. There's another, unrelated **MATHER'S** in Broughton St which is managing to keep its head above water in the city's grooviest thoroughfare by remaining pub-like and unpretentious.

239 **STEWART'S:** 14 Drummond St on the S side and just off S Br. Lino, beer,
D3 pensioners and folk who sing when in their cups. Few concessions to anything that has happened to the licensed trade since the 1960s. Until 12midnight Mon-Sat, 11pm Sun.

240 **ROYAL OAK:** Infirmary St. Tiny upstairs and not much bigger down. During the
D3 day, pensioners sip their pints (couple of real ales) while the cellar opens up later at night for its legendary folk sesh (293/LATE BARS). Open till 2am.

241 **THE CENTRAL BAR:** 7 Leith Walk. Once grand and still echoes its past, but now
D2 perhaps anachronistic. Tiled walls, ornate ceiling, green leather seats, cheap beer. It's been said before – if this was at the top of Leith Walk it would be yuppie paradise . . . but it's not. Worth a look though. Until 11pm daily.

242 **INTERNATIONAL BAR:** 15 Brougham Pl, Tollcross. A sprinkling of real ales in this
C4 locals' howf – some students given its location. No frills, but until 1am daily.

THE BEST REAL-ALE PUBS

Pubs on other pages may have or feature real ale, but the following are the ones where they take it seriously and/or have a good choice.

THE CUMBERLAND BAR: Cumberland St, corner of Dundonald St. After work this New Town bar attracts its share of irritating mobile phone addicts – but later the locals reclaim it and Camra (Campaign for Real Ale) supporters seek it out too. At any one time there's an average of 12 real ales on tap. Nicely appointed, decent pub lunches, unexpected beer grd. Mon-Wed until 11.30pm, Thurs-Sat to 12midnight. Sun opening in summer, may be extended.
243
C1

STARBANK INN: 64 Laverockbank Rd, Newhaven. On the seafront rd betw Newhaven and Leith. Usually 9 different ales on offer. Gr place to sit with pint in hand and watch the sun sink over the Forth. Also does food. Bar until 11pm Sun-Wed, 12midnight Thurs-Sat.
244
xC1

THE BOW BAR: 80 West Bow (halfway down Victoria St) they know how to treat drink in this excellent wee bar. Ask for a whisky – a fair few available – and there's no insane rigamarole about ice in the glass. Laphraoig, for example, comes straight as nature intended. Bliss. There are real ales you won't find anywhere else in the city. Until 11.30pm Mon-Sat, 11pm Sun.
245
D3

THE GUILDFORD ARMS: 1 W Register St. Just behind Burger King at E end of Princes St (opp Balmoral Hotel) and on same block as the Café Royal (221/GREAT 'EDINBURGH' PUBS). Lofty, ornate Victorian hostelry with loadsa good ales. Pub grub available on 'gallery' floor as well as bar. Sun-Wed until 11pm, Thurs-Sat until 12midnight.
246
D2

BERT'S: 29 William St. Rare ales, a suit and twinset crowd after work but a fair mix at other times in this faux Victorian bar. Decent pies for carnivores or veggies alike and a good place to escape from Princes St. shopping neurosis. Until 11pm Sun-Thurs, 12midnight Fri-Sat. More local **BERT'S** at 2 Raeburn Pl, Stockbridge.
247
B3/ B1

BANNERMAN'S: 212 Cowgate. Cellar-like stone-floored howf in the Old Town depths with decent selection of real ales, Sunday night folk (1882/FOLK MUSIC), a good bustle when busy and an eternal quality on those quiet winter evenings when you slump into one of the musty old chairs by the fire. Also does a good breakfast at w/ends 11am-4pm (209/SUN BREAKFAST). Till midnight, 1am Fri-Sat.
248
D3

THE CANNY MAN: 237 Morningside Rd. Officially known as the Volunteer Arms, but everybody calls it the Canny Man's. Good smorrebrod at lunch time (259/BEST FOOD), and wide range of real ales. Management have an attitude (problem).
249
xC4

KAY'S: 39 Jamaica St (off India St in the New Town). Go on an afternoon when gentlemen of a certain age talk politics, history and football over pints of real ale. The bow-tied barman patiently serves. All red and black and vaguely distinguished with a tiny snug – The Library. Until 11.45pm (11pm Sun).
250
B7

CASK & BARREL: 115 Broughton St. Wall-to-wall distressed wood, gr selection of real ales and the only bar in Edin where they've realised that samosas make ideal snacks. Also does pub grub, sometimes Thai-flavoured. Until 12.30am Sun-Wed, 1am Thurs-Sat.
251
D2

CLOISTERS: 26 Brougham St, Tollcross. Nine real ales on tap in this simple and unfussy bar with its wooden panelling and laid-back app. Same owners as Bow Bar (*above*). Basic pub grub at lunch times, bar closes 12midnight (12.30am Fri-Sat).
252
C4

CALEY SAMPLE ROOM: 5/8 Angle Park Terr. Half-owned by the nearby (independent) Caledonian Brewery, the CSR sells all the expected Caledonian real ales and a couple of guests besides. A neighbourhood bar most of the time, a haven for home and away fans before and after games at Tynecastle. Basic pub lunches Mon-Fri, drink served until 12midnight Sun-Thurs, 1am Fri-Sat.
253
A4

THE MERMAN: 42 Bernard St, Leith. Formerly Tod's Tap and hasn't changed much. Good range of real ales, real fire in the big rm through the back. Real pub really. Promotes itself as an antidote to orange and blue hip bar fatigue. Until 11pm (12midnight Fri-Sat).
254
xE1

CALEDONIAN BEER FESTIVAL: An annual event held around the first w/end in June at Edin's own – and independent – Caledonian Brewery, a red-brick Victorian
255

pile at 42 Slateford Rd (on rt-hand side going out of town). It's a gr site, 50 real ales from Adnams to Whitbread on tap, food and music (esp jazz) on the Thurs-Sat evenings and Sun afternoon in the brewery's own Festival Hall, a refurb bottling plant. See local press for details or call 337 1286. The Festival Hall also hosts ceilidhs every Sat (1892/CEILIDHS).

PUBS WITH THE BEST FOOD

257 ✚ **SHORE BAR:** 553 5080. 3 The Shore. A bistro/restau but the same
xE1 ♈ (blackboard) menu faster and friendlier in the bar (where you can smoke). Light meat dishes, lots of fish and always something vegn. Lunch and LO 10pm (65/BISTROS).

258 ✚ **KING'S WARK:** 554 9260. 36 The Shore, on the corner of Bernard St. Woody,
xE1 ♈ candlelit, absolutely fine. A business haunt at lunch times and a good informal restau-come-bar in the evenings. Scottish slant on the menu, incl excellent fish in beer batter and chips; also food at the bar and real ales. Lunch and LO 10pm. Bar open to 11pm, 12midnight Fri-Sat.

259 ✚ **THE CANNY MAN:** 447 1484. 237 Morningside Rd (aka The Volunteer Arms)
xC4 ♈ on the A702 via Tollcross, 7km from centre. Idiosyncratic renowned eaterie with a certain hauteur. Carries a complement of malts as long as a gr big long thing, serious wine list and excellent smorrebrod lunch attack (12noon-3pm daily). B-listed building with monkey-jacketed bar staff, cigars for sale – a shrine to the good life. No loonies or undesirables welcome (you may be tested). Until 12midnight Mon-Sat, 11pm Sun (249/REAL ALE).

260 **BLACK BO'S:** 557 6136. 57 Blackfriars St. Adj to vegn restau of same name, the bar
D3 offers good coffee, snacks and meals during the day with the restau taking over in the evening. Where to go for vegn haggis filos with rosemary and green ginger sauce. DJs at night. 11am-1am daily.

261 **CELLAR No. 1:** 220 4298. 1a Chambers St. Former bistro now knocking out a fine
D3 standard of bar food with a Med twist from its subterranean premises. Lunch and LO 10pm Mon-Sat, no food Sun. Thurs is flamenco night; Wed, Fri, Sat live jazz. Bar Mon-Thurs 12noon-1am, Fri-Sat 12noon-3am, Sun 6pm-1am. (Same people have opened new bistro on corner of Chambers St/S Br (downstairs v much preferred).

262 **OLD CHAIN PIER:** 552 1233. 1 Trinity Cres, on the Forth just W of Newhaven
xD1 Harbour. Rt on the waterfront, off the beaten track. Been here for yrs but now considerably smarter than it was – still v approachable with friendly staff. Well-kept real ale, gr bar snacks (stilton with oatcakes, interesting toasties) and excellent-value bar meals. LO food 8pm (but ask nicely after 8 and you never know). Bar 12noon-11pm Sun-Wed, to 12midnight Thurs-Sat.

263 **DRUM AND MONKEY:** 538 8111. 80 Queen St. Clubby, city suit kind of bar with
C2 odd lady taking coffee in the pm. Smarter than your average pub grub with occasional Mediterranean influences and Scottish faves. Jazz on Sat afternoons, food until 10pm, couple of real ales. Bar 11am-12midnight Mon-Thurs, to 1am Fri-Sat.

264 **SHEEP'S HEID:** 661 1020. Causeway, Duddingston Village. An 18th-century
xE4 coaching inn 10km from centre behind Arthur's Seat and reached most easily through the Queen's Park. Restaurant upstairs and decent pub food down, including alfresco dining in summer. The village and the nearby wildfowl loch should be strolled around if you have time. Food till 9pm incl Sun.

265 **THE GOLF TAVERN:** 229 3235. 31 Wright's Houses. Off Bruntsfield Pl facing on to
C4 the Links. V English country pub style with hearty food (beef 'n'ale pie, sausage and mash), couple of Chesterfields for slumping purposes; clientele can be a bit XR3i. LO food 7.30pm. Bar closes 12midnight daily.

266 **BENNET'S:** 229 5143. 8 Leven St, next to the King's Theatre. An Edin standby, it
C4 could be listed for several reasons (222/GREAT 'EDINBURGH' PUBS), not least for its honest-to-goodness (and cheap) pub lunch. À la carte (sausage, fish, steak pie etc) and daily specials under the enormous mirrors. Lunch only, 12midday-2pm.

267 **THE ABBOTSFORD:** 225 5276. 3 Rose St. A doughty remnant of Rose St drinking
D2 days of yore, and still the best pub lunch nr Princes St. Nothing fancy in the à la

carte of grills and mainly meaty entrées. Huge portions. LO in bar 3pm. Restau upstairs serves food in evening too LO 9.45pm. Bar until 11pm. Cl Sun.

THE DOME: 624 8624. 14 George St. Terribly big. Former bank and grandiose in the way that only a converted temple to Mammon could be. Main part sits 15 metres under the elegant domed roof with island bar and raised platform at back for diners (groovy stained glass with snake motif). Staff almost impeccable, pricey menu; you come for the surroundings more than the victuals (MED). Lunch 12noon-3pm, LO dinner 10pm daily. Also snack menu for casual diners away from roped-off posh nosh area. Adj real ale art deco bar Frazers was dreamed up by a marketing person having a bad concept day and may be changing as we go to press. Final bit, downstairs : Why not? a nightclub for over-25s: well, let us count the ways . . . Main bar Sun-Thurs until 11.30pm, Fri-Sat until 1am.   **268** *C2*

Outside Town

THE SUN INN, LOTHIANBURN: 663 2456. On a bend of the A7 nr t/off for Newtongrange, under mega viaduct, 18km S of city centre. Happy, homely pub in the unfashionable netherlands of Midlothian. Bistro-style food, lunch and LO 9.30pm. Always a couple of real ales – one from the Broughton Brewery. MED.INX   **269** *xE4*

THE BRIDGE INN/THE POP INN, RATHO, W LOTHIAN: 333 1320. 16km W of centre via A71, turning rt opp Dalmahoy Golf Club. Large choice of comforting food in canalside setting. Has won various awards, including accolades for its kids' menu. Restau, bar food and canal cruises with nosh. Pop Inn 12noon-9pm daily. Restau lunch daily and LO 9pm Mon-Sat. Bar until 11pm, 12midnight Fri-Sat. (161/KID-FRIENDLY.)   **270** *xA4*

DROVER'S INN, E LINTON: 01620 860298. 5 Bridge St. Off the A1, 35km S of city. Fair way to go for eats, but don't think about the A1, think about the food, much improved of late. A classic village pub with warmth and delicious meals in bistro beside bar or restau up top. Beer grd outback is o/looked and trains whoosh by, but on a sunny day, partake their excellent lunch here. Lunch and dinner (6-9.30pm) daily.   **271** *xE2*

THESE ARE HIP

INDIGO YARD: 220 5603. 7 Charlotte Lane, off Queensferry St. Tucked away in the W End, this spacious designer café bar (numero uno 1997) offers exposed brickwork, balcony tables, booths and babes in blue of both genders serving good food and drink. More Med than Mex cuisine with flexible menu, but possibly too loud later on for serious dining (63/BISTROS). Until 1am daily. Same people have **THE IGUANA** (*below*) and **MONTPELIERS** (74/CHAINS-U-LIKE).   **272** *B3*

TRAVERSE THEATRE BAR: Downstairs at the Traverse Theatre, Cambridge St. One of the first Edin bars to go in for designer furniture, rolling art exhibs and all that jazz. Still trendy if a bit arch. Catering handled by Henderson's (109/VEGN RESTAUS), 10am-8pm if no show, until 10pm when there's something on. Gr buzz pre- and post-performance. Bar until 12midnight Sun, Tues, Wed; 11pm Mon; 1am Fri-Sat. Much later during Festival when it's one of the nerve centres. Good place to meet nice people.   **273** *C3*

IGUANA: 220 4288. 41 Lothian St. From the makers of Montpeliers (74/CHAINS-U-LIKE) comes this self-consciously clubby café/bar over the road from Edin Univ's Bristo Sq buildings - so v studenty in term time. DJs (Thurs-Sat) play ambient/dub/dance later on. During the day people eat, drink or sip coffee in calm, cool surroundings (by Glasgow's Graven Images). Good all-day veggie breakfast, LO food 8.30pm. 9am-1am daily.   **274** *C3*

NEGOCIANTS: 225 6313. 45-47 Lothian St. (Pron 'Nigoshunts' by locals.) Mirrors, food, space and shooters (non-lethal variety) upstairs; dancefloor, DJs (every night), drink and more drink down. Range of clients from civilised bagel-nibblers mid-morning to Chimayed-out dance fiends in the wee small hours. Zanier and less pretentious than Iguana next door, claim the waitresses - but just as studenty. Table service lacks pace - but hey! LO food 2.30am. Open 9am-3am daily.   **275** *D3*

SIRIUS: 555 3344. 7-10 Dock Pl, Leith. 'Designed' without being dreadful - quite harmonious really and almost democratic in the clientele mix it attracts. Gr energy about the place on the night-out nights, cocktail pitchers abound - wet   **276** *xE1*

Wed afternoon muzak would be *Wonderwall*. Does coffee and food in that eclectic, flexible style (i.e. Med-Mex). Until 12midnight Sun-Wed, 1am Thurs-Sat.

277 **PO-NA-NA:** 226 2224. 43b Frederick St. A case of souk it and see in this popular N
C2 African theme bar - part of a chain but not obstrusively. Does v reasonable snacks, functions as a bar until 11pm, then it's more of a club with entry charge and DJs. 7 days until 3am. The fag machine is covered in zebra skin. Fun.

278 **THE OUTHOUSE:** 557 6668. 12a Broughton St Lane. Not an avowedly gay
D2 establishment, but happily mixed of an evening when there's a nice atmo in this v contemporary café/bar. Modish food available 12midday-4pm for self-conscious business diners and a regular Sun barbecue on the patio (not the greatest of views though). A Portishead remix kind of place. Until 1am.

279 **BAROQUE:** Broughton St. Once more into the breach for Med-Mex. Decor-wise,
D2 the designer was presumably given a few monographs on Matisse, some on Gaudí, a lot of drugs and told to do something extravagant. The result is the most orange and blue bar in Edinburgh but potty enough to be appealing. Our design consultant said: "Why have recessed low-voltage lights then turn them up bright?" Who cares? not here . . . LO food 7pm, bar until 1am daily.

280 **THE CATWALK CAFE:** 478 7770. 2 Picardy Pl on the 'Playhouse R/bout' at top of
D2 Broughton St. Concrete gray - maybe the new blue 'n' orange. Who knows because this latest addition to 'hip bars in Edin' opened as we went to press. Two levels, a catwalk. Food till 6pm, downstairs DJ. A design departure in the city, its future seems assured; at least until the next time. We'll see.

PUBS AND CLUBS WITH GOOD LIVE MUSIC

281 **TRON CEILIDH HOUSE:** 220 1550. 9 Hunter Sq, behind Tron Kirk. Three levels.
D3 Simple bar on ground floor with folk jam on Sat-Sun afternoons; labyrinth at basement one with similar folk jam sesh Sun-Thurs evenings (1882/FOLK MUSIC); basement 2 has comedy club, songwriters night and yet more folk. Some gr real ales – always something going on. Sun-Thurs to 12midnight, Fri-Sat to 1am.

282 **THE OYSTER BARS: ST JAMES:** 557 2925. Calton Rd opp St James Centre and off the
D2/ top of Leith Walk. One of 4 'Oyster Bars', this is the one with live music on Wed
C2 nights. Also does food daily LO 10pm. More music at the **QUEEN ST OYSTER BAR** (basement on the corner of Queen St and Hanover St). Wee bands Mon, Tues and Thurs (226 2530). Other Oyster Bars which are worth a visit if you like their style
xE1/ are at **THE SHORE** (Leith), the **WEST END** (W Maitland St). All open till 1am (LATE
B3 BARS, *p. 43*).

283 **THE VENUE:** 557 3073. Calton Rd behind the main post office and Waverley Stn.
D2 Edinburgh's major live music venue at club level with well-established dance clubs most nights like Pure and Tribal Funktion (1869/NIGHTCLUBS). For live music, it's on the UK club circuit, so often notable bands and the best of the Scottish wannabes. Watch for posters and flyers.

284 **LA BELLE ANGELE:** 225 2774. 11 Hasties Close behind the Kitchen and the Living
D3 Rm in the Cowgate (LATE BARS, *p. 43*). Combines its role as a DJ club and live music venue well. Rm has attitude and atmos.

285 **THE CAS ROCK:** 229 4341. 104 W Port. Nr art college. Musical oasis in Edinburgh's
C3 pubic triangle, the area full of bars with 'dancers'. No-nonsense, Indie/alternative thrashing in small space. Hot, sweaty, beery rock 'n' roll. Until 1am daily.

286 **THE LIQUID ROOM:** 225 2564. At the top of Victoria St. Formerly the Music Box,
D3 recently given a face lift. Enter at st level and descend to watch bands before they go on to greater things (or not). For details consult *The List*. Times vary. Also a major club venue for clubs called Evol and Liquid.

287 **SUBWAY:** 225 6766. Cowgate, under George IV Br. Cavernous grungey rock'n'
D3 rolling venue with bar. Fairly but not exclusively studenty, live music some nights, DJs on others playing all sorts from 1960s to cheesy dance. Open 5pm-
C3 3am daily. Also **SUBWAY WEST END**, 23 Lothian Rd. Much more a student haunt, glitzier than its Cowgate cousin – nothing live but DJs playing Indie, 1970s, 1980s and assorted. Lager, lager, lager etc.

NEGOCIANTS: 225 6313. 45 Lothian St. Basement DJs in a bar for the young dudes, dancefloor. Upstairs is a café bar, serving interesting food; bustling all day with studentish crowd, LO food 2.30am. Open 9am-3am daily. **IGUANA** next door also does cool tunes. Fuller report on both: 274/275/HIP. 288 D3

THE JAFFA CAKE: 229 7986. 28 King's Stables Rd. Hard drinking club for teenies. Six cheap vodkas, a snog in the toilets then some serial vomiting a bit later. Lots of pop/chart/dance cheese but this club is also home to FBI (alternate Sats), one of Edinburgh's top Indie nights. Open Thurs-Sat until 3am. Cheap admn. 289 C3

THE BEST LATE BARS

NEGOCIANTS: 45 Lothian St, by the Univ Union buildings. Civilised café/restau/bar upstairs and basement with DJs. Open till 3am every night. Further details: 288/LIVE MUSIC; 208/SUN BREAKFAST). 290 D3

PO-NA-NA: 43B Frederick St. More of a club than a bar later on perhaps but open to 3am daily. Think Morocco. Young crowd; queue at w/ends (277/HIP). 291 C2

THE LIVING ROOM: 235 Cowgate, next door to The Kitchen (*see below*). A pavement with a roof, a balcony and some designer twiddles with its share of lassies in microfrocks and proto-Damons and Liams who may manage a club later, or may not. 7pm-3am daily. Pretty dead until after 10-ish though. Commercial dance 7 nights. Dancefloor (handy that). Bit tense. (If you complain once more, you'll meet army of me. Bouncers, that is . . .) 292 D3

THE ROYAL OAK: Infirmary St nr the top and S Br. Run by ex-*White Heather Club* dancer Sandra Adams, this place is a folk institution. Locals drink in the tiny bar upstairs during the day, live sessions kick-off downstairs every night around 10pm with well-kent faces dropping in occasionally for the tunes and the singalong. Until 2am daily (240/'UNSPOILT' PUBS). 293 D3

IGUANA: 41 Lothian St. Oh-so-cool establishment with DJs spinning some v nice choons. Food until 8pm, bar daily to 1am (274/HIP; 207/SUN BREAKFAST). 294 C3

INDIGO YARD: 7 Charlotte Lane Major design statement. Heaving with 20/30 somethings, popular, food until late, bar until 1am (272/HIP). If you don't want to shout over the top of indie/dance crossover, try Mathers nearby (238/'UNSPOILT' PUBS), in every sense the opp corner. 295 B3

THE BASEMENT: Broughton St. It's gr to be straight? The place for hets to hang back late in Broughton St (a neighbourhood of many gay nightspots). Basementful of mixed groovers (though not much rm to move or shake). Until 1am. 296 D2

BAROQUE: Broughton St. Design-mania. Even more orange and blue than those above. Décor will keep you awake if nothing else. Till 1am (279/HIP). 297 D2

ST JAMES OYSTER BAR: Calton St off top of Leith Walk. Gr atmos, always busy, music on Weds (282/LIVE MUSIC). Nachos, other happy food, special beer/eats offers. This OB (and others on this page) owned and run by the estimable Brothers Donkin. All open 7 days till 1am. 298 D2

QUEEN ST OYSTER BAR: 16A Queen St, nr corner of Hanover St. Central, small; always buzzing. The luncheon-in-a-cave OB. Live music 3 nights (282/LIVE MUSIC). 299 C2

THE KITCHEN: 237 Cowgate. An ante-rm for the city's club scene, this is the place if you want a pint of 80/- before moving on. Taken over by S&N recently. DJs Thurs-Sat play hip hop, house and disco/funk/soul – loadsa students. Pub grub until 7pm daily. Bar 11am-1am daily. V different to The Living Rm (*see above*). 'We hate them,' said the barman. 300 D3

LEITH OYSTER BAR: 10 Burgess St, on the shore of Water of Leith. Front bit is quite restauranty. Just holds its end up among the much more chic local eateries. The 'ach, fancy a lasagne and a couple o' pints?' OB. 301 xE1

WEST END OYSTER BAR: 28 Maitland St, beyond Princes St at Haymarket. The big-screen television football-type OB. 302 B3

THE BOUNDARY BAR: 379 Leith Walk. Early rather than late – people really do turn up here at 5am for a drink because that's when it opens. Basic and unlovely old beer outlet on the old boundary betw Edin and Leith, and betw now and then. Does it really matter when it shuts? 303 E1

THE MAIN ATTRACTIONS

304
C3
✚ ✚ ✚ **EDINBURGH CASTLE:** Go to Princes St and look up. The main attraction, extremely busy in summer. Tartan tea cosies on sale in the shop rake in the bawbees. And yet. St Margaret's 12th-century chapel is simple and beautiful, the rolling history lesson that leads up to the display of Scotland's crown jewels is fascinating; the newly installed Stone of Destiny is a big deal to the Scots (though others may not see why). And, ultimately, the Scottish National War Memorial is one of the most genuinely affecting places in the country – a simple, dignified testament to shared pain and loss (1407/CASTLES). Last ticket 45mins before closing. Apr-Sep 9.30am-6pm, Oct-Mar 9.30am-5pm. HS

305
E2
✚ ✚ **HOLYROOD PALACE:** Foot of the Royal Mile. Queenie's N Brit time-share – she's here for a wee while at end June/beginning July every yr. Large parts of the palace are dull (Duke of Hamilton's loo, Queen's wardrobes) so only a dozen or so rms are open, most dating from 17th century but couple from the earlier 16th-century bit. Lovely cornices abound. Anomalous Stuart features, adj 12th century abbey ruins quite interesting. Upper-class shop, so get your souvenirs here. Apr-Oct: Mon-Sat 9.30am-5.15pm (last ticket), Sun 9.30am-4.30pm (last ticket). Nov-Mar: 9.30am-3.45pm (last ticket) daily. Now open New Year's Day. HS

306
C3
D3
E3
E4
✚ ✚ **THE ROYAL MILE:** The High St, the medieval main thoroughfare of Edin following the trail from the volcanic crag of Castle Rock and connecting the two landmarks above. Heaving during the Festival but if on a winter's night you chance by with a frost settling on the cobbles and there's no one around, it's magical. Always interesting with its wynds and closes (Dunbar's Close, Whitehorse Close, the secret grd opp Huntly House), but lots of tacky tartan shops too. See it on a walking tour – there are several esp at night (ghost/ghouls/witches etc). Some of the best actually take you under the st (1559/SPOOKY PLACES). Mercat Tours (661 4541) are pretty good. Also Robin's (661 0125) and Witchery (225 6745).

307
D3
✚ ✚ **ROYAL SCOTTISH MUSEUM:** Chambers St. From the big whale skeleton to archaeological artefacts, design exhibs to stuffed elephants, it's all here. Building designed by Captain Francis Fowkes, Royal Engineers, and completed in 1888. Ab fab atrium soars way up high. Extension (with the story of Scotland) has ETA of St Andrew's Day 1998 and is tipped to be one of the most important new buildings of the decade. 10am-5pm Mon-Sat, 12noon-5pm Sun. The huge and impressive new extension opens 1998.

308
C2
✚ ✚ **NATIONAL GALLERY** and **ROYAL SCOTTISH ACADEMY:** The Mound. The National is the rear of the 2 neoclassical buildings on Princes St and houses a superb collection of Old Masters in a series of hushed salons. Many are world famous, but you don't emerge goggle-eyed as you do from the National in London – more quietly elevated (FREE). The Playfair 'temple' on Princes St itself is the **RSA**; changing exhibitions which in early summer and midwinter show work from contemporary Scottish artists (ADMN). Both galleries 10am-5pm. Sun 2-5pm.

309
xA3
✚ ✚ **EDINBURGH ZOO:** 334 9171. Corstorphine Rd. 4km W of Princes St, buses from Princes St Gdns side. Whatever you think of zoos, this one is highly respected and its serious zoology is still fun for kids (organised activities in Jul/Aug). The penguins waddle out at 2pm daily and the melancholy, accusing eyes of the wolves connect with onlookers in a profoundly disconcerting manner. Open AYR. Mon-Sat 9am-6pm, Sun 9.30am-6pm. ADMN

310
xE4
✚ ✚ **ROYAL COMMONWEALTH POOL:** 667 7211. Dalkeith Rd. Hugely successful pool complex which includes a 50m main pool, a gym, sauna/steam rm/suntan suites and a jungle of flumes. Goes like a fair, morning to night. Some people find the water overtreated and too noisy, but Edin has many good pools to choose from; this is the one that young folk prefer. Some lane swimming. Mon-Fri 9am-9pm, Sat-Sun 10am-4pm (7pm in summer).

311
xA2
✚ ✚ ✚ **THE FORTH BRIDGE:** S Queensferry, 20km W of Edin via A90. First turning for S Queensferry from dual carriageway; don't confuse with signs for road br. Or train from Waverley to Dalmeny and walk 1km. Knocking on now and showing its age, the Bridge was 100 in 1990. But still . . . Can't see too many private finance initiative wallahs rushing in to do anything of similar scope these days – who would have the vision? An international symbol of Scotland, it should be seen. How about from the N Queensferry side?

THE OTHER ATTRACTIONS

✠ ✠ **ROYAL BOTANIC GARDEN:** 552 7171. Inverleith Row, 3km from Princes St. **312**
Bus nos 23, 27. Enter from Inverleith Row or Aboretum Pl. 70 acres of *B1*
ornamental grds, trees and walkways; a joy in every season. Tropical plant houses,
well-groomed rock and heath grd and enough space just to wander. New Chinese
Grd coming on nicely, precocious squirrels everywhere. Gallery with occasional
exhibs and café with outdoor terrace for serene afternoon teas (176/TEAROOMS).
But don't jog – or they'll getcha. The natural high. Open 7 days 10am-4pm (Nov-
Feb), 6pm (Mar-Apr/Sept-Oct) and till 8pm (May-Aug).

✠ ✠ **NATIONAL PORTRAIT GALLERY:** 556 8921. 1 Queen St. Sir Robert Rowand **313**
Anderson's fabulous and custom-built neo-Gothic pile houses paintings *D2*
and photos of the good, gr and merely famous. Danny McGrain hangs out next
to the Queen Mum and Nasmyth's familiar pic of Burns is here. Good venue for
photo exhibs, beautiful atrium with star-flecked ceiling and frieze of (mainly)
men in Scottish history from a Stone-Age chief to Carlyle. Splendid. Gr café
(166/TEAROOMS). Mon-Sat 10am-5pm, Sun 2-5pm.

✠ **GALLERY OF MODERN ART:** 556 8921. Belford Rd. Betw Queensferry Rd and **314**
Dean Village (nice to walk through). Best to start from Palmerston Pl and *xA2*
keep left. Former school with permanent collection from Impressionism to
Hockney and the Scottish painters alongside. An intimate space where you can fall
in love with paintings on winter afternoons. Important temporary exhibs. The café
is excellent (314/TEAROOMS). 10am-5pm, Sun 2pm-5pm.

✠ ✠ **MUSEUM OF CHILDHOOD:** 225 2424. 42 High St. Local authority-run **315**
shrine to the dreamstuff of tender days where you'll find everything *D3*
from tin soldiers to Lady Penelope on video. Full of adults saying, 'I had one of
them!' Child-size mannequins in upper gallery can foment an *Avengers*-era
spookiness if you're up there alone. Mon-Sat 10am-5pm. Cl Sun.

✠ **ST GILES' CATHEDRAL:** Royal Mile. Not a cathedral really, although it was **316**
once – the High Kirk of Edin, Church of Scotland central and heart of the *D3*
city since the 9th century. The building is mainly medieval with Norman
fragments and all encased in a Georgian exterior. Lorimer's oddly ornate Thistle
chapel and the 'big new organ' are impressive. Simple, austere design and bronze
of John Knox set the tone historically. Holy Communion daily and other regular
services. Good coffee shop in the crypt (178/TEAROOMS). Summer: Mon-Fri 9am-
7pm, Sat 9am-5pm, Sun 1pm-5pm. Winter: Mon-Sat 9am-5pm, Sun 1pm-5pm.

THE GEORGIAN HOUSE: 225 2160. 7 Charlotte Sq. Built in the 1790s, this town
house is full of period furniture and fittings. Not many rms, but the dining-rm and **317**
kitchen are drop-dead gorgeous – you want to eat and cook there. Delightful *B2*
ladies from the National Trust for Scotland answer your queries. Moderator of the
General Assembly of the Church of Scotland bides up the stair. Apr-Oct 10am-
5pm, Sun 2-5pm. Last adm 4.30pm.   NT

LAURISTON CASTLE: 336 2060. 2 Cramond Road S. 9km W of centre by A90,
turning rt for Cramond. Elegant architecture and gracious living from Edwardian **318**
times. A largely Jacobean tower house set in tranquil grounds o/look the Forth. *xA2*
The liveability of the house and the preoccupations of the Reid family make you
wish you could poke around for yourself, but there are valuable and exquisite
decorative pieces and furniture and it's guided tours only. You could always
continue to Cramond for the air (320/WALKS IN THE CITY). Apr-Oct 11am-5pm
(cl lunch, cl Fri); Nov-Mar 2-4pm, w/ends only.   ADMN

DEEP SEA WORLD/BUTTERFLY & INSECT WORLD: 1360/1357/ KIDS.

ARTHUR'S SEAT: 319/WALKS IN THE CITY.

THE PENTLANDS: 324/WALKS OUTSIDE THE CITY.

THE SCOTT MONUMENT/CALTON HILL: 331/329/BEST VIEWS.

THE BEST WALKS IN THE CITY

See p.10 for walk codes.

319 **ARTHUR'S SEAT**: Of many walks (*see* 330/BEST VIEWS), a good circular one taking in
E3 the wilder bits, the lochs and gr views starts from St Margaret's Loch at the far
end of the park from the palace. Leaving the car park, skirt the loch and head for
the ruined chapel. Pass it on your rt and, after 250m in a dry valley, the buttress
of the main summit rears above you on the rt. Keeping it to the rt, ascend over a
saddle joining the main route from Dunsapie Loch which appears below on the
left. Crow Hill is the other peak crowned by a triangular cairn – both can be
slippery when wet. From Arthur's Seat head for and traverse the long steep
incline of the Crags. Paths parallel to the edge lead back to the chapel.
(Incidentally, nae mt bikes off tarmac or Sgt Sobotnicki will have words.)

START: Enter park at palace at foot of the High St and turn left on main road for
1km; the loch is on the rt.

PARK: There are car parks beside the loch and in front of the palace (paths start
here too, across the rd).   5-8KM   CIRC   MT BIKE (RESTRICTED ACCESS)   2-B-2

320 **CRAMOND**: This is the charming village (not the suburb) on the Forth at the mouth
xA2 of the Almond with a variety of gr walks. (**A**) To the rt along the 'prom'; the trad
seaside stroll. (**B**) Across the causeway at low tide to Cramond Island (1km). Best
to follow the tide out; this allows 4hrs (tides are posted). People have been known
to stay the night in summer, but this is discouraged. (**C**) Cross the mouth of the
Almond in the tiny passenger boat which comes on demand (summer 9am-7pm,
winter 10am-4pm) then follow coastal path to Dalmeny House which is open to
the public in the afternoons (May-Sept, Sun-Thu); or walk all the way to S
Queensferry (8km). (**D**) Past the boathouse and up the R Almond Heritage Trail
which goes eventually to the Cramond Brig Hotel on the A90 and thence to the
old airport (3-8km). Though it goes through suburbs and seems to be on the
flight path of the London shuttle, the Almond is a real river with a charm and
ecosystem of its own. The Cramond Bistro (312 6555) on the riverside is not a
bad wee bistro and awaits your return. BYOB. Cl Mon.

START: Leave centre by Queensferry Rd (A90), then rt following signs for
Cramond. Cramond Rd N leads to Cramond Glebe Rd; go to end.

PARK: Large car park off Cramond Glebe Rd to rt. Walk 100m to sea.
                                          1/3/8KM   XCIRC   BIKE   BUS 41   1-A-1

321 **CORSTORPHINE HILL**: W of centre, a knobbly hilly area of birch, beech and oak,
xA2 criss-crossed by trails. A perfect place for the contemplation of life's little
mysteries and mistakes. Or walking the dog. It has a radio mast, a ruined tower,
a boundary with the wild plains of Africa (at the zoo) and a vast redundant
nuclear shelter that nobody's supposed to know about. See how many you can
spot. If it had a tearoom in an old pavilion, it would be perfect.

START: Leave centre by Queensferry Rd and 8km out turn left at lights, signed
Clermiston. The hill is on your left for the next 2km.

PARK: Park where safe, on or nr this rd (Clermiston Rd).
                                          1-7KM   CIRC   XBIKE   BUS 26.85   1-A-1

322 **WATER OF LEITH**: The indefatigable wee river that runs from the Pentlands
D2 through the city and into the docks at Leith can be walked for most of its length,
though obviously not by any circular route. (**A**) The longest section from Balerno
12km o/side the city, through Colinton Dell to the Tickled Trout pub car park on
Lanark Rd (4km from city centre). The 'Dell' itself is a popular glen walk (1-
2km).

START: A70 to Currie, Juniper Green, Balerno; park by High School. (**B**) Dean
Village to Stockbridge: enter through a marked gate opp Hilton Hotel on Belford
Rd (combine with a visit to Gallery of Modern Art). (**C**) Warriston, through the
spooky old graveyard (1512/GRAVEYARDS), to The Shore in Leith (plenty pubs to
repair to). Enter by going to the end of the cul-de-sac at Warriston Cres in
Canonmills; climb up the bank and turn left. Most of the Water of Leith Walkway
(A, B and C) is cinder track.
                                          8KM   (OR LESS)   XCIRC   BIKE   BUS 43.44   1-A-1

EASY WALKS OUTSIDE THE CITY

Buses mostly from St Andrew's Square. Info: 225 3858. See p.10 for walk codes.

HERMITAGE OF BRAID: Strictly speaking, this is still in town, but there's a real sense of being in a country glen and from the windy tops of the Braid hills there are some marvellous views back over the city. Main track along the burn is easy to follow and you eventually come to Hermitage House info centre; any paths ascending to the rt take to the ridge of Blackford Hill. In winter, there's a gr sledging place over the first br up to the left and across the main rd.

START: Blackford Glen Rd. Go S on Mayfield to main T jnct with Liberton Rd, turn rt (signed Penicuik) then hard rt immediately.

323
xD4

1-4KM   CAN BE CIRC   XBIKE   BUS 7   1-A-1

THE PENTLANDS: Alan Jackson, poet of this parish, once wrote: 'Look wifie, behind you, the wild Pentlands.' And wild they are – a serious range of hills rising to almost 2,000ft, remote in parts and offering some fine walking. There are many paths up the various tops and round the lochs and reservoirs. **(A)** A good start in town is made by going off the bypass at Colinton, follow signs for Colinton Village, then the left fork up Woodhall Rd. Second left up Bonaly Rd (signed Bonaly Scout Camp). Drive/walk as far as you can (2km) and park by the gate leading to the hill proper where there is a map showing routes. The path to Glencorse is one of the classic Pentland walks. **(B)** Most walks start from signposted gateways on the A702 Biggar Rd. There are starts at Boghall (5km after Hillend ski slope); on the long straight stretch before Silverburn (a 10km path to Balerno); from Habbie's Howe about 18km from town; and from the village of Carlops, 22km from town. **(C)** The most popular start is probably from the visitor centre behind the Flotterstone Inn, also on the A702, 14km from town (decent pub lunch and 6-10pm, all day w/ends); trailboard and ranger service. The remoter tops around Loganlea reservoir are worth the extra mile.

324
MAP 7
B2

1-20KM   CAN BE CIRC   MTBIKE   BUS 4 OR ST ANDR SQ   2-B-2

ROSLIN GLEN: Special: spiritual, historical and enchanting with a chapel (1494/CHURCHES), a ruined castle and woodland walks along the R Esk. **START:** A701 from Mayfield or Newington (or bypass, t/off Penicuik, A702 then fork left on A703 to Roslin). Some parking at chapel, 500m from corner of Main St/Manse Rd or follow B7003 to Rosewell (also marked Rosslynlee Hospital) and 1km from village the main car park is to left.

325
MAP 7
C2

1-8KM   XCIRC   BIKE   BUS ST ANDR SQ   1-A-1

ALMONDELL: A country park to W of city (18km) nr (and one of the best things about) Livingston. A deep, peaceful woody cleft with easy paths and riverine meadows. Fine for kids, lovers and dog walkers. Visitor centre with teashop. Trails marked (1220/COUNTRY PARKS).

START: Best app from Edin by A71 via Sighthill. After Wilkieston, turn rt for Camp (B7015) then follow signs. Or A89 to Broxburn past start of M8. Follow signs from Broxburn.

326
MAP 7
B2

2-8KM   XCIRC   BIKE   BUS ST ANDR SQ   1-A-1

BEECRAIGS & COCKLEROY HILL: Another country park W of Linlithgow with trails and clearings in mixed woods, a deer farm and a fishing loch. Gr adventure playground for kids. Best is the climb and extraordinary view from Cockleroy Hill, far better than you'd expect for the effort. From Ben Lomond to the Bass Rock; and the gunge of Grangemouth in the sky to the E.

327
MAP 7
A1

START: M90 to Linlithgow (26km), through town and left on Preston Rd. Go on 4km, park is signed, but for hill you don't need to take the left turn. The hill (and nearest car park to it), are on rt.

2-8KM   CIRC   MTBIKE   BUS ST ANDR SQ   1-A-1

BORTHWICK & CRICHTON CASTLES: Takes in 2 impressive castles, the first a posh hotel (42/HOTELS OUTSIDE TOWN) and the other an imposing ruin (1439/RUINS) on a ridge o/look the Tyne. A walk through dramatic Border Country steeped in lore. Path obvious at first in either direction, then peters out, but the castle you're going to is always in view. Nice picnic spots nr Crichton.

328
MAP 7
C2

START: From Borthwick: A7 S for 16km, past Gorebridge, left at N Middleton; signed. From Crichton: A68 almost to Pathhead, signed then 3km.

7KM   XCIRC   XBIKE   BUS ST ANDR SQ   1-B-2

THE BEST VIEWS OF THE
CITY AND BEYOND

329 ✠ ✠ **CALTON HILL:** Gr view of the city easily gained by walking up from E end
E2 of Princes St by Waterloo Pl, to the end of the buildings and then up
stairs on the left. The City Observatory and the Greek-style folly lend an elegant
backdrop to a panorama (unfolding as you walk round) where the view up
Princes St and the sweep of the Forth estuary are particularly fine. At night, the
city twinkles. Popular cruising area for gays – but be careful if that's your
intention; you are vulnerable. It's not a good idea.

330 ✠ ✠ **ARTHUR'S SEAT:** W of city centre. Best app through Queen's Park from
E3 the bottom of Canongate by Holyrood Palace. The igneous core of an
extinct volcano with the precipitous sill of Salisbury Crags presiding over the city
and offering fine views for the fit. Top is 251m and on a clear day you can see
100km. Surprisingly wild considering proximity to city. 3 lochs, incl
Duddingston (follow rd to rt from palace for 6km), a bird sanctuary. Various
climbs (less than an hr). 'Volunteers Walk' starts opp the car park on macadam
and continues on grass through 'Hunter's Bog' to the 'Piper's Walk' and the top.
For other specific walks, see p. 47.

331 **SCOTT MONUMENT:** Princes St. Design inspiration for Thunderbird 3. This 1844
D2 Gothic memorial to one of Scotland's best-kent literary sons rises 61.5m above the
capital's main drag and provides no end of scope for the vertiginous to come to
terms with their affliction. 287 steps means it's no cakewalk and narrow stairwells
weed out claustrophobics too. Those who make it to the top are rewarded with
fine views. Underneath, a statue of the mournful Sir Walter gazes across at Jenners.
Apr-Sep 9am-6pm; Oct-Mar 9am-3pm. Cl Sun.   ADMN

332 **CAMERA OBSCURA:** Castlehill, Royal Mile. At v top of st nr the castle entrance, a
C3 tourist attraction that, surprisingly, has been there for over a century. You ascend
through a shop, photography exhibits and holograms to the viewing area where
a continuous stream of small groups are shown the effect of the giant revolving
periscope thingie. All Edin life is visible – amazing how much fun can be had
from a pin-hole camera with a focal length of 8.6m. You could watch it all day.
Apr-Oct 9.30am-6pm, sometimes later. Nov-Mar 10am-5pm.   ADMN

THE PENTLAND HILLS: 324/WALKS OUTSIDE THE CITY.

BLACKFORD HILL/THE BRAIDS: 323/WALKS OUTSIDE THE CITY.

CASTLE RAMPARTS: 304/MAIN ATTRACTIONS.

NORTH BERWICK LAW/TRAPRAIN LAW: 1577/HILLS.

SOME GREAT SUNDAY RUNS

333 **PEEBLES:** A 45min drive S by A703. Plenty woody walks, gdns to visit and
MAP 8 Tweedy scenery; good choice of afternoon tea, pub grub, etc.
B2
WALKS: Tweedside walk (1613/GLEN AND RIVER WALKS). Forestry walks in
Glentress (on A72, 2km SE on A72) or Cadrona Forests (other side of river 6km
on B7062), both with trail boards at car parks.

GARDENS: Kailzie (1207/GARDENS); Dawyck (1201/GARDENS).

FOOD: KAILZIE GARDENS coffee shop (1108/TEAROOMS), **THE HORSESHOE**
(1055/BEST FOOD), **THE TRAQUAIR ARMS** (955/INNS), **CRINGLETIE HOUSE HOTEL** for
afternoon tea, Sun lunch or special dinner (698/BORDERS HOTELS).

334 **ABBEY ST BATHANS:** Scattered township in the bucolic vale of the Whiteadder,
MAP 8 about 1hr drive SE of Edin. A1 to Cockburnspath is fastest rd, but the B6365
B1 through the Lammermuirs via Haddington and Gifford is a more leisurely drive.

WALKS: Best walk is through village 1km to 'Toot' corner, into woods and
follow path, keeping to hill side to pass the Edenshall Brochs. Follow river
further to excellent swimming and picnic spot. Other walks from village incl part
of Southern Upland Way. See 1339/SWIMMING HOLES for other app.

FOOD: The only place in village happens to be v good. **THE RIVERSIDE** is more a
restau than a café (1116/TEAROOMS). Other suggestions are on the way back –
DROVER'S INN, E Linton (271/EDIN PUBS WITH FOOD); **THE WATERSIDE,**

Haddington; and **BONAR'S,** Gifford (714/713/<small>LOTHIANS HOTELS</small>).

EAST LOTHIAN COAST: Nearest place to Edinburgh for coastal walks, especially the **335** beaches, all within an hr from town. Inland, both N Berwick Law and Traprain <small>MAP 7</small> Law are easy climbs, and there are several interesting churches and churchyards . . . well, it is Sunday (1808/<small>CHURCHES</small>). And the Museum of Flight (1831/<small>MUSEUMS</small>).

WALKS: Longest beach walks at **ABERLADY** (nature reserve) just beyond village on A198 towards N Berwick or from other side at Gullane. Or **JOHN MUIR COUNTRY PARK** (1217/<small>COUNTRY PARKS</small>), just o/side Dunbar. Beaches at **YELLOW-CRAIGS** and **SEACLIFF** are an airy amble at any time of yr (341/362/<small>BEACHES</small>). For vertical walks, **N BERWICK LAW** and (slightly stiffer) **TRAPRAIN LAW** (1577/<small>HILLS</small>), or the **LAMMERMUIRS,** offer a variety of trails in an empty landscape (1587/<small>HILL WALKS</small>). See also 1633/<small>WOODLAND WALKS</small> for **WOODHALL DENE** and **HUMBIE WOODS**.

FOOD: Same places as Abbey St Bathans (*above*) and see <small>LOTHIANS HOTELS</small>, *pp.100-101;* also try **LUCA'S** (1145/<small>ICE CREAM</small>) and the **CAPRICE** for pizza (by the br, in the main st). Both in Musselburgh on the way back.

THE FIFE COAST: Over the Forth Rd Br (which might slow you up, esp on the way **336** back), by the M90 leaving at jnct 1 for **ABERDOUR** (1241/<small>COASTAL VILLAGES</small>), <small>MAP 5</small> **SILVER SANDS BEACH** (signed) and the walk to Burntisland, or jnct 3 for Kirkcaldy (45mins from Edin centre) and then to the **EAST NEUK VILLAGES**.

WALKS: See 1645/1646/<small>COASTAL WALKS</small>. Or go further to **ST ANDREWS** – it's another world. Hill walks in the **LOMONDS** (1584/<small>HILL WALKS</small>).

VISIT: THE SECRET BUNKER (1812/<small>MUSEUMS</small>); **KELLIE CASTLE** (1420/<small>CASTLES</small>).

FOOD: See <small>FIFE RESTAUS</small>, *p.101* and 1953/<small>ST ANDREWS</small>. Great fish'n'chips in Anstruther or Kirkcaldy (1084/1094/<small>FISH AND CHIPS</small>).

BEST OF THE SPORTS FACILITIES

For bus and transport info phone 0131 225 3858 from o/side Edin or 0800 232323 from the city and surrounding area.

SWIMMING AND INDOOR SPORTS CENTRES

337

COMMONWEALTH POOL: 667 7211. Dalkeith Rd. (310/<small>MAIN ATTRACTIONS</small>.) The *E4* biggest, but Edin has many others. Recommended are **WARRENDER** (447 0052) *xC3* Thirlestane Rd 500m beyond the Meadows S of centre; **LEITH VICTORIA** (555 4728) *xE1* in Jnct Pl off the main st in Leith, now refurb with Pulse centre; **GLENOGLE** (343 *C1* 6376) in Stockbridge, the New Town choice, v friendly. All these pools are old and tiled, 25yds long, seldom crowded and excellent for lane swimming – at certain times. All tend to have different sessions, so phone to check.

PORTOBELLO: Portobello Esplanade (*see* <small>BEACHES</small>, p.51). Similar to others – closed *xE1* for extensive refurb at time of writing but planning to reopen in late 1997. Splendid Turkish baths have gone apparently – shame. Phone Commonwealth Pool for info.

AINSLIE PARK: 551 2400. Pilton Drive off Ferry Rd, N of centre, 5km from Princes *xC1* St; and **LEITH WATERWORLD:** 555 6000. Foot of Leith Walk. Leisure centres with *xE1* water thrills for kids. Ainslie also has lane swimming and all the other indoor/outdoor sports facs like 5-a-side pitches etc.

MEADOWBANK: 661 5351. London Rd. City athletics stadium with courts for *xE2* squash and badminton (often booked), Pulse centre, weights room, 40ft indoor climbing wall, outdoor football/hockey pitches and velodrome. No pool.

MARCO'S: 228 2141. 51 Grove St. Labyrinthine commercial centre with aerobic *B3* classes, gym, squash and snooker. No pool. Little Marco's will look after your kids while you sweat.

UNIVERSITY GYM: 650 2585. The Pleasance. No-nonsense complex, v cheap. The *E3* best in town for weights (Nautilus/Universal) and circuit training. Squash, badminton, indoor tennis etc. Quiet in vacs, membership not required. For a reasonable fee, the Fitness and Sports Injury Centre (FASIC) is an excellent alternative to the 'take two asprin and go away' school of GP. Few fake suntans.

E1 **EDINBURGH CLUB:** 2 Hillside Cres. 556 8845. Probably the most civilised of non hotel-type clubs. Usually members only, longer-stay visitors may be able to negotiate a rate. Good weights (mainly universal), sauna/steam/sun/bistro. Good aerobics classes. And spinning, apparently. No pool.

B3 **DRUMSHEUGH BATHS CLUB:** 5 Belford Rd, W End. Private swimming club in elegant building above Dean Village that costs a fortune to join and has an 18-month waiting list (so nae chance readers). But gorgeous Victorian pool with rings and trapeze over the water, sauna, multigym and bar. Frequented by the quality. If you're chums with a law lord, get him to sign you in as a guest.

338 GOLF COURSES
There are several municipal courses (see phone directory under City of Edin Council) and nearby, esp down the coast, some famous names that aren't open to nonmembers. 3 of the best available are:

xC3 **BRAID HILLS:** 447 6666. Braid Hills app. 2 18-hole courses (no. 2 summer only). Thought to be the best in town. Never boring; exhilarating views. Booking usually not essential, except w/ends. Women welcome (and that ain't true everywhere round here).

MAP 7 D1 **GULLANE NO. 1:** 01620 842255. The best of 3 courses around this pretty, twee village (35km down the coast) that was built for golf. Now you are really golfing! (though not on Sat). (1653/GREAT GOLF.)

MAP 7 D1 **GLEN GOLF CLUB (aka N BERWICK EAST):** 01620 895288. Some say W is best (01620 892135) but most say E and few would argue that N Berwick on a fair day was worth the drive (36km, A1 then A198) from Edin. That's the Bass Rock out there, and Fidra. Open to women (1653/GREAT GOLF).

339 OTHER ACTIVITIES

B1 **TENNIS:** There are lots of private clubs though only the **GRANGE** (332 2148) has lawn tennis and you won't get on there easily. There are places you can slip on (best not to talk about that), but the municipal centres (Edin residents/longer-stay visitors should get a Leisure Access card [661 5351] allowing advance reservation) are:

xA4 **SAUGHTON:** 444 0422. Stevenson Drive. 8km W of city centre. 2 astroturf courts and one other. Also used for football, so phone to book.

xC4 **CRAIGLOCKHART:** 444 1969. Colinton Rd. 8km SW of centre via Morningside and Colinton Rd. 6 indoor courts, 7 outdoor and a 'centre court' – best to check/book by phone. Other separate sports facs include squash, badminton & gym, 443 0101. Centre open Mon-Fri 9am-11pm, Sat-Sun 9am-11pm.

xC4 **SKIING:** Artificial slopes at **HILLEND** on A702, 10km S of centre. 445 4433. Excellent facility with various runs. The matting can be bloody rough when you fall and the chairlift is a bit of a dread for beginners, but once you can ski here, St Anton is all yours. Tuition every evening (not Thur) and w/ends. Open till 10pm in winter, 9pm in summer. Now run by Midlothian Council: snowboarders surf on plastic mountain.

D4 **PONY-TREKKING: LASSWADE RIDING SCHOOL:** 663 7676. Lasswade exit from city bypass then A768, rt to Loanhead 1km and left to end of Kevock Rd. Full hacking and trekking facs and courses for all standards and ages.

xA4 **PENTLAND HILLS TREKKING CENTRE:** 01968 661095. At Carlops on A702 (25km from town) has sturdy, steady Icelandic horses who will bear you good-naturedly into the hills. Exhilarating stuff. Bus from St Andrew's Sq.

xA3 **ICE-SKATING: MURRAYFIELD ICERINK:** 337 6933. Riversdale Cres just off main Glas Rd nr zoo. Cheap, cheerful and chilly. It has been here forever and feels like a gr 1950s B movie . . . go round! Sessions daily from 2.30pm.

xD1 **ALIEN ROCK:** 552 7211. Old St Andrew's Church, Pier Pl, Newhaven. Indoor rock climbing in a converted kirk. Laid back atmos, bouldering rm and interesting 40-ft walls of various gnarliness to scoot up. Daily; phone for sessions. Have a pint after in **THE STARBANK** or **THE OLD CHAIN PIER** nearby (262/BEST FOOD).

xD1 **FORECORT LEISURE:** 555 4533. Ashley Pl, off Newhaven Rd (opp Comet). Keith says we have to put this in as it's his local and he's a sucker for watching MTV on the monitors while jogging on the treadmill. 5-a-side football pitch, multigym, fitness studios, kids' play area and basic café.

BEST BEACHES

PORTOBELLO: Edinburgh's town beach, 8km from centre by London Rd. When sunny – chips, lager, bad ice cream. When miserable – soulful dog walkers. Arcades, mini-funfair, long prom. A 'used to be' place. **340** *xE3*

YELLOWCRAIGS: Nearest decent beach (35km). A1 or bypass, then A198 coast rd. Left o/side Dirleton for 2km, park and walk 100m across Links to fairly clean strand and sea. Gets busy, but big enough to share. Hardly anyone swims, but you can. Scenic. **GULLANE BENTS,** a sweep of beach, is nearby and reached from village main st. Connects westwards with Aberlady Nature Reserve. **341** *xE2*

✚ **SEACLIFF:** The best beach, least crowded/littered; perfect for picnics, beachcombing, dreaming and gazing into rock pools. There is a harbour, still in use, which is also good for swimming. 50km from Edin, Seacliff is off the A198 out of N Berwick, 3km after Tantallon Castle. At a bend in the rd and a farm (Auldhame) there is an unsigned rd off to left. 2km on there's a barrier, costing 2 x 50p to get car through. Car park 1km then walk. From A1, take E Linton turn-off, go through Whitekirk towards N Berwick, then same. **342** *xE2*

BEST GALLERIES

Apart from those mentioned previously (OTHER ATTRACTIONS, *p.44*), *the following are always worth a look. Check* The List *magazine for details.*

CITY ART CENTRE: 529 3993. Market St. Quite big. This is the place the populist blockbuster exhibs come to as well as excellent social/educational displays. Sensibly curated city asset. Convenient if uninspiring café. **343** *D3*

THE FRUITMARKET GALLERY: Across the rd in Market St, a smaller, more ware-housey space for more contemporary collections, retrospectives, installations. Café (165/TEAROOMS) highly recommended for meeting and eating, watching the world go by. **344** *D3*

THE COLLECTIVE GALLERY: 220 1260. 22 Cockburn St. Innovative venue specialising in installations of Scottish and other young contemporary trailblazers. Members' work for sale – often interesting, won't break the bank. **345** *D3*

THE SCOTTISH GALLERY: 558 1200. 16 Dundas St. Guy Peploe's influential New Town gallery on 2 floors. Where to go to buy something painted, sculpted, thrown or crafted by up-and-comers or established names – everything from affordable jewellery to original Joan Eardleys at £10k plus. Or just look. **346** *C2*

OPEN EYE GALLERY: 557 1020. 75-79 Cumberland St. Excellent small private gallery in residential part of New Town. Always worth checking out for accessible contemporary painting and ceramics. Almost too accessible (take cheque book). **347** *C1*

THE PRINTMAKERS' WORKSHOP AND GALLERY: 23 Union St off Leith Walk nr London Rd r/bout. Workshops that you can look over. Exhibs of work by contemporary printmakers and shop where prints from many of the notable names in Scotland are on sale at reasonable prices. Bit of a treasure. **348** *D1*

BELLVUE GALLERY: 557 1663. 4 Bellvue Cres. Edinburgh's newset small gallery at the bottom of fashionable Broughton St. Selected contemporary work in light salons (gallery is part of a house). The one to watch, the openings to go to. Afternoons. **349** *D1*

PHOTOGRAPHY: Edin is blessed with two contemporary photo-art venues. **STILLS** 622 6200, 23 Cockburn St, recently closed for refurbishment, came back bolder, brighter in Oct 1997 with a café. **PORTFOLIO** 220 1911, 43 Candlemaker Row is a small 2-floor space in what used to be the city's left-wing bookshop. **350** *D3*

GOOD NIGHTLIFE

For the current programmes of the places recommended below and all other venues, consult The List magazine, on sale at most newsagents.

351 MOVIES

Multiplex chains apart, these ones take movies seriously:

C4 **THE CAMEO:** 228 4141. Home St in Tollcross. 3 screens showing important new films and cult classics. Some late movies at w/ends. Good bar.

C3 **FILMHOUSE:** 228 2688. Lothian Rd opp Usher Hall. 3 screens with everything from first-run art-house movies to subtitled obscurities and retrospectives. Home of the annual Film Festival; café/bar (until 11.30pm Sun-Thurs, 12.30am Fri-Sat) is a haven from the excesses of Lothian Rd. Open to non-cinephiles.

xC4 **THE DOMINION:** 447 2660. Newbattle Terr, off Morningside Rd. Friendly, family-run cinema with 3 screens (one of them's like sitting in a plane). Nice wee place to see big films with the kids. Luca's ice cream.

352 THEATRE

D3 The main city theatres are **THE FESTIVAL THEATRE:** 529 6000. Nicolson St. Edinburgh's showcase theatre re-created from the old Empire with a huge glass frontage of bars and a stage and screen dock large enough to accommodate the world's major companies. Eclectic programme AYR.

C4 **THE KING'S:** 229 1201. Leven St, Tollcross, and **THE LYCEUM:** 229 9697. Grindlay St, are both ornate and lately refurb theatres with wide-ranging popular programmes.

C3 **THE TRAVERSE:** 228 1404. Small but influential, dedicated to new work (though mainly touring companies) in modern Euro, v architectural 2-theatre premises in Cambridge St (behind Lyceum). Good rendezvous bar in theatre (273/HIP) also excellent adj restau (50/BEST RESTAUS) and café/bar (60/BISTROS).

B1 **THEATRE WORKSHOP:** 226 5425. 34 Hamilton Pl. A small neighbourhood theatre in Stockbridge with a wide reputation for vital, innovative work. Café bar run by the Helios people (113/VEGN RESTAUS).

353 CLASSICAL MUSIC

C3/ E4 Usually from one of Scotland's national orchestras at regular concerts in the **USHER HALL** 228 1155. Lothian Rd. Smaller ensembles more occasionally at **THE REID, ST CECILIA'S** or **THE QUEEN'S HALL.** See *The List* or Saturday's edition of the *Scotsman* newspaper.

354 JAZZ

C3 **THE QUEEN'S HALL:** 668 3456. Clerk St. Occasional 'concerts'; see press.

CELLAR NO ONE: 5225 7183. 1A Chambers St. Basement bistro and bar with light combos, where you will probably see all of Edin's best players at some time. Late.

xE1 **NOBLES:** 554 2024. 44A Constitution St. Dependable bar food and real ales in a fine-sized rm. Folk on Thurs, R&B Fri and jazz Sat, but phone to confirm.

LEITH JAZZ FESTIVAL/ EDINBURGH JAZZ FESTIVAL: Late May/ early Aug. Selected venues. Check *The List* for details or TO.

355 FOLK

See 1882/FOLK MUSIC and PUBS WITH MUSIC, p.42. Best bets on a regular basis are:

D3 **SANDY BELL'S** aka **THE FORREST HILL BAR:** Forrest Hill.

D3 **THE ROYAL OAK HALL:** Infirmary St (293/LATE BARS).

B3 **WEST END HOTEL:** 225 3656. Palmerston Pl.

D3 **THE TRON TAVERN and CEILIDH HOUSE:** 220 1550. Hunter Sq.

ROCK AND POP

See PUBS WITH MUSIC, *p.49 and* 1855/ROCK AND POP, *p. 242.*

CLUBS

See EDINBURGH BARS AND CLUBS, *p.42 and* 1885/ROCK AND POP, *p. 242.*

GAY NIGHTLIFE

See GAY SCOTLAND THE BEST, *p. 236.*

SHOPPING GAZETTEER

These are the shops that get it rt. SOUTH means S of a central area bisected by Princes St; EAST is E of the city centre, etc.

ESSENTIALS

Bakers
Bread: **JENNER'S**, See Dept Stores. Only Edin stockist of Fisher & Donaldson's Dr Floyd's bread (1129/BAKERS).
Bread/Italian: **VALVONA & CROLLA**, 19 Elm Row. 556 6066. EAST
Bread: **AULD ALLIANCE**, 32 Victoria St. 622 7080. SOUTH
Patisserie: **FLORENTIN**, 8 St Giles St. 225 6267. CENTRAL
Custard pies: **IRVINE'S**, 16 Clerk St. 667 0262. SOUTH
Italian: **FRANCHINO'S PASTICCERIA**, 14 Albert St. 554 7417. EAST
Italian: **ANGELO'S**, 20a Brougham Pl. SOUTH

Barbers
WOODS, 12 Drummond St. 556 6716.

Butchers
Free Range: **GEORGE BOWER**, 75 Raeburn Place. 332 3469. NORTH

Delicatessen
GLASS & THOMPSON, 2 Dundas St. 557 0909. CENTRAL
VALVONA & CROLLA, 19 Elm Row. 556 6066. EAST
PECKHAM'S, 159 Bruntsfield Pl. 229 7054. SOUTH
BENNTTTI'S, 9 Rendolf Pl. 225 6252. CENTRAL
Mexican: **LUPE PINTO'S**, 24 Leven St. Bruntsfield. 228 6241. SOUTH
Cheese: **IAIN MELLIS**, 30A Victoria St. 226 6215. CENTRAL & 205 Bruntsfield Pl, 447 7414. SOUTH
Cheese: **HERBIE**, 66 Raeburn Pl. 332 9888. NORTH

Department Stores
JENNERS, Princes St. 225 2442. CENTRAL
General: **JOHN LEWIS**, St James Centre. 556 9121. CENTRAL
Ironmongers: **GRAYS**, 89 George St. 225 7381. CENTRAL

Fishmonger
GEORGE ARMSTRONG, 80 Raeburn Pl. 315 2033. NORTH. Also at The Gyle Shopping Centre, way out WEST.
CLARK BROS, 2 Harbour New St, Musselburgh. 665 6181. EAST
LONGA FISH, 23 Leven St, Tollcross. 229 2160. SOUTH
SOMETHING FISHY, 16a Broughton St. 556 7614. NORTH
Seafood: **TSE'S FISH MARKET**, 2 Warrender Park Rd. 662 4207. SOUTH

Flowers
RAEBURN GROCERS, 23 Comely Bank Rd. 332 5166. NORTH
GRANTS THE FLORIST, 116 Nicolson St. 668 2660. SOUTH
FLOWERS BY MAXWELL, 32 Castle St. 226 2866. NORTH

Fruit & Veg
FARMER JACK'S, 5 Graham St. 553 6090. EAST
VALVONA & CROLLA, 19 Elm Row. 556 6066. Fresh from Milan. EAST
ARGYLE PLACE: Several shops for fresh produce in this st. SOUTH
Organic: **REAL FOODS**, 37 Broughton St. 557 1911. CENTRAL

Haggis
MACSWEENS, 118 Bruntsfield Pl, 229 9141. SOUTH. Also
MACSWEENS FACTORY, Dryden Rd, Bilston Glen, Loanhead. 440 2555. 10km S of city.

Hairdressers
CHEYNES, various branches. 225 2234. CENTRAL
CHARLIE MILLER, 13 Stafford St. 226 5550. CENTRAL

Late-night
General: Some 24hr general stores have opened in the last yr – main chains are **ALLDAYS** (Nicolson St, Raeburn Pl) and **COSTCUTTER** (Lothian Rd & elsewhere).
SAINSBURY'S SUPERMARKET, Blackhall. 332 0704. Open 24hrs on Fri night. NORTH
Late Chemists: **BOOTS**, 48 Shandwick Pl. 225 6757. Till 9pm. CENTRAL

Men's clothes
New labels: **CRUISE**, St Mary's St & 94 George St. 226 3524/556 2532. CENTRAL. Giorgio, Hugo, Ralph, Hughie [Hughie? Ed]
SMITHS, 124 High St. 225 5927. CENTRAL
Established Labels: **AUSTIN REED**, 39 George St. 225 6703. CENTRAL
Both: **JENNERS**, Princes St. 225 2442. CENTRAL
HOUSE OF FRASER, 145 Princes St. 225 2472. CENTRAL

Newspapers
INTERNATIONAL NEWSAGENTS, 367 High

St. 225 4827. CENTRAL
JOHN MENZIES, Esp 107 Princes St. 226 6214. CENTRAL

Oriental Grocers
PAT'S CHUNH YING CHINESE SUPERMARKET, 199 Leith Walk. 554 0358. EAST
SIN FUNG, 16 Bruntsfield Pl. 228 6007. SOUTH

Pasta
GOURMET PASTA, 52 Morningside Rd, 447 4750. SOUTH. Also 32 Raeburn Pl, NORTH

Shoes
Shoes That Last: **BARNETS,** 7 High St. 556 3577. CENTRAL.
Modish: **SCHUH,** 32 N Bridge. 225 6552 and 6 Frederick St. 220 0290. Both CENTRAL

Tobacco
THE PIPE SHOP, 92 Leith Walk. 553 3561. EAST

Wholefoods
REAL FOODS, 37 Broughton St. 557 1911. CENTRAL; 8 Brougham St. 228 1201. SOUTH
ROOTS, 60 Newington Rd. 668 2888. SOUTH

Wine & Beer
J. E. HOGG, 61 Cumberland St. 556 4025. NORTH
IRVINE ROBERTSON WINES, 10 N Leith sands 553 3521. EAST
PETER GREEN, 37a/b Warrender Park Rd. 229 5925. SOUTH
BOTTLE STOP, 49a Broughton St, 558 1674. NORTH
OASTS & TOASTS, 107-109 Morrison St, 228 8088. WEST

Women's clothes
New labels: **CORNICHE,** 2 Jeffrey St. 556 3707. CENTRAL
JANE DAVIDSON, 152 Thistle St. 225 3280. CENTRAL
Second-Hand: **HAND IN HAND,** 3 N W Circus Pl. 226 3598. NORTH
Hire a posh frock: **DRESS HIRE STUDIO,** 19 Grassmarket. 225 7391. CENTRAL

THE MOST INTERESTING SHOPS

Antiques
General: Grassmarket, Victoria St; Thistle St, St Stephen St, NW Circus Pl.
Bric-à-Brac: **BYZANTIUM,** 9 Victoria St. 225 1768. CENTRAL
UNICORN, 65 Dundas St. 556 7176. NORTH
Jewellery: **JOseph BONNAR,** 72 Thistle St.

226 2811. CENTRAL
Clothes: **HAND IN HAND,** 3 NW Circus Pl. 226 3598. NORTH

Bedding
AND SO TO BED, 22 Howe St. 225 6998. NORTH

Brushes
ROBERT CHESSER, 40 Victoria St. CENTRAL

Cards
General: **PAPER TIGER,** Stafford St. 226 5812, 53 Lothian Rd. CENTRAL
Funniest: **PJ's,** 60 Broughton St. NORTH
Playing/Tarot: **SOMERVILLES,** 82 Canongate. 556 5225. CENTRAL

Ceramics
WARE ON EARTH, 15 Howe St. 558 1276. NORTH
AZTECA, 5 Grassmarket. 229 9368; 16 Victoria St. CENTRAL

Clothes
General: See Shopping For Essentials
MACKENZIE, 2 Hunter Sq. 225 9359. CENTRAL
Old: **PADDIE BARRASS,** 15 Grassmarket. 226 3087. CENTRAL
ELAINE'S, 53 St Stephen St. NORTH
FLIP, 60 South Bridge. 556 4966. SOUTH
Outdoor: **GRAHAM TISO,** 13 Wellington Pl. 554 0804 and Rose St. EAST

Comics
DEAD HEAD COMICS, 27 Candlemaker Row. 226 2774. CENTRAL
FORBIDDEN PLANET, 3 Teviot Pl. 225 8613. CENTRAL

Cookbooks
CLARISSA DICKSON-WRIGHT'S COOK BOOKSHOP, Grassmarket. 226 4445. CENTRAL

Furniture
Modern: **INHOUSE,** 28 Howe St. 225 2888. NORTH
Traditional: **SHAPES,** 33 West Mill Rd. 441 7936. SOUTH
American: **THE GREAT AMERICAN INDOORS,** 14 Springvalley Gardens. 447 7445. SOUTH

Ice cream
LUCA'S, 34 High St. Musselburgh. 665 2237. EAST 20km

Jokes
AHA HA HA, 99 West Bow. 220 5252. CENTRAL

Junk
JUST JUNK, Broughton St. NORTH

SAM BURNS' YARD, Main rd to
Prestonpans. EAST 25km
UTILITIES Broughton St. CENTRAL

Luggage and bags
A D MACKENZIE, 34 Victoria St. 220
0089. CENTRAL

Models
MARIONVILLE MODELS, 42 Turnhouse
Rd. 317 7010. WEST
MAC'S MODELS, 168 Canongate. 557
5551. EAST
WONDERLAND, 397 Lothian Rd. 229
6428. CENTRAL

Presents
ROUND THE WORLD, 82 West Bow &
NW Circus Pl. 225 7086.
CENTRAL/NORTH
MANIC MANIC, Broughton St. 556 5366.
NORTH
NOMAD'S TENT, St Leonard's Lane. 662
1612. SOUTH
IMAGES OF NEPAL, 10 Grassmarket. 220
4208. CENTRAL
STUDIO ONE, 10 Stafford St. 226 5812.
BLACKADDER GALLERY, 5 Raeburn Pl.
332 4605. NORTH
GALERIE MIRAGES, 46a Raeburn Pl. 315
2603. NORTH

Rude Stuff
LEATHER & LACE, 8 Drummond St. 557
9413. SOUTH
WHIPLASH TRASH, 53 Cockburn St. 226
1005. SOUTH

Rugs
MIHRAB GALLERY, 297 Canongate. 556
6952. CENTRAL
WHYTOCK AND REID, Belford Mews. 226
4911. WEST

Sci-fi
FORBIDDEN PLANET, 3 Teviot Pl. SOUTH

Souvenirs
See below and **ANYWHERE ON THE HIGH ST.**
Tartan, Serious: **KINLOCH ANDERSON,**
Commercial St. 555 1371. EAST
HECTOR RUSSELL, Princes St./High St.
Tartan and tacky: Not hard to find.

Sports
MACKENZIE'S 17 Nicolson St. 667 2288.
SOUTH
MOMENTUM, 22 Bruntsfield Pl. 229 6665.
SOUTH (SURFING)
WHITE STUFF, Hanover St. 624 2424.
NORTH (SNOWBOARDING)
AITKEN AND NIVEN, 77-79 George St.
556 1866. CENTRAL

Sweets
CASEY JAMES, 52 St Mary's St. SOUTH

Video Rental
ALPHABET VIDEO, 22 Marchmont Rd.
229 5136. SOUTH
C & A VIDEO, 93 Broughton St. 556 1866.
CENTRAL

Woollies
JUDITH GLUE, 64 High St. 556 5443.
CENTRAL
NUMBER TWO, St Stephen Pl. 225 6257.
NORTH
BILL BABER, 66 Grassmarket. 225 3249.
CENTRAL
THE CASHMERE STORE, 2 St Giles St. 225
4055. CENTRAL
HILLARY ROHDE, 332 4147 (exclusive
cashmere; by appointment only)

SECTION 2

Glasgow

The telephone code for Glasgow is 0141
Refer to MAP B, *unless otherwise stated*

THE BEST HOTELS

357
xA1 **ONE DEVONSHIRE GARDENS:** 339 2001. 1 Devonshire Grds. Off Gr Western Rd (the A82 W to Dumbarton), to arrive by car you have to go round the back. 3 seperate houses in leafy Victorian terrace and after accolades and write-ups galore, the most notable urban hotel in Scotland. It's all down to detail and service, fab fitxures and fabrics: it's all down to DESIGN and Ken McCulloch. Every rm different but all with the things that we modern travellers look out for: CD players, big beds, huge baths, deep baths, big beds, deep carpets/towels/curtains (but could it be the breakfast OJ was . . .help ma boab, out of a carton). Some Ralph Lauren rms; the supersuits all in house 3 (rms 21, 27, 28) if you're Pavarotti or just celebrating. Restau a foodie experience in itself (403/THE BEST RESTAUS).
27RMS JAN-DEC T/T PETS CC KIDS LOTS

358
C2 **THE MALMAISON:** 221 6400. 278 W George St. Sister hotel of the one in Edin (10/INDIVIDUAL HOTELS) and same team as One Devonshire *(see above)* so no surprise that this is an outstanding hotel. The recent expansion, utilising the adj building, has more than tripled the accom and the addition of the Café Mal downstairs, has created a cool, sky-lit area in contrast to the woody, clubbiness of the brasserie next door (414/BISTROS). An improvement on what was already pretty good to begin with. Well proportioned rms (some suites), with CDs, cable etc. Stylish excellence.
73 RMS JAN-DEC T/T XPETS CC KIDS MED.EX

359
xA1 **THE DEVONSHIRE HOTEL:** 339 7878. 5 Devonshire Gardens. Confusingly perhaps for first-time visitors, this similarly sumptuous town house hotel is at the other end of the short block containing One Devonshire *(above)*. I say 'similarly' (pictures, plants, atmos etc.), but it is less de luxe, less designey and some may find more effortless. Dining-rm small and for residents only. All bedrms delightfully different.
14RMS JAN-DEC T/T PETS CC KIDS LOTS

360
C2 **GLASGOW HILTON:** 204 5555. 1 William St, app from the M8 slip rd (or from city centre via Waterloo St) it has a forbidding, Fritz Lang/Metropolis appearance which isn't really dispelled once inside. The clean lines of the atrium/lobby and the ubiquitous theme bar and bistro off it increase the sensation of being on a huge and expensive film set. But, hotel it is, and one of the best in the town with good service and appointments. Japanese people made esp welcome. Cameron's, the hotel's main restau, is present and correct; Minsky's bistro and Raffles bar not too special.
319RMS JAN-DEC T/T PETS CC KIDS LOTS

361
C3 **THE MARRIOTT:** 226 5577. 500 Argyle St nr motorway. Modern and functional business hotel where parking is a test for the nerves. Nevertheless, there's a calm, helpful attitude from the staff inside; for further de-stressing you can hypnotize yourself by watching the soundless traffic on the Kingston br o/side; or there's a pool to lap. No-smk floors.
298RMS JAN-DEC T/T PETS CC KIDS LOTS

362
D2 **THE COPTHORNE:** 332 6711. 50 George Sq. Situated on the sq which is the municipal heart of the city and next to Queen St Stn (trains to Edin and pts NE), Glas will be going on all about you and there's a conservatory terrace, serving breakfast and afternoon tea, from which to watch. Bedrms vary greatly; some perhaps overdone. Recently revamped and busy brasserie.
141RMS JAN-DEC T/T PETS CC KIDS LOTS

363
A2 **THE MOAT HOUSE:** 204 0733. Congress Rd. Beside the SECC, on the Clyde, this towering, glass monument to the 1980s feels like it's in a constant state of 'seige readiness'. The Marine Restau, in the lobby, has a good reputation and ring-side seating for the coming millennial developments, across the river. Somewhat removed from city centre (about 3km but you wouldn't want to walk), it's esp handy for SECC and Armadillo goings-on.
282RMS JAN-DEC T/T PETS CC KIDS LOTS

364
D2 **THE CENTRAL HOTEL:** 221 9680. Gordon St. Grande dame of Glasgow's hotels. Once the last word in gracious living, the elegance is now a little faded, although a certain atmos still remains in the sweep of the staircase and in the grandiose public rms. Rms are individual and you're at the hub of a gr city. Taxis easy to find, parking less so. New leisure centre.
221RMS JAN-DEC T/T PETS CC KIDS EXP

365
A1 **KELVIN PARK LORNE:** 314 9955. 923 Sauchiehall St. By no means in the superluxe league, but included because many of the rms, esp the suites, are individualistic, often rather grand. Location is handy for the W End (galleries/ restaus/Kelvingrove Park).
99RMS JAN-DEC T/T PETS CC KIDS EXP

THE BEST INEXPENSIVE HOTELS

✚ **CATHEDRAL HOUSE:** 552 3519. 28-32 Cathedral Sq/John Knox St. Next to the 366
Cathedral (some rms o/look) and close to the Merchant City, this detached E2
old building has been tastefully refurb and converted into a café bar (with
occasional live music), a separate and decent restaurant (Fri-Sat at time of going to
press), and comfortable bedrms above. Discreet and informal hospitality for the
traveller; much as it always has been here, in the ancient heart of the city.

7RMS JAN-DEC T/T PETS CC KIDS MED.EX

✚ **THE TOWN HOUSE:** 357 0862. 4 Hughenden Terr. Quiet st off Gr Western Rd 367
via Hyndland Rd, o/look the cricket grounds. These spacious rms have been xA1
faithfully restored and even if you don't happen to live in a well appointed town
house, on a gracious terrace yourself, you'll feel at home here. Close to the W
End.

10RMS JAN-DEC T/T XPETS CC KIDS MED.INX

✚ **CHARING CROSS TOWER:** 221 1000. 10 Elmbank Grds above Charing Cross 368
Stn in W End. Once an office block, now a vast city-centre budget hotel, C1
with no frills and no pretence, but a v adequate rm for the night – I mean it's not
a pile of charm and you wouldn't want to spend your holidays here, but its
functionalism, anonymity and sheer urban melancholy make it a kind of Euro-
Glas must. M8 rms less quiet.

276RMS JAN-DEC T/T XPETS CC KIDS MEDINX

✚ **THE BRUNSWICK:** 552 0001. 104-108 Brunswick St. V contemporary, slightly 369
spartan hotel in the Merchant City. The rms are bright and cheerful and E3
economically designed to make use of every inch of space; low Japanese-style
beds. A good base for nocturnal forays into pub and club land. Restau has had
mixed response; but breakfast v pleasant.

18RMS JAN-DEC T/T XPETS CC KIDS MEDINX

✚ **RAB HA'S:** 553 1545. 83 Hutcheson St. Rms above a pub (558/BEST FOOD) in 370
the urban heart of the Merchant City that have had a recent overhaul; new E3
central heating system for the winter, etc. Good place to get plumbed in, yourself.

4RMS JAN-DEC T/T PETS CC XKIDS MED.INX

✚ **THE COURTYARD HOTEL:** 552 2424. 52 Virginia St. Conversion of the old 371
Tobacco Merchants house (in Merchant City) that has managed to retain the D3
original staircase (ask the porter to take your bags, there's no lift). Surprisingly
quiet area, though in emerging gay-zone ; a stone's throw from all the chain stores
of Argyle St and more interesting Merchant City shops. A comfortable enough
place to recuperate from shopping. Breakfast best in rm.

34RMS JAN-DEC T/T PETS CC KIDS CHP

BABBITY BOWSTER: 552 5055. 16-18 Blackfriars St. This carefully renovated, late 372
18th-century town house, was pivotal in the redevelopement of the Merchant E3
City. Renowned for its hospitality; bar (542/REAL ALE) and beer grd, 'Schottische'
restau upstairs and simple accom above. A welcoming howff in new/old Glas.

6RMS JAN-DEC X/X XPETS CC XKIDS MED.INX

WICKETS HOTEL: 334 9334. 52 Fortrose St. Probably best app via Dumbarton Rd, 373
turning up Peel St before railway br. O/look W of Scotland Cricket Ground xA1
(hence title), this family-run hotel has been a Kelvinside secret for yrs. Decent
rms, conservatory restau and a large terraced beer grd, made for long summer
afternoons.

10RMS JAN-DEC T/T PETS CC KIDS MED.INX

KIRKLEE: 354 5555. 11 Kensington Gate. The Stevens keep a tidy house and most 374
notably a tidy grd (geraniums, lobelia, hydrangea etc.) in this leafy suburb nr the xA1
Botanics and the less botanical jungle of Byres Rd. They bother.

9RMS JAN-DEC T/T XPETS CC KIDS MED.INX

THE WHITE HOUSE: 339 9375. 12 Cleveden Cres. Not really a hotel, more self- 375
catering apartments nr Botanics. V civilised alternative, esp if there are a few of xA1
you and/or are staying a week.

8UNITS JAN-DEC T/T PETS CC KIDS MED.INX

NUMBER 52 CHARLOTTE ST: 553 1941. Serviced apartments in superb conversion 376
of the one remaining Georgian town house in historic (now decimated) st betw E3
the Barrows Market and Glas Green. V good rates for bedrm/lounge/ kitchen;
everything but breakfast.

6RMS JAN-DEC X/T XPETS CC KIDS MED.INX

THE VICTORIAN HOUSE: 332 0129. 214. Renfrew St. Expansive guesthouse which 377
has swallowed up adj houses in hill top terr behind Sauchiehall St nr Art School C1
(631/MACKINTOSH). Basic accom. Rms without facs cheaper but bathrms can be a

floor away. Location is the appeal.

36RMS JAN-DEC X/T PETS CC KIDS INX

378 **RENNIE MACKINTOSH HOTEL:** 333 9992. 218-220 Renfrew St. Taking advantage of
C2 the upcoming Yr of Architecture celebrations in 1999, this new and competitively
B2 run hotel, (and its soon-to-open partner the **GREEK THOMSON,** Elderslie St), have
cheekily borrowed the names of 2 of Glasgow's most famous sons. Never mind,
the Mockintosh isn't too overbearing, the service is friendly and helpful, and
there's alfresco breakfasting in the summer. How long before we get Hotel Ally
McCoist?
24RMS JAN-DEC T/T X/PETS CC KIDS INX

THE BEST CAMPING AND CARAVAN PARKS

379 **STRATHCLYDE PARK:** 01698 266155. 20km SE Glas. M74 at jnct 6 or M8/ A725. On
MAP 1 the edge of a large popular country park (1218/COUNTRY PARKS; 1391/BIRDS;
E3 1715/WATER SPORTS) and easily reached by motorway system. Go left just after
park entrance. Check in until 9.30pm. Stay up to 2 weeks. Usual but good
standard facs on site and many others nearby e.g. café, windsurfing, gym till
8.30pm, 500m away). Motorway close, so traffic noise, but no visual intrusion on
this well-managed, parkland site. Caravans and tents separate. Glasgow's most
accessible caravan park by car. 150 pitches. Apr-Oct.

380 **BARNBROCK, LOCHWINNOCH:** 01550 614791. 40km SW Glas via M8/A8 Pt Glas
MAP 1 then Kilmacolm rd A761, then B786; or via Johnstone A737, A760 to
C3 Lochwinnoch. Let's face it, it's not exactly convenient, but this beautiful, remote
site (camping only) is on the edge of the wild and wonderful Muirshiel Country
Park (1215/COUNTRY PARKS) and Lochwinnoch Nature Reserve (1400/WILDLIFE
RESERVES) and it's not far to go to leave the city behind completely. 15 tents.

381 **CLOCH CARAVAN PARK, GOUROCK:** 01475 632675. 45km W of Glas along the coast.
MAP 1 Take M8 then A8 through Greenock and Gourock; continue for 6km. This is a
C3 residential caravan park (no tents) with only a few touring pitches. Vast terraced
caravan land with shop etc. Best feature is that it o/look the historical Cloch Pt
Lighthouse and the glittering Clyde. 10 places only.

382 **TULLICHEWAN, BALLOCH:** 01389 759475. 40km NW of Glas. Once again a fair
MAP 1 distance from the city, but fast rds from this direction via A82 (dual carriageway
D2 all the way), or via Erskine Br and then M8. Best to leave the car here and take
frequent train service from Balloch Stn nearby; 30 mins to Glas Central Stn. This
park is nicely situated nr L Lomond and tourist centres and is well managed and
good fun for kids. Shop, laundrette, games rm, TV, sauna, sunbeds etc. Probably
the best park for holiday making hereabouts. 140 places.

383 **ARDLUI, LOCH LOMOND:** 01301 704243. Continue on A82 (from above). At the
MAP 1 other end of the loch in an ideal spot for exploring the remoter parts of this
D2 popular area by boat (they have hiring facs and a 100 berth marina), or on foot.
For self-catering, 6-8 berth caravans are available for hire and there's an on site
hotel (11 rms, 2 bars and 2 restaus) if your tent blows away in the night. Laundry,
children's play area, shop and all the boating facs you'll need. 97 places.

THE BEST HOSTELS

384 ✚ **S.Y. HOSTEL:** 332 3004. 7 Park Terrace. Close to where the old Glas hostel
B1 used to be in Woodlands Terr in the same area of the W End nr the univ and
Kelvingrove Park. This building was converted in 1992 from the Beacons Hotel,
which was where rock 'n' roll bands used to stay in the 1980s. Now the bedrms
are converted into dorms for 4-6 (some larger) and the public rms are common
rms with TV/games/café etc. Still feels more like a hotel than a hostel and is a gr
place to stay. Late opening. You must be a member of the YHA. Phone for info.

385 ✚ **BAIRD HALL, STRATHCLYDE UNIV:** 332 6415. 460 Sauchiehall St. The landmark
C2 Grade A-listed art deco building near the Art School and the W End.
Originally the Beresford Hotel, built 1937 and once Glasgow's finest (v Miami
Beach). 194 rms in vacs and 11 available all yr round. Spartan, almost drab,
though the rms are fine, like an American Y. Reeks of nostalgia as well as
disinfectant. Dining-rm, TV and reading rm. Lots of groovy places nearby such
as Nico's, Variety Bar, Baby Grand and the Griffin. All are listed further on.

CLYDE HALL, STRATHCLYDE UNIV: 221 1219. 318 Clyde St. A v central block, off-campus at the bottom of Union/Renfield St and almost o/look the river. 165 single and twin rms mainly in summer vac. Refectory and TV rm. Some smaller rms on lower floor are available cheaply as self-catering specifically for backpackers, and are a v good deal. **386** *D3*

MURRAY HALL, STRATHCLYDE UNIV: 552 4400 (ext 3560). Collins St. Modern, but not sterile block of single rms on edge of main campus and facing towards Cathedral. Part of large complex (also some student flats to rent by the week) with bar/shop/laundrette. Quite central, close Merchant City bars. Vacs only. **387** *E2*

QUEEN MARGARET HALL, GLASGOW UNIV: 334 2192. 55 Bellshaugh Rd. Off-campus (in fact, rather a long way from anything) but a big high-rise block of comfortable rms where there's a good chance of accom when more central halls are full. Get a bike. Vacs only. **388** *xA1*

CAIRNCROSS HOUSE, GLASGOW UNIV: 330 5385. Kelvinhaugh Pl off Argyle at Murphy's Pakora Bar. Nr Kelvingrove Park, Byres Rd and some good pubs and Indian restaus, a recently built student-hall complex not brickful of ambience, but well appointed and convenient. Vacs only. **389** *A2*

The SYH(A) is the Scottish Youth Hostel Association of which you have to be a member (or a member of an affiliated organisation from another country) to stay in their many hostels round Scotland. Phone 01786 451181 for details or contact any YHA hostel.

Note: Both Strathclyde and Glasgow Universities have several halls of residence available for short-term accom in the summer months. For those above (the best of them) and others, you may also phone:

GLASGOW: 330 5385

STRATHCLYDE: 553 4148 (central booking)

THE BEST HOTELS OUTSIDE TOWN

See also HOTELS IN ARGYLL, *p. 94, and* AYRSHIRE/CLYDE VALLEY, *p. 95. Refer to Map 1.*

✠ **GLEDDOCH HOUSE, LANGBANK, nr GREENOCK:** 01475 540711. M8/A8 to Greenock then B789 signposted Langbank/Houston, then 2km – hotel is signed. 30km W of centre by fast rd. A château-like country-house hotel, formerly the home of the Lithgow Shipping family. High above the Clyde estuary, there are spectacular views across to Dumbarton Rock and the Kilpatrick Hills. Rms not lavish but comfortable, only a few have the view. Reputable dining-rm strong on Scottish ingredients and cuisine. Pleasant conservatory. Excellent 18-hole golf course; health club, tiny pool. **390** *D3*

37RMS JAN-DEC T/T PETS CC KIDS TOS LOTS

✠ **CAMERON HOUSE, nr BALLOCH, LOCH LOMOND:** 01389 755565. A82 dual carriageway into W End or via Erskine Br and M8. 45km NW of centre. Highly regarded mansion-house hotel complex with excellent leisure facs in open grounds on the bonny banks of the loch. Sports incl 9-hole golf, good pool, tennis and a busy marina for sailing/ windsurfing etc. Notable restau (The Georgian Rm) and all-day brasserie. Many famous names from Gazza to Pavarotti have holed up here (but they wouldn't have Oasis). 68RMS JAN-DEC T/T XPETS CC KIDS TOS LOTS **391** *D2*

THE BLACK BULL HOTEL: 01360 550215. 2 The Sq, Killearn. A81 towards Aberfoyle, take the rt fork after Glengoyne Distillery, and the hotel is at the top end of the village next to the church. Recent change of hands; extensively refurb, this old hotel has been given a new lease of life. Open-plan bar/restau with good food, spacious conservatory with enclosed grd and tastefully decorated, comfortable rms *(and see 692/*CENTRAL HOTELS*).* **392** *D3*

11RMS JAN-DEC T/T PETS CC KIDS MED.EXP

BOWFIELD COUNTRY CLUB, HOWWOOD: 01505 705225. Jnct 29 off M8 for Howwood then 3km from Main St via steep Z-bend. 32km SW of centre. Farmhouse-like retreat in gentle hill country just beyond the conurbation. Rms in modern annex are comfortable and with the club facs (squash, gym, saunas etc.) and a large pool (open till 10pm), represent good value. Less earnest than usual health clubs and they've thought about those difficult teenagers. **393** *D3*

23RMS JAN-DEC T/T XPETS CC KIDS EXP

394 **BOTHWELL BRIDGE HOTEL, BOTHWELL:** 01698 852246. Uddingston t/off from M74
E3 15km SE. Main St. Nr castle and good pub (1433/RUINS; 531/'UNSPOILT' PUBS).
Comfortable, family run hotel with an Italian ambience. V kid friendly.
75RMS JAN-DEC T/T XPETS CC KIDS EXP

395 **CULCREUCH CASTLE HOTEL, FINTRY:** 01360 860228. Off B818 in Campsie Fells
D3 32km N of centre via A81 Milngavie rd from Glas. Fintry is well kept and
pastoral in valley betw the Fells and the Fintry Hills. Some fine walking (598/
WALKS OUTSIDE THE CITY). Ancestral home of the Galbraiths with many old features
incl a half-tester bed (whatever that is). Dungeons converted into bar/bistro.
Many weddings, so check w/ends. 8RMS JAN-DEC T/T PETS CC KIDS TOS MED.INX

396 **THE BALLOCH HOTEL, BALLOCH, LOCH LOMOND:** 01389 752579. 40km NW by fast
D3 rds (*see* Cameron House, *above*) or frequent and convenient train. Busy hotel (beer
grd and local bar) in tourist centre by loch side moorings. Goes like the Glas Fair
in summer. 14RMS JAN-DEC T/T PETS CC KIDS MED.INX

397 **THE INVERKIP HOTEL, INVERKIP:** 01475 521478. M8 from Glas then A8 and A78
C3 from Pt Glas heading S for Largs. 50km W centre. Inverkip is a wee bypassed
village now dominated from the other side of the main rd by the Kip Marina
(1718/WATER SPORTS). Hotel is in Main St; a family-run coaching inn with busy
pub downstairs. The most reasonable place to stay on this part of the Clyde coast.
5RMS JAN-DEC X/T PETS CC KIDS INX

398 **KIRKTON HOUSE:** 01389 841951. Darleith Rd. Cardross. A814, past Helensburgh
C3 to Cardross village then N up Darleith Rd. Kirkton House is 1km on rt. 18th-
century Scottish farmhouse that combines rustic charm with *every* mod con,
(check your web site). Informal and unpretentious, ('no hang-ups'), quality
home-cooking and a stone's throw from L Lomond. International clientele.
6 RMS JAN-DEC T/T PETS CC KIDS MEDINX.

THE BEST RESTAURANTS

✝ ✝ **YES:** 221 8044. 22 W Nile St. Downtown and downstairs (through street-level café bar is a good place to meet and the 'Brasserie Menu' one of the best value light meals in town) is the airy and uncluttered creation of Ferrier Richardson and currently the best restau in town. Poss down to chef Iain MacMaster who in the last edition of this book was at the Puppet Theatre. Some Asian/Pacific influence to superbly balanced dishes presented with flair and no fuss. Lunch and LO 11pm (upstairs 9pm). Both cl Sun. **399 D2** MED

✝ ✝ **THE BUTTERY:** 221 8188. 652 Argyle St. Central, but curious location for Glasgow's most consistently superb restau owned as the Rogano (*see below*) by Alloa Breweries. Occupying the only remaining tenement block in an area carved up by urban developers, the Buttery and its little brother downstairs, the Belfry, are best reached via the westerly extension of St. Vincent St then Elderslie St on the left, then left again at the church and down to the end. New chef Willie Deans kent face of the Scottish culinary Olympic team pepping up the menu but comfortable old-fashioned ambience remains. No changes should depose the winning sample-all-desserts option. 6 days lunch and 7-10pm, Cl Sun and Sat lunch. **400 B2** EXP

✝ **PUPPET THEATRE:** 339 8444. 11 Ruthven Lane. In a converted mews behind Byres Rd, one of Scotland's most stylish restaus. A series of intimate dining areas, the crescent-shaped conservatory, most popular and maybe tightly packed. Fixed price menus. Contemporary British with Scottish slant and impeccable ingredients and presentation. Lunch (not Sat); LO 11pm. Cl Mon. **401 A1** EXP

✝ **ROGANO:** 248 4055. 11 Exchange Pl. Betw Buchanan St and Queen St. An institution in Glas since the 1930s. Décor replicating a Cunard ship, the *Queen Mary*, is the major attraction. It's *the* place to take visiting friends or meet clients, even if just for cocktails. The restau is spacious and perennially fashionable with fish and seafood the specialities. Downstairs, the supper and luncheon rm has a lighter/cheaper menu, and though it's a bit sub-Rogano its informality is easier on the self-image and the pocket. Rogano is owned by Alloa Breweries. Restaurant: lunch and 6-10.30pm. Café Rogano: lunch and 6-11pm (Fri/Sat till midnight, Sun till 10pm). **402 D3** EXP/MED

✝ **ONE DEVONSHIRE GARDENS:** 339 2001. Glasgow's most stylish hotel (357/BEST HOTELS) has a restau which has won accolades in its own rt. Like the sumptuous surroundings, dishes on the fixed-price menu are contemoprary, voguish and seductive. Staff are young and friendly. All in all, a food experience that doesn't feel like hotel. **403 xA1** EXP

✝ **THE UBIQUITOUS CHIP:** 334 5007. 12 Ashton Lane. A cornerstone of Glasgow's culinary establishments. Two-storey, covered courtyard draped with vines, off a cobbled lane in the heart of the W End, heaped with accolades over 26yrs in residence.The main bit is still one of the most atmospheric of rms. The menu is based on exemplary fresh Scottish seafood, the best of game and beef and fine, original cooking. All complimented by an outstanding wine list. Daily lunch and 6.30-11pm. (423/BISTROS.) **404 A1** EXP

✝ **THE CABIN:** 569 1036. 996 Dumbarton Rd. New chef, David Dempsie, joins Denis Dwyer's capable team in the kitchen, and, if anything, the food is now even better than before. Beautifully cooked fresh seafood and Scottish game, home-made Irish soda bread and delicious puds. You'll probably have to linger after dinner, when Wilma, legendary waitress and *chanteuse*, does her diva thing. Unique. BYOB. Tues-Sat Lunch and 7.30-9.30pm. LO 9pm. **405 xA1** MED

✝ **STRAVAIGIN:** 334 2665. 28 Gibson St. 50m downhill from Glas University's Men's Union, that is to say, in the v heart of bohemia, is where you'll find this underground restau. Stravaigin has a constantly changing menu, with a range and diversity that is truly eclectic, mixing international cuisines esp Asian and Pacific Rim to an effect that Asian restaus themselves rarely achieve. Fresh ideas and the freshest of ingredients combine to put this restau in a class of its own. Mon-Thurs noon-midnight, Fri-Sat noon-1am, Sun 5pm-midnight. **406 A1** INX

✝ **TWO FAT LADIES:** 339 1944. 88 Dumbarton Rd along from Kelvingrove Museum nr the end of Byres Rd. Calum Mathieson's seafood bistro is not just any old pt in a storm; in Glas it's about the only pt in a storm if you want first-class seafood. Easy on the eye and palate (nothing too fancy) and for this **407 A1** integrity and reliability, easy on the pocket. Simple and sound. Tues-Sat LO 10pm, Lunch Fri/Sat only. Cl Sun. (467/SEAFOOD RESTAUS.)   MED

408
B1   ⚓ **THAI FOUNTAIN:** 332 2599 2 Woodside Cres, Charing Cross. Same ownership as Amber Regent (*below*), this is probably Glasgow's best Asian restau. Genuinely Thai and not at all Chinese. Innovative dishes with gr diversity of flavours and textures, so sharing several is best. Of course you will eat too much. Cl Sun.   MED

409
B1   ⚓ **LA PARMIGIANA:** 334 0686. 447 Gr Western Rd. Not just the best Italian for many (given convenient location nr Kelvin Br - you can usually park somewhere nearby), this is the favourite place to eat without the ceremony and dulcet tones. Contemporary, if perhaps predictable cuisine. Good atmos. For when you can't face anything that isn't lightly done in olive oil. LO 11pm. Cl Sun.   MED

410
C2   **BOUZY ROUGE:** 221 8804. 111 W Regent St. Sister retau of the B Rouge in Airdrie (01236 763853), this is an excellent unpretentious restau downtown bistro. Owned by the Brown family (Roman Camp, Callender 682/CENTRAL and the Whinsmuir 1037/BEST FOOD) with chef Paul Holmes, it repeats the Airdrie formula of eclectic, affordable contemporary food and wine list. Gr for breakfast and Sun lunch. 7 days, 9.30am-midnight. Sun 12-12. LO 10pm.   INX

411
xC1   **GINGERHILL:** 956 6515. Hillhead St, Milngavie. At the end of the pedestrianised centre of Milngavie (15km N of centre), an intimate, friendly upstairs parlour. Coffee shop/restau during the day and in the evening specialising in seafood with excellent fresh produce (Gigha-landed fish etc), thoughtfully prepared by Carol Thomson and Heather Andrew (and their all-female team). Tables are yours for the night from 7pm. BYOB (and 10% off booze if you buy at Oddbins nearby). Mon-Sat 11am-4pm. Thur-Sat 7pm onwards (468/SEAFOOD RESTAUS).   INX

412
B1   **NAIRNS:** 0141 353 0707. Woodside Cres. Nick Nairn's new 'populist' restau, of which much is anticipated, opening after publication. Expect a v good scran. MED

AMBER REGENT: 331 1655. 50 West Regent St (451/FAR EASTERN RESTAUS).

KILLERMONT POLO CLUB: 946 5412. 2002 Maryhill Rd (442/INDIAN RESTAUS).

THE BEST BISTROS AND CAFÉ BARS

413
B2   ⚓ **MITCHELLS:** 204 4312. 2 branches, both W. 157 N St on the left bank of the M8 at the Mitchell Library, next to the real-ale Bon Accord Bar. Ales here too, but notably *the* place for informal and v good food with a genuine bistro atmos. Intimate, more colourful version in busy Ashton Lane off Byres Rd (339 2220) has helpful BYOB, inexpensive pre-theatre menu and more laid-back atmos. Both have food till 11pm, bar till midnight. Cl Sun.   INX

414
C2   ⚓ **MALMAISON:** 221 6401. 278 W George St. The brasserie in the basement of the hotel (358/ BEST HOTELS), with the same set up in Edin (10/BEST HOTELS) and a v similar menu. Excellent brasserie ambience in meticulously designed woody salon. Seating lay out and busy waiters mean lots of buzz; also private dining-rms and the adjacent **CAFÉ MAL** in bright contrast. Fixed-menu lunch or dinner Mediterranean style with daily specials. 7 days, lunch and LO 10.30pm.   MED

415
C2   ⚓ **PAPINGO:** 332 6678. 104 Bath St. Bright bistro in a cool basement with an accomplished new chef and a fresh outlook. The food is Scottish/French and perfectly portioned, especially for pre-theatre dinner. Wines and waiters are esp well chosen. Daily till 10.30/11pm.   INX

416
D2   ⚓ **MOJO:** 331 2257. 158A Bath St. Discreet, comfortable bistro behind the curtains at the back of this busy, metropolitan basement bar. The menu features some Japanese dishes such as sushi/sashimi, which are just as confidently produced as the more trad steak/frites. Relaxed atmos; straight talking wine list. Mon-Sat noon-midnight, Sun 6pm-midnight.   INX

417
C2   ⚓ **BABY GRAND:** 248 4942. 3/7 Elmbank Gardens. Inviting haven amongst high-rise office blocks opp Charing Cross Tower Hotel; a downtown-USA location. (Go behind the King's Theatre down Elmbank St, rt at gas stn and look for the hotel.) Probably the best urban atmos on this page. Narrow rm with bar stools and banquettes, often with background music from the eponymous piano.

Light, eclectic menu from tapas to full meals materialise in the tiny gantry. Daily from 8am-midnight/1am. We'll say it again (they *did* like it), 'only real cities have places like this'.

CHP

COTTIER'S: 357 5827. 93 Hyndland Rd (576/LIVE MUSIC *for directions, it's not easy to find*). Converted church that encompasses a bar; regular live music and benches outside, a restau; with an interesting menu made up of light, spicy dishes mostly from S of the Mason-Dixon line and a theatre that stages a broad range of productions/music throughout the yr. An autonomous state really, (probably have their own football team). (485/SUN BREAKFAST and many other reasons.) 7 days.

418
xA1

INX

BLUE BANANA: 959 2722. 42 Munro Place. Through Anniesland Cross, going W on Gr Western Rd. Turn into first Esso garage on left (really!) and it's through the gateway on the left. Madeleine Valente's friendly, 'family kitchen' style bistro. A variety of Scottish/international dishes, combining the freshest of ingredients and the cooking expertise of her extended family. Mon-Sat Lunch and 6-11pm.

419
xA1

MED

THE BELFRY: 221 0630. 652 Argyle St. App via W extension of St Vincent St, Elderslie St and left at the conical church. The basement of the Buttery, one of Glasgow's finest restaus (400/BEST RESTAUS) in the one remaining tenement of an area savaged by the M8. Bistro version of the Scots/French cuisine served up top, in study-like cellar rms with dark wood and books. New star chef so eat the best for less. Mon-Sat lunch, 6-11pm. Cl Sun.

420
B2

INX

THE CUL DE SAC: 334 8899. 44 Ashton Lane, the main lane off Byres Rd with the Grosvenor Cinema and The Ubiquitous Chip. Perenially fashionable crêperie/diner dedicated to serving good, simple food with flair, even wit. The atmos is relaxed and conversational, the burgers are exceptional and the fresh exotic flowers add a final *touché* (486/SUN BREAKFAST). Daily noon-11pm (Fri/Sat midnight).

421
A1

CHP

BAR BREL: 342 4966. 39 Ashton Lane. The unstoppable Billy McAnnanie's latest wheeze - a Gallic bar/bistro across the lane from the Cul de Sac (*above*). Flagstone floor, metal tables and enormous doors that fold back when its sunny. No mistaking the Belgo er . . . Belgian, influence in the cooking; fat, crispy chips served with large bowls of steaming mussels, or with steak. No Belgian jokes, but Belgian beers and a good wine list. Daily 11am-11pm (Fri/Sat till 12).

422
A1

INX

UPSTAIRS AT THE CHIP: 334 5007. 12 Ashton Lane. At other end of lane from Cul de Sac (*above*) and upstairs from The Chip (404/BEST RESTAUS), this is the wine bar and cheap seats version of the celebrated restau. Some tables are around the gallery of the courtyard below. There's a different menu with some similar seafood and puds as well as bar-type salads and soups etc. The bill will be less and you still get the celebrated wine list. Lively atmos.

423
A1

INX

TRON CAFÉ-BAR: 552 8587. 63 Trongate. Attached to the important Tron Theatre (640/NIGHTLIFE), currently undergoing major face-lift. Café at the front for coffee and chat and buzzing bar/bistro at the back with New Glas clientele, decent house wines and an eclectic menu. Not always the best grub in the city, but definately up there for atmos. Food till 10.30/11pm. Cl Mon evening.

424
E3

CHP

BARGO: 552 2680. 80 Albion St. Huge, Merchant City, bar and bistro in demand for fashion shoots due to its lofty stylish design. Big windows though not much to watch. The menu is a bit of a contemporary mix and match, but ain't bad considering this is more of bar to be seen in (dreaming of Manhatten). Popular pre-club venue (562/PRE-CLUB BARS). 7 days 10am-midnight. LO for food 10pm.

425
E3

INX

THE BEST FRENCH RESTAURANTS

78 ST VINCENT: 221 7710. 78 St Vincent St. Impressive split-level rm with an enormously high ceiling and a big mural by Glasgow artist Donald McLeod. Stylish cuisine balancing the tried and tested with some touches of originality. Slightly formal with an atmos of discreet efficiency. Not bad wines. Lunch (not Sun) and LO 10.30pm (10.45pm Sat/Sun).

426
D2

MED

THE BRASSERIE: 248 3801. 176 W Regent St. Related to Rogano (402/BEST RESTAUS), so seafood is their forte and menu has seasonal note. Busy in evenings, but you can usually find a nook for that tête à tête. Here you will find a genuine steak tartare. Good wine-list, especially bin-ends and halves. Mon-Fri noon-11pm, Sat lunch and 6pm-11pm. Sun, parties only.

427
C2

MED

428 **FROGGIE'S:** 572 0007. 53 W Regent St. Café/bistro with French owners and
D2 French home-cooking app. Gone a bit cajun/creole of late, but there are still a few
reminders left, viz the classic Marseillaise, *soupe de poisson*. Bustling brasserie
atmos. Some reasonable wines and you can BYOB. Open every day, best to book
at w/ends. Mon-Sat 9am-1am; Sun 5pm-midnight.   INX

429 **PIERRE VICTOIRE:** 221 7565. 91 Miller St, and in the W End at 16 Byres Rd (339
D3 2544). These 2 extensions along the M8, of the empire that started in Edin
A3 (76/CHAINS-U-LIKE) will soon be by joined another in Hope St. Cheap, cheerful,
and still as French as Jacques Tati's hat. Of the 2 so far, Byres Rd is better, but is
a v small Pierre. Lunch and 5-10.30pm.   INX

THE BEST ITALIAN RESTAURANTS

430 ✚ ✚ **FRATELLI SARTI:** 248 2228. 133 Wellington St and 204 0440 (best number
D1   for bookings), 121 Bath St. Glasgow's famed emporio d'Italia combining
a deli in Wellington St, wine shop in Bath St and restaus in each. Gr bustling
atmos. Cultivated and celebrated by anyone who has ever managed to get a table
at lunchtime. Good pizza, specials change every day, *dolci* and *gelati* in super-
calorific abundance. LO 10.30pm. Cl Sun.   CHP

431 ✚ **LA PARMIGIANA:** 334 0686. 447 Gr Western Rd. Sophisticated ristorante that
B1   blends trad service and contemporary Italian cuisine into one, seamless
performance. Carefully chosen dishes and wine list; solicitous service. Milano
rather than Napoli. Expect to find Italians (who consider this to be one of the
city's gr restaus). Mon-Sat lunch and 6-11pm. Cl Sun.   MED

432 ✚ **LA FIORENTINA:** 420 1585. 2 Paisley Rd W. Not far from river and motor-way
B3   over Kingston Br, but app from Eglinton St (A77 Kilmarnock Rd). It's at the
Y-jnct with Govan Rd. Trad tratt in an imposing listed building with an angel on
top. Always busy, usually seafood specials and off-hand waiters that break into
the occasional aria. As Italian as you want it to be, gr atmos with enormous menu
and wine list. Mon-Sat lunch and 5.30-11pm (though LO 9.30pm). Cl Sun.   MED

433 **MASSIMO:** 332 3227. 57 Elmbank St. Downstairs and across the st from Kings
C2 Theatre. Family run café/bar/ristorante where they joke about our lengthy 'rainy
season' and serve good pasta/pizza with a 'sunny' attitude. 6 days 9.30-11.30, Cl
Sun.   INX

434 **RISTORANTE CAPRESE:** 332 3070. 217 Buchanan St. Basement café nr the Concert
D2 Hall. Glaswegians (and footballers) love this place judging by the rogues gallery
of happy smiling punters. Checked tablecloths and Dino crooning in the
background create the authentic 'mamma mia' atmos. Friendly service, constantly
mobbed (well, not *mobbed*). LO 10/11pm. Book at w/ends.   INX

435 **PAPERINO'S:** 332 3800. 283 Sauchiehall St. Of course when you look into the good
C2 Glas restaus of a type, you find they're often owned by the same people. That
explains why this ordinary-looking though quite smart restau is better than the
rest – it's the same family as La Parmigiana (*above*) and the Big Blue (553/BEST
FOOD). Pasta and pizza here are always just fine. 7 days. LO 11pm/midnight. INX

436 **CAFÉ DU SUD:** 332 2054. 8 Clarendon St. Recently opened, immediately popular
C1 little restau tucked away behind St Georges Cross. Mediterranean/Italian style
cooking from husband and wife team who run it with an emphasis on the
personal touch. Everything seems fresh and home-made. Better book. Mon-Sat
Lunch Noon-3pm. and 6pm-10.30pm. Cl Sun.   INX

437 **PIZZA EXPRESS:** 221 3333. 151 Queen St, nr George Sq. The first of several,
D2 stylishly designed PEs in Scotland. Peter Boizot's finely-tuned formula translated
here with moderate success. Occasional jazz and the gospel of good pizza heard
every evening. Pasta, but only 2; some salads. 7 days till 11.30pm.   INX

438 **ANTIPASTI:** 337 2737. 337 Byres Rd. Popular restau on 2 levels that spills onto the
A1 st in warm weather bringing a touch of *la dolce vita* to the corner of Observatory
Rd. Good pasta, shame that if you just want an espresso and dessert you can't
have it alfresco. Breakfast time till late (midnight w/ends).   INX

439 **TREVI:** 334 3262. 526 Gr Western Rd. Tiny family run tratt with celebrity photos
B1 next to Italia league memorabilia on the walls. The staff can get a bit distracted on
international fixture nights. Loyal clientele; specials change every day. Tasty
home-made focaccia. Mon-Fri lunch and 6-11pm, Sat/Sun 6-11pm.

VINO VINO: 332 7718. 51a W Regent Street. Unexpectedly large rm downstairs with murals and pillars presumably trying to give the impression that you're eating outdoors in a Tuscan courtyard. Extensive wine list, (as you would expect) ain't exp. This new addition to Glasgow's Italianos is more kid friendly and relaxed than most. Good pasta, quality espresso. Some Florentine efficiency. Mon-Thurs Noon-11pm. Fri/Sat till 11.30pm.

440
D2

INX

FAZZI'S: 332 0941. 67 Cambridge St. Across the rd from the Glas Thistle Hotel. This once gr deli/café (and some say it's gone rt down the pasta tube) incl here more for nostalgia than now. They still like to put their more glamourous customers by the window, well . . . it pays to advertise, so you might or might not get a good view of the neighbourhood as well as a decent cappuccino. 8am-10pm, Sun 11am-9pm.

441
D1

INX

THE BEST INDIAN RESTAURANTS

☧ KILLERMONT POLO CLUB: 946 5412. 2022 Maryhill Rd. The more genuine traditions of the days of the Raj are still in evidence at Killermont. Within a hill top restau, at the Milngavie end of Maryhill Rd, you will find courteous manners, attentive service and a clubby atmos in the front rm which is kept as a shrine to all things polo (and they do run their own team). The food is fresh, light and the spices are sprinkled with care. Here Indian cuisine is taken seriously and they experiment in their Sun-Tues buffet-dinner. Lunch (not Sun) and 5pm-midnight (LO 10.30pm).

442
xC1

MED

☧ MOTHER INDIA: 221 1663. 28 Westminster Terr nr the Kelvin Park Lorne Hotel. A kitchen style restau where 'on-the-bone', a touchstone of authentic Indian home cooking, is used to gr effect. Tired of the old trad buffet round they've devised a new app where you can make up your own buffet, as many dishes as you like all freshly prepared. Lots of vegn choice. V relaxed neighbourhood atmos. BYOB. 7 days lunch and LO 10.30pm.

443
B2

INX

CREME DE LA CREME: 221 3222. 1071 Argyle St. The biggest, the most flash (and god knows they love flash), in town or anywhere for that matter so *they* say. Still at the hot edge of all things curried with the intro of a newly extended Goanese style menu. Frequently busy with office parties and leaving-dos, which keeps the place buzzing. Behind the flambé and the razzmatazz this is a restau that is run with care and, dare we say, precision. 7 days lunch (not Sun) and LO 11pm.

444
B2

MED

ASHOKA ASHTON LANE: 357 5904. 19 Ashton Lane. Front line curry shop for students from Glasgow Univ, just up the lane. V popular, v customer-led, so the food is strong on flavour and generously portioned. Can do no wrong, some say, while . . . **ASHOKA WEST END:** 339 0936. 1284 Argyle St. Always been a good, simple and dependable place to go for a bite of curry, but now seeming pricey to the faithful and shock-horror, some are going elsewhere. Still the healthy option menu is a good idea and on Sun family night, kids eat free. Both 7 days, lunch and open till midnight (W End even later).

445
B2

INX

MR SINGH'S INDIA: 221 1452. 149 Elderslie St. In an up-and-coming part of town this restau has acquired a reputation for consistency and kilted (really!) affability and has so far avoided the buffet trap. Simply better than most. It's perfectly placed to take on all (new)comers. 7 days, lunch and LO 11.30pm.

446
B2

CAFÉ INDIA: 248 4074. 171 N St. Enormous brasserie, big on a glamour, that seems a bit time-warped now, but the food is pretty good and presented in a way to make *you* feel good too. (*Group hug.*) The extensive menu is busy with herbs and spices and is not merely hot. A night on the town kind of joint. Buffet Sun/Mon. 7 days lunch and LO 11.30/midnight.

447
B2

INX

SHISH MAHAL: 334 1057. 68 Park Rd. First generation Indian restau that still, after 30 yrs, remains one of Glasgow's faves rather than finest. Though it's been a long time since Billy Connolly immortalized the vindaloo here, faithful followers swear it's yet to be bettered. But changes afoot. Till 11pm/midnight.

448
B1

INX

KAMA SUTRA: 332 0055. 331 Sauchiehall St. Part of the Ashoka group, this new restau has built a reputation for good food. An extensive and adventurous menu where each dish comes with a breakdown of contents and region of origin. Extracts from the original Indian sex-guide dotted here and there are peered at, surreptitiously. If those positions don't put you off your dinner, the pointy bits will. 7 days lunch and till midnight (Fri/Sat till 1am).

449
C2

INX

THE BEST FAR EASTERN RESTAURANTS

450 ✠ **THAI FOUNTAIN:** 332 2599. 2 Woodside Cres. Charing Cross nr the motorway,
B1 ✝ Mitchell Library etc. Few Thai restaus in Glas; this one clearly the best (and probably the best in Scotland). Owned by Chinese Mr Chung (*see* Amber Regent, *below*), but the Thai chefs know a green curry from a red. Tom yam excellent and weeping tiger beef v popular with those who really just want a steak. Lots of prawn and fish dishes and real vegn choice. Lunch and LO 11pm. Cl Sun.   MED

451 ✠ **AMBER REGENT:** 331 1655. 50 W Regent St. Elegant Cantonese restau that
D2 ✝ prides itself on courteous service and the quality of its food. The menu is trad with dishes designed to be eaten using chopsticks, although cutlery, of course, is provided. Candle-lit booths, sumptuous decor and a creditable wine list. Quite romantic. In *Michelin* guide. Lunch, LO 11pm (Fri 11.30, Sat 12). Cl Sun.   MED

452 **HO WONG:** 221 3550. 82 York St in city centre nr river, betw Clyde St and Argyle
C3 St. Discreet, urbane Pekingese/Cantonese restau which relies on its reputation and makes few compromises. Décor dated now, but still up-market clientele; roomful of suits at lunch and Bolly, Moët and DP on the champagne list. Notable for seafood and duck. Also, best Szechuan in town (cool down with a sorbet). Lunch (not Sun) and LO 11.30pm.   MED

453 **PEKING INN:** 332 8971. 191 Hope St. The revolving hot-plate/server at the centre
D2 of the table was an innovation when first introduced here. Since then there has been many a slip 'twixt cup and lip in the course of lengthy, exploratory meals fueled by endless jugs of hot saki. Famous for its spicy, Szechuan specials and good times. Lunch and LO 11.15pm (w/ends 12.15am).   MED

454 **LOON FUNG:** 332 1240. 417 Sauchiehall St. One of Glasgow's most respected
C2 Cantonese restaurants. Traditionally the place where the local Chinese community meet for lunch with their families and on a Sun/Mon/Tues, the pace is fast and friendly while the food, as you would expect, is fresh and authentic. Everybody on chopsticks. 7 days noon-10/11pm.   MED

455 **THE NOODLE BAR:** 333 1883. 482 Sauchiehall St. Authentic, Chinese style noodle
C2 bar, 100 m from Charing Cross. Choose one of the four types of rice or egg noodles as a base, then decide whether you would like it prepared as a soup (yes, you would) add some meat or veg from the menu board, take a ticket and while you're translating the 'chinese script only' specials, your food will arrive. Truly groovy. 7days noon-5am. (479/LATE NIGHT RESTAUS).   CHP

456 **AMBER RESTAURANT:** 339 6121. 130 Byres Rd. Trad, Chinese restau with an
A1 informal attitude and helpful staff. Recently extended selection of vegn dishes. V popular takeaway/home-delivery service; their chow mien is the best in the W end. Lunch except Sat/Sun and 5pm-11.30pm.   INX

457 **PATTAYA:** 572 0071. 473 Sauchiehall St. A recent, and welcome addition to the
C2 cadre. The ambience is cool and calming, a long way from Bangkok. And any holidays in Pattaya are probably best forgotten. Lengthy menu requires 2- beers-worth of perusal to do it justice. All the old lemon grass favourites are available and some thought has gone into creating authentic, vegn alternatives. Mon-Fri lunch and 5.30-11.30, Sat/Sun 5.30-12am.   MED

458 **MATA HARI:** 332 9789. 17 W Princes St. Malaysian and Singaporean cuisine which
C1 is Hal Al. Less spicy than Thai, with the exotic flavours of star flower and fresh cinnamon present along with the more usual lemon grass and ginger. There are some meat dishes but the menu is split mainly between vegn and seafood with an authentic, street-vendors' noodle dish that's straight off Clarke Quay, Singapore. 7 days 5pm-11pm, Fri/Sat till 11.30pm.   INX

THE BEST MEXICAN RESTAURANTS

Glas has innumerable restaurants and café bars with Mexican choices on a menu that mixes food from all over (best to stick to the potato skins). The places below are best Mex:

PANCHO VILLAS: 552 7737. 26 Bell St. Bright, colourful restau free of the cluttered cantina stereotype, run by real, live Mexican, Maira Nunez. Menu in Spanish/ingredients in English. No burritos ('an American invention'). Plenty of veggie choices but you really have to try the Albondigas en salsa, (that's spicy meatballs). Mon-Sat Lunch and 6-11pm, Sun till 10pm. **459** *E3* INX

CANTINA DEL REY: 552 4044. 6 King's Court in E End nr St Enoch's glasshouse. Frozen margaritas a must in this spacious bar/restau which actually does feel like a cantina. Fajitas (with floury tortillas and spicy dips) a favourite amongst the comidas (which also includes blackened fish) and brought sizzling across the rm to your table. Free nachos; you keep on drinking. 7 days, noon till LO 10pm (Fri/Sat till 11pm). **460** *D3* INX

SALSA: 337 1416. 184 Dumbarton Rd. Western off-shoot of the Cantina (*above*), smaller, more neighbourhood friendly. Spicy salsas of the title and all the things they accompany. As with all Mexican places, food can vary with the chef, most of whom have never been N, never mind S of the Rio Grande, but here it's more conscientious than most. Good vegn choice. 7 days, noon-10pm (Fri 11pm). **461** *xA1* INX

THE BEST RESTAURANTS FROM ROUND THE WORLD

ATHENA TAVERNA: 424 0858. 778 Pollokshaws Rd. On the S Side about 2km from the river. A Greek Cypriot restau and, adj, a wine bar that's big on real ale. Usual kleftiĉos etc, many chicken dishes, rabbit, feta and olives, plus the salads you get sick of on holiday then hanker after when you get home. Main courses cheap; vegn options. Indifferent wine list includes the inevitable Demestica but never mind, there's always the Furstenberg. Mon-Sat lunch; LO vary 10pm-1am. Cl Sun. **462** *xC4* INX

CAFE SERGHEI: 429 1547. 67 Br St just over the Jamaica St (or Glas) Br. Greek island evenings on a bleak rd heading S, a restau in an interesting conversion of former bank with upstairs balcony beneath impressive cupola; tiles and woodwork. Friendly, talkative waiters advise and dispense excellent Greek grub, incl vegn dishes. Better moussaka than you'll find easily on your holidays. Fri is Greek dancing night. Lunch (not Sun) and 6-11pm, 7 days. **463** *D3* INX

MISKA: 334 0594. 1321 Argyle St. Out to the W end of town, near the Art Galleries. Hugely popular Austrian/Tuscan/ Slovenian restau with a bewildering choice of dishes on offer; best to order one of the set menus, sit back and enjoy an Alpen Tour. Totally unpretentious; good value for money, not easily forgotten. 7 days 12.30-10.15pm, Fri/Sat till 11.15pm. **464** *A2* INX

JUNKANOO: 248 7102. 111 Hope St. Opp Central Stn and hotel. Glasgow's original tapas bar has gone back to its Spanish roots and rt back on form. Plenty vegn dishes and an emphasis on organic/free-range ingredients. Real Mojitos, one of the best most moreish drinks in the world (using fresh mint and limes with Havana Club). 7 days, LO 11pm. **465** *D3* CHP

PRINCE ARMANY'S: 420 6660. 7 Clyde Place. Over Jamaica St Br and under the railway br on the rt. Glasgow's one and only Arabic restau that transforms itself into a nightclub (guest DJs), after midnight. Food is buffet-style; choose from at least 6 main courses; rack of lamb is a favourite, and afterwards, join in with the belly dancing, but only if you've got your chops down. Tues-Fri 5pm-Midnight, w/ends until 3am. Cl Mon. **466** *C3* CHP

STRAVAIGIN: 334 2665. 30 Gibson St (406/BEST RESTAUS). MED

SEAFOOD AND FISH RESTAURANTS

467
A1
✝ ✝ **TWO FAT LADIES:** 339 1944. 88 Dumbarton Rd. Informal and bright restau that's one of Glasgow's best unkept secrets. The quality and freshness of the seafood and imaginative cooking, in the hands of chef/proprietor Calum Mathieson, makes this place a reliably fine prospect whether you're a fishhead or not (curiously fewer in Glas than elsewhere). Not always open on Mon (depends on the fish dunnit?), so phone. Pre-theatre menu. Sensible short, wine list. Mon/Tues-Sat 6-10pm, Lunch Fri/Sat (407/BEST RESTAUS). MED

468
MAP 1
D3
✝ **GINGERHILL:** 956 6515. Hillhead St, Milngavie. Upstairs at the end of the main st in this northern suburb of Glas (you are at the start of the W Highland Way), is a restau run entirely by women mostly from the island of Gigha (like much of the seafood they serve). Fixed menu and daily specials depending on what's landed. Vegn options and some chargrilled meat. One dinner sitting only, Thu-Sat (other nights if there are more than 6 of you); light lunches Mon-Sat. BYOB, no corkage (412/BEST RESTAUS). MED

469
xA1
THE RED SNAPPER: 357 2186. 14 Hyndland Rd. Going W on Gr Western Rd. Take a left at the 2nd set of lights after Byres Rd; restau is in The Coach House Hotel, set in the Victorian terrace on rt. The bright rm and wicker furniture give the feeling of sitting on someone's porch. Although there are other options on the menu, emphasis is on seafood. The early evening table d'hote (6-7pm), is good value at less than £8 for 2 courses. Frequently changed and affordable wine list on the blackboard. 7 days. LO 10 pm. MED

THE BEST VEGETARIAN RESTAURANTS

Every café bar in town has its veggie options on the menu, however these are the real restaus and see below for other places with more than a token piece of crêpe.

470
B1
BAY TREE: 334 5898. 403 Gr Western Rd. Recently changed hands so no longer a feminist co-op, just an 'old-fashioned exploitative capitalist concern now' says a member of staff, in jest we hope. Fact is the place is cleaner, a lot less militant and the food is better with a wider range and some middle-eastern dishes (owners are Iranian). All is still vegan, the sole concession being a jug of milk marked 'cows'. 7 days till 9pm (Sun till 8pm). (484/SUN BREAKFAST.) CHP

471
B1
VEGVILLE DINER: 333 1771. 93-97 St Georges Rd nr Charing Cross. Media-friendly restau (TV people nearby) with poster paint decor and a lively atmos. A gr deal of thought has gone towards creating a menu that is both imaginitive and tempting for veggies and non-veggies alike, and with a drinks licence in the offing, the world will indeed be their oyster (mushroom). Mon 10am-7pm, Tues/Wed 10-10pm, Thurs-Sat 10am-11pm. Cl Sun. CHP

472
B3
THE 13TH NOTE: 553 1638. 80 Glassford St. Merchant City bar with candle-lit tables upstairs and regular live music down. All vegan à la carte (vegeburgers 100% less beef than McDonalds) incl chilli, stroganoff, keftedhes and daily specials (577/LIVE MUSIC). 7 days noon-7pm (bar LO midnight). CHP

473
B1
GRASSROOTS: 353 3278. 48 Woodlands Rd. The foremost emporium for all things organic in Glas. The range and variety of eco-friendly products, in one place, is now large enough to offer a serious alternative to that weekly trip to the supermarket. The deli-counter is the real thing, full of tasty, 'genetically un-improved' goodies and although there's no café at press time, one is planned.

474
A1
CAFÉ ALBA: 61 Otago St. Popular neighbourhood café with excellent, trad vegn food. Hot dishes of the day, good salads/dressings and home-made cakes, scones and slices. Hungry univ crowd, so there's not much left beyond 2.30pm. Mon-Sat 10am-5pm. CHP

475
B2
THE ASHA: 221 7144. Elderslie St. Intimate, vegn Indian restau with a *hunting horn* as a centrepiece! Why not! All dishes can be be made to order; your choice of sauce and chilli-ness. Three fixed price Thalis and a selection of starters that are moreish than most. Some wines, but a jug of lager is probably the answer here. Lunch (except Sun), and 5-11.30pm. INX

Restaurants serving good vegn food but which are not exclusively vegn:

THAI FOUNTAIN, THE UBIQUITOUS CHIP and **PUPPET THEATRE** (408/404/401/BEST RESTAUS).

CAFÉ MAL, BABY GRAND and **THE TRON CAFÉ BAR** (414/417/424/BISTROS).

PATTAYA, MATA HARI (457/458/FAR EASTERN RESTAUS).

MOTHER INDIA (443/INDIAN RESTAUS).

JUNKANOO (465/ROUND THE WORLD).

CAFÉ GANDOLFI and **CAFÉ ALBA** (507/509/TEAROOMS).

THE BEST LATE-NIGHT RESTAURANTS

See other pages, esp INDIAN RESTAUS *p. 67, for w/end late openings.*

✠ **INSOMNIA/CRISPINS DELI:** 332 5500. 38 Woodlands Rd. 24 hr café/deli that dispenses food, infusions, strong coffee and drinks to those who just *will not go to their beds*. In a rm full of higgeldy-piggeldy bits of furniture, baths full of goldfish and a clock noticable by its absence, Glasgow's demi-monde plot and sip tea into the wee hrs of the afternoon. 7 days, 24hrs.
476
B1

CHANGE AT JAMAICA: 429 4422. 11-17 Clyde Pl under railway br on S side of Jamaica Br. Owned by the folk who run Peckham's (1165/1166/DELIS), a café/ restau which really comes into its own after midnight on Fri/Sat. 'Breakfast' (anything from porridge to pizza) served till 5am to night owls and more exotic party animals – an essential slice of Glas nightlife. You may have to wait for a table once the club crowd arrive (from 3am onwards). Good music, good puds. Drinks till 1am, but pots and pots of tea. Also lunch and 7pm-midnight. Cl Sun.
477
D3

CANTON EXPRESS: 332 0145. 407 Sauchiehall St. A bit forlorn these days since their chef left for pastures new, but still open late and still serving hot, tasty food to those that know what they want and want it now. 7 days noon-4am.
478
C2

THE NOODLE BAR: 333 1883. 482 Sauchiehall St. And this is where the chef went, (across the rd next door to the The Garage). The real deal. Authentic, Chinese fast food, no frills, (ticket service and eezee-kleen tables). The noodle is 'king' here and they take their cooking quite seriously. 7 days noon-5am.
479
C2

KING'S CAFE: 332 0898. 71 Elmbank St. Been here for yrs, for that special, deep fried pizza, need that sometimes, (inexplicably), gets you at 3 am. Comfy booths, house wine and Bud. Restau closes at 11pm but the takeaway stays open till 4.30am, on Thurs/Fri/Sat.
480
C2

GUIDO'S CORONATION RESTAURANT: 55 Gallowgate. Nr the Barrowland (1886/ROCK AND POP) for as long as people have been going there. Fish and chips and home-made pizza/ice cream. Sit-In or takeaway. Sun-Thurs till 1am, Fri/Sat till 2am.
481
E3

PRINCE ARMANY'S: 420 6660. 7 Clyde Pl. Over Jamaica St Br and under the railway br on the rt adj Change at Jamaica (*above*). Glasgow's Arabic restau that transforms into a club with guest DJs, after midnight. Tues-Fri 5pm-Midnight, w/ends till 5am. Cl Mon (466/ROUND THE WORLD).
482
C3

FROGGIE'S: 332 8790. 53 W Regent St. You have to order by 11pm, but this French/cajun caff/bistro is open 7 days till 1am (428/FRENCH RESTAUS).

GOOD PLACES FOR SUNDAY BREAKFAST

483   ✚ **CAFÉ GANDOLFI:** 552 6813. 64 Albion St. Atmospheric rm, with soft daylight
E3   filtering through the stained-glass and the comforting, oversized wooden
furniture. This is a pleasant start to the day, made even better with some baked
eggs, a pot of tea and the Sunday papers. From 11am.

484   **BAY TREE:** 403 Gr Western Rd. This excellent caff (470/VEGN RESTAUS) provides
B1   another antidote to the toxins of Sat night. A hearty vegan breakfast is served all
day. From 11am.

485   **COTTIER'S:** 93 Hyndland St off Hyndland Rd (418/BISTROS; 418/LIVE MUSIC *for*
A1   *directions*). Deep in the hefty-mortgage belt of Hyndland, this converted church
probably gets more of a congregation now than it ever did. Eclectic menu from
fruit plate to the full monty and eggs benedict to cajun kedgeree. Noon-4pm.
Papers provided.

486   **CUL DE SAC:** 44 Ashton Lane, off Byres Rd (421/BISTROS). A smart relaxed place
A1   to phase into Sunday. Clubby staff, so revival may take till late afternoon. The
fry-up includes potato scones and comes in a vegn version, and there are the
better-than-average burgers and exotic crêpes. Brunch noon-4pm.

487   **NICO'S:** 332 5736. 379 Sauchiehall St. Long-established example of the French café
C2   bar abroad. Begins to look like a Manet painting in late afternoon light (*Oh,
c'mon Graeme!*). Croissants, cafetieres and comfy banquettes. Brunch: noon-4pm
(open till midnight).

488   **UPSTAIRS AT THE CHIP:** 334 5007. 12 Ashton lane. 'Sair heid' or not, their Bloody
A1   Marys are the best in town and combined with a veggie breakfast (gr potato
crowdie), famously restorative. Selection of papers. Unhurried. From 12.30pm.

THE BEST TAKEAWAY FOOD

489   ✚ **HUNGRYS:** 353 1889. 98 Bath St. 'American-style' deli/ sandwich shop in
D2   downtown Glas. It's a long way from 34th St, NYC, but it's much better than
most on these blocks as long lunch queues attest. Several kinds of bread, good
soup. Try a pepper and tuna mayo on herb focaccia. Mon-Fri 8am-4pm.

490   ✚ **MUNGO JERRI'S:** 552 7999. 25 Parnie St. At bottom of High St and nr the Tron
E3   and Tron Theatre. 30 or so sandwiches to choose from, most have an
American angle and there's also lox and bagels, BLTs, tortillas and lots on rye. Gr
veggie burgers. Sit-in or takeaway. Wish they delivered.

491   **NUMBER ONE SANDWICH ST:** 248 2050, 104 St Vincent St and 221 2002, 9 Waterloo
D2   St. 2 other downtown locations where office-workers and shop assistants descend
in droves for assembly-line and some bespoke sandwiches and baked potatoes.
Betw them they produce over 1,000 lunches a day. Mon-Fri 8am-4pm.

492   **SANSIRO:** 248 9553. 539 Sauchiehall St. Smart, little Italian lunch-box W of
B2   Charing Cross. Pizza, pasta, over-stuffed ciabatta, crostino and good coffee to
take away in this constantly changing part of Sauchiehall St. Mon-Fri 8am-4pm.

493   **LITTLE ITALY:** 339 6287. 205 Byres Rd. In Michelangelo's depiction of the
A1   Creation, God is reaching out to Man giving him the spark of life. In a v similar
painting, above the counter here, Man is being handed . . . a cup of coffee. Gr
pizza and pasta, freshly baked breads, ice cream, loadsa Italian wines and a
heavenly cup of coffee. Mon-Thurs 8am-10pm, Fri/Sat 8am-1am, Sun 5-10pm.

494   **LE PETIT PAIN:** 337 1118. 239 Byres Rd. Bright, little continental baguette/ciabatta
A1   shop all baked on the premises. Fillings usually made up of a combination of two
or three ingredients and the whole effect is . . . fresh. They do takeaway/deliveries
or you can sit at one of the benches in the window. Good coffee. Mon-Fri 8.30-
6pm, Sat 9-6pm, Sun 12-6pm.

495   **TOSCANA:** 956 4020. 46 Station Rd, Milngavie. It's a long way from town, so you'd
MAP 1   have to be in the area, but if you are this family-run Italian café also does gr
D3   takeaway pasta and pizza and home-made puds. Till 10pm.

GREAT CAFÉS AND GREASY SPOONS

UNIVERSITY CAFÉ: 87 Byres Rd. When your granny, in the lines of the well-known song, was 'shoved aff a bus', this is where she was taken afterwards and given a wee cup of tea to steady her nerves. People have been coming here for generations to sit at the 'kneesy' tables, share the salt and vinegar and eavesdrop on their neighbours' conversations. Run by the Verecchia family who administer advice, sympathy and pie, beans and chips with equal aplomb. A gem. Daily till 10pm (w/ends till 10.30pm). Cl Tues. Takeaway open later. **496 A1**

GROSVENOR CAFÉ: 35 Ashton Lane, behind Byres Rd nr Hillhead Stn. For over 30yrs they've been serving hot, filled rolls and bowls of steaming broth to students, and all the rest of us who have happily crammed into the wee booths. They've added a patio at the rear and are licenced to sell beer and wine now. More extensive suppery menu after 7pm. 7 days, 9am-11pm (Mon till 7pm, Sun till 5.30pm). **497 A1**

EQUI: 449 Sauchiehall St. This used to be a schoolboy hideout when the old High School was round the corner in Elmbank St. Dogging double maths for a bacon roll and a frothy coffee in the booth at the back seemed like a fair exchange at the time. Real formica. Few tables, erratic service; quite indispensable. Mon-Sat 10am-8pm. Cl Sun. **498 C2**

COIA'S CAFÉ: 473 Duke St. Since 1928, supplying this E End high st with ice cream, gr deal breakfasts and the kind of comforting lunch (you would call it dinner) café bar places just cannot do. There's a telly in the corner but it's really only there to spark off open debate. Sit-in or take away. Sweeties of all sorts; and Havana cigars. 7 days, 7.30am-9pm (LO 7.30pm); Sun from 11am. **499 xE2**

ALLAN'S SNACK BAR: 6 Storie St, Paisley. Off the High St, a chip shop with classic greasy spoon adj and a chips-with-everything menu in a Paisley days-gone-by atmos. So much better than anything on this or any other high st. Happy waitresses. Mon-Thu 11am-7pm, Fri/Sat 11am-8pm. Cl Sun. **500 xA4**

JACK McPHEES; 285 Byres Rd. Recent name-change, (it used to be Loreto's), but under the new coat of paint it's still the same. All day breakfast, big cups of tea, chippy next door and if you don't behave yourself you might get an old-fashioned 'clip round the ear'. Mon-Sat 8am-10pm, Sun 8am-7pm. **501 A1**

THE UNIQUE: 223 Allison St. Quite the best high-tea/fish 'n' chips. All the trad trimmings. Full report: 1085/FISH AND CHIPS.

KID-FRIENDLY PLACES

TASHA BLANKITT: 423 5172. 378 Cathcart Rd. Bit out of the way, but not far from Pollokshaws Rd on the S side. A friendly spot to take the kids, commandeer a comfy corner and have some macaroni cheese. High chairs and half portions (516/TEAROOMS). 7 days. 8.30am-5.30pm (Sun 10.30am-4.30pm). **502 xD4**

TGI FRIDAYS: 221 6996.113 Buchanan St. The Glas branch of the national chain adored by kids because of the way they get fussed over and are given, pretty much, a free run of the place. The food is from everywhere via America and when added, free-hand, to the crayon drawings on the tablecloth, can look quite spectacular. Huge range of cocktails available for parents who need them. 7 days 11am-11.30pm, Sun till11pm. **503 D2**

HARRY RAMSDEN'S: Paisley Rd W beside motorway flyover – not far from centre, but difficult without a car. Not a bad branch of the national chain that caters well for kids. Greasy, cooked in lard and in cheerfully tacky surroundings, the chips and peas, sausage and fishcakes come in kids' portions and there's a playground to throw them into before back in the car. **504 C3**

DI MAGGIO'S: 334 8560. 61 Ruthven Lane, off Byres Rd, W End; 632 4194 at 1038 Pollokshaws Rd on a busy corner S of the river; and 248 2111 at 21 Royal Exchange Sq. Bustling, friendly pizza joints with good Italian attitude to bairns. There's a choice to defy the most finicky kid. High chairs, special menu. 7 days. **505 A1**

JACK McPHEES; 285 Byres Rd. Squeaky booths, gingham table covers . . . Cuthbert, Dibble and grub. Kids' meal and drink £1.95 (501/GREAT CAFÉS). 6 days 8am-10pm, Sun-7pm. **506 A1**

THE BEST TEAROOMS AND
COFFEE SHOPS

506
D2
✚ ✚ **FRATELLI SARTI:** 248 2228. 133 Wellington St and 121 Bath St. Full report: 430/ITALIAN RESTAUS, but mentioned here just in case you want a light snack or an excellent cappuccino and you miss it. Open 8am-10pm. Cl Sun.

507
E3
✚ **CAFÉ GANDOLFI:** 552 6813. 64 Albion St, Merchant City nr City Halls. The vaguely bohemian, Europe-somewhere atmos, the stained glass and the heavy, over-sized wooden furniture create a unique ambience that has stood the fashionability test of recent times. The food is light and imaginative and served all day. May have to queue. 7 days, 9am-11.30pm, Sundays from noon.

508
D3
✚ **THE GRANARY:** 226 3770. 82 Howard St. Beside/behind the glass-pyramid of the St Enoch Centre towards river. A calm oasis away from the bustling shoppers on Argyle St that serves mainly vegn dishes but the emphasis is on home-baking. The apple pie is still the best in town. Hard to believe that this place exists in an area decimated by the mall-mongers. *Vive la resistance!* Mon-Sat 8.30am-6pm. Sun 11-5pm.

509
B1
✚ **CAFÉ ALBA:** 61 Otago St. Just after the dog-leg on this busy st that's always in danger of falling into the river you'll find this supremely unruffled little café. Fresh vegn fare, none of which exists much beyond lunch time and home-baked cakes that also have a tendency to disappear quickly. Draws a slightly arty (but not starving in garrets obviously) crowd. Mon-Sat 10am-5pm.

510
A1
THE METRO: Cresswell Lane, off Byres Rd nr Hillhead Stn. The huge sky-lights make this split-level rm a cheery rendezvous even on a dull day. There's a salad bar and a board for the day's hot dishes, lots of imported tortes and tarts and a weird counter system that defies description. Mon-Sat 8-6pm.

511
C2
THE WILLOW TEAROOMS: 217 Sauchiehall St. Another level (The Gallery), has been added upstairs, and a new sister tearoom has now opened at 97 Buchanan St. Both, under the discerning eye of proprietor Anne Mulhern, recreate the interiors of the original Miss Cranston's Tearooms, designed by C R Mackintosh. 30 blends of loose leaf tea, all manner of cakes, scones and sandwiches and now a wee glass of wine. (635/MACKINTOSH). Mon-Sat 9.30am-4.30pm.

512
xA4
EXHIBITION CAFÉ: 353 4799. 10 Dumbreck Rd. Bellahouston Park. On the ground floor of 'House for an Art Lover' (637/MACKINTOSH). This bright rm has a modern Spanish feel; tan leather couches, tubular steel chairs and gallery space. Nicely prepared, light, lunch menu that is without fussiness, like the surroundings. Excellent latte/espresso/cappuccino. Daily 10am-5pm.

513
C2
BRADFORDS: 245 Sauchiehall St. Coffee shop/restau upstairs from the flagship shop of this local and estimable bakery chain (1131/BAKERS). Not the speediest waitresses but the macaroni cheese is good and the cakes and pies from downstairs represent Scottish bakery at its best. Mon-Sat 9am-5.30pm.

514
C3
PICKERING AND INGLIS, THE CHAPTERHOUSE: 26 Bothwell St. A self-serve coffee shop at the back of a bookshop. Wholesome and home-baked; Busy, Christian rendezvous, behind the tracts and concordances. Mon-Sat 8.30am-4.30pm.

515
D3
THE JENNY TRADITIONAL TEAROOMS: 20 Royal Exchange Sq and opp new Gallery of Modern Art. Trad they are; inside, a chintzy parlour just as you might like to imagine it (though not perhaps of a main st in Glas). Sombrely lit and low-voiced for the serious business of taking tea (several varieties) with scones, cakes (not all home-made – tut-tut) and their famous fudge. Hot dishes and interesting sandwiches. Pavement tables in summer. Also suppers, Thu-Sat.

516
xD4
TASHA BLANKITT: 423 5172. 378 Cathcart Rd. An out-of-the-way and unusual gift/coffee shop/bistro south of the river with a loyal following. 'Hampstead in Govanhill' home-cooking that's truthful, often imaginative and selective; micro's only there to heat things up. Mon-Sat 8.30am-5.30pm, Sun 10.30am-4.30pm. Dinner w/ends only, 7-11pm.

517
C2
CCA: 350 Sauchiehall St. Within the Centre for Contemporary Arts where there's a bookshop, exhib space and usually gr stuff going on. Bar and bistro/coffee shop; interesting and interested folk. 9am-11pm/midnight. Cl Sun.

SOME GREAT 'GLASGOW' PUBS

Pubs that are notable for other specific reasons are on other pages. Pubs in Glas are licensed till midnight or 1am (and later only during special events).

✝ **VICTORIA:** 157 Bridgegate. 'The Vicky' is in the 'Briggait', one of Glasgow's oldest streets, nr the Victoria Br over the Clyde. Once a pub for the fishmarket and open odd hours, now it's a howff for all those who like an atmos that's old, friendly and uncontrived. Small interior; you can close the door on all that new Glas. Maclays, Theakstons and Greenmantle ales. Mon-Sat till midnight, Sun till 11pm.
518
D3

✝ **SCOTIA BAR:** 112 Stockwell St. Nr the Victoria, late 1920s Tudor-style pub with a low beamed ceiling and intimate, woody 'snug'. Long the haunt of folk musicians, writers and raconteurs. Music and poetry sessions, folk and blues. Daily till midnight.
519
D3

✝ **CLUTHA VAULTS:** 167 Stockwell St. This and the pubs above are part of the same family of trad Glas pubs. The Clutha (ancient name for the Clyde) has a Victorian style interior and an even longer history. Music. Same hrs.
520
D3

✝ **BLACKFRIARS:** 36 Bell St. Contemporary version of the 'old' city's public houses, essential as meeting places, because poky, tenement flats were not built for entertaining. Nowadays, there's more space, but the people are just as sociable and there's no back green. Ales, lagers old and new, all-day menu including 'nightbites' till midnight (557/BEST FOOD). Regular programme of live music (*see* 573/LIVE MUSIC). 7 days till midnight.
521
E3

✝ **THE HORSESHOE:** 17 Drury St. A mighty pub since 1884 (and before) in the small st betw Mitchell and Renfrew Streets nr the stn. Early example of this style of pub, (dubbed; 'gin palaces'). Island rather than horseshoe bar and an upstairs lounge where they serve high-tea. The food is amazing value (551/BEST FOOD). Caledonian and Maclays. Daily till midnight.
522
D2

✝ **THE HALT BAR:** 160 Woodlands Rd. On the old tram route W, this Edwardian pub remains largely unspoiled. Original counter and snug intact. Home to the Bud Neill Appreciation Society. Neill's surreal, 1950s cartoon characters have been immortalized, across the rd, in bronze. 'Mighty fine' (529/'UNSPOILT' PUBS; 575/LIVE MUSIC). Open till 11pm (midnight weekends). The Halt is handily close to:
523
B1

✝ **UISGE BEATHA**: 246 Woodlands Rd. 'Oo-i-skay Bay' (or something like that) means 'the water of life' and is a unique Highland outpost in the city. Shooting-lodge chic and cosy; more than a mere draught of the Gael. Good grub at lunch time. Related to one of the gr Highland bars, The Drover's Inn, Inverarnan (1003/BLOODY GOOD PUBS). Sun-Thu till 11pm, Fri/ Sat till midnight.
524
B1

BAR 10: 10 Mitchell Lane off Buchanan St. Mongrel furniture and sliced-brawn tiles, high ceiling and design (by Ben Kelly of Manchester's Hacienda fame), this place looks like it's been transported from Canal St, NYC. Good food, gossip and strong coffee served with a shot of iced water during the day; the place to go pre-club at night. Regular DJs at w/ends.
525
D2

THE LOUNGE, THE LIVING-ROOM, THE APARTMENT: W Regent St and Byres Rd. 2 bars and a club related, not necessarily in style, but by protagonist Colin Barr's entrepreneurial vision. The Lounge in W Regent St, is a beach-bar basement with football TV and a big Sunday breakfast. The Living Room at the bottom of Byres Rd is a 2 rm see-and-be-seen scenario with eclectic menu (till 8pm) and smooth music. The Apartment is a relaxed, stylish, after-hrs drinking club in Royal Exchange Sq (1868/nightclubs). Bars: 7 days till midnight.
526
C2
A1

LOCK 27: 1100 Crow Rd. At the v N end of Crow Rd beyond Anniesland, an unusual boozer for Glas: a canal side almost country pub in a v urban setting complete with gasometers. Pub on a lock of the Forth and Clyde Canal (596/CITY WALKS), unused these days. Good food; 4 ales. Gets busy. 7 days.
527
xA1

McPHABBS: 23 Sandyford Place. 2 blocks W of Charing Cross. Non-aligned boozer more of a 'shebeen' than anything else. *Laissez-faire* attitude. Postage-stamp patio at rear, tasty bar food, endorsed by local MP George Galloway (552/BEST FOOD). Good malts. 7 days, till midnight Fri/Sat.
528
B1

THE BEST OLD 'UNSPOILT' PUBS

Of course it's not necessarily the case that when a pub's done up it's spoiled, or that all old pubs are worth preserving but some have resisted change and that's part of their appeal. The following places don't have to recreate 'atmos'. Glas pubs close no later than midnight.

529
B1
✠ **HALT BAR:** 160 Woodlands Rd. Edwardian pub, that used to be an official stop on the old tram route W. In the classic trad of the stand-up bar with a 'snug' (for the ladies), behind a wooden partition, with 'pulpit' serving-hatch. Varied (free) live music through the back (575/LIVE MUSIC). Sun-Thu till 11pm, Fri/Sat till midnight. Music usually from 9pm.

530
C2
✠ **THE GRIFFIN (and the GRIFFINY and the GRIFFINETTE):** 266 Bath St. Corner of Elmbank St nr Kings Theatre. Built 1903 to anticipate the completion of the Theatre and offer the patrons a pre-show pie and a pint. Stand at the Edwardian Bar like generations of Glaswegians. Main bar still retains 'snug' with a posh, etched glass partition; booths have been added but the atmosphere is still 'Old Glasgow' (550/BEST FOOD). Sun-Thu till 11pm, Fri/Sat till midnight.

531
xE2
THE ROWAN TREE, UDDINGSTON: 12km SE of centre via M74. In Old Mill Rd off Main St where sign points (in opp direction) for Bothwell Castle. A cottagey pub in the shadow of the world-famous Tunnock's Caramel Wafers factory and long frequented by the wafermakers. Food at lunch time, coal fire in winter, folk music on Fridays. Maclays. Mon-Sat till 11.45pm, Sun till 11pm.

532
E3
THE SARACEN'S HEAD: Gallowgate, nr Barrowlands. An establishment of this name has existed in the neighbourhood since 1755, playing host to a multitude of colourful characters; not least Boswell and Johnson, on the return leg of their grand Highland tour. This, the most recent incarnation, opened in 1905 and is famous for its lethal 'White Tornado' cider. The atmos is more 'wild west' than E end, although the 'one singer, one song', rule still prevails. 7 days, but not open late (Fri/Sat till 9pm).

533
D3
THE MITRE: The lane of Brunswick St off Argyle St opp C&A. Untouched by the 'gentryfiers' and full of character. Gem of a bar, just quietly getting on with its business. Bit of music at w/ends, food at lunch, Belhaven; nothing fancy. 7 days till 11pm or midnight.

534
xC4
M J HERAGHTY: 708 Pollokshaws Rd. More than a touch of the Irish about this pub and easily more authentic than recent imports. A local with loyal regulars who'll make you welcome; old pub practices still hold in this howff in the S. Sun-Thu till 11pm, Fri/Sat till midnight.

535
B3
BRECHIN'S: 803 Govan Rd. Nr jnct with Paisley Rd W and motorway over-pass. Established in 1798 and, as they say, always in the same family. A former shipyard pub which, despite the proximity to Rangers FC, is not partisan. It's behind the statue of shipbuilder Sir William Pearce (which, covered in sooty grime, was known as the 'Black Man') and there's a feline 'rat-catcher' on the roof (making it a listed building). Unaffected neighbourhood atmos. Mon-Sat till 11pm, Sun till 6.30pm.

536
B3
THE OLD TOLL BAR: 1 Paisley Rd W. Opp the site of the original Parkhouse Toll where monies were collected for use of the 'turnpikes' betw Glas and Greenock. Opened in 1874, the original interior is still intact; the *fin de siècle* painted glass and magnificent old gantry preserved under order. A 'palace pub' classic. Real ale and some single malts. 7 days till 11pm.

537
D2
THE HORSE SHOE: 17 Drury St. The celebrated city-centre bar with the famous longest bar in the world and an assortment of Old and New Glaswegians all along it (522/GREAT 'GLASGOW' PUBS; 551/BEST FOOD).

538
E3

xA3
BAIRDS BAR and **THE DISTRICT:** 2 bars from opp sides of the gr divide. **BAIRDS** in the Gallowgate adj Barrowlands (643/NIGHTLIFE) is a Catholic stronghold green to the gills where, on days when Celtic play at home up the rd at Parkhead, you'd have to be in by 11am to get a drink. **THE DISTRICT,** 252 Paisley Rd W, Govan, nr Ibrox Park, is where Rangers supporters gather and rule in their own blue heaven. Both pubs give an extraordinary insight into what makes the Glas time bomb tick. Provided you aren't wearing the wrong colours (or say something daft), you'll be very welcome in either.

THE BEST REAL-ALE PUBS

Pubs on other pages may purvey real ale, but the following are the ones where they take it seriously and/or have a good choice.

♱ BON ACCORD: 153 N St. On a slip rd of the motorway swathe nr the Mitchell Library. One of the first real ale pubs in Glas. Over 100 malts as well as up to 18 beers; always Youngers 3, McEwan's 80/-, Theakston and Old Peculiar plus many guest ales on hand pump. Food at lunch time and light bites till 9pm. Light, easy-going atmos here, but they do take their ale seriously; there's even a 'tour' of the cellars if you want it. Mon-Sat till midnight, Sun till 11.30. **539** B2

♱ THREE JUDGES: 141 Dumbarton Rd opp the bottom of Byres Rd. Named after the triumverate of boxing judges that used to own it. These days you're more likely to find professors than practitioners of the 'gentlemanly art'. Maclays and 9 guest ales that change regularly (1,320 at last count). 7 days. **540** A1

TENNENTS: 191 Byres Rd. Nr the always-red traffic lights at Univ Ave, a big, booming watering-hole of a place where you're never far away from the horseshoe bar and its several excellent hand pumped ales incl Maclays, Caledonian and Theakston. Revamped to take it into the next century, but the 'old century' crowd will still be there. **541** A1

BABBITY BOWSTER: 16 Blackfriars St. In a pedestrianised part of the Merchant City and just off the High St, a highly successful pub/restau/hotel; but the pub comes first. Maclays is heavily featured and makes their own Babbity Thistle Ale, but there's always an English guest and lots of malts. Food all day (551/BEST FOOD), occasional folk music (esp Sun), o/side patio and exhibs. Proprietor Fraser Laurie has thought of everything. **542** E3

BOSWELL HOTEL: 27 Mansionhouse Rd. S side via Pollokshaws Rd, Langside Ave and rt just before the Battlefield Monument at the edge of Queen's Park. Though now passed from private hands to Tennents, purveyors of fizzy lagers, this remains a real-ale haven. 3 busy bars and notable for family pub food. Usually 3 or 4 regulars and 8 guest ales, all well looked after. Rms upstairs. Fine, unpretentious grub till 10pm. Kids and all non-believers welcome. Sun-Thu till 11pm, Fri/Sat till midnight. **543** xC4

THE CASK AND STILL: 154 Hope St. Formerly the Pot Still, there are up to 8 ales here (always Youngers 3, McEwan's 80/- and Old Peculiar), but it's also noted for a mind-boggling range of malts. They've got over 200. Mon-Sat till 11pm/midnight. Cl Sun. Same folk have the **RITZ BAR** at 241 N St nr the Bon Accord (*see above*). Large, friendly boozer with half a dozen ales and food to go with. Occasional music and quiz nights. 7 days but closed Sun lunch. **544** D2

THE BREWERY TAP: 1055 Sauchiehall St, nr Kelvingrove Park. Same management as Blackfriars (521/GREAT 'GLASGOW' PUBS) and Stoat and Ferret (*see below*). Since you can see the univ from the bar, local students treat it as an unofficial recreation rm. Gr music on tape (and regular live jazz) and ales on tap: Belhaven, Caledonian, Arrols, Tetleys and guests. **545** A1

THE STOAT AND FERRET: 1055 Sauchiehall St, 1534 Pollokshaws Rd. S side sister to The Tap/Blackfriars and ploughing a similar furrow. Regularly changed guest ales; featured beer of the month and live folk/jazz at the w/ends. **546** B2

THE ATHENA TAVERNA: 778 Pollokshaws Rd. Intimate wine bar/lounge adj decent Greek restau on the S side (462/ROUND THE WORLD) with 2 Czech beers on draft and a large selection of German wheat-beers. Restau hrs. **547** xC4

THE HORSESHOE: 17 Drury St. Gr for lots of reasons (522/GREAT 'GLASGOW' PUBS) not the least of which is its range of beers: Caledonian, Greenmantle, Maclays and Bass on hand pump. **548** D2

VICTORIA BAR: 157 Bridgegate. Another pub mentioned before (518/GREAT 'GLASGOW' PUBS) where FPA, Maclays and others can be drunk in a dark woody atmos enlivened by occasional trad music. **549** D3

PUBS WITH GOOD FOOD

Most of these pubs are also notable for other reasons. Glas bars usually close no later than midnight.

550
C2
THE GRIFFIN: 266 Bath St. On corner of Elmbank St across from King's Theatre. The Griffin, the Griffiny and the Griffinette: they're always there on that corner and your basic pie/chips/beans and a pint will not be bettered at this price (£2.50 at time of going to press, the equivalent 80yrs ago of 8 old pence). Other staples available and a more elaborate menu in the lounge or the Griffinette next door (incl Sun lunch). Food: noon-3pm and evenings till 7pm. Pub till midnight/1am.

551
D2
THE HORSESHOE: 17 Drury St. The classic pub to be recommended for all kinds of reasons. But lunch is a particularly good deal with 3 courses for £2.40 (pie and beans 80p), and old favourites on the menu like mushy peas, macaroni cheese, jelly and fruit. Lunch noon-2.30pm and all afternoon upstairs, including high-tea till 7.30pm (not quite the same atmos, but pure Glas). Pub open daily till midnight.

552
B1
McPHABBS: 221 0770. 23 Sandyford Pl. 2 blocks W of Charin Cross. Gr Scottish/Irish bar food; smoked haddies, salmon and steaks, beef and Guiness stew, etc. Given the 'parliamentary seal of approval' by local MP George Galloway who particularly rates the stew. 7 days, open till midnight at the w/ends (528/GREAT 'GLASGOW' PUBS).

553
B1
THE BIG BLUE: 445 Gr Western Rd. A modern bar/bistro in a gr uptown location literally on the (river) Kelvinside. Drinking drowns the eating later on, but till mid evening there's excellent Italian pub grub. Big Sun breakfast.

554
D2
THE DRUM AND MONKEY: 93 St Vincent St on corner of Renfield St. Cavernous but comfortable and particularly successful bar/bistro with a sombre gentlemen's club atmos – 'the odd libation for the overworked'. Comfort and more contemporary food with a bistro through the back which has an à la carte menu in the evening. Puds on blackboard. Also in Edin. 7 days till 11pm.

555
A2
MURPHY'S PAKORA: 1287 Argyle St. A good idea (long ago sold on) which solves the problem of what to drink with spicy Indian food (Murphy's Irish Stout). Pakora (best in mixed selections of 'thalis' or platters where you can choose any 3) are served all day; gram flour batter wrapped round anything you can think of (incl haggis) dipped in 3 sauces. Moist bits like aubergines and seafood work best. Table service and bar. 7 days, LO 11pm.

556
E3
BABBITY BOWSTER: 16 Blackfriars St. Already listed as a pub for real ale and as a hotel (there are rms upstairs), the food is mentioned mainly for its Scottishness (haggis and stovies) and all-day availability. It's also pleasant to eat o/side on the patio/grd in summer. Breakfast is served from 8am (542/REAL ALE; 372/INEXP HOTELS).

557
E3
BLACKFRIARS: 36 Bell St. Candleriggs in one of the focal points in the Merchant City. Gr Glas pub for all-round ambience, provision of real ale and music, and food available all day until midnight (but drinkers loud after 9pm). Menu changes slightly for evenings, but it's mainly pub-grub favourites such as the ubiquitous potato skins and Death by Chocolate. Specials vary with staff, who's cooking etc. (521/GREAT 'GLASGOW' PUBS; 573/LIVE MUSIC).

558
E3
RAB HA'S: 553 1545. 83 Hutcheson St. In an area bristling with pubs and eateries this old Merchant City howff has a reputation for good food. Well-chosen selection of bar meals incl organic veg specials. Restau downstairs in the evening.

559
C2
BRUNSWICK CELLARS: 353 0131. 239 Sauchiehall St. Across the st from the McLellan Galleries. Popular with clubbers/Xtreme sports fans at night and hungry office workers/art students (same crowd), during the day who dive into this dark, underground bar for a quick, cheap lunch. Freshly prepared enchiladas/salads/soups/sandwiches and, on Thursday, the cheapest pint you'll find on Sauchiehall St.

560
xA4
FOX AND HOUNDS, HOUSTON: On B790 village main st in Renfrewshire, 30km W of centre by M8 jnct 29 (A726), then cross back under motorway on B790. Village pub with real fire and dining-rm upstairs for family meals and suppers. Folk come from miles around. Sun roasts. Gr example of couthie cuisine. Food available daily at lunch time and from 6-10pm (all day Sat/Sun).

PRE-CLUB BARS

These bars all feature DJs at the weekends to get you up, and in the mood, for getting down with your 'bad self' at one of Glasgow's many clubs . . .

BAR 10: 221 8353. 10 Mitchell Lane. Half-way up Buchanan St pedestrian precinct on the left. There's an NYC look about this Ben Kelly designed joint that is so loved by its habitues, they make an exhibition out of themselves. Hang out, get your photo snapped and join the crowd (525/GREAT 'GLASGOW' PUBS). **561 D3**

BARGO: 552 2680. 80 Albion St. In the Merchant City, this spacious, designer-theque is much in demand for fashion shoots and, of course, high-glam posing on a Sat night. Can be attractively quiet during the day (425/BISTROS). **562 E3**

BAR MIRO: 353 0475. 36 Kelvingrove St. Nr Kelvingrove Park, off Sauchiehall St. Stylish bar on 2 floors that spills out onto the steps and a tiny forecourt in warm weather. **563 B1**

CUL DE SAC: 649 4717. 44 Ashton Lane. This upstairs bar is a perennial W End fave. Close to the underground for that last minute dash into town to beat club curfews (421/BISTROS). **564 A1**

MOJO'S: 331 2257. 158a Bath St. City centre, underground bar with comfy couches and a smart, urban atmos. Good food through the back (416/BISTROS). **565 C2**

MONKEY BAR: 353 2351. 100 Bath St. Colourful, underground bar, nr Mojo's (*see above*). Busy at the w/ends with a young professional/student crowd. **566 C2**

POLO LOUNGE: 553 1221. 84 Wilson St. Urbane and stylish bar/disco by the irrepressible Stephen King. Latest fave on the gay scene (1862/GAY SCOTLAND). **567 E3**

YO YO: 248 8484. 31 Queen St. Sports-themed, neon-lit, style bar for trendy young things. Next door to Archaos and with surprisingly good restau downstairs (1868/NIGHTCLUBS). **568 D3**

THE GATE: 333 0250. 408 Sauchiehall St. Intimate and smart, with a fondness for tartan and flavoured vodka. **569 C2**

PUBS AND CLUBS WITH LIVE MUSIC

Many other places have live music but programmes and policies can vary quickly. Best to look out for posters or consult The List *magazine, on sale fortnightly in the city-centre.*

✠ KING TUT'S WAH WAH HUT: 221 5279. 272 St Vincent's St. Every bit as good as its namesake in Alphabet City used to be; real, edgy, make-or-break atmos in the cramped rm upstairs where bands on the club circuit play to a damp and appreciative crowd. See flyers for bigger bands coming through. Doors open 8.30. Tickets at bar or Tower Records, Argyle St. **570 C2**

NICE 'N' SLEAZY: 333 9637. 421 Sauchiehall St at the W End. Not esp sleazy and fairly rock 'n' roll. Popular art school hang-out. Every flavour of alco-pop and voddie. Good indie juke-box and play station for hire. Bands downstairs (esp Thu-Sun) with a nominal entrance charge. Usually 9pm. Till midnight. **571 C2**

THE CATHOUSE: 248 6606. 15 Union St. Live rock club with mixed programme on various nights depending on availability of touring bands (other 'clubs' on other nights). Recent broadening of musical taste so no longer necessary to turn up with leather strides and pointy boots. Tickets in advance, as for King Tut's (*above*). **572 C3**

BLACKFRIARS: 552 5924. 36 Bell St. Merchant City pub with everything (522/GREAT 'GLASGOW' PUBS) which includes all kinds of live music and if you are a player, 'Glasgow songwriters' on Tuesday nights, features an open mic guest policy. Turn up early to book your spot. Free. **573 E3**

SCOTIA BAR and **THE CLUTHA VAULTS:** 552 8681/552 7520. Nr each other in the E End nr the river and under same management (112 and 167 Stockwell St). Integral part of the Glas folk scene for yrs, but also readings and other sessions (e.g. Clutha has bluegrass and country). Glas Folk Club on Wed at Scotia and always at w/ends. Free. (*See* 519/520/GREAT 'GLASGOW' PUBS; 1883/FOLK MUSIC.) **574 D3**

HALT BAR: 564 1527. 160 Woodlands Rd. Gr pub rock atmos with booked live acts on Thursday and 'open mic' spots on Wednesday and Saturday. Music starts around 9pm and admn is free. (529/'UNSPOILT' PUBS.) **575 B1**

576 **COTTIER'S:** 357 5825. 93 Hyndland St. In the densely populated quadrant betw
xA1 Dumbarton Rd and Byres Rd). A neighbourhood atmos to this converted church
(not in, but off the top of Hyndland St nr Highburgh Rd); it has the same
management as the Baby Grand (417/BISTROS) and Cathedral House (366/INEXP
HOTELS). Restau upstairs (418/BISTROS). Bar and theatre, on the ground level, serve
as a platform for local talent and cult-ish acts from abroad. Regularly features
special gigs with three or more bands on the bill and, occasionally, entire,
musically-themed, w/ends. Good programming.

577 **THE 13th NOTE:** 553 1638. 80 Glassford St. On similar circuit as King Tut's for up-
D3 and-coming (esp local) bands. V ambient candle-lit venue that puts on a variety of
indie/rock/jazz acts for a lively, studenty crowd, most nights of the week. (*See also*
472/VEGN RESTAUS.)

THE MAIN ATTRACTIONS

578 ✠ ✠ **KELVINGROVE ART GALLERY AND MUSEUM:** 287 2700. At westerly extension
A1 of Argyle St and Sauchiehall St by Kelvingrove Park. Huge Victorian
sandstone edifice with awesome atrium. On the ground floor is a natural history/
Scottish history museum. The upper salons contain the city's superb British and
European art collection. There are strong contemporary exhibs as well as the
permanent collection. Pipe-organ recitals every alternate Sun. Tearoom. The
Museum of Transport (584/OTHER ATTRACTIONS) is across the rd. Mon-Sat 10am-
5pm, Sun from 11am. (628/BEST ARCHITECTURE.)   FREE

579 ✠ ✠ **THE BURRELL COLLECTION** and **POLLOK PARK:** 649 7151. S of river via
xC4 A77 Kilmarnock Rd (over Jamaica St Br) about 5km, following signs
from Pollokshaws Rd. Set in rural parkland, this hugely successful attraction is an
award-winning modern gallery built to house the eclectic acquisitions of Sir
William Burrell. Showing a preference for medieval works, amongst the 8,500
items the magpie magnate donated to the city in 1944 are artefacts from the
Roman empire to Rodin. The building itself integrates old doorways and whole
rms reconstructed from Hutton Castle. Self-serve café and restau on the ground
floor. Pollok House and Grds further into the park (with works by Goya, El
Greco and William Blake) is worth a detour and has below stairs, the better
tearoom. Both open Mon-Sat 10am-5pm, Sun from 11am. Cl Tues. (596/CITY
WALKS.)   FREE

580 ✠ **GLASGOW CATHEDRAL/PROVAND'S LORDSHIP:** 552 8198/552 8819. High St.
xE2 Across the rd from one another they represent what remains of the oldest
part of the city which (as can be seen in the People's Palace, *below*) was, in the early
18th century, merely a ribbon of streets from here to the river. The
present Cathedral, though established by St Mungo in AD543, dates from the 12th century
and is a fine example of the v real, if gloomy, gothic. The House, built in 1471, is
a museum which strives to convey a sense of medieval life. Watch you don't get
run over when you re-emerge into the 20th century and try to cross the st. In the
background, the Necropolis piled on the hill invites inspection and offers a
viewpoint and the full gothic perspective (1511/GRAVEYARDS). Cl Tues.

581 ✠ **THE PEOPLE'S PALACE:** 554 0223. Closed for renovations until spring of 1998,
xE4 although the upstairs section, may open earlier. Best to call but if they're up
and running again, app via the Tron and London Rd, then turn rt into Glas Green.
This has been a folk museum *par excellence* wherein, since 1898, the history,
folklore and artefacts of a proud city have been gathered, cherished and
displayed. But this is much more than a mere museum; it is the heart and soul of
the city and together with the Winter Grds adj, shouldn't be missed if you want
to know what Glasgow's about. Tearoom in the Tropics, amongst the palms and
ferns of the Winter Grds, will still be part of the attraction for any visitor in the
future. Opening times will be as other museums (*see above*).   FREE

582 **ST MUNGO MUSEUM OF RELIGIOUS LIFE AND ART:** 553 2557. In the Cathedral precinct
xE2 or sq dubbed Ft Weetabix by Glas cabbies. Opened with some gnashing of teeth and
wringing of hands in 1993, it houses art and artefacts representing the world's six
major religions arranged tactfully in an attractive stone building with a zen grd in
the courtyard. The dramatic Dalì *Crucifixion* seems somehow lost, and the
assemblage seems like a good and worthwhile vision not quite realised. But if you
like your spirituality shuffled but not stirred, this is for you. The punters' comments
board is always . . . enlightening. Mon-Sat 10-5pm, Sun from 11am. Cl Tues.

HUNTERIAN MUSEUM AND GALLERY: 330 5431. Univ Av. On one side of the st, **583** Glasgow's oldest museum with geological, archaeological and social history *A1* displayed in a venerable building. The cloisters outside and the **UNIVERSITY CHAPEL** should not be missed. Across the st, a modern block contains part of Glasgow's exceptional civic collection – Rembrandt to the Colourists and the Glasgow Boys, as well as one of the most complete collections of any artist's work and personal effects to be found anywhere, viz that of Whistler. It's fascinating stuff even if you're not a fan. There's also a print gallery and the superb **MACKINTOSH HOUSE** (633/MACKINTOSH). Mon-Sat 9.30am-5pm. FREE

THE OTHER ATTRACTIONS

✝ ✝ **TRANSPORT MUSEUM:** 287 2700 . Off Argyle St behind the Kelvin Hall **584** and opp Art Gallery. May not seem your ticket to ride, but this is one of *A1* Scotland's most fascinating museums. Has something for everybody, esp kids. The reconstruction of a cobbled Glas st *circa* 1938 is an inspired evocation. There are trains, trams and unique collections of cars, motorbikes and bicycles. And model ships in the Clyde rm, in remembrance of a mighty river. Make a donation and the Mini splits in two. Mon-Sat 10am-5pm, Sun 11am-5pm. FREE

✝ ✝ **BOTANIC GARDENS AND KIBBLE PALACE:** 334 2422. Gr Western Rd. **585** Smallish park close to R Kelvin with river side walks (594/CITY WALKS), *xA1* and pretty much the 'dear green place'. Kibble Palace (built 1873) is the distinctive domed glasshouse with statues set amongst lush ferns and shrubbery from around the (mostly temperate) world. A wonderful place to muse and wander. Grds open till dusk; palace 10am-4.45pm.

✝ ✝ **GALLERY OF MODERN ART:** 331 1854. Queen St. Central, controversial **586** and housed in former Stirling Library, Glasgow's newest big visual arts *D2* attraction opened in a hail of art world bickering in 1996. Director Julian Spalding's choice of inclusion raised to record levels both the ire of critics and the interest of the public. This 'Modern Art' incl contemporary and populist from elsewhere, but little from the influential movements and bugger all from the Saatchi side in which many Glas artists have made notable contributions. Smart café up top. Check hrs.

✝ ✝ **THE BARROWS:** (pron 'Barras') The sprawling st and indoor market area **587** in the E End of the city around the Gallowgate. An experience, an *E3* institution, a slice of pure Glas. If you're only in town for one w/end, it's a must, and like no other market anywhere. Sat and Sun only (1798/MARKETS).

THE TENEMENT HOUSE: 333 0183. 145 Buccleuch St. Nr Charing Cross but can **588** app from nr the end of Sauchiehall St and over the hill. The typical 'respectable' *C1* Glas tenement kept under a bell-jar since Our Agnes moved out in 1965. She had lived there with her mother since 1911 and wasn't one for new-fangled things. It's a touch claustrophobic, with hordes of visitors, and is distinctly voyeuristic, but, well . . . your house would be interesting, too, in 50yrs time if the clock were stopped. Daily, Mar-Oct 2-5pm. ADMN

POLLOK LEISURE CENTRE: 881 3313. Cowglen Rd. Adj Pollok shopping centre in **589** S side. From city centre take Pollokshaws Rd, then rt fork (after 3km) to Pollok *xC4* Park and rt (after 1km) at r/bout along Barrhead Rd. Centre is 2km along on left at next r/bout. A place to take kids for water immersion thrills, slides etc in modern, safe leisurama. Mon-Fri 9.30am-9pm, Sat/Sun 10am-4pm.

GREENBANK GARDENS: 10km SW of centre via Kilmarnock Rd, Eastwood Toll, **590** Clarkston Toll and Mearns Rd. Then signposted (3km). A spacious oasis in the *xC4* suburbs; formal grds and 'working' walled grd, parterre and woodland walks around elegant, Georgian house. V Scottish. Grds open AYR dawn-dusk, shop/tearoom Apr-Oct 11-5 pm. NTS

MITCHELL LIBRARY: 287 2999. North St. On a slip rd and o/look the canyon of the **591** M8, the landmark domed edifice of Glasgow's main library. Named after Stephen *B2* Mitchell, tobacco lord (1789-1874), who wanted to leave a building 'worthy of the city', it opened in 1911. Interesting just to wander through the vast halls or upstairs to the quieter reading rms; the dome itself is astonishing. Theatre next door has a mixed theatre/music programme. Café till 4.30pm. Library: Mon-Fri 9am-9pm, Sat till 5pm. Cl Sun.

592 **THE CITY CHAMBERS:** 287 2000. George Sq. The hugely impressive building along
D2 the whole E end of Glasgow's municipal central sq. Let's face it, it's not often that
one could seriously recommend a visit to the District Council offices, but this is
a wonderfully over-the-top monument to the days when Glas was the second city
of the empire, a cross between an Italian Renaissance palace and an Escher marble
maze. Guided tours Mon- Fri, 10.30am and 2.30pm.

593 **FINLAYSTONE ESTATE:** 01475 540505. 30km W of city centre via fast M8/A8 signed
xA4 off dual-carriageway just before Pt Glas. Delightful grds and woods around
mansion house with many pottering places and longer trails (and ranger service).
Various 'attractions' e.g. that rare thing: a walled grd and Victorian laundry and
kitchen , etc. Visitor centre and conservatory tearoom. Much better family outing
than McDonalds or the grd centre. 7 days, 10.30am-5pm.

PAISLEY ABBEY: Paisley town centre, 15km from Glas (1524/ABBEYS).

BOTHWELL CASTLE, UDDINGSTON: 15km E, via M74 (1433/RUINS).

THE BEST CITY WALKS

See p. 10 for walk codes.

595 **KELVIN WALKWAY:** A path along the banks of Glasgow's other river, the Kelvin,
xA1 which enters the Clyde unobtrusively at Yorkhill but first meanders through
some of the most interesting parts and parks of the NW city. Walk starts at
Kelvingrove Park through the University and Hillhead district under Kelvin Br
and on to the celebrated Botanic Grds (585/OTHER ATTRACTIONS). The trail then
goes N, under the Forth and Clyde Canal (*see below*) to the Arcadian fields of
Dawsholm Park (5km), Killermont (posh golf course) and Kirkintilloch (13km
from start). Since the river and the canal shadow each other for much of their
routes, it's possible, with a map, to go by out one waterway and return by the
other (e.g. start at Gr Western Rd, return Maryhill Rd).

START: Usual start at the Eildon St (off Woodlands Rd) gate of Kelvingrove Park
or Kelvin Br. St parking only. 2-13+KM XCIRC BIKE 1-A-1

596 **FORTH AND CLYDE CANAL TOWPATH:** The canal, opened in 1790 and once a major
xA1 short cut for fishing boats and trade betw Europe and America, provides a
C1 fascinating look round the back of the city from a pathway that stretches on a
D1 spur from Pt Dundas just N of the M8 to the main canal at the end of Lochburn
Rd off Maryhill Rd and then E all the way to Kirkintilloch and Falkirk, and W
through Maryhill and Drumchapel to Bowling and the Clyde (60km). Much of
the route is through the forsaken or redeveloped industrial heart of the city, past
waste ground, warehouses and high flats, but there are open stretches and curious
corners and, by Bishopbriggs, it's a rural waterway. More info from British
Waterways (332 6936). Revitalising the whole Edin-Glas link will be a major
millennium project.

START: (1) Top of Firhill Rd (gr view of city from Ruchill Park, 100m further on,
606/BEST VIEWS). (2) Lochburn Rd (*see above*) at the confluence from which to go
E or W to the Clyde. (3) Top of Crow Rd, Anniesland where there is a canal side
pub, Lock 27 (527/GREAT 'GLASGOW' PUBS), with tables outside, real ale and food
(noon-7/8pm). (4) Bishopbriggs Sports Centre, Balmuildy Rd. From here it is
6km to Maryhill and 1km in other direction to the 'country churchyard' of
Cadder or 3km to Kirkintilloch. All starts have some parking.
ANY KM XCIRC BIKE 1-A-1

597 **POLLOK COUNTRY PARK:** The park that (apart from the area around the Gallery
xC4 and the House, 579/MAIN ATTRACTIONS) most feels like a real country park.
Numerous trails through woods and meadows. The leisurely Sun guided walks
with the park rangers can be educative and more fun than you would think (632
9299). Burrell Collection and Pollok House and Grds are obvious highlights.
There's an 'old-fashioned' tearoom in the basement of the latter. Enter by Haggs
Rd or by Haggs Castle Golf Course. By car you are directed to the entry rd off
Pollokshaws Rd and then to the car park in front of the Burrell. Train to
Shawlands or Pollokshaws W from Glas Central Stn.

598 **MUGDOCK COUNTRY PARK:** 956 6100. Not perhaps within the city, but one of the
xC1 nearest and easiest escapes (1216/COUNTRY PARKS). Park which includes
Mugdock Moor, Mugdock Woods (SSSI) and 2 castles is NW of Milngavie.

Regular train from Central Stn takes 20mins, then follow route of W Highland Way (1598/LONG WALKS) for 4km across Drumclog Moor to S edge of park. Or take Mugdock Bank bus from stn (not Sat) to end. By car to Milngavie by A81 from Maryhill Rd and left after Black Bull Hotel (on left) and before railway stn (over to rt) up Ellengowan Rd. Continue past reservoir then pick up signs for Park. 3 car parks, visitor centre is at second one. Many trails marked out and further afield rambles. This is a godsend betw Glas and the Highland hills.

5-20KM　CAN BE CIRC　BIKE　1-A-2

CATHKIN BRAES: On S edge of city with impressive views (604/VIEWS).

EASY WALKS OUTSIDE THE CITY

See p. 10 for walk codes. Refer to Map 1.

THE CAMPSIE FELLS: Range of hills 25km N of city best reached via Kirkintilloch or Cumbernauld/Kilsyth. Encompasses area that includes the Kilsyth Hills, Fintry Hills and Carron Valley betw. **(1)** Good app from A803, Kilsyth main st up the Tak-me-Doon (*sic*) rd. Park by the golf club and follow path by the burn. It's poss to take in the two hills to left as well as Tomtain (453m), the most easterly of the tops, in a good afternoon; views to the E. **(2)** Drive on to the jnct (9km) of the B818 rd to Fintry and go left, following Carron Valley reservoir to the far corner where there is a forestry rd to the left. Park here and follow track to ascend Meikle Bin (570m) to the rt, the highest peak in the central Campsies. **(3)** The bonny village of Fintry (395/HOTELS OUTSIDE TOWN) is a good start/base for the Fintry Hills and Earl's Seat (578m). 598 D3

10KM+　CAN BE CIRC　XBIKE　2-B-2

GLENIFFER BRAES, PAISLEY: Ridge to the S of Paisley (15km from Glas) has been a favourite walking-place for centuries. M8 or Paisley Rd W to town centre (many buses from Anderson Bus Stn/trains from Central Stn) then: **(1)** S via B775/ A736 towards Irvine or **(2)** B774 (Causewayside then Neilston Rd) and sharp rt after 3km to Glenfld Rd (Bus: Clydeside 24). For **(1)** go 2km after last houses, winding up ridge and park/start at Robertson Park (signed). Here there are superb views and walks marked to E and W. **(2)** 500m along Glenfield Rd is a car park/ranger centre. Walk up through grds and formal parkland and then W along marked paths and trails. Eventually, after 5km, this route joins **(1)**. 599 D3

2-10KM　CAN BE CIRC　MTBIKE　1-A-2

GREENOCK CUT: 45km W of Glas. Can app via Pt Glas but simplest route is from A78 rd to Largs. Travelling S from Pt Glas take first left after IBM, signed L Thom. Loch side 5km up winding rd. Park at Cornalees Bridge Centre. Walk left along loch side rd to Overton (5km) then path is signed. The Cut, an aqueduct built in 1827 to supply water to Greenock and its 31 mills, is now an ancient monument. Gr views from the Mast, over the Clyde. Another route to the right from Cornlees leads through a glen of birch, rowan and oak to the Kelly Cut. Both trails described on board at the car park. 600 C3

15/16KM　CIRC　MTBIKE　1-B-2

MUIRSHIEL: General name for vast area of 'Inverclyde' W of city incl Greenock Cut (*above*), Castle Semple Country Park and Lunderston Bay a stretch of coastline nr the Cloch Lighthouse on the A770 S of Gourock for littoral amblings. But best wildish bit is Muirshiel Country Park itself with trails, a waterfall and Windy Hill (1084ft). Nothing arduous, but a breath of air. From Pt Glas head S on A761 for Kilmacolm then S for Lochwinnoch on B786. 601 C3

THE WHANGIE: On A809 N from Bearsden about 8km after last r/bout and 2km after the Carbeth Inn, the car park, for the Queen's View (605/BEST VIEWS). Climb uphill towards the stand of conifers and over the stile. Of 2 paths, one leads along the top of the scarp, the other lower down, runs parallel to it and offers more protection from the elements. Both lead to the westerly end of the escarpment. Once you get to the summit of Auchineden Hill, take the path that drops down to the W, (a half-rt-angle) and look for crags on your rt. This is the 'back door' of The Whangie. The path then seems to disappear into the side of the hill but carry on and you'll suddenly find yourself in a deep cleft in the rock face with sheer walls rising over 10m on either side. The Whangie is more than 100m long and at one pt the walls narrow to less than 1m. As you emerge, take the lowest path, back along the face of the hill to the stile and then down to the car park. Local mythology has it that The Whangie was made by The Devil, who lashed his tail in anticipation of a witchy rendezvous somewhere in the N, and carved a slice through the rock, where the path now goes. 602 D3

5KM　CIRC　XBIKE　XDOGS 1-A-1

603 **CHATELHERAULT, nr HAMILTON:** Jnct 6 off M74, well signposted into Hamilton,
E3 follow rd into centre, then bear left away from main rd where it's signed for A723.
The gates to the 'château' are about 3km outside town. A drive leads to the
William Adam-designed hunting lodge of the Dukes of Hamilton, set amidst
ornamental grds with a notable parterre and extensive grounds. Tracks along the
deep, wooded glen of the Avon (ruins of Cadzow Castle) lead to distant glades.
Ranger service and good guided walks (01698 426213). 20km SE of city centre.
House open 10.30am-4.30pm, walks at all times. 2-7KM CIRC BIKE I-A-2

THE BEST VIEWS OF THE CITY
AND BEYOND

604 **CATHKIN BRAES, QUEEN MARY'S SEAT:** The southern ridge of the city on the B759
xC4 from Carmunnock to Cambuslang, about 12km from centre. Go S of river by
Albert Br to Aikenhead Rd which continues S as Carmunnock Rd. Follow to
Carmunnock, a delightfully rural village, and pick up the Cathkin Rd. 2km along
on the rt is the Cathkin Braes Golf Club and 100m further on the left is the park.
Marvellous views to N of the Campsies, Kilpatrick Hills, Ben Lomond and as far
as Ben Ledi. Walks on the Braes on both sides of the rd.

605 **QUEEN'S VIEW, AUCHINEDEN:** Not so much a view of the city, more a perspective
xC1 on Glasgow's Highland hinterland, this short walk and sweeping vista to the N
has been a Glaswegian pilgrimage for generations. On A809 N from Bearsden
about 8km after last r/bout and 2km after the Carbeth Inn which is a v decent pub
to repair to. Busy car park attests to its popularity. The walk, along path cut into
ridge side, takes 40-50mins to cairn at 634ft from which you can see The Cobbler
(that other Glas favourite (1570/HILLS), Ben Ledi and sometimes as far as Ben
Chonzie 50km away. The fine views of L Lomond are what Queen Victoria came
for. Further on is the Whangie (602/WALKS OUTSIDE THE CITY). I-A-1

606 **RUCHILL PARK:** An unlikely but splendid panorama from this overlooked, but
xC1 well-kept park to the N of the city nr the infamous Possilpark housing estate. Go
to top of Firhill Rd (past Partick Thistle football ground) over Forth and Clyde
Canal (595/CITY WALKS) off Garscube Rd where it becomes Maryhill Rd. Best
view is from around the flagpole; the whole city amongst its surrounding hills,
from the Campsies to Gleniffer and Cathkin Braes, becomes clear.

607 **BAR HILL at TWECHAR, nr KIRKINTILLOCH:** 22km N of city, taking A803 Kirkin-
xE1 tilloch t/off from M8, then the 'low' rd to Kilsyth, the B8023 and bearing left at
the 'black-and-white br'. Next to Twechar Quarry Inn, a path is signed for Bar
Hill and the Antonine Wall. Steepish climb for 2km, ignore the strange dome of
grass: this isn't it. Over to left in copse of trees is the remains of one of the forts
on the wall which stretched across Scotland in the first two centuries AD. Ground
plan explained on a board. This is a special place with strong history vibes and
airy views over the plain to the city which came a long time after. I-A-2

608 **BLACKHILL, nr LESMAHAGOW:** 28km S of city. Another marvellous outlook, but in
xE1 the opp direction from above. Take jnct 10/11 on M74, then off the B7078 signed
Lanark, take the B7018. 4km along past Clarkston Farm, head uphill for 1km and
park by Water Board mound. Walk uphill through fields to rt for about 1km.
Unprepossessing hill which unexpectedly reveals a vast vista of most of E central
Scotland. I-A-2

609 **PAISLEY ABBEY:** About one Saturday a month betw May and Oct (1-5pm) on
xA4 Abbey 'open days', the tower of this amazing edifice can be climbed
(1524/ABBEYS). The tower (restored 1926) is 150ft high and from the top there's a
grand view of the Clyde. Obviously this is a rare experience, but phone Tourist
Info (0141 889 0711) for details; next Sat could be your lucky day. M8 to Paisley;
frequent trains from Central Stn.

610 **LYLE HILL, GOUROCK:** Via M8 W to Greenock, then round the coast to relatively
MAP 1 genteel old resort of Gourock where the 'Free French' worked in the yards
C3 during the war. A monument has been erected to their memory on the top of Lyle
Hill above the town from where you get one of the most dramatic views of the gr
crossroads of the Clyde (Holy Loch, Gare L and L Long). Best vantage-point is
further along the rd on other side by trig pt. Follow British Rail stn signs, then
Lyle Hill. There's another gr view of the Clyde further down the water at **HAYLIE,
LARGS** the hill 3km from town reached via the A760 rd to Kilbirnie and Paisley

3km. The island of Cumbrae lies in the sound and the sunset.

CAMPSIE FELLS, GLENIFFER BRAES (598/599/WALKS OUTSIDE THE CITY).

BEST OF THE SPORTS FACILITIES

SWIMMING AND INDOOR SPORTS CENTRES
611

Well, surprise surprise, the best 2 pools, Arlington Baths (332 6021) and the Western Baths (339 1127), are both private. Temporary memberships may be negotiable.

WHITEHILL POOL: 551 9969. Onslow Dr parallel to Duke St at Meadowpark St in *xE3*
the E End nr Alexandra Park (phone for times but usually Mon-Fri till 8.30pm
and Sat/Sun till 1.45pm). 25m pool with sauna/multigym (universal).

NORTH WOODSIDE LEISURE CENTRE: 332 8102. Braid Sq. Not far from St George's *C1*
Cross nr Charing Cross at the bottom of Gr Western Rd. In a rebuilt area; follow
AA signs. Modern pool (25yds) and sauna/steam/sun centre. Open Mon-Fri
8/9am-7/8pm (Sat/Sun 10am-4pm).

THE POLLOK LEISURE CENTRE: 881 3313. Cowglen Rd. Not a do-your-lengths *xC4*
kind of a pool – more a family water outing (589/OTHER ATTRACTIONS).

GOUROCK BATHING POOL: 01475 631561. On rd S, an open-air heated pool on the MAP 1
Clyde. Gr prospect for summers like they used to be (1703/SWIMMING POOLS). C3

KELVIN HALL: 357 2525. Argyle St by Kelvingrove and Art Gallery. Major venue *A1*
for international indoor sports competitions, but open otherwise for weights/
badminton/tennis/athletics. Book hr-long sessions. No squash.

SCOTSTOUN LEISURE CENTRE: 959 4000. Danes Dr Huge, state-of-the-art sports *xA2*
multiplex. 10 lane pool, indoor halls and outdoor pitches. 9am-10pm. w/ends-
6pm.

MARCO'S: 554 7184. Templeton Business Centre (beside the fabulous Templeton *E3*
Carpet Factory), by Glas Green in the E End. Like the Edin one, a labyrinthine
and massively successful complex with squash/snooker/gym (universal and first
class)/indoor jogging track (even though it is next to the Green). Nonmembers
ok. Open 10am-10pm (Sat till 8pm). No pool.

ALLANDER SPORTS CENTRE: 942 2233. Milngavie Rd, Bearsden, 16km N of centre *xC1*
via Maryhill Rd. Best by car. Squash (2 courts) badminton/snooker and swimming pool (open late, but times vary; usually till 10.30 Tue/Thu/Fri and 9pm
Sat/Sun). Waiting list for gym.

GOLF COURSES
612

*Glas has a vast number of parks and golf courses. The following clubs are the best of those that
are open to nonmembers.*

CATHKIN BRAES: 634 0650. Cathkin Rd SE via Aikenhead Rd/Carmunnock Rd to *xC4*
Carmunnock village, then 3km. Best by car. Civilised, hill top course on the v
southern edge of the city. Nonmembers Mon-Fri (though probably not Fri
morning).

HAGGS CASTLE: 427 1157. Dumbreck Rd nr jnct 22 of the M8, go straight on to *xC4*
Clubhouse at first r/bout. Part of the grounds of Pollok Park; a convenient
course, perhaps overplayed, but not difficult to get on.

POLLOK GOLF CLUB: 632 1080. On the other side of the White Cart Water and *xC4*
Pollok House and rather more up-market. Well-wooded parkland course, flat and
well kept, but not cheap. Women not permitted to play.

GLEDDOCH, LANGBANK: 01475 540711. Excellent 18-hole course adj and part of MAP 1
Gleddoch House Hotel (390/HOTELS OUTSIDE TOWN). Restricted play. C3

TROON/IRVINE: 50km away but some of the best golfing to be had. By car on the MAP 1
A77 via Kilmarnock or train hourly from Central Stn. Glas Gailes, Western C4
Gailes and the Portland Course all eminently playable links (Royal Troon
difficult to get on). Portland: 01292 311555. Gailes courses (via Irvine and
requiring car to get there): 01294 311347 (1648/1647/GREAT GOLF).

TENNIS:
613

Public courts (Apr-Sep) membership not required: **KELVINGROVE PARK,** 6 courts, *A1*

BEST GALLERIES

Apart from those listed previously (see ATTRACTIONS, p. 80 and p. 81) the following galleries are always worth looking into. The Glasgow Gallery Guide, *free from any of them, lists all the current exhibs.*

615   ⚓   ⚓   **GLASGOW PRINT STUDIOS:** 552 0704. 22 King St. Influential and accessible
D3   upstairs gallery with print work on view and for sale from many of Scotland's leading and rising artists. Cl Sun. Print shop over rd.

616   ⚓   ⚓   **TRANSMISSION GALLERY:** 552 4813. 28 King St. Cutting edge and often
D3   off-the-wall work from contemporary Scottish and international artists. Reflects Glasgow's increasing importance as a hot spot of conceptual art. Stuff you might disagree with. Cl Sun/Mon.

617 **COMPASS GALLERY:** 221 6370. 178 W Regent St. Glasgow's oldest established
E2   commercial contemporary art gallery. Cl Sun. Their 'New Generation' exhib in July/Aug shows work from new graduates of the art colleges and has heralded many a career. Combine with the other Gerber gallery.

618 **CYRIL GERBER FINE ART:** 221 3095. 148 W Regent St. British paintings and esp the
C2   Scottish Colourists and 'name' contemporaries. Gerber, the Compass, and Art Exposure have Christmas exhibs where small, accessible paintings can be bought for reasonable prices. Cyril will know what's good for you. Cl Sun.

619 **ART EXPOSURE GALLERY:** 552 7779. 19 Parnie St. Behind the Tron Theatre.
E2   Showcase gallery with a friendly, down-to-earth attitude exhibiting the work of contemporary/graduate Scottish artists. Sort of 'affordable'. 11-6pm. Cl Sun.

620 **COLLINS GALLERY:** 552 4400 (ext 2558). 22 Richmond St. Part of Strathclyde Univ
E2   campus (betw George St and Cathedral St). Varied, often important exhibs. Cl Sun.

621 **GLASGOW 1999 CENTRE:** 227 1999. The Terrace, Princes Sq. Excellent, public
D3   access, multi-media exhibition space featuring work from across the spectrum.

622   ✚   ✚   **THE GLASGOW ART FAIR:** George Sq in tented pavilions. Held every yr
D2   (since 1996) in mid-April (1970/EVENTS). Most of the above galleries and many more (incl rest of Scotland and the UK) are represented; highly selective and good fun. I know a thing or two about this event: with Julian Spalding of Glasgow Museums, I helped to invent it. Do come 1998/99.

THE BEST ARCHITECTURE

There is a section entirely devoted to C R Mackintosh (p. 87/MACINTOSH TRAIL) who designed the Glasgow School of Art, one of the most celebrated buildings and although he casts a long shadow, his work is only one chapter in the story of Glasgow's architecture.

A short stroll along St. Vincent St in a westerly direction, starting from George Sq and returning via Douglas St and finally W George St, will give a good impression of how many quality 19th and 20th-century buildings there are in Glasgow's city centre. The variety of styles becomes more obvious on closer inspection and the buildings that employ the boldest mixtures of design seem to work the best. Here are the outstanding ones:

623 **BANK OF SCOTLAND:** 110-120 St Vincent St. (1927) Architect: James Miller.
C2   Monumental neo-classicism, or so I'm told (it's largely Greek to me), but the symmetry, betw the huge columns along the front and the tall windows up above, is cleverly designed to make you feel v small.

624 **THE HATRACK:** 142A-144 St Vincent St. (1899) Architect: James Salmon Jr. Just up
C2   the st, on the same side is an early example of narrow-frontage design. Ten storeys built on a single house plot with so many windows there's hardly any visible stonework. A v elegant solution to the perennial Scottish problem of lack of natural light.

THE ATHENEUM THEATRE: 179 Buchanan St. (1891) Architects: Burnet & Campbell. The inspiration for many buildings and the first of its kind in Glas. With a strange, narrow, asymmetrical frontage studded with arch and bay windows on one side and curious arrow-slits on the other, decorated with statuary and topped with an octagonal cupola, all vying for attention but somehow creating an eccentric, and typically Glaswegian whole.

625
D2

THE PEARCE INSTITUTE: 840 Govan Rd. (1903) Architect: Sir Rowand Anderson. Commissioned by shipbuilders, this is another example of eclectic design. The main façade is in the style of a 17th-century town building but where the eastern end is almost severe, the western end is flamboyantly Renaissance in character with its curvaceous gable and detailed, heraldic sculpture over the huge, mullioned window. Built at a time when, according to Anderson, architecture in Scotland was 'in a more vigorous and healthy state than in any other country in Europe'.

626
xA3

SCOTTISH CO-OPERATIVE: 95 Morrison St. (1897) Architects: Bruce and Hay. Just a big warehouse really, but when you're skimming past in your car, level with the top-floor, on the S side slip-rd off the Kingston Br, all of a sudden it becomes Gotham City . . . and at the other end of the br, on the city bound off ramp, you get the futuristic equivalent, gliding down between the twin glass monoliths of the **EAGLE BUILDING** (1990 Keppie Design), and the former **BRIT-OIL BUILDING** (1988) Architect: Hugh Martin, to land at the foot of **ALEXANDER THOMSON'S** spectacular church set on a massive plinth on the corner of Pitt St and St Vincent St. Awarded 'World Monument' status in 1997. (Rumour has it that this is the church setting used in Ian Banks' *Espedair St*).

627
C3

C2

C2

At the beginning of Woodlands Terrace there's a flight of 1850s moss-clad, stone steps that lead down into Kelvingrove Park on the rt. By following the path up to the Bruce monument you can take in the High Victorian sweep of **PARK CIRCUS** and then the view of Gilmorehill with **GLASGOW UNIVERSITY** (1870), Architects: Sir George Gilbert Scott and son John Oldrid Scott, at the top, with its towering spire and vaulted passageways, and the **ART GALLERY/MUSEUM** (1900) Architects: Sir J.W Simpson and Milner Allen, massive and grandiose, at the foot, seperated by the Kelvin R.

628

B1
A1
A1

Although it's a work of engineering, and therefore doesn't strictly belong here, **THE CLYDE NAVIGATION TRUSTEES CRANE No. 7**, better known as the 'Finnieston Cran', stands as a poignant reminder of Glasgow's maritime past and the many thousands of people who worked here in the shipyards. Perhaps one day you'll be able to sail up the Clyde again, and as you do you'll see the 'Cran' and beside it, the **GLASGOW CONFERENCE CENTRE** itself, also better known as the 'Armadillo', and you'll know you're nearing journey's end, the heart of Glas.

629
A2

A2

TEMPLETON'S CARPET FACTORY: Glas Green. Last, but not least. Where one can truly state, 'they don't build them like that anymore'.

630
E4

THE MACKINTOSH TRAIL

The gr Scottish architect and designer Charles Rennie Mackintosh (1868-1928) had an extraordinary influence on contemporary design. Glas is the best place to see his work.

GLASGOW SCHOOL OF ART: 353 4500. 167 Renfrew St. Mackintosh's supreme architectural triumph. It's enough almost to admire it from the st (and maybe best, since this is v much a working college) but there are guided tours at 11am and 2pm (Sat 10.30am) of the sombre yet light interior, the halls and library. You might wonder if the building itself could be partly responsible for it's remarkable output of acclaimed painters. The Tenement House (588/OTHER ATTRACTIONS) is nearby.

631
C2

QUEEN'S CROSS CHURCH: 870 Garscube Rd where it becomes Maryhill Rd (corner of Springbank St). Built 1896-99. Calm and simple, the antithesis of Victorian gothic. If all churches had been built like this, we'd go more often. The HQ of the Charles Rennie Mackintosh Society, which was founded in 1973 (phone 945 6600). Open Mon-Fri 10.30-5.30pm, Sun 2.30-5pm (1496/CHURCHES).

632
xC2

FREE

633
A1
MACKINTOSH HOUSE: 330 5431. Univ Avenue. Opp and part of the Hunterian Museum (583/MAIN ATTRACTIONS) within the univ campus. The Master's house has been transplanted and methodically reconstructed from the next st (they say even the light is the same). If you've ever wondered what the fuss is about, go and see how innovative and complete an artist, designer and architect he was, in this inspiring yet habitable set of rms. Mon-Sat, 9.30am-5pm (cl 12.30-1.30pm). FREE

634
C4
SCOTLAND STREET SCHOOL: 429 1202. 225 Scotland St. Opp Shields Rd underground and best app by car from Eglinton St (A77 Kilmarnock Rd over Jamaica St Br). Entire school (from 1906) preserved as museum of education through Victorian/Edwardian and wartimes. Original, exquisite Mackintosh features, esp tiling, and powerfully redolent of happy school days. This is a uniquely evocative time capsule. Café and temporary exhibs. Mon-Sat 10am-5pm, Sun 2-5pm. FREE

635
D1
WILLOW TEAROOM: Sauchiehall St. The café he designed (or what's left of it); certainly where to go for a tea break on the trail (511/TEAROOMS).

636
xA1
THE HILL HOUSE, HELENSBURGH: 01436 673900. Upper Colquhoun St. Take Sinclair St off Princes St (at Romanesque tower and TO) and go 2km uphill, taking left at Kennedy St and follow signs. A complete house incorporating Mackintosh's typical total unity of design, built for Walter Blackie in 1902-4. Much to marvel over and wish that everybody else would go away and you could stay there for the night. There's even a library full of books to keep you occupied. Tearoom; grds. Open Apr-Dec, 1.30-5.30pm. Helensburgh is 45km NW of city centre via Dumbarton (A82) and A814 up N Clyde coast. ADMN

637
xA4
HOUSE FOR AN ART LOVER: 353 4770. Bellahouston Park. 10 Dumbreck Rd. Take the M8 W, then the M77, turn rt onto Dumbreck Rd and it's on your left. These rms were designed, nearly a century ago, specifically, it would seem, for willowy women to come and go, talking of Michelangelo. Detail is the essence of Mackintosh, and there's plenty here, but the overall effect is of space and light and a complete absence of clutter. Design shop and Exhibitions Café (512/TEAROOMS) on the ground floor. Daily 10am-5pm. ADMN

GOOD NIGHTLIFE

For the current programmes of the places below and all other venues, consult The List magazine, on sale fortnightly at most newsagents.

638 CINEMA

There are all the usual multiplexes, but the best picture houses are:

C2 **GLASGOW FILM THEATRE:** 332 6535. Rose St at downtown end of Sauchiehall St. Known affectionately as GFT, has bar and 2 screens for essential art house flicks.

A1 **GROSVENOR:** 339 4928. Ashton Lane, off Byres Rd behind Hillhead Stn. Busy lane for eats and nightlife as well as this old cinema with 2 screens and a selected programme of mainly current hits.

639 THEATRE

*The trad theatres are the **KING'S,** 227 5511, Bath St, with popular shows like pantos, Gilbert and Sullivan and other musicals; and the **THEATRE ROYAL,** 332 3321, Hope St, home of Scottish Opera and with mainly high-brow diet of opera, dance and drama. There are several other v notable places though some suffering from recent cut backs. Look for info on:*

D3 **THE CITIZENS':** 429 0022. Gorbals St just over the river. Fabulous main auditorium and 2 small studios. Drama at its v best. One of Britain's most influential theatres, especially for design. In midst of lottery-funded renovations, but ready for the panto season 1997 - oh yes it is, the one we love.

xC4 **THE TRAMWAY:** 422 2023. 25 Albert Dr on S side. A theatre and vast performance space. Dynamic and widely influential with an innovative and varied programme from all over the world. Seasonal programme.

C2 **CCA:** 332 7521. Centre for Contemporary Arts, 350 Sauchiehall St. Central arts-lab complex, notable as a theatre for modern dance (esp in spring with its New Moves programme), but also has gallery and other performance space and a good café (517/TEAROOMS). Cl Sun.

✝ **THE ARCHES THEATRE:** 221 9736. Midland St betw Jamaica St and Oswald St. *D3*
Experimental and vital theatre on a tight budget in the railway arches under
the tracks of Central Stn. Andy Arnold will not lie down. Opening times vary.
W/end clubs among the best (1868/NIGHTCLUBS).

RSAMD: 332 4101. 100 Renfrew St. The Royal Scottish Academy of Music and *D2*
Drama. Part and wholly student productions often with guest directors. Eclectic,
often powerful mix.

THE TRON THEATRE: 552 4267. 63 Trongate. Contemporary Scottish theatre and *E3*
other interesting performance, esp music. Recent face lift. Gr café-bar with food
before and *après* (424/BISTROS).

CLASSICAL MUSIC 640

Scottish Opera at the **THEATRE ROYAL,** (332 3321) and National and International
orchestras at the **ROYAL CONCERT HALL,** top of Buchanan St (332 6633). Smaller
events and ensembles at the **CITY HALLS,** Candleriggs (287 5024), **HUTCHESONS'
HALL,** 158 Ingram St (552 8391), **RSAMD,** 100 Renfrew St (332 4101), and
GILMOREHILL CENTRE, Univ Ave (330 3838.)

JAZZ 641

For residencies and one-offs, see *The List* or *Live Scene,* a monthly freesheet available
at most music pubs and venues. The most consistent and coherent programme of
jazz gigs is in the **INTERNATIONAL JAZZ FESTIVAL** in early July (details 227 5511).
Most frequently used venues during rest of yr are pubs like **THE BABY GRAND, THE
BREWERY TAP** or **BLACKFRIARS.** Sunday afternoon jazz upstairs at the **PAISLEY
ARTS CENTRE,** New St (887 1010). Occasional performances at **PIZZA EXPRESS** 151
Queen St (221 3333) and concerts at the **MITCHELL THEATRE** (227 5033).

FOLK 642

Information as above.

Major concentration of gigs during **CELTIC CONNECTIONS** held every January in
the Royal Concert Hall (*see above*) and the **GLASGOW FOLK FESTIVAL** held at the
end of June (227 5511). Throughout the yr look for gigs at the **SCOTIA BAR** and
THE CLUTHA VAULTS, both Stockwell St, 552 7520 (519/520/GREAT GLASGOW
PUBS), and **BABBITY BOWSTERS,** Blackfriars St (Sun), **VICTORIA BAR,** Stockwell St
(Fri and Sat). Some of the best fun can be had at the **RIVERSIDE,** Fox St off Clyde
St, upstairs – ceilidh dance every Fri/Sat at 8pm (248 3144). Don't be late. For
more details *see p. 241/*FOLK MUSIC.

ROCK AND POP 643

See also ROCK 'N' POP, *p. 49*

✝ ✝ ✝ **BARROWLAND BALLROOM:** Gallowgate. When its lights are on, you *E3*
can't miss it. The Barrowland is world-famous and for many bands
one of their favourite gigs. It's tacky and a bit run-down, but distinctly venerable;
and with its high stage and sprung dance floor, perfect for rock'n'roll. The Glas
audience is one of the best in the world and many tours begin here to pick up on
the special atmos. We love it 'live'.

SECC: 248 3000. Finnieston Quay beyond the city centre and, for many, beyond *A3*
the pale as far as concerts are concerned (big shed, not big on atmos) but there are
3 different-sized halls for mainly arena-sized acts and everyone from Eric to Pav
and TAFKAP have played here. Glasgow's own, Wet Wet Wet currently hold the
record for numbers of nights sold.

*Neither of these venues has its own box office. For tickets and information check with 'Inside
Tickets', Tower Records, Argyle St. 204 5788.*

Concerts also take place regularly at the **PAVILION THEATRE,** Renfield St (332
1846), which is a cosier place to watch a band, and more occasionally at the
MITCHELL THEATRE behind the Mitchell Library. For live music in smaller venues,
see *p. 79 for* PUBS AND CLUBS WITH LIVE MUSIC.

For NIGHTCLUBS, *see p. 238, and for* GAY NIGHTLIFE, *see p. 237.*

SHOPPING GAZETTEER

This is a selection of useful shops that get it rt. South is S of a central area bisected by the river. E/W axis taken as Renfield St.

ESSENTIALS

Butchers
GILLESPIE'S, 1601 Gr Western Rd, Anniesland. 959 2015. WEST
JAMES ALLEN, 85 Lauderdale Gdns. 334 8973. WEST
MURRAY'S, 121 Royston Rd. 552 2201. EAST

Bakers
BRADFORDS, 245 Sauchiehall St and branches. 332 2057. CENTRAL
Bread: **BAKEHAUS**, 387 Gr Western Rd. 334 5501. WEST
Pâtisserie: **PÂTISSERIE FRANCOISE**, 138 Byres Rd. 334 1882/1351 Springburn Rd. 558 7377. WEST/EAST

Barbers
CITY BARBERS, 99 W Nile St. 332 7114. CENTRAL

BARNIE DICK'S, 99 W Nil123 Byres Rd. 339 4043. WEST

Delicatessen
FRATELLI SARTI, 133 Wellington St. 248 2228. CENTRAL
PECKHAMS, 100 Byres Rd/Central Stn/Clarence Dr. WEST/CENTRAL/WEST
COOKERY BOOK, 20 Kilmarnock Rd. 632 9807. SOUTH
TOSCANA, 44 Station Rd, Milngavie. 956 4020. NORTH
Kosher: **MORRISONS**, Sinclair Drive. 632 0998. SOUTH
Cheese: as above and Fazzi's, *see below.*

Department Stores
FRASERS, 45 Buchanan St. 221 3880. CENTRAL
General: **DEBENHAMS**, 97 Argyle St. 221 9820. CENTRAL
Ironmongers: **CROCKETS**, 136 W Nile St. 332 1041. CENTRAL

Fishmongers
ALAN BEVERIDGE, 188 Byres Rd/7 Station Rd, Milngavie. WEST/NORTH
FISH PLAICE, alley off Saltmarket by St Andrews St. 552 2337. EAST
MacCALLUMS, 944 Argyle St. 204 4456/455 Gr Western Rd. 334 5680. WEST

Flowers
ROOTS AND FRUITS AND FLOWERS, 451 Gr Western Rd. 334 5817. WEST
Dried: **INSCAPE**, 141 Gr Western Rd. 332 6125. WEST

Fruit & Veg
ROOTS AND FRUITS, 457 Gt Western Rd/355 Byres Rd. 339 5164/334 3530. WEST
NO. I FOR VALUE, 61 Candleriggs by City Hall. CENTRAL

Organic: as above and Grassroots, *see below.*

Fish 'n' Chips
UNIQUE, 223 Allison St. 423 3366. SOUTH
PHILADELPHIA, 445 Gt Western Rd. 339 2372. WEST
UNIVERSITY CAFE, 83 Byres Rd. 334 9813. WEST

Hairdressers
RITA RUSK, 49 W Nile St. 221 1472. CENTRAL
DLC, Mitchell Lane. 204 2020. CENTRAL
ALAN EDWARDS, The Briggait/56-58 Wilson St. 552 5232/552 5282. EAST/CENTRAL
GARY'S CUTTING CLUB, 76 Drymen Rd, Bearsden. 942 0393. NORTH

Hats
PANDORA'S HATS, 5 Sinclair Dr, Battlefield. 649 7714. SOUTH

Late-night
General: **GOODIES (and others adj)** 645 Gr Western Rd. 334 8848. WEST
FRIENDLY'S, Sauchiehall St. CENTRAL.
ALLDAYS, Kelvinbridge. WEST
Chemist: **SINCLAIRS**, 693 Gr Western Rd. 339 0012. WEST
C and M MACKIE, 1067 Pollokshaws Rd. 649 8915. SOUTH

Lingerie
SILKS, 675 Clarkston Rd. 633 0442. SOUTH
BRIEF ENCOUNTER, 78 Hyndland St.357 2383. WEST

Men's Clothes
New Labels:
CRUISE, 47 Renfield St. 248 2476. CENTRAL
SLATER MENSWEAR, 165 Howard St. 552 7171. CENTRAL
ITALIAN CENTRE, John St (Armani, Versace etc). CENTRAL
Established Labels: **HENRY BURTON**, 111 Buchanan St. 221 7380. CENTRAL

Newspapers
NEWSPAPER KIOSK, Buchanan St. 332 7355. CENTRAL
BARRETTS, 263 Byres Rd. 339 0488. WEST.
International Magazines: **JOHN SMITH**, 57 St Vincent St. 221 7472. CENTRAL

Pasta
FAZZI BROTHERS, 67 Cambridge St/230 Clyde St. 332 0941. CENTRAL
FRATELLI SARTI,133 Wellington St. 248 2228. CENTRAL

Shoes
Shoes That Last: **ROBERT JENKINS**, 183 Hyndland Rd. 334 8547. WEST. 14

Royal Exchange. 248 3743. CENTRAL
Modish: **SCHUH,** 45 Union St. 248 7319.
CENTRAL
ASPECTO, 20 Gordon St. 248 2532.
CENTRAL

Tobacco
TOBACCO HOUSE, 9 St Vincent's Pl. 226
4586. CENTRAL

Wholefoods
GRASSROOTS, 48 Woodlands Rd. 353
3278. WEST
QUALITY DELI, 123 Douglas St. 331 2984.
CENTRAL

Wine
UBIQUITOUS CHIP WINES, 12 Ashton
Lane. 334 5007. WEST
FRATELLI SARTI, 121 Bath St (also
Wellington St, above). CENTRAL
PECKHAM AND RYE, 21 Clarence Drive.
334 4312. WEST
LITTLE ITALY, 205 Byres Rd. 339 6287.
WEST

Women's Clothes
New Labels:
ITALIAN CENTRE, as above (also Mondi).
CENTRAL
CRUISE, 180 Ingram St. CENTRAL
MAXXI, 162 Fenwick Rd. 620 3133.
SOUTH
MOON, 10 Ruthven Lane. 339 2315. WEST
Labels: **FRASERS,** 45 Buchanan St. 221 3880.
CENTRAL

THE MOST INTERESTING SHOPS
One shopping precinct in Glas is referred
to many times below, namely **PRINCES
SQUARE,** an indoor shopping mall off the
middle of Buchanan St (Argyle St end)
and probably the single best
concentration of high-quality, interesting
shops in town. These include **KATHERINE
HAMNETT, CHRISTIAN LACROIX, LUSH,
NANCY SMILLIE, SHEILA MILLER** and
LINENS FINE. For a coffee break or snack,
D'ARCY'S or **IL PAVONE** on the basement
floor are excellent.

Antiques
General: **HERITAGE HOUSE,** Unit 39,
Yorkhill Quay. 357 4712. WEST
LANSDOWNE ANTIQUES 334 8469 and
RETRO, Otago St. WEST
Bric-à-brac: **ALL OUR YESTERDAYS,** 6 Park
Rd. 334 7788. WEST
Jewellery: **VICTORIAN VILLAGE, SARATOGA
TRUNK,** 57 W Regent St. 332 0808.
CENTRAL (*also for bric-à-brac, clothes
etc, see p. 229/*MARKETS)
Clothes: **STARRY STARRY NIGHT,** 19
Dowanside Lane. WEST

Art Supplies
MILLERS, 11 Clarendon Pl. 331 3203.
WEST.
ART STORE, 94 Queen St. 221 0266.
CENTRAL

Baby Goods and Kids Stuff
Clothes: **STRAWBERRY FIELDS,** 517 Gr
Western Rd. 339 1121. WEST
Toys: **THE SENTRY BOX,** 175 Gr George St.
334 6070. WEST

Cards and Gift Wrap
PAPYRUS, 374 Byres Rd. 334 6514/296
Sauchiehall St. WEST/CENTRAL
PHEONIXI GRAPHICS, 254 Sauchiehall St.
353 0102. CENTRAL
ILLUMINATI, Princes Sq. 204 2361.
CENTRAL

Ceramics
NANCY SMILLIE, Princes Sq. 248
3874/Cresswell Lane. CENTRAL/WEST
WARE ON EARTH, Italian Centre, Ingram
St. CENTRAL

Clothes
General: See SHOPPING FOR ESSENTIALS and
Princes Sq (above).
Hip: **MELLO,** 2659 Virginia St. 552 5656.
CENTRAL
HUSTLER AND PENELOPE'S PITSTOP,
Queen St. CENTRAL
Nearly New: **ALCHEMY,** 519 Gr Western Rd.
334 9610. WEST
Old: **BOEM SCIFRA,** Decourcey's Arcade,
Cresswell Lane. 357 1335. WEST
FLIP, 68 Queen St. 221 2041.
THE SQUARE YARD, Stevenson St West at
the BARRAS (587). EAST
Outdoor: **BLACK'S,** 254 Sauchiehall St. 353
2344. CENTRAL
TISO'S, 129 Buchanan St. 248 4877.
CENTRAL
CLEARWATER WORK & LEISURE, 1124
Argyle St. 334 2228. WEST.

Collectables
RELICS, Dowanside Lane. 341 0007. WEST
JADES, 1121 Maryhill Rd. 946 2920. WEST
KOLLECTABLES, 51 Parnie St.
552 2208. CENTRAL

Comics
FUTURESHOCK, 88 Byres Rd. 339 8184.
WEST
FORBIDDEN PLANET, 168 Buchanan St. 331
1215. CENTRAL

Furniture
Modern: **INHOUSE,** 26 Wilson St. 552 5902.
CENTRAL
TONY WALKER, 92 Woodside Terr. 332
2662. WEST
Traditional: **ADRIENNE'S,** 28 Park Rd. 334
5943. WEST

Games
GAMES WORKSHOP, 66 Queen St. 226
3762. CENTRAL
PC/Console Games:
C.A GAMES, De Courcey's Arcade,
Cresswell Lane. 334 3901. WEST
G FORCE, 77 Union St. 248 8272.
CENTRAL

Ice cream
COLPI, Milngavie centre, Newton Mearns
and Clydebank

QUEENS CAFÉ, 515 Victoria Rd. 423 2409.
WEST
UNIVERSITY CAFÉ, Byres Rd. WEST

Interiors
DESIGNWORKS, 38 Gibson St. 339 9520.
WEST
INHOUSE, 26 Wilson St. 552 5902.
CENTRAL

Jewellery
ARGYLE ST. ARCADE. Vast selection of
different shops.CENTRAL
SHEILA MILLER DESIGNER JEWELLERY,
Princes Sq. 221 1248. CENTRAL

Jokes
TAM SHEPHERD'S, 33 Queen St. 221 2310.
CENTRAL
THE PARTY SHOP, 201 Sauchiehall St. 332
3392. CENTRAL

Junk
THE BARRAS, 1798/MARKETS. EAST
BURNTHILLS DEMOLITION,
1803/JUNKYARDS. WEST

Presents
EVOLUTION, 396 Byres Rd. 334 3200.
WEST
NICE, HOUSE, Italian Centre (*see above*).
CENTRAL
PAST TIMES, 70 Buchanan St. 226 2277.
CENTRAL

Sports
NEVIS SPORT, 261 Sauchiehall St. 332
4814. CENTRAL
BOARDWISE, 1146 Argyle St. 334 5559.
CENTRAL

Tartan
Serious: **HECTOR RUSSELL,** 85 Renfield St.
332 4102. CENTRAL
GEOFFREY'S, 309 Sauchiehall St. 331 2388.
CENTRAL
Tacky: **ROBIN HOOD GIFT HOUSE,** 11 St
Vincent St. 221 7408. CENTRAL

Theatrical Costumes
THE PARTY SHOP, 201 Sauchiehall St. 332
3392. CENTRAL
DRESS U UP, 1011 Argyle St. 221 2087.
WEST

Woollies
JUMPERS, Princes Sq. 248 5775. CENTRAL

Sandwiches and Takeaway
See p. 72 for listings and report.

SECTION 3

Regional Hotels and Restaurants, including Aberdeen and Dundee

THE BEST HOTELS AND RESTAURANTS IN ARGYLL

See also 1946/CENTRES: OBAN. Refer to Map 1.

644
C1
AIRDS HOTEL, PORT APPIN: 01631 730236. 40km N of Oban 4km off A828. A gourmet experience awaits you here in this refined hotel in a charming corner of Scotland. Member of cosmopolitan *Relais et Châteaux* group (and in all the other guidebooks that count), some may find this small roadside hotel a bit formal, but the Allens are fastidious hosts and son Graeme who replaced Betty in the kitchen is every bit as superb a chef. There's a v nice short walk behind the house and staying here also has the v pleasing prospect of breakfast. The family guesthouse up the rd is a cheaper stopover. Lismore passenger ferry 2km away (1903/MAGIC ISLANDS). 14RMS MAR-DEC T/T XPETS CC KIDS LOTS/MED.INX

EAT One of the best meals you will find in the N (and S, E and W). EXP

645
C3
KILFINAN HOTEL, KILFINAN: 01700 821201. 13km from Tighnabruaich. On B8000 which, 7km further N, joins L Fyne at Otter Ferry and continues to Strachur. Coaching inn, nestling in terraced grds, comfortably furnished throughout. Quality is paramount to Lynne and Rolf Mueller and it comes over in everything, not least the food. Some folk seem to find them a bit shirty at first, but they're v nice really. JAN-DEC T/T PETS CC KIDS TOS MED.EXP

EAT Rolf works wonders with excellent local seafood and game; restau and barmeals. EXP

646
C2
TAYCHREGGAN, KILCHRENAN: 01866 833211. Signed off A85 just before Taynuilt, 30km from Oban and nestling on a bluff by L Awe in imposing countryside. Quay for the old ferry to Portsonachan is nearby with boats available. The Pauls have turned this long-established loch side inn into a fine and not too exp hotel with a restau where even locals take the long and winding (and enchanting) rd to eat. Pleasant rms and bar. That awesome loch is always there outside. Hotel part of Virgin marketing group. 20RMS JAN-DEC T/X PETS CC KIDS TOS MED.INX

EAT Nicely judged menu of consistently high standard. Euan's good wine list. EXP

647
B3
STONEFIELD CASTLE HOTEL, TARBERT (ARGYLL): 01880 820836. Just o/side town on the A83, a castle which evokes the 1970s more than preceding centuries. Splendid grds leading down to L Fyne. Unlikely (heated) open-air swimming pool. The surrounding luxurian grds are fabulous. Dining-rm with crazy carpet and staggering views. Friendly, flexible staff; overall, it seems quintessentially Scottish and ok, esp for families (976/KIDS) though style people may moan. 33RMS JAN-DEC T/T PETS CC KIDS MED.EX

648
C2
ARDENTINNY HOTEL, DUNOON: 01369 810209. 20km N via A880/A885. Trad, Clydeside inn by Glen Finart forest adj L Long. Gdn o/side bar with private cove. Famous food; rms seem pricey. Alternative access on L Goil Cruiser 'water taxi', 01301 703349. 11RMS MAR-NOV T/T PETS CC KIDS TOS EXP

649
B3
WEST LOCH HOTEL, TARBERT (ARGYLL): 01880 820283. Picturesque 1710 former coaching inn on the cusp of Kintyre, just o/side of Tarbert on A83. Within easy reach of ferries to Islay, Gigha and Arran. Lovely views of loch over rd, freshly furnished whilst retaining authentic features. Good food, relaxing though roadside rms may be noisy. Feel at home here (950/INNS). 7RMS FEB-DEC X/T PETS CC KIDS MED.INX

650
B3
COLUMBA HOTEL, TARBERT: 01880 820808. Ideal budget hotel on water front in this perfect Argyll town. New 'Net Store' bar v popular with yachties and locals. Bedrms seem constantly to be refurb; 3 huge superior rms ideal for families. Unusual gym and sauna. 11RMS JAN-DEC T/T PETS CC KIDS TOS MED.INX

651
B1
BARRIEMORE, OBAN: 01631 566356. Corran Esplanade. This hotel, the v last one in a st full of them along the coast to Ganavan, is a good bet if you're in Oban. Front rms have excellent views of Kerrera and Lorne. B&B only. 13RMS MAR-JAN X/X PETS CC KIDS INX

ARDANAISEIG, LOCH AWE: 01866 833333 (913/COUNTRY-HOUSE HOTELS).

ISLE OF ERISKA: 01631 720371. 20km N of Oban (905/COUNTRY-HOUSE HOTELS).

ARDSHEAL HOUSE: 01631 740227. 27km S of Ft William (915/COUNTRY-HOUSE HOTELS).

LOCH MELFORT: 01852 200233. 22km S of Oban (912/COUNTRY-HOUSE HOTELS).

RESTAURANTS

✚ **CREGGANS INN, STRACHUR:** 01369 860279. 2km N Strachur on A815 to **652**
Cairndow, a busy rd in summer along L Fyne. Road house bar/restau and **C2**
more formal dining-rm in a v successful combination of the popular and the more
particular. From burgers in the bar to Arran queenies eaten off crisp linen, to
cream teas in a coffee shop where you can sit o/side. The fiefdom of the late Sir
Fitzroy and Lady Maclean, the coffee shop sells their considerable canon of
books. Something for everybody, as they say.   CHP/MED/EXP

✚ **CHATTERS, DUNOON:** 01369 706402. 58 John St next to Safeway. Rosie **653**
Macinnes' excellent restau in town rather than on esplanade is, by itself, a **C3**
good reason for getting the ferry. The Cowal peninsula awaits your explorations
(and Benmore Grds 1196/GARDENS). Bar menu and à la carte, and a small grd for
drinks or lunch on a good day. All delightful. Mon-Sat 10-3pm; 6-10pm.   MED

✚ **THE KILBERRY INN:** 01880 770223. Superlative home-cooking in roadside pub **654**
betw Tarbert and Lochgilphead by the coastal route (B8024). Better than **B3**
many more highfalutin' restaus. Fuller report: 1033/BEST FOOD.   INX

THE BEST HOTELS AND RESTAURANTS
IN AYRSHIRE & CLYDE VALLEY

See also 1940/AYR. Refer to Map 1.

✚ ✚ **TURNBERRY HOTEL, TURNBERRY:** 01655 331000. Not just a hotel on the **655**
Ayrshire coast, more a way of life centred on golf. Looks over the 2 **C4**
courses which are difficult to get on unless you're a guest (1650/GREAT GOLF). All
that should be expected of a world-class hotel except, perhaps, the buzz; but
plenty of golf chat and time moving slowly. The spa complex adj has state-of-the-
art 'treatments', even exercise. Restau here has one of the best 'light' menus in
Scotland; main dining-rm looks over the courses to Ailsa Craig beyond – dinner
only, and epic Sun lunch.   132RMS JAN-DEC T/T PETS CC KIDS TOS LOTS
EAT The Bay is the light place to eat; pastas, risottos, etc. Also main restau. MED/EXP

✚ **GLEDDOCH HOUSE, LANGBANK, nr GREENOCK:** 01475 540711. 35km from Glas **656**
by fast rd – M8/A8 t/off marked Langbank/Houston after jnct 31, follow **C3**
signs. Set in extensive grounds (including 18-hole golf course), with commanding
view of Clyde by Dumbarton Rock (but only from a few rms). Small leisure club
adj. Excellent conservatory and dining-rms. Most civilised place to stay close to
Glas.   37RMS JAN-DEC T/T PETS CC KIDS
EAT Excellent restau with 2 AA rossettes. Scottish accents.   EXP

CHAPELTOUN HOUSE HOTEL, STEWARTON: 01560 82696. 12km from Irvine. **657**
Recently taken over by the Dobson family (as Montgreenan below) who are **D3**
refurbing as we speak, retaining the oakiness and charming grounds (but will they
improve the pictures?). Keen to raise from 2 to 3 AA rossettes, this is the dining-
rm to watch around here (sorry for the pressure Tom). Big improvement from
previous narky owners.   8RMS JAN-DEC T/T XPETS CC XKIDS TOS LOTS

MONTGREENAN, nr KILWINNING: 01294 557733. Take A736 (5km) from the A78 **658**
around Irvine and several r/bouts later you arrive in a surprisingly woody enclave **D4**
and a civilised country-house hotel (phone for directions). Woody and friendly
inside too, but awful pictures again. Not so 'going upmarket' as Chapeltoun
(above), but doing well by Ayrshire. A surprisingly 'Virgin' hotel.
                                21RMS JAN-DEC T/T PETS CC KIDS TOS LOTS

PIERSLAND HOTEL, TROON: 01292 314747. Craig End Rd opp Portland Golf **659**
Course which is next to Royal Troon (1648/GREAT GOLF). Mansion house of **C4**
some character and ambience much favoured for weddings. Wood-panelling,
open fires, lovely grds only a 'drive' away from the courses (no preferential
booking on Royal, but Portland usually poss) and lots of gr golf nearby. Notable
locally for bar meals.   23RMS JAN-DEC T/T PETS CC KIDS TOS EXP

LOCHGREEN HOUSE, TROON: 01292 313343. Elegant country-house hotel in golfing **660**
green Ayrshire (660/AYRSHIRE HOTALS). Astute owners, the Costleys, also have **C4**
the **BURNS MONUMENT HOTEL, ALLOWAY, nr AYR:** 01292 442466. Being wholly **D4**
refurb at time of going to press. On bank and by br over the Doon, and grds.

Good setting visited by hordes of tourists, since in this corner are also found the old Brig (at end of the grd), the Alloway Kirk and the v Monument (1551/LITERARY PLACES). Report next time.

RESTAURANTS

661
D4 ✚ **FOUTERS, AYR:** 01292 261391. 2A Academy St. Off Sandgate. The best meal in town. Proprietor Laurie Black, chair of Taste of Scotland scheme, cares much about food and wine and Scotland's efforts to do better. Despite commitments he's usually in the kitchen creatively cooking with the v best local ingredients. I was there on the first day of the new Ayrshire potatoes; I wonder who else in Ayrshire felt they simply *had* to have them? Tue-Sat: lunch and LO 10.30pm, Sun 7-10pm.

662
C3 ✚ **BRAIDWOODS, nr DALRY:** 01294 833544. Off main A78 coast rd, take Dalry Rd at Saltcoats, 6km along country rd: the Braidwood's whitewashed cottages and Keith's legendary cooking. This is better than most of Glas and much better value (incl wines). Wed/Sat lunch and dinner, and Sun lunch.   MED

663
C5 ✚ **WILDINGS, GIRVAN:** 01465 713481. 56 Montgomerie St opp·Ailsa Craig Hotel, off rd into Girvan from Ayr. Colourful, cosy restau effortlessly pre-eminent in the area. Big menu exceedingly well done. Tues-Sat: lunch and LO 9 pm.   MED

664
E3 ✝ **RISTORANTE LA VIGNA, LANARK:** 01555 664320. 40 Wellgate. Famously good Italian restau in a back st in Lanark. 7 days, lunch and dinner. Must book.
                                                                                MED

665
C3 **VICTORIA HOUSE, GOUROCK:** 01475 630351. Main st above the trad Victoria pub, an excl new restau; not yet in the foodie guides but growing local reputation. Wed-Sat.   INX

C3 **FINS, FAIRLIE, nr LARGS:** 01475 568989. 8 km S of Largs on A78. Excellent seafood bistro (1077/SEAFOOD RESTAUS).   MED

THE BEST HOTELS AND RESTAURANTS IN THE SOUTH-WEST

See also 1941/CENTRES: DUMFRIES. Refer to Map 9.

666
A4 ✚ ✝ **KNOCKINAAM LODGE, PORTPATRICK:** 01776 810471. Tucked away on dream cove, historic country house full of fresh flowers, gr food, sea air and informal, but v good service. Run by Canadians who know and love what they're doing. Their enjoyment is yours (908/COUNTRY-HOUSE HOTELS).
10RMS JAN-DEC T/T PETS CC KIDS TOS LOTS

EAT Probably the best meal in the S. Fixed menu – you won't mind.   EXP

667
C4 ✚ ✝ **COLLIN HOUSE, AUCHENCAIRN:** 01556 640292. Imposing pink-washed stone house high above bay with wide Solway views. Elegant rms, intimate atmos. Deserved big reputation for fine food.
6RMS JAN-DEC T/T PETS CC XKIDS TOS MED.INX

EAT John Woods: some guy in the kitchen! Excellent. Nonresidents must book. EXP

668
B3 **KIRROUGHTREE HOTEL, NEWTON STEWART:** 01671 402141 on A712. AA hotel of yr 1996/97. Built 1719, another of Burns' haunts. Extensive country house newly refurb with heavy drapes and plush atmos. Original panelled hall and stairs, spacious rms. Chef trained by Michel Roux. Golf at the Cally Palace, the other big hotel around here (our previous choice).   17RMS FEB-DEC T/T PETS CC KIDS TOS LOTS

669
C4 **BALCARY BAY, AUCHENCAIRN, nr CASTLE DOUGLAS:** 01556 640311. 20km S of Castle Douglas and Dalbeattie. Off A711 at end of shore rd. Watch fishermen casting their nets in the hazy bay. Ideal base for walking and birdwatching: hotel may be deserted by day. Ok period atmos; the clock ticks on. Gr hideaway spot.
17RMS MAR-NOV T/T PETS CC KIDS TOS EXP

670
C4 **CLONYARD HOUSE, COLVEND, nr ROCKCLIFFE, nr DALBEATTIE:** 01556 630372. On Solway Coast rd nr Rockcliffe and Kippford (1239/COASTAL VILLAGES; 1640/COSTAL WALKS) but not on sea. Later extension to house provides bedrms adj to patio grd with own private access. Family oriented: parrot inside, aviary and enchanted tree to play in o/side.   15RMS JAN-DEC T/T PETS CC KIDS TOS MED.INX

671
A3 **CORSEWALL LIGHTHOUSE HOTEL, STRANRAER:** 01776 853220. A718 to Kirkcolm 3km, B738 to Corsewall 6km. Wild location on cliff top. Cosily furnished in

summer house style – would you go out in winter? The adj fully functioning lighthouse (since 1817) makes for surreal evenings watching it and other lighthouse beams. Snug dining-rm. 6RMS JAN-DEC T/T PETS CC KIDS LOT

CORSEMALZIE HOUSE, PORT WILLIAM, nr NEWTON STEWART: 01988 860254. A714 **672** from main A75 S of Newton Stewart then B7005 through Bladnoch; follow signs *B4* after br (8km). Trad granite house with comfortable rms, hidden in beautiful bluebell woods. Fishing on R Bladnoch and their own loch, and 3 politically correct labradors. 15RMS MAR-JAN T/T PETS CC KIDS TOS EXP

COMLONGON CASTLE, CLARENCEFIELD, nr DUMFRIES: 013878 70283. 14km S of **673** Dumfries. Early 20th-century house beside 15th-century castle, set in lush *D3* acreage extending down to the Solway. Atmos, panelled rms, armour and weaponry. Popular wedding venue (200 a year!), 4-poster beds. The smell of apples when the ghost's around. 11RMS MAR-DEC T/T XPETS CC KIDS MED.EX

KIRKCUDBRIGHT: pronounced 'cur-coo-bree'; a gem of a town. 3 fine hotels. **674**
GLADSTONE HOUSE: 01557 331734, a 'Gleneagles' guesthouse with grds, is superb *C4* and v inexp; **GORDON HOUSE HOTEL:** 01557 330670 (12 rms, cheap and cheerful); and **THE SELKIRK ARMS:** 01557 330402 (16 rms, all mod cons, but not cheap). Selkirk Arms has the chef to watch (*see below*).

WELL VIEW, MOFFAT: 01683 220184. Ballplay Rd away from busy through rd. In **675** lots of guides, esp for food, but a pleasant stopover in town of many more av. *D2* Immaculate rooms with views, and owners. No smk – they'd be horrified! 6RMS JAN-DEC T/T XPETS CC KIDS MED.EX

EAT Janet in the kitchen. John on the wine list. When in Moffat, go here. EXP

ABBEY ARMS & CRIFFEL INN, NEW ABBEY, nr DUMFRIES: 01387 850489/850244. **676** Opp each other on village sq, comfy inns nr Sweetheart Abbey and Criffel *D3* (1575/HILLS) 12km S of Dumfries. CHP

RESTAURANTS

RIVERSIDE INN, CANONBIE, nr LANGHOLM: 01387 371295. 2km from border – you **677** get v good food here but they were a tad cool with our Emma so we've gone off *E3* them a bit. 8 rms upstairs (MED.EX). Open Mon-Sat. Bar food 7 days 7-9 pm (1039/BEST FOOD). Restau LO 8.30 pm. Cl Sun lunch. INX/MED

THE SELKIRK ARMS, KIRKCUDBRIGHT: 01557 330402 where Adam McKissnock is a **678** TV celebrity chef in the making – a star rising in the Solway (hope he's still here *C4* by the time you read this). Dinner 7-9.30pm, 7 days. INX/MED.

THE AULD ALLIANCE, KIRKCUDBRIGHT: 01557 330569 Solway scallops and salmon, **679** etc. 7 nights. (Easter-Oct) – no credit cards though. Also **BISTRO ROMA**, 01557 *C4* 331391. Ok Italiano in gr town. Cl Mon. Both restaus are central and easy to find.

CARLO'S, CASTLE DOUGLAS: 211 King Street, 01556 503977. Bustling atmos in **680** small rm with green tardis in case you need to phone for a ride home. Best Italian *C3* food in the S. Cl Mon. INX

THE BEST HOTELS AND RESTAURANTS IN CENTRAL SCOTLAND

See also 1948/CENTRES: STIRLING. Refer to Map 6.

Note: Some of Scotland's best hotels and restaus are in this region.

✚ ✚ **CROMLIX HOUSE, DUNBLANE:** 01786 822125. 3km from A9 and 4km from **681** town on B8033; first follow signs for Perth, and then Kinbuck. A long *D3* drive through an old estate with splendid mature trees to this spacious, not gloomy Victorian house, meticulously redecorated by Ailsa and David Assenti. Now unquestionably one of the gr country-house hotels in Scotland with excellent service and attention to detail. Staff ratio 2:1 and a happy crew. Who wouldn't be in these glorious Perthshire acres with fishing lochs (the House Loch nearby complete with swans and solitude) and Craig Brown's sure touch in the kitchen? 14RMS (8 SUITES) FEB-DEC T/T PETS CC KIDS LOTS

EAT Nonresidents: drive that drive for dinner (or Sun lunch)! Gr conservatory. EXP

✚ ✚ **THE ROMAN CAMP, CALLANDER:** 01877 330003. Behind the main st (at E or **682** Stirling end), away from the tourist throng and with extensive grds on *C3* the R Teith; another, more elegant world. Roman ruins nearby, but the house was built for the Dukes of Perth and has been a hotel since the war. Rms low-ceilinged and snug; period furnishings; some rms small, many magnificent. O/side, the corridors do creak. Delightful drawing rm and conservatory. Dining-rm has new sympatico extension. Private chapel should a prayer come on. Rods for fishing – and the river swishes the lawn.The v lucky Brown family preside.

14RMS JAN-DEC T/T PETS CC KIDS TOS LOTS

EAT Dining-rm effortlessly the best food in town (with chef Ian McNaught). EXP

683 ✠ ⚓ **GEAN HOUSE, ALLOA:** 01259 219275. On edge of town on B9096 to Tullibody
D4 (turn up by Town Hall). Untypical Scottish manor house, Edwardian and reminiscent of Lutyens' Greywalls at Gullane, and turned into a hotel which is the epitome of stylish comfort. Warm, wood-panelled and furnished in simple good taste; cosy inglenook fireplace. Comfy bedrms, terraced grds. Chef Douglas Imrie does oysters and greenlip mussels and other New World-meets-old variations. Old Ochils not far away.

7RMS JAN-DEC T/T PETS CC KIDS TOS LOTS

684 **STIRLING HIGHLAND, STIRLING:** 01786 475444. Reasonably sympathetic
D4 conversion of former school (with modern accom block) in the historic section of town on rd up to castle. Serviceable modern hotel in prime location; light 17m pool. 'Sophisticated' Scholars restau up top; the Italian Bistro, Rizzios at st level, is not so *al dente,* but pleasant enough.

76RMS JAN-DEC T/T PETS CC KIDS MED.EX/EXP

685 **BLAIRLOGIE HOUSE, STIRLING:** 01259 761441. 7km E of town centre on A91. A
D3 Victorian house truly nestling at the foot of the hills, in this case the splendid Ochils (1586/HILL WALKS). Well-kept grds (with azaleas and bluebells in spring) tumble to the rd. Cosy and accommodating (nice) family home; bright dining-rm (by Pete Clark). Much better value than many self-conscious country-house hotels. Views over Forth flood plain. Wallace Monument is nearby.

7RMS JAN-DEC T/T PETS CC KIDS MED.INX

686 **LAKE HOTEL, PORT OF MENTEITH:** 01877 385258. A v lake side hotel on the Lake
C3 of Menteith in the purple heart of the Trossachs. Good centre for touring and walking. The Ichmahome ferry leaves from nearby (1538/MARY, CHARLIE AND BOB). Only a few rms o/look lake (3 newer ones carry supplement, but are worth the extra). Splendid conservatory for sunset supper. Romantic or what?

16RMS JAN-DEC T/T PETS CC KIDS TOS MED.EX

687 **DUNBLANE HYDRO, DUNBLANE:** 01786 822551. One of the huge hydro hotels left
D3 over from the last health boom, this one is part of the Stakis chain. Nice views for some and a long walk down corridors for most. Exercise also in the gym and the pool. It's a dinner-dance world.

215RMS JAN-DEC T/T PETS KIDS CC TOS EXP

688 **INVERARNAN HOTEL/THE DROVER'S INN, INVERARNAN:** 01301 704234. N of Ardlui
A2 on L Lomond and 12km S of Crianlarich on the A82. Much the same as it was when it began in 1705; bare floors, open fires, shared facs and heavy drinking (1003/BLOODY GOOD PUBS). Highland hoolies here much recommended (Hogmanay millennium already booked up). A wild place in the wilderness.

20RMS JAN-DEC X/X PETS CC KIDS CHP

689 **HOTELS IN KILLIN:** Killin is on the corner of the old 'Central' region, but is a v
C2 Highland sort of a place. Famous for the Falls of Dochart, the rocky course of the river that runs through the town, and with mighty Ben Lawers nearby, it is a good gateway for pts N and W. There are 2 good inexp hotels. **THE KILLIN HOTEL:** 01567 820296. V Scottish, tartan everywhere, pleasant old-fashioned feel; conservatory on front. **DALL LODGE:** 01567 820217. Smaller, more personal, many *objets*. Both hotels on main st.

32/10RMS JAN-DEC T/T PETS CC KIDS MED.INX

RESTAURANTS

690 ✠ ✠ **BRAEVAL OLD MILL, ABERFOYLE:** 01877 382711. Just E of Aberfoyle on
B3 A873 for Port of Menteith and Stirling. Small, converted 'mill' on edge of golf course. Nick and Fiona Nairn's place. Probably Scotland's most sought-after meal, since Nick's TV career took off and I for one, who never knows what I'm doing far enough in advance to book and get in here, haven't had the pleasure this summer. Nick not flaming over the hot stove nowadays, but he has them well-trained. It's just v good. Lunch and dinner Wed-Sat and Sun lunch. Weekday lunches easier.

EXP

♣ **THE UNICORN INN, KINCARDINE:** 01259 730704; 15 Excise St. Nr Kincardine 691
♦ Br in village (Stirling 20km, M9 5km jnct 7). I always get lost and ask at the E4
petrol stn. Unique spot in this part of the world; bistro atmos, most excellent
food. Light, Mediterranean app (and Spanish music). Seafood medley is a
signature dish (there are live lobsters in a tank downstairs). Best use of samphire
I've had in Scotland. Gr cheeseboard. Nice people, chef Brian Ainslie taught by a
maestro.   MED

♣ **BLACK BULL, KILLEARN:** 01360 550215. Good-looking village, 30mins N of 692
♦ Glasgow betw L Lomond (Drymen) and the Campsies. Excellent pub food B4
and conservatory restau. Good service (owners had hotel in US); waiters have ear
pieces! Imaginative cuisine way beyond usual pub standard. Excellent puds. Live
jazz.   MED

CREAGAN HOUSE, STRATHYRE: 01877 384638. End of the village on main A84 for 693
Crianlarich. Creagan House is the place to eat in Rob Roy country and there are C2
some wonderful walks pre and *après* (1572/HILLS). They have 5 inexp rms and the
Gunn's are an extremely congenial bunch. Gordon Gunn is also an innovative
and individualist chef and ingredients come local, incl the grd. Never v sure about
the decorations, esp the pictures, but the sale of work section of the dining-rm
when I was there, reflects their local commitment. Cl Feb.   MED

CROSS KEYS HOTEL AND BAR, KIPPEN: 01786 870293. Main st of couthie town 694
15km W of Stirling by A811. Notable omission from previous editions since this C4
excellent pub-food place has been here and winning accolades for yonks. Gr for
families and generally for informal unpretentious food (1038/BEST FOOD).   INX

KIPLINGS, BRIDGE OF ALLAN: 01786 833617. Well Rd off the main st and up the hill 695
towards Sherriffmuir in dreaming and amazingly well-heeled suburb of D3
Stirling/Bridge of Allan. Even the birds twitter politely. Like much of this, the
restau probably looks better from the o/side. But Stirling comes over.   EXP

♣ **THE ALLAN WATER CAFÉ, BRIDGE OF ALLAN:** Caff that's been here for ever at 696
♦ the end of the main st in Bridge of Allan. Original features, gr feel, gr fish 'n' D3
chips and, of course, the ice cream (1099/CAFÉS). 7 days, 9am-9pm.   CHP

THE BEST HOTELS AND RESTAURANTS IN THE BORDERS

See also 1944/CENTRES: HAWICK AND GALASHIELS, p. 262. Refer to Map 8.

♣ ♦ **SUNLAWS HOUSE, nr KELSO:** 01573 450331. Easily the best country-house 697
♦ hotel in the Borders. Owned by the Duke and Duchess of Roxburghe, D3
who have a personal input. Some recent refurb, incl 4-poster beds, etc.
Reliable wine list (by the Duke) and menu (safe and satisfying). The recently-
added 18-hole golf course has broadened appeal. Clearly improving all round and
compared with other country-house hotels, good value. A taste of the high life
without being stuffy.   22RMS JAN-DEC T/T PETS CC KIDS TOS EXP
EAT Where to go to dine and wine in the E Borders. Chef David Bates.   EXP

♣ **CRINGLETIE HOUSE, PEEBLES:** 01721 730233. Country house 5km from town 698
♦ just off A703 Edin rd (35km). Late 19th-century Scottish baronial house in B2
28 acres. The Maguire family delight in the place, offering their home-made
honey for breakfast, and fruit and veg from the walled grd at dinner. Huge
geraniums from the glasshouse in the conservatory restau. Welcome to a more
civilised gone-by world.   13RMS MAR-DEC T/T PETS CC KIDS TOS MED.EX
EAT Gracious dining in 2 formal rms. Friendly.   MED

♣ **BURTS, MELROSE:** 01896 822285. In Market Sq/main st, some (double-glazed) 699
♦ rms o/look. Busy bars, esp for food, The dining-rm is *where to eat* in this C3
part of the Borders. Trad, but comfortably modernised small town hotel.
Convenient location. Good service (1529/ABBEYS; 1585/HILL WALKS;
1206/GARDENS).   21RMS JAN-DEC T/T PETS CC KIDS TOS MED.EX
EAT Jolly and busy bar, or more refined dining-rm. Chef Gary Moore.   EXP

DRYBURGH ABBEY HOTEL, nr ST BOSWELLS: 01835 822261. Secluded, elegant 19th- 700
century house in Abbey grounds banking R Tweed. Peaceful atmos; good C3
swimming pool, and walks for contemplations.

                                            26RMS JAN-DEC T/T PETS CC KIDS TOS EXP

701 **THE LEY, nr INNERLEITHEN:** 01896 830240. 3km from village up Leithen Water
B2 through golf course. Doreen and Willy McVicar don't advertise that they run an
unconventional 'hotel' in their 1861 turreted country house - those in the know
return regularly to enjoy the well-judged menu, wine list and woodlands.

3RMS APR-SEPT X/X XPETS XCC XKIDS MED.EX

702 **EDNAM HOUSE, KELSO:** 01573 224168. Just off town sq, o/look R Tweed; a majestic
D3 Georgian mansion with original features. Dated in a comfy way, fishing regalia
dotted around; the restau's river view is poss its main attraction.

32RMS JAN-DEC T/T PETS CC KIDS TOS MED.INX

703 **THE CROOK INN, TWEEDSMUIR:** 01899 880272. Historic country inn on the A701
A3 Moffat–Edin rd in the hill country nr head of the Tweed, 32km S of Peebles.
Unlikely 1930s features in some of the rms. Nr Dawyck Gardens (xxxx/
GARDENS).

8RMS JAN-DEC X/X PETS CC KIDS MED.INX

RESTAURANTS

EATING IN MELROSE:

704 **MARMIONS:** 01896 822245. Buccleuch St nr the abbey. Established local fave
C3 bistro, now level pegging with its culinary neighbours. Not sampled this time
round, but locals say standard varies. Cl Sun.

INX

705 **MELROSE STATION RESTAURANT:** 01896 822546.TOS. Another French-inspired
C3 eaterie, in stn conversion. Jostles for bistro slot with Marmions. But **BURTS** (*see
above*) is where to go for the really good meal or the pub grub version. Locals
swear by the **KING'S HEAD** for pub food in the main st. Here, rugby is everything.

INX

706 **CULTER MILL, nr ABINGTON:** 01899 220950. A respite from the frustration of
A3 crawling along in a convoy on the A702 (the main Edin – S route). Neatly
converted mill – delicious fuel for the rd (fresh fish in batter is perfection). Cl
Mon-Tue. Lunch , LO 9pm (10pm Sat). Book at w/ends.

INX

THE BEST HOTELS AND RESTAURANTS
IN THE LOTHIANS

See section 1 for Edin. Refer to Map 7.

707 ⚓ ⚓ **GREYWALLS, GULLANE:** 01620 842144. On the coast, 36km E of Edin off
D1 A198 just beyond golfers' paradise of Gullane. O/looks Muirfield, the
championship course (no right of access) and nr Gullane's 3 courses and N
Berwick's 2 (1652/1653/GREAT GOLF). No grey walls here but warm sandstone and
light, summery public rms in this Lutyens-designed manor with grds attributed to
Gertrude Jekyll. It's the look that makes it special and the roses are legendary.
Sculpture grd in July and literary w/ends. Library like a London club, and service.
Golf ain't everything.

22RMS APR-OCT T/T PETS CC XKIDS TOS LOTS

EAT Fine and subtle dining in elegant rm adj course; chef Paul Baron is a confident
player. Wine list has depth and character.

EXP

708 **GREEN CRAIGS, ABERLADY:** 01875 870301. Individual hotel in superb setting on
D1 Edin side of Aberlady (A198, 8km A1). Décor may be iffy for some, but overall
it's comfortable and cared about. They get you to the golf in 'style'. Sun lunch
recommended.

6RMS JAN-DEC T/T PETS CC KIDS EXP

709 **MARINE HOTEL, NORTH BERWICK:** 01620 892406. The grand old seaside hotel of N
D1 Berwick reeks of holidays gone by – you almost expect to see Margaret
Rutherford on the putting green. Snooker, open-air swimming pool. O/looks
Links and Fidra. Good for kids and golf.

83RMS JAN-DEC T/T PETS CC KIDS EXP

710 **OPEN ARMS, DIRLETON:** 01620 850241. Dirleton is 4km from Gullane towards N
D1 Berwick. Comfortable if pricey hotel in centre of village, opp ruins of castle.
Location means it's a golfers' paradise and special packages are available. Restau
has two AA whatsits.

10RMS JAN-DEC T/T PETS CC KIDS TOS LOTS

711 **THE OLD ABERLADY INN:** 01875 870503. Main St. Straightforward drop inn with
D1 simple, well-kept rms, a good farmhouse-style bistro with interesting menu and a
trad howff for drinks and bar food. Popular with golfers – ok for anyone.

8RMS JAN-DEC T/T PETS CC KIDS MED.INX

TWEEDDALE ARMS, GIFFORD: 01620 810240. One of two inns in this heart of E 712
Lothian village 9km from the A1 at Haddington, within easy reach of Edin. Set D2
among rich farming country, Gifford is conservative and couthy. Some bedrms
small, but public rms v pleasant. Smells like a country inn should.

16RMS JAN-DEC T/T PETS CC KIDS MED.INX

JOHNSTOUNBURN HOUSE: 01875 833696. An excellent and relaxing country-house
hotel within easy reach of town (43/HOTELS OUTSIDE TOWN).

RESTAURANTS

✝ ✝ **LA POTINIÈRE, GULLANE:** 01620 843214. E Lothian's best restau still in a
league of its own (51/BEST RESTAUS). MED

✝ **BONARS, GIFFORD:** 01620 810264. Main St. Within months of opening, chef 713
Douglas Bonar and his wife Annabel gained 2 AA rosettes for this intimate D2
wee restau. It provides rich and flamboyant big-league cuisine in an unexpected
location. Strong wine list. 7 days, lunch and dinner, LO 9.30pm. MED

✝ **THE WATERSIDE, HADDINGTON:** 01620 825674. 115 Waterside. On the river, opp 714
side of the pedestrianised old br from St Mary's (1508/CHURCHES). Upstairs D1
restau is more of a pink napkin affair, bistro/bar down has various rms. Separate
vegn menu. Château Musar 1989 on the wine list usually wins our vote, but this is
the reliable Lothian bistro. Daily lunch/supper, LO 10pm. INX

THE GRANGE, NORTH BERWICK: 01620 895894. 35 High St. Restau with a classic but 715
modern design feel and lots of nice touches like mega flowers and well-chosen D1
antique 'bits'. Grd bar, candlelit salon and main rm. Food what you might term
'contemporary Scots' and good with it. Gr cheeses. Lunch Tues-Sun, dinner Tues-
Sat. LO 10.30pm. Management changes imminent. MED

QUADRANT, NORTH BERWICK: 01620 895110. 7/9 Quality St. As soon as it opened 716
in June 1997, this became E Lothian's hippest café/bar. It has all the design values D1
of its nearby capital cousins, a kind of Negociants *au bord de la mer* (275/HIP),
with a spacious feel, cocktail menu and stylish food, although the soundtrack tends
to VH-1 rather than trip hop. 7 days; food always available. LO 10pm; bar 11pm. INX

POLDRATE'S, HADDINGTON: 01620 826882. On B6369 out of Haddington to 717
Lennoxlove and Gifford. Converted mill; bistro atmos, blackboard menu and D1
small, selected wine list changes frequently. Tue-Sun lunch and LO 9.30pm. INX

THE CREEL, DUNBAR: 01368 863279. On corner nr restored harbour area of old 718
resort and pt. Modern bistro with open kitchen, so you can see the honest, unfussy E1
cuisine marché being prepared. Sensible range of choices including seafood. Friendly
folk before and after. Just rt! Tue-Sun lunch, Tues-Sat 7-9pm. INX

THE OLD CLUBHOUSE, GULLANE: 01620 842008. E Links Rd behind main st, on 719
corner of Green. Large woody clubhouse; a bar/bistro serving food all day till D1
10pm. Gr busy atmos. Surprising wine selection; the puds are bought in. INX

DROVER'S INN, EAST LINTON: 01620 860298. Nr A1 (271/BEST FOOD). INX

CHAMPANY'S, nr LINLITHGOW: 01506 834532 (152/BURGERS). INX/EXP

THE BEST HOTELS AND RESTAURANTS
IN FIFE

*See also 1942/CENTRES: DUNFERMLINE AND KIRKCALDY, p. 260; 1953/HOLIDAY CENTRES: ST
ANDREWS, p.271. Refer to Map 5.*

✝ ✝ **OLD COURSE, ST ANDREWS:** 01334 74371. This world-famous hotel is the 720
one you come to first on the A91 from N or W. Unlike many de luxe D2
hotels in the UK, this has lightness to it and accessibility – it is after all surrounded
by greens and full of golfers coming and going. Most rms o/look the famous
course and sea (immaculate and tastefully done with no fac or expense spared), as
do the Conservatory and less informal Road Hole Grill up top. Bar here also for
lingering views and whisky in the glass. Truly gr for golf, but anyone could
unwind here, towelled in luxury. 125RMS JAN-DEC T/T PETS CC KIDS LOTS
EAT Rd Hole Grill for spectacular dinner esp in late light summer. Mark Boxer's
Gourmet Menu excels over TDH. Young, keen v exp wine list. EXP

721 ✚ **BALBIRNIE HOUSE, MARKINCH:** 01592 610066. Signed from the rd system
C3 around Glenrothes (3km) in surprisingly silvan setting of Balbirnie Country
Park. One of the most sociable and comfortable country-house hotels in the land
(and Taste of Scotland Hotel of the Yr 1996), with high standards in service and
décor that's easy to be at home with. Elegant restau and more informal downstairs
bistro (lunch only). New Orangery extension 1998. No leisure facs, but good golf
in the park. Wake to the thwack of balls!
36RMS JAN-DEC T/T PETS CC KIDS TOS LOTS
EAT Elegant hotel dining and bistro for lunch. 2 AA rosettes.   EXP

722 **RUFFLETS, ST ANDREWS:** 01334 472594. 4km from centre via Argyle St opp W Pt
D2 along Strathkinness Low Rd past univ playing fields. Serene feel to this country-
house hotel on edge of town. The celebrated grds are a joy to walk in after dinner
. . . or after getting married.   20RMS JAN-DEC T/T PETS CC KIDS TOS EXP

723 **KILCONQUHAR CASTLE ESTATE, nr ELIE:** 01333 340501. On B942 nr Colinburgh,
D3 3km from Elie (that famously nice town). Mainly time-share villas, but 'club rms'
available in castle itself with access to all facs incl pool, tennis, golf and esp riding.
Daily rates poss.   13RMS JAN-DEC T/T PETS CC KIDS MED.INX

724 **CAMBO ESTATE, nr CRAIL:** 01333 450054. 2km E of Crail on A917. Huge country
E3 pile in glorious grds on the coastal rd betw St Andrews and Crail. Only 2/3 rms,
but this is B&B in the grand manner. Rattle around, pretend you're house guests
and be grateful you don't have to pay the bills.
2RMS JAN-DEC X/X PETS CC KIDS MED.INX

725 **THE GOLF HOTEL, ELIE:** 01333 330209. Earlsferry end of favourite village
D3 (1240/COASTAL VILLAGES) o/look not bad golf. Recent improvements make this a
good value and friendly billet.   22RMS MAR-OCT T/T PETS KIDS MED.INX

726 **THE HERMITAGE, ANSTRUTHER:** 01333 310909. Small B&B-type family house in the
E3 essential East Neuk town. Tasteful (unlike most round here) and friendly. The
Cellar (*see below*) for the treat of your stay. 4RMS JAN-DEC X/X XPETS CC KIDS INX

727 **WOODSIDE HOTEL, ABERDOUR:** 01383 860328. Refurb inn in main st of pleasant
B4 village with prize-winning rail stn, castle and church (1502/CHURCHES), coastal
walk and nearby beach. This is where to come from Edin (by train, of course) with
your bit on the side.   20RMS JAN-DEC T/T PETS CC KIDS MED.INX

728 **FORTH VIEW, ABERDOUR:** 01383 860402. Brilliant setting by a jagged jetty on the
B4 Forth beneath a cliff for airy walks (and famed for rock-climbing). On foot by
path from harbour; or car from corner of Silver Sands beach car park, by extreme
track. Accom is basic in family house, but you wake up with Edin over the sea.
Novel still waiting to be written here.   5RMS APR-OCT X/X PETS CC KIDS CHP

SANDFORD HILL: 01382 541802. 7km S of Tay Br. Underrated country-house hotel
in N Fife nr Dundee. Report: 916/COUNTRY-HOUSE HOTELS.

RESTAURANTS

729 ✚ ✚ **THE PEAT INN, nr CUPAR and ST ANDREWS:** 01334 840206. At a crossroads
D3 of the county, the hamlet of Peat Inn (signed from all over) and of Scottish
cuisine, this restau was one of the first gr Scottish restaus and David Wilson our
first outstanding chef. Standards have improved immeasurably and now you don't
need to go 50 miles to be sure of superb food. But on occasion come here – it is
still an epicurean experience and should you not care to navigate the backrds of
Fife, there are 8 rms for staying the night and looking forward to breakfast. 3 AA
rosettes. Tue-Sat 1-3pm and 7-9.30pm.   EXP

730 ✚ ✚ **THE CELLAR, ANSTRUTHER:** 01333 310378. Off courtyard behind Fisheries
E7 Museum in this busy E Neuk town (1240/COASTAL VILLAGES) – you'd call
this entrance unassuming. As is the whole app, though seafood here is among the
v best you'll find in Scotland. Peter Jukes sources the best produce and then let's
it do its own thing. So simple, so invariably spot-on. Tue-Sat lunch and 7-9pm (7
days high season though not Mon lunch (1071/SEAFOOD RESTAUS).   MED

731 ✚ **OSTLER'S CLOSE, CUPAR:** 01334 655574. Down a close at the narrow part of the
D2 main st, Amanda and Jimmy Graham run a bistro/restau that has Cupar on
the gastronomic map. But no pretence here about 'fine cuisine'; this is honest with
thought and flair. Couldn't eat this time round. Tue-Sat 1-3pm; 7-9.30pm.   MED

BOUQUET GARNI, ELIE: 01333 330374. High St of genteel town **732** (1240/COASTAL VILLAGES). Here for nearly 10yrs with consistently good **D3** dining and accolades (3 AA rosettes). However, may change hands, so check if Andrew Keracher still here (his family are famous for fish). Lunch and 7-9pm. Cl Sun. No smk.

MED

OLD RECTORY, DYSART: 01592 651211. 2km E of Kirkcaldy (5km centre); still 'the **733** best restuarant in W Fife' despite the fact that foodie critic Gillian Glover rather **C4** disagreed with me. You'll just have to go E darling! Tue-Sun lunch; Tue-Sat dinner.

MED

CHANNEL RESTAURANT, NORTH QUEENSFERRY: 01383 412567. Main st on way to **734** harbour or lure of Deep Sea World (1360/KIDS). The rail br, however, is the real **B5** attraction (311/MAIN ATTRACTIONS) and provides stunning backdrop to this informal bistro with young, innovative owners. Their mum grows organic ingredients. Just opened at press time, this place is gonna be good. Wed-Sat lunch/dinner, Sun afternoons.

INX

VALENTE'S, KIRKCALDY & THE ANSTRUTHER FISH BAR: 2 gr fish 'n' chip shops with queues every day, but hang about for the real Saturday night (1084/1094 FISH AND CHIPS).

CHP

THE BEST HOTELS AND RESTAURANTS IN PERTHSHIRE AND TAYSIDE

See also DUNDEE HOTELS AND RESTAURANTS, *p. 116; 1947/CENTRES: PERTH, p. 266; and 1915/HOLIDAY CENTRES: PITLOCHRY. Refer to Map 4.*

FARLEYER HOUSE, nr ABERFELDY: 01887 820332. 4km town on B846 to **735** Tummel Br. Cool country house in grounds with fine trees and 6-hole **B3** golf course, nr Castle Menzies. Excellent dining-rm and informal bistro. Library for whiling away afternoons. Homely with light, yet sophisticated touch. Serve yourself bar after hrs. A Virgin hotel.

11RMS+COTT JAN-DEC T/T PETS CC KIDS LOTS

EAT Almost like a city bistro, except woody acres o/side. Open to nonresidents. Blackboard menu. Most exquisite food in the area.

INX

BALLATHIE HOUSE, nr PERTH: 01250 883268. 20km N of Perth and more **736** fully reported in the town section (1947/PERTH), but a true country- **C3** house hotel on the Tay that you fall in love with. Good dining, good fishing; good for the w/end away.

28RMS JAN-DEC T/T PETS CC KIDS TOS LOTS

EAT Award-winning chef Kevin McGillvray. Gr local produce esp beef/lamb. EXP

KINFAUNS CASTIE, PERTH: 01738 620777. A90 Dundee rd (Perth 7km). **737** Not long ago a walkers' hostel, a lavish restoration has turned this **C4** Scottish baronial pile into a sumptuous country-house hotel too recently opened at time of going to press to judge, but these people used to have Adranaiseig on L Awe and that was a superb retreat. No expense spared on the staircase, the marble fireplaces and the Famous Grouse suite (and may my Internet site be with you). Haven't dined, but we must. Seems refreshingly informal.

16RMS FEB-DEC T/T PETS CC KIDS LOTS

NEWMILN COUNTRY ESTATE, GUILDTOWN, nr PERTH: 01738 552364. A93 **738** Blairgowrie rd (Perth 10km). Driveway assumes you've got a Range **C3** Rover and certainly fishermen will be in their element here; but so might the rest of us. More like a houseparty with excellent dining at the end of a day in the river, or countryside (or Perth). The McFarlanes will make you v welcome.

12RMS JAN-DEC T/T PETS CC KIDS EXP

EAT 3 AA rosettes for chef Paul Burns; haven't tried, this treat awaits.

INX

DUNKELD HOUSE, DUNKELD: 01350 727771. Former home of Duke of Atholl, **739** a v large impressive country house on the banks of the R Tay just outside **C3** Dunkeld. Leisure complex with good pool etc and many other activities laid on. V decent menu. Fine for kids. Pleasant walks. Not cheap but often good deals available. Managed by Stakis chain. Gets full: 3000 enquiries after TV holiday show was aired.

92RMS JAN-DEC T/T PETS CC KIDS LOTS

740 ✚ **ROYAL HOTEL, COMRIE:** 01764 679200. Central sq of cosy town, a sympathetic
B4 and stylish upgrading of trad small-town hotel. Excellent restau with good
light and superb pub out back with real ale and atmos (1020/REAL ALES). Bravely
light carpet with exquisite rugs. A pleasing bit of style in the county bit of the
country. 11RMS JAN-DEC T/T XPETS CC KIDS MED.EX

741 KINLOCH HOUSE, nr BLAIRGOWRIE: 01250 884237. 5km W on A923 to Dunkeld.
C3 A country house with open views to the Sidlaw Hills. Panelled and galleried, and
rather formally attired and run – definitely one for snobs rather than slobs. You
have to fit the bill, then of course you pay it. 21RMS JAN-DEC T/T PETS CC KIDS EXP

742 CASTLETON HOUSE, EASSIE, nr GLAMIS: 01307 840340. 13km W of Forfar, 25km N
D3 of Dundee. App from Glamis, 5km SW on A94. Family-run country-house hotel
with good restau. Not over-pricey or stuffy; bar meals as well as dining-
rms/conservatory. Popular Sun lunch. 6RMS JAN-DEC T/T PETS CC KIDS TOS EXP

743 PINE TREES HOTEL, PITLOCHRY: 01796 472121. A safe haven in visitor-ville – it's
C3 above the town and above all that (there are many mansions here). Take
Larchwood Rd off W end of main st (signed for golf course). Woody grds, woody
interior. There's a piano-player at dinner (Tues/ Thur/Sat). Scots owners – now
there's a change. 20RMS FEB-DEC T/T XPETS CC KIDS MED.EX

744 KILLIECRANKIE HOTEL, KILLIECRANKIE: 01796 473220. 5km N of Pitlochry. Village
D2 inn ambience; cosy rms of individual character. Carefully run. Gr food. Plenty
walks round about. 10RMS MAR-DEC T/T PETS CC KIDS TOS EXP
EAT V fine home-cooking in restau and bar (LO 9.30pm). In every guide book
that counts. Pop over from Pitlochry. INX

745 KENMORE HOTEL, KENMORE: 01887 830205. Nr ancient coaching inn in quaint
B3 conservation village. Excellent prospect for golfing (at Taymouth Castle adj,
(1676/GOLF IN GREAT PLACES) and fishing. On river (Tay) itself with terrace.
Comfy rms. 35RMS JAN-DEC T/T PETS CC KIDS MEDINX

746 CLOVA HOTEL, GLEN CLOVA: 01575 550222. Nr end of Glen Clova, one of the gr
D2 Angus Glens (1270/GLENS), on B955 25km N of Kirriemuir. A walk/climb/
country retreat hotel with multifarious activities thought up by Graham Davie.
Hot soup, warm stove, warm welcome. Superb walking nearby. Often full.
 7RMS JAN-DEC T/T PETS CC KIDS INX

747 HOTEL COLL EARN, AUCHTERARDER: 01764 663553. Off main st. Extravagant
C4 Victorian mansion with exceptional stained glass. Comfy rms, huge beds.
 9RMS JAN-DEC T/T XPETS CC KIDS .EXP

748 GUINACH HOUSE, ABERFELDY: 01887 820251. On A826 Crieff rd and among the
B3 famous 'Birks' (1623/WOODLAND WALKS). Small mansion in pleasant grd. Chef
prop Bert Mackay has 2 AA rosettes. 7RMS JAN-DEC X/T PETS CC KIDS MED.EX

749 ATHOLL ARMS, BLAIR ATHOLL: 01796 481205. Main st opp castle, the major
B2 attraction hereabouts (1412/CASTLES) and part of the estate. Recent refurb has
improved rms and tartanised downstairs. Excellent chef Martin Hollis now
installed in magnificent lofty dining-rm, the old ballrm for the castle. A v
Highland experience. 30RMS JAN-DEC T/T PETS CC KIDS INX

GLENEAGLES: 01764 662231 (906/COUNTRY-HOUSE HOTELS).

KINNAIRD HOUSE: 01796 482440 (904/COUNTRY-HOUSE HOTELS).

AUCHTERARDER HOUSE: 01764 663646 (909/COUNTRY-HOUSE HOTELS).

OLD MANSION HOUSE, AUCHTERHOUSE: 01382 320366 (878/DUNDEE HOTELS).

B2 CRIEFF HYDRO, CRIEFF: 01764 655555. Superb for many reasons, esp kids.
Quintessentially Scottish (919/KIDS).

RESTAURANTS

750 ✚ ✚ **LET'S EAT, PERTH:** 01738 643377. Corner of Kinnoul St. Tony Heath and
C4 Shona Drysdale's perfect county town eaterie. Cuisine without the
trappings, but all the rt trimmings. Extremely good value and instantly the place
to eat here when they left the Dee (Courtyard, Aberdeen) and came to the Tay.
 MED

THE BUT 'N' BEN, AUCHMITHIE, nr ARBROATH: 01241 877223. 2km off A92 N **751** from Arbroath, 8km to town or 4km by cliff-top walk. Village perched on **E3** cliff top where ravine leads to small cove and quay. Adj cottages converted into cosy restau open noon-3pm for lunch, 4-5.30pm for high-tea (2 sittings Sun), 7-10pm for dinner. Cl Tue. Menus vary but all v Scottish and informal with emphasis on fresh fish/seafood, brilliant value – Margaret Horn continues to provide a Scottish experience for her ain folk and all others. INX

CARGILLS, BLAIRGOWRIE: 01250 876735. Cosy wine bar ambience, busy à la carte **752** menu and blackboard. Serviceable, reliable. Unprepossessing frontage, but on **C3** river side. Adj coffee shop/gallery. The place to eat in these valleys beneath the ski zone. INX

3 GOOD RESTAURANTS AT KINROSS: Close to jnct 6 of the M90, but excellent in any **753** case. **CARLIN MAGGIE'S:** 01577 863652. 191 High St. Scots cuisine with Oz **C4** influence (chef Tom McConnell) real pavlova to real Perthshire (with kangaroo). Cl Sun/Mon and March. MED

CROFTBANK HOUSE: 01577 863819. Stn Rd; 1km on main rd from motorway jnct. **754** Discreet hotel with notable dining-rm (2 AA rosettes). Also bar meals (5RMS). Cl Mon (MED). **GROUSE AND CLARET:** 01557 864212. Heatheryford on other (W) side of jnct, about 1km. On fishing lochans, converted farm buildings with popular pleasant restau and 3 rms. INX

LOCHSIDE LODGE, LINTRATHEN: 01575 560340 (886/DUNDEE EAT AND DRINK).

THE BEST HOTELS AND RESTAURANTS IN THE NORTH-EAST

Excludes Aber, but see also 1954/CENTRES: Ballater. Refer to Map 3.

PITTODRIE HOUSE, PITCAPLE: 01467 681444. Large 'family' mansion **755** house on estate in one of the best bits of Aberdeenshire with Bennachie **C3** above. 40km Aber but 'only 30mins from airport' via A96. Follow signs off B9002. Tennis courts, croquet lawn, billiards and lots of comfortable rms. Exquisite walled grd 500m from house. Fine menu, veg from grd; good esp French wine list. 27RMS JAN-DEC T/T PETS CC KIDS TOS LOTS

DARROCH LEARG, BALLATER: 01339 755443. On main A93 at edge of **756** town. Nigel Franks has carefully brought this hotel (long in the family) **B4** forward. With superior standards, but a relaxed ambiance and an excellent dining-rm, it is now the best in this hotel-studded town. Change of chef since last edition, but have quickly regained 3 AA rosettes. Comfortable rather than opulent with attentive and considerate staff. No bar, but civilised drinks before and *après*. Good base for touring. 18RMS JAN-DEC T/T PETS CC KIDS TOS LOTS
EAT Conservatory dining-rm and one of best restaus in NE; Chef David Mutter deserves a name-check too. Nice grd view, fab food. EXP

OLD MANSE OF MARNOCH: 01466 780873. On B9117, 1km from A97, the **757** Huntly to Banff rd. Exactly as you'd imagine it, a charming old manse nr the **C2** banks of R Deveron. Bucolic surroundings; bright and healthy breakfast.
5RMS JAN-DEC X/X PETS CC XKIDS TOS MED.EX
EAT Keren Carter's imaginative 4-course menu (2 choices only) changes daily. May seat round the one table, like a dinner party. Must book. 2 AA rosettes. MED

CRAIGELLACHIE HOTEL, CRAIGELLACHIE: 01340 881204. The quintessential **758** Spey-side hotel, off A941 Elgin to Perth and Aber rd by the br over Spey. **B2** Esp good for fishing, but well placed for walking (Speyside Way runs along bottom of grd, *see* 1600/LONG WALKS) and distillery visits (1191-5/WHISKY). Informal; some fab rms. Nice snug and, of course, this is where to drink the drink. 29RMS JAN-DEC T/X XPETS CC KIDS TOS MED.EX

ROTHES GLEN, ROTHES: 01340 831254. 5km N of Rothes on A941 Elgin-Perth **759** rd. Big house in whisky country (nr Glen Grant distillery and grd). Mr **B2** MacKenzie and Mr Symonds run a tight and tidy ship with flair and ambition. A tad OTT? You may not notice. 16RMS JAN-DEC T/T PETS CC XKIDS TOS LOTS

UDNY ARMS, NEWBURGH: 01358 789444. A975 off A92. Village pub with gr **760** **D3**

food and character run by the Craig family for over 10yrs. Rms tasteful and individually furnished. Folk come from Aber (28km) to eat here. Golf course Cruden Bay (1657/GREAT GOLF) 16km N and walks beside Ythan estuary (1398/WILDLIFE).   26RMS JAN-DEC T/T XPETS CC KIDS TOS MED.INX

EAT Excellent grub in bar or dining-rm. Good ambience. Lunch; LO 9.30pm.
MED

761 ✚ **STAKIS ROYAL DEESIDE, BALLATER:** 013397 55858. On the Braemar rd (A93).
B4 ┃ Part of a country-club/time-share operation (Craigendarroch) with elegant dining, good leisure facs and discreet resort-in-the-woods feel. Good service, 2 restaus, one by pool (though more chlorine than cuisine) and the conscientiously up-market Oak. Lodges can be available on short lets, a good idea for a group holiday or w/end.   44RMS JAN-DEC T/T XPETS CC KIDS TOS LOTS

762 **MELDRUM HOUSE, OLD MELDRUM:** 01651 872294. 1km from village, 30km N of
D3 Aber via A947 Banff rd. Reopened with new owners after lapse. Comfortable granite country house with many fires, spacious grounds and nice feel to bedrms. Regrettably, couldn't stay or try dinner, but this is a noteworthy hotel. Golf course (still) in the making at press time. 9RMS JAN-DEC T/T PETS CC KIDS LOTS

763 **THE MANSION HOUSE, ELGIN:** 01343 548811. In town centre (beneath the left hand
B2 of the statue on the hill). Comfortable and elegant town house in a comfortable and gentle town with 'leisure facs', incl pool/gym and drop-in bistro. Good dining-rm.   22RMS JAN-DEC T/T XPETS CC KIDS TOS LOTS

764 **MANSEFIELD HOUSE, ELGIN:** 01343 540883. Refurb hotel on edge of town centre
B2 considered locally to be the place to eat. Haven't stayed (or eaten), but do what the Elginites do.   20RMS JAN-DEC T/T XPETS CC KIDS TOS MED.INX

765 **BANCHORY LODGE HOTEL, BANCHORY:** 01330 822625. A sporting-lodge hotel nr
D4 town centre, but superbly situated on the banks of the Dee. No longer hold fishing rts, but can arrange. Public rms and many bedrms o/look the river. Sporty rather than staid atmos. People come back like the fish.
22RMS FEB-DEC T/T PETS CC KIDS EXP

766 **RAEMOIR HOUSE, BANCHORY:** 01330 824884. 5km from town via A980 off main st.
D4 Mansion in the country with old-fashioned (1970s going on Victorian) feel, so fairly relaxed. 9-hole golf and tennis. Stable annex. I haven't stayed or eaten, but it is recommended (and Cliff liked it).   20RMS JAN-DEC T/T PETS CC KIDS LOTS

767 **DELNASHAUGH INN, BALLINDALLOCH, nr GRANTOWN ON SPEY:** 01807 500255.
B2 Road-side and Speyside (actually the Avon, pron 'Arn') inn, comfy, unpretentious. On bend of A95 betw Craigellachie and Grantown nr confluence of main rds and rivers. Laura Ashley/Sarah Churchill décor, not minimalist, but simple. Food also. Much ado about fishing.
9RMS MAR-NOV T/T PETS CC KIDS EXP

768 **CASTLE HOTEL, HUNTLY:** 01466 792696. Behind Huntly Castle ruin; app from
D2 town through castle entrance and then over R Deveron up impressive drive. Large but family-scale lodge-house; former seat of the Dukes of Gordon. Rms have character and views. Fishing fixed. 30RMS JAN-DEC T/T PETS CC KIDS MED.INX

769 **BAYVIEW HOTEL, CULLEN:** 01542 841031. 50m off main A98 Banff to Elgin rd,
C1 o/look harbour. Some rms have gr views of a gr bay (1260/BEACHES). Also a gr walk nearby (1643/COASTAL WALKS). Good pub food, incl the local smoked fish soup, Cullen Skink. LO 9pm.   6RMS JAN-DEC T/T PETS CC KIDS MED.INX

770 **ARCHIESTOWN HOTEL, ARCHIESTOWN:** 01340 810218. Main st of small village in
B2 heart of Speyside nr Cardhu Distillery (1194/WHISKY). A village inn with comfortable rms and celebrated food in bistro setting (LO 8.30pm). Fishers and locals.   9RMS JAN-DEC T/T PETS CC KIDS MED.EX

771 **WATERSIDE INN, PETERHEAD:** 01779 71121. Edge of town on A952 to Fraserburgh
E2 on tidal R Ugie. Standard, well-run modern hotel, recommended for its service and convenience and because it's the best option around. Good for kids (929/KIDS).   110RMS JAN-DEC T/T PETS CC KIDS MED.EX

772 **GRANT ARMS, MONYMUSK:** 01467 651226. The village inn in delightful rural
D3 Aberdeenshire, a good centre for walking (1582/HILLS), close to the 'Castle Trail' (1408/CASTLES; 1476/COUNTRY HOUSES) and with fishing rts on the Don.
10RMS JAN-DEC X/T PETS CC KIDS MED.INX

EAT Best pub food for miles, and dining. Daily lunch, 6.30-9pm.   INX

RESTAURANTS

✚ ✚ **THE OLD MONASTERY, nr BUCKIE:** 01542 832660. This is *the* place to eat on a long stretch of coast. Off main A98; instead of going into Buckie, follow small rd marked for Drybridge. The converted church is 5km on the left with gr views of the distant Moray coastline. Lunch in the Cloisters Bar (with views) and dinner in the church itself. Fairly simple menu using fresh local ingredients and careful attention. The view and the grd in summer, the wood-stove in winter. Often booked: don't set out without phoning. Tue-Sat. **773 C2** EXP

✚ **THE GREEN INN, BALLATER:** 01339 755701. On the green in touring centre of Royal Deeside, a restau with rms (3, above the shop). Rms often booked, but phone for availability, then you get an excellent start to the day as well. Jeff Purves' generally healthy and PC app to food means it's good all the way through. The salmon will be wild, the scallops dived; no-fry policy and heather honey instead of sugar, etc., but no preciousness here, just efficiency and quality. **774 B4** MED

✚ **BRUNO'S RESTAURANT, BALLATER:** 01339 755346. Another restau with (guesthouse-type) rms. 34 Victoria Rd (head from sq to golf course) – a totally Italian experience in unlikely suburban setting. Bruno won't tell you, but when the Royals are up the rd at Balmoral, they get him over to knock them up his exceptional pasta, made for him in the old country. Good value and warm welcome in this family house. 8rms are INX; ristorante open Apr-Sept. Cl Mon-Tues; not lunch. **775 B4** INX

WHITE COTTAGE, ABOYNE: 01339 886265. Just before Aboyne going W on A93 the Royal Deeside rd. Cottage it is, but not quite white. Laurie Mill's straightforward app – simply good food, simply pleasant surroundings. Undeniably worthwhile stop on the rd; nice with kids. Lunch and dinner LO 9pm. Cl Mon. **776 C4** MED

MILTON RESTAURANT: 01330 844566. On main A93 Royal Deeside rd 4km E of Banchory opp the entrance to Crathes (1199/GARDENS; 1477/COUNTRY HOUSES). Roadside and surprisingly contemporary café/restau in old steading. Pottery adj. Light and exceedingly pleasant space. Snack/hot food menu by day and dinner at night. 7 days, not Sun even. **777 C4** INX

FAGINS, WHITEHILLS nr BANFF: 01261 861321. Loch St on rt as you app this coastal village 3km W of Banff off B9139. Long-standing local reputation for surf 'n' turf suppers cooked in galley kitchen in corner of dining-rm above an unpromising pub. Honest to goodness food with some flair. Fri-Sun lunch, Wed-Sat 7-10pm. **778 C1** INX

✚ ✚ **LAIRHILLOCK, nr STONEHAVEN:** 01569 730001. 15km S of Aber off A92. Excellent country pub and restau, good for kids. Full report 845/ABER RESTAUS; 1034/GREAT FOOD. **D4**

TOLBOOTH, STONEHAVEN: 01569 762287 (1076/SEAFOOD RESTAUS).

THE BEST HOTELS AND RESTAURANTS IN THE HIGHLANDS

See also Ft William, p. 261; Ullapool, p. 268; Skye, p. 751; Western Isles, p. 252. Refer to Map 2.

✚ ✚ **INVERLOCHY CASTLE, FORT WILLIAM:** 01397 702177. 5km from town on A82 Inverness rd, Scotland's flagship Highland (*Relais et Châteaux*) hotel. Now owned and refurb by a Malaysian company, the castle continues to play host to visiting luminaries and royalty, but is less inhibiting than before. Everything you expect of a 'castle'; the epitome of grandeur and service. Huge colourful, comfortable rms, set in acres of rhododendrons with rainbow trout in the lake and the big Ben over there. **779 C4** 16RMS JAN-DEC T/T PETS CC KIDS LOTS

✚ ✚ **CLIFTON HOUSE, NAIRN:** 01667 453119. Seafield St off A96 to Inverness. A suburban mansion o/look park and seafront of genteel town nr Inverness. For over 50yrs (can it really be 50yrs?) one of the most distictly individual hotels in the Highlands run by the inimitable J Gordon MacIntyre and full of his good taste. Last time I was there he was working in the grd from which herbs and glorious flowers come. Sometimes he chefs though his son does most. Excellent wine list. In winter there are musical and theatrical evenings and Mrs Mac has an antiques and ceramics gallery adj. Every rm is a different experience; **780 D3** dinner is not merely a meal. It's a house party and demonstrates that all the management training, spas and gyms, trouser-presses and unctuous waiters in the world will never make up for style. 12RMS JAN-DEC X/X PETS CC KIDS EXP

EAT Dining never dull, often dramatic. Hand-picked excellent value wine list.
EXP

781
D3
CULLODEN HOUSE, INVERNESS: 01463 790461. 5km E of town nr A9, follow signs for Culloden village, not the Battlefield. Hugely impressive, Georgian mansion and lawn on edge of suburbia and, of course, history. The most conscientiously de luxe hotel hereabouts. Some fab grd suites. Excellent chef. Part of Virgin marketing group. 25RMS JAN-DEC T/T PETS CC KIDS TOS LOTS

782
D3
DOWER HOUSE, nr MUIR OF ORD: 01463 870090. On A862 between Beauly andDingwall, 18km NW of Inverness and 2km N of village. Charming, personal place; you feel like a house guest. Cottagey-style small country house, with comfy public rms. Also lodge house accom.
5RMS JAN-DEC T/T PETS CC XKIDS EXP

EAT Michelin chef Robyn Aitchison, simple, sophisticated. Fixed menu. MED

783
C3
LOCH TORRIDON HOTEL, L TORRIDON, nr KINLOCHEWE: 01445 791242. At the end of the glen (Torridon) in immense scenery. Highland lodge atmos; hills to climb. Report: 965/GET-AWAY-FROM-IT-ALL. 22RMS JAN-DEC T/T PETS CC XKIDS LOTS

784
D3
POLMAILY HOUSE, DRUMNADROCHIT, LOCH NESS: 01456 450343. 5km from Drumnadrochit on A831 to Cannich in Glen Urquhart and nr awesome Glen Affric (1265/GLENS). Unpretentious country-house retreat in lived-in unmanicured grounds. Many walks; tennis, riding and covered-in pool. Small, comfy public rms, individual bedrms. Sensible dinner and wine list. Everything on hand for kids (920/KIDS), but ok for those without. The house and the glen are yours. 14RMS JAN-DEC T/T PETS CC KIDS EXP

785
D3
DUNAIN PARK, INVERNESS: 01463 230512. 6km SW town on A82 Ft William rd. Mansion-house just off the rd, a quiet and more civilised alternative to hotels in town, esp for those on business. Nice grds, small pool in outhouse; real countryside beyond. Notable restau/dining-rm with sound Scottish menu; lots of creamy puds. Excellent wine and malt list. Fresh donuts for breakfast.
14RMS JAN-DEC T/T PETS CC KIDS TOS EXP

EAT Ann Nicholl's no-nonsense menu and sideboard of delicious puds. MED

786
C2
THE SUMMER ISLES HOTEL, ACHILTIBUIE: 01854 622282. 40km from Ullapool with views over the isles; Stac Polly and Suilven are close by to climb. V popular restau, comfortable rms above; with *Swiss Family Robinson* log cabins in grds. Adj pub offers similar quality food at half the price.
13RMS APR-OCT T/X PETS CC XKIDS TOS EXP

EAT Fairly formal dining, but awfully good. All would-be restaurateurs should be shown this cheeseboard. Seafood lunches and bar meals a must if nearby. MED.EX

787
D3
BUNCHREW HOUSE, nr INVERNESS: 01463 234917. On A862 Beauly rd only 5km from Inverness yet completely removed from; on the wooded shore of the Beauly Firth. Dining-rm and some bedrms o/look water; you might see Ben Wyvis. Gr club bar, esp for late dram. 11RMS JAN-DEC T/T PETS CC KIDS TOS EXP

788
D3
COUL HOUSE, CONTIN, nr STRATHPEFFER: 01997 421487. Comfortable country-house hotel on the edge of the wilds with some elegant public rms. Family-run with nice dogs. Well-kept lawns where a piper plays in summer (Fri evenings). V Taste of Scotland menu. 20RMS JAN-DEC T/T PETS CC KIDS TOS MED.EX

789
C4
ONICH HOTEL, ONICH, by FORT WILLIAM: 01855 821214. 16km S on main A82, one of 3 roadside and, in this case, loch side hotels which are more attractive than many in town. Onich is the best value and about half its rms o/look L Linnhe. Busy bars and grassy terrace. 27RMS JAN-DEC T/T PETS CC KIDS MED.EX

790
C4
LODGE ON THE LOCH, ONICH: 01855 821237. As above and the other hotel of note. More exp, but there are 4 rms not *en suite*, which are better value.
18RMS MAR-OCT T/T PETS CC KIDS TOS EXP

791
C1
KINLOCHBERVIE HOTEL, KINLOCHBERVIE: 01971 521275. Serviceable hotel on hill o/looking important fishing pt (go see evening fish market). 1970s kind of rms and restau, bar and bistro. 14RMS JAN-DEC T/T PETS CC KIDS EXP

792 **SUTHERLAND ARMS HOTEL, LAIRG:** 01549 402291. Town hotel o/look L Shin. Not such gr value, but in a wide swathe of big country, this is the best option. Go fish.   D2

27RMS   APR-OCT   T/T   PETS   CC   KIDS   MED.INX

KNOCKIE LODGE, LOCH NESS: 01456 486276 (910/COUNTRY-HOUSE HOTELS).

ARISAIG HOUSE, ARISAIG: 01687 450622 (985/SCOTTISH HOTELS).

ACKERGILL TOWER, nr WICK: 01955 603556 (964/GET-AWAY-FROM-IT-ALL).

RESTAURANTS

✝ ✝ **THE CROSS, KINGUSSIE:** 01540 661166. Off main st at traffic lights, head   793
200m uphill then left into glen. Perfect setting for the best restau in the ski   D4
zone, part of 'restau with rms' hotel in converted tweed mill (799/INEXP
HIGHLANDS HOTELS). Airy rm, doesn't feel like Kingussie. Ruth Hadley, master
chef, works wonders in the kitchen and Tony talks you through amazing wine list
and the cheese, both fastidiously selected with gr flair and enthusiasm. Best to stay
the night after this. Mar-Nov. Cl Tue.   EXP

✝ ✝ **OLD PINES, nr SPEAN BRIDGE:** 01397 712324. Medium-priced dining in   794
inexp hotel and one of the best meals in the Highlands. How Sukie   C4
Barbour does it with all those kids, God knows, but the food can be brilliant.
Some doubt at time of going to press whether local licensing will allow
continuation of dinner being available to nonresidents. That would be a gr pity.
Phone to check. See also 814/INX HIGHLAND HOTELS.   MED

✝ **LA RIVIERA at the GLEN MORISTON HOTEL & RIVA, INVERNESS:** 01463 230512   795
& 237377. Italian restaus in Inverness owned by the same people and   D3
probably best food in town (but see **CAFÉ NUMBER ONE**). La Riviera is dining-rm,
Riva is riverside downtown café/tratt and not exp. Fuller reports: 1945/
INVERNESS.   EXP/INX

GOOD INEXPENSIVE HOTELS IN THE HIGHLANDS

Refer to Map 2.

✝ ✝ **THE CEILIDH PLACE, ULLAPOOL:** 01854 612103. Jean Urquhart's   796
unconventional app and individual hotel still out in front; an oasis up-N.   C2
What started out 27yrs ago as a coffee/exhibition shop in a boat shed, has spread
along this row of cottages now comprising a restau, bookshop, self-serve
wholefood/coffee area, and bedrms upstairs. In winter food is served in front of the
roaring fire in the Parlour Bar. Bunkhouse across the rd is to be refurb and offers
cheaper accom. Live music and events throughout the yr, or you can simply sit on
the lounge/terrace upstairs and wonder about Ullapool.

23RMS   JAN-DEC   T/X   PETS   CC   KIDS   EXP

EAT Coffee shop/bistro 8am-11pm. Restau informal, but urbane.   MED

✝ ✝ **THE ALBANNACH, LOCHINVER:** 01571 844407. 2km up rd to Baddidarach   797
as you come into Lochinver on the A837, at the br. Lesley and Colin   C2
have created a unique and comfortable haven in their 18th-century house. The
byre in the grds has recently been converted into a suite; the croft walk behind
has gr views over the water to Suilven. After one of Lesley's winning dinners you
get the sun on the terrace o/looking the grd (you have to go there to smoke) and
drink the tranquility; and their whisky.   MAR-DEC   X/X   XPETS   CC   XKIDS   INX

EAT When in Assynt, eat at The Albannach. Simple.   MED

✝ **AUCHENDEAN LODGE, DULNAIN BRIDGE, nr GRANTOWN ON SPEY:** 01479   798
851347. An urbane enclave in an area of stunning scenery nr Aviemore skiing   E3
and Whisky Trail. Tastefully and cosily furnished Edwardian lodge with log fires,
good malts and cellar, and books. Food with flair and imagination – they know
their oysters and their mushrooms.   7RMS   JAN-DEC   X/T   PETS   CC   KIDS   TOS   MED.INX

EAT Most imaginative menu in wide area of S Speyside, incl Aviemore.   ME

✝ **THE CROSS, KINGUSSIE:** 01540 661166. Inexp but tastefully done hotel in   799
converted tweed mill by river which gurgles o/side most windows. Restau   D4
not cheap, but superb.
EAT To stay, you're expected to eat; you'd be mad not to (793/HIGHLANDS
HOTELS).   9RMS   MAR-NOV   T/X   XPETS   CC   XKIDS   MED.INX

800 ⚓ **GLENGARRY CASTLE, INVERGARRY:** 01809 501254. The MacCallum family are
D4 approaching their 40th anniversary here and prove not only that a friendly
welcome and relaxed ambience need not be forced, but also that value for money
can still be found. A real castle; large bedrms. Extensive grounds, where forests
come down to the loch. Tennis, fishing and a good base for touring the 'Ness'
area. And check out the 15th Earl. 26RMS APR-OCT T/T PETS CC KIDS MED.EX

801 ⚓ **GLENFINNAN HOUSE HOTEL, GLENFINNAN:** 01397 722235. Victorian mansion
C4 with lawns down to L Shiel and the Glenfinnan Monument over the water.
No shortbread-tin twee or tartan carpet here; instead a warm welcome from the
MacFarlanes, who'll entertain your requests on assorted musical instruments.
Excellent value (987/SCOTTISH HOTELS).
20RMS APR-OCT X/X PETS CC KIDS MED.INX

802 **BALLACHULISH HOUSE, BALLACHULISH:** 01855 811266. Surprisingly spookyless
C5 considering it's reputed to be one of the most haunted houses in Scotland (mind
you, I was there in the gloamin'; it may be different in the dark). N wing newly
refurb, lovely hill views. Billiard rm and games, 'trust' bar, and Liz Grey's
expertise at the Aga. 6RMS JAN-DEC T/X PETS CC KIDS MED.EX

803 **LOCH MAREE HOTEL, TALLADALE:** 01445 760288. On A832 15km from Kinlochewe
C2 and rt by the loch side (1292/LOCHS). A Highland fishing hotel catering for
discriminating tourists (incl Queen Victoria) since 1872. All fishing arrangements
made including ghillies. A good base for walking in Torridon. Nr Inverewe
(1198/GARDENS) and Gairloch. Unpretentious comfort, good value.
32RMS MAR-NOV T/T PETS CC KIDS MED.INX

804 **BEN LOYAL HOTEL, TONGUE:** 01847 611216. Good small hotel on the N coast nr
D1 Ben Loyal. Friendly hosts and lovely views of the sweeping country all around
you. Not all rms are en suite; the adj bungalow is cheaper still but more basic.
Dinner, B&B. 12RMS MAR-NOV X/T PETS CC KIDS TOS MED.EX

805 **TIGH-AN-EILEAN, SHIELDAIG:** 01520 755251. Lovely freshly-furnished hotel on
C3 waterfront o/look Scots Pine island on loch. Good food and pub make this an
ideal base to explore from; the marquetry compass on the hall floor may pt you
in the rt direction. 12RMS APR-OCT X/X PETS CC KIDS EXP

806 **EDDRACHILLES HOTEL, nr SCOURIE:** 01971 502080. Not the friendliest of places but
C2 the rms are ok and the setting is exceptional; if you're a nice couple and you keep
your traps shut, you'll be all rt. Handy for Handa Island (1380/BIRDS). S of
Scourie on A894. 11RMS MAR-OCT T/T XPETS CC XKIDS MED.INX

807 **SUTHERLAND ARMS HOTEL, GOLSPIE:** 01408 633234. Roadside inn at N end of
D2 town nr Dunrobin Castle and Big Burn Walk (1611/GLEN WALKS). First coaching
inn in Scotland now run by Kiwis, it's a good stopover on the route N.
16RMS JAN-DEC T/T PETS CC KIDS INX

808 **DORNOCH CASTLE HOTEL, DORNOCH:** 01862 810216. Atmos 16th-century castle in
D2 main st. Dinner in the dungeons (huge stone fireplace) and drinks upstairs in the
turreted bar o/look cathedral. Bedrms in old part and new wing. Beach and golf
nearby (1659/GREAT GOLF). 17RMS APR-OCT T/T PETS CC KIDS MED.EX

809 **ROYAL HOTEL, CROMARTY:** 01381 600217. Marine Terr on seafront nr harbour.
D3 Unfussy hostelry o/look Cromarty Firth with its oil stuff and dolphins in this gr
wee town at the end of the rd in the Black Isle (1267/COASTAL VILLAGES).
Conservatory, busy bar, afternoon teas. 10RMS JAN-DEC X/T PETS CC KIDS MED.INX

810 **LOVAT ARMS, BEAULY:** 01463 782313. Best hotel of many in main st of market town
D3 20km from Inverness. Relaxed, welcoming family-run hotel with gr bar meals
and comfy public rms. Much tartan upstairs.
23RMS JAN-DEC T/T PETS CC KIDS INX

811 **TOMICH HOTEL, TOMICH, nr DRUMNADROCHIT:** 01456 415399. The inn of a quiet
C4 conservation village, part of an old estate on the edge of Guisachan Forest. Nr
fantastic Plodda Falls (1277/WATERFALLS) and Glen Affric (1265/GLENS). Basic
facs, but use of pool nearby in farm steading (9am-9pm); esp good for fishing
holidays. 25km drive from Drum by A831. 8RMS JAN-DEC T/T PETS CC KIDS MED.INX

812 **FORT AUGUSTUS ABBEY:** 01320 366233. A real abbey, home to a community of
D4 Benedictine monks, once a school, and now open to visitors with 'heritage centre'
and some accom. Backpackers hostel separate, but also rms in main building,

singles, twins, etc. Still feels like school; admin can be chaotic and it still feels v basic but v cheap. L Ness (with boat trips) at end of grounds. Abbot's Table restau, but I'd breakfast only. You don't have to pray (but I hear it can help).

32RMS JAN-DEC X/X XPETS KIDS CHP

THE LOVAT ARMS, FORT AUGUSTUS: 01320 366206. Old-fashioned gem; a mansion house above the town at the end of L Ness. Original features, gr furnishings; some rms unchanged, but even new ones OK. Refurb bar, the rest as was. **813 D4**

21RMS JAN-DEC T/T PETS CC KIDS MED.INX

✚ **OLD PINES, nr SPEAN BRIDGE:** 01397 712324. 3km Spean Br via B8004 for Garlochy at Commando Monument. This 'restau with rms' is a home from home. Open-plan pine cabin with log fires, games, enough books for a public library and bedrms each named after a flower and furnished accordingly. Enjoy Sukie Barber's exceptional cooking and the ducks on the stream (921/ KIDS; 749/HIGHLAND HOTELS). **814 C4**

8RMS JAN-DEC X/X XPETS CC KIDS TOS MED.INX

PORT-NA-CON, nr DURNESS: 01971 511367. Ken and Lesley Black's guesthouse on this idyllic shore is gr value. Comfortable rms (1 en suite), 600 books in the library and mts all around waiting to be climbed, ensure guests return regularly. Seafood from the loch (where Ken mans the lighthouse) often on the dinner menu (INX). Nonresidents should book. **815 D1**

3RMS APR-OCT X/X PETS CC KIDS CHP

BALCRAGGAN HOUSE, nr FESHIE BRIDGE, nr KINCRAIG: 01540 651488. On the B970 rd betw Kingussie and Kincraig and Inverdruie nr Aviemore, a family house and B&B rather than hotel, though dinner is available. Modern house on bend of rd 1km Feshiebridge, only 2 rms, but of a standard too good not to mention. **816 D4**

2RMS APR-OCT X/X PETS XCC KIDS INX

HEATHBANK HOUSE, BOAT OF GARTEN: 01479 831234. Quirky taste in wall decorations, lots of fans and odd pictures; but individual. Colonial-type house in neat village nr skiing and osprey reserve (1387/BIRDS). The Mackintosh conservatory continues their idiosyncratic thing. No smk. **817 D3**

7RMS DEC-OCT X/X XPETS XCC KIDS TOS CHP

GLENELG INN, GLENELG: 01599 522273 (947/INNS).

TOMDOUN HOTEL, NR INVERGARRY: 01809 511218 (953/INNS).

GOOD INEXPENSIVE RESTAURANTS IN THE HIGHLANDS

Refer to Map 2.

✚ **CAFÉ NUMBER ONE, INVERNESS:** 01463 226200. Castle St. New favourite spot to eat in the Highland capital. See 1945/INVERNESS for full report. **D3** INX

✚ **OLD STATION, SPEAN BRIDGE:** 01397 712535. Richard and Helen Bunney have cracked the popular railway stn restau-conversion; the food is of a standard that will endure long after the trend. Their single AA rosette (1997) should be 2. W coast seafood, E coast crab and rather good duck jostle on a menu, which incl their now popular, but unsurpassed, white chocolate cheesecake. Apr-Oct 7days, dinner only: 6.30-9pm. **818 C4** MED

✚ **SEAGREEN, KYLE OF LOCHALSH:** 01599 534388. Café by day (incl patio tables at the back) and dinner at night. Eclectic eco-atmos with wholefood products to buy, art exhibitions and books ranging from Erica Jong to M C Beaton. Dinner menu of interesting wholefood, organic ale, local cheeses and handmade chocolates with your decaff. Restau May-Sept; LO 9pm; café AYR 10am-6pm (1057/VEGN RESTAUS). **819 C3** MED

✚ **BIADH MATH, KYLE OF LOCHALSH:** 01599 534813. In among the busy port, off the rd to Skye and with *that* br in the distance. Seafood (with unusual dressings; 'raspberry and poppy seed') and vegn selection. Apr-Oct: lunch Mon-Fri 10am-3pm; dinner 7 days 6.30-9pm (pron 'bee-ach ma'). **820 C3** MED

✚ **OFF THE RAILS, PLOCKTON:** 01599 544423. On the platform of this working railway stn; but no droopy sandwiches here, just good home-baking and snacks in the day; 10.30am-5pm. Blackboard specials and evening menu 6.30-9.30pm. Good spot on edge of perfect little Plockton (1233/COASTAL VILLAGES). **821 C3** INX

822 ✚ **LA MIRAGE, HELMSDALE:** 01431 821615. Dunrobin St nr the Br Hotel. A little
E2 piece of Las Vegas in Caithness; this glitterati parlour is a novelty in this wee
village by the sea. Snacks of every kind all day; with life-size photos of the
inimitable proprietor Nancy Sinclair and various celebs gracing the walls – you
never know who might pop over! Daily noon-8.45pm (Dec-Apr, noon-7pm).
Good family fare.   INX

823 **THE BOATHOUSE, KINCRAIG:** 01540 651394. 2km from village towards Feshiebridge
D4 along L Insh. Part of L Insh Water sports (1721/WATER SPORTS), a balcony restau
o/look beach and loch. Fine setting and ambience, friendly young staff, incl
Australians. Some vegn. Salmon from the loch. Bar menu and home-baking till
6pm; supper till 9pm. Apr-Oct.   CHP

824 **THISTLES, CROMARTY:** 01381 600471. Church St. Only decent restau in an
D2 interesting town well worth a visit (1235/COASTAL VILLAGES). Mixed reviews, but
Georgia says it's ok and that's good enough for me. Unpretentious menu: twice-
baked Stilton souffle puffed among the omlettes. Lunch , dinner LO 9pm. Cl Sun
night, Mon lunch.   INX

825 **OLD LIBRARY LODGE, ARISAIG:** 01687 450651. Nr the end of the infamous 'Road
C4 to the Isles' just as they start to hove into view. Converted stables with bedrms
(MED.INX) above and behind. Hot and cold lunch snacks (INX) 11.30am-2.30pm.
Good selection of not only seafood but also meat and veg for the evening table
d'hôte (MED) 6.30-9.30pm, booking advisable. Quay and beach nearby (with boats
to Rum, Eigg and Muck), bask in the sunset behind them.   INX

826 **OLD SCHOOL, RHICONICH, nr KINLOCHBERVIE:** 01971 521383. Halfway betw the
C1 A894 rd from the N coast to Scourie and Lochinver, and Kinlochbervie on the
scenic B801. Not exactly converted but *adapted*, which is what makes it atmos
(the huge ruler on the wall helps too). Snacks and kids menu in day; 3 courses at
night with nursery puds. The world map from 1945 makes interesting reading.
Daily 12-2pm and 6-8pm. Also accom. Open AYR.   INX

827 **RIVERSIDE BISTRO, LOCHINVER:** 01571 844356. On way into town on A837. Self-
C2 serve during day; vast array of Ian Stewart's home-made pies and calorific cakes.
You can eat in, sit out at the picnic tables, or take away. Conservatory restau
beside river serves v popular meals at night; using local seafood, venison, vegn –
something for everyone incl, apparently, Michael Winner (though don't let that
put you off). Daily lunch and 6-9pm.   MED

828 **THE OYSTERCATCHER, PORTMAHOMACK, nr TAIN:** 01862 871560. On promontory
D2 of the Dornoch Firth (Tain 15km) this hidden seaside village could bring back
childhood memories (even somebody else's). Brightly coloured murals adorn the
caff, fish swim in lit tanks. Locals come for Charlotte's snacks in the day and
bistro at night. We come further, because it's quite wonderful here. Open AYR
(not Feb) 11am-6pm and 7-8.30pm. Cl Mon.   CHP

829 **MORANGIE HOUSE, TAIN:** 01862 892281. On way into/out of Tain from A9.
D2 Popular locally for its food; there's a huge menu with pages of food (grills, roasts,
etc.) catering for everyone. You scoff in the conservatory, quaff in the pine and
tartan lounge; a good choice for Sun lunch. Lunch and 6-9.30pm.   MED/INX

830 **FALLS OF SHIN COFFEE SHOP, nr LAIRG:** Self-serve café/restau in the visitor centre
D2 and shop across the rd from the Falls of Shin on the Achany Glen rd 8km S of
Lairg (1291/WATERFALLS). Excellent basic food, among best I've seen in similar
situations. Somebody there cooks and cares. Mar-Oct 7days, LO 5.30pm.   CHP

831 **THE DUNNET HEAD TEA-ROOM, DUNNET HEAD, nr THURSO:** 01847 851774. 15km N
E1 of Thurso on the coast rd via Castletown. A cliff side café serving snacks, meals,
puddings and a good selection of kids' faves. John has now retired to his radio
shack out the back, but can sometimes be seen looking for puffins or distributing
his newsletter about the the weather and the wildlife. Only 3km from the famous
Head; it's a good stop. 7 days; 3-8pm (Apr-Oct).   INX

832 **KYLESKU HOTEL, nr KYLESTROME:** 01971 502231. On A894; tucked down beside
C2 L Glencoul where the boat leaves to see Britain's 'highest waterfall'
(1282/WATERFALLS). Gr pub seafood, delicious desserts; with similar formal menu
in adj restau. Both o/look loch; windswept/sunstroked atmos. Good value.   INX

THE BEST PLACES TO STAY IN AND AROUND ABERDEEN

It's been said before, but in oil city, hotels are expensive. But remember, though full during the week, many places offer surprisingly good w/end deals.

✝ ✝ **MARCLIFFE OF PITFODELS:** 01224 861000. N Deeside Rd (*en route* to Royal Deeside 5km from Union St). Aberdeen's premiere hotel. A member of the Small Luxury Hotels of the World group, it is a successful mix of the intimate and the spacious, the old (mansion house) and the new (1993 refurb). Personally run by Stewart and Sheila Spence, the sort of hoteliers whom no detail or face escapes. 2 excellent restaus, breakfast in light conservatory. Often dinners and dos attended by the gr and the good Aberdonians; always efficient and friendly service. **833**
42RMS JAN-DEC T/T PETS CC KIDS TOS LOTS

✝ **MARYCULTER HOUSE HOTEL, MARYCULTER:** 01224 732124. Another out-of-town hotel, in the same direction as above (and same owners) but 7km further on. Excellent situation on banks of Dee with river side walks and an old graveyard and ruined chapel. Newer annex; 8/9 rms o/look river. Poacher's Pocket and dining-rm. Cocktail bar impressive. Friendly and comfortable. 20mins to town; my choice! **834**
23RMS JAN-DEC T/T XPETS CC KIDS TOS EXP

✝ **ARDOE HOUSE, BLAIRS:** 01224 867355. 12km SW of centre on the S Deeside (it's poss to turn off the A92 from Stonehaven and the S at the first br and get to the hotel avoiding the city). The Dee is on other side of rd from hotel, but nearby. A goodly chunk of Scottish Baronial with few, but more individual rms and a newer annex where most rms have pleasant countryside views. Frequent weddings, but good w/end rates. **835**
71RMS JAN-DEC T/T XPETS CC KIDS TOS LOTS

THE PATIO HOTEL: 01224 633339. Beach Boulevard. New hotel in the developing Beach pleasure zone, not such a bad place to be. Leisure Centre, Virgin Multiplex and Really Big Disco nearby; and the long beach and seafront. This place, part of an emerging UK chain, wins no architectural plaudits from the o/side, but is comfortable and contemporary in its inner courtyard. Lightsome though bedrms have curiously wee windows. Own pool etc. Not far to Silver Darlings for dinner (846/ABER RESTAUS). **836**
92RMS JAN-DEC T/T PETS CC KIDS EXP/LOTS

CALEDONIAN THISTLE HOTEL: 01224 640233. Victorian edifice on Union Terr. Of several city centre hotels just off Union St, this always seems the most easy to deal with, the most calm and efficient. All the facs you'd expect; 2 restaus. **837**
80RMS JAN-DEC T/T PETS CC KIDS TOS LOTS

ATHOLL HOTEL: 01224 323505. 54 King's Gate. W towards Hazelhead, an Aber stalwart, the sort of place you put your rellies and join them for dinner or a bar meal. I've never stayed, but people say this is the best among many mansions. Hotel says it's 'in a class of its own'. **838**
35RMS JAN-DEC T/T XPETS CC KIDS MED.EX

THE BRENTWOOD HOTEL: 01224 595440. 101 Crown St. In an area of many hotels and guesthouses to the S of Union St, this one is surprisingly commodious and a better prospect than most. An adequate business hotel on a budget. Close to Union St and bars/restaus. Bar meals recommended and the ale is real. **839**
65RMS JAN-DEC T/T PETS CC KIDS MED.INX

THE CULTS HOTEL, CULTS: 01224 867632. 9km from centre on A93 Deeside rd so well-placed for touring/Castle Trail and nr Faradays to eat (848/ABER RESTAUS). Refurb of this roadside pub/hotel seems a bit dated now, but it's still good value and decent value is hard to find. **840**
6RMS JAN-DEC T/T PETS CC KIDS MED.IN

WATERWHEEL INN, BIELDSIDE: 01224 861659. 12km centre also via A93 N Deeside Rd. Busy (Toby) roadhouse with various bars/restaus though rms at back are reasonably quiet. **841**
21RMS JAN-DEC T/T PETS CC KIDS MED.EX

BIELDSIDE INN, BIELDSIDE: 01224 867891. Once again on A93 N Deeside Rd betw Cults and Peterculter, 10km SW of centre. Literally on the roadside, but with pastoral views out the back. Rms above the pub with shared facs. Mentioned here because it's cheap. **842**
7RMS JAN-DEC X/X PETS CC KIDS INX

HOSTELS: SY H: 8 Queen's Rd, an arterial rd to W. Grade 1 hostel 2km from centre (plenty buses). No café. Rms mainly for 4 to 6 people. You can stay out till 2am. Other hostels and self-catering flats c/o Univ, of which the best is probably the **ROBERT GORDONS**, 01224 2621344. Northern College have self-catering flats **843**

all over (check Aberdeen TO). Campus in Old Aberdeen which is good place to be though 6km city centre has univ halls accom 01224 272664. All vacs only.

844 **CAMPING AND CARAVAN PARK:** Only one I recommend is at **HAZELHEAD**, 8km W of centre. Follow signs from ring rd. Swimming pool nearby. Grassy.

THE BEST RESTAURANTS IN ABERDEEN

TOPS

845 ✠ ☗ **THE LAIRHILLOCK INN:** 01569 730001. Not in the city at all, but a roadside inn at a country crossroads to the S, reached off either the rd to Stonehaven or the S Deeside Rd W. Easiest is: head S on main A92, turn off at 'Durris' then 5km. Long-famous for its pub food and informal atmos (1034/BEST FOOD), now the same restau is becoming increasingly recognised as one of the best in the NE. Captain Budd runs a tight ship and shows what can be done even when location is not up your st. The quarterly newsletter is a model of friendly marketing. Restau: Mon-Sat dinner and Sun lunch. LO 9.30pm. Inn: 7days lunch and LO 10.30pm.
MED/INX

846 ✠ ☗ **SILVER DARLINGS:** 01224 576229. Didier Dejean's breakthrough bistro now going 11yrs in this perfect spot. Not so easy to find – head for Beach Esplanade, the lighthouse and harbour mouth (Pocra Quay). The light winks and boats glide past. Inside the rm is simple, the seafood superb. Mostly chargrilled; the smell pleasantly pervades. Different menu for lunch and dinner, changes seasonally and depends on the catch. Apposite wines, wicked desserts. Expansion upstairs imminent at time of writing. Mon-Fri lunch and Mon-Sun dinner 7-9pm.
EXP

847 ☗ **Q BRASSERIE:** 01224 595001. 9 Alfred Place, just beyond W end of Union St above the College Bar. In former church building, this is probably Aber's most stylishly top nosh, it's lofty space put to good use. Fans and Q branding everywhere, incl signature big clock (lighting less effective and pictures not well hung – well, we can be picky, this is supposed to be entirely chic). However, all only combines to give authentic 'brasserie' feel and chef Paul Whitecross is the only one in town to get 2 AA whatsits (1997). Good service. Cl Sun.
MED

848 ☗ **FARADAYS:** 01224 869666. Kirkbrae, Cults. 8km W on A93, turning uphill opp Kelly's. John Inches' assured dinner menu and superior versions of comfort food for lunch, e.g. mince with skirlie and peas, stew with doughboys. Intimate bistro ambience in former hydro-electricity station. Aber's reliably good repast. Tue-Sat lunch, Mon-Sat 7-9.30pm.
EXP

SEAFOOD

849 ☗ **THE ASHVALE:** 01224 596981. 46 Gt Western Rd nr Union St and branches (incl Elgin, Br of Don, Inverurie and Brechin). The famous Ashvale fish 'n' chip shop, the NE equivalent, I suppose, of Harry Ramsden's, but we'd say better, esp here at original branch. Sit in (room for 300) or take away. Long, varied menu; you'd be daft not to have fresh fried fish (1086/ FISH AND CHIPS).
INX

850 ☗ **ATLANTIS at the MALACCA HOTEL:** 01224 591403. 349 Gr Western Rd. Thosethat know where to go in Aber for excellent fish and seafood may not necessarily go to Silver Darlings or the Ashvale, but come here. Hotel dining-rm atmos is not too evident (tables in conservatory) and the fish v good. Moderately priced wines. Lunch (not Sat) and dinner LO 9.30pm .
MED

ITALIAN

851 **LITTLE ITALY:** 01224 515227 or 512240. 79 Holburn St nr W end of Union St. The authentic good-fun and esp late-night Italian eaterie. Usual pasta/pizza mix. Can be raucous. Food till midnight Mon-Wed, till 2am Thur-Sat.
MED

852 **BORSALINO:** 01224 732902. Peterculter on main A93 (after Rob Roy Br), 15km W of city centre but famously worth the drive. For over 20yrs Franco's unlikely cantina in a roadside cottage. Here is a remote corner of Tuscany: pasta, the (awful) veal, tiramisu. Morning coffee, lunch and LO 10.30pm.
MED

853 **CARMINE'S PIZZA:** 01224 624145. 32 Union Terr. This tiny slice of a rm for *the best* pizza in town and on the wall, a few famous faces who've eaten them (well . . . Adam Faith). Noon-5.30pm. Cl Sun.

GIO'S: 01224 622300. Nethergate behind M&S (and less interesting off-shoot at Inn on the Park Hotel). Popular arriviste Italian with dark, theatrical uptown atmos. Pasta and steak. Book w/ends. 7 days, lunch (not Sun) and LO 10pm. **854**

POLDINO'S: 01224 647777. 7 Little Belmont St. The other favourite Italian haunt of the Aberdonians. Good Italian home-cooking, incl puddings. City centre, always buzzy. Mon-Sat lunch and 6-10.45pm. **855**
INX

EASTERN

THE ROYAL THAI: 01224 212922. Crown Terr (off Crown St which is off Union St). Now going 6yrs, the first and many say best of the welcome Asian invasion. 'Banquets' with sample dishes are a good idea. Good service, moody lighting. Daily lunch and 7-11pm. **856**
MED

DIM SUM INN: 01224 636750. 303 George St. Way down this long st off Union (about 1km), but the Chinese of choice for calm interior and good Cantonese cookery. 7 days, lunch and LO 10.30pm. **857**
INX

YU: 01224 580138. 347 Union St. Central, stylish, airy and relaxed Peking Chinese. Good fish; light, imaginative sauces. Daily lunch and 7-11pm. **858**
MED

FRENCH

GERARDS: 01224 639500. 50 Chapel St. The longest-established major restau in city. Trad French and *très* exp (set meal a good idea). Good ambience and the discreet charm of the bourgeoisie. Open 7 days. **859**
EXP

THE BARBIZON: 01224 640340. 3 Golden Sq. Similar, but a bit up-market and certainly upstairs from **PIERRE VICTOIRE** (which is in the basement). Bistro food and informal atmos at corner of pleasant city sq. Mon-Sat, lunch and LO 11pm. **860**
INX

LA BONNE BAGUETTE: 01224 644445. Off Union St down steps at side of graveyard. *Très* popular and quite French café. Pâtisserie, snacks (baguettes, etc.) and specials. Daytime only 8.30am-5pm. Cl Sun. **861**
CHP

BISTROS

OWLIES: 01224 649267. Littlejohn St. All-day brasserie in warehouse setting, a long-time Aber fave. Plain French fare (with provincial and more cosmo variations e.g. gado gado, couscous and good vegn menu). Mon-Sat LO 10pm (11 w/ends). Good atmos, good attitude. **862**
INX

THE WILD BOAR: 01224 625357. 19 Belmont St. Narrow, intimate and usually buzzing bar-bistro. From big cake selection to steaks; gallery setting with changing exhibitions. Owned by Alloa Breweries, who are good at this sort of thing. 7 days, food LO 8pm (10pm w/ends). **863**
INX

THE LEMON TREE: 01224 642230. 5 W North St. From E end of Union St heading for beach, W North is off King St. Excellent arts centre with café-bar/restau downstairs. Food ok rather than fantastic, but gr ambience. Lunch: Wed-Sun. INX **864**

THE BEST PUBS AND CLUBS IN ABERDEEN

PUBS WITH ATMOSPHERE AND ATTITUDE

THE PRINCE OF WALES: 7 St Nicholas Lane, just off Union St at George St. **865**
An all-round gr pub always mentioned in guides and one of the best places in the city for real ale: Old Peculiar, Caledonian 80/-, Youngers 3 and guest beers. V cheap self-service food at lunchtime. Lots of wood, flagstones, booths. Large area but gets v crowded. 7 days, 11am-11pm.

THE BLUE LAMP: Gallowgate. Snug pub with nice ambience and long-established **866** clientele and up the st large stone-floored lounge (The Blue Lampie) with gr atmos and live music w/ends (so open 1am).

MA CAMERON'S INN: Little Belmont St. The 'oldest pub in the city' (though the **867** old bit is actually a small portion of the sprawling whole – but there's a good snug). No nonsense oasis in buzzy street. Food: lunch and early evening. Cl Sun.

THE GLOBE: 13 N Silver St. Urban and urbane bar in single rm – a place to drink **868** coffee as well as lager, but without self-conscious, pretentious 'café bar' atmos. Known for its food at lunch and 5-7.45pm (not w/ends).

869 **UNDER THE HAMMER:** 11 N Silver St. Basement bar along the st from above, v intimately Aberdonian and a good place to meet them. Slightly older and mixed crowd. Only open evenings (till midnight) and best late on. My kind of place.

870 **THE LEMON TREE:** 5 W North St. A theatre (upstairs) and a spacious bar/restau on st level where there's lunchtime food (864/ABER RESTAUS) and a mixed programme of entertainment. Phone (01224 642230) or watch for fliers, but prog will include comedy, jazz, folk, pop and cabaret. No membership required.

CONTEMPORARY PUBS

871 **COLLEGE:** Alfred Pl at W end of Union St. Hugely popular 'sports' and MTV kind of bar underneath Q Brasserie (847/ABER RESTAUS) with similar stylish interior. Screens hanging everywhere for the footie, boxing, and other bodies disporting and competing just like around the bar.

872 **THE OLD TOWN SCHOOL:** Little Belmont St as Ma Cameron's above, but the v up-to-date equivalent with everything from themed interior, balcony and patio to many ales, gr wine selection (by glass), malts and grub. All works, gets busy.

873 **CAFÉ SOCIETY:** 9 Queens Rd. An enduring nitespot on the oil slick circuit where an older crowd can dispose of their income and some of their sexual angst. Sub-Steven Conroy pictures and fake chandeliers 'create' a lounge-lizard atmos; the o/side patio is nice of a summer evening. Food served till 10pm, bar midnight.

874 **THE PUBS IN JUSTICE MILL LANE:** Many to choose from in this short st parallel to Union St. They go in and out of fashion, but at time of writing : **BEX** was hippest; **WORD & WEB** gets the décor prize; **BELLS** best for oldies and companion-seekers.

CLUBS

With more ready cash than most, the Aberdonian has many clubs to choose from. Once again we tried loads, those below are the ones we recommend. Clubs close at 2pm (at time of writing).

875 ✚ **MINISTRY OF SIN:** 01224 211611. 16 Dee St off Union St. Converted church and, after all these yrs still a good bet mainly because proprietor Mike Wilson put it together properly in the first place. Studenty but a pleasant mix – in Aber they generally don't mind oldies on the dancefloor. Remarkably open 7 days (at time of writing) with different music policies (e.g. Sun guest DJs); call 01224 211611.

876 **THE WORKS:** 9 Belmont St. Underneath a vodka bar, a zinc-lined, corrugated kind of a clubland disco with gr lay out and a young jumpy crowd (you could say enthusiastic). Thur (some live nights) and Fri/Sat till 2am.

877 **THE PELICAN at the METRO HOTEL:** Market St. Funky subterranean beatbox in the basement of this plastic hotel with good indie attitude and live bands. Guest DJs and live local bands (Thur). Underground atmos. Thu-Sat.

See also 1865/GAY BARS AND CLUBS.

THE BEST HOTELS IN AND AROUND DUNDEE

878 ✚ **THE OLD MANSION HOUSE, AUCHTERHOUSE:** 01382 320366. 15km NW of centre on B954 to Alyth (take Coupar Angus rd from ring route). Every important Scot in history is reputed to have stayed in this 16th-century castellated hse. It hasn't changed a lot; but what would William Wallace make of the surprising outdoor pool? We loved it.   6 RMS JAN-DEC T/T PETS CC KIDS TOS EXP

EAT: Elegant dining in the green world beyond Dundee.   EXP

✚ **SANDFORD HILL:** 01382 541802. Excellent rural retreat over the water 7km S of Tay Br via A92/914 (916/COUNTRY-HOUSE HOTELS).

SWALLOW HOTEL: 01382 641122. Modern, all-purpose hotel chain on town ring rd, but good for families (930/KIDS).

879 **THE SHAFTESBURY:** 01382 669216. 1 Hyndford St just off Perth Rd (about 3km from city centre). A suburban (jute baron's) mansion converted into a comfortable hotel with neat back grd. All rms different; loungeable lounge. Decent value.   12RMS JAN-DEC T/T PETS CC KIDS INX

DRUMNACREE HOUSE HOTEL, ALYTH: 01828 632194. St. Ninians Rd. Take A923 off 880 ring rd in Dundee; follow signs for Alyth B954: 12km. Quiet house in residential rd of a sleepy farming town. Frilly decor, friendly hosts.

6RMS APR-DEC T/T PETS CC KIDS TOS MED.INX

EAT: All home-grown veg, local produce cooked traditionally or exotically - you choose (Cajun twist when I was there). 7pm onwards. Must book first. 2 AA rosettes.

MED

THE QUEENS HOTEL: 01382 322515. Nethergate/Perth Rd. Convenient location 881 with parking round the back. Old-style Victorian city hotel popular with those of a certain age who favour how things used to be done - last of the (good but not home-made) summer wine.

47RMS JAN-DEC T/T PETS CC KIDS MED.EX

HOTEL BROUGHTY FERRY, BROUGHTY FERRY: 01382 480027. 16 W Queen St. On 882 main rd into the 'Ferry' (*see above*). Cleanly refurb inside, with conservatory. Pool and snooker rm lurking surprisingly in the basement. On busy corner, but calm inside. Bar/restau. No smk.

11RMS JAN-DEC T/T XPETS CC KIDS MED.EX

WOODLANDS, BROUGHTY FERRY: 01382 480033. From Broughty Ferry main st, 883 take left after 1.5km into Abercromby St, second left into Panmure Terr. High falutin' house in substantial acreage. One of the 'Bett Inn' chain, popular out-of-town wedding venue quite complete with small swimming pool and gym.

17RMS JAN-DEC T/T PETS CC KIDS MED.EX

FORT HOTEL, BROUGHTY FERRY: 01382 737999. 58 Fort St. The 'Ferry' is easily 884 reached by bus/train or Arbroath A92, then A930. About 8km along Tayside and a pleasant, less urban place with good pubs and restaus. This recently modernised rooming house is in main area, above the Fort Bar. Basic but adequate.

10RMS JAN-DEC T/T PETS CC KIDS MED.INX

HOSTELS: There is no S.Y.H. in the area, although in summer months univ hall accom is available – info from TO. 01382 434664. **THE WHITE HOUSE** 01382 455788. 208 Broughty Ferry Rd. Caters for backpackers.

CAMPING AND CARAVANNING: 01382 552334. Most are on the Carnoustie route.

RIVERVIEW CARAVAN PARK: 01382 535471. Take A92 Arbroath rd, 3 miles along 885 take 3rd sign for Monifieth and follow caravan signs. **TAYVIEW EAST HOLIDAY PARK** : 01382 532837. Union St. Monifieth has gr sea views. Good site also at **TAYPORT:** across Tay Br, 8km SE of centre. 100 pitches on sandy/grassy site nr Tentsmuir (1402/WILDLIFE).

THE BEST PLACES TO EAT AND DRINK IN DUNDEE

✝ **LOCHSIDE LODGE, BRIDGEND OF LINTRATHEN:** 01575 560340. A schlep from 886 town, but worth it. 9km from Alyth towards Glenisla on B954 past Reekie Linn (1287/WATERFALLS), or via Kirriemuir. Converted stone steading beside loch; gr setting, gr food. Accom available mid 1998 (3rms). Lunch/dinner LO 9pm. Cl Mon.

MED

SOUTH KINGENNIE HOUSE: 01382 350562 Also out of town. Take Claypott Rd out 887 of Broughty Ferry, then B978 to Kellas (2km). At app to village, restau signed to rt (1km along). Major Sun lunch destination for Dundonians needing a lungful of air, an eyeful of green fields and a stomach full of sublime roast beef with all the trimmings. Similar hearty menu at other times. Cl Sun evening and Mon.

INX

THE SHIP INN: 01382 779176. On front at Broughty Ferry. Weathered by the R 888 Tay since the 1800s, this cosy pub has sustained smugglers, fishermen and foody folk alike. Upstairs restau's Scottish menu has earned them their solid reputation. Lunch and 5-10.30pm, w/ends noon-10.30pm.

CHP

CUL DE SAC: Tay Square, off S Tay St next to Repertory Theatre (also has good 889 foyer theatre café, **THE HET**). New café/bar/restau with chilled atmos. A happening place at time of going to press. Noon - 10.30pm.

INX

CAFÉ BUONGIORNO: 01382 221179. 11 Bank St. Recently moved into town from 890 Franco's Cantina at Monifeith; the same crew continue to delight with all things Italiano. Café by day and restau from 7-10pm.

MED

VISOCCHI'S: 01382 779297. 40 Gray St, Broughty Ferry. More of a café than the 891 original Kirriemuir branch caff. After almost 70yrs they're still making mouthwatering Italian flavoured ice creams (*amaretto, cassata* etc.) alongside home-made pasta and snacks. CHP

892 **BEIDERBECKES:** 304 Perth Rd. Jazz influenced pizzas (there's a Satchmo and a Hoagy Carmichael) with topping and base proportioned evenly for a change. Dundee-wise they've hit the rt note. Laid-back sounds. 10.30am-5pm; Sun 12-5pm. CHP

893 **RAFFLES:** 01382 226344. 18 Perth Rd. Old fave now made trendy by new management, but some would say café lunches pre-packed with clingfilm is not the way ahead. Downstairs Sun brunch a highlight. Tue-Sun LO 9pm; w/ends 10.30pm. INX

894 **PIERRE VICTOIRE:** Castle St. Revitalised by new management. Largest P V in Scotland: 250 seats in old print works. Live music Thur-Sat. LO10pm CHP

895 **THE NAWAB:** 01382 731800. 43a Gray St, Broughty Ferry. Mint coloured exterior set back from st, large low-lit interior with obligatory waterfall. Stands out in a stack of Indians with varied menu and staff to guide you through. Charcoaled meat a speciality. Till midnight. INX

896 **THE AGACAN:** 01382 644227. 113 Perth Rd. Fabled bistro for Turkish eats and wine. Art on the walls. Even non-meaties might like the bohemian ambience. Cl Mon.

897 **MANDARIN GARDEN:** 01382 227733. 40 S Tay St. Formerly 'The Riverside' now renamed. Low key decor, peaceful atmos; food is the thing. Excellent seafood and different meats covered in every type of sauce. Lunch and 5-11pm. Cl Sun. INX

898 **ROYAL OAK:** 01382 229440. 167 Brook St nr W Pt. Excellent pub food with an Indian emphasis that's satisfyingly quirky. Bar and dining-rm. Lunch and LO 9pm. INX

PUBS

899 **THE FISHERMAN'S TAVERN:** 12 Fort St, Broughty Ferry. Good pub lunches here, but notable for real ales. Listed 17th-century fisherman's cottage, snug portside atmos. 6 rms above if you want to B&B. 11am-midnight.

900 **LAINGS:** Roseangle, off Perth Rd. V popular with 20s-30s crowd. Beer gdn gets crowded in summer, typical pub food to fill you up with yummy Banoffee pie. 11am-11.30pm.

901 **MERCANTILE BAR:** Commercial St. Huge newly fashioned trad style pub with circular gallery brimming with regulars. Food till 7pm. V mixed crowd.

902 **TAYBRIDGE BAR:** 129 Perth Rd. Legendary drinking place. Est 1867: smell of spit and sawdust still lingers; women are present, but usually accompanied by their 'man'.

903 **PUBS IN THE WEST PORT: THE GLOBE, TALLYS etc:** Popular student hang-outs in W Pt (end of S Tay St & off Marketgait; behind univ) Irish influence more authentic than usual. CHP

SECTION 4

Particular Places to Eat and Stay throughout Scotland

SUPERLATIVE COUNTRY-HOUSE HOTELS

Houses (both large and small, grand and intimate) in the country that have been turned into hotels. Usually family-run/owner-occupied, expensive but stress-free.

904
MAP 4
C3
✚ ✚ **KINNAIRD HOUSE, DUNKELD:** 01796 482440. 12km N of Dunkeld (Perth 35km) via A9 and B898 for Dalguise. In bucolic setting beneath woody ridge of Tay Valley, a country house which envelops you with good taste and comfort. Good, unobtrusive service; impeccable detail. The CDs are Domingo/Cole/Beethoven, the books are ones you'd want to read, the postcards are Scottish Wildlife Trust. You get a teddy on your bed and there's a stylish 'K' on everything. Gr snooker rm. Elegant dining with John Webber's sure touch. Silently beyond the grounds and river, endless traffic ploughs N and S on the A9. One day you'll have to join it again. Until then, live Kinnaird. Also 8 superb individual cottages (esp 'Castle Peroch') on the estate.

9RMS(8COTT) JAN-DEC T/T PETS CC KIDS LOTS

✚ ✚ **CROMLIX HOUSE, DUNBLANE:** 01786 822125. Improved and perfected over the last few years – full report (681/CENTRAL HOTELS), but now unquestionably one of the best country-house hotels in the UK. Fabulous grounds, fastidious service, excellent food.

905
MAP 1
B1
✚ ✚ **ISLE OF ERISKA, LEDAIG:** 01631 720371. 20km N of Oban. As you drive over the Victorian iron br onto the isle (a real island), you enter a more tranquil world. Its 300 acres are a sanctuary for wildlife; you are not the only guests. The famous badgers, for example, come almost every night to the door of the bar for their milk. This baronial house continues to improve its service and facs and like other hotels on this page can take on an increasingly demanding world. Great 17m pool in grounds and gym, 9-hole golf, putting, tennis and clay shooting; it's all there if you feel like action, but it's v pleasant just to stay still. Dining, with a Scottish flavour and impeccable local ingredients from a rich backyard and bay, has 2 AA rosettes. 16RMS JAN-DEC T/T PETS CC KIDS TOS LOTS

906
MAP 4
C4
✚ ✚ **GLENEAGLES, AUCHTERARDER:** 01764 662231. On A824 and rather difficult to miss. Scotland's truly luxurious resort hotel. For facs on the grand scale others pale into insignificance; and it competes on an international level. Only the sun and an open-air pool are missing, but the famous golf (3 courses), the Equestrian Centre, Shooting School, Falconry Centre and Country Club make up for the climate. Strathearn Restau is a foodie heaven but fabulously expensive; 6 sommeliers mull over your wine. When you are in love and rich go here; there are no cheap w/ends. 236RMS JAN-DEC T/T PETS CC KIDS TOS LOTS

907
MAP 2
C2
✚ ✚ **ALTNAHARRIE INN, ULLAPOOL:** 01854 633230. 2km from town, but other side of L Broom. They come in a launch to get you and intimacy is immediately established with one's fellow travellers. Hotel unique in every sense, a comfortable haven in a wild setting; some rms in the natural grds. Wester Ross is behind you. Gunn Eriksen's dinners are legendary with their extraordinary attention to detail. 8RMS APR-OCT X/X PETS CC KIDS LOTS

908
MAP 9
A4
✚ ✚ **KNOCKINAAM LODGE, PORTPATRICK:** 01776 810471. An ideal place to lie low; an historic Victorian house nestled between two hills, on its own cove. The Irish coastline is the only thing on the horizon, apart from your considerate Canadian hosts proferring discreet service, excellent food (chef Tony Pierce excels with his tastings menu), drink (over 400 wines and eclectic malts) and calm congeniality. 15km S of Stranraer off A77, nr Lochans.

10RMS MAR-DEC T/T PETS CC KIDS LOTS

909
MAP 4
C4
✚ **AUCHTERARDER HOUSE, AUCHTERARDER:** 01764 663646. Off B8062 Crieffrd 3km from this village more commonly associated with Gleneagles. In contrast, it is intimate, sumptuous and merely relaxing. Proprietor, the inimitable Ian Brown, was moving on at time of going to press, so for the moment we wait and see. Much loved by not very right-on politicians, the Reagans came and the Majors (remember them) and the week I was there, F W de Klerk; probably not the Blairs. I've always had the average rms, but there are big suites in there somewhere. Public rms formal verging on gloomy; conservatory bar exquisite.

15RMS JAN-DEC T/T PETS CC KIDS TOS LOTS

910
MAP 7
D4
✚ **KNOCKIE LODGE, nr FORT AUGUSTUS, LOCH NESS:** 01456 486276. 3km down rd/track from B862, the quiet E bank rd round L Ness (1314/SCENIC ROUTES); 15km Ft Augustus. Rambling mansion on bluff o/looking loch, set among

farmland with wide open views. Recently changed hands, which is just as well since the previous owner and his military precision were not conducive to happy holidays. Haven't visited since, but incl here for location and high expectation.

10RMS MAY-SEPT T/X PETS CC XKIDS LOTS

✠ **BALLATHIE HOUSE, KINCLAVEN, nr BLAIRGOWRIE and PERTH:** 01250 883268. Superb situation on R Tay; culinary delights, comfortable, relaxing: a chance to enjoy the finer things in (Perthshire) life. Merits longer mention than this, but because it is handy for Perth and probably the best place to stay nr the town. Full report and codes: 1947/PERTH.

911
MAP 4
C3

✠ **LOCH MELFORT, ARDUAINE, nr OBAN:** 01852 200233. 22km S of Oban on the A816 and on one of the most commanding sites on this picturesque coast. The fabulous view is not everything, but the rms and the restau make the most of it. 20 rms in an annex have either patios or (better) balconies. Large light dining-rm with notable seafood; Chartroom Bar with more informal bistro fare. The wonderful Arduaine Gardens (1203/GARDENS) run by the NTS are on your doorstep.

912
MAP 1
B2

26RMS MAR-DEC T/T PETS CC KIDS EXP

✠ **ARDANAISEIG, LOCH AWE:** 01866 833333. 16km from Taynuilt signed from main A85 to Oban down beautiful winding rd and 7km from Kilchrenan. In sheltered landscaped gardens dotted with funny *faux* Roman statuary and sculptures that burst from the rhododendrons. Nice to wander in even if you're not a guest – go for afternoon tea or lunch. On a promontory of the loch. New management, new chef. Remains to be seen, but this hotel has gr charm.

913
MAP 1
C2

14RMS APR-OCT T/T PETS CC XKIDS TOS LOTS

✠ **ARISAIG HOUSE, ARISAIG:** 01687 450622. On A830, rd to the Isles from Ft William to Mallaig. 2km before Arisaig and 18km from Mallaig in stunning countryside on one of Scotland's most romantic coasts. The grds are a joy. Civilised and relaxed. Fuller report: 985/SCOTTISH HOTELS.

914
MAP 2
C4

14RMS JAN-DEC T/T XPETS CC XKIDS TOS EXP

✠ **ARDSHEAL HOUSE, KENTALLEN:** 01631 740227. 27km S of Fort William. 2km along private track off A828. Neil Sutherland grew up in the house and has returned here with his family to share its peace and beauty with you. Set on a farmland promontory o/looking L Linnhe and the hills. The warm house is comfortably furnished; with antiques, china and paintings. Philippa's delicious cooking in the conservatory. Not all rms have the views but extensive grounds to walk. Rm service and trouser presses don't exist here; you won't need them. Great value.

915
MAP 2
C5

5RMS MAR-NOV T/X PETS CC KIDS TOS MED.EXP

✠ **SANDFORD HILL, nr WORMIT (nr DUNDEE & ST ANDREWS):** 01382 541802. 7km S of Tay Bridge via A92 and A914, 100m along B946 to Wormit. In an unpromising landscape of quarries and pigfarms, a civilised withdrawal from the jams of Dundee and bunkers of St Andrews. An austere mansion with unusual layout and mullioned windows looking out to gorgeous grds. Wild but romantic tennis court, pub lunches. 750 acres adj farmland of 'activities' – clay-pigeon shooting, fishing in Farm Loch, off-road driving.

916
MAP 5
D2

16RMS JAN-DEC T/T PETS CC KIDS TOS EXP

✠ **FLODIGARRY COUNTRY HOUSE, SKYE:** 01470 552203. Nr Staffin, 32km N of Portree. Set on a the face of a hill with amazing views across Staffin bay and the mighty Quirang behind. Gr crack in the bar (sessions at the drop of a fiddle) and lounge; the piano is often played. When I was there locals were playing charades. Flora MacDonald's cottage in the grounds with its tastefully refurbished bedrooms offers a rare opportunity actually to stay in a romantic place redolent of this island's history. Relaxed atmos; breakfast at your leisure with gr sky and Skye on your doorstep.

917
MAP 7
B3

16RMS JAN-DEC X/T PETS CC KIDS TOS EXP

✠ **CORROUR HOUSE, AVIEMORE:** 01479 810220. Small country house 3km from the concrete moor of Aviemore, handy for the ski slopes. Without airs but not without graces, this family-run hotel is extremely good value. Since I first mentioned it I have never once been able to get back in, but I've never had a single complaint.

918
MAP 2
D4

8RMS JAN-DEC X/T PETS CC KIDS MED.INX

HOTELS THAT WELCOME KIDS

919
MAP 4
B2

CRIEFF HYDRO, CRIEFF: 01764 655555. A national institution and still a family business and where your family is part of theirs. App via High St, turning off at Drummond Arms Hotel uphill then follow signs. Vast Victorian pile with activities for everybody from bowlers to babies. Still run by the Leckies from hydropathic beginnings but with recent refurbs, incl the fabulous winter gardens moving graciously with the times. Gr tennis courts, riding school, Lagoon Pool. Tiny cinema shows smut-free movies (Thu/Sun after dinner); nature talks, donkey rides. Kids endlessly entertained (even while you eat). Beyond are the Trossachs.

JAN-DEC   T/T   PETS   CC   KIDS   MEDIN.EX

920
MAP 2
D3

POLMAILY HOUSE, nr DRUMNADROCHIT: 01456 450343. 5km from main L Ness rd at Drumnadrochit via A831 to Cannich (and glorious Glen Affric), a good country-house hotel for adults that is excellent for kids. The Whittington-Davis's have 4 themselves. Their lucky kids and yours have lots to do in the grds – trout pond where older kids can fish, pet rabbit run, bikes, indoor swimming pool, friendly pet goat. Tree house and swing up the back esp popular. Separate kids' meal time; special rates.

12RMS   JAN-DEC   T/T   PETS   CC   KIDS   MED.EX

921

OLD PINES, nr SPEAN BRIDGE: 01397 712324. 3km Spean Br via B8004 for Garlochy at Commando Monument. Bill and Sukie Barber have 7 kids so will be unfazed by the demands of yours. Amazing value: £5 per child! One level pine log cabin - all bedrms individually furnished; bunk beds with wee teddies to cuddle and take home. Playrm with books, videos and games for kids of all ages, and the Barber brood are also on hand to play with. Menagerie of animals around the stream (tame ducks everywhere) and Sukie's legendary cooking (794/HIGHLANDS HOTELS).

8RMS   JAN-DEC   X/X   XPETS   CC   KID TOS   MED.INX

922

GLENFINNAN HOUSE, GLENFINNAN: 01397 722235. Just off the 'Road to the Isles' (the A830 from Ft William to Mallaig). V large Highland 'hoos' with so many rms and such large grds you can be as noisy as you like and no one will hear you. Great intro to the Highland heartland; music, scenery and local characters will create a lasting impression for you – and the bairns (801/INEXP HIGHLAND HOTELS).

20RMS   APR-OCT   X/X   PETS   CC   KIDS   MED.INX

923
MAP 2
B2

BAILE-NA-CILLE, TIMSGARRY, UIG, HARRIS: 01851 672242. 58km W of Stornoway, a long way to go, perhaps, and although this isolation might be more usually sought by adults, the beach here is one that kids will remember all their lives – wide, safe, untouched. Kids eat earlier and they will be tired. General air of anything goes (except smoking). And it feels unpolluted.

9+3RMS   MAR-OCT   X/X   PETS   CC   KIDS   MED.INX

924
MAP 1
C2

DRIMSYNIE: 01301 703247. Lochgoilhead, Argyll. Hotel/chalet/caravan/leisure complex – a holiday village, in fact, on the loch and on the rd to Carrick Castle. Every activity you could poss want (pool, ponies, golf and boating) to divert attention from the scenery. Chalets best for larger families – then you don't have to eat in the restau. The delights of the Sheep and Wool Centre may not detain you long.

8RMS+CHALETS   JAN-DEC   X/X   PETS   CC   KIDS   MED.INX

925
MAP 8
B2

PEEBLES HYDRO, PEEBLES: 01721 720602. Innerleithen Rd. One of the first Victorian hydros, now more Butlins than Bath. Huge grounds, corridors (I got lost immediately!) and floors of rms where kids can run around. Water fun downstairs in small pool. Entertainment and baby-sitting services. V traditional and refreshingly untrendy. Rms vary.

137RMS   JAN-DEC   T/T   PETS   CC KIDS   TOS   MED.INX/EXP

926
MAP 1
B3

STONEFIELD CASTLE HOTEL, TARBERT: 01880 820836. O/side Tarbert on A83 on slopes of L Fyne with wonderful views. A real castle with 60 acres of woody grounds to explore and a gr open-air pool. Full report and codes: 647/ARGYLL HOTELS.

927
MAP 2
C5

ISLES OF GLENCOE HOTEL, BALLACHULISH: 01855 811602. Beside the A82 Crianlarich to Ft William: a modern hotel and leisure centre jutting out onto L.Leven. New adventure playground o/side and nature trails. Conservatory restau o/looking the water, adj. to refurb lounge. 'Mysteryworld' centre in grds with its spooky actors retelling the local Celt history and 'astromyths' is fairly awful. Snacks in the restau all day, new age gift shop (*sic*). Glencoe and 2 ski areas nearby.

39RMS   JAN-DEC   T/T   PETS   CC   KIDS   MED.INX/EXP

COYLUMBRIDGE HOTEL, nr AVIEMORE: 01479 810661. 8km from Aviemore Centre on B970 rd to ski slopes and nearest hotel to them. A bit tacky now, but best of the oft-criticised Aviemore hotels; and the most facs. 2 pools of decent size, sauna, etc., kids' play park, video games. some organised kids' activities. Plenty to do in summer and winter (1606/WALKS; 1371/KIDS). Aviemore timewarp better for kids than adults.
928
MAP 2
D6
175 (INCL FAMILY)RMS JAN-DEC T/T PETS CC KIDS MED.EX

WATERSIDE INN, PETERHEAD: 01779 471121. Edge of town on A952 to Fraserburgh. Modern hotel with pool etc and some activities for kids. Aden Country Park nearby (1369/KIDS). Kids' menu and meal times and family rms. Ugie and Deedee (the bears) are a gr success., but you wouldn't want to take them to bed. Adventure playground. Go-karts. Sometimes special family w/ends.
929
MAP 3
E2
110(30 FAMILY)RMS JAN-DEC T/T PETS CC KIDS TOS MED.EX

SWALLOW HOTEL, DUNDEE: 01382 641122. Conveniently placed on the edge of town, just off ring rd system and the rd in from Perth. A link in the commercial chain; but pleasantly sprawling with surprisingly lush grds, nature trails and leisure facs. Deals available.
930
MAP 4
D3
110RMS JAN-DEC T/T PETS CC KIDS EXP

THE BEST HOSTELS

For hostels in EDINBURGH, *see p.17; for* GLASGOW, *see p.61.* SYHA *Info:* 01786 451181.

✝ ✝ ✝ **CARBISDALE CASTLE, CULRAIN, nr BONAR BRIDGE:** 01549 421232. The flagship hostel of the SYH, an Edwardian castle in terraced grds o/looking the flood plain of a river on the edge of the Highlands. Once the home of the exiled King of Norway, it still contains original works of art (nothing of gr value though the sculptures are elegant). The library, ballrm, lounges are all in use and it's only a few quid a night. Shared dorms as usual but no chores. Kitchens and café. Bike hire in summer; lots scenic walks. Stn (from Inverness) 1km up steep hill. Buses: Inverness/Thurso/Lairg. 80km Inverness, 330km Edin 226 beds.
931
MAP 2
D2

✝ **STIRLING:** 01786 473442. Modern, superb conversion. Gr part of town, close to castle, adj ancient graveyard and with fine views from some rms. One of the new hotel-like hostels with student-hall standard and facs. Café (open 8-8.30am and 6-6.30pm) or self-catering. Access till 2am.
932
MAP 6
D4

✝ **LOCH LOMOND S.Y.H.:** 01389 850226. Alexandria, Dumbarton. Built in 1866 by George Martin, the tobacco baron (as opposed to the other one who produced the Beatles), this is hosteling on the grand scale. Towers and turrets, galleried upper-hall, space for banqueting and a splendid view across the loch, of where you're going tomorrow. 30km Glas. Stn (Balloch) 4km. Buses 200m. 184 beds.
933
MAP 1
D2

THE BORDERS
934
MAP 8
C3

There are some ideal wee hostels in this hill-walking tract of Scotland (where it all began) and one major one:

MELROSE: 01896 822521. Grade 1, 90 beds, v popular. Well-appointed mansion looking across to the Abbey; student-hall standard.

BROADMEADOWS: 01750 76262. 8km from Selkirk off A7, the first hostel in Scotland (1931) is a cosy howff with a stove and a view.

SNOOT: 01450 880259. 10km S of Hawick, Snoot is cute; a country church by the Borthwick Water converted into bunkrooms. Pastoral.

The 3 hostels above are all within an easy day's walk of one another.

INVERNESS STUDENT HOSTEL: 01463 236556. Independent hostel opp the SYH at 8 Culduthel Rd, uphill from town centre (some dorms have views). Run by same folk who have the great Edin one (29/HOSTELS), with similar laid-back atmos and camaraderie. Another has opened down st.
935
MAP 7
D3

ROWARDENNAN, LOCH LOMOND: 01360 870259. The hostel at the end of the rd up the E (less touristy) side of L Lomond from Balmaha and Drymen. Large, well managed and modernised and on a water-side site. On W Highland Way and obvious base for climbing Ben Lomond (1589/MUNROS). Good all-round activity centre.
936
MAP 6
B3

HOSTELLING IN THE HEBRIDES: Simple hostelling in the crofting communities of Lewis, Harris and the Uists. Run by a trust to maintain standards in the spirit of Highland hospitality with local crofters acting as wardens, all hostels are about
937
MAP 2

Grade 3 SYH. 2 in Lewis, 2 in Harris and one each in N and S Uist. No advance bookings necessary or accepted (suggests they will always fit you in). No smk and no Sun arrival or departure. Check local TO's for details (1936/WESTERN ISLES).

938 **TOBERMORY, MULL:** 01688 302481. Looks out to Tobermory Bay. Central but
MAP 1 simple island hostel (grade 3), the only hassle, as usual, being that it's closed
B1 during the day. Members' kitchen. Nr ferry to Ardnamurchan, but main Oban ferry is 35km away (1237/COASTAL VILLAGES).

939 **GLENCOE:** 01855 811219. Deep in the glen itself, 3km off A82/4km by back rd
MAP 2 from Glencoe village and 33km from Ft William. Modern timber house o/looking
C5 river; especially handy for climbers and walkers. Clachaig pub, 2km for good food and crack. (Also 1304/SCENIC ROUTES; 1558/SPOOKY PLACES; 1533/BATTLEGROUNDS; 1008/PUBS; 1689/SKIING; 1603/SERIOUS WALKS.).

940 **RATAGAN:** 01599 511243. 29km from Kyle of Lochalsh, 3km Shiel Br (on A87) A
MAP 1 much-loved Highland hostel on the shore of L Duich and well situated for
C4 walking and exploring some of Scotland's most celebrated scenery e.g. 5 Sisters of Kintail/Cluanie Ridge (1605/SERIOUS WALKS), Glenelg (1305/SCENIC ROUTES; 1464/PREHISTORIC SITES), Falls of Glomach (1276/WATERFALLS). From Glenelg there's the short and dramatic crossing to Skye through the Kylerhea narrows (continuous, summer only), quite the best way to go.

941 **INDEPENDENT HOSTELS IN SKYE: DUN FLODIGARRY, nr STAFFIN:** 01470 552212. In
MAP 2 far N 32km from Portree beside Flodigarry Country-House Hotel, whose pub is
B3 one of the best on the island and has great ceilidhs (1935/SKYE), and amidst big scenery. O/looks sea. Bunkrms for 2-6 (holds up to 66) and great refectory. Open AYR.

942 **SKYE BACKPACKERS GUEST HOUSE, KYLEAKIN:** 01599 534510. Convenient guest
MAP 2 house with mainly 4-bunk rms and smallish gantry/lounge nr br for last/first stop
B3 on what used to be the island. Open AYR.

943 **GLEN FESHIE, nr AVIEMORE:** 01540 651323. Privately-run hostel in farmhouse by
MAP 1 the rd-side in Glen Feshie, signed Achlean from Feshiebridge on the B970. A
D6 walkers' refuge which has a genuine, friendly atmos. Store sells basics; free porridge, but also meals provided. Good base for Cairngorm walking (1606/SERIOUS WALKS). Open AYR.

THE BEST ROADSIDE, SEASIDE AND COUNTRYSIDE INNS

944 ✚ **PIERHOUSE, PORT APPIN:** 01631 730302. An inn at the end of the rd (the
MAP 2 minor rd that leads off the A825 Oban to Ft William) and at the end of the
B1 'pier', where the tiny passenger ferry leaves for Lismore (1903/MAGIC ISLANDS). New 50-seat rotunda restau with gr seafood (1082/SEAFOOD RESTAUS) and jazzy lounge. Informal atmos courtesy of the MacLeod's (and the hyperactive Calum!), refurb-ed comfortable rms. Note: management may be changing.

11RMS   JAN-DEC   T/T   XPETS   CC   KIDS   MED.EX

945 ✚ **CLUANIE INN, GLENMORISTON:** 01320 340238. On main rd to Skye 15km
MAP 2 before Shiel Br, a trad inn surrounded by the mt summits that attract the
C4 walkers and travellers who frequent the place. Recent refurb to unusually good standard. Gym, sauna – even a sunbed so the folks back home believe you when you tell them it didn't rain! The Cluanie Ridge and the 5 Sisters await you in the morning (1605/SERIOUS WALKS).

13RMS   JAN-DEC   T/X   PETS   CC   KIDS   MED.EX

946 ✚ **APPLECROSS HOTEL, APPLECROSS:** 01520 744262. Judy Fish hails from
MAP 2 Yorkshire and now runs this Gaelic inn at the back of beyond. No one comes
C3 here unless they mean to (and can traverse the heights of the legendary 'Pass of the Cattle' road (1306/SCENIC ROUTES), or the delights of the lengthy coastal route from Shieldaig). All rms (none en suite) have sea views and the beer grd over the rd gets busy in summer,with guests enjoying the views of Skye as they eat the seafood that swims past the front door (969/GET-AWAY-FROM-IT-ALL).

5RMS   JAN-DEC   X/X   PETS   CC   KIDS   INX

947 ✚ **GLENELG INN, GLENELG:** 01599 522273. At the end of that gr rd over the hill
MAP 2 from Shiel Br on the A87 (1305/SCENIC ROUTES) . . . well, not quite the end
C3 because you can drive further round to ethereal L Hourn, but this halt is a v civilised hostelry of fame and infamy. Decent food, good drinking, snug lounge.

Grd with tables and views. Charming rms. From Glenelg, take the best route to
Skye (1961/FAVOURITE JOURNEYS).

6RMS APR-OCT X/X PETS XCC KIDS MED.EXP

WEEM HOTEL, WEEM, nr ABERFELDY: 01887 820381. 2 km from Aberfeldy on the
rd to Glen Lyon which is a rd worth taking (1266/GLENS) and points N to L
Rannoch. Old coaching inn, good base for some gr scenery and L Tay fishing.
Friendly Yorkshire couple offer Highland hospitality.

948
MAP 4
B7

14RMS JAN-DEC X/T PETS CC KIDS INX

FORTINGALL HOTEL, FORTINGALL, nr ABERFELDY: 01887 830367. Same area as
above, 15km from Aberfeldy but close to the Glen. Trad inn, incl. flock wallpaper
and other such furnishings. Often booked. The 'oldest tree' in Europe is next
door in the churchyard. Good for fishing and walking and kids are welcomed.

949
MAP 4
B3

9RMS MAR-OCT T/T PETS CC KIDS INX

WEST LOCH HOTEL, TARBERT: 01880 820283. Beside A83 just W of Tarbert; ideal
stopover en route to the islands. Comfortably furnished; with original features
sympathetically retained. Board games and books dotted around, children
welcome in relaxed, friendly atmos. 9-hole golf course across the rd. Good value,
but roadside rms may be noisy.   7RMS FEB-DEC X/T PETS CC KIDS MED.INX

950
MAP 4
B3

KILDRUMMY INN, KILDRUMMY, nr BALLATER: 01975 571227. 30km N of Ballater via
A97 off main A93 Deeside Rd. Nr Kildrummy Castle and Kildrummy Castle
Hotel and grds. Roadside inn with nice walks around. Basic but basically fine;
and v Scottish.   4RMS JAN-DEC X/X PETS CC KIDS CHP

951
MAP 4
B3

GLENISLA HOTEL, KIRKTON OF GLENISLA: 01575 582223. 20km NW of Kirriemuir
via B951 at head of this secluded story-book glen. A home from home: hearty
food, real ale and local colour. Fishers, stalkers, trekkers and walkers all come by.
Miles from the town literally and laterally. Got home and saw it advertised for
sale in the 'paper! – so it may be different soon.

952
MAP 4
D2

6RMS JAN-DEC X/X PETS CC KIDS INX

TOMDOUN HOTEL, nr INVERGARRY: 01809 511218. 20km from Invergarry, 12km
off the A87 to Kyle of Lochalsh. A 19th-century coaching inn that replaced a
much older one; off the beaten track but perfect (we do mean perfect) for fishing,
walking (L Quoich and Knoydart have been waiting a long time for you) and
naturalising. Superb views over Glengarry and Bonnie Prince Charlie's country.
Excellent value; old-fashioned style.   10RMS MAR-OCT X/X PETS CC KIDS CHP

953
MAP 2
C4

ST MICHAEL'S INN, nr ST ANDREWS: 01334 839220. On A919 towards Dundee,
10km from St Andrews. At crossrds, a 200-year-old inn, seems Englishy, often
busy, with pub food and restau. Plenty of golf and other attractions within reach.
Good bet given cost of board in St Andrews.

954
MAP 5
C2

8RMS JAN-DEC X/T PETS CC KIDS INX

TRAQUAIR ARMS, INNERLEITHEN: 01896 830229. 100m from the A72 Gala –Peebles
rd towards Traquair, a popular village and country inn that caters for all kinds of
folk (and, at w/ends, large numbers of them). Notable for bar meals, real ale and
family facs. Rms recently refurb.   10RMS JAN-DEC T/T PETS CC KIDS MED.INX

955
MAP 8
B3

THE KAMES HOTEL, TIGHNABRUAICH: 01700 811489. Frequented by passing
yachtsmen who moor alongside and pop in for lunch. Good base for all things
offshore; marine cruises or a nostalgic journey on a 'puffer', with a gr selection of
malts to warm you up before or after. 10RMS JAN-DEC X/T PETS CC KIDS MED.INEX

956
MAP 1
C3

BRIDGE OF CALLY HOTEL, BRIDGE OF CALLY: 01250 886231. Exemplary roadside
pub on a bend of the road betw Blairgowrie and Glenshee/Braemar (the ski zone
and Royal Deeside). Cosy and inexpensive betw gentle Perthshire and the wilder
Grampians.   9RMS JAN-DEC T/T PETS CC KIDS INX

957
MAP 4
C3

CLACHAIG INN, GLENCOE: 01855 811252. Basic accom but you will sleep well, esp
after walking/climbing/drinking, which is what most people are doing here. Gr
atmos both inside and out.   19RMS JAN-DEC X/X XPETS XCC KIDS CHP

958
MAP 2
C5

MOULIN HOTEL, PITLOCHRY: 01796 472196. Kirkmichael Rd; at the landmark
crossrds on the A924. Rms above and beside notable pub for food and esp ales –
they brew their own out the back. (1019/REAL ALES).   17RMS JAN-DEC T/T MED.INX

959
MAP 4
C3

CULFAIL HOTEL: 01852 200274. On A816 20 km S of Oban and nr a gr bit of W
Highland coast that includes Seil Island, Luing etc. The bar of this hotel is *the*
watering hole for the neighbourhood and people travel serious distances for the

960
MAP 1
B2

privilege. A gantry full of choice single malt whiskies and bar food provided as and when. A friendly hotel.

9RMS JAN-DEC X/T PETS CC KIDS INX

961 **GALLEY OF LORNE, ARDFERN:** 01852 500284. Roadside/seaside inn in yachty haven
MAP 1 of Ardfern. Salts, locals and other worthies mingle at the bar and the restau/bistro
B2 is good for families early in the evening and for drinking much wine later on. Rms
basic, but Ardfern is a good berth.

JAN-DEC X/T PETS XCC KIDS INX

962 **GLENMORISTON ARMS HOTEL, INVERMORISTON, LOCH NESS:** 01320 351206. On
MAP 2 main A82 betw Inverness (45km) and Ft Augustus (10km) at the Glen Moriston
D4 corner, and quite the best corner of this famous loch side to explore. Busy local
bar, fishermen's tales and window-boxes on your sill. Bar meals look ok and
extensive malt list - certainly a good place to drink them.

8RMS JAN-DEC T/T PETS CC KIDS MED.INX

THE OLD ABERLADY INN: 01875 870503 (711/LOTHIANS HOTELS).

THE GREAT GET-AWAY-FROM-IT-ALL HOTELS

963 ✞ ✞ ✞ **SKIBO CASTLE, DORNOCH:** 01862 894600. A vast estate once home to
MAP 1 the formidable Carnegies (that hall in N Dunfermline, etc.). They
D2 declared it to be 'heaven on earth' which may be your sentiment too. Now like
an Edwardian 'gentleman's' club you can sample the atmos once, but to return
you join the club. Some club! The sumptuous castle retains its original
furnishings (silk wallpaper, panelling, etc.) and the service from your discreet
'hosts' is exemplary. Lodges in the grds offer more privacy, with the obligatory
golf course, spa, gym and beach, all oases of relaxing indulgence – vintage Rolls
Royces take you around. It is world class, but you may need to win the lottery
before you can experience this kind of fairy land. Phone for details. LOTS AND LOTS

964 ✞ ✞ **ACKERGILL TOWER, nr WICK:** 01955 603556. One of the most genuine
MAP 2 Highland-castle-hoolly thingies I've come across. Usually the sole
E1 domain of corporate hospitality shindigs, available to individuals 4 times a yr for
the house party w/ends. Set in sumptuous acres: miles of sandy beach, woods to
whirl in, and the 15th-century castle perched next to the sea. The whole
household greets you on arrival and makes you feel part of it all. The Wick band
pipe their way down the drive as they arrive for your ceilidh, Catriona indulges
you with her afternoon teas and Craig proudly cooks up a storm using
ingredients from the grd; you eat inside or out – wherever the season takes you.
All food, drink, activities and surprises incl in the tariff. Spontaneity no extra
charge.

LOTS

965 ✞ **LOCH TORRIDON, GLEN TORRIDON, nr KINLOCHEWE:** 01445 791242.
MAP 2 Impressive former hunting lodge on lochside, surrounded by majestic mts.
C2 The atmos o/side can be affected by the weather, and within by the mood of your
hosts. Dressing for dinner is expected; if not entirely necessary in this
comfortable but cosy baronial house. Numerous walks poss for all abilities,
fishing and Diabeg nearby (1243/COASTAL VILLAGES).

22RMS JAN-DEC T/T PETS CC XKIDS LOTS

966 ✞ **MONACHYLE MHOR, nr BALQUHIDDER:** 01877 384622. Not so very remote,
MAP 6 butseems so once you've negotiated the stretch of rd alongside Loch Voil
B2 from Balquhidder (only 11km from the A84 Callander-Crianlarich rd) and Rob
Roy's now famous grave (1518/GRAVEYARDS). Farmhouse o/looking L Voil from
the magnificent Balquhidder Braes. Friendly, cosy and inexp; a place to relax in
summer or winter. Rms in courtyard annex are best (4), but all have character.
Fishing. Informal meals.

10RMS JAN-DEC SOME T/T PETS CC KIDS INX

967 ✞ **CLOVA HOTEL, GLEN CLOVA, nr KIRRIEMUIR:** 01575 550222. Well, not that nr
MAP 4 Kirriemuir; 25km N to head of glen on B955 and once you're there there's
D2 nowhere else to go except up. Proprietor Graham Davie arranges all kinds of
activities, however, from parachuting to falconry, so there's never a dull moment
and there is superb walking hereabouts (e.g. L Brandy and the classic path to L
Muick). An inexp get-away-from-it all.

7RMS JAN-DEC T/T PETS CC KIDS ·INX

968 ✞ **THE PIER HOUSE, INVERIE, KNOYDART:** 01687 462347. Currently the only
MAP 2 restau on this far-away peninsula, though another imminent at the pub

nearby (1006/BLOODY GOOD PUBS). Accessible on foot (*sic*) from Kinlochourn C4 (25km) or Bruce Watt's boat from Mallaig (Mon, Wed, Fri). Friendly couple offer warm hospitality in their home and surprisingly good cooking for somewhere so remote; rovers often return. When the Pier House is full, you can stay at the big hoose (1km from village), but it's pretty basic (01687 462331). A better option is the **DOUNE STONE LODGE** 01687 462667; 5km up the single rd (MED.INX). We couldn't stay, but it comes much recommended. 4RMS JAN-DEC X/X PETS XCC KIDS CHP

APPLECROSS HOTEL, APPLECROSS: 01520 744262. At the end of the rd (the 969 Pass of the Cattle which is often snowed up in winter, so you can really MAP 2 disappear) N of Kyle of Lochalsh and W of Strathcarron. Report:946/INNS. C3

5RMS JAN-DEC X/X PETS CC KIDS INX

TOMICH HOTEL nr CANNICH: 01456 415399. 8km from Cannich which is 20km 970 from Drumnadrochit. Reminded that this place was 'remote' on recent whistle- MAP 2 stop visit to Plodda Falls which are nearby (1277/WATERFALLS). Cosy country inn D3 in conservation village with added bonus of use of swimming pool in nearby steading. Good base for outdoorsy w/end. Glen Affric across the way.

8RMS JAN-DEC T/T PETS CC KIDS INX

MULLERDOCH HOUSE, nr CANNICH, nr DRUMNADROCHIT: 01456 415460. Leaving L 971 Ness at Drumnadrochit up Glen Urquhart to Cannich (20km), then follow R MAP 2 Cannich to head of glen (12km) where it's blocked by the mighty Mullerdoch D3 Dam. Almost tangible pressure as this cosy Edwardian shooting lodge lies below it, but only herds of red deer wander here and with 11 Munros within 20mins, it's a good place to wander, too. Good for hunters/shooters/fishers. Fixed dinner at 8pm. 7RMS JAN-DEC X/T PETS CC KIDS MED.INX

ARDEONAIG, LOCH TAY: 01567 820400. On S Loch Tay rd midway betw Kenmore 972 and Killin. Recommended by a reader, Margaret McGraw, we set off from MAP 4 Kenmore (20km narrow rd) in a hurry, but this is no way to go. Once you arrive B3 you forget all that. An airy roadside inn by the water opp Ben Lawers. Friendly staff and many dogs. Upstairs library, good food, gr scenery – you won't miss the telly. 14RMS MAR-NOV T/X PETS CC KIDS MED.EX

CAPE WRATH HOTEL, nr DURNESS: 01971 511212. 3km S Durness just off A838; on 973 rd to Cape Wrath Ferry (1637/COASTAL WALKS) which takes you to Britain's MAP 2 farthest-flung corner and the Cliffs of Clo Mor. O/looking the loch, the hotel is D1 popular with fishermen; passing tourists also shoal up for lunch. Fishing on 3 rivers including the celebrated Dionard and lochs. Durness Golf nearby (1680/GOLF) and there's some of Britain's most spectacular and undisturbed coastline to wander. Annex cheaper. 19RMS APR-OCT X/X PETS CC KIDS MED.INX

SPRINGBANK COTTAGE, ST ABBS: 018907 71477. Centre of the village next to St 974 Abbs harbour, 5km from the A1. Not a hotel, certainly a B&B but definitely a gr MAP 8 place to get away. Small and friendly cottage (no smk) with an outdoors tea grd E1 open all year, popular with divers - bring a wetsuit when raining. Walk in St Abbs Head nature reserve (1397/WILDLIFE RESERVES). Few rms so often full in summer.

3RMS FEB-DEC X/T PETS ?CC KIDS CHP

THE MILL HOUSE, TEMPLE: 01875 830253. Temple is on the B6372, 5km off the A7 975 S of Edin (yes folks, this is Keith's idea of a get-away-from-it-all w/end). Turn rt MAP 7 after the village sign then down a driveway by the kirk. Gorgeous wee cottage in C2 riverside gdens. Cordon bleu cooking. The only place in the Lothians we would call 'idyllic'. 3RMS APR-SEP T/T XPETS XCC XKIDS TOS MED.EX

TUSHIELAW INN, ETTRICK VALLEY: 01750 62205. Further down the valley (15 miles 976 Selkirk) a v cosy retreat. Only 3 rms and exceptionally good value. Both this hotel MAP 8 and the place above are close to Edin. 3RMS JAN-DEC X/T PETS CC KIDS CHP B3

KNOCKINAAM LODGE, nr PORTPATRICK: 01776 810471 (666/SW BEST HOTELS).

CORSEMALZIE HOUSE, nr WIGTOWN: 01988 860254 (671/SW BEST HOTELS).

SOME HIGHLAND AND ISLAND PLACES TO CAMP

In Scotland the Best! we don't do caravan life style. In fact, because we spend a lot of time behind them on Highland roads, WE HATE CARAVANS, but wild camping is a different matter. Although it's probably irresponsible to encourage it greatly, it's a good and inexp way to experience Scotland, provided you are sensitive to the environment and respect the rights of farmers and other landowners.

977 **KINTRA, ISLAY:** Bowmore-Port Ellen rd, take Oa turn-off then follow signs 7km.
MAP 1 Restau and bar at end of rd with long beach one way, wild coastal walk the other.
A3 Camping (room also for a few caravans) on grassy strand looking out to sea; not a formal site but facs available. Also bunkhouse.

978 **LOCHAILORT:** A 12km stretch S from Lochailort on the A861, along the southern
MAP 2 shore of the sea loch itself. A flat, rocky and grassy foreshore with a splendid
C4 seascape and backed by brooding mtns. Nearby is L nan Uamh where Bonnie Prince Charlie landed (1544/MARY, CHARLIE AND BOB). Once past the salmon farm laboratories, you're in calendar scenery; the Glenuig Inn at the southern end is a fine pub to repair to. No facs except the sea.

979 **MULL:** Calgary Beach 10km from Dervaig, where there are toilets; also S of
MAP 1 Kilchronan on the gentle shore of L Na Keal where there is nothing but the sky
B1 and the sea. Ben More is in the background (1592/MUNROS).

980 **GLEN ETIVE, nr BALLACHULISH and GLENCOE:** One of Scotland's gr unofficial
MAP 2 camping grounds. Along the rd/river side in a classic glen (1268/GLENS) guarded
C5 where it joins the pass into Glencoe by the awesome Buachaille Etive Mor. Innumerable grassy terraces and small meadows on which climbers and walkers have camped for generations, and pools to bathe in (1336/SWIMMING HOLES). The famous Kingshouse Pub is 2km from the foot of the glen for sustenance, malt whisky and comparing midge bites.

981 **OLDSHOREMORE, nr KINLOCHBERVIE** and **ACHMELVICH, nr LOCHINVER:** 2 superb
MAP 2 beaches with grassy links and nr villages for supplies, the pub etc. Achmelvich has
C1/C2 official campsite, Oldshoremore (and neighbouring coves) has only you.

THE BEST VERY SCOTTISH HOTELS

982 ⚜ ⚜ **THE CEILIDH PLACE, ULLAPOOL:** 01854 612103. Off main st near pt forthe
MAP 2 Hebrides, this place more than any other in the Highlands encapsulates
C2 Scottish trad culture and hospitality and interprets it in a contemporary manner. Caters for all sorts: there's an excellent hotel above (with a truly comfortable lounge – you help yourself to drinks) and a stylish restau below. A bar with occasional live music and gr bar meals. A bunkhouse across the way with cheap and cheerful (though thin-walled) accom and a bookshop where you can browse through the best new Scottish literature. Scottish-ness is all here and nothing embarrassing in sight.   23RMS JAN-DEC T/X PETS CC KIDS EXP/CHP

983 ⚜ ⚜ **THE ALBANNACH, LOCHINVER:** 01571 844407. 2km up rd to Baddidarach
MAP 2 as you come S into Lochinver on A837, at the br. Lovely 18th-century
C2 house in one of Scotland's most scenic areas, Assynt, where the mtns can take your breath away even without going up them (1567/1568/FAVOURITE HILLS). Arty atmos for creative professionals needing to unwind; which you will do in these tasteful, informal surroundings. The food is the best for miles. No smk.
5RMS MAR-DEC X/X XPETS CC XKIDS INX

984 ⚜ **KILDRUMMY CASTLE HOTEL, nr ALFORD, ABERDEENSHIRE:** 01975 571288. 60km
MAP 3 W of Aberdeen via A944, through some fine bucolic scenery and the green
B3 Don valley to this spectacular location with the real aura of the Highlands. Well placed if you're on the 'Castle Trail', this comfortable chunk of Scottish Baronial has the redolent ruins of Kildrummy Castle on the opposite bluff and a gorgeful of gardens betw. Some rms small, but all v Scottish. Romantic in autumn when the grds are good. J/tie for dinner.   16RMS FEB-DEC T/T PETS CC KIDS TOS EXP

985 ⚜ **ARISAIG HOUSE, ARISAIG:** 01687 450622. Another hotel in Bonnie Princ
MAP 7 Charlie country on the 'Road to the Isles'; here there's a cave at the foot of
C4 their fields (and wonderful gdns) where he once hid – it's very near where he landed (1544/MARY, CHARLIE AND BOB). Of course it's not just any other hotel,

but an elegant country house which succeeds in the apparently rare combination of refinement and r&r. Good manners, but very Scots. *Relais and Châteaux*.

14RMS APR-OCT T/T XPETS CC XKIDS TOS EXP

✝ **EILEAN IARMAIN, SKYE:** 01471 833332. Situated in Sleat area on S of island, this snug Gaelic inn nestles in the bay and is the classic island hostelry. A dram in your rm awaits you; from the hotel's adj whisky company. Bedrms in cottage across from hotel ensure you'll not be bothered by the crack from the pub. Food real good. Mystic shore walks. Gallery and shop nearby.

986
MAP 2
C4

12RMS JAN-DEC T/T PETS CC KIDS MED.EX

✝ **GLENFINNAN HOUSE, GLENFINNAN:** 01397 722235. Off the Road to the Isles (A830 Ft William to Mallaig). The MacFarlanes recently celebrated a quarter century of running their hotel in this historic house (1545/MARY, CHARLIE & BOB). Newly refurb without losing its charm, the huge rms remain intimate and cosy with open fires. Legendary sessions and ceilidhs wherever there's a gathering in the house and you get piped into dinner. Solitude is still achievable in the huge grounds, or fishing on L Shiel (boat available). Day trips to Mull and Skye nearby.

987
MAP 2
C4

20RMS APR-OCT X/X PETS CC KIDS MED.INX

✝ **BALLACHULISH HOUSE, BALLACHULISH.** 01855 811266. On rd A828 betw Obanand (just S of) Ft William a family house steeped in history and the folklore of the Highlands. Said to be the most haunted house in Scotland, your close encounters are more likely to be with your hospitable hosts bringing vegetables and flowers in from the gdn for dinner. More of a guesthouse than a hotel (802/INEXP HIGHLAND HOTELS).

988
MAP 2
C5

6RMS JAN-DEC T/X PETS CC KIDS MED.EX

CRIEFF HYDRO, CRIEFF: 01764 655555. The quintessential Scottish family hotel. (919/HOTELS FOR KIDS).

STONEFIELD CASTLE, TARBERT: 01880 820836 (639/ARGYLL HOTELS).

REAL RETREATS

✝ ✝ ✝ **SAMYE LING, ESKDALEMUIR, nr LOCKERBIE/DUMFRIES:** 01387 373232. Bus or train to Lockerbie/Carlisle then bus (Mon/Wed/Sat) to Boreland (01345 090510) or taxi (01576 470480). 2km from village, community consists of an extraordinary and inspiring temple, main house (with some accom), dorm and guesthouse blocks, a café (open 7 days 9am-5pm) and shop. On the hill and out of bounds the area where people really retreat; available for short retreats (up to a yr) and conferences. Much of Samye Ling, a world centre for Tibetan Buddhism, is still under construction, but they offer daily and longer stays (£15-25) and many courses in all aspects of Buddhism, meditation, tai chi, Alexander Technique, etc. Daily timetable, from prayers at 6am and work period. Breakfast/lunch and soup, etc. for supper at 6pm; all vegn. Busy, thriving community atmos; some space cases and holier-than-thous, but rewarding and unique and thriving. Probably Britain's most must-do retreat – lots of famous names. Their recent acquisition, **HOLY ISLAND**, off Arran, requires much work to turn it into a place for longer retreats. Boats leave from the pier at Lamlash, accom limited. Phone Samye Ling for details.

989
MAP 9
E2

✝ ✝ **PLUSCARDEN, between FORRES and ELGIN:** 01343 890257. Signed from main A96 (11km from Elgin) in a sheltered glen S-facing with a background of wooded hillside, this is the only medieval monastery in the UK still inhabited by monks. It's a deeply calming place. The (Benedictine) community keep walled gdns and bees. 7 services a day in the glorious chapel (1573/ABBEYS) which visitors can attend. Retreat for men (15 places) and women (separate, self-catering) with no time limit and no obligatory charge. Men eat with monks (mainly vegn). Restoration/building work always in progress (of the abbey and of the spirit).

990
MAP 3
B2

✝ ✝ **FINDHORN COMMUNITY, FINDHORN, nr FORRES:** 01309 690311. The world-famous spiritual community (now a foundation) begun by Peter Caddy and Dorothy Maclean in 1962, a village of mainly caravans and cabins on the way into Findhorn on the B9011. Open as an ordinary caravan park and visitors can join the community as 'short-term guests' eating and working on-site but probably staying at recommended B&Bs. Also full programme of courses and residential workshops in spiritual growth/dance/healing, etc. Accom mainly at Cluny Hill College in Forres. Many other aspects and facs available in this

991
MAP 3
A2

cosmopolitan and well-organised new-age township. Excellent shop (1164/DELIS).

992 **COLLEGE OF THE HOLY SPIRIT, MILLPORT, ISLAND OF CUMBRAE:** 01475 530353.
MAP 1 Continuous ferry service from Largs (hourly in winter), then 6km bus journey to
C3 Millport. Off main st through gate in the wall, into grounds of the Cathedral of the Isles (1498/CHURCHES) and another more peaceful world. A retreat for the Episcopal Church since 1884, there are 19 simple but comfortable rms in the college next to the church with B&B or full board (£17-30). No set schedule but Matins/Eucharist/Evensong each day and occasional concerts in summer. Warden available for direction and spiritual counselling. Fine library. Bike hire. Phone 'the Provost'. Try the island's gr café (1111/CAFÉS).

993 **ST BENEDICT'S ABBEY, FT AUGUSTUS:** 01320 366233. Ask for Father Stephen.
MAP 2 Benedictine Monastry and former school at the head of L Ness, now a tourist
D4 attraction, inexp hotel (812/HIGHLAND HOTELS) and a retreat (if that coexistence is poss), the latter more likely in the winter months. The scenery is wonderful, the appointments are gothic and edifying, the monks are charming. Mixed.

994 **CARBERRY TOWERS, MUSSELBURGH, nr EDINBURGH:** 0131 665 3135. Sitting in
MAP 7 extensive, well-kept grounds 3km S of Musselburgh, parts of this fine old house
C2 date back to the 15th century. Now a Christian residential and conference centre, most accom is in new block 50m away; student-hall standard. Courses for church workers/group weekends which visitors may sometimes join. Not a quiet retreat but inexp for a break; high on 'renewal', low on rock 'n' roll.

995 **NUNRAW ABBEY, GARVALD, nr HADDINGTON:** 01620 830228. Cistercian community
MAP 7 earning its daily bread with a working farm in the land surrounding the abbey –
D1 but visitors can come and stay for a while and get their heads together in the Sancta Maria Guesthouse (a house for visitors is part of their doctrine). Payment by donation. V Catholic monastic ambience throughout. Guesthouse is 1km from the monastery, a modern complex built to a trad Cistercian pattern. Services open to visitors.

996 **SALISBURY CENTRE, EDINBURGH:** 0131 667 5438. 2 Salisbury Rd. 'Community and
MAP A creative resource' in Georgian house on capital's Southside, est 1973 by Dr
xE4 Winifred Rushforth, psychotherapist and dream specialist. Not a retreat in the isolated sense, although 'w/end retreats' are possible. Classes during week and w/end workshops in meditation, healing, aromatherapy, massage, yoga, shiatzu, tai chi and pottery. Organic garden, therapy rm, some basic accom.

997 **CAMAS ADVENTURE CENTRE, MULL:** 01681 700404. Part of Iona Community (2
MAP 1 others on Iona; this one is aimed at youngsters) near to Fionnphort in S of island
A1 (good bus service). No electricity, cars, TV or noise except the waves and the gulls. Outdoor activities (e.g. canoeing, hillwalking). 2 dorms; share chores. Week-long stays. You'll probably have to relate.

GET-AWAY WEEKENDS

LOCHAWESIDE

WHERE TO STAY

TAYCHREGGAN (646/ARGYLL HOTELS); **ARDANAISEIG** (913/ HOTELS).

WHERE TO EAT AND DRINK

LOCK 16, CRINAN HOTEL (1070/SEAFOOD); **KILCHREGGAN INN, FORD HOTEL.**

WHERE TO VISIT

THE WOODS (1619/WOODLAND WALKS); **TEMPLE WOOD** (1461/PREHISTORIC SITES).

TARBERT, ARGYLL

WHERE TO STAY

STONEFIELD (647/ARGYLL HOTELS; 926/KIDS); **THE COLUMBA** (650/ARGYLL HOTELS); **WEST LOCH** (649/ARGYLL HOTELS).

WHERE TO EAT AND DRINK

THE ANCHORAGE (1075/SEAFOOD RESTAUS); **WEST LOCH** (*as above*); **KILBERRY INN** (1033/BEST FOOD); **AN TAIRBERT CENTRE** W on A83 (*see below*).

WHERE TO VISIT

The **VILLAGE** itself; **ISLAY/JURA** (by ferry from Kennacraig, 7km S, *see p250*); **GIGHA** (by ferry from Tayinloan 14km SW); **ARRAN** (by ferry from Claonaig 9km SE) **TARBERT CASTLE** (1436/RUINS) & **SKIPNESS CASTLE**; **AN TAIRBERT CENTRE** for kids.

SPEYSIDE

WHERE TO STAY

CRAIGELLACHIE, ROTHES GLEN, DELNASHAUGH, MANSION HOUSE (p. 105).

WHERE TO EAT AND DRINK

MANSEFIELD HOUSE HOTEL, ELGIN: 764/NE hotels

ARCHIESTOWN HOTEL BISTRO: 01340 810218. Well-known spot locally for good (2 AA rosettes) informal dining. LO 8.30pm.

AUCHENDEAN LODGE: a bit further S (nr Grantown) but imaginative cuisine (798/INEXP HIGHLAND HOTELS).

WHERE TO VISIT

DISTILLERIES: p. 150; **SPEYSIDE WAY:** 1600/LONG WALKS; **BALLENDALLOCH CASTLE:** on A95 midway betw Grantown and Craigellachie. Family big house with pleasant Speyside grds. Apr-Sept 10am-5pm.; **ELGIN CATHEDRAL:** 1429/RUINS; **JOHNSONS:** 1769/WOOLIES; **CHRISTIES OF FOCHABER:** 1794/GARDEN CENTRES; **JUST ART:** 1846/INEX ART

EAST NEUK OF FIFE

WHERE TO STAY

See p. 101 FIFE HOTELS /RESTAUS. Note also; **THE BELVEDER:** way back at **WEST WEMYSS** (*see* KIRKCALDY, *p. 260*); **ANSTRUTHER, THE HERMITAGE:** 01333 310909; **THE SPINDRIFT:** 01333 310573; **THE SMUGGLERS:** 01333 310506; **ELIE, THE ELMS:** 01333 330404; **ELIE, GOLF HOTEL:** 01333 330209 (725/FIFE HOTELS).

WHERE TO EAT AND DRINK

THE CELLAR, ANSTRUTHER (1071/SEAFOOD RESTAUS); **THE ANSTRUTHER FISH BAR** or **RESTAU** (1094/FISH AND CHIPS); **THE PEAT INN** (729/FIFE BEST RESTAUS); **OSTLER'S CLOSE, CUPAR** (731/FIFE BEST RESTAUS); **THE BOUQUET GARNI, ELIE** (732/FIFE BEST RESTAUS); **THE SHIP, ELIE** (732/PUB FOOD); **OLD RECTORY, DYSART** (733/FIFE BEST RESTAUS).

WHERE TO VISIT

THE SECRET BUNKER (1812/MUSEUMS); **WALKS FROM CRAIL** (1645/COASTAL WALKS); **CRAIL POTTERY** (1739/CRAFTS); **THE COURTYARD GALLERY, CRAIL** (INEXP ART, *p. 235*); **GOLF, ST ANDREWS** (the town and its attractions, *see p. 271*); **FISHERIES MUSEUM, ANSTRUTHER** (1828/MUSEUMS); **ISLE OF MAY** (1383/BIRDS).

PARTICULAR PLACES TO EAT AND STAY   131

BLOODY GOOD PUBS

Pubs in EDIN, GLAS, ABER *and* DUNDEE *are listed in their own sections.*

1003
MAP 6
A2

✚ ✚ **DROVER'S INN, INVERARNAN:** A famously Scottish drinking den/hotel on the edge of the Highlands just N of Ardlui at the head of L Lomond and 12km S of Crianlarich on the A82. Smoky, low-ceilinged rooms, open ranges, whisky in the jar, stuffed animals in the hall and kilted barmen; this is nevertheless the antithesis of the contrived Scottish tourist pub.

1004
MAP 2
C4

✚ ✚ **CLUANIE INN:** 01320 340257. On A87 at head of L Cluanie 15km before Shiel Br on the long rd to Kyle of Lochalsh. A trad wayside inn with good pub food, a restau and MED.INX refurb-ed accom. Perfect base for climbing/walking (esp the Five Sisters of Kintail, 1605/SERIOUS WALKS). A cosy refuge.

1005
MAP 6
D4

✚ **BORESTONE BAR, BANNOCKBURN nr STIRLING:** Bloody fine pub on r/about 2km from centre of Stirling. Lounge bar, but mainly notable for the public bar where you will find no wine and usually no women – and the best whisky collection in Scotland.

1006
MAP 2
C4

✚ **OLD FORGE, INVERIE, KNOYDART:** A warm haven for visitors to this remote peninsula. Drying rack above the open fire for walkers' sodden clothes, real ales and real character courtesy of the locals. Adj. conservatory restau in the offing. Stay along the rd.

1007
MAP 1
B2

TIGH-AN-TRUISH, CLACHAN, ISLE OF SEIL: 01852 300242. Beside the much-photographed 'Bridge over the Atlantic' which links the 'Isle' of Seil to the 'mainland'. On B884, 8km from B816 and 22km S of Oban. Country pub with rms/apartments above (with views of br). A place where no one cares how daft your hair looks after a hard day's messing about on boats. Food LO 8.30pm.

1008
MAP 2
C5

✚ **CLACHAIG INN, GLENCOE:** Deep in the glen itself down the rd signed off the A82, 8km from Glencoe village. Both the pub with its wood-burning stove and the lounge are woody and welcoming. Real ale and real climbers and walkers. Handy for hostel 2km down rd. Decent food and good, inexp accom.

1009
MAP 1
B1

✚ **THE MISHNISH, TOBERMORY:** Proper bar lunches, shirt and tie bar staff, new pool table, ashtrays changed every half-hour. What goes on? The Mish has had a refit, and there's competition in the air. 7 days till late. Usually live music.

1010
MAP 2
A4

POLLACHAR INN, SOUTH UIST: Southern tip; on the shore looking over to Barra. It's a long way from Brighton. The Saturday night discos are a long way from Manchester. Just a thought. Hell, who cares about anywhere else!

1011
MAP 2
A4

CASTLEBAY BAR, BARRA: Adj Castlebay Hotel. Brilliant bar. All human life is here. More Irish than all the Irish makeovers on the mainland. Occasional live music, frequent conversations with complete strangers.

1012
MAP 2
D3

PHOENIX, INVERNESS: 108 Academy St. Trad horseshoe bar. Always lively. Back lounge has become Jock Tamson's, a brewery 'old Scottish pub' makeover. Though tastefully done, it would perhaps go down better in, well, Ireland. The real pub is at the front.

1013
MAP 8
B3

TIBBIE SHIELS INN: Off A708 Moffat-Selkirk rd. Occupies its own particular place in Scottish culture, esp literature (1555/LITERARY PLACES) and in the Border hills SW of Selkirk where it nestles between 2 romantic lochs. On Southern Upland Way (1285/WATERFALLS) a good place to stop and refuel.

1014
MAP 9
C4

THE MURRAY ARMS and **THE MASONIC, GATEHOUSE OF FLEET:** 2 adj, unrelated pubs that just fit perfectly into the life of this gr wee town. Murray has accom and home-style food (the profiteroles looked sinful) that's popular with the locals.

1015
MAP 2
D4

LOCH INN, FORT AUGUSTUS: Busy canalside (Caledonian Canal which joins L Ness in the distance) pub for locals and visitors. Good grub (you should book for the upstairs restau), reasonable malts. Food LO 9pm. Some live music.

1016
MAP 6
D4

SETTLE INN, STIRLING: St Mary's Wynd off Broad St which leads up to the castle. Interesting 18th-century pub (up/downstairs) with great atmos and good mix of drinkers. Estimable Wallace Ale; whisky selection that directly mirrors mine.

GREAT PUBS FOR REAL ALE

✠ **FISHERMAN'S TAVERN, DUNDEE:** In Broughty Ferry, but not too far to go for gr atmos and the best collection of ales in the area. In Fort St near the seafront. Belhaven/Maclays/Theakston and guests. Low-ceilinged and friendly (899/DUNDEE PUBS). **1017 MAP 4 D3**

✠ **THE PHEASANT, HADDINGTON:** On corner where main st divides. Old-style, real-ale howf claiming to have the best selection in E Lothian. No arguments from us. Rare guests on tap, and local Belhaven brewed along the road in Dunbar. Busy market-town atmos; snooker and folk club upstairs Wed. Mind the parrot. **1018 MAP 7 D1**

✠ **MOULIN INN/HOTEL, PITLOCHRY:** 2km uphill from main st on rd to Br of Cally, an inn at a picuresque crossrds since 1695. Some rms and restau, but notable mainly for cosy bar and brewery out back from which comes 'the Braveheart' and the 'Old Remedial'. Live music some Sun. Food LO 9.30pm. **1019 MAP 4 C3**

✠ **ROYAL HOTEL, COMRIE:** Main sq; public bar is behind hotel. By same people who have the Bow Bar and Cloisters in Edin, a rare combination of stylish and right-on ambience, sort of city meets the country. Guests and regulars, which incl Earthquake Ale (made by Caledonian), exclusive to pub. Live music. **1020 MAP 3 B4**

✠ **ROYAL HOTEL, KINGUSSIE:** Main St. Busy local with all sorts of folk, juke box, snooker; gr lively atmos. Amazing range of malts packed along the shelves and about 8 ales on hand-pump. Makes you wonder who drinks them all in this small town. At their annual beerfest, any pint for a quid. **1021 MAP 2 D4**

✠ **THE FOUR MARYS, LINLITHGOW:** Main st nr rd up to palace so handy for a pint after schlepping around the historical attractions. Mentioned in most beer guides. Half a dozen ales on tap incl various guests. Notable malt whisky collection and very popular locally for lunches (daily) and evening meals (Thurs-Sat, LO 8.45pm). Open 7 days. **1022 MAP 7 B1**

THE TAPPIT HEN, DUNBLANE: By the cathedral and with a small inexp hotel upstairs (The Chimes, 4 rms, 01786 822164). Good ales (incl the Wallace), atmos and live music. **1023 MAP 6 D3**

MARINE HOTEL, STONEHAVEN: Popular local on great harbour front with seats o/side; pool tables, juke box and bar meals inside. Youngish crowd. 6 ales incl McEwans 80/-, Taylor's Landlord. Loungs/restau upstairs. Open all day. **1024 MAP 3 D4**

GIRSEY NICOL'S, BO'NESS: 5 Corbiehall. Curious collision of the ancient and modern with distressed wood all over, half a dozen real ales but a margarita machine and karaoke nights as well. Drinks promos, big breakfasts, live music - you can't say they don't put their heart into their work. Bar lunches. **1025 MAP 6 E4**

THE WOOLPACK, TILLICOULTRY: Via Upper Mill St from main st on your way to the Ochils. They come far and wide to this ancient pub. Bar food and a changing selection of ales which they know how to keep. So no change here chaps. **1026 MAP 6 E3**

CLACHNAHARRY INN, INVERNESS: On A862 Inverness-Beauly rd just outside Inverness o/looking firth with beer grd. Long list of regulars posted, 5/6 on tap. tomintoul Stag and Wildcat when we visited. They like kids. **1027 MAP 2 D3**

THE GROG AND GRUEL, FORT WILLIAM: Main st (pedestrianised). 15 ales in cellar and at least 6 on at a time upstairs. Skye and Fraoch Heather most notable. Tex-Mex, pasta food.11am to midnight/1am. **1028 MAP 2 C4**

THE OLD INN, GAIRLOCH: Southern app on A832 nr golf course, an 'old inn' across an old br; a goodly selection of malts. 12 real ales in the cellar; 2 on tap each day. Specialise in English ales, and exclusive 'Flowerdale' from Skye. **1029 MAP 2 C3**

BETTY NICOL'S, KIRKCALDY: 299 High St at the E end. Moved over from Edin (where they had the Malt Shovel), innkeepers who know and love their ales. Gr selection with usually 8 posted. Live music. Open 7 days. **1030 MAP 5 C4**

DREEL TAVERN, ANSTRUTHER: On busy rdside corner as you come into village from W (Kirkcaldy side). Low-ceilinged old pub with beer grd in summer for claustrophobic quaffers. Calder Ales, Orkney Dark, Border Ramparts and other visitors. **1031 MAP 5 E3**

ISLE OF SKYE BREWERY, UIG, SKYE: 01470 542477. Angus MacRuary brews the legendary Cuillin ales. Shop. Maybe if you ask him nicely he'll open a pub. **1032 MAP 2 B3**

SECTION 5

Good Food and Drink

PUBS THAT SERVE THE BEST FOOD

Pubs in EDIN, GLAS, ABER *and* DUNDEE *are listed in their own sections.*

1033
MAP 1
B3
✠ ✠ **KILBERRY INN, KILBERRY, nr TARBERT:** 01880 770223. On B8024 from W Loch Tarbert, the coast rd of Knapdale, 22km Tarbert/32km Lochgilphead – and you might whizz past. Down to earth good honest Yorkshire home cooking! Huge blackboard menu with a plethora of pies and Kath Leadbetter's pastry that really does melt in the mouth. Eat in the parlour of a roadside inn; you'll wish you lived nearer (though there are 2 inexp rms). Home-made jams and chutneys. Lunch and 6.30-9pm. Book w/ends. Cl Sun.

1034
MAP 3
D4
✠ ✠ **LAIRHILLOCK, nr NETHERLEY, STONEHAVEN:** 01569 730001. Here forever for gr pubfood, open evenings – LO 9.30pm – and Sun lunch (845/ABER RESTAUS). Inn more informal and downright friendly. Pub and conservatory. Fine for kids. Superb cheese selection, notable malts and ales. Can app from S Deeside Rd, but simplest direction for strangers is: 15km S of Aber by main A92 towards Stonehaven, then signed Durris, go 5km to country crossrds.

1035
MAP 6
E4
✠ ✠ **UNICORN INN, KINCARDINE:** 01259 730704. More a restau in a former pub than a pub with food, and unquestionably the best place to eat hereabouts. Worth coming from Stirling for. Light, Mediterranean-style dishes in bistro atmos. Best to book at w/ends. Report: 691/CENTRAL HOTELS. Cl Mon and Sun lunch.

1036
MAP 8
D2
✠ **THE WHEATSHEAF, SWINTON, betw KELSO and BERWICK:** 01893 523188. A hotel pub in an undistinguished village about halfway betw the 2 towns (18km) on the B6461. In deepest, flattest Berwickshire, Alan and Julie Reid serve up the best pub grub you've had since England. Open noon-2pm and 6-9pm. Cl Mon.

1037
MAP 6
E3
✠ **THE WHINSMUIR COUNTRY INN, POWMILL, nr DOLLAR:** 01577 840595. A hotel/roadhouse and pub recently refurb by the Brown family who run the prestigious Roman Camp in Callander (682/CENTRAL HOTELS) and apart from the accom, a v decent place for an informal and civilised meal; gr wine list etc. On A977 Kinross (12km – M90, jnct 6) – Kincardine Br. 7 days. LO 9pm.

1038
MAP 6
C4
✠ **THE CROSS KEYS, KIPPEN:** 01786 870293. Another inn missed last edition (I think we've got them all now), though here forever in this quiet backwater town off the A811 15km W of Stirling. Bar meals by coal fire, à la carte and family restaus. A real pub food haven, and about the only thing Egon Ronay has got right around here. LO 8.45pm.

1039
MAP 9
E3
✠ **RIVERSIDE INN, CANONBIE:** 013873 71512. 2km from Border off A7 S of Langholm. Superb pub food (with restau/accom) in this calendar pub o/looking meadows of the Esk. The first/last gr pub meal in Scotland. Impeccable, but owners were snooty with our Emma. Mon-Sat, lunch and 7-9pm.

1040
MAP 1
D4
✠ **WHEATSHEAF INN, SYMINGTON, nr AYR:** 01563 830307. 2km A77. Pleasant village off the unpleasant A77 with this busy coaching inn opposite church. Folk come from miles around to eat (book at w/ends) honest-to-goodness pub fare in various rms (roast beef every Sunday). Menu on boards. LO 10pm.

1041
MAP 2
C2
✠ **KYLESKU HOTEL, KYLESKU:** 01971 502231. Off A894 betw Scourie and Lochinver in Sutherland. A hotel and pub with a gr quayside location on L Glencoul where boats leave for trips to see the 'highest waterfall in Europe' (1282/WATERFALLS, 832/INEXP HIGHLAND RESTAUS). A friendly atmos with local fish, seafood (esp with legs) and yummy desserts. Noon-9.30pm.

1042
MAP 6
E3
✠ **STRATHALLAN HOTEL, DOLLAR:** Chapel Pl. All round gr pub (with 4 inexp rms above) in back st of couthie and tidy town. Ales, malts, a games selection and beer grd. Food, after going through a lean patch, is back to being probably the best in town. Definitely worth a visit after doing the glen (1609/GLEN AND RIVER WALKS).

1043
MAP 6
C3
MYRTLE INN, CALLANDER: On way in/out of town A84 S, the Doune and Stirling rd. This was always an unlikely good place to eat on the way in or out of a town lined with many indifferent restaus (sorry Callander, if truth hurts). New management at time of press, but augers well. LO 9pm.

SHIP INN, ELIE: Pub on the bay at Elie, the perfect toon in the picturesque East Neuk of Fife (1240/COASTAL VILLAGES). Bar and rm through back, but food mainly in refurb-ed boathouse next door and bistro above (good view, book w/ends). Same menu throughout and blackboard specials. Real popular place esp in summer when terrace o/looking the beach gets like Bondi. LO 9.30pm.

1044
MAP 5
D3

HUNTING LODGE HOTEL, FALKLAND : 01337 857226. Main st of much visited town in central Fife, opp the fabulous Palace (1410/CASTLES). All day menu of mainly stalwarts like 80/- Ale steak pie and macaroni cheese. Beer grd a bit removed. Open 7 days. LO 8pm.

1045
MAP 5
C3

GOBLIN HA' HOTEL, GIFFORD. 01620 810244. Twee village in the boondocks; one of 2 hotels (712/LOTHIANS HOTELS). This, the one with the gr name, serves a decent pub lunch and supper (6-9pm; 9.30pm on Fri and Sat) in lounge and more basic version in the pub. Conservatory out back and grd in summer with kids' play area.

1046
MAP 7
D2

DROVER'S INN, E LINTON: 01620 860298. A village off A1, 35km from Edin. A notable E Lothian eatery within reach of city – food recently much improved. Restau upstairs, blackboard specials down. Can eat alfresco in summer with trains whooshing by (271/BEST FOOD).

1047
MAP 7
D1

TORMAUKIN INN, GLENDEVON: 01259 781252. On A823 through wooded Glen to Auchterarder, 36km E of Stirling, 16km W of M90 at jnct 6/7. Rdside inn with very pleasant accom (10 rms/MED.INX), restau and fine pub meals. À la carte and daily specials with vegn dishes. W/ends busy. Lunch and 5.30-9.30pm.

1048
MAP 4
C4

THE BYRE, BRIG O' TURK: 01877 376292. On A821 from Callander at end of the village adj Dundarroch Hotel. Country inn (with new friendlier owners) in deep Trossachs. Blackboard table d'hôte in bar or (no smk) restau. Lunch and 6-9pm.

1049
MAP 6
B3

OLD BRIDGE INN, AVIEMORE: Off Coylumbridge rd at S end of Aviemore as you come in from A9 or Kincraig. 100m main st but sits in hollow. Recent expansion, but an old inn like it says with basic à la carte and more interesting blackboard specials. Kids' menu, ski-bums welcome. Lunch and 6-9pm.

1050
MAP 2
D4

THE CROWN, PORTPATRICK: 01776 810261. Pub on harbour with tables o/side in summer. Light, airy conservatory at back serving freshly caught fish. 12rms above. Locals and Irish who sail over for lunch (sic). LO 10pm.

1051
MAP 9
A4

OLD SMUGGLERS, AUCHENCAIRN: 01556 640331. An alternative place to stay to the Balcary Bay and Collin House Hotels in this old smuggling stretch of the Solway coast (though only 3 rms). Good pub grub and village crack. LO 10pm.

1052
MAP 9
C4

THE ANCHOR, KIPPFORD: The place to eat on the 'Scottish Riviera', esp if you've walked over from Rockcliffe (2km). In summer, tables o/side look (over the rd) to the silted Solway. Elbow to elbow inside with all ages enjoying grub.

1053
MAP 9
C4

THE SHIP INN, BROUGHTY FERRY: Excellent seafront (Tay estuary) snug pub with food upstairs and down (best tables at window upstairs). Famous for clootie dumpling (but not in summer). 7 days, lunch and 5-10pm (888/DUNDEE EAT AND DRINK).

1054
MAP 4
D3

HORSESHOE INN, EDDLESTON, nr PEEBLES: 5km N on A703 to Edin, this rdside inn is more a restau than just a pub, serving food from 7.30am right through to 3pm, and then dinner in the evenings. Now with 8 bedrms.

1055
MAP 8
B2

THE AULD CROSS KEYS INN, DENHOLM, nr HAWICK: 01450 870305. Not a lot of eating places to recommend in Hawick (in fact, none), so Peter and Heather Ferguson's old faithful is worth the 8km journey on the A698 Jedburgh rd. On the Green, with pub and dining lounges through the back. Blackboard menu, heaps of choice and food. Big on Sun high tea (4-6.30pm). No food Mon.

1056
MAP 8
C3

FOX AND HOUNDS, HOUSTON: 01505 612448 (560/BEST FOOD)

OLD CLUBHOUSE, GULLANE: 01620 842008 (719/LOTHIANS HOTELS).

THE BEST VEGETARIAN RESTAURANTS

Not surprisingly, perhaps, there are precious few completely vegetarian restaus in Scotland. But there are lots in EDIN (see p. 26) and some in GLAS (see p. 70).

1057   **SEAGREEN, KYLE OF LOCHALSH:** 01599 534388. On edge of town, rd
MAP 2   toPlockton. Café/bookshop/wholefood during the day (open AYR); in
C3   another rm is a seafood restau at night (May-Sept). Not your run-of-the-mill tofu; Fiona Begg's varied and artistic menu demonstrates just how innovative vegn cookery can be. vegan selection. No whiff of bacon sarnies here among the books. No smk. Organic ale. 7 days.   MED

1058   **HELIO'S at FINDHORN COMMUNITY, FINDHORN:** You will go a long way in the
MAP 3   N to find real vegn food, so it may be worth the detour from the main A96
A2   Inverness–Elgin rd (the Culloden Pottery restau nr Nairn, was undergoing major refurb at press time), to Findhorn and the famous commune (991/RETREATS) where there is a gr deli (1164/DELIS) and a pleasant caff by the 'Hall'.

1059   **TAIGH-NA-MARA, nr ULLAPOOL:** 01854 655282. A vegan cottage guesthouse
MAP 2   on the quiet shore of L Broom opposite Ullapool (25km) and 5km from br
C2   at head of the loch. Invisible from the rd (phone first for directions) accessible only by walking down through field to loch-side; this is a vegn haven. Nature all around and all things *au naturel* from Tony and Jackie's kitchen. The fount of Scottish wholefood info, their new cookbook is quite fruity.   CHP

1060   **BEN TIANAVAIG, PORTREE, SKYE:** 01478 612152. 5 Bosville Terr, just up from main
MAP 2   st on Staffin rd. Upstairs bistro mainly vegn; may need to reserve not just your
B3   table but also your main course because limited availability (due to all home cooking on modest premises). Lunch w/ends, dinner Tue-Sun 6-9.30pm.   INX

1061   **AN TUIREANN, PORTREE, SKYE:** Off Dunvegan rd (at the Co-op). Name keeps
MAP 2   changing – known locally as the Anvil Café. Now being extended to incorporate
B3   conservatory (for evening recitals) and craft shop at front, with gallery and exhib rm: all sounds gr and will enhance this already friendly foody caff. Mon-Sat 10am-5pm. Cl Sun.   CHP

1062   **THE MOUNTAIN RESTAURANT, GAIRLOCH:** 01445 712316. Restau with conser-vatory
MAP 2   and tables outside with mt view. Bookshop and adj Nature Shop with every kind
C3   of spiritual whatsits you may want. 40 fruit teas and mt-themed wholefood in various formations. Scones can be rock-like. All day; 'Candlelit' dinners 6.30pm-9pm.   INX

THE BEST VEGETARIAN-FRIENDLY PLACES

Edin and Glas cafés and restaus are mentioned in their own sections, see p. 26 and p. 70.

1063   **ORKNEY/ SHETLAND**

WOODWICK HOUSE, EVIE, ORKNEY: 01856 751330. B&B, seals, music and woodland.

BURRASTON HOUSE, WALLS, SHETLAND: 01595 809307. Good value lunches and set dinners.

BAYANNE HOUSE, SELLAFIRTH YELL, SHETLAND: 01957 744219. A croft by the sea. Accom.

1064   **HIGHLANDS**

THE CEILIDH PLACE, ULLAPOOL: 01854 612103 (796/INEXP HIGHLAND HOTELS).

CAFÉ NUMBER ONE, INVERNESS: 01463 226200 (1945/ INVERNESS).

RIVER CAFÉ, INVERNESS: 01463 714884 (1945/ INVERNESS).

DUNNET HEAD TEAROOM, nr THURSO: 01847 851774 (831/INEXP HIGHLAND RESTAUS).

THREE CHIMNEYS, SKYE: 01470 511258 (1920/ISLAND RESTAUS).

BIADH MATH, KYLE OF LOCHALSH (820/INEXP HIGHLAND RESTAUS).

RIVERSIDE BISTRO, LOCHINVER: 01571 844356 (827/INEXP HIGHLAND RESTAUS).

Q BRASSERIE, ABERDEEN: 01224 595001 (847/ABER RESTAUS).

LEMON TREE, ABERDEEN: 01224 642230 (864/ABER RESTAUS).

OWLIES, ABERDEEN: 01224 649267 (862/ABER RESTAUS).

MILTON RESTAURANT: 01330 844566 (777/NE HOTELS)

GREEN INN, BALLATER: 01339 755701 (774/NE HOTELS).

GORDON ARMS HOTEL, KINCARDINE O'NEIL, DEESIDE: 01339 884236. Halfway betw Ballater and Aberdeen. Hotel with ok-ish pub food. Organic wine list.

ARGYLL

THE CLIFTON COFFEE SHOP, TYNDRUM: 01838 400271 (1111/TEAROOMS).

THE BOXTREE, OBAN: 01631 563542 (1946/OBAN).

ARISAIG HOUSE HOTEL, ARISAIG: 01687 450622 (914/COUNTRY-HOUSE HOTELS).

AN TAIRBEART HERITAGE CENTRE, TARBERT: 01880 820190. On A83 S. Family fare.

FIFE AND LOTHIANS

OSTLER'S CLOSE, CUPAR: 01334 655574 (731/FIFE RESTAUS).

THE VINE LEAF, ST ANDREWS: 01334 477497 (1953/ST ANDREWS).

BRAMBLES and **THE MERCHANT HOUSE, ST ANDREWS** (1127/TEAROOMS).

SUNFLOWER CAFE, KIRKCALDY: 01592 646266. 39 Whytecauseway, nr the High St. Open AYR. 8.30am-4.30pm.

WATERSIDE BISTRO, HADDINGTON: 01620 825674 (714/LOTHIANS RESTAUS).

DROVER'S INN, EAST LINTON: 01620 860298 (1043/BEST FOOD).

CENTRAL:

FARLEYER HOUSE nr ABERFELDY: 01887 820332 (735/PERTHSHIRE RESTAUS).

LET'S EAT, PERTH: 0101738 643377 (750/PERTHSHIRE RESTAUS).

UNICORN INN, KINCARDINE: 01259 730704 (691/CENTRAL RESTAUS).

MYRTLE INN, CALLANDER: 01877 330919 (1043/BEST FOOD). New owners, reports please.

MONACHYLE MHOR nr BALQUHIDDER: 01877 384622 (966/GET-AWAY-FROM-IT-ALL).

KILLIECRANKIE HOTEL BAR, KILLIECRANKIE: 01796 473220 (744/PERTHSHIRE HOTELS).

SOUTH AND SOUTH WEST:

MARMIONS, MELROSE: 01896 822245 (704/BORDERS HOTELS).

OPUS, DUMFRIES: 95 Queensbury St. Popular daytime salad bar.

THE BEST SEAFOOD RESTAURANTS

For seafood restaus in EDINBURGH, *see p. 25; for* GLASGOW, *see p. 70.*

1070
MAP 1
B2
✠ ✠ **LOCK 16, CRINAN HOTEL, CRINAN:** 01546 830261. 8km off A816. On coast, 60km S of Oban (Lochgilphead 12km) at head of the Crinan Canal which joins L Fyne with the sea. This is the third-floor rm where you drink in the sunset over the Sound of Jura (from where your dinner has come) as well as a glass or two of perfectly complementary white wine. O/side on the quay is the boat which has landed those massive prawns, sweet clams and other creatures with legs or valves, which are cooked v simply and brought on heaped tureens to your table. Ground-floor restau serves similar fare but not only seafood. Here I had the best Dover sole I've ever tasted. It is all as it should be. EXP

1071
MAP 5
E3
✠ ✠ **THE CELLAR, ANSTRUTHER:** 01333 310378. The best in SE Scotland. Behind Fisheries Museum in busy East Neuk of Fife town. Fish and shellfish from beyond the harbour wall, some meat options. Cosy French bistro atmos. Full Report: 730/FIFE RESTAUS. MED

1072
MAP 3
B3
✠ ✠ **SILVER DARLINGS, ABERDEEN:** 01224 576229. Down by harbour. For many yrs one of the best restaus in the city and the NE. Exquisite chargrilled seafood. report: 846/ABER RESTAUS. MED

1073
MAP 7
B3
✠ **LOCHBAY SEAFOOD, SKYE:** 01470 592235. 14km N Dunvegan; A850 to Portree, B886 Waternish peninsula coastal route. Another scenic Skye drive leads you to the door of this small cottage at end of the village row. O/looks water where your shellfish, skate or even shark have come from. Main dishes served unfussily with chips or baked potatoes. Comforting puds and Irish coffee. Simply v good – you'll need to book. Apr-Oct; lunch & LO 8.30ish. Cl Sat. MED

1074
MAP 1
C2
✠ **LOCH FYNE SEAFOOD AND SMOKERY:** 01499 600264. On A83 the L Lomond to Inveraray rd, 20km Inveraray/11km Rest and Be Thankful. Rdside smokery which is not merely a net across the end of the loch to catch tourists. In summer you may well have to book or wait; people come from afar for the oysters and the smokery fare, esp the kippers. Spacious, though the booths can seem cramped. House white (other whites and whisky) well chosen. Same menu all day, no 'meal times'. Shop sells every conceivable packaging of salmon, etc., 9am-9pm. Though some readers complain of indifferent service, it is busy so on balance this is a notable spot. It's always been fyne by me, something to look forward to on the long road home. INX

1075
MAP 1
B3
✠ **THE ANCHORAGE, TARBERT:** 01880 820881. New owners Mediterranean refurb is in perfect sync with light touch displayed at the stoves. Complementary wines, desserts and coffee – an all round experience. Authentic location on busy quay of quintessential Highland port. Lunch and 7pm-10pm. MED

1076
MAP 3
D4
✠ **THE TOLBOOTH, STONEHAVEN:** 01569 762287. On corner of harbour, one of the best restaus in the area in a great setting. Upstairs bistro with interesting seafood menu served with flair and integrity; good wine list, some real bargains. Tue-Sun 6-9.30pm. Sun lunch. MED

1077
MAP 1
C3
✠ **FINS, FAIRLIE, nr LARGS:** 01475 568989. On main A78 8km S of Largs a seafood bistro, smokery, shop and craft/cookshop that I neglected last edition. My regret because this place is altogether good. Chef Gillian Dick uses exemplary restraint and the wine list is similarly to the point. Lunch and dinner. Cl Mon. INX

1078
MAP 1
C4
✠ **CREELERS, BRODICK, ARRAN:** 01770 302810. Just outside Brodick on rd N to castle in a modern tourist plaza-plex. Even with their other Creelers doing so well in Edin (102/SEAFOOD RESTAUS) Tim and Fran James still manage to keep this excl island bistro tip-top (and get the boat out). Lunch LO 10pm. Cl Mon. MED

1079
MAP 7
C4
✠ **MOREFIELD HOTEL, ULLAPOOL:** 01854 612161. Neptune's seafood, vegn and Indian food all on offer in this quirky popular restau on a kind of housing estate. The conserv restau was closed the night I went; but it is rhapsodised over. Bar meals are great and selection of seafood amazing; close your eyes and enjoy. The people at the next table had driven 100 miles for this meal – nuff said. INX/MED

1080
MAP 7
C4
CRANNOG, FORT WILLIAM: 01397 705589. The original branch of a family tree which spread, but didn't quite take root in Edin and Glas. This, however, remains your best bet in Ft William. Finlay Finlayson's converted smokehouse is where the Cal

140   GOOD FOOD AND DRINK

Mac boats used to dock. Usual fresh fish and seafood from surrounding islands. Limited puds do incl walnut tart. Service can be slow if you're hurrying to the ferry at Mallaig.

MED

SEAFOOD CAFÉ, TARBET, nr SCOURIE: 01971 502251. Charming conservatory restau on cove where boats leave for Handa Island bird reserve (1380/BIRDS). Julian catches your seafood from his boat (he'll also take you on a cruise) and Jackie cooks it; some take photos of the results. Cheesecake for dessert. It's so peaceful here you'll want to stay and can do so in adj self-catering barn. Located at end of unclassified rd off the A894 between Laxford Br and Scourie; best phone to check openings. Apr-Sept: Mon-Sat 12-8pm. Some Sun in summer.

1081
MAP 2
C1

INX

THE PIERHOUSE, PORT APPIN: 01631 730302. At the end of the minor rd and 3km from the A828 Oban–Ft William rd in Pt Appin village rt by the tiny 'pier' where the passenger ferry leaves for Lismore. The MacLeod's continue to cater for every kind of visitor. Locally caught seafood (Lismore oysters, Mallaig flatfish, hand-dived shellfish) is handed over fresh to the door by boat. Lively atmos, wine and wonderful view (944/INNS).

1082
MAP 2
B1

INX

NO. 33, PERTH: 01738 633771. George St nr art gallery. Seafood lounge long time one of the best restaus in town, with bar area for oysters (incl after-theatre supper). Restau: lunch and LO 9.30pm; bar: 10.30pm+. Cl Sun/Mon.

1083
MAP 4
C4

MED

THE BEST FISH AND CHIP SHOPS

✤ ✤ **VALENTE'S, KIRKCALDY:** 01592 205774. 73 Overton Rd (not downtown version). Ask directions to this superb chippy in E of town; worth the detour and worth the queue when you get there. Phone if you're lost. Till 11pm. Cl Wed.

1084
MAP 5
C4

✤ ✤ **THE UNIQUE, GLASGOW:** 223 Allison St. Not exactly central, but if you're on the S-side you'll find the best fish 'n' chips in town here. Through the curtain in the café, they serve lunches, fish teas and spam fritters. Veg oil used. Old-fashioned hours, viz 8.15am-1.15pm, 3.45-9pm. That's right, 9pm – closed.

1085
MAP 8
xD4

✤ ✤ **THE ASHVALE, ABERDEEN, ELGIN, INVERURIE** and **BRECHIN:** Original restau (1985) at 46 Gt Western Rd nr Union St, and 2 other city branches. Restau and takeaway complex à la Harry Ramsden (and they steadfastly stick to dripping). Various sizes of haddock, sole, plaice. Home-made stovies, etc., all served fresh and fast. Open 7 days, noon-1am; restau noon-11pm Sun-Thu; till midnight Fri/ Sat.

1086
MAP 3

✤ ✤ **THE NEW DOLPHIN, ABERDEEN:** Chapel St. Despite the pre-eminence of the Ashvale in Aberdeen, many would rather swear by this small, always busy place just off Union St. Few tables, superb takeaway. Till 1am and 3am w/ends.

1087
MAP 3
D3

✤ **L'ALBA D'ORO, EDINBURGH:** Henderson Row, nr corner with Dundas St. Large selection of deep-fried goodies, incl many vegn savouries. Inexpensive proper pasta, real pizzas and even the wine's ok. A lot more than your usual fry-up – as several plaques on the wall attest (incl *Scotland the Best!*). Open until midnight.

1088
MAP A
D1

✤ **THE RAPIDO, EDINBURGH:** 77 Broughton St. Fine chips. Popular with late-nighters stumbling back down the hill to the New Town, and the flotsam of the 'Pink Triangle.' 1.30am (3.30am Fri/Sat).

1089
MAP A
D2

✤ **THE DEEP SEA, EDINBURGH:** Leith Walk, opp Playhouse. Open late and often has queues but these are quickly dispatched. The haddock has to be 'of a certain size'. Trad menu. Still one of the best fish suppers you'll ever feed a hangover with. 2am-ish (3am Fri/Sat).

1090
MAP A
D2

✤ **DEEP SEA, DUNDEE:** 81 Nethergate at bottom end of Perth Rd; v central. The Sterpaio family have been serving the Dundonians excellent fish 'n' chips since 1939; gr range – lemon sole, scampi, haddock, cod etc in veg oil. Café with aproned waitress service is a classic. V trad, so . . . oo tasty. Mon-Sat, 11.30am-6.40pm.

1091
MAP 4
D3

✤ **PEPPO'S, ARBROATH:** 51 Ladybridge St next to the harbour where those fish come in. Fresh as that and chips in dripping. Peppo has been here since 1951; John and Frank Orsi are now carrying on the gr family trad and feeding the hordes. Mon-Fri 4-10pm, Sunday 4-8pm. Cl Sat, so they can go and watch Arbroath FC get beat again.

1092
MAP 4
E3

1093
MAP 3
D5
✠ **THE BERVIE CHIPPER, INVERBERVIE:** Main st as you come in from Stonehaven (and they do). Refurb after 35yrs with sit-in area up and downstairs and take-away. Gets through enormous amounts of haddock and cod. Lard used. 7 days; May-Sept noon-11pm; rest of year 4-11pm.

1094
MAP 5
E3
✠ **THE ANSTRUTHER FISH BAR:** On the front in Fife seaside town (1240/COASTAL VILLAGES); just look for the queue. Get a gr fish supper and walk round the harbour. Lard used. 7 days till 11pm. There's also the **FISH RESTAURANT** further along the front for sit-in sole, etc. (and pizzas). The takeaway wins.

1095
MAP 1
C3
✠ **WEST END, ROTHESAY:** 1 Gallowgate. Winner of awards (recently the Seafish Fryers Quality) and unmissable if you're on Bute. Only haddock, but wide range of other fries and fresh pizza. Uses expensive groundnut oil. Summer: 12-12am (Sun 4-11pm); winter 12-12am ,Cl 2-4pm. Café in summer till 8pm. Cl Mon.

1096
MAP 9
D3
BALMORAL, DUMFRIES: Balmoral Rd. Seems as old and essential as the Bard himself. Now using groundnut oil, hence the best chip in the south. 7 days.

1097
MAP 1
B1
ONORIO'S, OBAN: George St. Legendary but this is where the wifie patiently told me, 'Anyone who says you can fry good chips in vegetable oil is having you on, son.' This is bollocks, missus (*see above*). But their lardy chips are good and you're near the seafront to eat and walk off the grease. Lunch/4-11.30pm. (Cl Sun winter.)

MAP 6
E4
CORVI'S, BO'NESS: Just squeezing on this page, a new entry for its fine fish supper, and gr home-made ice cream (1158/ICE CREAM).

GREAT CAFÉS

For *cafés* in EDIN, *see* p. 71, GLAS, p. 64.

1098
MAP 1
C3
✠ ✠ ✠ **NARDINI'S, LARGS:** 01475 674555. The Esplanade, Glas side. An institution. The epitome of the seaside cafeteria and all the nostalgia of Doon the Watter days. This airy brasserie with cake, ice cream and chocolate counters and in the back a trad tratt with full Italian à la carte and OK wines has a timeless formula which works as well today as it ever did. The light fittings like almost everything else are true originals. Summer evenings with the long light and a bowl of ice cream and the place busy with all kinds of folk is life-affirming stuff. Get you down there. High tea (4-6pm) is always a good idea. Summer till 10.30pm/winter 8pm. (1155/ICE CREAM.). No sign of Daniella now.

1099
MAP 6
D3
✠ **ALLAN WATER CAFÉ, BRIDGE OF ALLAN:** Henderson St (main st) beside the eponymous br. Real whiff of nostalgia along with the fish'n'chips and the ice cream, which are the best around. Worth coming over from Stirling (8km) for a takeaway or a seat in the comforting woody caff – and a reminisce of the life before the mall and the burgering of your high st. 7 days, 8am-9pm.

1100
MAP 1
C3
✠ **THE RITZ CAFÉ, MILLPORT:** See Millport, see the Ritz. Since 1906 and now in its fourth generation, the classic café on the Clyde. Somewhat overshadowed by Nardini's (*see above*) and a short ferry journey away (from Largs, continuous; then 6km), but it should be an essential part of any visit to this part of the coast, and Millport is not without charm. Food 'n' chips, frothy cappuccino, famous home-made ice cream (esp with melted marshmallow), Millport rock and, of course, the hot peas. 7 days, 10am-10pm forever.

1101
MAP 1
C4
✠ **TOGS, TROON:** Templehill nr main crossrds. There are 2 seaside caffs in downtown Troon (the other, the pleasingly named Venice Café, is also good), but this is the one that did it for me – it even smells like a café should. Snacks and stuff and brilliant rock. 7 days 9am- 6 or 8pm (from 10am on Sun).

1102
MAP 1
C3
CAFÉ MELBOURNE, SALTCOATS: 72 Hamilton St, opp Safeways along from main st. More caff culture in Ayrshire than anywhere else, this one is unchanged over years and has all the 1950s nostalgia you could want. A very good sandwich roll is served with milky coffee and v green drinks. 9am-5.30pm. Frying adj.

1103
MAP 1
E3
THE MARKET BAR AND RESTAURANT, LANARK MARKET: Hyndford Rd. Betw the auction rings and only on auction days (e.g. Mon), a café from a bygone era. Farmers' sons of farmers' sons still cram the tables and the seats by the counter for the canteen cooking that's always hit the spot. Jam roly-poly, jelly, apples and custard after your mince and chips. The walls creak. The waitresses josh with the regulars; there's a cakestand on every table. Till 6 (or 8pm on special days).

THE CASTLE RESTAURANT, INVERNESS: On rd that winds up to the castle from the main st, nr the TO and the hostels. No pandering to tourists here, but this great caff has been serving chips with everything for 37 years. Recent redecoration, but not poshed up. Pork chops, prawn cocktail, perfect fried eggs. They work damned hard. 8am-8.30pm. Cl Sun. | 1104 MAP 2 D3

THE CAFÉ IN BRIG O'TURK IN THE TROSSACHS: 01877 376267. Hanging baskets of flowers o/side this shack are what you notice from the rd (the A821 12km W of Callander) in the heart of the afternoon tea belt of the Trossachs. But more substantial high teas are served: Highland stew, Cullen skink, whisky spice cake. Book for evening. Always so busy, Ann Park hates any more mentions. Sorry. | 1105 MAP 6 B3

BEN LEDI CAFE, CALLANDER: Main st nr sq. Fish teas, and a sq meal that's better than . . . well loads better, actually, than most of what's on offer in the poncier places on the tourist strip. Take away or sit in. The best ice cream for miles around. It is always worth a stop in Callander. Cl Thu. | 1106 MAP 6 C3

THE BEST TEAROOMS AND COFFEE SHOPS

For EDIN, *see p. 31; for* GLAS, *p. 74.*

✠ ✠ **TUDOR RESTAURANT, AYR:** 8 Beresford Terr, nr Odeon and Burns Monument Sq. For over 25yrs a tearoom and restau, a classic of its type: roomy, well-used, full of life. Bakery counter at front (sausage rolls and 'fly cemeteries' as they're supposed to be) and waitress service in the body of the kirk. Breakfast 9-11am, high tea 3.15-8pm (9pm July/Aug) and lunch(eon) in betw. Open Sun in season. Trad without being tacky. | 1107 MAP 1 D4

✠ ✠ **KAILZIE GARDENS TEAROOMS, PEEBLES:** On the way out of town towards Traquair (1207/GARDENS) this v civilised courtyard coffee shop is nr the Garden entrance. Superior sort of home-baking – the apple cake should be famous and it's hard to choose from the rest. Open 7 days, till 4pm Mon-Fri and 5pm at w/ends (5.30pm in summer). Apr-Oct. They also do w/end dinners. | 1108 MAP 8 B2

✠ ✠ **THE GRANARY, COMRIE:** Main st parlour with gr home-bakes arranged on an old-fashioned counter. TLC coconut biscuits, tiffin, brill bics, major cakes – come with appetite. Jams/chutneys/ice cream. No smk. Mar-Oct 10-5pm. Cl Mon. Also **FARM FOOD BAR,** 2km W on A85 to Lochearnhead. Highly recommended roadside coffee shop/diner with hot dishes, salads, etc. Open till 9pm. Apr-Oct. | 1109 MAP 4 B4

✠ ✠ **THE POWMILL MILKBAR, nr KINROSS:** On the A977 Kinross (on the M90, jnct 6) to Kincardine Br rd, a real milkbar and a real slice of Scottish cack and cake. Apple pie and moist fly cemeteries – an essential stop on the Sunday run whatever day of the week you're passing. The paper plates do little justice to the confections they bear, but are part of the deal. Hot meals and salads. Good place to take kids. 7 days, 9am-5pm (6pm w/ends, earlier in winter). (1610/GLEN AND RIVER WALKS.) | 1110 MAP 4 C4

✠ ✠ **THE CLIFTON COFFEE SHOP, TYNDRUM:** On A82, a strategically placed pit-stop on the drive to Oban or Ft William (just before the rd divides), with a Scottish produce shop and the 'Green Welly Shop' selling outdoor gear. Fast (Scottish) food to an unusually good standard and emporium packed with Scottish produce, from whisky to videos. Here you get the picture and the flavour of the land – this is Scotland, ken? 7 days, 8.30am-5.30pm. | 1111 MAP 6 A2

✠ **THE BLACK-FACED SHEEP, ABOYNE:** 01339 887311. Nr main Royal Deeside rd through Aboyne (A93) and TO, this excellent coffee shop/gift shop is well-loved by locals but is thankfully missed by the bus parties hurtling towards Balmoral. Home-made breads and cakes, snacks; good coffee. 10.30-5pm, Sun from 11am. | 1112 MAP 3 C4

✠ **NORTH BEACHMORE FARM RESTAURANT, nr MUASDALE:** on A83 Tarbert–Campbeltown rd. Signposted up a steep track, 2km off the rd and into the hills. Matt and Eileen McInnes' home-cooking is v popular locally; you see why. Stunning views of the Sound of Gigha, (and on a clear day Ireland). Food excl too. Open AYR 10am-11pm. | 1113 MAP 1 B3

1114 ⚓ **THE GREEN BARN, TOBERMORY, MULL:** Up the hill at the edge of town 500m
MAP 1 off Dervaig rd, 2km centre. Run by (and part of) the dairy farm of the people
B1 who make the excellent Mull cheddar (which you can 'win' with this book, *see
p.12*), but that's not the reason I'm recommending it. Rather, it's just gr what
they've done with it – go see! A glass barn full of plants, hearty soup, farm bakes.
Walk from the village – it will do you good. May-Sep; Mon-Fri (Cl w/end) 10am-
4pm.

1115 ⚓ **PUDDLEDUCKS, BLAIRLOGIE, nr STIRLING:** On main A91 in tiny village.
MAP 6 Couple of hot dishes at lunch but mainly delicious cakes, and I do mean
D3 delicious cakes. 3 ladies make 'em. Stock up on the way to the Ochils. 7 days
10.30-4.30pm.

1116 **THE RIVERSIDE, ABBEY ST BATHANS:** 01361 840312. By the trout farm, nr R
MAP 8 Whiteadder in the middle of this rustic hamlet on the Southern Upland Way. A
D1 welcome place for a café (though it's more of a restau really) with friendly
service, hearty grub, incl pheasant pie, various savoury flans and puddings which
will need a bit of walking off. Tue-Sun 11am-5pm and bank holiday Mon.

1117 **THE OLD BANK, DUMFRIES:** 95 Irish St, off High St. Coffee shop in converted bank
MAP 9 (revolving doors and cornices remain) on st where Burns lived. Delicate snacks,
D3 good puds and cakes. Mon-Sat 10am-5pm.

1118 **PEEL FARM COFFEE& CRAFT SHOP nr ALYTH:** B954 to Lintrathen (3km N. of
MAP 4 Reekie Linn (1287/WATERFALLS). Farmhouse fare and handcrafted knits, pottery,
D3 jewellery. Traditional, cosy, mumsie. 9am-5pm Easter-mid Oct daily.

1119 **AN CARRAIG TEAROOM, STRATHYRE:** Main st on A84 as you leave towards
MAP 6 Crianlarich (and after Munro Hotel). Look out for it, because it's quite discreet.
C2 Some hot dishes but becoming renowned for cakes, like a great tearoom should.
Excellent lentil soup. Jams and provisions. Daytime only. Cl Tues.

1120 **THE SMITHY, NEW GALLOWAY:** Nr end of main st, a bookshop/coffee shop/ general
MAP 9 centre for the village and walkers/wanderers in this neck of the Galloway woods.
C3 V harmonious – this is the way tourist-type café/gift shops should look in
Scotland (but rarely do). Home-baking and now large range of local cheeses to
go with gr oatcakes. Meals all day till 6pm (till 9pm June-Aug; 8pm Sept).
Licensed. Now you can hire a bike here to work of your excesses! Cl Nov-Feb.

1121 **THE WHITEHOUSE OLD SCHOOL TEAROOM, by KENNACRAIG:** Nr the ferry terminal
MAP 1 to Islay, 14km S of Tarbert; 100m off the main A83 rd to Campbeltown. A small
B3 schoolhouse in a neat cottage grd serving home-baked goodies and light snacks.
10.30am-7pm. Cl Tue.

1122 **THE CHATTERBOX, NEWTON STEWART:** Main st nr corner on A75. The *only* place
MAP 9 in town for a good cup of tea (huge selection) and slice of home-made cake.
B3 Lunch menu v popular and snacks too. Mon-Sat, 9am-5pm.

1123 **COFFEE HOUSE, GRANTOWN-ON-SPEY:** 35 High St. Surprisingly authentic Italian
MAP 2 café with genuine Italian cakes, ice cream and espresso. They serve stew as well
E7 as pretty good pasta. Nice people run this place. Till 5pm.

1124 **THE COFFEE SHOPPE, FRASERBURGH:** 30 Cross St. Small front-room-of-
MAP 3 somebody's-hoose-type place. Scottish and imported cakes (e.g. carrot cake,
E1 pavlova) all home made. Mum's soup, scones and rowies. Mon-Sat, 9am-4.30pm.
Cl Wed.

1125 **BINNIE'S TEAROOM, CROMARTY:** In great wee village in Black Isle 30km NE of
MAP 2 Inverness (1235/COASTAL VILLAGES) on corner of Church St. Home-baking and
D3 some snacks. Country Kitchen opp has, in my opinion, better scones and better
jam, but my contacts say . . . it has to be Binnie's. Only till 4pm. Cl Fri.

1126 **KIND KYTTOCK'S KITCHEN, FALKLAND:** Folk come to Falkland (1410/CASTLES;
MAP 5 1849/INEXP ART; 1584/HILL WALKS) for many reasons, not least for afternoon tea.
C3 Several choices, this the longest established. Omelettes, toasties, baked potatoes,
baking. Good service. No smk upstairs. 10.30am-5.30pm. Cl Mon.

1127 **MERCHANT'S HOUSE, ST ANDREWS:** S St in the middle. Self-serve restau-cum-
MAP 5 coffee shop with urbane, relaxed, yet busy atmos. Conservatory through back
D2 though not all the plants are real! Next, but by no means least, another place:
BRAMBLES: 5 College St. Similar ambience. Both have good home bakes, hot
dishes and good vegn choices. St Andrews is lucky to have these wholesome

options, but then it is that kind of a town. Both 7 days till 5/5.30pm.

DUN WHINNY'S, CALLANDER: Off main st at Glas rd, a welcoming wee (but not twee) tearoom; not run by wifies. Banoffee pie kind of thing and clootie dumpling. I'll be incognito here, because they don't like me in Callander. Contrary to reports, I do like it, though I won't be retiring there. 10am-5.30pm.

1128
MAP 6
D3

DUNNET HEAD TEAROOM nr THURSO: 15km N (831/INEXP HIGHLAND RESTAUS).

THE BEST SCOTCH BAKERS

✠ ✠ **FISHER & DONALDSON, DUNDEE/ST ANDREWS/CUPAR:** Main or original branch in Cupar and 3 in Dundee. Superior contemporary bakers along trad lines - surprising (and a pity) that they haven't gone further, although they do supply a few selected outlets (e.g. Jenners in Edin with pastries and the most excellent Dr Floyd's bread which is as good as anything you could make yourself). Main sq, Cupar; Church St, St Andrews; Whitehall St, 300 Perth Rd; and Lochee, Dundee, which is v well served with decent bakers, for example:

1129
MAP
4/5

✠ **GOOD-FELLOW AND STEVEN** and **WALLACE'S, DUNDEE:** G&S have several branches in Dundee and Fife. Wallaces are famous for their pies and massive bridies, and have branches in Crichton St and Faraday St.

1130
MAP
4/5

✠ **BRADFORD'S:** 245 Sauchiehall St, Glas, and suburban branches in selected areas, i.e. they have not over-expanded; for a bakery chain, some lines seem almost home-made. Certainly better than all the industrial 'home'-bakers around. Individual fruit pies, for example, are uniquely yummy, and the all-important Scotch pie pastry is exemplary. (513/TEAROOMS.)

1131
MAP 8
C 2

✠ **WATERSIDE BAKERY, STRATHAVEN, nr LANARK:** 01357 521260. Specialising in huge array of savoury breads: sunflower, Bavarian, sourdough, black bun and, at Christmas, stollen. They also make all their flavoured shortbreads and oatcakes. Good wholesome stuff! Mon-Sat 8am-5.30pm (Sat from 7am!)

1132
MAP 1
E4

✠ **SCOTCH OVEN, CALLANDER:** Opp Royal Hotel in busy touristy main st and one of the best things about it. Good bread, rolls, cakes, the biggest, possibly the best, tattie scones and sublime doughnuts. Also featuring what may be the perfect Scotch pie pastry. This is where to stock up for your walk on the Braes, the other great thing about Callander. Open 7 days.

1133
MAP 6
C3

✠ **McINTYRE'S, PERTH:** Main branch at 2 Main St on corner of Perth Br (overTay) and main A93. Home of the best morning rolls in Scotland and also estimable for their Black Bun (the trad Scots bannock, a necessary component of Hogmanay celebrations) and many staples. In their well-scrubbed bakery downstairs, flour dusted bakers work the nights away. The mural on the end wall awaits this new edition, for a touch up I think.

1134
MAP 4
C4

✠ **BLACK'S OF DUNOON:** aka Cowal Cottage Bakery at 144 Argyll St, the main st of Dunoon. Popular for eons and still influenced by the American base that used to be nearby; loads of doughnuts and muffins. The old favourites shortbread, potato scones and the like still draw the queues.

1135
MAP 1
C3

HOUSTON'S OF HAWICK: Nothing too mould-breaking about old Houston's; just honest Border baking. They're at 16 Bourtree Pl as you come into Hawick from the Jedburgh rd just as they've always been. It's where I came in, too, to go to school, and I have incl the place where I found an alternative to school dinners, mainly for nostalgic reasons. They do make the best Selkirk bannocks.

1136
MAP 8
C7

BREADALBANE BAKERY, ABERFELDY: 37 Dunkeld St. On rd out of town to Grantully opp petrol stn. Home of Aberfeldy Whisky Cake (a rich fruit job with single malt flavour) and Holyrood Tarts (no, not Hollywood) and brill home-made biscuits, etc.

1137
MAP 4
B3

THE DORNOCH BAKERY, DORNOCH: Behind cathedral, a busy town bakery with a couple of tables in front of the ovens. Great selection of pies (esp fruit pies) and bread (esp milk bread). Often has queues.

1138
MAP 2
D2

ASHER'S, NAIRN: 2 branches at either end of Main St and also in Inverness (Church St) and Forres. Baking on the Moray Firth for 100 years and has esp good bread and rolls. Coffee shops attached.

1139
MAP 2
D3

PILLANS AND SONS, KIRKCALDY: Nr Harbour and end of High St. Here for 100yrs

1140

MAP 5
C4
or so turning out their Scottish rolls and cakes and unconventional Scotch pies (let's hope the scions of the family can put up with the early rising). Neat trios of cakes in the window. Nostalgia and good Scots baking.

1141 **ADAMSON'S IN FIFE: PITTENWEEM, ELIE, CRAIL, ANSTRUTHER and CUPAR:** Baking in
MAP 5 the kingdom since 1887, Adamson's is one of the few places that keeps trad bakery going, not succumbing to the creaming, or industrial yeasting of everything. Where else can you find puggy buns, Hedderwick buns or raggy biscuits? Mainly small neighbourhood shops – the one in Elie is out of *Dr Finlay's Casebook*. Original bake-house in Pittenweem. Go see!

1142 **THE BAKERS IN CROMARTY:** Bank St. It used to be called Mathesons now run by
MAP 2 some Canandians, it's better than ever. A Mr Don Coutts, a local resident, wrote
D3 to rave about the place. He enclosed one of their estimable vegetable pies. By the time it got to me, it was in no fit state. No nasty preservatives.

1143 **AITKENS, ABERDEEN:** Glenbervie Rd and Menzies Rd, Torry (a district of Aber
MAP 3 over the br) and 202 Holburn St in city centre. They do fancy cakes, pies and all the usual, but are mainly notable as the place to get your rowies, the buttery rolls which are the Aberdonian contribution to breakfast considered by many to give the croissant a run for it's money. Aitkens rowies send Aberdonians into rapures all over the world.

1144 **McLARENS, FORFAR:** Town centre next to Queens Hotel. There are others in the
MAP 4 town, but this is the best place to sample the famous Forfar bridie, a meat-and-
D3 potato shortcrust pastie that'll may keep you going all the way to Aber.

THE BEST ICE CREAM

1145 ✚ ✚ **LUCA'S, MUSSELBURGH, nr EDINBURGH:** 32 High St. Queues out the door
MAP 7 ✝ ✝ in the middle of a Sun afternoon in February are testament to the
C1 enduring popularity of this almost-legendary ice cream boutique. 3 classic flavours (vanilla, choc and strawberry) and pure ingredients attract folk from Edin (14km) though there is a branch in the nearby suburb of Craigmillar. Café through the back has basic snacks and ice cream in its sundae best, but you might have to wait when it gets busy. Mon-Sat 9am-10pm, Sun 10.30am-10pm.

1146 ✚ ✚ **MANCINI'S, THE ROYAL CAFÉ, AYR:** 11 New Rd, the rd to Prestwick. Ice
MAP 1 ✝ ✝ cream that's taken seriously, entered for competitions and usually wins
C4 one category or another. Family biz for aeons. 101 flavours (though not all at the same time). Now (and first) with the formidable 'ice cream toastie'. These Mancini's genuinely love ice cream. 9.30am-11.30pm; Cl Thu in winter.

1147 ✚ **THE CHOCOLATE BOX, BIGGAR:** The Taylors had been making ice cream here
MAP 8 ✝ before the Italians thought of it: the original 'family blocks' are in the café
A2 across the square, but the real vanilla scoop is here in their confectionery shop (where the additional variety of home-made tablet, fudge and chocolates is waist expanding). 7 days, 9-5pm (opens at 1pm Sun).

1148 ✚ **JANETTA'S, ST ANDREWS:** 31 South St. Family firm since 1908. There are two
MAP 5 ✝ Janetta's, but the one to adore is opp the Byre Theatre. Once only vanilla,
D2 Americans up for the Open asked for other flavours. Now there are 52, incl the favourites, ginger, hokey-pokey and the famous irn-bru sorbet. Also frozen yogs. Janetta's is another good reason for being a student at St Andrews. 7 days 9am-6pm.

1149 ✚ **CALDWELL'S, INNERLEITHEN:** On the High St in this ribbon of a town
MAP 8 ✝ between Peebles and Gala they've been making ice cream since 1911. Purists
B2 will approve of the fact that they still make only vanilla – chocolate powder on top if you want. The shop sells everything from Blue Nun to bicycles. Mon-Fri till 8.30pm, Sat/Sun 7.30pm.

1150 **VISOCCHI'S, BROUGHTY FERRY/KIRRIEMUIR:** Orig from St Andrews; ice-cream
MAP 4 makers for 30 years and still with the café they opened in Kirriemuir in 1953. On
D3 the main drag of the Angus town (1270/GLENS), it's a hang-out for everybody. Broughty Ferry (Dundee's seaside suburb) more middle-class, with a contemporary menu; home-made pasta as well as the peach melba. But whatever comes and goes, the ice cream will go on forever. 7 days (891/DUNDEE EAT AND DRINK).

CASA MARCHINI, ABERDEEN: 333 King St, heading out of town for A92 N but only 500m from end of E end of Union St. Superior ice cream in multi flavours and ice-cream cakes to superior trad Italian recipes. This place should be more widely recognised; it licks all the others in Aber. 7 days, till 10pm.
1151
MAP 3

THE ALLAN WATER CAFÉ, BRIDGE OF ALLAN: An old-fashioned café in an old-fashioned town, near the eponymous br in the main st since 1902. Fabulously good fish 'n' chips and ice cream. The former now dispensed from a modernised shop next door. Ice cream (only vanilla) in the old woody café that smells like a real caff should. 7 days, 8am-9pm.
1152
MAP 6
D3

COLPI'S, MILNGAVIE, GLASGOW: Opp Black Bull in Milngavie centre (pron Mullguy) and there since 1928. Many consider this to be Glas's finest. Only vanilla at the cone counter but strawb/choc flake/amaretto/honeycomb to take home. There's another branch in Clydebank. Till 9pm, 7 days.
1153
MAP 8
xC1

TORTOLANO'S, UDDINGSTON: 29 Main St. 15km E of city via M74, Uddingston t/off, at the lights where you turn for Bothwell Castle (1433/RUINS). Tiny confectioners/ice-cream shop with proper biscuit cones as an option and 5 flavours (try the 'double cream') all home made by Montecassino's Mr Tortolano. Their loss, definitely our weight gain.
1154
MAP 1
D3

NARDINI'S, LARGS: On the Esplanade. The debate about best ice cream continues and this, from the celebrated Nardini empire in particular (1098/CAFÉS.), but summer 1997 I had a pistachio and vanilla doublescoop on the esplanade one balmy evening as the boat came in from Cumbrae; all was well with the world. This ice cream was part of the magic.
1155
MAP 1
C3

DRUMUIR FARM, COLLIN, nr DUMFRIES: 5km off A75 (Carlisle/Annan) rd E of Dumfries on B724 (nr Clarencefield). A real farm producing real ice cream - 'the original' still the most popular (it's creamier than vanilla). Apr-Sept 12 -5.30pm. Cl Mon. W/ends only in winter.
1156
MAP 9
D3

CREAM O' GALLOWAY, RAINTON, nr GATEHOUSE OF FLEET: 01557 814040 A75 take Sandgreen exit 2km, then left at sign for Carrick. Originally a dairy farm producing cheese, now you can watch them making the creamy concoctions which you find all over in 'good shops' Nature trail and playground. Apr-Oct 11am-6pm.
1157
MAP 9
C4

CORVI'S, BO'NESS: Seaview Pl, opp car park with tourist info. Downhome fish 'n' chip shop that serves home-made vanilla or strawberry ice cream in premises that look like an extended version of someone's parlour. Eat in or take away - the fish supper is the local choice. Mon-Tues 11am-6.30pm, Thurs-Sat 11am-7.30pm.
1158
MAP 6
E4

CAPALDI'S, BRORA: Louis has retired but his legacy lives on! Drift away on a blue cloud and take away an ice cream cake. 7 days; 9.30am-9pm (Sun from 8am!).
1159
MAP 2
E2

BEN LEDI CAFÉ, CALLANDER: Main St (1106/CAFÉS).

THE REALLY GOOD DELIS

1160
MAP A
E1
♦ ♦ ♦ **VALVONA AND CROLLA, EDINBURGH:** 19 Elm Row, nr top of Leith Walk. Since 1934, an Edin institution, the shop you show visitors. Full of smells, genial, knowledgeable staff and a floor-to-ceiling range of cheese (Ital/Scot, etc.), meats, oils, wines and more. Fresh veg now trucked in from Milan markets, on-premises bakery, great caffe/bar (87/ITALIAN RESTAUS). Also demos, tastings, Fringe venue. Second to none.

1161
MAP A
xC4
B4
♦ **GOURMET PASTA, EDINBURGH:** 52 Morningside Rd and 32 Raeburn Pl. As the name suggests, these pasta kitchens/shops in the dense dinner-party zones of Stockbridge and Morningside sell mainly freshly-made pasta and various sauces, as good as (or better than) you can make yourself. Also tortes, tarts and roulades, sweet or savoury and by the slice. Your guests will never know. Cl Sun.

1162
MAP A
♦ **GLASS & THOMPSON, EDINBURGH:** 2 Dundas St. Important and contemporary New Town provisioner. Selective choice of Mediterranean – style goodies to eat or take away and bread/pâtisserie and dinner party essentials. Report: 175/TEAROOMS.

1163
MAP B
D2
♦ **FRATELLI SARTI, GLASGOW:** 113 Wellington St. The people who used to own Fazzi's (see below) re-create their Italian empire with a deli/tratt here and another eating place/wine shop in Bath St (441/ITALIAN RESTAUS). Feels like Italy.

1164
MAP 3
A2
♦ **FINDHORN COMMUNITY SHOP, FINDHORN:** Serving the new age township of the Findhorn Community and therefore pursuing a conscientious app, this has become an exemplary and v high quality deli, worth the detour from the A96 Inverness-Elgin rd even if you have apprehensions about their 'thing'. Packed and carefully selected shelves; as much for pleasurable eating as for healthy. You may wish this shop was nearer you. Till 6pm. (w/ends 5pm.) Cl Tue am.

1165
MAP B
D3
PECKHAM'S, CENTRAL STATION, GLASGOW: Best of several branches, most remarkable for its location in Glas's main station. From early train times to 11pm (midnight Fri/Sat, 10pm Sun), they've got everything you need from staples to fine wines and cheeses and a good range of up-market nibbles and quick meals.

1166
MAP A
C4
PECKHAM'S EDINBURGH branch – also nae half bad – is at 155 Bruntsfield Pl and opens to 12midnight daily.

FAZZI'S, GLASGOW: Main branch at 232 Clyde St and also 67 Cambridge St where there is a caff (441/ITALIAN RESTAUS).

1167
MAP B
B1
GRASSROOTS, GLASGOW: 48 Woodlands Rd, nr Charing Cross. First-class vegn food and provisions store, everything chemically unaltered and enviromentally-friendly. Gr breads and sandwiches for lunch and the best organic fruit/veg range in town. 7days till 6pm (7pm Thur, 3pm Sun).

1168
MAP 4
C4
ELLERY'S, PERTH: 2 Mill St, behind Marks & Spencer. Every county town should have a place like Ellery's, an antidote to the monotony of the modern High St. This is full of good things – not only the usual foody delights, but many home-cooked meats, pies, tortes, cakes, gr range of cheeses, esp Scottish. Innovative vegn, incl appetising loafs and tortes. Mon-Sat 9am-5.30pm.

1169
MAP 6
E3
NESBITS, DOLLAR: Main st of cosy town which nestles round its Academy and its glorious glen (1609/GLEN AND RIVER WALKS). Sort of town you'd expect a half-decent deli and this is it. Usual stuff mainly, but hot bread and cheese selection. Academy kids pig out on too much pocket money. Till 8pm.

1170
MAP 3
B2
GORDON AND MACPHAIL, ELGIN: South St. Purveyors of fine wines, cheeses, meats, Mediterranean goodies, unusual breads and other epicurean delights to the good burghers of Elgin for nigh on a century. Traditional shopkeeping, in the style of the 'family grocer', which will surely make a comeback as we weary of supermarkets. G & M are widely known as bottlers of lesser-known high-quality malts ('Connoisseurs' range) – on sale here. Mon-Sat 9am-5.15pm.

1171
MAP 7
D1
THE FOOD HAMPER, HADDINGTON: Town centre, nr clock tower. Formerly Gastronomes, now refurb-ed and under new management – but for locals and visitors, shopping here is still preferable to driving to Edin. Cl Sun.

1172
MAP 8
B2
THE OLIVE TREE, PEEBLES: 7 High St. Small emporium packed with wide selection of European groceries plus local delicacies: beer, honey, cheese *ad infinitum* – specialises in farmhouse and unpasteurised cheeses.

SCOTTISH CHEESES

MULL or TOBERMORY CHEDDAR: From Sgriob-Ruadh Farm (pron 'Skibrua'). **1173**
Comes in big 50lb cheeses and 1lb truckles. Good, strong cheddar, one of the v
best in the UK. The **INGLE SMOKEHOUSE** in Perth make a fine oak-smoked
cheddar. **LOCH ARTHUR** from Beeswing in Dumfries is a tangy organic cheddar.

DUNSYRE BLUE/LANARK BLUE: Made by Humphry Errington at Carnwath. Next **1174**
to Stilton, Dunsyre (made from the unpasteurised milk of Ayrshire cows) is the
best blue in the UK. It is soft, rather like Dolcelatte. Lanark, the original, is
Scotland's Roquefort and made from ewes' milk. Both can vary but are excellent.
Go on, live dangerously – unpasteurise.

BONCHESTER/TEVIOTDALE: From John Curtis at E Weems Farm in the Borders. **1175**
Bonchester is a Camembert-style cheese hand-made from Jersey milk, creamy-
rich with an orange tang. Teviotdale is firmer and has a fuller flavour.
STICHILL/KELSAE: Hand-made hard cheeses from Brenda Leddie near Kelso.
Rich, hard and crumbly cheeses, found only on the more informed cheese-
boards. My own favourites of the new Scottish cheeses.

CABOC/CROWDIE/GRUTH DHU: Widely available and established soft cheeses from **1176**
Highland Fine Cheeses in Tain (*see below*). Crowdie is traditional cottage or
crofters cheese, v basic; others made from double cream rolled in oatmeal/pepper.
Rich and delicious; usually avail in wee 'logs'.

CAIRNMORE: A hard, tangy, cheddary cheese from Sorbie in Wigtownshire **1177**
surprisingly made from ewes' milk, smoked or unsmoked.

And where to find them

All the delis mentioned will have good selections (esp Valvona's). Also:

✞ ✞ **IAIN MELLIS, EDINBURGH & GLASGOW:** 30A Victoria St & 205 Bruntsfield **1178**
Pl (Edin) and 492 Gr Western Rd (Glas). A real cheesemonger. Smell and MAP A
taste before you buy. Cheeses from all over the UK in prime condition. Daily and D3/C4
seasonal specials. Cl Sun. MAP B
B1

✞ ✞ **THE BIG CHEESE, ABERDEEN:** 22 Belmont St. Linda Davidson's rather fab **1179**
deli and cheese shop where v big cheeses from Scotland and the UK are MAP 3
piled up around you. New snacky bar with good crusty breads and fondues
opening after going to press, but will obviously be excellent. 9.30am-5.30pm
(later Thur). Cl Sun.

✞ **HERBIE, EDINBURGH:** 66 Raeburn Pl. Excellent selection. Clarissa Dickson- **1180**
Wright is a big fan. As usual she's right. As with Scottish cheeses, it's MAP A
practically impossible here to find a Brie or a blue in less than perfect condition. B1
All too moreish.

ISLAND CHEESES, ARRAN: 5km Brodick, rd to castle and Corrie. Excellent selection **1181**
of their own (the well-known cheddars but many others esp crowdie with garlic MAP 1
and hand-rolled cream cheeses) and others. See them being made. 7 days. C4

WEST HIGHLAND DAIRY, ACHMORE, nr PLOCKTON: 01599 577203. Excellent farm **1182**
dairy shop selling variety of their own cheeses from ewes'/goats'/cows' milk; MAP 2
yogurt, ice cream and cheesecakes. Open AYR 'dawn to dusk'. Signed from C3
village.

HIGHLAND FINE CHEESES, TAIN: 01862 892034. Follow signs off A9 for industrial **1183**
estate, nr Ferries Kitchens, adj to Burgess Plumbers, it's a white- chimneyed MAP 2
building (yes, it's difficult to find!). Open AYR Mon-Fri 9am-5pm. Caboc, D3
Crowdie, Galic. Yum!

PECKHAMS, GLASGOW: Other branches (incl Central Stn) at 100 Byres Rd and 43
Clarence Dr, and 155 Bruntsfield Pl, Edin.

JENNERS DEPARTMENT STORE, EDINBURGH: Princes St, top-floor food dept.

HOUSE OF BRUAR nr BLAIR ATHOLL: Roadside food, etc. emporium (1751/CRAFT
SHOPS).

PETER MACLENNAN, FORT WILLIAM: 28 High St.

SCOTTISH SPECIALITY FOOD, NORTH BALLACHULISH: By Leven Hotel.

WHISKY
The Best Distillery Tours

The process is basically the same in every distillery, but some are more atmospheric and some have more interesting tours, like these:

1184
MAP 1
A3
THE ISLAY MALTS: In one day you can visit several of Scotland's most impressive distilleries and sample infamous malts. The distilleries here look like distilleries ought to. **LAGAVULIN** (01496 302400) and **LAPHROAIG** (01496 302418) are both nr Pt Ellen. They offer fascinating tours, by appointment, where your guide will lay on the anecdotes as well as the process and you get a feel for the life and history as well as the product of these world-famous places. At Laphroaig you can join their 'Friend' scheme (free) and own a piece of their hallowed ground. **BUNNAHABHAIN** and **CAOL ILA** nr Pt Askaig, **BRUICHLADDICH** on rd to Pt Charlotte, will all show you around by arrangement too. **BOWMORE** has professional, more commercial, 1hr tours regularly (incl video show and the usual dram). All these distilleries are in settings that entirely justify the romantic hyperbole of their advertising. Worth seeing from the o/side as well as the floor.

1185
MAP 3
C2
STRATHISLA, KEITH: 01542 783044. The oldest working distillery in the Highlands, literally on the strath of the Isla river and methinks the most evocative atmos of all the Speyside distilleries. Recent refurb makes this an even classier halt. Used as the 'heart' of Chivas Regal, the malt not commonly available is still a fine dram. March-Nov, Mon-Sat 9.30am- 4pm; Sunday 12.30-4pm.

1186
MAP 2
B3
TALISKER, CARBOST, ISLE OF SKYE: From Sligachan-Dunvegan rd (A863) take B8009 for Carbost and Glen Brittle along the S side of L Harport for 5km. Skye's only distillery; since 1830 they've been making this classic after-dinner malt from barley and the burn that runs off the Hawkhill behind. A dram before the informative 40min tour. New visitor centre. No coach parties. Apr-Oct 9am-4.30pm (winter 2-4.30pm). Cl w/ends. Gr gifts nearby (1749/CRAFT SHOPS).

1187
MAP 7
D2
GLENKINCHIE, PENCAITLAND, nr EDINBURGH: 01875 342004. Only 25km from city centre (via A68 and A6093 before Pathhead), so popular. Founded in 1837 in a peaceful, pastoral place (it's 3km from the village) with its own bowling green; a country trip as well as a whisky tour. They have occasional 'silent seasons', so check since all you'd see then is a video. New visitor centre opened Dec 1996. May-Sep tours daily until 4pm, Oct-Mar Mon-Fri until 4pm.

1188
MAP 4
C2
EDRADOUR, nr PITLOCHRY: Claims to be the smallest distillery in Scotland, producing single malts for blends since 1825 and limited quantities of the Edradour (since 1986) as well as the House of Lords' own brand. Guided tour of charming cottage complex every 20min. 4km from Pitlochry off Kirkmichael rd, A924; signed after Moulin village. Feb-Nov 10.30-4pm.

1189
MAP 4
B4
GLENTURRET, nr CRIEFF: 2km from town off A85 to Comrie. A village has almost been built around this quaint distillery, the oldest in Scotland (1775) with award-winning visitor centre. Continuous tours, restau and shop with superior range of branded products and exemplary marketing. Self-service and waitress restau. The whisky itself has a smoky, roasted aroma; it's superb in its older bottlings, e.g. 1967-72. Open AYR Mon-Sat 9.30am-4.30pm, and Sun from noon. Jan-Feb, Mon-Fri 11.30am-2.30pm.

1190
HIGHLAND PARK, KIRKWALL, ORKNEY: 2km from town on main A961 rd S to S Ronaldsay. The whisky is great and the tour one of the best. The most northerly whisky in a class and a bottle of its own. You walk through the floor maltings and you can touch the warm barley and fair smell the peat. Good combination of the industrial and trad Mar-Dec w/days (2-3.30pm only in winter).

THE BEST OF THE SPEYSIDE WHISKY TRAIL: *Well signposted but bewildering number of tours, though by no means at every distillery. Many are in rather featureless industrial complexes and settings. These are the best along with Strathisla (see above):*

1191
MAP 3
B3
THE GLENLIVET, MINMORE: 01542 783220. Starting as an illicit dram celebrated as far S as Edin, George Smith licensed the brand in 1824 and founded this distillery in 1858, registering the already mighty name so that anyone else had to use a prefix. After various successions and mergers, independence was lost in 1978 when Seagrams took over. The famous Josie's Well, from which the water springs, is underground and not shown, but small parties and a walk-through which is not on a gantry make the tour as satisfying and as popular, esp with Americans, as the

product. Excellent new reception centre with bar/restau and shop. Apr-Oct, 10am-4pm; till 6pm July/Aug. Sundays 12.30-4pm.

GLENFIDDICH, DUFFTOWN: O/side town on the A941 to Craigellachie by the ruins of Balvenie Castle. Well-oiled tourist operation and the only distillery where you can see the whisky bottled on the premises; indeed, the whole process from barley to bar. Also the only major distillery that's free (incl dram). AYR 9.30am-4.30pm not w/ends in winter. On the same rd there's a chance to see a whisky-related industry/craft that hasn't changed in decades. The **SPEYSIDE COOPERAGE** is 1km from Craigellachie. You watch those poor guys from the gantry (no chance to slack). 9.30am-4.30pm.

1192
MAP 3
B2

GLEN GRANT, ROTHES: In Rothes on the A941 Elgin to Perth rd. A distillery tour with an added attraction viz the grds and orchard reconstructed around the shallow bowl of the glen of the burn that runs through the distillery. Tour vouchers can be used there to take a dram in the delightful Dram Pavilion. Apr-Oct 10-4pm (till 5pm June-Sept), from 11.30pm on Sun.

1193
MAP 3
B2

CARDHU, CARRON: Off B9102 from Craigellachie to Grantown through deepest Speyside, a small is charming distillery with its own community, a millpond, picnic tables, etc. Owned by United Distillers, Cardhu is the 'heart of Johnny Walker' (which, amazingly, has another 30 malts in it). 9.30am-4.30pm, winter 11-4pm Sat/Sun only.

1194
MAP 3
B2

DALLAS DHU, nr FORRES: Not really nr the Spey (3km S of Forres on B9010) and no longer a working distillery (ceased 1983), but instant history provided by HS and you don't have to go round on a tour. The wax workers are a bit spooky; the product itself is more life-like. Cl Thu afternoons/Fri in winter.

1195
MAP 3
A2
HS

Where to Find the Best Selection of Malts

GLASGOW

THE CASK AND STILL: 154 Hope St.

THE BON ACCORD: 153 North St.

EDINBURGH

BENNETS: 8 Leven St by Kings Theatre.

KAYS BAR: 39 Jamaica St.

THE BOW BAR: 80 West Bow.

CADENHEADS: 172 Canongate. The shop with the lot.

CANNY MAN'S: 237 Morningside Rd.

SCOTCH MALT WHISKY SOCIETY: The Vaults, 87 Giles St, Leith. Your search will end here. More a club (with membership) but visitors welcome.

THE BORESTONE BAR, STIRLING: St Ninians, Bannockburn rd 2km from centre. Staggering range of malts in truly authentic bar on a r/bout o/side Stirling. Even if few folk seem to drink them here, this v typical Scottish pub should be a must on any whisky trail or (if I've got anything to do with it) Whisky Festival.

LOCHSIDE HOTEL, BOWMORE, ISLAY: More Islay malts than you ever imagined in friendly local near the distillery. Malt whisky w/ends.

ARISAIG HOTEL, ARISAIG, nr MALLAIG: On the seafront. Small, civilised lounge and busy local. 100 malts move betw the bars.

KNOCKINAAM LODGE, PORTPATRICK: Comfortable country-house hotel; esp good lowland selection incl the (extinct) local Bladnoch (666/SW HOTELS).

CROMLIX HOUSE HOTEL, DUNBLANE: Excl and not overly expensive whisky list after dinner in civilised setting (681/CENTRAL HOTELS).

SETTLE INN, STIRLING: Carefully selected shelf of malts that almost exactly matches the list I have recommended. Several Balvenies for example (1016/BLOODY GOOD PUBS).

OBAN INN, OBAN: Good mix of customers, whisky and ale.

FISHERMAN'S TAVERN, BROUGHTY FERRY: (899/DUNDEE EAT AND DRINK).

LOCK INN, FORT AUGUSTUS: Canalside setting, good food and plenty whisky.

CLACHAIG INN, GLENCOE: Over 100 malts to go with the range of ales and the range of folk that come here to drink after the hills (1008/ BLOODY GOOD PUBS).

THE DROVER'S INN, INVERARNAN: Same as above, with over 100 to choose from and the rt atmos to drink them in (1003/BLOODY GOOOD PUBS).

DUNAIN PARK HOTEL, INVERNESS: After dinner in one of the best places to eat hereabouts, there's a serious malts list to mull over (785/HIGHLAND HOTELS).

THE BAR AT THE CRAIGELLACHIE HOTEL: Whiskies arranged around the cosy bar of this essential Speyside hotel and the river below (758/NE HOTELS).

ROYAL HOTEL, KINGUSSIE: Main st of small town S of Aviemore. Gr local (1021/REAL ALE) and astonishing range of whiskies.

HOTEL EILEAN IARMAIN, SKYE: Also known as the Isleornsay Hotel (1905/ISLAND HOTELS); not the biggest range but one of the best places to drink (it).

LOCH FYNE WHISKIES, INVERARAY: Beyond the church on the A83 a shop with 400 malts to choose from in various sizes and disguises; and whisky ware.

SLIGACHAN HOTEL, SKYE: 01478 650204. On A87 (A850) 11km S of Portree. 81 malts in Seamus' huge cabin bar. Good real-ale selection; mid-Apr, Sept festivals. Adj bunkhouse, shop, laundry, mt exhibition due for 1998.

GORDON & MACPHAIL, ELGIN: *The* whisky provisioner and bottlers of the Connoisseurs brand you see in other shops and bars all over. From these humble beginnings over 100yrs ago, they now supply their exclusive and rarity range to the world. 9am-5.15pm. Cl Sun.

THE WHISKY SHOP, DUFFTOWN: The whisky shop in the main st (by the clock-tower) at the heart of whisky country. Within a few miles of numerous distilleries and their sales operations, this place stocks all the product (incl many halfs). Apr-Oct 10am-9pm, Sun afternoons.

CAIRNGORM WHISKY CENTRE, INVERDRUIE, nr AVIEMORE: On main rd from Aviemore, nr Coylumbridge and adj Rothiemurcus Vistor Centre. Whisky emporium with over 500 for sale. Tasting rm (most afternoons). Open 7 days.

The Best Malts and When to Drink Them

Obviously, opinions vary. The following list is compiled from the consensus of several whisky buffs and 'authorities', and God knows there are plenty of them. Vintages make a discernible difference to the connoisseur; the whiskies here are fine in any of their readily available forms.

BEFORE DINNER

Bruichladdich	ISLAY	(pron 'Brew ich laddie')
Caol Ila	ISLAY	(pron 'Coal eela')
Glenmorangie	SPEYSIDE	
Tomintoul-Glenlivet	SPEYSIDE	

AFTER DINNER

Aberlour	SPEYSIDE	
Ardbeg	ISLAY	
Bowmore	ISLAY	
Bunnahabhain	ISLAY	(pron 'Bun a havan')
Glenfarclas	SPEYSIDE	
Highland Park	ORKNEY	
Lagavulin	ISLAY	(pron 'Laga voolin')
Laphroaig	ISLAY	(pron 'La froig')
Talisker	SKYE	
Tamdhu	SPEYSIDE	(pron 'Tam do')

ANYTIME

Balvenie	SPEYSIDE
Cragganmore	SPEYSIDE
Glenfiddich	SPEYSIDE
Glenkinchie	LOWLAND
Glenlivet	SPEYSIDE
Linkwood	SPEYSIDE
Macallan	SPEYSIDE
Springbank	CAMPBELTOWN

SECTION 6

Outdoor Places

THE BEST GARDENS

1196
MAP 1
C7
✚ ✚ **THE YOUNGER BOTANIC GARDEN, BENMORE:** 12km Dunoon on the A815 to Strachur. An 'outstation' of the Royal Botanic in Edin, gifted to the nation by Harry the Younger in 1928, but the first plantations dating from 1820. Walks clearly marked through formal grds, woody grounds and the 'pinetum' where the air is often so sweet and spicy it can seem like the v elixir of life. Redwood avenue, terraced hill sides, views; a grd of different moods and fine proportions. Café. Apr-Oct 10-6pm. ADMN

1197
MAP 1
C2
✚ ✚ **CRARAE, INVERARAY:** 16km SE on A83 to Lochgilphead. The famous grds on the wooded banks of L Fyne were lanscaped long ago around the gushing glen, and now seem as vast and lush as Borneo. 3 routes are marked (easiest takes 45mins). Riotous rhodies in May, gigantic hogweed in August and arbour after arbour in every season. Open AYR. Summer 9am-6pm, winter daylight hrs. ADMN

1198
MAP 2
C2
✚ ✚ **INVEREWE, POOLEWE:** on A832, 80km S of Ullapool. The world-famous grds on a promontory of L Ewe. First started in 1862, Osgood Mackenzie made it his life's work in 1883 and it continues with large crowds coming to admire his efforts. Helped by the ameliorating effect of the Gulf Stream, the 'wild' grd became the model for many others. The guided tours (1.30pm Mon-Fri) are probably the best way to get the most out of this extensive gdn. No 'keep off the grass' signs but you feel you should anyway. Open AYR. ADMN

1199
MAP 3
D4
✚ ✚ **CRATHES, nr BANCHORY, ROYAL DEESIDE:** 25km W of Aber and just off A93. One of the most interesting tower houses (1477/COUNTRY HOUSES) surrounded by exceptional topiary and walled grds of inspired design and tranquil atmos. Keen gardeners will be in their scented heaven. The Golden Garden (after Gertrude Jekyll) works particularly well and there's a wild grd beyond the old wall that many people miss. All in all, a v *House and Garden* experience. Grounds open AYR 9am-sunset. NTS   ADMN

1200
MAP 4
B4
✚ ✚ **DRUMMOND CASTLE GARDENS, MUTHILL, nr CRIEFF:** Signed from A822, 2km from Muthill and then up a long avenue, the most exquisite formal grds viewed first from the terrace by the house. A boxwood parterre of a vast St Andrew's Cross in yellow and red (esp antirrhinums and roses), the Drummond colours, with extraordinary sundial centrepiece; 5 gardeners keep every leaf in place. These are the grds in the *Rob Roy* movie – didn't they look gr at night? 7 days May-Oct 2-5pm. House not open to the public. ADMN

1201
MAP 8
A2
✚ **DAWYCK, STOBO, nr PEEBLES:** On B712 Moffat rd off the A72 Biggar rd from Peebles, 2km from Stobo. Another outstation of the Edin Botanics; a 'recent' acquisition, though tree planting here goes back 300 yrs. Sloping grounds around the gurgling Scrape burn which trickles into the Tweed. Landscaped woody pathways for meditative walks. Famous for shrubs and blue Himalayan poppies. The chapel is closed. Mar-Oct 10am-6pm. ADMN

1202
MAP 1
C1
✚ **ANGUS' GARDEN, TAYNUILT:** 7km from village (which is 12km from Oban on the A85) along the Glen Lonan rd. Take first rt after Barguillen Grd Centre. A grd laid out by the family who own the centre in memory of their son Angus, a soldier, who was killed in Cyprus. On the slopes around a small loch brimful of lilies and ducks. An informal mix of the tended and the uncultivated, a more poignant remembrance is hard to imagine as you while an hr away in this peaceful place. Open AYR. HONESTY BOX

1203
MAP 1
C2
✚ **ARDUAINE GARDEN, nr KIMELFORD:** 28km S of Oban on A816, one of Argyll's undiscovered arcadias recently gifted to the NTS and brought to wider attention. Creation of the microclimate in which the rich, diverse vegetation has flourished, influenced by Osgood Mackenzie of Inverewe and its restoration a testimony to 20yrs hard labour by the Wright brothers. Let's hope that the ongoing wrangle betw the surviving Wright brother and the NTS might be resolved. Enter/park by L Melfort hotel, gate 100m. Until dusk.

1204
MAP 1
B3
ACHAMORE GARDENS, ISLE OF GIGHA: 1km from ferry. Walk or cycle from ferry (bike hire at post office at top of ferry rd); an easy day trip. The 'big house' on the island set in 65 acres. Lush tropical plants mingle with rhodies that flourish early (Feb-March): all due to the mild climate and head gardener Malcolm McNeill's devotion. 2 marked walks (40mins/2hrs) start from the walled gdn (green route

takes in the sea view of Islay and Jura). The sheer density and variety of shrubs, pond plants and trees is revealed as you meander around this enchanting spot. Leaflet guides in jam jar at entrance. Open AYR. (1898/MAGICAL ISLANDS.) ADMN

LOGAN BOTANICAL GARDENS, nr SANDHEAD, S of STRANRAER: 16km S of Stranraer by A77/A716 and 2km on from Sandhead. Remarkable outstation of the Edin Botanics amongst sheltering woodland in the mild SW. Compact and full of pleasant surprises. Less crowded than other 'exotic' grds. The Gunnera Bog is quite extraterrestrial. Mar-Oct; 7 days, 10am-6pm. ADMN

1205
MAP 9
A4

PRIORWOOD, MELROSE: Next to Melrose Abbey, a tranquil secret grd behind high walls which specialises in growing flowers and plants for drying. Picking, drying and arranging is continuously in progress. Samples for sale. Run by enthusiasts on behalf of the NTS, they're always willing to talk stamens with you. Also includes an historical apple orchard with trees through the ages. Heavenly jelly on sale. Mon-Sat 10am-5.30pm; Sun 1-5.30pm. NTS ADMN

1206
MAP 8
C3

KAILZIE GARDENS, PEEBLES: On B7062 Traquair rd. Informal woodland grds just out of town; not extensive but eminently strollable. Old-fashioned roses and wilder bits. Some poor birds in cages and the odd peacock. Excellent courtyard teashop (1108/TEAROOMS). Kids' corner. Apr-Oct. ADMN

1207
MAP 8
B2

PITMEDDEN GARDEN, nr ELLON: 35km N of Aber and 10km W of the main A92. Formal French grds recreated in 1950s on site of Sir Alex Seaton's 17th-century ones. The 4 gr parterres, 3 based on designs for grds at Holyrood Palace, are best viewed from the terrace. Charming farmhouse 'museum' has also been somewhat transplanted. For lovers of symmetry and an orderly universe only. May-Sept 10am-5.30pm. NTS ADMN

1208
MAP 3
D3

CANDACRAIG GARDENS, STRATHDON: On A944 from Kildrummy to Alford which follows the Don through deep Aberdeenshire. A private walled cottage grd and secret world in the wild country. Gallery has changing exhibits on a horticultural theme. A nice place to while away an afternoon (and 2 cottages for accom if you want to stay longer). May-Sept 10am-5pm, Sun 2-6pm.

1209
MAP 3
B3

PITTODRIE HOUSE nr INVERURIE: An exceptional walled grd in the grounds of Pittodrie House Hotel at Chapel of Garioch in Aberdeenshire (755/NE HOTELS). 500m from house and largely unvisited by most of the guests, this secret and sheltered haven is both a kitchen grd and a place for meditations and reflections (and possibly wedding photos).

1210
MAP 3
D7

ARDKINGLAS WOODLAND, CAIRNDOW: Off the A83 L Lomond to Inveraray rd. Through village to signed car park and these mature woodlands in the grounds of Ardkinglas House on the southern bank nr the head of L Fyne. Fine pines include the 'tallest tree in Britain'. Magical at dawn or dusk. HONESTY BOX

1211
MAP 1
C2

DAMSIDE GARDEN, nr LAURENCEKIRK, S of STONEHAVEN: Signed off A92 15km N Montrose and 5km from rd. Also off A94 N of Laurencekirk; take Johnshaven t/off (also 5km). A herb grd on an ambitious and expanding scale, and a pinetum (acres) of mixed native and exotic species. A private botanical dream grd laid out as a series of themed 'rooms' e.g. Roman/ Egyptian/Celtic/Monastic/a camomile lawn etc. Mar-Dec 10am-5pm. Self-service restau. ADMN

1212
MAP 3
D5

There's another place specialising in herbs at **BRIN SCHOOL FIELDS** at Flichity S of Inverness (1790/GARDEN CENTRES).

THE HYDROPONICUM, ACHILTIBUIE: The 'Garden of the Future'; a weird indoor waterworld. Geraniums cluster round the pond by the café and other plants thrive in the microclimates. Apr-Sep. Tours: 10am/noon/2pm/5pm. Growing kits to buy; so you can have strawberries at Christmas. ADMN

1213
MAP 2
C2

ROYAL BOTANIC GARDEN, EDINBURGH: 312/OTHER ATTRACTIONS.

BOTANIC GARDEN AND KIBBLE PALACE, GLASGOW: 585/OTHER ATTRACTIONS.

THE BEST COUNTRY PARKS

1214 ✚ **DRUMLANRIG CASTLE, THORNHILL, nr DUMFRIES:** 01848 330248. On A76, 7km
MAP 9 N of Thornhill in the W Borders in whose romance and history it's steeped,
C2 much more than merely a country park, but included here because it's the sort of
place you could spend a good day, both inside the castle and in the grounds.
Apart from the art collection (Rembrandts, Leonardos, Holbeins) and the Craft
Courtyard (1762/CRAFT SHOPS), the outdoor delights include: woodland and
riverside walks, an adventure playground, the Falconry with flying
demonstrations (1pm/3pm, not Thu) and bike hire for further afield explorations
along the Nith etc. Open May-Aug; Mon-Sun 11am-4.15pm. Cl Thu.

1215 ✚ **MUIRSHEIL, nr LOCHWINNOCH:** Via Largs (A760) or Glas (M8, jnct 29 A737
MAP 1 then A760 5km S of Johnstone). N from village on Kilmacolm rd for 3km
C3 then signed. Muirshiel is name given to wider area, but park proper begins 6km
on rd along the Calder valley. Despite proximity of conurbation (Pt Glas is over
the hill), this is a wild and enchanting place for walking/picnics etc. Trails marked
to waterfall and summit views. Escape! (380/CAMPING.)

1216 **MUGDOCK COUNTRY PARK, nr MILNGAVIE:** Another marvellous park v close to
MAP 1 Glas reached by train to Milngavie then bus, or by car to either of 3 car parks
D3 around the vast site. Highly recommended. *For more info and directions, see*
597/CITY WALKS.

1217 **JOHN MUIR COUNTRY PARK, nr DUNBAR, EAST LOTHIAN:** Named after the 19th-
MAP 7 century conservationist who founded America's National Parks (and the Sierra
D3 Club) and who was born in Dunbar. This swathe of coastline to the W of the
town (known locally as Tyninghame) is an important estuarine nature reserve but
is good for family walks and beachcombing. Can enter via B6370 off A198 to N
Berwick or by 'cliff-top' trail from Dunbar (1399/WILDLIFE).

1218 **STRATHCLYDE PARK, between HAMILTON and MOTHERWELL:** 15km SE of Glas. Take
MAP 1 M8/A725 interchange or M74/jnct 5 or 6. Scotland's most popular country park,
E3 esp for water sports on the 'man-made' lake. Everything from canoeing to
parascending and you can hire all the gear there (1715/WATER SPORTS). Also;
excavated Roman bath house, playgrounds, sports pitches and now that the trees
are beginning to mature, some pleasant walks too. Nearby Baron's Haugh
(1391/BIRDS) and Dalzell Country Park more notable for their nature trails and
grds. (379/CAMPING; 1482/MONUMENTS.)

1219 **FINLAYSTONE ESTATE, LANGBANK nr GREENOCK:** A8 to Greenock, past Langbank,
MAP 1 then signed. Grand mansion home to Chief of Clan Macmillan set in formal grds
C3 in wooded estate. Leafy walks, walled grd. Rare magic.

1220 **ALMONDELL, nr EAST CALDER:** 12km from Edin city bypass. Well-managed park
MAP 7 in the valley of the R Almond set amidst an area of redundant industrial sprawl.
B2 If you've just spent light yrs trying to exit from Livingston's notorious rd system,
you'll need this green oasis with its walks through woods, meadows and along
cinder tracks. Picnic sites, visitor centre with refreshments, kids' areas and river
meadows. A71 from bypass (Kilmarnock), then B7015 (Camp) for 7km. Park on
rt just into E Calder village. Walk ahead into woods, not to rt.

1221 **MUIRAVONSIDE COUNTRY PARK:** 5km W of Linlithgow on B825. Also signposted
MAP 7 from J4 of the M9 Edin/Stirling. Former farm estate now run by the local
A1 authority providing 170 acres of woodland walks, parkland, picnic sites and a
visitor centre for school parties or anyone else with an interest in birds, bees and
badgers. Ranger service does guided walks Apr-Sep. Gr place to walk off that
lunch at the not-too-distant Champany Inn (152/BURGERS).

1222 **EGLINTON nr IRVINE:** Beside main A78 Largs to Ayr rd signed from
MAP 1 Irvine/Kilwinning intersection. Spacious lungful of Ayrshire nr new town nexus
C4 and traffic tribulations. Visitor centre with interpretation of absolutely
everything; network of walks. Not much left of the house. A factory makes
'ambient foods'. All a bit of a construct, but some parts are peaceful.

TENTSMUIR, nr TAYPORT: Estuarine park like John Muir, on Tay (1399/WILDLIFE).

ADEN, MINTLAW, nr PETERHEAD: 1369/KIDS.

HADDO HOUSE, ABERDEENSHIRE: Beautiful grounds and walks (1466/CO HOUSES).

KELBURNE COUNTRY CENTRE, LARGS: 1359/KIDS.

THE BEST TOWN PARKS

✝ ✝ **PRINCES ST GARDENS, EDINBURGH:** S side of Princes St. The greenery that launched a thousand postcards - millions probably - it's Edin. This former loch - drained around the time the New Town was built - is divided by the Mound. The eastern half has pitch and putt and the Scott Monument (331/BEST VIEWS), the western has its much-photographed fountain, open-air café and space for locals and tourists to sprawl on the grass when sunny. You'll also find the the Ross Bandstand here - heart of Edinburgh's Hogmanay (1989/ANNUAL EVENTS) and the International Festival's gobsmacking fireworks concert (1982/ANNUAL EVENTS). Louts with lager, senior citz on benches, Italian teens with daft wee rucksacks - all our lives are here. Till dusk.
1223
MAP A
C3

✝ ✝ **HAZELHEAD PARK, ABERDEEN:** Via Queens Rd, 3km centre. Extraordinary park where the mysterious gardening skills of the Aberdonians are magnificently in evidence. Many facs incl a maze, mini-zoo, wonderful tacky tearoom and there are lawns, memorials and botanical splendours aplenty esp azalea garden in spring and roses in summer. Gr sculpture (a leaflet describes).
1224
MAP 3
D3

✝ **DUTHIE PARK, ABERDEEN:** Riverside Dr along R Dee from the br carrying main A92 rd from/to Stonehaven. The other large well-kept park with duck pond, bandstand, hugely impressive rose grds in summer, carved sculptures and the famous, though now somewhat shabby Winter Grd of subtropical palms/ferns etc (10am-almost dusk).
1225
MAP 3
D3

✝ **PITTENCRIEFF PARK, DUNFERMLINE:** The extensive park alongside the Abbey and Palace ruins gifted to the town in 1903 by Carnegie. Open areas, glasshouses, pavilion (more a function rm) but most notably a deep verdant glen criss-crossed with pathways. Lush, full of birds, good after rain.
1226
MAP 5
B2

BEVERIDGE PARK, KIRKCALDY: Also in Fife, another big municipal park with a duck and boat pond, wide-open spaces and many amusements (e.g. bowling, tennis, putting, paddling). **RAVENSCRAIG** a coastal park on the main rd E to Dysart is an excellent place to walk. Gr prospect of town and Firth, coves and skerries.
1227
MAP 5
C4

WILTON LODGE PARK, HAWICK: Hawick is perhaps not overfull of visitor attractions, but it does have a pretty nice park with facs and diversions enough for everyone e.g. the civic gallery, rugby pitches (they quite like rugby in Hawick), a large kids' playground, a café and lots of riverside walks by the Teviot. Lots of my school friends lost their virginity in this park (yes Mr Angry who wrote, I can say that). All-round open-air recreation centre. S end of town by A7.
1228
MAP 8
C3

ROUKEN GLEN AND LINN PARK, GLASGOW: Both on S side of river. Rouken Glen via Pollokshaws/Kilmarnock rd to Eastwood Toll then rt. Good place to park is second left, Davieland Rd beside pond. Across park from here (or beside main Rouken Glen rd) is main visitor area with grd centre, a Chinese restau and 'Butterfly Kingdom'. Linn Park via Aikenhead and Carmunock rd. After Kings Park on left, take rt to Simshill Rd and park at golf course beyond houses. A long route there, but worth it; this is one of the undiscovered Elysiums of a city which boasts 60 parks. Ranger Centre.
1229
MAP B
xC4

VICTORIA PARK, GLASGOW: Just N of the Clyde at Whiteinch on the Clydeside Expressway, another of Glasgow's lesser-known but notable parks. In its SW corner there's a surprising gem of a rock grd enclosing a fossil grove, Glasgow's 'oldest attraction': 300 million-yr-old tree trunks (or so they reckon) discovered during excavations of the walkways. Pavilion open every day. Cl noon-1pm and dusk in winter.
1230
MAP B
A2

CAMPERDOWN PARK, DUNDEE: Calling itself a country park, Camperdown is the main recreational breathing space for the city and hosts a plethora of distractions (a golf course, a wildlife complex, mansion house etc). Situated beyond Kingsway, the ring-route; go via Coupar Angus rd t/off. Best walks across the A923 in the Templeton Woods.
1231
MAP 4
D3

GRANT PARK, FORRES: Forres, is a frequent winner of the Bonny Bloom competitions. Grant Park, with its balance of ornamental grds, open parkland and woody hill side, is the carefully tended rose in its crown. Good municipal facs like pitch and putt, playground. Cricket in summer and topping topiary. Through woods at top of Cluny Hill, a tower affords gr views of the Moray and Cromarty Firths and surrounding forest from which the town takes its name.
1232
MAP 3
A2

THE MOST INTERESTING
COASTAL VILLAGES

1233 ✠ **PLOCKTON, nr KYLE OF LOCHALSH:** A Highland gem of a place 8km over the
MAP 2 ⊤ hill from Kyle, clustered around inlets of a wooded bay on L Carron.
C3 Cottage grds down to the bay and palm trees! Some gr walks (1639/COASTAL
WALKS). Haven Hotel (01599 544233) is best place to eat. Plockton Hotel (CHP,
pub grub) or Creag nan Darach (INX, 01599 544 222) beside the Haven are both
fine and it's not hard to feel connected with the village. (1757/CRAFT SHOPS.)
Hamish was here.

1234 ✠ **STROMNESS, ORKNEY MAINLAND:** 24km from Kirkwall and a different
⊤ kettleof fish. Hugging the shore and with narrow streets and wynds, it has
a unique atmos, both maritime and European. Some of the most singular shops
you'll see anywhere and the Orkney folk going about their business. Park nr
harbour and walk down the cobbled main st if you don't want to scrape your
paintwork (1938/ORKNEY; 1837/GALLERIES).

1235 ✠ **CROMARTY, nr INVERNESS:** At end of rd across Black Isle from Inverness
MAP 2 ⊤ (45km NE), but worth the trip. Village with dreamy times-gone-by atmos,
D3 without being twee. Lots of kids running about and a pink strand of beach.
Delights to discover include: the kirk, plain and aesthetic with countryside
through the windows behind the altar; Hugh (the geologist) Miller's
house/museum; Binnie's (1125/TEAROOMS); the shore and cliff walk
(1644/COASTAL WALKS) and of course the dolphins (1395/DOLPHINS). Royal Hotel
is inexp and good (809/INEXP HIGHLAND HOTELS).

1236 **CULROSS, nr DUNFERMLINE:** By A994 from Dunfermline or jnct 1 of M90 just over
MAP 5 Forth Rd Br (15km). Old centre conserved and being restored by NTS. Mainly
A4 residential and not awash with craft and coffee shops. More historical than merely
quaint; a community of careful custodians lives in the white, red-pantiled houses.
Footsteps echo in the cobbled wynds. Palace and Town House open Easter-Sept,
11-5pm. Pamphlet by Rights of Way Society available locally, is useful.

1237 **TOBERMORY, MULL:** Not so much a village, rather the main town of Mull, set
MAP 1 around a hill on superb Tobermory Bay. Ferry pt for Ardnamurchan, but main
B1 Oban ferry is 35km away at Craignure. Usually a bustling harbour front with
quieter streets behind; a quintessential island atmos. Some good inexp hotels (and
quayside hostel) well situated to explore the whole island. (1937/MULL;
1908/ISLAND HOTELS; 938/BEST HOSTELS.)

1238 **PORT CHARLOTTE, ISLAY:** A township on the 'Rinns of Islay', the western
MAP 1 peninsula. By A846 from the pts, Askaig and Ellen via Bridgend. Rows of
A3 whitewashed, well-kept cottages along and back from shoreline. On rd in, there's
a creamery, an island museum and a coffee/bookshop. Also a 'town' beach and
one between PC and Bruichladdich (and esp the one with the war memorial
nearby). Quiet and charming not quaint. (1934/ISLAY; 1916/ISLAND HOTELS)

1239 **ROCKCLIFFE, nr DUMFRIES:** 25km S on Solway Coast rd, A710. On the 'Scottish
MAP 9 Riviera', the rocky part of the coast around to Kippford (1640/COASTAL WALKS).
D4 A good rock-scrambling foreshore and a village with few houses and Baron's
Craig hotel; set back with gr views. Good pub at Kippford (1053/BEST FOOD).

1240 **EAST NEUK VILLAGES:** The quintessential quaint wee fishing villages along the bit
MAP 5 of Fife that forms the mouth of the Firth of Forth, **CRAIL, ANSTRUTHER,**
D3/ **PITTENWEEM, ST MONANCE** and **ELIE** all have different characters and attractions
E3 esp Crail's harbour, Anstruther as main centre and home of Fisheries Museum
(*see also* 1904/FISH AND CHIPS; 726/FIFE HOTELS; 1383/BIRDS) and perfect Elie
(1731/WINDSURFING; 725/FIFE HOTELS; 1044/BEST FOOD; 1661/GREAT GOLF). Or
See St Andrews p. 271. Cycling good, traffic in summer not.

1241 **ABERDOUR:** Betw Dunfermline and Kirkcaldy and nr Forth Rd Br (10km E from
MAP 5 jnct 1 of M90) or, better still, go by train from Edin (frequent service: Dundee or
B4 Kirkcaldy); before Railtrack it used to win the 'best-kept station' award. Walks
round harbour and to headland, Silver Sands beach 1km, castle ruins.
(1502/CHURCHES; 728/ FIFE HOTELS.)

1242 **MORAY COAST FISHING VILLAGES:** From Speybay (where the Spey slips into the
MAP 3 sea) along to Fraserburgh, some of Scotland's best coastal scenery and many
C1/D1 interesting villages in cliff/cove and beach settings. Esp notable are **PORTSOY** with

17th-century harbour (1706/SWIMMING POOLS); **SANDEND** with its own popular beach and a fabulous one nearby (1243/BEACHES); **PENNAN** made famous by the film *Local Hero* (the hotel/pub is cosy and cheap: 01346 561201); **GARDENSTOWN** with a walk along the water's edge to **CROVIE** (pron 'Crivee') the epitome of a coast-clinging community; and **CULLEN,** which is more of a town and has a gr beach. (769/N E HOTELS.)

DIABEG, WESTER ROSS: On N shore of L Torridon at the end of the unclassified rd from Torridon on one of Scotland's most inaccessible peninsulas. Diabeg (pron 'Jee-a-beg') is simply beautiful. Fantastic rd there and then walk!
1243
MAP 2
C3

DUNURE, AYR: 15km S of Ayr on A719, the coast rd past the Heads of Ayr (cliff walks) 10km from Culzean (1409/CASTLES). Only a few cottages, a pub, an old harbour and the dramatic ruins of Dunure Castle, once the scene of horrific tortures, now a kids' playground.
1244
MAP 1
C4

ISLE OF WHITHORN: Strange faraway village at end of the rd, 35km S Newton Stewart, 6km Whithorn (1459/PREHISTORIC SITES). Mystical harbour where low tide does mean low, saintly shoreline, a sea angler's pub (Steam Packet) and McWilliams' amazing leaning stores. Ninian's chapel less uplifting, but you can see why he landed.
1245
MAP 9
B4

CORRIE, ARRAN: Last but not least, the bonniest bit of Arran, best reached by bike from Brodick (1933/ARRAN). I'd like a memorial bench on that shoreline.
1246
MAP 1
C3

FANTASTIC BEACHES AND BAYS

✝ ✝ **KILORAN BEACH, COLONSAY:** 9km from quay and hotel, past Colonsay House: parking and access on hill side. Described as the finest beach in the Hebrides, it does not disappoint, even in the rain. Craggy cliffs on one side, negotiable rocks on the other and, in betw, tiers of grassy dunes. The island of Colonsay was once bought as a picnic spot. This beach was probably the reason why.
1247
MAP 1
A2

✝ ✝ **MACHRIHANISH:** At the bottom of the Kintyre peninsula 10km from Campbeltown. Walk N from Machrihanish village, or from the car park on the main A83 to Tayinloan and Tarbert at pt where it hits/leaves the coast. A joyously long strand (8km) of unspoiled orange-pink sand backed by dunes and facing the 'steepe Atlantic Stream' all the way to Newfoundland (1667/GOLF IN GREAT PLACES).
1248
MAP 1
B4

✝ ✝ **SANDWOOD BAY, KINLOCHBERVIE:** This mile-long sandy strand with its old 'Stack', is legendary, but therein lies the problem since now too many people know about it and you may have to share in its glorious isolation. Inaccessibility is its saving grace, a 7km walk from the sign off the rd at Balchrick (nr the cattle grid), 6km from Kinlochbervie; allow 3hrs return plus time there. More venturesome is the walk from the N and Cape Wrath (1637/COASTAL WALKS).
1249
MAP 2
D1

✝ **OLDSHOREMORE:** The beach you pass on the rd to Balchrick, only 3km from Kinlochbervie. It's easy to reach and a beautiful spot: the water is clear and perfect for swimming, and there are rocky walks and quiet places. **POLIN,** 500m N, is a cove you might have to yourself.
1250
MAP 2
D1

✝ **ISLAY: SALIGO, MACHIR BAY** and **THE BIG STRAND:** The first two are bays on NW of island via A847 rd to Pt Charlotte, then B8018 past L Gorm. Wide beaches; remains of war fortifications in deep dunes. They say 'no swimming'. The Big Strand on Laggan Bay: along Bowmore-Pt Ellen rd take Oa t/off, follow Kintra signs. There's a restau/bar, accom, camping and gr walks in either direction, 8km of glorious sand and dunes (contains the Machrie Golf Course). An airy amble under a wide sky. (1666/GOLF IN GREAT PLACES; 1635/COASTAL WALKS.)
1251
MAP 1
A3

✝ **OSTAL BEACH/KILBRIDE BAY, MILLHOUSE, nr TIGHNABRUAICH:** Down rd from 'Millhouse corner' on B8000, a track to rt at a white house (there's a church on the left) marked 'Private Road, No Cars' (often with a chain across to restrict access). Park and walk 1km, turning rt at lochan. You arrive on a perfect white sandy crescent known locally as Ostal and, apart from stranded jellyfish and the odd swatch of sewage, in certain conditions, a mystical secret place to swim and picnic. The N coast of Arran is like a Greek island in the bay.
1252
MAP 1
C3

✝ **SOUTH UIST:** Deserted but for birds, an almost unbroken strand of beach running for miles down the W coast; the machair at its best early summer. Take any rd off the spinal A865; usually less than 2km. Good spot to try is t/off at Tobha Mor; real black houses and a chapel on the way to the sea.
1253
MAP 2
A3

1254 ⚓ **SCARISTA BEACH, SOUTH HARRIS:** On main rd S of Tarbert (15km) to Rodel.
MAP 2 The beach is so beautiful that people have been married there. Hotel over the
B2 rd is worth staying just for this, but is also a gr retreat (1907/ISLAND HOTELS).
Golf course on links (1672/GOLF IN GREAT PLACES). Fab in early evening. The sun
also rises.

1255 ⚓ **LUNAN BAY, nr MONTROSE:** 5km from main A92 rd to Aber and 5km of deep
MAP 4 red crescent beach under a wide northern sky. But'n'Ben, Auchmithie, is an
E3 excellent place to start or finish (751/PERTHSHIRE HOTELS) and good app (from S),
but best viewpoint from Boddin Farm 3km S Montrose and 3km from A92
signed 'Usan'. Often deserted – pity that this mention may help to change that.

1256 **JURA, LOWLANDMAN'S BAY:** Not strictly a beach (there is a sandy strand before the
MAP 1 headland) but a rocky foreshore with ethereal atmos; gr light and space. Only
B3 seals break the spell. Go rt at 3-arch br to first group of houses (Knockdrome),
through yard on left and rt around cottages to track to Ardmenish. After deer
fences, bay is visible on your rt, 1km walk away.

1257 **VATERSAY, OUTER HEBRIDES:** The tiny island joined by a causeway to Barra. Twin
MAP 2 crescent beaches on either side of the isthmus, one shallow and sheltered visible
A4 from Castlebay, the other an ocean beach with rollers. Dunes/machair; safe
swimming. There's a helluva hill betw Barra and Vatersay if you're cycling.

1258 **BARRA, SEAL BAY:** 5km Castlebay on W coast, 2km after Isle of Barra Hotel
MAP 2 through gate across machair where rd rt is signed Taobh a Deas Allathasdal. A
A4 flat, rocky Hebridean shore and skerries where seals flop into the water and eye
you with intense curiosity. The better-beach beach is next to the hotel.

1259 **WEST SANDS, ST ANDREWS:** As a town beach, this is hard to beat; it dominates the
MAP 5 view to W. Wide swathe not too unclean and sea swimmable. Golf courses behind.
D2 In 1997 only Scottish beach to get 'the blue flag', but beach buffs may prefer
Kinshaldy (1402/WILDLIFE), Kingsbarns (10km S), or Elie (28km S).

1260 **MORAY COAST:** Many gr beaches along coast from Spey Bay to Fraserburgh,
MAP 3 notably **CULLEN** and **LOSSIEMOUTH** (town beaches) and **NEW ABERDOUR** (1km
C1/ from New Aberdour village on B9031, 15km W of Fraserburgh) and **ROSE-**
D1 **HEARTY** (8km W of Fraserburgh) both quieter places for walks and picnics. One
of the best-kept secrets is the beach at **SUNNYSIDE** where you walk past the
incredible ruins of Findlater Castle on the cliff top (how did they build it? And
what a place, on its grassed-over roof, for a picnic) and down to a cove which on
my sunny day was quite simply perfect. Take a left going into Sandend 16km W
of Banff and follow rd for 2km, turning rt and park in the farmyard. Walk from
here past dovecote, 1km to cliff. See also1643/COASTAL WALKS.

1261 **NORTH COAST:** To the W of Thurso, along the N coast, are some of Britain's most
MAP 2 unspoiled and unsung beaches. No beach bums, no Beach Boys. There are so
D1 many gr little coves, you can have one to yourself even on a hot day, but those to
mention are: **STRATHY** and **ARMADALE** (35km W Thurso), **FARR** and **TORRISDALE**
(48km) and **COLDBACKIE** (65km). My favourite (which may be called
Ceannabeinne after the hill above it, but **PETE'S BEACH** is easier to remember) is
further along where L Eriboll comes out to the sea and the rd hits the coast again
7km E of Durness. It's a small 100m cove flanked by walls of oyster-pink rock
and shallow turquoise sea; perfect.

1262 **SANDS OF MORAR, nr MALLAIG:** 70km W of Ft William and 6km from Mallaig,
MAP 2 these easily accessible beaches may seem overpopulated on summer days and the
C4 S stretch nearest to Arisaig may have one too many caravan parks, but they go on
for miles and there's enough space for everybody. The sand's supposed to be
silver but in fact it's a v pleasing pink. Lots of rocky bits for exploration. One of
the best beachy bits is (coming from Mallaig) the next bay after the estuary; park
on the rd. And the bit nr the youth hostel, Camusdarroch (where *Local Hero* was
filmed), further from rd, is quieter and a v good swathe of sand.

1263 **THE BAY AT THE BACK OF THE OCEAN, IONA:** Easy 2km walk from frequent ferry
MAP 1 from Fionnphort, S of Mull (1895/MAGICAL ISLANDS) or hire a bike from the store on
A2 your left as you walk into the village. Paved rd most of way. John Smith, who is
buried beside the abbey, once told me that this was one of his favourite places. Me too.

1264 **DORNOCH** and **EMBO BEACHES:** The wide and extensive sandy beach of this
MAP 2 pleasant town at the mouth of the Dornoch Firth famous also for its golf links.
D2 4km N, Embo Sands starts with caravan city, but walk N towards Golspie.

THE GREAT GLENS

✝ ✝ ✝ **GLEN AFFRIC:** Starts beyond Cannich at the end of Glen Urquhart **1265**
A831, 20km from Drumnadrochit on L Ness. A beautiful, dramatic MAP 2
gorge that strikes westwards into the wild heart of Scotland. Superb for rambles C3
(1608/GLEN AND RIVER WALKS), expeditions, Munro-bagging (further in, beyond
L Affric) and even just tootling through in the car. Shaped by the Hydro Board,
L Benevean nevertheless adds to the drama. Cycling good (bike hire in Cannich)
as is the detour to Tomich and Plodda Falls (1277/WATERFALLS). Stop at Dog Falls.

✝ ✝ ✝ **GLEN LYON, nr ABERFELDY:** One of Scotland's crucial places both **1266**
historically and geographically, much favoured by fishers/walkers/ MAP 4
Munro-baggers. Wordsworth and Tennyson, Gladstone and Baden Powell all B3
sang its praises. The Lyon is a classic Highland river tumbling through corries,
gorges and riverine meadows. Several Munros are within its watershed and rise
gloriously on either side. Rd all the way to the loch side (30km). Eagles soar over
the remoter tops at the head of the glen. Fishing permits from Fortingall Hotel
on the way there (949/INNS, 01887 830367). The 'oldest tree' in Europe, a rather
scraggy yew, is by the church next to the hotel.

✝ ✝ **GLEN NEVIS, FORT WILLIAM:** Used by many a film director; easy to see **1267**
why. Ben Nevis is only part of magnificent scenery. Many walks and MAP 7
convenient facs (1283/WATERFALLS; 1604/SERIOUS WALKS). Not sure about the C4
Braveheart car park or the 'legend' of Samuel's Stone; other-wise, it's a national
treasure.

✝ ✝ **GLEN ETIVE:** Off from more exalted Glencoe (and the A82) at **1268**
Kingshouse, as anyone you meet in those parts will tell you, this truly is MAP 7
a glen of glens. And, as my friends who camp and climb here implore, it needs no C5
more advertisement.

STRATHCARRON, nr BONAR BRIDGE: You drive up the N bank of this Highland **1269**
river from the br o/side Ardgay (pron 'Ordguy') which is 3km over the br from MAP 2
Bonar Br. Rd goes 15km to Croick and its remarkable church (1506/CHURCHES). D2
The river gurgles and gushes along its rocky course to the Dornoch Firth and
there are innumerable places to picnic, swim and stroll further up. Quite heavenly
on a warm day.

THE ANGUS GLENS: Glen Clova/Glen Prosen/Glen Isla. All via Kirriemuir. Isla to **1270**
W is a woody, approachable glen with a deep gorge, on B954 nr Alyth (1287/ MAP 4
WATERFALLS) and the lovely Glenisla Hotel (952/INNS). Others via B955, to D2
Dykehead then rd bifurcates. Both glens stab into the heart of the Grampians.
'Minister's Walk' goes betw them from behind the kirk at Prosen village over the
hill to B955 above Clova village (7km). Glen Clova is a walkers' paradise esp
from Glendoll 24km from Dykehead; limit of rd. Viewpoint. 'Jock's Rd' to
Braemar and the Capel Mounth to Ballater (both 24km). Campsite and SYH.
Also gr hotel at Clova (746/PERTHSHIRE HOTELS) and famous 'Loops of Brandy'
walk (2hrs, 2-B-2); stark and beautiful.

GLENDARUEL: The Cowal Peninsula on the A886 betw Colintraive and Strachur. **1271**
Humble but perfectly formed glen of R Ruel, from Clachan in S (a kirk and an MAP 1
inn) through deciduous meadowland to more rugged grandeur 10km N. Easy C3
walking and cycling. W rd best. Views L Fyne and Argyll from W ridge. 2-B-2

GLEN LONAN, nr TAYNUILT: Betw Taynuilt on A85 and A816 S of Oban. Another **1272**
quiet wee glen, but all the rt elements for walking, picnics, cycling and fishing or MAP 1
just a run in the car. Varying scenery, a bubbling burn (the R Lonan), some C1
standing stones and not many folk. Angus' Garden at the Taynuilt end should not
be missed (1202/GARDENS). No marked walks; now get lost! 2-B-2

GLEN TROOL, nr NEWTON STEWART: 26km N by A714 via Bargrennan which is on **1273**
the S Upland Way (1599/LONG WALKS). A gentle wooded glen of a place around MAP 9
L Trool. One of the most charming, accessible parts of the Galloway Forest Park. B3
(1546/MARY, CHARLIE, BOB.) Start of the Merrick climb (1576/HILLS).

THE SMA' GLEN, nr CRIEFF: Off the A85 to Perth, the A822 to Amulree and **1274**
Aberfeldy. Sma' meaning small, this is the valley of the R Almond where the MAP 4
Mealls (lumpish, shapeless hills) fall steeply down to the rd. Where the rd turns B3
away from the river, the long distance path to L Tay begins (28km). Sma' Glen,
8km, has good picnic spots, but they get busy and midgy in summer.

1275 **STRATHFARRAR, nr BEAULY or DRUMNADROCHIT:** Rare unspoiled glen accessed
MAP 2   from A831 leaving Drumnadrochit on L Ness via Cannich (30km) or S from
D3   Beauly (15km). Signed at Struy. Arrive at gatekeeper's house. Access restricted to
25 cars per day (Cl Tue and mid Aug-Oct); you must be out by 7pm. 22km to
head of glen past lochs. Good climbing, walking, fishing. Peace be with you.

THE MOST SPECTACULAR WATERFALLS

One aspect of Scotland that really is improved by rain. All the walks to these falls are graded
I-A-I *unless otherwise stated (see p. 10 for walk codes).*

1276 ✝ ✝ **FALLS OF GLOMACH:** 25km Kyle of Lochalsh off A87 nr Shiel Br, past
MAP 2   Kintail Centre at Morvich then 2km further up Glen Croe to br. Walk
C3   starts other side; there are other ways, (e.g. from the SY Hostel in Glen Affric), but
this is most straightforward. Allow 5/7 hrs for the pilgrimage to one of Britain's
highest falls. Path is steep but well trod. Glomach means gloomy and you might
feel so, peering into the ravine; from precipice to pool, it's 200m. But to pay tribute,
go down carefully to ledge. Vertigo factor and sense of achievement both fairly
high. (940/HOSTELS.)   2-C-3

1277 ✝ ✝ **PLODDA FALLS, nr TOMICH, nr DRUMNADROCHIT:** A831 from L Ness to
MAP 2   Cannich (20km), then 7km to Tomich, a further 5km up mainly woodland
C3   track to car park. 200m walk down through woods of Scots Pine and ancient
Douglas Fir to one of the most enchanting woodland sites in Britain and the
Victorian iron br over the brink of the 150m fall into the churning river below. The
dawn chorus here must be amazing (I'll never hear it). Freezes into winter
wonderland (ice climbers from Inverness). Good hotel in village (784/HIGHLANDS
HOTELS).

1278 ✝ **FALLS OF BRUAR, nr BLAIR ATHOLL:** Close to the main A9 Perth-Inverness rd,
MAP 4   12km N of B Atholl nr new House of Bruar shopping experience. (1751/CRAFT
B2   SHOPS). Consequently, the short walk to lower falls is now v consumer-led but less
crowded than you might expect. The lichen-covered walls of the gorge below the
upper falls (1km) are less ogled and more dramatic. Circular path is well marked but
steep and rocky in places. Tempting (1345/SWIMMING HOLES).

1279 ✝ **GLENASHDALE FALLS, ARRAN:** 5km walk from br on main rd at
MAP 1   WhitingBay.Signed up the burn side, but uphill and further on than you think,
C4   so allow 2hrs (return). Short series of falls in a rocky gorge in the woods with paths
so you get rt down to the brim and the pools. Swim here, swim in heaven!   I-B-I

1280 **EAS FORS, MULL:** On the Dervaig to Fionnphort rd 3km from Ulva Ferry; a series of
MAP 1   cataracts tumbling down on either side of the rd. Easily accessible. There's a path
B1   down the side to the brink where the river plunges into the sea. On a warm day
swimming in the sea below the fall is a rare exhilaration.

1281 **EAS MOR, SKYE:** Glen Brittle nr end of rd. 24km from Sligachan. A mt waterfall
MAP 2   with the wild Cuillins behind and views to the sea. App as part of a serious
B3   scramble or merely a 30-min Cuillin sampler. Start at the Memorial Hut, cross the
rd, bear rt, cross burn and then follow path uphill.   2-C-2

Another impressive torrent of wild mt water is the **LEALT FALLS** about 20km N of
Portree on the A855. Beside rd; park and peer.

1282 **EAS A' CHUAL ALUINN, KYLESKU:** 'Britain's highest waterfall' nr the head of Glencoul,
lAP 2   is not easy to reach. Kylesku is betw Scourie and Lochinver off the main A894.
C2   20km S of Scourie. There are 2hr cruises at 11am/2pm May-Sept (and 4pm
July/Aug) outside hotel (832/INEXP HIGHLAND RESTAUS). Falls are a rather distant
prospect, but you may be able to alight and get next boat. The captain's rap will keep
you going. There's also a track to the top of the falls from 5km N of the Skiag Br on
the main rd (4hrs return), but you will need to take directions locally. The water
freefalls for 200m, which is 4 times further than Niagara (take pinch of salt here).
There is a spectacular pulpit view down the cliff, 100m to rt.   2-C-3

283 **STEALL FALLS, GLEN NEVIS, FORT WILLIAM:** Take Glen Nevis rd at r/bout o/side
P 2   town centre and drive 'to end' (16km) through glen. Start from the second car
C4   park you come to, following path marked Corrour, uphill through the woody
gorge with R Ness thrashing below. Glen eventually and dramatically opens out
and there are gr views of the long veils of the Falls. Precarious 3-wire br for which
you will also need nerves of steel. One day in Jan, of 10 of us, 2 couldn't do it. I

am one (sad person). I blamed a hangover.

CORRIESHALLOCH GORGE/FALLS OF MEASACH: Jnct of A832 and A835, 20km S of
Ullapool; possible to walk down into the gorge from both rds. Most dramatic app
is from the car park on the A832 Gairloch rd. Staircase to swing br from whence
to consider how such a wee burn could make such a deep gash. V impressive.

1284
MAP 2
C3

THE GREY MARE'S TAIL: On the wildly scenic rd betw Moffat and Selkirk, the
A708. About halfway, a car park and signs for waterfall. The lower track takes
10/15mins to a viewing place still 500m from falls; the higher, on the other side of
the Tail burn, threads betw the austere hills and up to L Skene from which the
falls overflow (45/60mins). Mountain goats cast a wary eye.

1285
MAP 9
E2

THE FALLS OF CLYDE, NEW LANARK, nr LANARK: Dramatic falls in a long gorge of
the Clyde. New Lanark, the conservation village of Robert Owen the social
reformer, is signed from Lanark. It's hard to avoid the 'award-winning' tourist
bazaar, but I'd recommend getting out of the village and along the riverbank ASAP.
The path to the Power Station is about 3km, but the route doesn't get interesting
till after it, a 1km climb to the first fall (Cora Linn) and another 1km to the next
(Bonnington Linn). Swimming above or below them is not advised (but it's gr).
Certainly don't swim on an 'open day', when they close the station and divert all
the water back down the river in a mighty surge (about once a month in summer
on Sundays; details from TO: 01555 661661). There is a gr Italian restau in Lanark
(664/AYRSHIRE HOTELS) by the way.

1286
MAP 1
E3

REEKIE LINN, ALYTH: 8km N of town on back rds to Kirriemuir on B951 betw Br
of Craigisla and Br of Lintrathen. A picnic site and car park on bend of rd leads
by 200m to the wooded gorge of Glen Isla with precipitous viewpoints of defile
where Isla is squeezed and falls in tiers for 100ft. Can walk further along the glen.
Excellent loch side restau nearby (886/DUNDEE EAT AND DRINK) and tearoom
(1118/TEAROOMS).

1287
MAP 4
D3

FALLS OF ACHARN nr KENMORE, LOCH TAY: 5km along S side of loch on unclass rd.
Walk from opp engineering plant in township of Acharn; falls are signed. Steepish
start then 1km up side of gorge; waterfalls on other side.

1288
MAP 4
B3

FALLS OF ROGIE, nr STRATHPEFFER: Car park on A835 Inverness-Ullapool rd, 5km
Contin/10km Strathpeffer. Accessibility makes short walk (250m) quite popular
to these hurtling falls on the Blackwater R. Br (built by T Army) and salmon
ladder (they leap in summer). Woodland trails marked, include a circular route
to Contin (1630/WOODLAND WALKS).

1289
MAP 2
D3

FOYERS, LOCH NESS: On southern route from Ft Augustus to Inverness, the B862
(1314/SCENIC ROUTES) at the village of Foyers (35km from Inverness). Park next
to shops and cross rd, go through fence and down steep track to viewing places
(slither-proof shoes advised). R Foyers falls 150m into foaming gorge below and
then into L Ness throwing clouds of spray into the trees (you may get drenched).
Occasionally the Hydro 'turn the water off' and it just stops.

1290
MAP 2
D4

FALLS OF SHIN, nr LAIRG, SUTHERLAND: 6km E of town on signed rd, car park and
falls nearby are easily accessible. Not quite up to the splendours of others on this
page, but an excellent place to see salmon battling upstream (best June-Aug).
Visitor centre with extensive shop; the café/restau here is surprisingly good
(830/HIGHLANDS HOTELS).

1291
MAP 2
D2

THE LOCHS WE LOVE

✝ ✝ **LOCH MAREE:** A832 betw Kinlochewe and Gairloch. Dotted with islands
covered in Scots pine hiding some of the best examples of Viking graves
and apparently a money tree in their midst. Easily viewed from the rd which
follows its length for 15km. Bienn Eighe rises behind you and the omniscient
presence of Slioch is opposite. Aultroy Vistor Centre (5km Kinlochewe), fine
walks from car park further on, good accom and fishing at L Maree Hotel
(803/HIGHLANDS HOTELS).

1292
MAP 2
C3

✝ ✝ **LOCH AN EILEAN:** An enchanted loch in the heart of the
RothiemurchusForest (1620/WOODLAND WALKS) for directions. There's a
good visitor centre. You can walk rt round the loch (5km, allow 1.5hrs). This is
classic Highland scenery, a landscape of magnificent Scots pine. It was one of
Wainwright's favourites.

1293
MAP 2
D4

1294
MAP 2
C4
✠ LOCH ARKAIG: 25km Ft William. An enigmatic loch long renowned for itsfishing. From the A82 beyond Spean Br (at the Commando Monument) cross the Caledonian Canal, then on by single track rd through the Clune Forest and the 'Dark Mile' past the 'Witches Pool' (a cauldron of dark water below cataracts), to the loch. Bonnie Prince Charlie came this way before and after Culloden; one of his refuge caves is marked on a trail.

1295
MAP 6
B2
LOCH LUBHAIR, nr CRIANLARICH: The loch you pass (on the rt) on the A85 to Crianlarich (4km), in Glen Dochart, the upper reaches of the Tay water system. Small, perfect, with bare hills surrounding and fringed with pines and woody islets. Beautiful scenery that most people just go past in the car heading for Oban or Ft William. Enquire locally for kayak hire.

1296
MAP 6
B3
LOCH ACHRAY, nr BRIG O' TURK: The small loch at the centre of the Trossachs betw **LOCH KATRINE** (on which the SS *Sir Walter Scott* makes thrice-daily cruises: 01877 376316) and **LOCH VENACHAR.** The A821 from Callander skirts both Venachar and Achray (picnic sites). Ben Venue and Ben A'An rise above: gr walks (1571/HILLS) and views. A one-way forest rd goes round the other side of L Achray thro Achray Forest (enter and leave from the Duke's Pass rd betw Aber- foyle and Brig O' Turk). Details of trails from forest vistor centre 3km N Aberfoyle. Bike hire at L Katrine/ Callander/ Aberfoyle - it's the best way to see these lochs.

1297
MAP 3
B4
LOCH MUICK, nr BALLATER: At head of rd off B976, the S Dee rd at Ballater. 14km up Glen Muick (pron 'Mick') to car park, visitor centre and 100m to loch side. Lochnagar rises above (1594/MUNROS) and walk also begins here for Capel Mounth and Glen Clova (1270/GLENS). 3hr walk around loch and any number of ambles. The lodge where Vic met John is at the furthest pt (well it would be). Open aspect with grazing deer and not too much forestry.

1298
MAP 2
D1
LOCH ERIBOLL, NORTH COAST: 90km W of Thurso. The long sea loch that indents into the N coast for 15km and which you drive rt round on the main A838. Deepest natural anchorage in the UK, exhibiting every aspect of loch side scenery including, alas, fish cages. Ben Hope stands nr the head of the loch and there is a perfect beach (my beach) on the coast (1261/BEACHES). Walks from Hope.

1299
MAP 9
B3
✠ LOCH TROOL, nr NEWTON STEWART: The small, celebrated loch in a bowl of the Galloway Hills reached via Bargrennan 14km N via A714 and 8km to end of rd. Woodland visitor centre/café on way. Good walks but best viewed from Bruce's Stone (1546/MARY, CHARLIE AND BOB) and the slopes of Merrick (1576/HILLS). An idyllic place.

1300
MAP 2
C4
LOCH MORAR, nr MALLAIG: 70km W of Ft William by the A850 (a wildly scenic route). Morar village is 6km from Mallaig and a single track rd leads away from the coast to the loch (only 500m but out of sight) then along it for 5km to Bracora. It's the prettiest part with wooded islets, small beaches, loch side meadows and bobbing boats. The rd stops at a turning place but a track continues to Tarbet and it's poss to connect with a post boat and sail back to Mallaig on L Nevis. L Morar, joined to the coast by the shortest river in Britain, also has the deepest water. There is a spookiness about it and just possibly a monster called Morag.

1301
MAP 4
B3
LOCH TUMMEL, nr PITLOCHRY: W from Pitlochry on B8019 to Rannoch (and the end of the rd), L Tummel comes into view, as it did for Queen Victoria, scintillating beneath you, and on a clear day with Schiehallion beyond (1331/VIEWS). This N side has good walks (1627/WOODLAND WALKS), but the S rd from Faskally just o/side Pitlochry is the one to take to get down to the lochside to picnic etc. Great caravan park on B8019 at Ardquallich and a hotel, **THE QUEENS VIEW,** 01796 473291, with great views (10 rms, cl Feb, MED.INX).

1302
MAP 2
C6
LOCH LUNDAVRA, nr FORT WILLIAM: Here's a secret loch in the hills, but not far from the well-trodden tracks through the glens and the sunny streets of Ft William. Go up Lundavra Rd from r/bout at W end of main st, out of town, over cattle grid and on (to end of rd) 8km. You should have it to yourself; good picnic spots and gr view of Ben Nevis.

LOCH LOMOND: The biggest, maybe not the bonniest (1955/BIG ATTRACTIONS).

LOCH NESS: The longest; you haven't heard the last of it (1958/BIG ATTRACTIONS).

THE SCENIC ROUTES

✝ ✝ ✝ **ROTHESAY–TIGHNABRUAICH:** A886/A8003. The most celebrated part **1303** of this route is the latter, the A8003 down the side of L Riddon to MAP 1 Tighnabruaich along the hill sides which give the breathtaking views of Bute and C3 the Kyles, but the whole way, with its diverse aspects of loch side, riverine and rocky scenery, is supernatural. Includes short crossing betw Rhubodach and Colintraive.

✝ ✝ ✝ **GLENCOE:** The A82 from Crianlarich to Ballachulish is a fine drive, **1304** but from the extraterrestrial L Ba onwards, there can be few rds MAP 2 anywhere that have direct contact with such imposing scenery. After Kinghouse C5 and Buachaille Etive Mor on the left, the mts and ridges rising on either side of Glencoe proper are truly awesome. The visitor centre, well signposted 8km from Glencoe village, sets the topographical and historical scene. (1008/BLOODY GOOD PUBS; 1603/SERIOUS WALKS; 1533/BATTLEGROUNDS; 1558/SPOOKY PLACES; 939/HOSTELS.)

✝ ✝ **SHIEL BRIDGE–GLENELG:** The switchback rd that climbs from the A87 (Ft **1305** William 96km) at Shiel Br over the 'hill' and down to the coast opp the MAP 2 Sleat Peninsula in Skye (short ferry to Kylerhea). As you climb you're almost as C4 high as the surrounding summits and there's the classic view across L Duich to the 5 Sisters of Kintail. Coming back you think you're going straight into the loch! It's really worth driving beyond Glenelg to Arnisdale and ethereal L Hourn (16km).

✝ **APPLECROSS:** 120km Inverness. From Tornapress nr Lochcarron for 18km. **1306** Leaving the A896 seems like leaving civilisation; the winding ribbon heads MAP 2 into monstrous mts and the high plateau at the top is another planet. It's not for C3 the faint-hearted and Applecross is a relief to see with its campsite/coffee shop and a friendly, faraway inn (946/INNS).

✝ **THE GOLDEN ROAD, SOUTH HARRIS:** The main rd in Harris follows the W **1307** coast, notable for bays and sandy beaches (1254/BEACHES). This is the other MAP 2 one, winding round a series of coves and inlets with offshore skerries and a B2 treeless rocky hinterland – the classic Hebridean landscape, esp Finsbay. Tweed is woven in this area; you can visit the crofts but it would be impolite to leave without buying some gloves or something (1756/CRAFT SHOPS).

SLEAT PENINSULA, SKYE: The unclassified rd off the A851 (main Sleat rd) esp **1308** coming from S, i.e. take rd at Ostaig nr Gaelic College; it meets coast after 9km. MAP 2 Affords rare views of the Cuillins from a craggy coast. Returning to 'main' rd S B4 of Isleornsay, pop into the gr hotel pub there (1905/ISLAND HOTELS).

LOCHINVER–ACHILTIBUIE: Achiltibuie is 40km from Ullapool; this is the route **1309** from the N; 28km of winding rd/unwinding Highland scenery; through glens, MAP 2 mts and silver sea. Known locally as the 'wee mad rd' (it is maddening if you're C2 in a hurry). Passes Achin's Bookshop (1746/CRAFT SHOPS), the path to Kincraig Falls and the mighty Suilven.

LOCHINVER–DRUMBEG: The coast rd N from Lochinver (20km) is also marvellous; **1310** essential Assynt. Actually best travelled N–S so that you leave the splendid vista MAP 2 of Eddrachillis Bay and pass through lochan, moor and even woodland, touching C2 the coast again by sandy beaches (at Stoer a rd leads 7km to the lighthouse and the walk to the Old Man of Stoer, 1638/COASTAL WALKS) and app Lochinver with one of the classic long views of Suilven.

LEADERFOOT–CLINTMAINS, nr ST BOSWELLS: The B6356 betw the A68 and the **1311** B6404 Kelso-St Boswells rd. This small rd, busy in summer, links Scott's View MAP 8 and Dryburgh Abbey (1526/ABBEYS; best found by following Abbey signs) and C3 Smailholm Tower, and passes through classic Border/Tweedside scenery. Don't miss Irvine's View if you want to see the Borders (1329/VIEWS).

BRAEMAR–LINN OF DEE: 12km of renowned Highland river scenery along the **1312** upper valley of the (Royal) Dee. The Linn (rapids) is at the end of the rd, but MAP 3 there are river walks and the start of the gr Glen Tilt walk to Blair Atholl A4 (1606/SERIOUS WALKS). Deer abound.

BALLATER-TOMINTOUL: This is the ski road to the Lecht (1690/SKIING), the A939 **1313** which leaves the Royal Deeside rd (A93) W of Ballater before it gets really royal. MAP 3 A ribbon of road in the bare Grampians, past the sentinel ruin Corgarff (open to B4 view, 250m walk) and the valley of the trickling Don. Rd proceeds seriously uphill and main viewpoints are S of the Lecht. There is just nobody for miles. Walks in Glenlivet estates S of Tomintoul. Good hotel here.

1314 **FORT AUGUSTUS–DORES, nr INVERNESS:** The B862 often single-track rd that
MAP 2 follows and, for much of its length, skirts L Ness. Much quieter and more
D4 interesting than the main W bank A82. Starts off in rugged country and follows the extraordinary straight rd built by Wade to tame the Highlands. Reaches the loch side at Foyers (1290/WATERFALLS) and goes all the way to Dores (15km from Inverness). There are paths to the shore of the loch. Fabulous untrodden woodlands nr Errogie (marked) and the spooky graveyard adj Boleskin House where Aleister Crowley did his dark magic and Jimmy Page of Led Zeppelin may have done his. 35km total; worth taking slowly.

1315 **THE DUKE'S PASS, ABERFOYLE–BRIG O'TURK:** Of the many rds through the
MAP 6 Trossachs, this one is spectacular though gets busy; numerous possibilities for
B3 stopping, exploration and gr views. Good viewpoint 4km from L Achray Hotel, above rd and lay-by. One-way forest rd goes round L Achray. Good hill walking starts (1571/1572/1573/ FAVOURITE HILLS) and L Katrine Ferry (2km) 3 times a day Apr-Sept (01877 376316). Bike hire at L Katrine, Aberfoyle and Callander.

1316 **GLENFINNAN–MALLAIG:** The A830, Road to the Isles. Through some of the most
MAP 2 impressive and romantic landscapes in the Highlands, splendid in any weather (it
C4 does rain rather a lot) to the coast at the Sands of Morar (1262/ BEACHES). This is deepest Bonnie Prince Charlie country (1545/MARY, CHARLIE and BOB) and demonstrates what a misty eye he had for magnificent settings. The rd is shadowed for much of the way by the West Highland Railway, which is an even better way to enjoy the scenery (1964/FAVOURITE JOURNEYS).

1317 **LOCHAILORT–ACHARACLE:** Off from the A830 above at Lochailort and turning S
MAP 2 on the A861, the coastal section of this gr scenery is superb esp in the setting sun.
C4 This is the rd to Castle Tiorem, which should not be missed (1428/RUINS); Michael McGregor's new wildlife centre nearby shouldn't be either (1379/KIDS).

1318 **AMULREE–KENMORE:** The unclassified single track and often v narrow rd that
MAP 4 leads from the hill-country hamlet of Amulree to cosy Kenmore. Past L Freuchie,
B3 a steep climb takes you to a plateau ringed by magnificent (distant) mts and, by the time you descend to L Tay, you may be completely intoxicated with the scenery. But don't forget to close the gates.

1319 **PURE PERTHSHIRE, MUTHILL–COMRIE:** A route you won't find in any other
MAP 4 guidebook. It takes you through some of the best scenery in central Scotland and
B4 ends up (best this way round) in Comrie with its teashops and other pleasures (1109/TEAROOMS; 1344/PICNICS). Leave Muthill by Crieff rd turning left (2km) into Drummond Castle grounds up a glorious avenue of beech trees (gate open 2-5pm). Visit grd (1200/GARDENS) then continue through estate. At gate, go rt, following signs for Strowan. v quiet rd; we have it to ourselves. First jnct, go left following signs (4km). At T-jnct, go left to Comrie (7km).

THE CLASSIC VIEWS

For views of and around Edin and Glas see p. 48 and p. 84. No views from hill or mt tops are included here.

1320 ♆ ♆ ♆ **THE QUIRANG, SKYE:** Best app is from Uig direction taking the rt-hand
MAP 2 unclassified rd off the hairpin of the A855 above and 2km from town
B3 (more usual app from Staffin side is less of a revelation). View (and walk) from car park, the massive rock formations of a towering, contorted ridge. Solidified lava heaved and eroded into fantastic pinnacles. Fine views also across Staffin Bay to Wester Ross. (1930/ISLAND WALKS.)

1321 ♆ ♆ ♆ **The views of AN TEALLACH and LIATHACH:** An Teallach, that gr
MAP 2 favourite of Scottish hill walkers (40km S of Ullapool by the
C2 A835/A832), is best viewed from the side of little L Broom or the A832 just before you get to Dundonald.

The classic view of the other great Torridon mts (Beinn Eighe and Liathach together, 100km S by rd from Ullapool), for those who can't imagine how (or why) you would attempt to go up them, is from the track around L Clair which is reached from the entrance to the Coulin estate off the A896, Glen Torridon rd (be aware of stalking). These mts have to be seen to be believed.

✝ ✚ **From RAASAY:** There are a number of fabulous views looking over to Skye 1322
from Raasay, the small island reached by ferry from Sconser MAP 2
(1893/MAGICAL ISLANDS). The panorama from Dun Caan, the hill in the centre of B3
the island (444m) is of Munro proportions, producing an elation quite
incommensurate with the small effort required to get there. Start from the rd to the
'N End'.
2-B-2

✝ ✚ **THE REST AND BE THANKFUL:** On A83 L Lomond-Inveraray rd where it's 1323
met by the B828 from Lochgoilhead. In summer the rest may be from MAP 1
driving stress and you may not be thankful for the camera-toting masses, but this C2
was always one of the most accessible, rewarding viewpoints in the land.
Surprisingly, none of the encompassing hills are Munros but they are nonetheless
dramatic. There are mercifully few carpets of conifer to smother the grandeur of
the crags as you look down the valley.

✚ **ELGOL, SKYE:** End of the rd, the B8083, 22km from Broadford. The classic 1324
view of the Cuillins from across L Scavaig and of Soay and Rum. Cruises MAP 2
(Apr-Oct) in the *Bella Jane* 01471 866244, (or *Nicola p. 1396*) to the famous corrie B4
of L Coruisk, painted by Turner, romanticised by Walter Scott; with 45mins
ashore.

✚ **THE SUMMER ISLES, ACHILTIBUIE:** The Summer Isles are a scattering of islands 1325
seen from the coast of Achiltibuie (and the lounge of the Summer Isles Hotel MAP 2
786/HIGHLANDS HOTELS)and visited by boat from Ullapool. But the best place to C2
see them, the stunning perspective of this western shore is on the road to
Altandhu, possibly to the pub there. On way to Achiltibuie, turn rt thro Polbain,
on about 2.5km. There's a bench. Sit on it, drink in the sunset.

CAMAS NAN GEALL, ARDNAMURCHAN: 12km Salen on B8007. 4km from Ardna- 1326
murchan's Natural History Centre (1379/KIDS) 65km Ft William. Coming esp MAP 2
from the Kilchoan direction, a magnificent bay appears below you, where the rd B4
first meets the sea. Almost symmetrical with high cliffs and a perfect field (still
cultivated) in the bowl fringed by a shingle beach. Car park viewpoint and there
is a path down. Deer graze around here.

GLENGARRY: 3km after Tomdoun t/off on A87, Invergarry-Kyle of Lochalsh rd. 1327
Lay-by with viewfinder. An uncluttered vista up and down loch and glen with MAP 2
not a house in sight (pity about the salmon cages). Distant peaks of Knoydart are C4
identified, but not L Quoich nestling spookily and full of fish in the wilderness
at the head of the glen. Bonnie Prince Charlie passed this way.

SCOTT'S VIEW, ST BOSWELLS: Off A68 at Leaderfoot Br nr St Boswells, signed 1328
Gattonside. 'The View', old Walter's favourite (the horses still stopped there long MAP 8
after he'd gone), is 4km along the rd (Dryburgh Abbey 3km further; C3
1526/ABBEYS). Magnificent sweep of his beloved Border country, but only in one
direction. If you cross the rd, climb through the gate and head up the hill towards
the jagged standing stone that comes into view, you reach . . .

IRVINE'S VIEW: The full panorama from the Cheviots to the Lammermuirs. This, 1329
the finest view in southern Scotland, is only a furlong further. This is where I'd MAP 8
like my bench – you now the kind of thing: a wee plaque saying 'He loved the C3
Borders' view.

THE LAW, DUNDEE: Few cities have such a single good viewpoint. To N of the 1330
centre, it reveals the panoramic perspective of the city on the estuary of the MAP 4
silvery Tay. Best to walk from town; the one-way system is a nightmare. Get D3
chips at Luigi's (ask a local) on the way up: Dundee in a poke.

QUEEN'S VIEW, LOCH TUMMEL, nr PITLOCHRY: 8km on B8019 to Kinloch Ran- 1331
noch. Car park and 100m walk to rocky knoll where pioneers of tourism, Queen MAP 4
Victoria and Prince Albert, were 'transported into ecstasies' by the view of L B2
Tummel and Schiehallion (1301/LOCHS; 1627/WOODLAND WALKS).

CALIFER, nr FORRES: 7km from Forres on A96 to Elgin, turn right for 'Pluscarden', 1332
follow narrow rd for 5km. Viewpoint is on rd and looks down across Findhorn MAP 3
Bay and the wide vista of the Moray Firth to the Black Isle and Ben Wyvis. B2
Fantastic light. We didn't visit in 1997, but readers wrote to say . . . 'it's really
nice'.

THE MALCOLM MEMORIAL, LANGHOLM: 3km from Langholm and signed from 1333

MAP 9
A3
main A7, a single-track rd leads to a path to this obelisk raised to celebrate the military and masonic achievements of one John Malcolm. The eulogy is fulsome esp compared with that for Hugh MacDiarmid on the cairn by the stunning sculpture at the start of the path (1490/MEMORIALS). Views from the obelisk, however, are among the finest in the S, encompassing a vista from the Lakeland Fells and the Solway Firth to the wild Border hills. Path 1km.

1334 DUNCRYNE HILL, GARTOCHARN, nr BALLOCH: Gartocharn is betw Balloch and
MAP 1   Drymen on the A811, and this view, was recommended by writer and
D2   outdoorsman Tom Weir as 'the finest viewpoint of any small hill in Scotland'. Turn up the rd at the E end of village and park 1km on left by a small wood (a sign reads 'Woods reserved for Teddy bears'). The hill is only 470ft high and 'easy', but the view of L Lomond and the Kilpatrick Hills is superb.

SUMMER PICNICS AND GREAT SWIMMING HOLES

Lest it needs to be said: gr care should be taken when swimming in rivers; don't take them for granted. Kids should be watched. Most of these places are trad local swimming and picnic spots where people have swum for yrs, but rivers continuously change their course and their nature. Wearing sandals or old sports shoes in the water is a good idea.

1335 **THE FAIRY POOLS, GLEN BRITTLE, SKYE:** On a hot day, this is one of the best
MAP 2   places on Skye to head for; swimming in deep pools with the massif of
B3   the Cuillins around you. One pool has a stone br you can swim under. Head off A863 Dunvegan rd from Sligachan Hotel (1186/WHISKY) then B8009 and Glenbrittle rd. 7km down just as rd begins to parallel the glen itself, you'll see a river coming off the hills. Park in lay-by on rt. 1km walk, follow this up.

1336 **THE POOLS IN GLEN ETIVE:** Glen Etive is a wild, enchanted place where
MAP 2   people have been camping for yrs to walk and climb in the Glencoe area.
C5   There are many grassy landings at the river side as well as these perfect pools for bathing. The first is about 6km from the main Glencoe rd, the A82 at Kingshouse, but just follow the river and find your own. Take midge cream for evening wear.

1337 **FESHIEBRIDGE:** At the br itself on the B970 betw Kinussie and Inverdruie
MAP 2   nr Aviemore. 4km from Kincraig. Gr walks here into Glen Feshie and in
D4   nearby woodland, but under br a perfect spot for Highland swimming. Go down to left from S. Rocky ledges, clear water. One of the best.

1338 **ROB ROY FALLS, nr INVERARNAN:** A82 N of Ardlui and 3 km past The
MAP 6   Drover's Inn (1003/BLOODY GOOD PUBS). Sign on the rt (Picnic Area),
A2   height restriction so watch your Landcruiser. Park, then follow the path to the main waterfall where you'll be able to glimpse a secluded upper pool, through the trees. There's an overhanging rock face on one side and smooth slabs at the edge of the falls. Natural suntrap in summer, but the water is 'Baltic' at all times.

1339 **NEIDPATH, PEEBLES:** 2km from town on A72, Biggar rd; sign for castle. Park
MAP 8   on rd in lay-by 100m further on, or down track by castle (gates shut at 5pm
B2   and they get shirty if you're still parked). Idyllic setting of a broad meander of the Tweed, with medieval Neidpath Castle, a sentinel above (open to public Apr-Sept). Two 'pools' (3m deep in av summer) linked by shallow rapids which the adventurous chute down on their backs. Usually a rope-swing at upper pool. TAKE CARE. Tweedside Walk passes by (1613/GLEN AND RIVER WALKS).

1340 **THE WHITEADDER, nr ABBEY ST BATHANS:** Can walk in from village or from
MAP 8   Toot corner (1587/HILL WALKS); past Edenshall brochs follow river (pron
D1   'Whit-adir'). Easier via A6112 to Duns (6km from A1 at Granthouse), rd to rt marked Abbey St Bathans, go 500m to first corner, then rough track signed for brochs for 1km to river side at swing br. 3 superb rocky pools with the br above. Midges can be menacing, so take the lotion; river shoes useful.

1341 **RANDOLPH'S LEAP nr FORRES:** Spectacular gorge once again on the mythical
MAP 3   Findhorn which carves out some craggy scenery on its way to a gentle coast.
A2   This secret glade and fabulous swimming hole are behind a wall and it's difficult to describe how to find them succinctly (*see 1618/WOODLAND WALKS for directions*), but it's S of Forres and Nairn and nr Logie Steading, a courtyard of good things (1856/GALLERIES). One Randolph of course once leapt here; we just bathe and lie under the trees dreaming of gods (and maybe satyrs).

STRATHMASHIE, nr NEWTONMORE: On A86 Newtonmore/Dalwhinnie (on A9) to Ft William rd 7km from Laggan, watch for Forest sign, small off rd car park and lay-by. River follows rd. Last time I was there it was one of the hottest days of the summer; this is a pool of brilliant water. **1342** MAP 2 D4

DOG FALLS, GLEN AFFRIC: Ross. Half-way along Glen Affric rd before you come to the loch, a well-marked picnic spot and gr place to swim in the peaty waters surrounded by the Caledonian Forest (with trails). Birds well sussed to picnic potential (some of the most voracious tits in the world) can be positively Hitchcockian (1608/GLEN AND RIVER WALKS). **1343** MAP 2 C3

Nr COMRIE: 2 great pools of different character nr the neat little town in deepest Perthshire. **THE LINN,** the town pool: go over humpback br from main A85 W to Lochearnhead, signed The Ross. After 2km there's a parking place on left. River's relatively wide, v pleasant spot. For more adventurous, **GLENARTNEY** is 5km on rd to Cultybraggan training camp (follow signs), continue past camp and then MoD range on left until a ruined cottage on rt. Park and walk down to river in glen. What with the twin perils of the Army and the Comrie Angling Club, you might feel you have no right to be here, but you do and this stretch of river is quite marvellous; you should have it to yourself. **1344** MAP 4 B4

FALLS OF BRUAR, nr BLAIR ATHOLL: Just off A9, 12km N of Blair Atholl. 250m walk from car park and new visitor centre to lower fall (1778/WATERFALLS) where there is an accessible large deep pool by the br. Cold, fresh mt water in a woody gorge. The water sprites probably packed their bags when the shopping arrived. **1345** MAP 4 B2

THE OTTER'S POOL, NEW GALLOWAY FOREST: A clearing in the forest reached by a track, 'The Raider's Rd', running from 8km N of Laurieston on the A762, for 16km to Clatteringshaws Loch. The track, which is only open Apr-Oct, has a toll of £1.50 and gets busy. It follows the Water of Dee and halfway down the rd you come to the Otter's Pool. A bronze otter used to mark the spot (it got nicked) and it's a place mainly for kids and paddling; but when the dam runs off it can be deep enough to swim. Rd closes 9pm. (1628/WOODLAND WALKS.) **1346** MAP 9 C3

ANCRUM: A secret place on the quiet Ale Water (out of village towards Lilliesleaf, 3km out 500m from farm sign to Hopton – a recessed gate on the rt and a rough track). A meadow, a Border burn, a surprising 3m pool to swim. Arcadia! **1347** MAP 8 D3

THE COBBY, KELSO: A stretch of the Tweed with wide grassy banks, a tradl picnic/swimming spot with Floors Castle in the background. Rd to Floors and left to river. Fairly deep and wide at this point; good swimmers only. **1348** MAP 8 D3

'THE PIER', DOUNE: Where the tiny Ardoch flows into the Teith (a river which makes a more prominent appearance at Callander), a swimming place on a river meadow known for no obvious reason as 'The Pier'. Walk downhill from Doune Castle past the sewage works (no, really!) and on for 100m. Gr for active picnics. **1349** MAP 6 D3

PARADISE, SHERIFFMUIR, nr DUNBLANE: A pool at the foot of an unexpected leafy gorge on the moor betw the Ochils and Strathallan. Here the Wharry Burn is known locally as 'Paradise', and for good reason. Take rd from 'behind' Dunblane or Br of Allan to the Sheriffmuir Inn; head downhill (back) towards Br of Allan and park nr the hump back br. Walk downsteam for 1km. It can be midgy and it can be perfect. The inn (01786 823285), built in the same yr as the battle (1715), has ales, food (6-8.45pm) and a warm welcome. **1350** MAP 3 D3

POTARCH BRIDGE & CAMBUS O'MAY on the DEE: 2 places on the 'Royal' Dee, the first by the reconstucted Victorian br (and nr the hotel) 3km E of Kincardine O'Neill. Cambus another stretch of river E of Ballater (6km), stop perhaps at The Willows for tea, or park by the river. Locals swim, picnic on rocks, etc, and there are forest walks on the other side of rd. **1351** MAP 3 C4

STRATHCARRON, nr BONAR BRIDGE: Dream river, pick your spot (1269/GLENS).

INVERMORISTON: On main L Ness rd A82 betw Inverness and Ft Augustus, this is the best bit. R Moriston tumbles under an ancient br. Perfectly Highland. Ledges for picnics, invigorating pools, ozone-friendly. **1352** MAP 2 D4

DULSIE BRIDGE, nr NAIRN: 16km S of Nairn on the A939 to Grantown, this locally revered beauty spot is fabulous for summer swimming. The ancient arched br spans the rocky gorge of the Findhorn and there are ledges and even sandy beaches for picnics and from which to launch yourself or paddle into the peaty waters. **1353** MAP 2 D3

GOOD PLACES TO TAKE KIDS

CENTRAL:

1354
MAP 7
C1
✚ ✚ **EDINBURGH ZOO:** 0131 334 9171. Corstorphine Rd. 4km W of Princes St. A large and long-established zoo, where the natural world from the poles to the plains of Africa is ranged around Corstorphine Hill. Enough huge/exotic/ghastly creatures and friendly, amusing ones to fill an overstimulated day. The penguins and the seals do their stuff at set times. More familiar creatures hang out at the 'farm'. Café and shop stocked with environmentally ok toys and souvenirs. Open 7 days, 9am-6pm (till dusk in winter).

1355
MAP A
xC1
CHILDREN'S FESTIVAL, EDINBURGH: 0131 554 6297 for info. Annual event held sometime in May somewhere in the capital, possibly in tents. Yes, you guessed, there were changes afoot when the book was being written but the kids' fest will take place. A week of shows from around the world.

1356
MAP A
D3
✚ ✚ **MUSEUM OF CHILDHOOD, EDINBURGH:** 0131 5294142. 42 High St. An Aladdin's cave oftoys through and for all ages. Much more fascinating than computer games - allegedly (315/OTHER ATTRACTIONS).

1357
MAP 7
C2
✚ **BUTTERFLY FARM, nr DALKEITH and EDINBURGH:** 0131 663 4932. On A7, signed Eskbank/Galashiels from ring rd (1km). Part of a big complex which includes a grd centre and the revamped and rather swish **BIRDS OF PREY CENTRE** (flying displays; kids get to handle some of the birds, phone for details 0131 654 1720). As for the bugs, the butterflies are delightful but 'orrible children will be far more impressed with the scorpions, locusts and other assorted uglies on show. Red-kneed tarantula not for the faint-hearted. 7 days, 10am-5pm.

1358
MAP 4
B4
AUCHINGARRICH WILDLIFE CENTRE, nr COMRIE: 4km from main st turning off at br then signed. Recent coralling in picturesque Perthshire Hills that's especially good fun for kids mainly because of its easy-going atmos. Lots of baby fluffy things, some of which you can hold. Don't ask what happens to them when they grow up! Good place to start sex education. New emus and meerkats. Open AYR 10am-dusk. Coffee shop till 5pm.

1359
MAP 1
C3
KELBURN COUNTRY CENTRE, LARGS: 2km S of Largs on A78. Riding school, grds, woodland walks up the Kel Burn and a central visitor/consumer section with shops/exhibits/cafés. Wooden stockade for clambering kids; commando assault course for exhibitionist adults and less doddering dads. Falconry displays (and long-suffering owl). Kelburn continues to develop its range of attractions: the Secret Forest has appeared in the woods. Combine with Vikingar (1695/LEISURE CENTRES) for an exhausting day. Stock up with chips and Nardini's ice cream (1155/ICE CREAM). 7days 10am-6pm.

FIFE AND DUNDEE:

1360
MAP 5
B5
✚ **DEEP SEA WORLD, N QUEENSFERRY:** 01383 411411. The massively successful aquarium in a quarry which must make life hell in N Queensferry at the w/end (park'n'ride system and buses from Edin, or better still by *Maid of the Forth* from S Queensferry (1963/FAVOURITE JOURNEYS). Habitats are viewed from a conveyor belt where you can stare goggle-eyed at the goggle-eyed fish teeming around and above you. Poor old Moby the whale's skull is now displayed (he got into trouble in the Forth in 1997) along with Amazonian fish in a 'rainforest habitat'. Maximum hard sell to this all-weather attraction, but kids like it even when they've been queueing for aeons. In my view the best thing is the view from the canteen. Open AYR 7 days: summer 10am-6.30pm; winter 11am-5pm.

1361
MAP 5
D2
✚ **CRAIGTON PARK, ST ANDREWS:** 01334 473666. 6km SW of St Andrews on the Pitscottie rd. An oasis of fun: bouncy castles, trampolines, putting, crazy golf, boating lake, a train thro the grounds, adventure playgrounds and glasshouses. A perfect day's amusement esp for nippers. Easter-Sept; 10.30am-6.30pm, 7 days.

1362
MAP 4
D2
CAMPERDOWN PARK, DUNDEE: The large park just off the ring-road system (the Kingsway and via A923 to Couper Angus) with a wildlife centre and a nearby play complex. Animal-handling at w/ends, but watch out: that gorilla does eat babies. 'Over 80 species'. Open AYR, but centre 10am-4.30pm, earlier in winter (1231/ TOWN PARKS).

SOUTH AND SOUTH WEST:

✤ **GO BANANAS, PRESTWICK:** 01292 475215. Off main st at Station rd, past stn to beach and to rt. Big shed that's a soft play area for kids. Everything that the little blighters will like in the throwing-themselves-around department. Shriek city and a non-parent nightmare zone. They never had anything like this in my day, only trees (he said, Day-Glo green with envy). 7 days 9.30am-7pm. **1363 MAP 4 D3**

LOUDON CASTLE, nr GALSTON: Recent theme park in S of Glas hinterland. Just off A71 Kilmarnock-Edin rd (go from Glas via A77 Kilmarnock rd). Behind the ruins of the said Loudon Castle (burned out in 1941), a fair-ground which includes the 'largest carousel in Europe' and massive 'chairy plane', has been transplanted in the old walled grd. Nice setting; well kids may not notice the setting, but they won't forget the chairy plane. Open AYR 10am-dusk. **1364 MAP 1 D3**

PALACERIGG COUNTRY PARK, CUMBERNAULD: 01236 720047. 6km E of Cumbernauld. 740 acres of parkland; ranger service, nature trails, picnic area and kids farm. 18-hole golf course and putting green. Exhib area with changing exhibits about forestry, conservation etc. Open AYR: 7 days; daylight hrs. Visitor centre and tearoom till 6.30pm in summer, 4.30pm winter. **1365 MAP 1 E3**

THE TWEEDHOPE SHEEPDOG CENTRE, MOFFAT: 01683 221471. Viv Billingham Parkes has competed in numerous sheep trials and now shepherds the public in to watch her skilful demos: Easter-Oct; 11am/3pm or by appointment. W/ends and winter by appointment only. **1366 MAP 9 D2**

TEDDY MELROSE, TEDDY BEAR MUSEUM, MELROSE: 01896 822464. The Wynd. Charming teddy cornucopia: small rm displaying Pooh, Rupert and friends, with origin and history details alongside. Downstairs you can watch teddies being made, then ponder over which teddy keepsake to buy in the shop. Yummy cream teas in the courtyard. Open AYR: 10am-5pm. Small theatre behind for grown-ups in the evening (1877/THEATRES). **1367 MAP 8 C3**

DRUMLANRIG CASTLE, nr DUMFRIES: 1214/COUNTRY PARKS.

NORTH-EAST

✤ **MACDUFF AQUARIUM:** On seafront E of the harbour, a new family attraction for this underrated Moray Firth port. Underrated perhaps because neighbouring Banff gets much more attention from tourists, but Duff House (1836/GALLERIES) gets much fewer visitors than this user and child-friendly sea life centre. All the fish seem curiously happy with their lot and content to educate and entertain. Open AYR 10-5pm (till 8pm in summer). **1368 MAP 3 D2**

✤ **ADEN, MINTLAW, nr PETERHEAD:** (pron 'Ah-den'). Country park just beyond Mintlaw on A950 16km from Peterhead. Former grounds of mansion with walks and many organised activities and events. Farm buildings converted into Heritage Centre (kids free), café etc. Adventure playground, 'working farm'. Open AYR. **1369 MAP 3 D2**

✤ **STORYBOOK GLEN, nr ABERDEEN:** Fibreglass fantasy land in verdant glen 16km S of Aber via B9077, the S Deeside rd, a nice drive. Characters from every fairy tale and nursery story dotted around 20-acre park. Their fixed manic stares give them a spooky resemblance to people you may know, but kids presumably don't find them so real. Older kids may find it tame – no guns, no big technology. New 'indoor play area'. Mar-Oct 10-6pm. Nov-Feb w/ends only 11-4pm. **1370 MAP 3 D4**

HIGHLANDS

✤ **THE CAIRNGORM REINDEER HERD nr AVIEMORE:** At Glenmore Forest Park on rd from Coylumbridge 12km from Aviemore. Real reindeer aplenty in reasonably authentic free-ranging habitat. Possibly too poignant when it's snowing. They've come a long way from Sweden in 1952. Transport to slope and meal for handfeeding. 1hr 30min trip. They are so . . . small. 11am AYR plus 2.30pm in summer. **1371 MAP 2 D4**

✤ **LEAULT FARM nr KINCRAIG:** Actually on fast bit of the main A9, but easier to find by looking for sign 1km S of Kincraig on the B9152. Working farm with daily sheepdog trials where Neal Ross demonstrates his extraordinary facility with dogs and sheep (and ducks). By all accounts this is gr spectacle and is totally authentic in this setting. Usually noon and 4pm (May-Oct, also 10 and 2pm July/Aug). Cl Sat. **1372 MAP 2 D4**

1373 **THE HIGHLAND WILDLIFE PARK, KINCRAIG:** On B9152 betw Aviemore and
MAP 2 Kingussie. Large drive-through 'reserve' run by Royal Zoological Society with
D4 wandering herds of deer, bison etc and pens of other animals. 'Habitats', but
mostly cages. Must be time to bring back some of these bears and wolves - sort
out the deer and liven up the caravan parks. Open 10-5pm.

1374 **HIGHLAND AND RARE BREEDS FARM, ELPHIN, nr ULLAPOOL:** 01854 666204. Bridie
MAP 2 and Russell Pursey's charming croft with over 30 'breeds' from the Soay sheep of
D4 St Kilda to Tamworth pigs; many feathered friends. A genuine working farm set
on either side of the rd (A835 26km N of Ullapool) that's v hooves and hands-on.
There's always a baby something to pet. Farmwork demos and tours. The sun
seems to shine here all day. May-Sept, 10am-5pm; 7 days.

1375 **LANDMARK CENTRE, CARRBRIDGE:** 01479 841614. A purpose-built tourist centre
MAP 2 with audiovisual displays and a gr deal of shopping. Gr for kids messing about in
C2 the woods on slides, in a 'maze' etc, in a large adventure playground. The Tower
may be too much for Granny but there are fine forest views. Open AYR 7 days.

MAP 2 **ISLAY WILDLIFE INFO & FIELD CENTRE, PORT CHARLOTTE:** 01496 850288.
D3 Fascinating wildlife centre for all ages. Activity rm and organised day trips.
(1404/WILDLIFE; 1934/ISLAY).

1376 **SEALIFE CENTRE, OBAN:** 16km N on the A828. On the shore of L Creran this is
MAP 1 one of a number of UK waterworlds (another in **ST ANDREWS**) now spreading to
B1 Europe too. Environmentally conscientious they 'rescue' seals and house
numerous aquatic life. The new 'World of the Jellyfish' is the ultimate lava lamp
of baby moon-jellys floating around their glass cylinder. Café/shop/adventure
playground. Open Feb-Nov, 9am- 6pm.

1377 **RARE BREEDS FARM, OBAN:** 4km from town via Argyll Sq, then S (A816), bearing
MAP 1 left at church and on past golf course. A weird and wonderful collection of
B1 animals in hill side pens and runs, who seem all the more peculiar because they're
versions of familiar ones – but are they sheep or dogs or goats or what? Leaving
the caging questions aside, it's a funny farm for kids and the creatures seem keen
enough for the attention and the far too many crumbs from the tearoom table.
Open 7 days in season.

1378 ⚓ **ARGYLL WILDLIFE PARK, INVERARAY:** 4km W of town on A83. Another zoo-
MAP 1 ✝ type place, but with many native animals in more or less their natural habitat.
C2 Lots of them just wander and waddle about. Set amongst pinewoods on the braes
of L Fyne, there are probably even a few animals (e.g. mink and foxes), trying to
get in. Of the many badgers, wildcats, deer and multifarious wildfowl, only one
old boar has so far escaped. Apr-Oct, 10-5pm, 7days.

1379 **NATURAL HISTORY CENTRE, ARDNARMURCHAN:** 01972 500209. A861 Strontian,
MAP 2 B8007 Glenmore 14km. Photographer Michael McGregor's award winning
B4 interactive exhib; a bit of a surprise out here. Kids will enjoy, adults may be
impressed. Tearoom. Mon-Sat; 10.30am-5.30pm. Sun; 12-5.30pm.

THE BEST PLACES TO SEE BIRDS

See p. 175 for WILDLIFE RESERVES, *all of which are bird reserves, too.*

✝ ✝ **HANDA ISLAND, nr SCOURIE, SUTHERLAND:** Take the boat from Tarbet **1380**
Beach 6km off A894 5km N of Scourie and land on a beautiful island run MAP 2
by the Scottish Wildlife Trust as a sea bird reserve. Boats (Apr-mid Sept though C1
fewer birds after Aug) are continuous depending on demand (01971 502077/340).
Crossing 15mins. Small reception hut and 2.5km walk over island to cliffs which
rise 350m and are layered in colonies from fulmars to shags. Allow 3 to 4hrs.
Perhaps you can persuade the boatman to go to see the cliffs and the formidable
stack from below. Though you must take care not to disturb the birds, you'll be
eye to eye with seals and bill to bill with razorbills. No boats on Sun. Eat at the
seafood café on the cove when you return (1081/SEAFOOD RESTAUS).

✝ ✝ **CAERLAVEROCK, nr DUMFRIES:** 17km S on B725 nr Bankend, signed from **1381**
rd. Park at 'The Wildlife and Wetlands Centre'. Admn to observation MAP 9
towers and walkways betw embankments into which hides have been built at D3
intervals allowing fine views of surrounding wetlands. Large assemblies of numerous species; sightings posted. Gr success story for Barnacle Geese now
wintering from Spitzbergen in many thousands. A well-managed site where it is
poss to get so close to the birds that it's hard to imagine that they don't know
you're there. Barn owl watch and special toads. Oct-April 10am-5pm. ADMN

✝ ✝ **LUNGA** and **THE TRESHNISH ISLANDS:** Off Mull. Sail from Iona or **1382**
Fionnphort or Ulva ferry on Mull to these uninhabited islands on a 5/6hr MAP 1
excursion which probably takes in Staffa and Fingal's Cave. Best months are A1
May-July when birds are breeding. Some trips allow 3hrs on Lunga. Razorbills,
guillemots and a carpet of puffins oblivious to your presence. This will be a
memorable day. Boat trips (01688 400242) or check Tobermory TO (01688
302182) who will advise of other boatmen. All trips dependent on sea conditions.

✝ ✝ **ISLE OF MAY, FIRTH OF FORTH:** Island at mouth of Forth off Crail/ **1383**
Anstruther reached by daily boat trip from Anstruther Harbour (01333 MAP 5
310103), May-Sept 9am-2.30pm depending on tides. Boats hold 40-50; trip 45mins; C3
allows 3hrs ashore. Island (including isthmus to Rona) 1.5km x 0.5km. Info centre
and resident wardens. See guillemots, razorbills and kittiwakes on cliffs and shags,
terns and thousands of puffins. Most populations increasing. This place is strange as
well as beautiful. The puffins in early summer are, as always, engaging.

✝ **THE LAGOON, MUSSELBURGH:** On E edge of town behind the racecourse **1384**
(follow rd round), at the estuarine mouth of the R Esk. Waders, sea birds, MAP 7
ducks aplenty and often interesting migrants on the mudflats and wide littoral. C1
The 'lagoon' itself is a man-made pond behind and attracts big populations (both
birds and binocs). This is the nearest diverse-species area to Edin (15km) and in
recent yrs has become one of the most significant migrant stopovers in the UK.

✝ **FOWLSHEUGH, nr STONEHAVEN:** 8km S of Stonehaven and signed from **1385**
A92with path from Crawton. Sea bird city on spectacular cliffs where you MAP 3
can lie on your front and look over. The cliffs are 75m high; take gr care. 80,000 D4
pairs of 6 species esp guillemots, kittiwakes, razorbills and also fulmar, shag,
puffins. Poss to view the birds without disturbing them and see the 'layers' they
occupy on the cliff face. Or go by boat twice weekly in summer from Stonehaven
Harbour (check TO for details 01569 762806). Best seen May-July.

✝ **LOCH OF THE LOWES, DUNKELD:** 4km NE Dunkeld on A923 to Blairgowrie. **1386**
Properly managed (Scottish Wildlife Trust) site with double-floored hide and MAP 4
permanent binocs. Main attractions are the captivating ospreys (from early Apr- C3
Aug/Sept). Nest 100m over loch and clearly visible. Their revival is well
documented, including diary of movements, breeding history etc;

✝ **LOCH GARTEN, BOAT OF GARTEN:** 3km village off B970 into Abernethy Forest. **1387**
Famous for the ospreys and so popular that access may be restricted until MAP 2
after the eggs have hatched. 2 car parks: the first has nature trails through Scots D4
pine woods and around loch; other has the main hide 300m away. Extraordinary
palaver considering there's only one pair and there are no fish in the loch so they
don't feed there (anyhow fishfarms are easier). Och, but they are magnificent.

✝ **ISLAY, LOCH GRUINART, LOCH INDAAL:** RSPB reserve. Take A847 at **1388**
Bridgendthen B8017 turning N and rt for Gruinart. The mudflats and fields MAP 1
at the head of the loch provide winter grazing for huge flocks of Barnacle and A3

Greenland geese. They arrive, as do flocks of fellow bird-watchers, in late Oct. Hides and good vantage points near rd. The Rhinns and the Oa in the S sustain a huge variety of bird life.

1389 ✝ **MARWICK HEAD, ORKNEY MAINLAND:** 40km NW of Kirkwall, via Finstown and Dounby; take left at Birsay after L of Isbister cross the B9056 and park at Cumlaquoy. Spectacular sea bird breeding colony on 100m cliffs and nearby at the Loons Reserve, wet meadowland, 8 species of duck and many waders. Orkney sites include the Noup cliffs on Westray, North Hill on Papa Westray and Copinsay, 3km E of the mainland. The remoter, the merrier.

1390 **ORKNEY PUFFINS:** 'Wildabout' tour's dusk puffin patrol (01856 851011). Or go solo at Costa Head, Brough of Birsay and Westray; check Kirkwall TO for latest.

1391 **BARON'S HAUGH, MOTHERWELL:** nr Strathclyde Park. From Motherwell Civic
MAP 1 Centre, take rd for Hamilton then left (1km) up Leven St, bearing rt to end (there
E3 are signs). RSPB reserve of woodland, marsh and scrub by R Clyde; a sanctuary in a heavily built-up area. Furthest of 4 hides is 1.5km walk. The wide variety of habitats offers a surprising range of species esp in winter. Dalzell Country Park adj, has trails.

1392 **THE BASS ROCK, off NORTH BERWICK:** 01620 892838. 'Temple of gannets'. A
MAP 7 gr-guano encrusted spaceship take-off ramp sticking out of the Forth and where
D1 Davie Balfour was imprisoned in RLS's *Catriona* (aka *Kidnapped II*). Weather-dependent boat trips available May-Sep courtesy of Mr Marr, from N Berwick harbour (also to nearby Fidra). Phone for details.

1393 **LOCH OF KINNORDY, KIRRIEMUIR:** 4km W of town on B951, an easily accessible site
MAP 4 with 2 hides o/look loch and wetland area managed by RSPB. Geese in winter,
D3 gulls aplenty; always tickworthy.

1394 **STRATHBEG, nr FRASERBURGH:** 12km S off main Fraserburgh-Peterhead rd, the
MAP 3 A952 and signed 'Nature Reserve' at Crimond. Wide, shallow loch v close to
E2 coastline, a 'magnet for migrating wildfowl' and from the (unmanned) reception centre at loch side it's poss to get a v good view of them. Marsh/fen, dune and meadow habitats. In winter 30,000 geese/widgeon/mallard/swans and occasional rarities like cranes and egrets. Binocs in centre and 2 other hides; marked route around.

WHERE TO SEE DOLPHINS, WHALES AND PORPOISES

1395 ✝ ✝ *The coast around the N of Scotland offers some of the best places in Europe from which to see whales and dolphins and, more ubiquitously, seals. You don't have to go on boat trips, though of course you get closer, the boatman will know where to find them and the trip itself can be exhilarating. A list of operators is given below. Dolphins are most active on a rising tide esp May-Sept.*

MORAY and CROMARTY FIRTHS, nr INVERNESS and CROMARTY:

The best area in Scotland. The population of bottlenose dolphins in this area well exceeds 100 and they can be seen AYR.

THE DOLPHIN WATCH and MARINE RESEARCH STATION: Just N of the Kessock Br on the A9 and adj the Tourist Information Centre. Underwater microphones pick up the chatterings of dolphins and porpoises and there's always somebody there to explain. Apr-Nov, 7 days 10am-7.30pm.

CROMARTY: Any vantage around the town is good and an old lighthouse cottage has been converted into a research base here. Other sites in this area with helpful marker boards at **FOULIS FERRY**, W end of car park; **BALINTORE**, opp Seaboard Memorial Hall; **TARBERT NESS beyond PORTMAHOMACK,**end of path through reserve; and esp **CHANONRY POINT**, E end of pt beyond lighthouse. Sightings further out along the Moray Firth poss at **BURGHEAD, LOSSIEMOUTH and BUCKIE, SPEY BAY and PORTKNOCKIE.**

NORTH WEST

On the W coast, esp nr Gairloch the following places may offer sightings of orcs, dolphins and minke whales mainly in summer.

RUBHA REIDH nr GAIRLOCH: 20km N by unclassified rd beyond Melvaig. Nr the Carn Dearg Youth Hostel W of Lonemore where rd turns inland is good spot.

GREENSTONE POINT N of LAIDE on the A832 nr Inverewe Gardens and Gruinard Bay. Harbour porpoises here Apr-Dec and minke whales May-Oct.

RED POINT of GAIRLOCH: by unclassified rd via Badachro. High ground looking over N Minch and S to L Torridon. Harbour porpoises often along this coast.

OTHER PLACES

MOUSA SOUND, SHETLAND: 20km S of Lerwick (1449/PREHISTORIC SITES).

ARDNAMURCHAN, THE POINT: The most westerly point (and lighthouse) on this wildly beautiful peninsula. Go to end of rd or park nr Sanna Beach and walk round. Sanna Beach is worth going to just to walk the strand. New visitor centre with tearoom and toilets.

STORNOWAY, ISLE OF LEWIS: Heading out of town for Eye Peninsula, at Holm nr Sandwick S of A866 or from Bayble Bay (all within walking distance).

BOAT TRIPS TO SEA LIFE

FROM CROMARTY: DOLPHIN ECOSSE (01381 600323); **SEABOARD MARINE** (01381 871254).

FROM INVERNESS: DOLPHIN CRUISES (01463 717900); **MACAULAY CHARTERS** (01463 717337).

ON THE ISLANDS: SEA-LIFE CRUISES, MULL (01688 400223); **GORDON MACKINNON, SKYE:** (01471 866236) L Coruisk in the Cuillins; **WILDABOUT, ORKNEY:** (01856 851011) puffin patrols at dusk.

MINCH CHARTERS, MALLAIG: 01687 462304. Every kind of mammal in all kinds of scenery: L Coruisk, Corryvreckan, St Kilda (1999/SEVEN THINGS).

LAXFORD CHARTERS: 01971 502251. Unusual islands and skerries of L Laxford (nr Handa Island); seals, birds and gr seafood back on land (1081/SEAFOOD RESTAUS).

SUMMER ISLES CRUISES: 01854 622200. The islets and seal colony. Angling if you like.

WILDLIFE CRUISES: 01955 611353. From John o' Groats; puffins, seabirds, seals. June-Aug.

. . . And OTTERS   1396

Otters can be seen all over the NW Highlands in sheltered inlets, esp early morning and late evening and on an ebb tide. Skye is one of best places in Europe to see them. Otter watch at **KYLERHEA:** 3km from ferry (from Glenelg), signposted. **OTTER SURVIVAL FUND AND VISITOR CENTRE, BROADFORD** (01471 822487) organise guided walks for all wildlife and might pt you in the rt direction.

GREAT WILDLIFE RESERVES

These wildlife reserves are not merely bird-watching places. Most of them are easy to get to from major centres; none requires permits.

ST ABBS HEAD, nr BERWICK: 22km N Berwick, 9km N Eyemouth and   1397
only 10km E of main A1. Spectacular cliff scenery (1641/COASTAL   MAP 8
WALKS), a huge sea bird colony, rich marine life and a varied flora make this a place   E1
of fascination and diverse interest. Good view from top of stacks, geos and cliff face full of serried ranks of guillemot, kittiwake, razorbill etc. Hanging grds of grasses and campion. Behind cliffs, grassland rolls down to the Mire L and its varied habitat of bird, insect and butterfly life and vegetation. Superb.

SANDS OF FORVIE and THE YTHAN ESTUARY, NEWBURGH: 25km N of Aber.   1398
Cross br o/side Newburgh on A975 to Cruden Bay and park. Path   MAP 3
follows Ythan estuary and, bearing N, enters the largest dune system in the UK   E3
undisturbed by man. Dunes in every aspect of formation. Collieston, a 17/18th-century fishing village arranged in terraces on the cliffs, is 5km away. The various coastal habitats support the largest population of eiders in UK (esp June) and huge numbers of terns. Plenty to see even from main rd lay-bys; also hides.

JOHN MUIR COUNTRY PARK, DUNBAR: The vast park betw Dunbar and N Berwick   1399

MAP 7
E1
named after the naturalist/explorer who was born in Dunbar and who, in founding Yellowstone National Park in the US, is regarded as the father of the Conservation movement. Includes estuary of the Tyne (park also known as Tyninghame), cliffs, sand spits and woodland, it covers a wide range of habitats. Many bird species (e.g. 30 waders), crabs, lichens, sea and marsh plants. Enter at E extremity of Dunbar at Belhaven, off the B6370 from A1; or off A198 to N Berwick 3km from A1. Or better, walk from Dunbar by 'cliff top trail' (2km).

1400 **LOCHWINNOCH:** 30km SW of Glas via M8 jnct 29 then A737 and A760 past
MAP 1 Johnstone. Also from Largs 20km via A760. Reserve is just o/side village on loch
C3 side and comprises wetland and woodland habitats. A serious 'nature centre' incorporating an observation tower. Hides and marked trails; and a birds-spotted board. Shop and coffee shop. Good for kids. Centre 10am-5pm.   RSPB

1401 **INSH MARSHES, KINGUSSIE:** 4km from town along B970 (after Ruthven Barracks,
MAP 2 1441/RUINS), a reserve run by RSPB but with much more than just birds to see.
D4 Trail (3km) marked out through meadow and wetland and a note of species to look out for (including 6 types of orchid). Also 2 hides (250m and 450m) high above marshes, vantage points to see waterfowl, birds of prey, otters and deer.

1402 **TENTSMUIR, betw NEWPORT and LEUCHARS:** The northern tip of Fife at the mouth
MAP 5 of the Firth of Tay, reached from Tayport or Leuchars via the B945. Follow signs
D2 for Kinshaldy Beach taking rd that winds for 4km over flat and then forested land. Park amongst Corsican pine plantation (car park closes 9pm in summer) and cross dunes to broad strand which many consider to be a better beach than the W Sands, St Andrews. Walks in both direction: W back to Tayport, E towards Eden Bird Sanctuary. Also 4km circular walk of beach and forest. Hide 2km away at Ice House Pond. Seals often watch from waves and bask in summer. Lots of butterflies. Waders aplenty and, to E, one of UK's most significant populations of eider. Most wildfowl offshore on Abertay Sands.

1403 **VANE FARM:** RSPB reserve on S shore of L Leven, beside and bisected by B9097
MAP 5 off jnct 5 of M90. Easily reached and v busy visitor centre with observation
B3 lounge and education/orientation facs. Hide nearer loch side reached by tunnel under rd. Nature Trail on hill behind through heath and birchwood (2km circ). Good place to introduce kids to nature watching. Recent upgrading.

1404 **ISLAY WILDLIFE INFO & FIELD CENTRE, PORT CHARLOTTE:** Jam-packed info centre
MAP 1 that's v 'hands-on' and interactive. Up-to-date displays of geology, natural
A3 history (rocks, skeletons, sealife tanks). Recent sightings of wildlife, flora and fauna lists, video rm, reference library. Kids area and activity days when staff take you on a tour around the surrounding areaj157.

1405 **BALRANALD, NORTH UIST, WESTERN ISLES:** W coast of N Uist reached by the rd
MAP 2 from Lochmaddy, then the Bayhead t/off at Clachan Stores (10km N). Sadly, we
A3 were pushed for time (and you can't be pushed for time in a nature reserve), so we couldn't do this place justice. Nor did we hear the corncrake, this being one of its last strongholds. Many species; many different habitats.

SECTION 7

Historical Places

THE BEST CASTLES

NTS: *Under the care of the National Trust for Scotland. Hrs vary.* HS: *Under the care of Historic Scotland. Standard hrs are: Apr-end Sept Mon-Sat 9.30am-6.30pm; Sun 2-6.30pm. Oct-Mar Mon-Sat 9.30am-4.30pm; Sun 2-4.30pm.*

1406
MAP 6
D4
✝ ✝ ✝ **STIRLING CASTLE:** Some would say that Stirling is 'better' than Edin: perched on its rock above the town, it is instantly comparable. And like Edin, it's a timeless attraction that can withstand waves of tourism as it survived the centuries of warfare for which it was built. Despite this primary function, it does seem a v civilised billet, with peaceful grds and rampart walks from which the views are excellent (esp the aerial view of the Royal Grds, 'the cup and saucer' as they're known locally). The renovation of the Gr Hall will recreate the jewel in Stirling's crown demonstrating how magnificent the banquets must have been in the court of James. It should be ready for the millennium. Appropiate and pleasant café. HS

1407
MAP A
C3
✝ ✝ ✝ **EDINBURGH CASTLE:** Edin city centre. Impressive from any angle and all the more so from inside. Despite the tides of tourists and time, it still enthralls. Superb perspectives of the city and of Scottish history. Recently arrived Stone of Destiny up there with the Crown Jewels as Big Attraction. Café and restau (superb views) with efficient, but uninspiring catering operation; open only castle hrs and to castle visitors (304/MAIN ATTRACTIONS). HS

1408
MAP 3
A2
✝ ✝ **BRODIE CASTLE, nr NAIRN:** 12km E of Nairn off main A96. More a (Z plan) tower house than a castle, dating from 1567 and still lived in by the 'Brodie of Brodie'. With a minimum of historical hocum, this 16/17th-century, but mainly Victorian, country house is furnished from rugs to moulded ceilings in the most excellent taste. Every picture (v few gloomies) bears examination. The nursery and nannie's rm, the guest rms, indeed all the rms, are eminently habitable. I could live in the library. There are regular musical evenings (01309 641371 for event programme). Tearoom and informal walks in grounds. An avenue leads to a lake; in spring the daffodils are famous. Apr-Sept 11am-5.30pm; Sun 1.30-5.30pm. W/ends in Oct. Grounds open AYR till sunset. NTS

1409
MAP 1
C4
✝ ✝ **CULZEAN CASTLE, MAYBOLE:** 24km S of Ayr on A719. Impossible to convey here the scale and the scope of the house and the country park. Allow some hrs esp for the grounds. Castle is more like a country house and you examine from the other side of a rope. From the 12th century, but rebuilt by Robert Adam in 1775, a time of soaring ambition, its grandeur is almost out of place in this exposed cliff-top position. It was designed for entertaining, and the oval staircase is magnificent. Wartime associations (esp with President Eisenhower, which will interest Americans) plus the enduring fascination of the aristocracy. 560 acres of grounds including cliff top walk, formal grds, walled grd, Swan Pond (a must) and Happy Valley. Harmonious home farm is visitor centre with café, exhibits and shop etc. Open Apr-Oct 10am-5pm. Culzean is pron 'Cullane'. NTS

1410
MAP 5
C3
✝ ✝ **FALKLAND PALACE, FALKLAND:** Middle of farming Fife, 15km from M90 at jnct 8. Not a castle at all, but the hunting palace of the Stewart dynasty. Despite its recreational rather than political role, it's one of the landmark buildings in Scottish history and in the 16th century was the finest Renaissance building in Britain. They all came here for archery, falconry and hunting boar and deer on the Lomonds; and for Royal Tennis which is displayed and explained. Still occupied by the Crichton-Stewarts, the house is dark and rich and redolent of those days of 'dancin and deray at Falkland on the Grene'. Apr-Oct 11-5.30pm, Sun 1.30-5.30pm. Gr walks from village (1584/HILL WALKS). NTS

1411
MAP 1
D3
✝ **CAWDOR CASTLE, CAWDOR, nr NAIRN and INVERNESS:** The mighty Cawdor of *Macbeth* fame. The family clear off for the summer and leave their romantic yet habitable castle, sylvan grounds and gurgling Cawdor Burn to you. Pictures from Claude to John Piper and Conroy, a modern kitchen as fascinating as the enormous one of yore. Even the 'tartan passage' is nicely done. The burn is the colour of tea. An easy drive (25km) to Brodie (1408/CASTLES) means you can see two of Scotland's most appealing castles in one day. Grds are gorgeous. May-early Oct, 7 days, 10am-5.30pm, 9-hole golf.

1412
MAP 4
B2
✝ **BLAIR CASTLE, BLAIR ATHOLL:** Impressive from the A9, the castle and the landscape of the Dukes of Atholl; 10km N of Pitlochry. Hugely popular; almost a holiday camp atmos. Numbered rms chock-full of 'collections':

costumes, toys, plates, weapons, stag skulls, walking sticks – so many things! Upstairs, the more usual stuffed apartments including the Jacobite bits. Walk in the policies (which is more than the current Duke does v often). Apr-Oct 10am-5pm.

✚ **GLAMIS, FORFAR:** 8km from Forfar via A94 or off main A929, Dundee-Aber rd (t/off 10km N of Dundee, a picturesque app). Fairy-tale castle in majestic setting. Seat of the Strathmore family (Queen Mum spent her childhood here) for 300 yrs; every rm an example of the interior of a certain period. Guided tours (continuous/50mins duration). Restau/gallery shop haven for tourists. Mid Apr-mid Oct, 10.30am. Last admn 4.45pm.

1413
MAP 4
D3

✚ **BRODICK CASTLE, ARRAN:** 4km from town (bike hire 01770 302868/302460). Impressive, well-maintained castle, exotic formal grds and extensive grounds. Goat Fell in the background and the sea through the trees. Dating from 13th century and until recently the home of the Dukes of Hamilton. An over-antlered hall leads to liveable rms with portraits and heirlooms, an atmos of long-ago afternoons. Tangible sense of relief in the kitchens now all the entertaining is over. Robert the Bruce's cell is not so convincing. Easter-Oct 11.30-5pm; Oct Sat/Sun only. Marvellous grounds open AYR.

1414
MAP 1
C4

NTS

✚ **DUART CASTLE, MULL:** 13th-century ancestral seat of the Clan Maclean who take up residence for the summer and clan gatherings. Quite a few modifications over the centuries as methods of defence grew in sophistication but with walls as thick as a truck and the sheer isolation of the place it must have made any prospect of attack seem doomed from the outset. Of course the only attacking that gets done these days is on scones in the tearoom but some scent of the old bloodthirst still remains. May-Sept 10.30am-6pm.

1415
MAP 1
B1

TOROSAY CASTLE, MULL: 3km from Craignure and the ferry. A Victorian arriviste in this strategic corner where Duart Castle has ruled for centuries. Not many apartments open but who could blame them – this is a family home, endearing and eccentric esp their more recent history (like Dad's Loch Ness Monster fixation). The heirlooms are valuable because they have been cherished and there's a human proportion to the house and its contents which is rare in such places. The grds, attributed to Lorimer, are fabulous, esp the Italianate Statue Walk, and are open AYR. The Mull Light Railway from Craignure is one way to go. Tearoom. Apr-Oct 10.30am-5.30pm.

1416
MAP 1
B1

DUNVEGAN CASTLE, SKYE: 3km Dunvegan village. Romantic history and setting, though more baronial than castellate, the result of mid-19th-century restoration that incorporated the disparate parts. Necessary crowd management leads you through a series of rms where the Fairy Flag, displayed above a table of exquisite marquetry, has pride of place. Grds down to the loch, where boats leave the jetty 'to see the seals'. Busy café and gift shop at gate side car park.

1417
MAP 2
B3

EILEAN DONAN, DORNIE: On A87, 13km before Kyle of Lochalsh. A calendar favourite, often depicted illuminated; but with the airport runway lights on the new br behind, it's even more like Coney Eilean. Inside it's a v decent slice of history for the price. The Banqueting Hall with its Pipers' Gallery must make for splendid dinner parties for the Macraes. Much military regalia amongst the bric-à-brac, but also the impressive Raasay Punchbowl partaken of by Johnson and Boswell. Mystical views from ramparts.

1418
MAP 2
C3

CASTLE MENZIES, WEEM, nr ABERFELDY: In Tay valley with spectacular ridge behind (there are walks here in the Weem Forest, part of the Tummel Valley Forest Park; separate car park). On B846, 7km W of Aberfeldy, through Weem. The 16th-century stronghold of the Menzies (pron 'Ming-iss'), one of Scotland's oldest clans. Sparsely furnished with odd clan memorabilia, the house nevertheless conveys more of a sense of Jacobite times than many more brimful of bric-à-brac. Bonnie Prince Charlie stopped here on the way to Culloden. Open farmland situation, so manured rather than manicured grounds. Apr-Oct 10.30am-5pm, Sun 2-5pm. Tearoom. Gr woodland walks nearby.

1419
MAP 4
B3

KELLIE CASTLE, nr PITTENWEEM, FIFE: Major castle in Fife. Dating from 14th century restored by Robert Lorimer, his influence evidenced by magnificent plaster ceilings and furniture. The grds, nursery and kitchen recall all the old Victorian virtues. The old-fashioned roses still bloom for us. Easter and May-Sept 1.30-5.30pm, w/ends only Oct. Grounds open AYR.

1420
MAP 5
E3

ADMN

CRAGIEVAR, nr BANCHORY: 15km N of main A93 Aber-Braemar rd betw Banchory

1421

MAP 3
D3 and Aboyne. A classic tower house, perfect like a porcelain miniature. Random windows, turrets, balustrades. Set amongst sloping lawns and tall trees. Limited access to halt deterioration (only 8 people at a time) means you are spared the shuffling hordes, but don't go unless you are respecter of the NTS conservation policy. Check local TOs for latest opening hrs, but probably May-Sept 1.30pm. Last Entry 4.45pm.

NTS

1422 **DRUM CASTLE (the IRVINE ANCESTRAL HOME), nr BANCHORY:** 1km off main A93
MAP 3 Aber-Braemar rd betw Banchory and Peterculter and 20km from Aber centre.
D4 For 24 generations this has been the seat of the Irvines. Our lot! Gifted to one William De Irwin by Robert the Bruce for services rendered at Bannockburn, it combines the original keep, a Jacobean mansion and Victorian expansionism. I have twice signed the book in the Irvine Rm and wandered through the accumulated history hopeful of identifying with something. Hugh Irvine, the family 'artist' whose extravagant self-portrait as the Angel Gabriel raised eyebrows in 1810, seems more interesting than most of my soldiering forebears. Give me a window seat in the library! Grounds have a peaceful walled rose grd (Apr-Oct 10-6pm). House: Easter-Sept 1.30-5.30 (July/Aug opens 11am), Oct w/ends only.

NTS

1423 **BALMORAL, nr BALLATER:** On main A93 betw Ballater and Braemar. Limited
MAP 3 access to the house (i.e. only the ballrm - public functions are held here when
B4 *they're* in residence) so grounds (open May-July) with Albert's wonderful trees are more rewarding. For royalty rooters only, and if you like Landseers . . . Crathie Church along the main rd has a good rose window, an altar of Iona marble. John Brown is somewhere in the old graveyard down track from new vistor centre (but I couldn't find him), the memorial on the hill is worth a climb for a poignant moment and the view of the policies. The Crathie services haven't been quite the same Sunday attraction since Di and Fergie on a prince's arm.

1424 **DUNROBIN CASTLE, GOLSPIE:** The largest house in the Highlands, the home of the
MAP 2 Dukes of Sutherland who once owned more land than anyone else in the British
D2 Empire. It's the first Duke who occupies an accursed place in Scots history for his inhumane replacement, in these vast tracts, of people with sheep. His statue stands on Ben Bhraggie above the town (1486/MONUMENTS). Living the life of English grandees, the Sutherlands transformed the castle into a *château* and filled it with their obscene wealth. Once there were 100 servants for a house party of 20 and it had 30 gardeners. Now it's all just history. The grds are still fabulous. The castle and separate museum are open May-mid Oct. Check 01408 633177 for times.

ADMN

CRATHES, nr BANCHORY: 1199/GARDENS; 1477/COUNTRY HOUSES.

FYVIE, ABERDEENSHIRE: 1476/COUNTRY HOUSES.

FASQUE, nr STONEHAVEN: 1468/COUNTRY HOUSES.

FLOORS CASTLE, KELSO: 1472/COUNTRY HOUSES.

TRAQUAIR, INNERLEITHEN: 1470/COUNTRY HOUSES.

THIRLESTANE, LAUDER: 1475/COUNTRY HOUSES.

THE MOST INTERESTING RUINS

HS: *Under the care of Historic Scotland. Standard hrs are: Apr-end Sept Mon-Sat 9.30am-6.30pm; Sun 2-6.30pm. Oct-Mar Mon-Sat 9.30am-4.30pm, Sun 2-4.30pm. 'Friends of Historic Scotland' membership: 0131 668 8600 or any of the manned sites (annual charge but then free admn).*

✝ ✝ ✝ **LINLITHGOW PALACE:** Impressive from the M9 and the S app to this the most agreeable of W Lothian towns, but don't confuse the magnificent Renaissance edifice with St Michael's Church next door, topped with its controversial crown and spear spire. From the richly carved fountain in the courtyard, to the Gr Hall with its adj huge kitchens, you get a real impression of the lavish lifestyle of the court. Apparently 'underperforms' as an attraction for Historic Scotland, so some titivation may be underway.

1425
MAP 7
B1

HS

✝ ✝ **CAERLAVEROCK, nr DUMFRIES:** 17km S by B725. Follow signs for Wetlands Reserve (1381/BIRDS), but go past rd end. Fairy-tale fortress within double moat and manicured lawns, the daunting frontage being the apex of an uncommon triangular shape. Since 1270, the bastion of the Maxwells, the Wardens of the W Marches. Destroyed by Bruce, besieged in 1640; now only waiting to be turned into a movie.

1426
MAP 9
D3

HS

✝ **DUNNOTTAR CASTLE, nr STONEHAVEN:** 3km S of Stonehaven on the coast rd just off the A92. Like Slains further N, the ruins are impressively and precariously perched on a cliff top. Historical links with Wallace, Mary Queen of Scots (the odd night) and even Oliver Cromwell, whose Roundheads besieged it in 1650. Mel Gibson's *Hamlet* was filmed here (bet you don't remember that). 400m walk from car park. Can walk along cliff top from Stonehaven (2km). Mar-Oct 9am-6pm, Sun 2-5pm. Nov-Mar Fri only 9-dusk.

1427
MAP 3
D4

✝ **CASTLE TIORAM, nr ACHARACLE:** Romantic, ruin where you don't need the saga to sense the place, and maybe the mystery is better than the history. 5km from A861 just N of Acharacle. A sign on the foreshore says 'Don't get stranded'; the walk across a short causeway adds to the experience. Recently and controversially, up for sale, but you'll still be able to go over whatever happens to it next. Pron 'Cheerum'. Musical beach at nearby Kentra Bay (1642/COASTAL WALKS).

1428
MAP 2
C4

✝ **ELGIN CATHEDRAL, ELGIN:** Follow signs in town centre. Set in a meadow by the river, a tranquil corner of this busy market town, the scattered ruins and surrounding graveyard of what was once Scotland's finest cathedral. The nasty Wolf of Badenoch burned it down in 1390, but there are some 13th-century and medieval renewals. The octagonal chapterhouse is especially revered, but this is an impressive and evocative slice of history. Guided tours are v good.

1429
MAP 3
B2

HS ADMN

✝ **KILDRUMMY CASTLE, nr ALFORD:** 15km SW of Alford on A97 nr the hotel (984/SCOTTISH HOTELS) and across the gorge from its famous grds. Most complete 13th-century castle in Scotland, an HQ for the Jacobite uprising of 1715 and an evocative and v Highland site. Here the invitation in HS advertising to 'bring your imagination' is truly valid. Apr-Oct 10-5pm.

1430
MAP 3
B3

HS

✝ **KISIMULL CASTLE, ISLE OF BARRA:** The medieval fortress, home of the MacNeils that sits on a rocky outcrop in the bay 200m offshore. Originally built in the 11th century, it was burnt in the 18th and restored by the 45th chief, an American architect, but was unfinished when he died in 1970. An essential pilgrimage for all MacNeils, it is fascinating and atmospheric for the rest of us, a grim exterior belying an unusual internal layout - a courtyard that seems unchanged and rms betwixt renovation and decay. The boatman John Allan will show you round on Mon/Wed/ Sat afts. Go to the quay or phone 01871 810449. See it before H S removes the weeds and the true ravages of time.

1431
MAP 2
A4

EDZELL CASTLE, EDZELL: 2km village off main st, signed. Pleasing red sandstone ruin in bucolic setting – birds twitter, rabbits run. Notable walled parterre grd created by Sir David Lindsay way back in 1604. The wall niches are nice. Mary Queen of Scots was here (of course).

1432
MAP 4
D2

HS

BOTHWELL CASTLE, UDDINGSTON, GLASGOW: 15km E of city via M74, Uddingston t/off into main st and follow signs. Hugely impressive 13th-century ruin, the home of the Black Douglases, o/look Clyde (with fine walks). Remarkable considering proximity to city that there is hardly any 20th-century intrusion except yourself. 1km from car park. Pay to go inside.

1433
MAP 1
D3

HS

1434 FORT GEORGE, nr INVERNESS: On promontory of Moray Firth 18km NE via A96
MAP 2 by village of Ardersier. A vast site and 'one of the most outstanding artillery
D3 fortifications in Europe'. Planned after Culloden as a base for George II's army
and completed 1769, it has remained unaltered ever since and allows a v complete
picture. May provoke palpitations in the Nationalist heart, but it's heaven for
militarists and altogether impressive. It's hardly a ruin of course, and is still
occupied by the army. HS

1435 DUNOLLIE CASTLE, OBAN: Just o/side town via Corran Esplanade towards
MAP 1 Ganavan. Best to walk to or park on Esplanade and then walk 1km. (No safe
B1 parking on main rd below castle.) Bit of a scramble up and a slither down, but the
views are superb. More atmospheric than Dunstaffnage and not commercialised.
You can climb one flight up, but the ruin is only a remnant of the gr stronghold
of the Lorn Kings that it was. The Macdougals, who took it over in the 12th
century, still live in the house below.

1436 TARBERT CASTLE: Tarbert, Argyll. Strategically and dramatically o/look the
MAP 1 sheltered harbour of this epitome of a West Highland pt. Unsafe to clamber over,
B3 it's for the timeless view rather than an evocation of tangible history that it's
worth finding the way up. Steps on Harbour Rd next to dental surgery.

1437 KILCHURN CASTLE, LOCH AWE: The romantic ruin at the head of L Awe, visited
MAP 1 either by a short walk (1km) from car park off the main A85 5km E of Lochawe
C2 village (betw the Stronmilchan t/off and the Inveraray rd) or by boat from village
(don't let boatman tell you it's a *long* walk in). Pleasant spot for loch reflections.

1438 ST ANDREWS CATHEDRAL: The ruins of the largest church in Scotland before the
MAP 5 Reformation, a place of gr influence and pilgrimage. St Rule's Tower and the
D2 jagged fragment of the huge W Front in their striking position at the convergence
of the main streets and o/look the sea, are remnants of its gr glory.

1439 CRICHTON CASTLE, nr PATHHEAD: 6km W of A68 at Pathhead (28km S Edin) or via
MAP 7 A7 turning E, 3km S of Gorebridge. Massive Border keep dominating the Tyne
C2 valley on knoll with church ruin nearby. Spectacular 'range' built late 16th
century. 500m walk from Crichton village. Good picnic spot. ADMN HS

1440 TANTALLON CASTLE, NORTH BERWICK: 5km E of town by coast rd; 500m to
MAP 7 dramatic cliff top setting with views to Bass Rock. Dates from 1350 with massive
D1 'curtain wall' to see it through stormy weather and stormy history. The Red
Douglases and their friends kept the world at bay. Wonderful beach nearby
(342/BEACHES). ADMN HS

1441 RUTHVEN BARRACKS, KINGUSSIE: 2km along B970 and visible from A9 esp at night
MAP 2 when it's illuminated, these former barracks built by the English Redcoats as part
D4 of the campaign to tame the Highlands after the first Jacobite rising in 1715, were
actually destroyed by the Jacobites in 1746 after Culloden. It was here that
Bonnie Prince Charlie sent his final order, 'Let every man seek his own safety',
signalling the absolute end of the doomed cause. Life for the soldiers is well
described and visualised. Open AYR. HS

1442 URQUHART CASTLE, DRUMNADROCHIT, LOCH NESS: 28km S of Inverness on A82.
MAP 2 The classic Highland fortress on a promontory o/look L Ness visited every yr by
D4 bus loads and boat loads of tourists. Photo opportunities galore amongst the
well-kept lawns and extensive ruins of the once formidable stronghold of the
Picts and their scions, finally abandoned in the 18th century. ADMN HS

1443 DOUNE CASTLE, DOUNE: Follow signs from centre of village which is just off A84
MAP 6 Callander-Dunblane rd. O/look the R Teith, the well-preserved ruin of a late
D3 14th-century courtyard castle with a Gr Hall and another draughty rm where
Mary Queen of Scots once slept. Walk in the meadow (1349/PICNICS).
ADMN HS

444 SLAINS CASTLE, betw NEWBURGH and CRUDEN BAY: 32km N of Aber off the A975
\P 3 perched on the cliffs. Obviously because of its location, but also because there's
E3 no reception centre/postcard shop or guided tour, this is a ruin that talks. Your
imagination, like Bram Stoker's (whom was inspired after staying here, to write
Dracula), can be cast to the winds. The seat of the Earls of Errol, it has been
gradually disintegrating since the roof was removed in 1925. Once, it had the
finest dining-rm in Scotland. The waves crash below, as always. Be careful!

THE BEST PREHISTORIC SITES

✝ ✝ ✝ **SKARA BRAE, ORKNEY MAINLAND:** 32km Kirkwall by A965/966 via 1445
Finstown and Dounby. Can be a windy walk to this remarkable
shoreline site, the subterranean remains of a compact village 5,000 yrs old. It was
engulfed by a sandstorm 600yrs later and lay perfectly preserved until uncovered
by another storm in 1850. Now it permits one of the most evocative glimpses of
truly ancient times in the UK.
ADMN HS

✝ ✝ **THE STANDING STONES OF STENNESS, ORKNEY MAINLAND:** Together with 1446
the Ring of Brodgar and the great chambered tomb of Maes Howe, all
within walking distance of the A965, 18km from Kirkwall, this is as impressive a
ceremonial site as you'll find anywhere. From same period as Skara Brae. The
individual stones and the scale of the Ring are v imposing and deeply mysterious.
The burial cairn is the finest megalithic tomb in the UK. Seen together, they will
stimulate even the most jaded sense of wonder.
HS

✝ ✝ **THE CALLANISH STONES, ISLE OF LEWIS:** 24km from Stornoway. Take 1447
Tarbert rd and go rt at Leurbost. The best preserved and most unusual MAP 2
combination of standing stones in a ring around a tomb, with radiating arms in B2
cross shape. Dating from 4000BC, they were unearthed from the peat in the mid-
19th century and have become the major historical attraction of the Hebrides.
Other configurations nearby. At dawn there's nobody else there (except camping
New-Agers). Vistor centre is out of sight (and interesting; with good caff). Free.
HS

✝ **THE CLAVA CAIRNS nr CULLODEN nr INVERNESS:** Here long before the most 1448
infamous battle in Scottish and other histories; well worth finding. Not so MAP 2
well marked but continue along the B9006 towards Cawdor Castle, that other gr D3
historical landmark (1411/CASTLES), taking a rt at the Culloden Moor Inn and
follow signs for Clava Lodge (holiday homes), picking up HS sign to rt.
Chambered cairns in grove of trees. Really just piles of stones, but the death rattle
echo from 5,000yrs ago is perceptible to all esp when no one else is there.
Remoteness inhibits new age attentions and allows more private meditations in
this extraterrestrial spot.
HS

✝ **THE MOUSA BROCH, SHETLAND:** On small island of Mousa, off Shetland 1449
mainland 20km S of Lerwick, visible from main A970; but to see it properly,
take boat (01950 431367). Isolated in its island fastness, this is the best preserved
broch in Scotland. Walls are 13m high (originally 15m) and galleries run up the
middle, in one case to the top. Solid as a rock, this example of a uniquely Scottish
phenomenon would have been a v des res at the turn of the millennium.
JARLSHOF in the far S next to Sumburgh airport has remnants and ruins from
Neolithic to Viking times - 18th century, with esp impressive 'wheelhouses'.
ADMN

TOMB OF THE EAGLES, ORKNEY MAINLAND: 33km S of Kirkwall at the foot of S 1450
Ronaldsay; signed from Burwick. A 'recent' discovery, the excavation of this cliff
cave is on private land. You should call in at the house first and they'll tell you the
whole story. Then there's a 2km walk. Allow time; this is ethereal stuff. ADMN

CAIRNPAPPLE HILL, nr LINLITHGOW, WEST LOTHIAN: App from the 'Beecraigs' rd 1451
off W end of Linlithgow main st. Go past the Beecraigs t/off and continue for MAP 7
3km. Cairnpapple is signed. Cairn and remnants of various rings of stones evince A1
the long sequence of ceremonial activities that took place on this high, windy hill
betw 2800 and 500BC. Atmos even more strange by the very 20th-century
communications mast next door. Go into the tomb.
ADMN HS

CAIRNHOLY, between NEWTON STEWART/GATEHOUSE: 1km off main A75. Signed 1452
from rd, a pleasant walk up the glen side. A mini Callanish of standing stones MAP 9
around a burial cairn on v human scale and in a serene setting with views of B4
Wigtown Bay, the S Uplands behind.

THE BROWN-AND-WHITE CATERHUNS, KIRKTON OF MENMUIR, nr BRECHIN: 5km 1453
uphill from war memorial at Kirkton, then signed 1km. Lay-by with obvious path MAP 4
to both on either side of the rd. White easiest (500m uphill). These iron-age hill E2
top settlements give tremendous sense of scale and space and afford an impressive
panorama of the Highland line. Colours refer to the heather-covered turf and
stone of one and the massive collapsed ramparts of the White. The Picts, on the
other hand, were blue (you know, like Mel Gibson).

1454 **EAST AQUHORTHIES STONE CIRCLE, nr INVERURIE, nr ABERDEEN:** Signed from B993
MAP 3 from Inverurie to Monymusk. A circle of pinkish stones with 2 grey sentinels
D3 flanking a huge recumbent stone set in the rolling countryside of the Don Valley
with Bennachie in the background (1582/HILLS).

1455 **LOANHEAD OF DAVIOT STONE CIRCLE, nr INVERURIE/ABERDEEN:** Head for the village
MAP 3 of Daviot on B9001 from Inverurie; or Loanhead, signed off A920 rd betw Old
D3 Meldrum and Insch. The site is 500m from top of village. Impressive and spooky
circle of 11 stones and one recumbent from 4000/5000BC. Unusual second circle adj
encloses a cremation cemetery from 1500BC. Remains of 32 people were found here.
Obviously, an important place for God-knows-what rituals.

1456 **ARCHAEOLINK nr INSCH, ABERDEENSHIRE:** Geographically betw the 2 sites above
MAP 3 and within an area of many prehistoric remnants, a spanking new state of the art
D3 interpretative centre. Impressively modern app to history both from exterior and
within, where interactive and audiovisual displays bring the food hunter-gatherer
past into the culture hunter-gatherer present. Mar-Oct 9.30-5pm, winter 10-4pm.
From 11am at w/ends.   ADMN

1457 **THE GREY CAIRNS OF CANSTER, nr WICK:** 20km S of Wick, a v straight rd (signed
MAP 2 for Cairns) heads W from the A9 for 8km. The cairns are instantly identifiable nr
E1 the rd and impressively complete. The 'horned cairn' is the best in the UK. In
2500BC these stone-piled structures were used for the disposal of the dead. You can
crawl inside them if you're agile. Nearby, also signed from A9 is:

1458 **HILL O' MANY STANES, nr WICK:** Aptly named place with extraordinary number of
MAP 2 small standing stones; 200 in 22 rows. If fan shape was complete, there would be 600.
E1 Their v purposeful layout is enigmatic and strangely stirring.

1459 **THE WHITHORN DIG, WHITHORN:** 1986 excavations are still ongoing at the medieval
MAP 9 priory, the shrine of St Ninian and home of the earliest church in Scotland. Not
B4 much to see but a serene spot behind main st of a forgotten town. Go further
(1239/COASTAL VILLAGES).

1460 **THE MOTTE OF UR, nr DALBEATTIE:** Off B794 N of Dalbeattie and 6km from main
MAP 9 A75 Castle Douglas to Dumfries rd. Most extensive bailey earthwork castle in
C3 Scotland dating from 12th century. No walls or excavation visible but a gr sense
of scale and place. Go through village of Haugh (good pub with food) and on for
2km. Looking down to rt at farm buildings the minor rd crosses a ford; park here,
cross footbridge and head to rt – the hillock is above the ford.

1461 **TEMPLE WOOD, nr KILMARTIN, nr LOCHGILPHEAD:** 2km S of Kilmartin and 1km
MAP 1 (signed) from A816, 2 distinct stone circles from a long period of history betw
B2 3000-1200BC. Story and speculations described on boards. Pastoral countryside
and wide skies. There are other sites in the vicinity. The Centre for Archeology
and Landscape Interpretation, beside the kirk, goes into it in more detail.   HS

1462 **CRANNOG CENTRE, ABERFELDY:** Adj Croft-Na-Caber Water Sports Centre on L
MAP 4 Tay (1712/WATER SPORTS). Reconstruction of iron-age dwelling (there are several
B3 under the loch). Credible and worthwhile archeological project. Open Apr-Oct.

1463 **BAR HILL, nr KIRKINTILLOCH:** A fine example of the low ruins of a Roman fort on
MAP 1 the Antonine Wall which ran across Scotland for 200 yrs early AD. Gr place for
D3 an out-of-town walk (607/VIEWS).

1464 **THE BROCHS, GLENELG:** 110km from Ft William. Glenelg is 14km from the A87 at
MAP 2 Shiel Br (1305/SCENIC ROUTES). 5km from Glenelg village in beautiful Glen Beag.
C4 The 2 brochs, Dun Trodden and Dun Telve, are the best preserved examples on
the mainland of these mysterious 1st-century homesteads. Easy here to
distinguish the twin stone walls that kept out the cold and the more disagreeable
neighbours. Free.   HS

1465 **BARPA LANYASS, NORTH UIST:** 8km S Lochmaddy, visible from main A867 rd, like
MAP 2 a hat on the hill (200m away). A 'squashed' beehive burial cairn dating from
A3 1000BC, the tomb of a chieftain. It's largely intact and you can explore inside,
crawling through the short entrance tunnel and down through the yrs.

GREAT COUNTRY HOUSES

✝ ✝ **HADDO HOUSE:** Designed by William Adam for the Earl of Aberdeen, the **1466**
Palladian-style mansion well known for its musical evenings. Not so MAP 3
much a house, more a leisure land in the best poss taste, with country park to D2
wander, a pleasant café, estate shop and gentle education. Austere inside perhaps,
but the basements are the place to ponder. The window by Burne-Jones in the
chapel is glorious. Excl programme of events, both NTS and Haddo House Trust.
Tickets avail in Aber (01224 641122). Enjoy some good life!

✝ ✝ **MOUNT STUART, BUTE:** 01700 503877. Unique Victorian Gothic house; **1467**
echoes 3rd Marquis of Bute's passion for mythology, astronomy, MAP 1
astrology and religion. Amazing splendour and scale, but atmos intimate and C3
romantic. Beautiful Italian antiques, notable paintings and fascinating attention to
detail with surprising humourous touches. Equally grand grds, with walks and
sea views. After a day here you still won't have taken it in. May-Oct 11am-5pm.
Cl Tue/Thu.

✝ ✝ **FASQUE, betw STONEHAVEN and MONTROSE:** W of A92 at Laurencekirk **1468**
and through Victorian Fettercairn to Fasque, one of the most fascinating MAP 3
old houses you'll ever be permitted to wander through on your own (or C4
accompanied by the enthusiastic custodian). Home of Gladstone (4 times Prime
Minister) whose descendants still live in the W wing. Shut down in 1939 till the
1970s, the world before and betw the wars was preserved and is still there for
faded-grandeur connoisseurs to savour and all of us to sense. Methinks, best
below stairs. May-Sept 7days 11-5.30pm (till 8pm June-Aug). Take no souvenirs.

✝ **MANDERSTON, DUNS:** Off A6105, 2km down Duns-Berwick rd. Described as **1469**
the swan-song of the Gr Classical House, one of the finest examples of MAP 8
Edwardian opulence in UK. All the more fascinating because the family still live D2
there. Below stairs as fascinating as up; sublime grds (don't miss the woodland
grd on other side of the lake, or the marble dairy). Open May-Sept, Thu/Sun 2-
5.30pm.

✝ **TRAQUAIR, INNERLEITHEN:** 01896 830323. 2km from A72 Peebles-Gala rd. **1470**
Archetypal romantic Border retreat steeped in Jacobite history. Human MAP 8
proportions, liveability and lots of atmos (those peacocks calling are spooky at B2
dusk). An enchanting house and a maze in the grd. Traquair ale still brewed. 1745
cottage tearoom, pottery and candlemaking. Major crafts and music fair held in
grounds in early Aug. Apr-Sept and afternoons in Oct, Fri-Sun.

GOSFORD HOUSE nr ABERLADY, EAST LOTHIAN: On A198 betw Longniddry and **1471**
Aberlady, the Gosford estate is behind a high wall and strangely stunted MAP 7
vegetation. Imposing house with centre block by Robert Adam and the wing you D1
visit by William Young who did Glas City Chambers. The Marble Hall houses
the remarkable collections of the unbroken line of the Earls of Wemyss.
Botticellis, Rubens and Canalettos and important portraits in delightfully
informal display (hand-written cards). No tearoom or paraphenalia here, but the
grounds with ornamental ponds and their Hansel and Gretel curling and ice
houses are superb picnic spots. Only open Wed/ Sat/Sun 2-5pm, June and July.

FLOORS CASTLE, KELSO: 01573 223333. More vast mansion than old castle, the **1472**
ancestral home of the Duke of Roxburghe, o/look with imposing grandeur the MAP 8
town and the Tweed. 18th-century with later additions. You're led round lofty D3
public rms past family collections of fine furniture, tapestries and porcelain.
Priceless; spectacularly impractical. Good grd centre (1791/GARDEN CENTRES).

MELLERSTAIN, nr GORDON/KELSO: 01573 410225. Home of the Earl of Hadding- **1473**
ton, signed from B6089 (Kelso-Gordon) or A6105 (Earlston-Greenlaw). One of MAP 8
Scotland's gr Georgian houses, begun by Wm Adam in 1725, completed by D3
Robert. Outstanding decorative interiors esp the library. May-Sept 12.30-5pm.

PAXTON, nr BERWICK: 01289 386291. Off B6461 rd to Swinton and Kelso about **1474**
6km from A1. Adam mansion with Chippendales, Trotters and a picture gallery MAP 8
which is an outstation of the National Gallery. They've made a very good job of E2
the wallpapering. Newly restored Victorian boathouse and salmon fishing
museum on the R Tweed. Tours (lasting 1hr) every 45mins, Apr-Oct 11am-5pm.

THIRLESTANE, LAUDER: 01578 722430. 2km off A68. A castellate/baronial seat of **1475**

MAP 8
C2
the Earls and Duke of Lauderdale and family home of the Maitlands; it must take some upkeeping. Extraordinary staterooms, esp plaster work; the ceilings must be seen to be believed. In contrast, the nurseries (with toy collection), kitchens and laundry are more approachable. May, June, Sept open Sun, Mon, Wed, Thur 2-5pm. July, Aug 2-5pm every day except Sat.

1476 FYVIE, ABERDEENSHIRE: 40km NW Aber, an important stop on the 'Castle Trail' which links the gr houses of Aberdeenshire. Before opulence fatigue sets in, see this pleasant baronial pile first. It was lived-in until the 1980s so feels less remote than most. Fantastic roofscape and ceilings. The *best* tearoom. Tree-lined acres; loch side walks. July/Aug 1.30-5.30pm. Grounds open AYR.

MAP 3
D2

1477 CRATHES, nr BANCHORY: 25km W of Aber on A93. Amidst superb grds (1199/GARDENS) a 'fairy-tale castle', a tower house which is actually interesting to visit. Up and down spiral staircases and into small but liveable rms. The notable painted ceilings and the Long Gallery at the top are all worth lingering over. 350yrs of the Burnett family are ingrained in this oak. Apr-Oct 11am-5.30pm. Grounds open AYR 9am-dusk.

MAP 3
D4

ABBOTSFORD, nr MELROSE: Home of Walter Scott (1556/LITERARY PLACES).

GREAT MONUMENTS, MEMORIALS AND FOLLIES

These sites are open at all times and free unless otherwise stated.

1478 THE AMERICAN MONUMENT, ISLAY: On the SW peninsula of the island, known as the Oa (pron 'Oh'), 13km from Pt Ellen. A monument to commemorate the shipwrecks in nearby waters, of 2 American ships, the *Tuscania* and the *Ontranto,* both of which sank in 1918 at the end of the war. The obelisk o/look this sea – which is often beset by storms – from a spectacular headland, the sort of disquieting place where you could imagine looking round and finding the person you're with has disappeared. Take rd from Pt Ellen past Maltings marked Mull of Oa 9km, through gate and left at broken sign. Park and walk 1.5km steadily uphill to monument. Bird life good in Oa area. 1-A-2

MAP 1
A3

1479 WALLACE MONUMENT, STIRLING: Visible for miles and with gr views, though not as dramatic as Stirling Castle. App from A91 or Br of Allan rd. 150m walk from car park and 246 steps up. Victorian gothic spire marking the place where Scotland's gr patriot swooped down upon the English at the Battle of Stirling Br. Mel Gibson has increased visitors though his face on the new Wallace statue is a sad joke. In the 'Hall of Heroes' the new heroines section requires a feminist leap of the imagination. The famous sword is v big. Cliff top walk through Abbey Craig woods is worth detour. Monument open daily 10am-5pm(or later),w/ends in winter till 4pm. ADM

MAP 6
D3

1480 THE GRAVE OF FLORA MACDONALD, SKYE: Kilmuir on A855, Uig-Staffin rd, 40km N of Portree. A 10ft-high Celtic cross supported against the wind, high on the ridge o/look the Uists from whence she came. Long after the legendary journey, her funeral in 1790 attracted the biggest crowd since Culloden. The present memorial replaced the original, which was chipped away by souvenir hunters. Dubious though the whole business may have been, she still helped to shape the folklore of the Highlands.

MAP 2
B3

1481 CARFIN GROTTO, MOTHERWELL: A723 just outside Motherwell 4km from M8, on left after 2nd garage. A homage to Lourdes, built largely by striking miners in 1921. (God's) acre of grds and pathways with reliquaries, shrines, a glass pavilion and chapel; the ghost of Ravenscraig is always in the background. Spiritual sustenance, despite the throngs, for the true believers; something of a curiosity for the rest of us. Pilgrimage centre and tearoom. Open at all times.

MAP 1
C3

1482 HAMILTON MAUSOLEUM, STRATHCLYDE PARK: Off (and visible from) M74 at jnct 5/6, 15km from Glas (1218/COUNTRY PARKS). Huge, over-the-top/over-the-tomb (though removed 1921) stone memorial to the 10th Duke of Hamilton. Guided tours daily (Easter-Sept at 3pm and, even better, evenings in July-Aug at 7pm; winter Sat/Sun at 3pm). Eerie and chilling and with remarkable acoustics – the 'longest echo in Europe'. Give it a shout or take your violin.

MAP 1
D3

1483 PENIEL HEUGH, nr ANCRUM/JEDBURGH: (pron 'Pinal-hue'.) An obelisk visible for miles and on a rise which offers some of the most exhilarating views of the

MAP 8
D3

Borders. Also known as the Waterloo Monument, it was built on the Marquis of Lothian's estate to commemorate the battle. It's said that the woodland on the surrounding slopes represents the positions of Wellington's troops. From A68 opposite Ancrum t/off, on B6400, go 1km past 'Woodland Centre' up steep, unmarked rd to left for 150m. Park, walk up through woods.

THE HOPETOUN MONUMENT, ATHELSTANEFORD nr HADDINGTON: The needle atop a rare rise in E Lothian and a gr vantage point from which to view the county from the Forth to the Lammermuirs and Edinburgh over there. Off A6737 Haddington to Aberlady rd on B1343 to Athelstaneford. Car park and short climb. Tower usually open and viewfinder boards at top. Good gentle 'ridge' walk E from here. **1484 MAP 7 D1**

THE PINEAPPLE, AIRTH: From Airth N of Grangemouth, take A905 to Stirling and after 1km the B9124 for Cowie. It sits on the edge of a walled grd at the end of the drive. 45ft high, it was built in 1761 as a grd retreat by an unknown architect and remained 'undiscovered' until 1963. How exotic the fruit must have seemed in the 18th century, never mind this extraordinary folly. Open AYR; oddly enough, you can stay there (2 twin rms, 01628 825925). **1485 MAP 6 D4**

THE MONUMENT ON BEN BHRAGGIE, GOLSPIE: Atop the hill (pron 'Brachee') that dominates the town, the domineering statue and plinth (over 35m) of the dreaded first Duke of Sutherland; there's been a fierce debate recently raging in the local press over whether it should be demolished. Climb from town fountain on marked path. The hill race go up in 10mins but allow 2hrs return. His private view along the NE coast is superb (1423/CASTLES; 1817/MUSEUMS). **1486 MAP 2 D2**

McCAIG'S TOWER or FOLLY, OBAN: Oban's gr landmark built in 1897 by McCaig, a local banker, to give 'work to the unemployed' and as a memorial to his family. It's like a temple or coliseum and time has mellowed whatever incongruous effect it may have had originally. The views of the town and the bay are magnificent and it's easy to get up from several points in town centre. (*See* OBAN, *p. 265.*) **1487 MAP 1 B1**

THE VICTORIA MEMORIAL TO ALBERT, BALMORAL: Atop the fir-covered hill behind the house, she raised a monument whose distinctive pyramid shape can be seen peeping over the crest from all over the estate. Desolated by his death, the 'broken-hearted' widow had this memorial built in 1862 and spent so much time here, she became a recluse and the Empire trembled. Path begins at shop on way to Lochnagar distillery, 45mins up. Forget Balmoral (1423/CASTLES), all the longing and love for Scotland can be felt here, the gr estate laid out below. **1488 MAP 3 B4**

THE PROP OF YTHSIE, nr ABERDEEN: 35km NW city nr Ellon to W of A92, or pass on the 'Castle Trail' since this monument commemorates one George Gordon of Haddo House nearby, who was prime minister 1852-55 (the good-looking guy in the first portrait you come to in the house). Tower visible from all of rolling Aberdeenshire around and there are reciprocal views should you take the easy but unclear route up. On B999 Aber-Tarves rd and 2km from entrance to house. Take rd for the Ythsie (pron 'icy') farms, 100m. Stone circle nearby. **1489 MAP 3 D2**

THE MONUMENT TO HUGH MacDIARMID, LANGHOLM: Brilliant piece of modern sculpture by Jake Harvey on the hill above Langholm 3km from A7 at beginning of path to the Malcolm obelisk from where there are gr views (1333/VIEWS). MacDiarmid, our national poet, was born in Langholm in 1872 and, though they never liked him much after he left, the monument was commissioned and a cairn beside it raised in 1992. The bare hills surround you. The motifs of the sculpture were used by Scotland's favourite Celtic rock band, Runrig, on the cover of their 1993 album, *Amazing Things.* **1490 MAP 9 E3**

MURRAY MONUMENT, nr NEW GALLOWAY: Above A712 rd to Newton Stewart about halfway betw. A fairly austere needle of granite to commemorate a 'shepherd boy', one Alexander Murray, who rose to become a professor of Oriental Languages at Edinburgh Univ in early 19th century. 10min walk up for fine views of Galloway Hills; pleasant waterfall nearby. Just as he, barefoot … **1491 MAP 9 B7**

SMAILHOLM TOWER, nr KELSO and ST BOSWELLS: The classic Border tower; plenty of history and romance and a v nice place to stop, picnic whatever. Good views. Nr main rd B6404 or off smaller B6937 – well signposted. Open Apr-Sept 9.30-6.30 (Sun from 2pm). But fine to visit at any time (1311/SCENIC ROUTES). **1492 MAP 8 D3**

SCOTT MONUMENT, EDINBURGH: 331/VIEWS.

THE MOST INTERESTING CHURCHES

All 'generally open' unless otherwise stated; those marked (*) have public services.

1493
MAP 1
C1
*ST CONAN'S KIRK, LOCH AWE: A85 33km E of Oban. Perched amongst trees on the side of L Awe, this small but spacious church seems to incorporate every ecclesiastical architectural style. Its building was a labour of love for one Walter Campbell who was perhaps striving for beauty rather than consistency. Though modern (begun by him in 1881 and finished by his sister and a board of trustees in 1930), the result is a place of ethereal light and atmos, enhanced by and befitting the inherent spirituality of the setting. There's a spooky carved effigy of Robert the Bruce, a cosy cloister and the most amazing flying buttresses. A place to wander and reflect.

1494
MAP 7
C2
*ROSSLYN CHAPEL, ROSLIN: 12km S of Edin city centre. Take A702, then A703 from ring-route rd, marked Penicuik. Roslin village 1km from main rd and chapel 500m from village crossroads above Roslin Glen (325/WALKS OUTSIDE THE CITY). Freemason central: stories abound of the Holy Grail hidden in the walls and for the next few yrs there's a metal hood to protect the roof. For such a wee chapel, visitors can spend hrs wandering around working the place out with help from copious guidance notes. Founded by a 15th-century Sinclair, Prince of Orkney, who reinterred his illustrious 13th-century ancestor here (the latter just happened to be a Grand Prior of the Knights Templar). All holy meaningful stuff in a *Foucault's Pendulum* sense. But a special place. Episcopalian.

1495
THE ITALIAN CHAPEL, ORKNEY MAINLAND: 8km S of Kirkwall at Lamb Holm and the first causeway on the way to St Margaret's Hope. In 1943, Italian PoWs brought to work on the Churchill Barriers transformed a Nissen hut, using the most meagre materials, into this remarkable ornate chapel. The meticulous *trompe l'oeil* and wrought-iron work are a touching affirmation of faith. At the other end of the architectural scale, **ST MAGNUS CATHEDRAL** in Kirkwall is a gr edifice, but also filled with spirituality.

1496
MAP 8
xB1
QUEEN'S CROSS CHURCH, GLASGOW: 870 Garscube Rd where it becomes Maryhill Rd at Springbank St. C R Mackintosh's only church. Fascinating and unpredictable in every part of its design. Some elements reminiscent of The Art School (built in the same year 1897) and others, like the tower, evoke medieval architecture. Bold and innovative, now restored and functioning as the headquarters of The Mackintosh Society. Mon -Fri 10.30-5pm, Sun 2.30-5pm. No services. (632/MACKINTOSH.)

1497
MAP 9
D2
*DURISDEER PARISH CHURCH, nr ABINGTON AND THORNHILL: Off A702Abington-Thornhill rd and nr Drumlanrig (1214/COUNTRY PARKS). If I lived in this village in the hills, I'd go to church more often. It's exquisite and the history of Scotland is writ on the stones. The Queensberry marbles (1709) are displayed in the N transept and there's a cradle roll and a list of ministers from the 14th century. The plaque to the two brothers who died at Gallipoli is especially touching.

1498
MAP 1
C3
*CATHEDRAL OF THE ISLES, MILLPORT ON THE ISLAND OF CUMBRAE: Frequent ferry service from Largs is met by bus for 6km journey to Millport. Lane from main st by Newton pub, 250m then through gate. The smallest 'cathedral' in Europe, one of Butterfield's gr works (other is Keble Coll, Oxford). Here, small is outstandingly beautiful. (992/RETREATS; 1100/CAFÉS.)

1499
MAP 2
B2
ST CLEMENTS, RODEL, SOUTH HARRIS: Tarbert 40km. Classic island kirk in Hebridean landscape (as long as the Super Quarry is never built). Simple cruciform structure with tower, which the adventurous can climb. Probably influenced by Iona. Now an empty but atmospheric shell, with blackened effigies and important monumental sculpture. Goats in the churchyard graze amongst the headstones of all the young Harris lads lost at sea in the Gr War. There are other fallen angels on the outside of the tower.

1500
MAP 2
A4
*ST MICHAEL'S CHAPEL, ERISKAY, nr SOUTH UIST/BARRA: That rare example of an ordinary modern church without history or grand architecture, which has charm and serenity and imbues the sense of well-being that a religious centre should. The focal pt of a relatively devout Catholic community who obviously care about it. Alabaster angels abound. O/look Sound of Barra. A real delight whatever your religion.

1501
*ST ATHERNASE, LEUCHARS: The parish church on a corner of what is essentially

an Air Force base spans centuries of warfare and architecture. The Norman bell tower is remarkable.

MAP 5
D2

*ST FILLAN'S CHURCH, ABERDOUR: Behind ruined castle in this pleasant seaside village (1502/COASTAL VILLAGES), a more agreeable old kirk would be hard to find. Restored from a 12th-century ruin in 1926, the warm stonework and stained glass create a v soothing atmos (church may be closed, but nice graveyard).

1502
MAP 5
B4

*DUNBLANE CATHEDRAL: A huge nave of a church built around a Norman tower (from David I) on the Allen Water and restored 1892. The wondrously bright stained glass is mostly 20th-century. The poisoned sisters buried under the altar helped change the course of Scottish history. This cathedral made more recently famous and seen on TV all over the world during the Dunblane tragedy.

1503
MAP 6
D3

HS

*ST MACHAR'S CATHEDRAL, ABERDEEN: The Chanonry in 'Old Aberdeen' off St Machar's Dr about 2km from centre. Best seen as part of a walk round the old 'village within the city' occupied mainly by the university's old and modern buildings. Cathedral's fine granite nave and twin-spired W Front date from 15th century, on site of 6th-century Celtic church. Noted for heraldic ceiling and 19/20th-century stained glass. Seaton Park adj has pleasant Don-side walks and . . . unexpected pleasures. Church open daily 9am-5pm.

1504
MAP 3
D3

*THE EAST LOTHIAN CHURCHES at ABERLADY, WHITEKIRK, ATHELSTANEFORD: 3 charming churches in bucolic settings; quiet corners to explore and reflect. Easy to find. All have interesting local histories and in the case of Athelstaneford, a national resonance - a 'vision' in the sky nr here became the flag of Scotland, the saltire. An innovative audiovisual display explains. Aberlady my favourite.

1505
MAP 7
D1

CROICK CHURCH, nr BONAR BRIDGE: 16km W of Ardgay, which is just over the river from Bonar Br and through the splendid glen of Strathcarron (1269/GLENS). This humble and charming church is chiefly remembered for its place in the history of the Highland clearances. In May 1845, 90 folk took shelter in the graveyard around the church after they had been cleared from their homes in nearby Glencalvie. Not allowed even in the kirk, their plight did not go unnoticed and was reported in *The Times*. The harrowing account is there to read, and the messages they scratched on the windows. Sheep graze all around.

1506
MAP 2
D2

*THOMAS COATES MEMORIAL CHURCH, PAISLEY: Built by Coates (of thread fame), an imposing edifice, one of the grandest Baptist churches in Europe. A monument to God, prosperity and the Industrial Revolution. Open Apr-Sept Mon/Wed/Fri 2-4pm, service on Sun at 11am.

1507
MAP 1
D3

*THE LAMP OF THE LOTHIANS, ST MARY'S COLLEGIATE, HADDINGTON: Follow signs from E main st. At the risk of sounding profane or at least trite, this is a church that's really got its act together, both now and throughout ecclesiastical history. It's beautiful and in a fine setting on the R Tyne, with good stained glass and interesting crypts and corners. But it's obviously v much at the centre of the community, a lamp as it were, in the Lothians. Guided tours, brass rubbings (Sat), summer recitals (Sun afternoon). Coffee shop and gift shop. Don't miss Lady Kitty's grd nearby, including the secret medicinal grd, a quiet spot to contemplate (if not sort out) your condition. Apr-Sept Mon-Sat 10-4pm.

1508
MAP 7
D1

*DUNKELD CATHEDRAL: In town centre by lane to the banks of the Tay at its most silvery. Medieval splendour amongst lofty trees. Notable for 13th-century choir and 15th-century nave and tower. Parish church open for edifying services.

1509
MAP 4
C3

RUTHWELL CHURCH, RUTHWELL: 10 miles SE Dumfries, B724 nr Clarencefield. Collect keys from Mrs Coulthard, Kirkyett House in village; she's the fount of all knowledge concerning this important building. Unique 18ft Runic Cross within Church, dating from 7th century. Carvings depict Biblical scenes with monk's inscription of 'The Holy Rood' poem. Fascinating history of its creation, preservation during the religious troubles of 1640, and subsequent restoration in 1823 by the community.

1510
MAP 9
D3

ST GILES CATHEDRAL, EDINBURGH: 316/OTHER ATTRACTIONS.

GLASGOW CATHEDRAL/UNIVERSITY CHAPEL: 580/583/MAIN ATTRACTIONS.

THE MOST INTERESTING GRAVEYARDS

1511 ✝ ✝ **GLASGOW NECROPOLIS:** The vast burial ground at the crest of the ridge,
MAP 8 running down to the river, that was the focus of the original settlement
E4 of Glas. Everything began at the foot of this hill and, ultimately, ended at the top
where many of the city's most famous (and infamous) sons and daughters are
interred within the reach of the long shadow of John Knox's obelisk. Generally
open (official times), but best if you can get the full spooky experience to
yourself. Check with the TO 0141 204 4400. (580/MAIN ATTRACTIONS.)

1512 **EDINBURGH: CANONGATE:** On left of Royal Mile going down to Palace. Adam
MAP A Smith and the tragic poet Robert Fergusson revered by Robbie Burns (who raised
E2 the memorial stone in 1787 over his pauper's grave) are buried here in the heart
of Auld Reekie. Tourists can easily miss this one. **GREYFRIARS:** A place of ancient
mystery, famous for the wee dog who guarded his master's grave for 14yrs, for
the plundering of graves in the early 18th century for the Anatomy School and
for the graves of Allan Ramsay (prominent poet and burgher), James Hutton (the
father of geology), William McGonagall (the 'world's worst poet') and sundry
serious Highlanders. Annals of a gr city are written on these stones. **WARRISTON:**
Warriston Rd by B&Q or end of cul-de-sac at Warriston Cres (Canonmills), up
bank and along railway line. Overgrown, peaceful, steeped in atmos. Gothic
horrorland (some of those guys like that sort of thing).

1513 **ISLE OF JURA:** Killchianaig graveyard in the N. Follow rd as far as it goes to
MAP 1 Inverlussa, graveyard is on rt, just before hamlet. Mairi Ribeach apparently lived
B2 until she was 128. In the south at Keils (2km from rd N out of Craighouse,
bearing left past Keils houses and through the deer fence), her father is buried and
he was 180! Both sites are beautiful, isolated and redolent of island history, with
much to reflect on, not least the mysterious longevity of the inhabitants.

1514 **CAMPBELTOWN CEMETERY:** Campbeltown. Odd, but one of the nicest things
MAP 1 about this end-of-the-line town is the cemetery. It's at the end of a row of
B4 fascinating posh houses, the original merchant and mariner owners of which will
be interred in the leafy plots next door. Still v much in use after centuries of
commerce and seafaring disasters, it has crept up the terraces of a steep and lush
overhanging bank. Guess you could do worse than see Campbeltown and die.

1515 **KIRKOSWALD KIRKYARD nr MAYBOLE and GIRVAN:** On main rd through village
MAP 1 betw Ayr and Girvan. The graveyard around the ruined Kirk famous as the burial
C5 place of the characters in Burns' most famous poem and a must for Burns fans and
thrall seekers. Tam O'Shanter, Souter Johnie and Kirkton Jean all lie here.

1516 **HUMBIE CHURCHYARD:** Humbie, E Lothian 25km SE of Edin via A68 (t/off at
MAP 7 Fala). This is as reassuring a place to be buried as you could wish for; if you're set
C2 on cremation, come here and think of earth. Deep in the woods with the burn
besides; after-hrs the sprites and the spirits must have a hell of a time.

1517 **ANCRUM GRAVEYARD, nr JEDBURGH:** The quintessential country churchyard; away
MAP 8 from the village (2km along B6400), by a lazy river (the Ale Water) crossed to a
D3 farm by a humpback br and a chapel in ruins. Elegiac and deeply peaceful
(1347/PICNICS).

1518 **BALQUHIDDER CHURCHYARD:** Chiefly notable as the last resting place of one Rob
MAP 6 Roy Macgregor who was buried in 1734 after causing a heap of trouble
C2 hereabouts and raised to immortality by Sir Walter Scott and Michael Caton-
Jones. Despite well-trodden path, setting is poignant. For best reflections head
along L Voil to Inverlochlarig. Sunday evening concerts in kirk July/Aug.

1519 **LOGIE OLD KIRK, nr STIRLING:** A crumbling chapel and an ancient graveyard at the
MAP 6 foot of the Ochils. The wall is round to keep out the demons, a burn gurgles
D3 beside and there are some fine and v old stones going back to the 16th century.
Take rd for Wallace Monument off A91, 2km from Stirling, then first rt. The old
kirk is beyond the new.

1520 **CHISHOLM GRAVEYARD, nr BEAULY:** Last resting place of the Chisholms and 3 of
MAP 2 the largest Celtic crosses you'll see anywhere, in a secret and atmospheric
D3 woodland setting. 10km S Beauly on A831 to Struy, 1km before Cnoc Hotel opp
Erchless Estate and through a white iron gate on rt. Walk 250m.

1521 **TUTNAGUAIL, DUNBEATH:** An enchanting cemetery 5km from Dunbeath, Neil
MAP 2 Gunn's birthplace, and found by walking up the 'Strath' he describes in his book
E2

Highland River (1554/LITERARY PLACES). With a white wall around it, this graveyard, which before the clearances once served a valley community of 400 souls, can be seen for miles. Despite isolation, it's still used.

THE GREAT ABBEYS

✠ ✠ **IONA ABBEY:** This hugely significant place of pilgrimage for new age and old age pilgrims and tourists alike is reached from Fionnphort, SW Mull, by frequent Calmac Ferry (5min crossing). Walk 1km. Here in 563BC St Columba began his mission for a Celtic Church that changed the face of Europe. Cloisters, graveyard of Scottish kings and, marked by a modest stone, the inscription already faded by the weather, the grave of John Smith father of our Blair New World. Regular services. Good shop (1748/CRAFT SHOPS). Residential courses and retreats (MacLeod Centre adj, 01681 700404) include a 'Christmas house party' (1895/MAGICAL ISLANDS). **1522 MAP 1 A1**

✠ ✠ **PLUSCARDEN ABBEY, betw FORRES and ELGIN:** A fully working monastic community (990/RETREATS) in one of the most spiritual of places. Founded by Alexander II in 1250 and being restored since 1948. Benedictine services (starting with Matins at 5am through Prime-Terce-Sext-None-Vespers at 6pm and Compline at 8.05pm) open to public. The ancient honey-coloured walls, the brilliant stained glass, the monks' Gregorian chant: the whole effect is a truly uplifting experience. The bell rings down the valley. Open at all times. **1523 MAP 3 B2**

✠ ✠ **PAISLEY ABBEY:** Town centre. An abbey founded in 1163, razed (by the English) in 1307 and with successive deteriorations and renovations ever since. Major restoration in the 1920s brought it to present-day cathedral-like magnificence. Exceptional stained glass (the recent window complementing the formidable Strachan E Window), an impressive choir and an edifying sense of space. Sunday Services (11am/6.30pm) are superb, esp full-dress communion and there are open days (about one Sat a month, phone TO: 0141 889 0711) with coffee in the cloisters, organ music and the tower open for climbing. Otherwise Abbey open AYR 10am-3.30pm. Café/shop. **1524 MAP 1 D3**

✠ ✠ **JEDBURGH ABBEY:** The classic abbey ruin; conveys the most complete impression of the Border abbeys built under the patronage of David I in the 12th century. Its tower and remarkable Catherine window are still intact. Excavations have unearthed first example of a 12th-century comb (worth half a million quid!). It's now displayed in the excellent visitor centre which brilliantly illustrates the full story of the abbey's amazing history. Best view from across the Jed in the 'Glebe'. Apr-Sep 9.30am-6.30pm, Oct-Mar until 4.30pm. **1525 MAP 8 D3** HS

✠ **DRYBURGH ABBEY, nr ST BOSWELLS:** One of the most evocative of ruins, an aesthetic attraction since the late 18th century. Sustained innumerable attacks from the English since its inauguration by Premonstratensian Canons in 1150. Celebrated by Sir Walter Scott, buried here in 1832 (with his biographer Lockhart at his feet), its setting, amongst huge cedar trees on the banks of the Tweed is one of pure historical romance. 4km A68. (1328/VIEWS.) **1526 MAP 8 C3** HS

CROSSRAGUEL ABBEY, MAYBOLE: 24km S of Ayr on A77. Built 1244, one of first Cluniac settlements in Scotland, an influential and rich order, stripped in the Reformation. Now an extensive ruin of architectural distinction, the ground plan v well preserved and obvious. Open daily. **1527 MAP 1 C4** HS

SWEETHEART, NEW ABBEY nr DUMFRIES: 12km S by A710. The endearing and enduring warm red sandstone abbey in the shadow of Criffel, so named because Devorguilla de Balliol, devoted to her husband (he of the Oxford College), founded the abbey for Cistercian monks and kept his heart in a casket which is buried with her here. No roof, but the tower is intact. (676/SW HOTELS.) **1528 MAP 9 D3** HS

MELROSE ABBEY: Another romantic setting, the abbey seems to give an atmos to the whole town. Built by David I (what a guy!) for Cistercian monks from Rievaulx from 1136, there wasn't much left, spiritually or architecturally, by the Reformation. Once, however, it sustained a huge community, as evinced by the widespread excavations. There's a museum of abbey, church and Roman relics; soon to include Robert the Bruce's heart, recently excavated in the grds. **1529 MAP 8 C3** HS

ARBROATH ABBEY: 25km N of Dundee. Founded in 1178 and endowed on an unparalleled scale, this is an important place in Scots history. It's where the Declaration was signed in 1320 to appeal to the Pope to release the Scots from the **1530 MAP 4 E3**

yoke of the English (you can buy facsimiles of the yellow parchment; the original is in Charter House in Edin). It was to Arbroath that the Stone of Destiny (on which the Kings of Scotland were traditionally crowned) was returned after being 'stolen' from Westminster Abbey in the 1950s and is now at Edinburgh Castle. HS

THE GREAT BATTLEGROUNDS

Chosen for accessibility and sense of history as well as historical significance.

1531
MAP 2
D3
CULLODEN, INVERNESS: Signed from A9 and A96 into Inverness and about 8km from town. Extensive battlefield on either side of the rd before you even get to the (v full-on) visitor centre. Positions of the clans and the troops marked out across the moor; flags enable you to get a real sense of scale. If you go in spring you see how wet and miserable the Moor can be (the battle took place on 16 April 1746). No matter how many other folk are there wandering down the lines, a visit to this most infamous of battlefields can still leave a pain in the heart. Centre 9am-6pm (winter 10am-4pm). Ground open at all times for more personal Cullodens. NTS

1532
MAP 2
B3
BATTLE OF THE BRAES, SKYE: 10km Portree. Take main A850 rd S for 3km then left, marked 'Braes' for 7km. Monument is on a rise on rt. The last battle fought on British soil and a significant place in Scots history. When the clearances, uninterrupted by any organised opposition, were virtually complete and vast tracts of Scotland had been depopulated for sheep, the Skye crofters finally stood up in 1882 to the Government troops and said enough is enough. A cairn has been erected nr the spot where they fought on behalf of 'all the crofters of Gaeldom', a battle which led eventually to the Crofters Act which has guaranteed their rights ever since. At the end of this rd at Peinchorran, there are fine views of Raasay (which was devastated by clearances) and Glamaig, the conical Cuillin, across L Sligachan.

1533
MAP 2
C5
GLENCOE: Not much of a battle, of course, but one of the most infamous massacres in British history. Much has been written (John Prebble's *Glencoe* and many recent interpretations) and the visitor centre provides the audiovisual scenario. There's the Macdonald monument nr Glencoe village and the walk to the more evocative Signal Rock where the bonfire was lit, now a happy wood-land trail in this doom-laden landscape. About 4km return from centre. (1558/ SPOOKY PLACES.)

1534
SCAPA FLOW, ORKNEY MAINLAND and HOY: Scapa Flow, surrounded by various of the southern Orkney islands, is one of the most sheltered anchorages in Europe. Hence the huge presence in Orkney of ships and personnel during both wars. The Germans scuttled 54 of their warships here in 1919 and many still lie in the bay. The *Royal Oak* was torpedoed in 1939 with the loss of 833 men. Much still remains of the war yrs (especially if you're a diver, 1728/DIVING): the rusting hulks, the shore fortifications, the Churchill Barriers and the ghosts of a long-gone army at Scapa and Lyness on Hoy.

1535
MAP 8
C3
LILLIARD'S EDGE, nr ST BOSWELLS: On main A68, look for Lilliard's Edge Caravan Park 5km S of St Boswells; park and walk back towards St Boswells to the brim of the hill (about 500m), then cross rough ground on rt along ridge, following whin hedge. Marvellous view attests to strategic location. 200m along, a cairn marks the grave of Lilliard who, in 1545, joined the Battle of Ancrum Moor against the English 'loons' under the Earl of Angus. 'And when her legs were cuttit off, she fought upon her stumps'. An ancient poem etched on the stone records her legendary . . . feet.

1536
MAP 4
C2
KILLIECRANKIE, nr PITLOCHRY: The first battle of the Jacobite Risings where, in July 1689, the Highlanders lost their leader Viscount (aka Bonnie) Dundee, but won the battle, using the narrow Pass of Killiecrankie. One escaping soldier made a famous leap. Well-depicted scenario in visitor centre; short walk to 'The Leap'. Battle viewpoint and cairn is further along rd to Blair Atholl, turning rt and doubling back at Little Chef and on, almost to A9 underpass (3km from visitor centre). You get the lie of the land from here. Many good walks in this area.

1537
MAP 6
D4
BANNOCKBURN, nr STIRLING: 4km town centre via Glas rd (it's well signposted) or jnct 9 of M9 (3km), behind a rather sad hotel. Some visitors might be perplexed as to why 24 June 1314 was such a big deal for the Scots and, apart from the 50m walk to the flag-pole and the huge statue, there's not a lot doing. But the visitor centre does bring the scale of it to life, the horror and the glory. The battlefield

itself is thought to lie around the orange building of the High School some distance away, and the best place to see the famous wee burn is from below the magnificent Telford Br. Ask at centre for directions (5km by road).

MARY, CHARLIE AND BOB
Mary Queen of Scots 1542-87

LINLITHGOW PALACE: Where she was born (1425/RUINS).

HOLYROOD PALACE, EDINBURGH: And lived (305/MAIN ATTRACTIONS).

INCHMAHOME PRIORY, PORT OF MENTEITH: The ruins of the Priory on the island in Scotland's only lake, where the infant Queen spent her early years in the safe keeping of the Augustinian monks. Short journey by boat from quay nr lake hotel. Signal the ferryman by turning the board to the island, much as she did. 7 days, 9.30am-6pm (Sun from 2pm). Delights of the Trossachs surround you. HS
1538 MAP 6 B3

MARY QUEEN OF SCOTS' HOUSE, JEDBURGH: In grds via Smiths Wynd off main st. Historians quibble but this long-standing museum claims to be 'the' house where she became ill in 1566, but somehow made it over to visit the injured Bothwell at Hermitage Castle 50km away. Tower house in good condition; displays and well-told saga. Easter-Nov 10am-4.45pm, Sun 4.30pm.
1539 MAP 8 D3

LOCH LEVEN CASTLE, nr KINROSS: The ultimate in romantic penitentiaries; on the island in the middle of the loch and clearly visible from the M90. Not much left of the ruin to fill out the fantasy, but this is where Mary spent 10 months in 1568 before her famous escape and her final attempt to get back the throne. Sailings Apr-Sept, 9.30am-5pm in small launch from Kirkgate Park. 7min trip, return as you like.
1540 MAP 4 C4

DUNDRENNAN ABBEY, nr AUCHENCAIRN and KIRKCUDBRIGHT: Mary Queen of Scots got around and there are innumerable places, castles and abbeys where she spent the night. This, however, was where she spent her last one on Scottish soil. She left next day from Pt Mary (nothing much to see there except a beach – it's 2km along the rd that skirts the sinister MoD range – the pier's long gone and . . . well, there's no plaque). The Cistercian abbey of Whitemonks (established 1142), which harboured her on her last night, is now a tranquil ruin. HS
1541 MAP 9 C4

'In my end is my beginning,' she said, facing her execution which came 19yrs later. Her 'death mask' is displayed at **LENNOXLOVE HOUSE, nr HADDINGTON;** it does seem on the small side for someone who was supposedly 6 feet tall!
1542

Bonnie Prince Charlie 1720-88

PRINCE CHARLIE'S BAY, ERISKAY: The uncelebrated, unmarked and beautiful beach where Charlie first landed in Scotland to begin the Jacobite Rebellion. Nothing much has changed and this crescent of sand with soft machair and a turquoise sea is still a secret place. 1km from township heading S. (1900/MAGICAL ISLANDS.)
1543 MAP 2 A4

LOCH NAN UAMH, nr ARISAIG, THE PRINCE'S CAIRN: 7km from Lochailort on A830, 48km Ft William. Signed from the rd, a path leads down to the left. This is the 'traditional' spot (pron 'Loch Na Nuan') where Charlie embarked for France in Sept 1746, having lost the battle and the cause. The rocky headland also o/look the bay and skerries where he'd landed in July the year before to begin the campaign. This place was the beginning and the end and it has all the romance necessary to be utterly convincing. Is that a French ship out there in the mist?
1544 MAP 2 C4

GLENFINNAN: The place where he 'raised his standard' to rally the clans to the Jacobite cause. For a while on that August day in 1745 it had looked as if only a handful were coming. Then they heard the pipes and 600 Camerons came marching from the valley (where the viaduct now spans). That must have been one helluva moment. Though it's thought that he actually stood on the higher ground, there is a powerful sense of place and history here. The vistor centre has an excellent map of Charlie's path/flight through Scotland – somehow he touched all the most alluring places! Tower can be climbed. NTS
1545 MAP 2 C4

CULLODEN, nr INVERNESS: 1531/BATTLEGROUNDS.

Robert the Bruce 1274-1329

BRUCE'S STONE, GLEN TROOL, nr NEWTON STEWART: 26km N by A714 via Bargrennan (8km to head of glen) which is on the S Upland Way (1599/LONG
1546 MAP 9 B3

WALKS). The fair Glen Trool is a celebrated spot in the Galloway Forest Park (1273/GLENS). The stone is signed and marks the area where Bruce's guerrilla band rained boulders down on the pursuing English in 1307 after they had routed the main army at Solway Moss. Good walking, incl Merrick (1576/HILLS).

1547 **BANNOCKBURN, nr STIRLING:** The climactic battle in June 1314, when Bruce
MAP 6 decisively whipped the English and got himself the kingdom (though Scotland
D4 was not recognised as independent until 1328, just before his death). The scale of the skirmish can be visualised at the visitor centre, but not so readily 'in the field' (1537/BATTLEGROUNDS).

1548 **ARBROATH ABBEY:** Not much of the Bruce trail here, but this is where the famous
MAP 4 Declaration was signed that was the attempt of the Scots nobility united behind
E7 him to gain international recognition of the independence they had won on the battlefield. What it says is stirring stuff; the original is in Edin (1530/ABBEYS).
HS

1549 **DUNFERMLINE ABBEY CHURCH:** Here, at last, some tangible evidence, his tomb.
MAP 5 Buried in 1329, his remains were discovered wrapped in gold cloth, when the site
B2 was being cleared for the new church in 1818. Many of the other gr kings, the Alexanders I and III, were not so readily identifiable (Bruce's ribcage had been cut to remove his heart). With gr national emotion he was reinterred underneath the pulpit. The church (as opposed to the ruins and Norman nave adj) is open Apr-Sept 9.30am-5pm. Gr café in Abbot House thro graveyard (1814/MUSEUMS).

1550 **MELROSE ABBEY:** On his deathbed Bruce asked that his heart be buried here after
MAP 8 it was taken to the Crusades to aid the Army in their battles. The lead casket
C3 containing it has recently been excavated from the chapter house and, after inspections in Edin by HS, it'll be displayed here.
HS

BRUCE'S CAVE: 1990/MOBILE MOMENTS.

THE IMPORTANT LITERARY PLACES

1551 **ROBERT BURNS (1759–96), ALLOWAY, AYR AND DUMFRIES:** Black-and-white signs
MAP showing the bard's nut mark a heritage trail through his life and haunts in Ayr-
1/9 shire and Dumfriesshire. His howff at Dumfries is v atmospheric. Best is at **ALLOWAY:** The Auld Brig o' Doon and the Auld Kirk where Tam o' Shanter saw the witches dance are more evocative than the Monument and surrounding grds or, 1km up the rd, the cottage (his birthplace; little atmos) and the state-of-the-art Tam o' Shanter Experience where you are 'transported back to 18th-century Ayrshire by 20th-century technology' (I don't think he'd have been overimpressed).

1552 **AYR:** The Auld Kirk off main st by river; graveyard with diagram of where his
friends are buried; open at all times. **DUMFRIES:** House where he spent his last yrs and mausoleum 250m away at back of a kirkyard stuffed with extravagant masonry. 10km N of Dumfries on A76 at **ELLISLAND FARM** is the most interesting of all the sites. The farmhouse with genuine memorabilia e.g. his mirror, fishing-rod, a poem scratched on glass, original manuscripts. There's his favourite walk by the river where he composed 'Tam o' Shanter' and a strong atmos about the place. Farmer/curator Les Byers will let you in to see when he's at home. **BROW WELL, nr RUTHWELL** on the B725 20km S Dumfries and nr Caerlaverock (1381/BIRDS), is a quiet place, a well with curative properties where he went in the latter stages of his illness. Not many folk go to this one.

1553 **LEWIS GRASSIC GIBBON (1901–34), ARBUTHNOT, nr STONEHAVEN:** Although James
MAP 3 Leslie Mitchell left the area in 1917, this is where he was born and spent his
D4 formative years. Visitor centre (01561 361668; Apr-Oct 7 days 10am-4.30pm) at the end of the village (via B967, 16km S of Stonehaven off main A92) has details of his life and can point you in the direction of the places he writes about in his trilogy, *The Scots Quair*. The first part, *Sunset Song*, is generally considered to be one of the gr Scots novels and this area, the **HOWE OF THE MEARNS**, is the place he so effectively evokes. Arbuthnot was 'Kinraddie' and the churchyard 1km away on the other side of rd still has the atmos of that time of innocence before the war which pervades the book. His ashes are here in a grave in a corner. From 1928 to when he died 6yrs later at the age of only 33, he wrote an incredible 17 books.

1554 **NEIL GUNN (1891–1973), DUNBEATH, nr WICK:** Scotland's foremost writer on
MAP 8 Highland life, only now receiving the recognition he deserves, was brought up in
E2

this NE fishing village and based 3 of his greatest yarns here, particularly *Highland River,* which must stand in any literature as a brilliant evocation of place. The **STRATH** in which it is set is below the house (a nondescript terraced house next to the Stores) and makes for a gr walk (1612/GLEN AND RIVER WALKS). There's a commemorative statue by the harbour, not quite the harbour you imagine from the books. Gunn also lived for many yrs nr **DINGWALL** and there is a memorial on the back rd to Strathpeffer and a wonderful view in a place he often walked (on A834, 4km from Dingwall).

JAMES HOGG (1770–1835), ST MARY'S LOCH, ETTRICK: 'The Ettrick Shepherd' who wrote one of the great works of Scottish literature, *The Confessions of a Justified Sinner,* was born, lived and died in the valleys of the **YARROW** and the **ETTRICK**, some of the most starkly beautiful landscapes in Scotland. **ST MARY'S LOCH** on the A708, 28km W of Selkirk: there's a commemorative statue looking over the loch and the adj and supernatural seeming L of the Lowes. On the strip of land betw is **TIBBIE SHIELS** pub (and hotel), once a gathering place for the writer and his friends (e.g. Sir Walter Scott) and still a notable hostelry. Across the valley divide (11km on foot, part of the S Upland Way (1599/LONG WALKS), or 25km by rd past the Gordon Arms Hotel is the remote village of **ETTRICK**, another monument and his grave (and Tibbie Shiels') in the churchyard. He was born, lived, died and was buried within this one acre.

1555
MAP 8
B3

SIR WALTER SCOTT (1771–1832), ABBOTSFORD, MELROSE: No other place in Scotland (and few anywhere) contains so much of a writer's life and work. This was the house he rebuilt from the farmhouse he moved to in 1812 in the countryside which he did so much to popularise. The house is still lived in by his descendants and the library and study are pretty much as he left them, including 9,000 rare books, antiquarian even in his day. There are pleasant grounds and topiary and a walk by the Tweed which the house o/look. His grave is at **DRYBURGH ABBEY** (1526/ABBEYS). House open Apr-Oct 10am-5pm; Sun 2-5pm.

1556
MAP 8
C3

ROBERT LOUIS STEVENSON (1850–94), EDINBURGH: Though Stevenson travelled widely – lived in France, emigrated to America and died and was buried in Samoa – he spent the first 30 yrs of his short life in Edin. He was born and brought up in the New Town, living at **17 HERIOT ROW** from 1857-80 in a fashionable town house which is still lived in (not open to the public). Most of his youth was spent in this newly built and expanding part of the city in an area bounded then by parkland and farms. Both the **BOTANICS** (312/OTHER ATTRACTIONS) and **WARRISTON CEMETERY** (1512/GRAVEYARDS) are part of the landscape of his childhood. However, his fondest recollections were of the **PENTLAND HILLS** and, virtually unchanged as they are, it's here that one is following most poignantly in his footsteps. The 'cottage' at **SWANSTON** (a delightful village with some remarkable thatched cottages reached via the city bypass/Colinton t/off or from Oxgangs Rd and a br over the bypass; the village nestles in a grove of trees below the hills and is a good place to walk from), the ruins of **GLENCORSE CHURCH** (ruins even then and where he later asked that a prayer be said for him) and **COLINTON MANSE** can all be seen, but not visited. The fact is, Edinburgh has no Stevenson Museum (though his lifetime was relatively recent and his acclaim international). You can always stay at the **HAWES INN** in South Queensferry and dream of *Kidnapped.*

1557
MAP 7
B2

IRVINE WELSH (c1958 -): Literary immortality awaits confirmation. Tours (*that* toilet etc) likely any day. **ROBBIES BAR:** might suffice (235/'UNSPOILT' PUBS).

THE REALLY SPOOKY PLACES

HIDDEN VALLEY, GLENCOE: The secret glen where the ill-fated Macdonalds hid the cattle they'd stolen from the Lowlands and which became (with politics and power struggles) their undoing. A narrow wooded cleft takes you betw the imposing and gnarled '3 Sisters' Hills and over the threshold (God knows how the cattle got there) and into the huge bowl of Coire Gabhail. The place envelops you in its tragic history, more redolent perhaps than any of the massacre sites. Park on the A82 5km from the visitor centre 200m to the E of 2 white buildings on either side of the rd (Alt-na-reigh). Cross rd and follow clear path down to and across the R Coe. Ascend keeping burn to left; 1.5km further up, it's best to ford it. Allow 3hrs. (1533/BATTLEGROUNDS.)

1558
MAP 1
C5

2-B-2

1559 **UNDER EDINBURGH OLD TOWN:** Two mentions here - Mary King's Close, a
MAP A medieval st under the Royal Mile closed in 1753; and the Vaults under North Br
- built in the 18th century and sealed up around the time of the Napoleonic Wars.
History underfoot for unsuspecting tourists and locals alike. Mercat Tours (0131
661 4541) will take you both places. Glimpses of a rather smelly subterranean life
way back then. It's dark during the day, but at night . . .

1560 **THE YESNABY STACKS, ORKNEY MAINLAND:** A cliff top viewpoint that's so wild, so
dramatic and, if you walk near the edge, so precarious that its supernaturalism
verges on the uneasy. Shells of lookout posts from the war echo the melancholy
spirit of the place. ('The bloody town's a bloody cuss/No bloody trains, no
bloody bus/And no one cares for bloody us/In bloody Orkney' – first lines of a
poem written then, a soldier's lament.) Nr Skara Brae, it's about 30km from
Kirkwall and way out west.

1561 **THE FAIRY GLEN, SKYE:** A place so strange, it's hard to believe that it's merely a
MAP 1 geological phenomenon. Entering Uig on the A856 from Portree, there's a turret
B3 on the left (Macrae's Folly) and, shortly before, a bus shelter on the rt with a rd
beside it. Take this rd for 2km and you enter an area of extraordinary conical hills
which, in certain conditions of light and weather, seems to entirely justify its
legendary provenance. Your mood may determine whether you believe they were
good or bad fairies, but there's supposed to be an incredible 365 of these grassy
hillocks, some 35m high – how else could they be there?

1562 **CLAVA CAIRNS, nr CULLODEN, INVERNESS:** Nr Culloden (1531/ BATTLEGROUNDS)
MAP 1 these curious chambered cairns in a grove of trees nr a river in the middle of 20th-
D3 century nowhere can be seriously X-Files (1448/PREHISTORIC SITES for details).

1563 **THE CLOOTIE WELL on the road betw TORE on the A9 and AVOCH:** Spooky spooky
MAP 2 place on the rd towards Avoch and Cromarty 4km from the r/bout at Tore N of
D3 Inverness. Easily missed, but it's on the rt side of the rd going E. What you see is
hundreds of rags (actually pieces of clothing) hanging on the branches of trees
around the spout of an ancient well. They go way back up the hill behind and
have probably been here for decades. Don't wish you were here. This has what
you'd call strong (but strange) vibrations.

1564 **BURN O' VAT, nr BALLATER:** This impressive and rather spooky glacial curiosity
MAP 3 on Royal Deeside is a popular spot and well worth the short walk. 8km from
B4 Ballater towards Aberd on main A93, take A97 for Huntly for 2km to a rd side
info kiosk at the Muir of Dinnet nature reserve. Some scrambling to reach the
huge cavern from which the burn flows to L Kinord. Can go further.

1565 **CRICHOPE LINN, nr THORNHILL:** A supernatural sliver of glen inhabited by water
MAP 9 spirits of various temperaments. Take rd for Cample on A76 Dumfries to Kilmar-
D2 nock rd just S of Thornhill; at village (2km) take left for 2km. Discreet sign and
gate in bank on rt is easy to miss, but quarry for parking 100m further on, on left,
is more obvious. Follow path upsteam on trickling Cample water for 1km until
you're at the gorge. Hope you come back.

1566 **SALLOCHY WOOD, LOCH LOMOND:** B837, N of Balmaha, look for Sallochy Wood
MAP 1 car park on the left. Cross back over the rd, away from L Lomond, and follow
D2 the trail signs, up the hill. After the large Cedar tree, the path takes you into the
woods. Slippery going (on the exposed tree roots) then an unexpected clearing in
middle of dense undergrowth. This is the ruined hamlet of Wester Sullochy.
Surrounded by gloomy conifers, the roofless buildings still stand, awaiting the
return of their long-dead tenants. Not a place to visit at night, but some do, and
they leave their mark . . .

THE NECROPOLIS, GLASGOW: 1511/GRAVEYARDS.

HAMILTON MAUSOLEUM, STRATHCLYDE PARK: 1482/MONUMENTS.

LOANHEAD OF DAVIOT, nr OLD MELDRUM, ABERDEENSHIRE: 1455/PREHISTORIC
SITES.

SECTION 8

Strolls, Walks and Hikes

FAVOURITE HILLS

Popular and notable hills in the various regions of Scotland but not including Munros or difficult climbs. Always best to remember that the weather can change v quickly. Take an OS map on higher tops. See p. 10 for walk codes.

1567   **SUILVEN, LOCHINVER:** From close or far away, this is one of Scotland's
MAP 2   awe-inspiring mountains. The 'sugar loaf' can seem almost
C2   insurmountable, but in good weather it's not so difficult. Route from Inverkirkaig 5km S of Lochinver on rd to Achiltibuie, turns up track by Achin's Bookshop (1746/CRAFT SHOPS) on the path for the Kirkaig Falls; once at the loch, you head for the Bealach, the central waistline through an unexpected dyke and follow track to the top. The slightly quicker route from the N (Glencanisp) following a stalkers' track that eventually leads to Elphin, also heads for the central breach in the mt's defences. Either way it's a long walk in; 8km before the climb. Allow 8hrs return. At the top, the most enjoyable 100m in the land and below – amazing Assynt. 731m. Take OS map.   2-C-3

1568   **STAC POLLAIDH/POLLY, nr ULLAPOOL:** The hill which is described
MAP 2   variously as 'perfect', 'preposterous' and 'gr fun', certainly has character
C2   and, rising out of the Sutherland moors on the rd to Achiltibuie off the A835 N from Ullapool, demands to be climbed. The route everyone takes is from the car park by L Lurgainn 8km from main rd. Head for the central ridge which for many folk is enough; the path to the pinnacles is exposed and can be off-putting. Best half day hill climb in the N. 613m. Allow 3-4hrs return.   2-B-3

1569   **GOAT FELL, ARRAN:** Starting from the car park at Cladach before Brodick
MAP 1   Castle grounds 3km from town, or from Corrie further up the coast (12km).
C3   Worn path, a steady climb, rarely much of a scramble but a rewarding afternoon's exertion. Some scree and some view! 874m. Allow 5hrs.   2-B-2

1570   **THE COBBLER (BEN ARTHUR), ARROCHAR:** Perennial favourite of the Glas hill
MAP 1   walker and, for sheer exhilaration, the most popular of 'the Arrochar Alps'. A
C2   motorway path ascends from the A83 on the other side of L Long from Arrochar (park in lay-bys nr Succoth rd end; there are always loads of cars) and takes 2.5-3hrs to traverse the up'n'down route to the top. Just short of a Munro at 881m, it has 3 tops of which the N peak is the simplest scramble (central and S peaks for climbers). Way isn't marked; consult map or other walkers.   2-B-3

FOUR MAGNIFICENT HILLS IN THE TROSSACHS

1571   **BEN VENUE and BEN A'AN:** 2 celebrated tops in the Highland microcosm of
MAP 6   the Trossachs around L Achray, 15km W of Callander; strenuous but not
B3   difficult and with superb views. Ben Venue (727m) is the more serious; allow 4-5 hrs return. Start from Kinlochard side at Ledard or more usually from behind L Achray Hotel: 100m along 'Forest Path' go left and then it's waymarked. Ben A'An (415m) starts with a steep climb from the main A821 along from the old Trossachs Hotel (now time-share flats). Scramble at top. Allow 2 to 3hrs.   2-B-3

1572   **BEINN ANT-SIDHIEN, STRATHYRE:** (pron 'Ben Shian'). Another Trossachs favourite
MAP 6   and not taxing. From village main rd (the A74 to Lochearnhead), cross bridge opp
B2   Monro Hotel, turn left after 200m then 500m to steep start through woods. O/look village and views to Crianlarich and Ben Vorlich. 600m. 1.5hrs.   2-B-3

1573   **DOON HILL, THE FAERIE KNOWE, ABERFOYLE:** Legendary hillock in Aberfoyle,
MAP 4   only 1hr up and back, so a gentle elevation into faerie land. The tree at the top is
B3   the home of the 'People of Quietness' and there was once a local minister who had the temerity to tell their secrets (in 1692). Go round it 7 times and your wish will be granted, go round it backwards at your peril (well, you wouldn't would you?). Go from end of main st and opp jnct of Trossachs/Callander rd take small rd past hotel for 2km, veering left. Better still, ask!   1-B-1

1574   **THE GOLDEN HILL, BEN OUR, LOCH EARN:** A relatively easy climb which feels like
MAP 4   a real mountain walk and with dramatic vews of the big hills around it, Ben
B3   Vorlich and the Ben Lawyers group and the Balquhidder Braes. Starts S of Lochearnhead on the S Lochearn rd 1.5km from its jnct with the A84. Park after white castle and church before crossing the R Ample. Follow river track for 1.5km to a footbridge then another past Glenample Farm. Curve round to the back of Ben Our, the path peters out nr the top. 3hrs return.   2-B-2

CRIFFEL, NEW ABBEY, nr DUMFRIES: 12km S by A710 to New Abbey, which Criffel dominates. It's only 569m, but seems higher. Exceptional views from top as far as English lakes and across to Borders. Granite lump with brilliant outcrops of quartzite. The annual race gets up and back to the Abbey Arms in under an hr; you can take it easier. Start 3km S of village, t/off A710 by a curious painted bus shelter signed for Ardwell Mains Farm. Park before the farm buildings and get on up.

1575
MAP 9
D3

2-A-2

MERRICK, nr NEWTON STEWART: Go from bonnie Glen Trool via Bargrennan 14km N on the A714. Bruce's Stone is there at the start (1546/MARY, CHARLIE AND BOB). The highest peak in S Scotland (843m), it's a strenuous though straightforward climb in glorious scenery. 4hrs.

1576
MAP 9
B3

2-B-3

NORTH BERWICK LAW: The conical volcanic hill, a beacon in the E Lothian landscape. **TRAPRAIN LAW** nearby, is higher, tends to be frequented by rock climbers, but has major prehistorical significance as a hillfort citadel of the Goddodin and a definite aura. NBL is easy and rewarding - leave town by Law Rd, path marked beyond houses. Views 'to the Cairngorms' (!) and along the Forth.

1577
MAP 7
D1

BOTH 1-A-1

RUBERSLAW, DENHOLM, nr HAWICK: The smooth hummock that sits above the Teviot valley and affords views of 7 counties, incl Northumberland. At 424m, it's a gentle climb taking about 1hr from the usual start at Denholm Hill Farm (private land, be aware of livestock). Leave Denholm at corner of Green by shop and go past post office. Take left after 3km to farm.

1578
MAP 8
C3

2-A-2

TINTO HILL, nr BIGGAR and LANARK: A favourite climb in S/Central Scotland with easy access to start from A73 nr Symington, 10km S of Lanark. Park 100m behind Tinto Hills farm shop, after stocking up with rolls and juice. Good track, though it has its ups and downs before you get there. Braw views. 707m. Allow 3hrs.

1579
MAP 1
E4

2-A-2

CONIC HILL, BALMAHA, LOCH LOMOND: An easier climb than the Ben up the rd and a good place to view it from, Conic, on the Highland fault line, is one of the first Highland hills you reach from Glas. Stunning views also of L Lomond from its 358m peak. Ascend thro woodland from the corner of Balmaha car park. Watch for buzzards and your footing on the final crumbly bits. 1.5hrs up.

1580
MAP 6
B4

2-A-2

KINNOULL HILL, PERTH: Various starts from town (the path from beyond Branklyn Grds on the Dundee Rd is less frequented) to the wooded ridge above the Tay with its tower and incredible views to S from the precipitous cliffs. Surprisingly extensive area of hill side common and it's not difficult to get lost. The leaflet/map from Perth TO helps. Local lurv spot after dark.

1581
MAP 4
C4

1-A-1

BENNACHIE, nr ABERDEEN: The pilgrimage hill, an easy 528m often busy at w/ends but never a let-down. Various trails take in 'the Taps'. Trad route from Rowan Tree nr Chapel of Garioch (pron 'Geery') signed Pittodrie off A96 nr Pitcaple. Also from Essons car park on rd from Chapel-Monymusk, which is steeper. Or from other side the Lord's Throat rd, a longer, more forested app from banks of the Don. All car parks have trail-finders. From the fortified top you see what Aberdeenshire is about. 2hrs. Bennachie's soulmate, **TAP O' NOTH**, is 20km W. Easy app via Rhynie on A97 (then 3km).

1582
MAP 3
C3

2-B-2

MORVEN, BERRIEDALE, nr WICK: The gr hill of Caithness from which you can see the whole county and from Orkney to the Moray Firth. 3 routes, but main two are (1) The Braemore rd from Dunbeath (Wick 32km) on the coast, to Braemore Lodge (9km), park and walk; about 5km return and a 2hr climb. The adj hill, the Maiden's Pap, really does look like a tit from this angle. (2) From further down coast take the rd from Berriedale (Helmsdale 15km) to the cottage at the Wag (15km). Less steep but longer route; depends how far you can get a car up the track. In either case check with the keepers, esp Aug-Oct. (01593 731371) 706m.

1583
MAP 2
E2

2-C-3

HILL WALKS

Apart from the mainly isolated hill tops mentioned previously, the following ranges of hills offer walks in various directions and more than one summit. They are all accessible and fairly easy. See p. 10 for walk codes.

1584 **LOMOND HILLS, FIFE, nr FALKLAND:** The conservation village lies below a
MAP 5 prominent ridge easily reached from the main st esp via Back Wynd (off which
C3 there's a car park) – just head on up. More usual app to both E and W Lomond,
the main tops, is from Craigmead car park 3km from village towards Leslie where
there is a trail-finder board. The celebrated Lomonds (aka the Paps of Fife), aren't
that high (West is 522m), but they can see and be seen for miles. Also start from
radio masts up rd from A912 E of Falkland.　　　3-10KM　CIRC　XBIKES　2-A-2

An easy rewarding single climb is Bishop's Hill. Start opp the church in Scotland-
well. A steep path veers left and then there are several ways up. Allow 2hrs. Gr
view of L Leven, Fife and a good swathe of Central Scotland. Gliders glide over.

1585 **THE EILDONS, MELROSE:** The 3 much-loved hills or paps visible from most of the
MAP 8 Central Borders and easily climbed from the town of Melrose which nestles at
C3 their foot. Leave main sq by rd to stn (the Dingleton rd), after 100m a path begins
betw 2 pebble-dash houses on the left. You climb the smaller first, then the
highest central one (422m). You can make a circular route of it by returning to the
golf course. Allow 1.5hrs.　　　3KM　CIRC　XBIKES　1-A-2

1586 **THE OCHILS:** Most usual app from the 'hillfoot towns' at the foot of the glens that
MAP 6 cut into their S-facing slopes, along the A91 Stirling-St Andrews rd. Alva,
D3 Tillicoultry and Dollar all have impressive glen walks easily found from the main
streets and, from there, there are tracks marked (1609/GLEN AND RIVER WALKS).
Good start nr Stirling from the Sheriffmuir rd uphill from Br of Allan or, from
the old graveyard (1519/GRAVEYARDS), take the steep rd up. From last houses
about 3km, there's a lay-by on the rt and a reservoir just visible on the left. There
are usually other cars here. A stile leads to the hills which stretch away to the E
for 40km and afford gr views for little effort. Highest point is Ben Cleuch, 721m.
Swimming place nearby called Paradise (1350/PICNICS).
　　　2-40KM　SOME CIRC　XBIKES　1/2-B-2

1587 **THE LAMMERMUIRS:** The hills SE of Edin that divide the rich farmlands of E
MAP 7 Lothian and the valley of the Tweed in the Borders. Mostly a high wide moor
E2 land but there's wooded gentle hill country in the watersheds of the southern
rivers and spectacular coastal scenery betw Cockburnspath and St Abbs Head.
(1397/WILDLIFE; 1641/COASTAL WALKS.) The eastern part of the S Upland Way
follows the Lammermuirs to the coast (1599/LONG WALKS). Many moorland
walks begin at the car park at the head of Whiteadder Reservoir (A1 to
Haddington, B6369 towards Humbie, then E on B6355 through Gifford), a
mysterious loch in the bowl of the hills. Excellent walks also centre on Abbey St
Bathans to the S Head off A1 at Cockburnspath. Through village
(1116/TEAROOMS) to Toot Corner (signed 1km) and off to left, follow path above
valley of Whiteadder to Edinshall Broch (2km). Further on, along river (1km), is
a swing bridge and a fine place to swim (1340/PICNICS). Circular walks possible;
ask in village.　　　5-15KM　SOME CIRC　MTBIKES　1/2-B-2

1588 **THE CHEVIOTS:** Not strictly in Scotland, of course, but they straddle the border and
MAP 8 Border history. There are many fine walks starting from Kirk Yetholm (incl the
D3 Pennine Way which stretches 400km S to the Peak district) incl an 8km circular
route of typical Cheviot foothill terrain that follows the actual border for half its
route (leaflet available in the pub). Most forays start at Wooler 20km from
Coldstream and the border. Cheviot itself (2,676ft) has wide boggy plateau,
Hedgehope via the Harthope Burn usually more fun.

THE CAMPSIE FELLS, nr GLASGOW: 598/WALKS OUTSIDE THE CITY.

THE PENTLAND HILLS, nr EDINBURGH: 324/WALKS OUTSIDE THE CITY.

SOME GREAT MUNROS

There are almost 300 hills in Scotland over 3,000ft as tabled by Sir Hugh Munro in 1891. Munro-bagging has become v popular and there are numerous books which give route details. The Munros selected here have been chosen for their relative ease of access both to the bottom and thence to the top. They all offer rewarding climbs, but none should be attempted without proper clothing (esp boots) and sustenance for the journey. You may also need an OS map. Always remember that the weather can change quickly in the Scottish mts.

BEN LOMOND, ROWARDENNAN, LOCH LOMOND: Many folk's first Munro, given proximity to Glas (soul and city). It's not too taxing a climb and has rewarding views (in good weather). 2 main ascents: 'tourist route' is easier, from toilet block at Rowardennan car park (end of rd from Drymen), well-trodden all the way; or 500m up past Youth Hostel, a path follows burn – the 'Ptarmigan Route'. Circular walk poss. 974m. 3hrs up.
1589 MAP 6 A3

AN TEALLACH, TORRIDON: Sea-level start from Dundonnell on the A832 S of Ullapool, so easy to find. This, one of the most awesome peaks in Scotland is not the ordeal it looks. Path well trod and once up there are gr scrambling opportunities for the nimble. Peering over the pinnacle of Lord Berkeley's Seat down to L na Sheallag is a jaw-drop. Take a day (a good day). 1,062m.
1590 MAP 2 C2

BEINN ALLIGIN, TORRIDON: The other gr Torridon trek - you may as well go for it! Car park by br on rd to Inveralligin and Diabeg, walk thro woods over moor by tumbling river. Left at fork then a steepish pull up onto the Horns of Alligin. You can cover 2 Munros in a circular route that takes you across the top of the world, up there with mighty Liathach and Beinn Eighe. 985m.
1591 MAP 2 C2

BEN MORE, MULL: The 'cool, high ben' sits in isolated splendour, the only Munro, bar the Cuillins, not on the mainland. Has a sea-level start from a lay-by on the coast rd B8073 that skirts the southern coast of L Na Keal, then a fairly clear path through the bleak landscape. Can be slightly tricky nr the top (don't think about it without good boots), but there are fabulous views across the islands, even as far as Ireland. 966m.
1592 MAP 1 B1

BEN WYVIS, nr GARVE: Standing apart from its northern neighbours, you can feel the presence of this mt from a long way off. Just to N of main A835 rd from Inverness-Ullapool and v accessible from it, park 6km N of Garve (48km from Inverness) and follow marked path by stream and through the forest. Vast plantations all around but you leave them behind and the app to the summit is by a soft and mossy ridge. Magnificent 1,046m.
1593 MAP 2 D3

LOCHNAGAR, nr BALLATER: Described as a fine, complex mt, its nobility and mystique apparent from afar, not least Balmoral Castle. App via Glen Muick (pron 'Mick') rd from Ballater to car park at L Muick (1297/LOCHS). Path to mt well signed and well trodden. 18km return, allow 6-8hrs. Steep at top. Apparently on a clear day you can see the Forth Br. 1,155m.
1594 MAP 3 B4

BLA BHEINN, SKYE: The magnificent massif, isolated from the other Cuillins, has a sea-level start and seems much higher than it is. The Munro Guide describes it as 'exceptionally accessible'. It has an eerie jagged beauty and – though some scrambling is involved and it helps to have a head for exposed situations – there are no serious dangers. Take A881 from Broadford to Elgol through Torrin and park 1km S of the head of L Slapin, walking W at Allt na Dunaiche along N bank of stream. Bla Bheinn (pron 'Blahven') is an enormously rewarding climb and permits rapid descent for scree runners to shorten the usual time of 8hrs. 928m.
1595 MAP 1 B4

BEN LAWERS, between KILLIN and ABERFELDY, PERTHSHIRE: The massif of 7 summits includes 6 Munros that dominate the N side of L Tay. They are linked by a twisting ridge 12km long that only once falls below 800m and, if you're v fit, it's poss to do the lot in a single day starting from the N or Glen Lyon side. The Munro beginner or non-bagger should start and plan route at the visitor centre 5km off the A827 nr Lawers.
1596 MAP 4 B7

MEALL NAN PTARMIGAN: The part of the ridge to the W, which takes in a Munro and several tops, is not arduous and is immensely impressive. In 3hrs you can get up, along some of it and back, and feel gr for the rest of the week. Start 1km further on from visitor centre down 100m track and through gate. Head up to saddle, paths indistinct, but just climb. At the top the path becomes clear, as does your reason for being here.
1597 MAP 4 B3

LONG WALKS

Once again, these walks require preparation, route maps, v good boots etc. But don't carry too much. Sections are always poss. See p. 10 for walk codes.

1598
MAP
1/2
THE WEST HIGHLAND WAY: The 150km walk which starts at Milngavie 12km o/side Glas and goes via some of Scotland's most celebrated scenery to emerge in Glen Nevis before the Ben. The route goes: Mugdock Moor-Drymen-L Lomond-Rowardennan-Inversnaid-Inverarnan-Crianlarich-Tyndrum-Br of Orchy-Rannoch Moor-Kingshouse Hotel-Glencoe-The Devil's Staircase-Kinlochleven. The latter part from Br of Orchy is the most dramatic. The Inveroran Hotel, Br of Orchy (01838 400220) and Kingshouse (01855 851259), both historic staging posts, are recommended, as is the Drover's Inn, Inverarnan (688/CENTRAL HOTELS). It's a good idea to book accom (allowing time for muscle fatigue) and don't take too much stuff. Info leaflet/pack from shops or Scottish Natural Heritage (01397 704716).

START: Officially at Milngavie (pron 'Mull-guy') Railway Stn (reg service from Glas Central, also buses from Buchanan St Bus Stn), but actually from Milngavie shopping precinct (Douglas St) 500m away; an inauspicious ramp down to Allander River by the side of Victoria Wine and then behind Presto supermarket. However, the countryside is close. Start from other end 1km down Glen Nevis rd from r/bout on A82 N from Ft William. Way is well marked, but you must have a route map.   2-B-3

1599
MAP
8/9
SOUTHERN UPLAND WAY: 350km walk from Portpatrick S of Stranraer across the Rhinns of Galloway, much moorland, the Galloway Forest Park, the wild heartland of Southern Scotland, then through James Hogg country (1555/LITERARY PLACES) to the gentler E Borders and the sea at Pease Bay (official end, Cockburnspath). Route is Stranraer-N Luce-Dalry-Sanquhar-Wanlockhead-Beattock-St Mary's L-Melrose-Lauder-Abbey St Bathans. The first and latter sections are the most obviously picturesque but highlights include L Trool, the Lowther Hills, St Mary's L, R Tweed. Usually walked W to E, the SU Way is a formidable undertaking . . . think about it! Info SNH as above.

START: Portpatrick by the harbour and up along the cliffs past the lighthouse. or Cockburnspath. Map is on side of shop at Cross.   2-B-3

1600
MAP 3
SPEYSIDE WAY: The walk that follows R Spey from the coast at Speybay betw Buckie and Lossiemouth to Ballindalloch (there have been plans to extend much further S to Boat of Garten) with side spurs to Dufftown from Craigellachie up Glenfiddich (5km) and to Tomintoul follow the R Avon (pron 'A'rn') regarded currently as the end of the walk (24km). Main section from coast to Ballindalloch through Fochabers and Craigellachie is about 50km and closely follows the river. Much less strenuous than SU or WH Ways. Tomintoul spur has more hill walking character and a gr viewpoint at 600m. Throughout walk you are in whisky country with opportunities to visit Cardhu, Glenlivet and other distilleries nearby (1191/1194/WHISKY). Trail criss-crosses river.

START: Usual start is from coast end. Speybay is 8km N of Fochabers; the first marker is by the banks of shingle at the river mouth.   1-A-3

1601
MAP 2
GLEN AFFRIC: In enchanting Glen Affric and L Affric beyond (1608/GLEN AND RIVER WALKS; 1265/GLENS; 1343/PICNICS), some serious walking begins on the 32km Kintail trail. Done either W-E starting at the Morvich Outdoor Centre 2km from A87 nr Shiel Br, or E-W starting at the Affric Lodge 15km W of Cannich. Route can include one of the approaches to the Falls of Glomach (1276/WATERFALLS). In mid-June, this strenuous walk is the first part of an Iron Man-type race called the Highland Cross where 600 self-confessed crazies complete the trail W-E with a 50km cycle dash to Beauly in 3.5hrs. Poss stopover at one of Scotland's remotest (and, amongst walkers, most celebrated) hostels, the recently refurb 'Allt Beithe'. Otherwise allow 10hrs.   2-C-3

SERIOUS WALKS

None of these should be attempted without OS maps, proper equipment and preparation. Hill or ridge walking experience may be essential.

THE CUILLINS, SKYE: Much scrambling and, if you want it, serious climbing over these famously unforgiving peaks. The Red ones are easier and many walks start at the Sligachan Hotel on the main Portree-Broadford rd. Every July there's a hill race up Glamaig; the conical one which o/look the hotel, 'Billy Whizz' from Ft William currently holds the record. Most of the Black Cuillins incl the highest, Sgurr Alasdair (993m), and Sgurr Dearg, 'the inaccessible pinnacle' (978m), can be attacked from the campsite or the youth hostel in Glen Brittle. A good guide is *Introductory Scrambles from Glen Brittle* by Charles Rhodes, available locally, but you will need something. (1956/BIG ATTRACTIONS; 941/942/HOSTELS; 1781/WATERFALLS; 1595/MUNROS; 1335/PICNICS.) **1602 MAP 2 B3**
3-C-3

AONACH EAGACH, GLENCOE: One of several poss major expeditions in the Glencoe area and one of the world's classic ridge walks. Not for the faint-hearted or the ill-prepared. It's the ridge on your rt for almost the whole length of the glen from Altnafeadh to the visitor centre (where you might consult over the route). Start from the main rd and once you're up and have hopped across, do resist the descent from the last summit (Sgorr nam Fiannaidh) to the welcoming bar of the Clachaig Hotel. On your way, you'll have come close to heaven, seen Lochaber in its immense glory and reconnoitred some fairly exposed edges and pinnacles. Go with somebody good. (1304/SCENIC ROUTES; 1008/BLOODY GOOD PUBS; 939/HOSTELS; 1533/BATTLEGROUNDS.) **1603 MAP 2 C5**
3-C-3

BEN NEVIS: Start on Glen Nevis rd, 5km Ft William town centre by br opp youth hostel or from vistor centre (4km town) over br and past Achintee Farm (gentler start). These paths lead to the same main route which continues to the top (many consider the tourist route to be v dull, but it is the safest). Allow the best part of a day (and I do mean the best – the weather can turn quickly here). Many people are killed every yr, even experienced climbers. It is the biggest, though not the best; you can see 100 Munros on a clear day (i.e. about once a yr.) You climb it because . . . well, because you have to. Go prepared (but you can hire boots etc on Glen rd). **1604 MAP 2 C4**
2-B-3

THE FIVE SISTERS OF KINTAIL and **THE CLUANIE RIDGE:** Both generally started from A87 along from Cluanie Inn (1004/BLOODY GOOD PUBS) and they will keep you rt; usually walked E to W. Sisters is an uncomplicated but inspiring ridge walk, taking in 2 Munros and 2 tops. Not as strenuous as it looks, though it's a hard pull up and you descend to a point 8km further up the rd (so arrange transport). Many side spurs to vantage-points and wild views. The Cluanie or S ridge is a classic which covers 7 Munros. Starts at inn; 2 ways off back onto A876. Both can be walked in a single day (Cluanie allow 9hrs). (940/HOSTELS.) **1605 MAP 2 C4**
3-C-3

From the Kintail Centre at Morvich off A87 nr Shiel Br another long distance walk starts to Glen Affric (1601/LONG WALKS).

GRAMPIAN WALKS: The mainly E-W routes through the mts linking R Dee at Braemar via the Linn of Dee (1312/SCENIC ROUTES) with the gr central Highland river systems (the Spey). Many walk guides available. App from W and A9: **1606 MAP 3 A4**

(1) **GLEN TILT:** starting at Blair Atholl (1607/GLEN AND RIVER WALKS); about 35km of superb Highland scenery. Converges with routes below.

(2) **GLEN FESHIE:** from Feshiebridge (starting at the br); 40km. **MAP 4 C7**

(3) **GLEN MORE FOREST PARK:** from Coylumbridge and L Morlich; 32km. (2) joins (3) beyond L Morlich and both go through the Rothiemurchus Forest 1620/WOODLAND WALKS) and the famous **LAIRIG GHRU**, the ancient Rt of Way through the Cairngorms which passes betw Ben Macdui and Braeriach. Ascent is over 700m and going can be rough. This is one of the gr Scottish trails. At end of June, the Lairig Ghru Race completes this course E-W in 3.5hrs, but generally this is a full-day trip. The famous shelter, Corrour Bothy betw 'Devil's Point' and Carn A Mhaim, can be a halfway house. Nr Linn of Dee, routes (1) and (2/3) converge and pass through the ancient Caledonian Forest of Mar. Going E-W is less gruelling and there's Aviemore to look forward to! **MAP 7 D4 /E4**

GLEN AFFRIC: Or rather beyond Glen Affric and L Affric (1608/GLEN WALKS; 1265/GLENS), the serious walking begins (1601/LONG WALKS).

GLEN AND RIVER WALKS

See also GREAT GLENS, *p. 161. Walk codes are on p. 10.*

1607 **GLEN TILT, BLAIR ATHOLL:** A walk of variable length in this classic Highland glen,
MAP 4 easily accessible from the caravan park off the main A9 in Blair Atholl. Trail
C2 leaflet from park office and local TOs. Fine walking and unspoiled scenery begins
only a short distance into the deeply wooded gorge of the R Tilt, but to cover the
circular route it's necessary to walk to 'Gilbert's Br' (9km return) or the longer
trail to Gow's Br (17km return). Begin here also the gr route into the Cairngorms
leading to the Linn of Dee and Braemar, joining the track from Speyside which
starts at Feshiebridge or Glenmore Forest (1606/SERIOUS WALKS).

UP TO 17KM   CIRC   XBIKE   1-B-2

1608 **GLEN AFFRIC, CANNICH, nr DRUMNADROCHIT:** Easy short walks are marked and
MAP 2 hugely rewarding in this magnificent glen well known as the first stretch in the gr
C3 E-W route to Kintail (1605/SERIOUS WALKS) and the Falls of Glomach
(1276/WATERFALLS). Starting pt of this track into the wilds is at the end of the rd
at L Affric; there are many short and circular trails indicated here. Car park is
beyond metal rd 2km along forest track towards Affric Lodge (cars not allowed
to lodge itself). Track cl in stalking season. Easier walks amongst famous Affric
pine/birch forest from car park at Dog Falls, 7km from Cannich. Waterfalls and
spooky tame birds. Good idea to hire bikes at Drumnadrochit or Cannich
(Caravan Park). Don't miss Glen Affric (1265/GLENS).

5/8KM   CIRC   BIKE   1-B-2

1609 **DOLLAR GLEN, DOLLAR, nr STIRLING:** The classic fairy glen in Central Scotland,
MAP 6 positively hoaching with water spirits, reeking of ozone and euphoric after rain.
E3 20km from Stirling by A91, or 18km from M90 at Kinross jnct 6. Start from top
of tree-lined av on either side of burn or from further up rd signed Castle
Campbell where there's a car park and a path down into glen. The Castle at head
of glen is open 7 days till 6pm (Oct-Mar till 4pm), and has boggling views. There's
a circular walk back or take off for the Ochil Tops, the hills that surround the
glen. There are also first-class walks (less frequented) up the glens of the other
hillfoot towns, Alva and Tillicoultry; they also lead to the hills (1586/HILL
WALKS).

3KM + TOPS   CIRC   XBIKE   1-A-2

1610 **RUMBLING BRIDGE, nr DOLLAR:** Formed by another burn running off the same
MAP 6 hills, an easier short walk in an Ochil Glen with something of the chasmic
E3 experience and the added delight of the unique double br (built 1713). There's a
pt here at the end of one of the walkways under the br where you are looking into
a Scottish jungle landscape as the Romantics imagined. Nr Powmill on A977 from
Kinross (jnct 6, M90) then 2km. Nearby is **BRIDGE BYGONES,** an antique/coffee
shop (w/ends till 5pm) and esp **THE POWMILL MILKBAR** serving excellent home-
made food for 35 yrs. It's 5km W on the A977. Open 7 days till 5pm (6m
weekends) (1110/TEAROOMS). Go after your walk! **GARTWHINZEAN HOTEL,** 1km
further on, is a roadhouse with superior bar food all day.

1611 **THE BIG BURN WALK, GOLSPIE:** A non-taxing, perfect little glen walk through lush
MAP 2 diverse woodland. Variations poss, but start just beyond Sutherland Arms
D2 (807/HIGHLAND INEXP HOTELS) in the garage yard which is just off the A9 before
Dunrobin Castle. Go past derelict mill and under aqueduct following river. A real
supernature trail unfolds with ancient tangled trees, meadows, waterfalls, cliffs
and much wildlife. 3km to falls, return via route to castle woods for best all-round
intoxication.

6KM   CIRC   XBIKE   1-B-1

1612 **THE STRATH AT DUNBEATH:** The glen or strath so eloquently evoked in Neil
MAP 2 Gunn's *Highland River* (1554/LITERARY PLACES), a book which is as much about the
E2 geography as the history of his childhood. A path follows the river for many
miles. A leaflet from the Dunbeath Heritage Centre points out places on the way.
It's a spate river and in summer becomes a trickle; hard to imagine Gunn's salmon
odyssey. It's only 500m to the broch, but it's worth going into the hinterland
where it becomes quite mystical (1521/GRAVEYARDS).

1-A-1

1613 **TWEEDSIDE, PEEBLES:** The river side trail that follows the R Tweed from town
MAP 8 (Hay Lodge Park) past Neidpath Castle (1339/PICNICS) and on through classic
B2 Border wooded countryside crossing river either 2.5km out (5km round trip) at
Manor Bror 6km out (Lyne Footbridge – 12km). Local pamphlet, *The Bridges of
Peebles*, worth finding at TO.

5/12KM   CIRC   XBIKE   1-A-1

Other good Tweedside walk between Dryburgh Abbey and Bemersyde House grounds. Start at either end.

GLEN LEDNOCK, nr COMRIE: Can walk from Comrie or take car further up to monument or drive further into glen to reservoir (9km) for more open walks. From town take rt off main A85 (to Lochearnhead) at Deil's Cauldron restau. Walk and Deil's Cauldron (waterfall and gorge) are signed after 250m. Walk takes less than 1hr and emerges on rd nr Lord Melville's monument (climb for gr views back towards Crieff, about 25 mins). River below in woody gorge. **1614 MAP 4 B4**

BRIDGE OF ALVAH, BANFF: Details: 1629/WOODLAND WALKS, mentioned here because the best bit is by the river and the br itself. The single span crossing was built in 1772 and stands high above the river in a sheer-sided gorge. The river below is deep and slow. In the rt light it's almost Amazonian. **1615 MAP 3 C2**

THE GANNOCHY BRIDGE AND THE ROCKS OF SOLITUDE, nr EDZELL: 2km N of village on B966 to Fettercairn. There's a lay-by after br and a wooden door in wall. Through it is another green world and a path above the rocky gorge of the R North Esk (1km). Huge sandstone ledges over dark peaty pools. You don't have to be alone (or maybe you do). **1616 MAP 4 E2**

Nr TAYNUILT: A walk recommended by the Richards family which takes in education with recreation. It goes via Bonawe Ironworks (1827/MUSEUMS) and L Etive along the river side to a swing br and thence to Inverawe Smokehouse (open to the public; café). Walk back less interesting but all v nice. Ask in Taynuilt for start. **1617 MAP 1 C1**

10 KM CIRC BIKE 1-A-1

WOODLAND WALKS

RANDOLPH'S LEAP nr FORRES: Tricky to explain how to find this spectacular gorge of the plucky little Findhorn lined with beautiful beechwoods and a gr place to swim or picnic (1341/PICNICS), so listen up. Go either: 10km S of Forres on the A940 for Grantown, then the B9007 for Ferness and Carrbridge. 1km from the sign for Logie Steading (1856/INEXP ART) and 500m from the narrow stone br, there's a pull-over place on the bend. The woods are on the other side of the rd. Or: take the A939 S from Nairn or N from Grantown and at Ferness take the B9007 for Forres. Approaching from this direction, it's about 6km along the rd; the pull-over is on your rt. If you come to Logie Steading you've missed it; don't - you will miss one of the silvan secrets of the N. **1618 MAP 3 A2**

LOCHAWESIDE: Unclassified rd on N side of loch betw Kilchrenan and Ford, centred on Dalavich. Illustrated brochure available from local hotels around Kilchrenan and Dalavich post office, describes 6 walks in the mixed, mature forest all starting from car parking places on the rd. 3 starting from the Barnaline car park are trail-marked and could be followed without brochure. Avich Falls route crosses R Avich after 2km with falls on return route. Inverinan Glen is always nice and the track from the car park N of Kilchrenan on the B845 back to Taynuilt isn't on the brochure, may be less travelled and also fine. **1619 MAP 1 C2**

2-8KM CIRC
XBIKE 2-A-2

ROTHIEMURCHUS FOREST, nr AVIEMORE: The place to experience the magic and the majesty of the gr Caledonian Forest and the beauty of Scots pine. App from B970, the rd that parallels the A9 from Coylumbridge to Kincraig/Kingussie. 2km from Inverdruie nr Coylumbridge follow sign for L an Eilean; one of the most perfect lochans in these or any woods. Loch circuit 5km (1293/LOCHS). **1620 MAP 2 D4**

ARIUNDLE OAKWOODS: Strontian. 35km Ft William via Corran Ferry. Walk guide brochure at Strontian TO. Many walks around L Sunart and Ariundle: rare oak and other native species (esp on the wetter ground). You see how v different was the landscape of Scotland before the Industrial Revolution used up the wood. Start over town br, turning rt for Polloch. Go on past Cosy Knits, with good home-baking café and park. 2 walks; well marked. **1621 MAP 2 C4**

5KM CIRC MTBIKE 1-A-2

BALMACARRA: 5km S Kyle of Lochalsh on A87. A woodland walk around the shore of L Alsh, centred on Lochalsh House. Mixed woodland in fairly formal grd setting where you are confined to paths. Views over to Skye. A fragrant and verdant amble. **1622 MAP 2 C3**

3KM CIRC XBIKE 1-A-1

THE BIRKS O' ABERFELDY: Circular walk through oak, beech and the birch (or birk) woods of the title, easily reached and signed from town main st (1km). **1623 MAP 4 B3**

Steep-sided wooded glen of the Moness Burn with attractive falls esp the higher one spanned by br where the 2 marked walks converge. This is where Burns 'spread the lightsome days' in his eponymous poem. 3KM CIRC XBIKE 1-A-2

1624 THE HERMITAGE, DUNKELD: On A9 2km N of Dunkeld. Popular, easy, accessible
MAP 4 walks along the glen and gorge of R Braan with pavilion o/look the Falls and,
C3 further on, 'Ossian's Cave'. Several woody walks around Dunkeld/Birnam - good leaflet from TO. 2KM CIRC XBIKE 1-A-1

1625 GLENMORE FOREST PARK, nr AVIEMORE: Along from Coylumbridge (and adj
MAP 2 Rothiemurchus) on rd to ski resort, the forest trail area centred on L Morlich
D4 (sandy beaches, good swimming, water sports). Visitor centre has maps of walk and bike trails and an activity programme.

1626 ABOVE THE PASS OF LENY, CALLANDER: A walk through mixed forest (beech, oak,
MAP 6 birch, pine) with gr Trossachs views. Start from MAIN car park on A84 4km N
C3 of Callander (the Falls of Leny are on opp side of rd, 100m away) on path at back, to the left - path parallels rd at first (don't head straight up). Way-marked and boarded where marshy, the path divides after 1km to head further up to crest (4km return) or back down (2km). 2 OR 4KM CIRC XBIKE 1-A-2

1627 LOCH TUMMEL WALKS, nr PITLOCHRY: The mixed woodland N of L Tummel
MAP 4 reached by the B8019 from Pitlochry to Rannoch. Visitor centre at Queens View
B3 (1331/VIEWS) and walks in the Allean Forest which take in some historical sites (a restored farmstead, standing stones) start nearby (2-4km). There are many other walks in area and the Forest Enterprise brochure is worth following (available from visitor centre and local TOs). (1301/LOCHS.)

1628 THE NEW GALLOWAY FOREST: Huge area of forest and hill country with every type
MAP 9 and length of trail incl section of S Upland Way from Bargrennan to Dalry
C3 (1599/LONG WALKS). Visitor centres at Kirroughtree (5km Newton Stewart) and Clatteringshaws L on the 'Queen's Way' (9km New Galloway) with easy routes around them. Glen and L Trool are v fine (1273/GLENS); the 'Retreat Oakwood' nr Laurieston has 5km trails. The Smithy in New Galloway has walk books and walk food (1120/TEAROOMS). There's a river pool on the Raiders' Rd 1346/PICNICS). One could ramble on . . .

1629 DUFF HOUSE, BANFF: Duff House itself is the major attraction around here
MAP 3 (1836/PUBLIC GALLERIES), but if you've time it would be a pity to miss the
C2 wooded policies and the meadows and riverscape of the Deveron. An illustrated map on the back of the free brochure for the house (available from local TOs) shows the route. To the Br of Alvah where you should be bound is about 7km return. *See also* 1615/GLEN AND RIVER WALKS.

1630 TORRACHILTY FOREST and ROGIE FALLS nr CONTIN and STRATHPEFFER: Enter by
MAP 2 old br just o/side Contin on main A835 W to Ullapool or further along (4km) at
D3 Rogie Falls car park. Shame to miss the falls (1289/WATERFALLS), but the woods and gorge are pleasant enough if it's merely a stroll you need. Ben Wyvis further up the rd is the big challenge (1593/MUNROS).

1631 ABERNETHY FOREST nr BOAT OF GARTEN: 3km from village off B970, but hard to
MAP 2 miss because the famous ospreys are signposted from all over (1387/BIRDS).
E3 Nevertheless this woodland reserve is a tranquil place among native pinewoods around the loch with dells and trails. Many other birdies twittering around your picnic. They don't dispose of the midges.

1632 FOCHABERS on main A98 about 3km E of town are some excellent woody and
MAP 3 winding walks around the glen and Whiteash Hill(2-5km). Further W on the
D2 **MORAY COAST: CULBIN FOREST -** head for Cloddymoss or Kentessack off A96 at Brodie Castle 12km E of Nairn. Acres of Sitka in sandy coastal forest.

1633 THE BEST WOODLAND WALKS NR EDINBURGH

DALKEITH COUNTRY PARK: 15km SE by A68. Enter via end of Main St.

VOGRIE COUNTRY PARK: 25km S by A7 then B6372 6km from Gorebridge.

ROSLIN GLEN: 18km S by A702/703 (325/WALKS OUTSIDE THE CITY).

CARDRONA FOREST/GLENTRESS, nr PEEBLES: 40km S to Peebles, 8km E on A72.

DAWYCK GARDENS, nr STOBO: 10km W of Peebles (1201/GARDENS). Follow glen.

HUMBIE WOODS: 25 km SE by A68 t/off at Fala. Follow signs for church. Most open woods (beech) beyond car park, through paddock. See churchyard (1516/GRAVEYARDS).

SMEATON GARDENS, EAST LINTON: the secret lake walk (1796/GARDEN CENTRES).

WOODHALL DENE, nr DUNBAR: A1 Dunbar bypass, E to Spott then rd to left, 5km. Small car park in river hollow. Follow river to important ancient woodland site (2km). Can be damp. Few people.

THE BEST WOODLAND WALKS NR GLASGOW

1634

BOTHWELL CASTLE, UDDINGSTON: M74 jnct 4 or 5. Main St then signs. Walk down to Clyde and follow river side trails to Blantyre.

CHATELHERAULT, nr HAMILTON: M74 jnct 6, 3km from town (603/WALKS OUTSIDE THE CITY).

MUGDOCK COUNTRY PARK: 25km NW via Milngavie (597/CITY WALKS).

WHERE TO FIND SCOTS PINE

Scots pine, along with oak and birch etc, formed the gr Caledonian Forest which once covered most of Scotland. Native Scots pine is v different from the regimented rows of pine trees that we associate with forestry plantations and which now drape much of the countryside. It is more like a deciduous tree with reddish bark and irregular foliage; no two ever look the same. The remnants of the gr stands of pine that are left are beautiful to see, mystical and majestic, a joy to walk among and no less worthy of conservation perhaps than a castle or a bird of prey. Here are some places you will find them:

ROTHIEMURCHUS FOREST: 1620/WOODLAND WALKS.

GLENTANAR, ROYAL DEESIDE: Nr Ballater, 10-15km SW of Aboyne.

Around **BRAEMAR** and **GRANTOWN-ON-SPEY**.

STRATHYRE, nr CALLANDER: S of village on rt of main rd after L Lubnaig.

ACHRAY FOREST, nr ABERFOYLE: Some pine nr the Duke's Pass rd, the A821 to L Katrine, and amongst the mixed woodland in the 'forest drive' to L Achray.

BLACKWOOD OF RANNOCH: S of L Rannoch, 30km W of Pitlochry via Kinloch Rannoch. Start from Carie, fair walk in. 250-year-old pines; an important site.

ROWARDENNAN, L LOMOND: End of the rd along E side of loch nr Ben Lomond. Easily accessible pines nr the loch side, picnic sites etc.

Shores of **LOCH MAREE** and around **LOCH CLAIR, GLEN TORRIDON:** Both nr the Beinn Eighe National Park. Woodland centre on A832 N of Kinlochewe.

GLEN AFFRIC, nr DRUMNADROCHIT: 1265/GLENS. Remnants of the Caledonian Forest in classic glen. Many strolls and hikes poss. Try Dog Falls (on main rd) for Affric introduction.

Native pinewoods aren't found S of Perthshire, but there are fine plantation examples in southern Scotland at:

GLENTRESS, nr PEEBLES: 7km on A72 to Innerleithen. Mature forest up the burn side, though surrounded by commercial forest.

SHAMBELLIE ESTATE, nr DUMFRIES: 1km from New Abbey beside A710 at the Shambellie House, 100yds sign. Ancient stands of pine over the wall amongst other glorious trees; this is like virgin woodland. Planted 1775-1780. Magnificent.

COASTAL WALKS

1635 ✠ ✠ **KINTRA, ISLAY:** On Bowmore-Pt Ellen rd take Oa t/off: then Kintra signed
MAP 1 7km. Good restau/bar with B&B in season, a place to camp
E3 (977/HIGHLAND CAMPING), a fabulous beach (1251/BEACHES) which runs in opp
direction and a notable golf course behind it (1666/GOLF IN GREAT PLACES). This
walk leads along N coast of the Mull of Oa, an area of diverse beauty, sometimes
pastoral, sometimes wild, with a wonderful shoreline. In café a detailed route map
has been annotated with pictures.   ANY KM   XCIRC   XBIKE   2-B-2

1636 ✠ ✠ **THE BULLERS OF BUCHAN, nr PETERHEAD:** 8km S of Peterhead on A975
MAP 3 rd to/from Cruden Bay. Park and walk 100m to cottages. To rt is
E2 precarious and spectacular cliff top walk to Cruden Bay (3km), to left the walk to
Longhaven Nature Reserve, a continuation of the dramatic cliffs and more sea
bird city. The Bullers is at start of walk, a sheer-sided 'hole' 75m deep with an
outlet to the sea thro a natural arch. Walk round the edge of it, looking down on
layers of birds (who might try to dive-bomb you away from their nests); it's a
wonder of nature on an awesome coast. Take gr care.

1637 ✠ ✠ **CAPE WRATH** and the **CLIFFS OF CLO MOR:** Britain's most NW point
MAP 2 reached by ferry from 1km off the A838 4km S of Durness by Cape
C1 Wrath Hotel; a 10min crossing then 40min minibus ride to Cape. Ferry holds 14
and runs May-Sept, 9.30am-4.30pm (01971 511376). At 280m Clo Mor are the
highest cliffs in UK; 4km round trip from Cape. MoD range – access may be
restricted. In other direction, the 28km to Kinlochbervie is one of Britain's most
wild and wonderful coastal walks. Beaches incl Sandwood (1249/BEACHES).
While in this NW area: **SMOO CAVE** 2km E of Durness is good. 200m down from
main A838.

1638 **OLD MAN OF STOER, nr LOCHINVER:** The easy, exhilarating walk to the dramatic
MAP 2 sea stack, 3km from lighthouse off unclassified rd 14km N Lochinver. Park and
C2 follow sheep tracks; cliffs are high and steep.   1-B-2

1639 **PLOCKTON:** Plockton is a v special wee place and best seen on foot (1233/COASTAL
MAP 2 VILLAGES) rather than on the telly. There's a gr view to start, from Frithard Hill
C3 up from the end of the st, about 1km and taking path to rt just before the new
houses. The shore/beach walk starts beyond the airstrip; follow rd round High
School playing fields at top of village and then follow 'Beach Access'. Gr walks
also from Achmore 8km away, from end of rd past West Highland Dairy, which
is signed.   8KM RETURN OR 5 FROM SCHOOL   1-A-2

1640 **ROCKCLIFFE TO KIPPFORD:** An easy stroll along the 'Scottish Riviera' through
MAP 9 woodland nr the shore (2km) past the 'Mote of Mark' a Dark Age hill ft with
D4 views to Rough Island. The better cliff top walk is in the other direction to
Castlepoint, but Kippford has The Anchor to look forward to (1053/BEST FOOD;
1239/COASTAL VILLAGES).

1641 **ST ABBS HEAD:** The most dramatic coastal scenery in S Scotland, scary in a wind,
MAP 8 rhapsodic on a blue summer's day. Extensive wildlife reserve and trails through
E1 coastal hills and vales to cliffs. Cars can go as far as lighthouse, but best to park
at visitor centre nr farm on St Abbs village rd 3km from A1107 to Eyemouth and
follow route (1397/WILDLIFE).   5-10KM   CIRC   XBIKE   1-B-2

1642 **SINGING SANDS, ARDNAMURCHAN:** Park at Arivegaig 3km Acharacle and cross
MAP 2 wooden br, following track round side of Kentra Bay. Follow signs for
B4 Gorteneorn, and walk through forest track and woodland to beach. As you
pound the sands they should 'sing' to you whilst you bathe in the beautiful
views of Rum, Eigg, Muck and Skye (and just possibly the sea). Check at TO for
directions and other walks booklet.   6KM   XCIRC   BIKE   1-B-1

1643 **EAST FROM CULLEN on the MORAY COAST:** This is the same walk mentioned with
MAP 3 reference to Sunnyside (1260/BEACHES) a golden beach with a fabulous ruined
C1 castle (Findlater) that might be your destination, if you walk in the easterly
direction from Cullen. Town itself has wide beach, but this walk has range of
superb coastal features and aspects. Take track E along from Harbour. 2hrs
return.   8KM   XCIRC   XBIKE   1-A-1

1644 **CROMARTY, THE SOUTH SOUTARS:** The walk from Cromarty village (1235/COASTAL
MAP 2 VILLAGES; 1125/TEAROOMS) round the tip of the S promontory at the narrow
D3 entrance to the Cromarty Firth. Starting at bowling green, follow the shoreline

then climb through woods of Scots pine over the headland; path may be indistinct – easier to drive some way up farm. Deserted wartime ruins give best views across to the cave-pocked cliffs of opp headland and out to sea.

5KM   CIRC   XBIKE   1-A-1

AROUND CRAIL

(1) **FIFE NESS:** From village go E along foreshore then on to cliff top – drive through Sauchope caravan site and park to avoid dismal start.

8KM   CIRC 2

(2) **TO ANSTRUTHER/PITTENWEEM:** In other direction to the East Neuk's 'main' town (or in reverse). Only fields betw path and coast rd, but a much more civilised way to go. Not circular, but regular buses back. Path starts from bottom W Braes, a cul-de-sac off main rd just before the last new houses towards Anstruther. Some erosion. Waymarking being improved. 6/8KM   XCIRC   XBIKE   1-A-1

THE CHAIN WALK, ELIE: A unique and adventurous way to get round this headland at the W end of Elie (and Earlferry), this walk (and clamber) is exhilarating and gr fun but not for anyone with vertigo, a dog, young kids, inagility. Walk along beach/around golf course, across boulder field, and around cliff following path using hand- and footholds carved into rock with chains to haul yourself up. Watch tide; don't go alone. If you're careful, it's a breeze. Allow 2hrs. If you're nervous, walk to top and meet your more intrepid friends there.

2-B-2

1645
MAP 5
E3

1646
MAP 5
D3

SECTION 9

Sports

SCOTLAND'S GREAT GOLF COURSES

Those listed are open to nonmembers and are available to visitors (incl women) at most times, unless otherwise stated. Always phone. Handicap certificates may be required.

Ayrshire (MAP 1)

1647 **GLASGOW GAILES/WESTERN GAILES:** 01294 311347/311649. Superb links courses
C4 next to one another, 5km S of Irvine off A78.

1648 **ROYAL OLD COURSE, TROON:** V difficult to get on. No wimmen. Staying at Marine
C4 Highland Hotel (01292 314444) helps. Easier is **THE PORTLAND COURSE:** Across
rd from Royal. Both 01292 311555. And 659/AYRSHIRE HOTELS for the adj
Piersland House Hotel.

1649 **OLD PRESTWICK:** 01292 477404. Original home of the Open and 'every challenge
D4 you'd wish to meet'. Hotels opp (eg the Golf View 01292 671234) cost less than
a round. Unlikely to get on w/ends.

1650 **TURNBERRY:** 01655 331000. Ailsa (championship) and Arran. Sometimes poss by
C4 application. Otherwise you must stay at hotel. (655/AYRSHIRE HOTELS.). Superb.

1651 **BELLEISLE, AYR:** 01292 441258. Good parkland course. Easy to get on.
D4

East Lothian (MAP 7)

Note: There is a gr booklet available at the local TO, entitled 'Golf in East Lothian'.

1652 **GULLANE NO.I:** 01620 842255. One of 3 varied courses surrounding charming
D1 village on links and within driving distance (35km) of Edin. Muirfield is nearby,
but you need intro. Gullane is okay most days except Sat. (Handicap required for
no.1 only - under 24 men, 30 ladies.) No.3 best for beginners. Visitor centre acts
as clubhouse for nonmembers on nos. 2 / 3. Clubhouse for members/no.1 players
only.

1653 **NORTH BERWICK EAST AND WEST:** E (officially the Glen Golf Club) has stunning
D1 views. A superb cliff-top course and is not too long, 01620 895288. W more
taxing (esp the classic 'Redan') used for Open qualifying; a v fine links. Also has
9-hole kids' course, 01620 892135.

1654 **MUSSELBURGH:** The original home of golf (really: golf recorded here in 1672), but
D1 this local authority-run 9-hole links is not exactly top turf and is enclosed by
Musselburgh Racecourse. Nostalgia still appeals though. **ROYAL MUSSELBURGH**
nearby compensates. It dates to 1774, fifth-oldest in Scotland. Busy early
mornings and Fri afternoons, 01875 810139.

North-East (MAP 3)

1655 **CARNOUSTIE:** 01241 853789. 3 good links courses; even poss (with handicap cert)
MAP 4 to get on the championship course (though w/ends difficult). Every hole has
E3 character. Buddon Links is cheaper and often quiet. Combination tickets
available. A well-managed and accessible golfing must. Hosting 1999 Open.

1656 **MURCAR, ABERDEEN:** 01224 704354. Getting on Royal Aber Course is difficult for
MAP 3 most people, but Murcar is a testing alternative, a seaside course 6km N of centre
D3 off Peterhead rd signed at r/bout after Exhibition Centre. Handicap cert needed.
Municipal course at Hazlehead (good course, ish condition).

1657 **CRUDEN BAY, nr PETERHEAD:** 01779 812285. On A975 40km N of Aber. Designed
MAP 3 by Tom Simpson and ranked in UK top 50, a spectacular links course with the
E2 intangible aura of bygone days. Quirky holes epitomise old-fashioned style.
W/ends difficult to get on.

1658 **NAIRN:** 01667 452787. Traditional seaside links course and one of the easiest
MAP 2 championship courses to get on. Good clubhouse, friendly folk. Nairn Dunbar
D3 on other side of town also has good links.

1659 **ROYAL DORNOCH:** 01862 810219. Sutherland championship course laid out by Tom
MAP 2 Morris in 1877. Amongst top 10 courses in UK, but not busy or incessantly
D2 pounded. No poor holes. Stimulating sequences. Probably the most northerly gr
golf course in the world – and where else could you get on so easily?

ST ANDREWS: 01334 475757. The home and Mecca of golf, v much part of the town (1953/HOLIDAY CENTRES) and probably the largest golf complex in Europe. Old Course most central, celebrated. Application by ballot the day before (handicap cert needed). For Jubilee (1897, upgraded 1989) and Eden (1914, laid out by Harry S. Holt paying homage to the Old with large, sloping greens), apply the day before. New Course (1895, some rate the best) easiest access. Less demanding are the new Strathtyrum and Balgove (upgraded 9-hole for beginners) courses. All 6 courses contiguous and 'in town'; and much is expected of the newest. Dukes Course (part of Old Course Hotel) is 3km away. Phone for reservations (and ballot). There's a whole lot of golf to be had - get your money out! **1660 D2**

ELIE: Book 01333 330301. Splendid open links maintained in top condition; can be windswept. The starter has his famous periscope and may be watching you. Adj 9-hole course, often busy with kids, is fun. **1661 D3**

CRAIL: 01333 50960. Originally designed by the legendary Tom Morris, links and park; all holes in sight of sea. Not exp; easy to get on. **1662 E3**

LUNDIN LINKS: 01333 320202/ladies 320832. Challenging seaside course used as Open qualifier. Some devious contourings. There is a separate course for women. **1663 D3**

LADYBANK: 01337 830814. Best inland course in Fife; Tom Morris-designed again. V well kept and organised. Good facs. Tree-lined and picturesque. **1664 C3**

GOOD GOLF COURSES IN GREAT PLACES

All these courses are open to women, nonmembers and inexpert players (except Luss).

⛳ **LOCH LOMOND GOLF CLUB, LUSS:** On A82 1km from conservation village of Luss. Exclusive American-owned club; membership only 5000 bucks! We can buy a cheaper season ticket to see the annual World Invitational tournament (early July; tickets 0990 661661); but no access to plebs to clubhouse. 18 holes of scenic golf by the Loch, with Jack Nicklaus due to design additional course soon. This is golfing for gold. **1665 MAP 1 D2**

⛳ **MACHRIE:** 01496 302310. Isle of Islay. 7km Pt Ellen. Worth going to Islay (BA's airstrip adj course or Calmac ferry from Kennacraig nr Tarbert) just for the golf. The Machrie (Golf) Hotel does deals. Old-fashioned course to be played by feel and instinct. Splendid, sometimes windy isolation with a warm bar and restau at the end of it. The notorious 17th, 'Iffrin' (it means Hell), vortex shaped from the dune system of marram and close-cropped grass, is one of many gr holes. 18. **1666 MAP 1 A3**

⛳ **MACHRIHANISH:** 01586 810213. By Campbeltown (10km). Amongst the dunes and links of the glorious 8km stretch of the Machrihanish Beach (1248/BEACHES). The Atlantic provides thunderous applause for your triumphs over a challenging course. 9/18. **1667 MAP 1 B4**

⛳ **SOUTHERNESS, SOLWAY FIRTH:** 01387 880677. 25km S of Dumfries by A710. A championship course on links on the silt flats of the Firth. Despite its prestige, it's not difficult to get on. Under the wide Solway sky, it's not just the name of a place – southerness is what you feel. 18. **1668 MAP 9 D6**

⛳ **ROSEMOUNT, BLAIRGOWRIE:** 01250 872622. Off A93, S of Blairgowrie. An excellent, pampered and well-managed course in the middle of green Perthshire, an alternative perhaps to Gleneagles, being much easier to get on (most days) and rather cheaper (though not at w/ends). 18. **1669 MAP 4 C3**

GLENCRUITTEN, OBAN: 01631 562868. Picturesque course on the edge of town. Head S (A816) from Argyll Sq, bearing left at church. Course is signed. Quite tricky with many blind holes. Can get busy, so phone first. 18. **1670 MAP 1 B1**

GAIRLOCH: 01445 712407. Just as you come into town from the S on A832, it looks over the bay and down to a perfect, pink, sandy beach. Small clubhouse with honesty box. Not the world's most agonising course; in fact, on a clear day with views to Skye, you can forget agonising over anything. 9/18. **1671 MAP 2 C3**

HARRIS GOLF CLUB, SCARISTA, ISLE OF HARRIS: 01859 511218 (the captain, but no need to phone). Just turn up on the rd betw Tarbert and Rodel and leave £5 in the **1672 MAP 2 B2**

box. First tee commands one of the gr views in golf and throughout this basic, but testing course, you are looking out to sea over Scarista beach (1254/BEACHES) and bay. The sunset may put you off your swing.

1673 NEW GALLOWAY: Local course on S edge of this fine wee toon. Almost all on a
MAP 9 slope but affording gr views of L Ken and the Galloway Forest behind. No
C3 bunkers and only 9 short holes, but exhilarating play. Easy on, except Sun. Just turn up. Clubs can be hired at The Smithy coffee shop in the village.

1674 MINTO, DENHOLM: 01450 870220. 9km E Hawick. Spacious parkland in Teviot
MAP 8 valley.
C3

1675 VERTISH HILL, Hawick: 01450 372293. A more challenging hill course. Both among
MAP 8 the best in Borders. 18.
C3

1676 TAYMOUTH CASTLE, KENMORE: 01887 830228. Spacious green acres around the
MAP 4 enigmatic empty hulk of the castle. Well-tended and organised course betw A827
B3 to Aberfeldy and the river. Inexp, and guests at the Kenmore Hotel (745/PERTHSHIRE HOTELS) get special rate. 18.

1677 GIFFORD: 01620 810267. Dinky inland course on the edge of a dinky village,
MAP 7 bypassed by the queue for the big E Lothian courses and a guarded secret among
D2 the regulars. (Can't play after 4pm Tues/Wed/Sat or Sun afternoons). 9/11.

1678 STRATHPEFFER: 01997 421219. V hilly (and we do mean hilly) course full of
MAP 2 character and with exhilarating Highland views. Small-town friendliness. You are
D3 playing up there with the gods and some other old codgers. 18.

1679 ELGIN: 01343 542884. 1km from town on A941 Perth rd. Many memorable holes
MAP 34 on moorland/parkland course in an area where links may lure you to the coast
B2 (Nairn, Lossiemouth). 18.

1680 DURNESS: 01971 511364. The most N golf course on mainland UK, on the wild
MAP 2 headland by Balnakeil Bay, looking over to Faraid Head. The last hole is 'over the
D1 sea'. Only open since 1988, it's already got cult status. 2km W Durness village. 9.

1681 BOAT OF GARTEN: 01479 831282. Challenging, picturesque course in town where
MAP 2 ospreys have been known to wheel overhead. Has been called the 'Gleneagles of
D6 the North'; certainly the best round around, though not for novices. 18.

1682 ROTHESAY: 01700 503554. Sloping course with breathtaking views of Clyde.
MAP 1 Visitors welcome. What could be finer than taking the train from Glas to Wemyss
C3 Bay for the ferry over (1959/FAVOURTIE JOURNEYS) and 18 holes. Finish up with fish 'n' chips at The W End (1095/FISH AND CHIPS) on the way home.

1683 TRAIGH, ARISAIG: 01687 450337. A830 Ft William-Mallaig rd, 2km N Arisaig.
MAP 2 Pronounced 'try'- and you may want to. The islands are set out like stones in the
C4 sea around you and there are 9 hilly holes of fun.

THE BEST SLEDGING PLACES

Locals will know where the best slopes are. Here's my suggestions for main centres:

1684 EDINBURGH
MAP A **THE BRAID HILLS:** The connoisseur's choice, you sledge down friendly and not-
xC4 too-challenging slopes in a crowded L S Lowry landscape that you will remember long after the thaw. Off Braid Hills Drive at the golf course. Can walk in via
xA3 Blackford Glen Rd. **CORSTORPHINE HILL:** Gentle broad slope with woodland at top and trails (321/CITY WALKS) and a busy rd at the bottom. App via Clermiston
A3 Rd off Queensferry Rd. **QUEEN'S PARK:** The lesser slopes that skirt Arthur's Seat, and further in around Hunter's Bog for the more adventurous or less sociable sledger.

1685 GLASGOW
MAP B **KELVINGROVE PARK:** At Park Terr side. No long runs but a winter wonderland
B1 when the rime's in the trees. **GARTNAVEL HOSPITAL GROUNDS:** In W end (Hynd-land) off Gr Western Rd. You can play safe sledging into the playing field, or
xC1 more adventurously through the woodlands. **QUEEN'S VIEW:** On A809 N of Bearsden 20km from centre. A v popular walk (605/BEST VIEWS) is also a gr place to sledge. Variable slopes off the main path. The Highlands can be seen on a clear
C4 day. **RUCHILL PARK:** In N of city (606/BEST VIEWS) and **QUEEN'S PARK** in S.

BEST OF THE SKIING

In a good yr the Scottish ski season can extend from Dec (or even Nov) till the 'lambing snow' of late April. And on a good day it can be as exhilarating as anywhere in Europe. Here's a summary (distances in km):

	GLEN-SHEE	CAIRN-GORM	AONACH MOR	GLEN-COE	THE LECHT
DIST/EDIN	130	215	215	165	200
GLASGOW	170	235	200	150	160
NR CENTRE	PERTH 65	INVERN 45	FT WILL 8	FT WILL 40	ABERDEEN
NR TOWN	BRAEMAR 20	AVIEM 15	FT WILL 8	BALLACHU-LISH 20	TOMINTOUL 11
NO OF RUNS	38	28	18	15	17
BEGINNERS	10	11	5	3	6
INTERMED	26	15	12	11	10
BLACKS	2	2	1	1	1
NO OF TOWS	26	17	12	7	12
CAFES	3	4	3	1	1
GOOD FOR	*Size*	*Size*	*Uplift*	*Fewer crowds*	*Fewer crowds*
	Access from rd	*Non-skiing*	*Access*	*Nr road*	*Nr road*
	Views Glas Maol	*Views*	*Views/Sunsets*	*Views*	*Families*
	2 distinct areas	*Beginners*	*Ski School*	*Most alpine*	*Near NE*
	Snowboarding	*Snowboarding*	*Café*		

GLENSHEE

BASE STATION: 013397 41320. **SCHOOL:** 013397 41331 or 01250 885 216.

1686

MAP 4

C2

WHERE TO STAY

DALMUNZIE HOUSE: 01250 885 226. 9km S. Country house. Golf. Family-run. MED.EX

BRIDGE OF CALLY HOTEL: 01250 886231. 36km S. **GLENISLA, KIRKTON OF GLENISLA:** 01575 582223. 32km SE (957/INNS). INX

SPITTAL OF GLENSHEE: 01250 885204. 8km S. Cheap'n'cheerful. MED.INX

COMPASS CHRISTIAN CENTRE: 01250 885209. 12km S. Recommended hostel not only for Jesus freaks. Dorm-type accom. CHP

WHERE TO EAT

CARGILLS BISTRO, BLAIRGOWRIE: 01250 87673 (752/PERTHSHIRE HOTELS). **DALMUNZIE/BRIDGE OF CALLY HOTEL/GLENISLA:** as above.

APRES-SKI

BLACKWATER INN: 17km S on main rd. A good all-round pub. Occasional live music.

SKI HIRE

BRIDGE OF CALLY SKI HIRE: Opp hotel (phone as above). On the way. **BLACKWATER SKI HIRE:** Also on main rd to slopes, but nearer.

CAIRNGORM

BASE STATION: 01479 861261. **SCHOOL:** 01479 810296/ 810655.

1687

MAP 2

D4

WHERE TO STAY

CORROUR HOUSE: 01479 811220. 11km W (918/COUNTRY-HOUSE HOTELS). INX

COYLUMBRIDGE: 01479 810661. 10km W. Nearest and best of modern Aviemore hotels. 2 pools/sauna. Ski hire. Okay restau. Comfort when you need it. MED.EX

CAIRNGORM, AVIEMORE: 01479 810630. Main st of main town. Busy bar. Rms not unreasonably priced and lots of them. INX

THE OSPREY, KINGUSSIE: 0540 661510. 32km S. Good value tho kitsch. MED.INX

WHERE TO EAT

THE CROSS, KINGUSSIE: 01540 661166 (793/HIGHLANDS HOTELS).

THE BOATHOUSE, KINCRAIG: 01540 651394 (823/INEXP HIGHLANDS HOTELS).

THE OLD BRIDGE, AVIEMORE: Welcoming, good atmos (1050/BEST FOOD).

APRES-SKI

THE WINKING OWL, AVIEMORE: At end of main st. Owl's Nest.

ROYAL HOTEL, KINGUSSIE: Real ales (8) and malts (1021/REAL ALE).

SKI HIRE

COYLUMBRIDGE HOTEL: 01479 810661. Behind hotel, run by Caird Sport (major operators) and nearest to slopes. Open mornings and 4–6.30pm.

1688 AONACH MOR/THE NEVIS RANGE

MAP 2 **BASE STATION:** 01397 705825. **SCHOOL:** 01397 705825.

C4 WHERE TO EAT and STAY

See **FORT WILLIAM,** *p. 261.*

APRES-SKI

No pub in immediate vicinity. Nearest all-in ski centre is **NEVIS SPORT, FORT WILLIAM:** 01397 704921. Bar (side entrance) till 11pm. Self-serve café all day till 5pm. Bookshop and extensive ski/outdoor shop on ground floor. Also ski hire.

SKI HIRE

As above (01397 704921), also Ellis Brigham (01397 706220), and base stn.

1689 GLENCOE

MAP 2 **BASE STATION:** 01855 851226. **SCHOOL:** 01855 851226.

C3 WHERE TO EAT and STAY

See **FORT WILLIAM,** *p. 261, and also:*

ISLES OF GLENCOE HOTEL, BALLACHULISH: 01855 811602. Modern development leisure centre incl pool. Good touring base (927/KIDS).

CLACHAIG INN, GLENCOE: 01855 811 252. Famous 'outdoor inn' for walkers, climbers etc with pub (1008/BLOODY GOOD PUBS), pub food and inexp accom.

KINGSHOUSE HOTEL: 01855 851259. The classic travellers' inn 1km from A82 through Glen and nr slopes (8km). Pub with food/whisky. Inexp rms.

APRES-SKI

As above, especially **CLACHAIG INN** and **KINGSHOUSE**

SKI HIRE

At base stn.

1690 THE LECHT

MAP 3 **BASE STATION:** 019756 51440. **SCHOOL:** 019756 51440.

B3 WHERE TO STAY

Nearest town (28km S) with big choice of hotels is Ballater.

RICHMOND ARMS, TOMINTOUL: 01807 580777. Also on sq. Trad hotel, log fires. Recent refurb now a v good prospect. 24 rms.   MED.INX

DARROCH LEARG, BALLATER: 013397 55443 (756/NE HOTELS).   MED.INX

GLENAVON HOTEL, TOMINTOUL: 01807 580218. On sq in nearest town.   CHP

WHERE TO EAT

GREEN INN, BALLATER: 013397 55701 (774/NE HOTELS).   MED

THE WHITE COTTAGE, nr ABOYNE: 01339 886265 (1954/HOLIDAY CENTRES).   MED

TOMINTOUL HOTELS above.   INX

APRES-SKI

GLENAVON HOTEL, TOMINTOUL: Good large bar for skiers, walkers (S end of Speyside Way is here) and locals.

ALLARGUE HOTEL, COCKBRIDGE: On rd S to Ballater 5km from slopes and o/look Corgarff Castle and the trickle of the R Don. Rms also.

SKI HIRE

From ski school, 019756 51440.

Weather and Road Reports

Dial 0891 654 then:

655 CAIRNGORM; 656 GLENSHEE; 658 GLENCOE; 660 NEVIS RANGE; 657 THE LECHT

OTHER SKI HOTLINES (ALL AREAS) ARE: 0891 654654 or 0891 500440.

THE BEST LEISURE CENTRES

PERTH LEISURE POOL: 01738 630535. A perfect example of the mega successful water-based leisure-land; makes you wonder where everyone went before they existed. Large, shaped pool with o/side section (open also in winter, when it's even more of a novelty); 2 flumes, 'wild water channel', whirlpools etc. 25m 'training' pool for lengths (sessions). Outdoor kids' area. Excellent facility. I go often (because it's open late). Daily 10am-10pm.
1691 MAP 4 C4

AQUADOME, INVERNESS: 01463 667500. Inverness's new all-weather attraction. Leisure waters; incl 3 flumes, wave machine and toddler area. Huge competition pool for serious swimming and luxurious health suites; massages, hydrotherapy and (ladies) that essential bikini line wax. All in all, a bigger splash. Phone for opening hrs.
1692 MAP 2 D3

DUNBAR POOL: 01368 865456. Model of its kind, o/look old harbour (where folks used to swim on a summer's day) and castle ruins. Cool, modern design amidst the warm red sandstone. Flumes and wave machine that mimics the sea o/side; lengths just possible in betw (though it's often v crowded). 7 days till 8pm (6pm at w/kends).
1693 MAP 7 E1

MAGNUM CENTRE, IRVINE: 01294 278381. From Irvine's throughway system, follow signs for Harbourside, then Magnum. Same report as last time - sorry couldn't go back. In an unalluring 'big shed', this phenomenally successful pleasuredrome provides every conceivable diversion from the monotony of my namesake o/side. From soothing bowls to frenetic skating, pools, cinema, cafés, courses, you name it. Secrete endorphins and other hormones - feel better.
1694 MAP 1 D4

VIKINGAR!, LARGS: Suddenly fulfilled all the needs and gaps in this busy visitor area of the Clyde coast - a pool and sports centre, a theatre, an indoor attraction and a dab of heritage. Got the award. But hey . . . it works. It won't exercise your intellect, but the other bits will do just fine. 7 days. 10.30am-6pm (till 4pm in winter).
1695 MAP 1 C3

THE TIME CAPSULE, MONKLANDS: 01236 449572. They say Monklands, but where you are going is downtown Coatbridge about 15km from Glas via M8. Known rather meanly as the 'Tim Capture' (local joke – you don't want to know!). Essentially a leisure (rather than swimming) pool and ice-rink lavishly fitted out on prehistoric monster theme. Even if you haven't been swimming for yrs, this is the sort of place you force the flab into the swimsuit. Cafés and view areas. Facs of the clean-up-your-act variety (e.g. squash, sauna, sun, steam, gym). 'Courses'. 10am-10pm.
1696 MAP 1 D3

DOLLAN AQUA CENTRE, TOWN CENTRE PARK, EAST KILBRIDE: 01355 260000. EK: The 'Great Experiment' in New Town planning, which just celebrated its 50th birthday, now boasts a qaulity leisure centre. 50m pool, fitness facs, soft play area and Scotland's first inter-active flume, (aquatic pin ball machine with you as the ball!) - there had to be a twist. Mon-Wed 7.30am-10pm, Thurs/Fri 8am-10pm, Sat/Sun 8am-6pm. Last sessions 2hrs before closing.
1697 MAP 1 D3

SCOTSTOUN LEISURE CENTRE: 0141 9594000. From town take Gr Western Rd to Anniesland Cross; Anniesland Rd on left. Danes is left again after 1km. If 'modernity is suburban' this state of the art. 10 lane pool, sports halls, heath suite, dance studio and gym. Outdoor footie and tennis - it's enormous. Call for times, but open till 10pm. Tues is women only from 6pm.
1698 MAP B xA2

EAST SANDS LEISURE CENTRE, ST ANDREWS: 01334 476506. From S St take rd for Crail then follow signs. About 2km from centre. Bright and colourful centre o/look
1699 MAP 5 D2

the E Sands, the less celebrated beach of St Andrews. Mainly a fairly conventional pool with 25m lane area as well as 50m water slide, toddlers' pool etc. Also 2 squash courts, gym with Pulsestar machines, 'remedial suite', bar and café. 7 days 7.30/8.30pm; Sat/Sun till 5pm. Times may vary.

1700 **BEACON LEISURE CENTRE, BURNTISLAND:** 01592 872211. On the front of quietly-
MAP 5 getting-on with-it Fife town nr Kirkcaldy. New family fun pool centre from Fife
C4 Enterprise drawing board (meeting) with 'landmark' beacon thing and external flume tubes. Once again it does work. Loadsa kids and 'waves' do come, but latest swimming in area (check times). 7 days.

1701 **BEACH LEISURE CENTRE, ABERDEEN:** 01224 655401. Beach Esplanade across rd
MAP 2 from beach itself. Multisports facility with bars and cafés. 'Leisure' Pool isn't
D3 much use for swimming (Aber has many others, 1709/SWIMMING POOLS) but it's fun for kids with flumes etc. Linx Ice Arena is adj for skating, curling, ice hockey. Multigym in foyer area has Universal Stns. Sessions vary. O/side is the long long beach and the N Sea.

THE BEST SWIMMING POOLS AND SPORTS CENTRES

For EDINBURGH, *see p.49; for* GLASGOW, *see p.85. And see Leisure Centres p 217.*

1702 ⚓ **STONEHAVEN OUTDOOR POOL, STONEHAVEN:** The 'Friends of Stonehaven
MAP 3 Out-door Pool' won the day (eat your hearts out N Berwick) and they've
D4 saved a gr pool that should go from length to strength. Fabulous 1930s Olympic-sized heated salt-water pool. There's a midnight swim every Wed from mid-June (is that cool, or what?). Summer only: 11am-7.30pm (10-6pm w/ends).

1703 ⚓ **GOUROCK BATHING POOL:** 01475 315611. The only other open-air (proper)
MAP 1 pool in Scotland that's still open! On coast rd S of town centre 45km from
C3 central Glas. 1950s-style leisure. Heated, so it doesn't need to be a scorcher (brilliant, but crowded when it is). Open 'in season' 10am-8pm, Sun till 5pm.

1704 ⚓ **PORTSOY OPEN-AIR POOL:** One of the most engaging of the villages on this N
MAP 3 Aberdeenshire coast 7km W of Banff with a pool flushed by the sea in an
C1 idyllic setting. Run by local swimming club with changing facs and great wee tearoom, it's only open Jun-Aug but take advantage of it on any sunny day. 50th anniversary in 1996. Long may it chill us out. Head W from centre or main A98.

1705 ⚓ **CARNEGIE CENTRE, DUNFERMLINE:** 01383 723211. Pilmuir St. Excellent all-
MAP 5 round sports centre with many courses and classes. 2 pools (ozone-treated),
B2 25m, and kids' pool. Lane swimming lunch time and evenings. Authentic Turkish and Aeretone Suite with men's, women's and mixed sessions. Large gym with Powersport stations etc. Badminton, squash, aerobic classes. Usually open till 9pm (including pool), but check. Keeping Dunfermline fitter then most of us.

1706 ⚓ **BISHOPBRIGGS SPORTS CENTRE, GLASGOW:** 0141 772 6391. 147 Balmuildy Rd.
MAP B At the N edge of Glas, best reached by car or 1km walk from stn; adj Forth
xE1 and Clyde Canal walkway (595/CITY WALKS). Large, modern, efficient with 33.3m pool, gym, sauna, bar, café etc. Open 9am-10pm (pool hours vary).

1707 ⚓ **LINLITHGOW POOL :** 01506 652783. On edge of pleasant town off rd to
MAP 7 Lanark. Modern light and airy sports centre with sauna and steam room at
B1 the pool side and W Lothian outside the windows. Excellent community facility, well designed and laid out. All towns should enjoy this quality of life. This pool is where I go.

1708 **GALASHIELS POOL:** 01896 752154. An award winning pool in the Central Borders
MAP 8 on the edge of parkland with picture windows bringing the outside in. No
C3 leisurama nonsense, just a good deck-level pool (25m). Pool in Hawick also good. Phone for opening hrs.

1709 **ABERDEEN BATHS:** 01224 587920. City well served with swimming pools. 3 in
MAP 3 suburbs are not esp easy to find, though Hazlehead (01224 310062) is signed from inner ring road to W of centre. Bon Accord Baths are a fine example of a municipal pool; recently refurbished, they're centrally situated behind the W end of Union St. Annie Lennox learned to swim here. The newer Beach Leisure Centre has just about thought of everything (1701/LEISURE CENTRES).

1710 **GOLSPIE SWIMMING POOL:** 01408 633437. A neat little pool (20m) next to the

High School. Nothing too high tech, but a friendly atmos and a friendly mural at one end. Hrs vary.

MAP 2
D2

MACTAGGART CENTRE, BOWMORE, ISLAY: 01496 810767. Eco-friendly pool (heated by adj distillery) o/look bay. Interesting whisky cask shaped ceiling and good fitness suite. Laundry facs. Cl Mon.

1711
MAP 1
A3

THE BEST WATER SPORTS CENTRES

✝ ✝ **CROFT-NA-CABER, nr KENMORE, LOCH TAY:** 01887 830588. S side of loch, 2km from village. Purpose-built water sports centre with instruction and hire of windsurfers, canoes, kayaks, dinghies, motor boats as well as waterskiing, river rafting (down the Tay through Taymouth Castle grounds to white water at Grandtully: pure exhilaration), parascending, archery and clay shooting. A v good all-round activities centre in a gr setting. Chalet accom and restau.

1712
MAP 4
B3

✝ **LINNHE MARINE:** 01631 730227. Lettershuna, Port Appin. 32km N of Oban on A828 nr Portnacroish. Established, personally run business in a fine sheltered spot for learning and ploutering. They almost guarantee to get you windsurfing over to the island in 2hrs. Individual or group instruction. Wayfarers, Luggers and fishing-boats. New laser clay pigeon shooting. Moorings. Castle Stalker and Lismore are just round the corner; the joy of sailing. May-Oct.

1713
MAP 1
C1

✝ **PORT EDGAR, SOUTH QUEENSFERRY:** 0131 331 3330. At end of village, under and beyond the Forth Road Br. Major marina and water sports centre. Berth your boat, hire anything from a Wayfarer to a canoe or just use the jetty to kick off some windsurfing or jet-skiing. Big tuition programme for kids. Easter-Oct.

1714
MAP 7
B1

✝ **STRATHCLYDE PARK:** 01698 266155. Major water sports centre 15km SE of Glas and easily reached from most of Central Scotland via M8 or M74 (jnct 5 or 6). 200-acre loch and centre with instruction on sailing, canoeing, windsurfing, rowing, water-skiing and hire facs for canoes, Mirrors and Wayfarers, windsurfers and trimarans. Sessions: summer 9.30am-10pm; winter 9.30am-5pm.

1715
MAP 1
D3

GREAT GLEN WATER PARK: 01809 501381. 3km S Invergarry on A82. On shores of tiny L Oich and L Lochy in the Gr Glen. Wonderful spot, with many other lochs nearby. Day visitors welcome with windsurfers, Wayfarers, kayaks, canoes and also mountain bikes and fishing rods for hire. Mainly, however, a chalet park with all the usual condo/timeshare facs (you can rent by the week).

1716
MAP 2
C4

CASTLE SEMPLE COUNTRY PARK, LOCHWINNOCH: 01505 842882. 30km SW Glas M8 jnct 29, A737 then A760 past Johnstone. Also 25km from Largs via A760. Loch (nr village) is 3km x 1km and at the Rangers Centre you can hire windsurfers, dinghies, canoes etc. Bird Reserve on opp bank (1400/WILDLIFE). Peaceful place to learn.

1717
MAP 1
C3

KIP MARINA, INVERKIP: 01475 521485. Major sailing centre on Clyde coast 50km W of Glas via M8, A8 and A78 from Pt Glas heading S for Largs. A yacht heaven as well as haven of Grand Prix status. Sails, charters, pub/restau, chandlers and myriad boats. Diving equipment jet skis and dinghies for hire.

1718
MAP 1
C3

SCOTTISH NATIONAL WATERSPORTS CENTRE, LARGS AND CUMBRAE: 01475 674666. Centre for all kinds of water sports in a doon-the-water situation, mainly at Millport on Cumbrae, but with general sports centre on mainland. Ferry betw.

1719
MAP 1
C3

LOCHORE, nr LOCHGELLY: 01592 414300. From Dunfermline-Kirkcaldy motorway take Lochgelly t/off into town and follow signs for Lochore Country Park. Small, safe loch for learning and perfecting. Canoes, dinghies and esp windsurfing. Instruction and hire. Park contains a good adventure playground.

1720
MAP 5
B4

LOCHINSH WATERSPORTS, KINCRAIG: 01540 651272. On B970, 2km from Kincraig towards Kingussie and the A9. Marvellous loch side site launching from gently sloping dinky beach into forgiving waters of L Inch. Hire of canoes, dinghies (Mirrors, Toppers, Lasers, Wayfarers) and windsurfers as well as rowing boats; river trips. An idyllic place to learn. Watch the others and the sunset from the balcony restau above (823/INEXP HIGHLAND HOTELS). Sports 8.30am-5.30pm.

1721
MAP 2
D4

LOCH MORLICH WATERSPORTS nr AVIEMORE: 01479 861221. By Glenmore Forest Park, part of the plethora of outdoor activities hereabouts (skiing, walking etc). This is the loch you see from Cairngorm and just as picturesque from the woody shore. Canoes/kayaks/rowing boats and dinghies (Wayfarers, Toppers, Optimists) with instruction in everything. Evening hire poss.

1722
MAP 2
D4

1723 **LOCHEARNHEAD WATERSPORTS:** 01567 830330. On A85 nr jnct with A84 is a water
MAP 6 sports centre where they suggest you'll never be out of your depth. Certainly the
C2 loch is wide open and (usually) gently lapping. Kayaks, Canadian canoes and
dinghies. Water-skiing, jet-biking and mountain bike hire. Café.

1724 **RAASAY OUTDOOR CENTRE, nr SKYE:** 01478 660266. Good place! Day visits or
MAP 2 holidays.
B3

1725 **WIGBAY SAILING CENTRE, STRANRAER:** 01776 703535. Tuition and powerboating.
MAP 9
A3

THE BEST DIVE SITES

*Scotland's seas are primal soup, full of life and world-class sites as hard core divers
already know. The E coast can be tricky if the wind is blowing from the N or E,
therefore the W coast is preferable (the further N the better). Thanks to the Gulf
Stream it's not cold, even without a dry suit, and once you're down it's like flying
thro the Botanics (says Tim McQuire). So when you see all those crazies walking
into the sea, remember, they may know something that you don't know. Some day
I will go down! This page due to Tim.*

1726 **WEST COAST**

MAP 1 **THE OUTER HEBRIDES:** excellent with fantastic visability esp of the W coast of
HARRIS where you can plop in virtually anywhere.

ST KILDA: offers the best diving in the UK, but it's the hardest to get to. On the edge
of the Continental Shelf and the whale migration route, it has huge drop-offs and
upwellings of life. Book boat and board well in advance.

THE SUMMER ISLES: from Ullapool harbour. Wrecks, lee shores and unpolluted
waters.

OBAN: Scuba central with lots of sites in the neighbourhood and easy access to the
isles. Charter a boat and search for scallops in **THE GARVELLACH** or dive the wrecks
in the **SOUND OF MULL.** Somewhere off **TOBERMORY** there is reputedly, one of
Scotland's most enigmatic wrecks, a Spanish galleon. Easier to find are dolphins off
the coasts of **ISLAY & TIREE** and see 1395/DOPHINS for other likely spots.

1727 **EAST COAST**

MAP 8 **ST ABBS HEAD:** Accessible from the shore (1641/COASTAL WALKS) or by boat from
EYEMOUTH, a marine reserve, so leave the lobsters alone. The spectacular Cathedral
Rock is encrusted with green and yellow dead men's fingers and in August /Sept is
a sanctuary for breeding fish (this cathedral is as beautiful as St Giles and is
distinctly non-denominational). Nearby shore-based diving at **DUNBAR** is shallow,
safe and simple.

THE ISLE OF MAY: across the Forth is more advanced. Take a boat from Anstruther
(1383/BIRDS). Main site is Picadilly Circus, a central atrium fed by gullies, full of
friendly seals.

1728 **ORKNEY**

SCAPA FLOW: The world-famous underwater burial site where the Germans scuttled
their fleet in 1918. Think Gaudalcanal, but colder. Although the scrappies have
been in, there are still dozens and cruisers down there. Most lie in 35-40m deep, so
plan carefully. Majorly eerie!

DIVE OPERATORS (Don't leave home without one).

1729 NATIONAL

Dive Scotland. 0131 441 2001. Andrew Adams and James Hogg. Friendly,
knowledgeable and resourceful. Will organise trips and training anywhere and to
suit all levels of experience.

1730 LOCAL

OBAN: Oban. Nervous Wrecks 01631 566000. Oban Divers 01631 566618.
Alchemy 01631 720337.

ULLAPOOL: Ullapool. Atlantic Diving Services (Achiltibuie) 01854 622261.

ORKNEY: Diving Cellar 01856 850055. Dolphin Scuba 01856 731269. Scapa Flow
Scuba 01856 851218.

THE BEST WINDSURFING

FOR BEGINNERS AND INSTRUCTION (*see also* WATER SPORTS).

1731

STRATHCLYDE PARK, nr MOTHERWELL and GLASGOW: 01698 266155.

CROFT-NA-CABER, KENMORE, LOCH TAY: 01887 830588.

LINNHE MARINE, nr OBAN: 01631 730227.

LOCH WINNOCH, between PAISLEY and LARGS: 01505 842882.

LOCHORE MEADOWS, LOCHGELLY, FIFE: 01592 860264.

TIGHNABRUAICH SAILING SCHOOL, TIGHNABRUAICH: 01700 811396.

SCOTTISH NATIONAL WATERSPORTS CENTRE, CUMBRAE AND LARGS: 01475 674666.

STRATHCLYDE PARK, nr MOTHERWELL and GLASGOW: 1218/COUNTRY PARKS. Lots to do in this recreational zone of the conurbation. Water may not be so turquoise.

✟ **ELIE, EAST NEUK OF FIFE:** 01333 330962. Small, friendly windsurfing and water sports operation on the beach (beyond the Ship Inn). Sheltered lagoon and open sea. Elie is an attractive, genteel sort of place (1044/BEST FOOD; 732/FIFE HOTELS; 1259/BEACHES; 1661/GREAT GOLF). Water skis and mountain bikes.

WINDSURFING SPOTS

WEST COAST

1732

MACHRIHANISH: Wave-sailing, fabulous long beach (159/BEACHES). Mainly at Air Force base end. MAP 1

PRESTWICK/TROON: Town beaches.

ISLAND OF CUMBRAE: Millport beach.

MILARROCHY BAY, LOCH LOMOND: 8km from Drymen (45km N of Glas). W/end centre run by 7th Wave. Second beach up from Balmaha. Picturesque.

EAST COAST

1733

FRASERBURGH: Town beach.

LUNAN BAY: 12km N of Arbroath. Also surfing.

CARNOUSTIE: Town beach.

ST ANDREWS: W Sands.

LONGNIDDRY/GULLANE: 25/35km E of Edin via A1 and A198.

PEASE BAY: 14km S of Dunbar, 60km S of Edin via A1 (1738/SURFING).

NORTH COAST

1734

THURSO: Many beaches nr town and further W to choose from (1261/BEACHES).

FOR ENTHUSIASTS

1735

ISLAND OF TIREE: The windsurfing capital of Scotland. 40km W of Mull. Countless clean, gently sloping beaches all round island (and small inland loch) allowing surfing in all wind directions.'Wave Classic', a major windsurfing event held in October. Tiree Lodge Hotel (01879 220368), Kirkapol Guest House (01879 220 729) or self-catering (Oban TO 01631 563122). Loganair fly every day except Sunday (0141 889 1311) and Calmac run ferries from Oban 3 or 4 times a week (01475 650100). MAP 1

INFORMATION/BOARD HIRE:

MACH, GLASGOW: 3146 Argyle St. 0141 334 5559.

MACH, EDIB: Lady Lawson St. 0131 229 5887.

THE BEST SURFING

A surprise for the sceptical: Scotland has some of the best surfing beaches in Europe. Forget the bronzed beachboys and lemon bleached hair, surfing in Scotland is titanium-lined, rubber and balaclavas, and you get an ice cream head even encased in the latest technology. The main season is Sept-Dec. Surfees probably don't divulge their favourite beach, but the following are good bets. Don't surf alone. This page is based on information from Neil Butler.

1736 WEST COAST

MAP 2
B1
ISLE OF LEWIS: Probably the best of the lot. Go N of Stornoway, N of Barvas, N of just about anywhere. Leave the A857 and your day job behind. Not the most scenic of sites, but the waves have come a long way, further than you have. Derek at Stornoway Surf and Sports (01851 705862) will tell you when and where to go.

MAP 1
B4
MACHRIHANISH: Nr Campbelltown at the foot of the Mull of Kintyre. Long strand to choose from (1248/BEACHES). Jamie at Clan Skates in Glasgow (0141 339 6523) usually has an up-to-date satellite map and a idea of both the W and (nearest to central belt) Pease Bay (*see below*).

1737 NORTH COAST

MAP 2
D1
STRATHY BAY: Nr Bettyhill on the N coast hafway betw Tongue and Thurso on the A836. Go past the village, park at the graveyard. Once in the foam, paddle to the rt. From here to Cape Wrath the power and quality of the waves detonating on the shore justify comparisons with Hawaii.

MAP 2
E1
THURSO: Surf City, well not quite, but it's a good base to find your own waves. Esp to the E of town at Dunnet Bay - a 5km long beach with excellent reefs at the N end.

MAP 2
E1
WICK: On the Thurso rd at Ackergill to the S of Sinclair's Bay (964/GET-AWAY-FROM-IT-ALL). Find the ruined castle and taking care, clamber down the gully to the beach. A monumental reef break, you are working against the backdrop of the decaying ruin drenched in history, spume and romance.

1738 EAST COAST

MAP 3
D3
NIGG BAY: Just S of Aberdeen (not to be confused with Nigg across from Cromarty) and off the vast beach at Lunan Bay (1255/BEACHES) betw Arbroath and Montrose.

MAP 7
E1
PEASE BAY: S of Dunbar nr Cockburnspath on the A1. The nearest surfie heaven to the capital. The caravan site has parking and toilets. V consistent surf here.

SECTION 10

Shopping

See also the SHOPPING *sections of Edin (pp. 54-56) and Glas (pp. 90-92) for other ideas.*

THE BEST CRAFT SHOPS

See also INEXPENSIVE ART AND CERAMICS, *p. 235.*

1739
MAP 5
E3
CRAIL POTTERY, CRAIL, FIFE: At the foot of Rose Wynd, signposted from mainst (best to walk). In a tree-shaded Mediterranean courtyard and upstairs attic is a cornucopia of brilliant, useful, irresistible things. Open 10.30am-5pm (Cl lunch, Sun 2-5pm). Don't miss the harbour nearby, one of the most romantic neuks in the Neuk. Pity there's nowhere decent in Crail for tea.

1740
MAP 2
D3
ANTA FACTORY SHOP, FEARN, nr TAIN: Off B9175 from Tain to the Nigg ferry, 8km through Hill of Fearn, on corner of disused airfield. The small shop adj to the factory is usually missed by those who go to the larger outlet in Tain. Much tartan curtain fabric; many rugs, throws and pots. You can commission furniture to be covered in their material. Free to wander round the pottery; no organised tours. Open AYR: Mon-Sat 10am-5pm (Sun 10am-4pm; June-Sep).

1741
MAP 2
C2
HIGHLAND STONEWARE, LOCHINVER and **ULLAPOOL:** On rd to Baddidarach as you enter Lochinver on A837; and in Mill St, Ullapool, on way N beyond centre. A modern large-scale pottery business incl a shop/warehouse and studios that you can walk round (Lochinver is more *engagé*). Similar to the 'ceramica' places you find in the Med, but not too terracota – rather, painted and patterned stoneware in set styles. Gr selection, pricey - but you may have luck rummaging in the Lochinver discount section. Mail-order service. Open AYR.

1742
MAP 2
B3
EDINBANE POTTERY, EDINBANE, SKYE: 500m off A850 Portree (22km) – Dunvegan rd. Long-established and reputable working pottery where all the various processes are often in progress. Earthy pots of every shape and size; unusual 'lantern' plant holders. Open AYR 9am-6pm. 7 days in summer.

1743
MAP 2
D4
KILN ROOM POTTERY AND COFFEE SHOP, LAGGAN: On main A86 rd (off A9 betw Pitlochry and Inverness), E-W route to Ft William and Skye. Simple, usable pottery made by the long wood-fired kiln method, with distinctive warm colouring. Selected knitwear, other stuff. Home-made cakes. 9am-6pm, 7 days.

1744
MAP 2
D1
BALNAKEIL, DURNESS, SUTHERLAND: From Durness and the main A836 rd, take Balnakeil and Faraid Head rd for 2km W. Founded in the 1960's in what one imagines was a haze of hash, this craft village is still home to those seeking to 'downshift'. Varied paintings, pottery, fruit wine and weaving in the different prefab huts where the community members live and work (the site used to be an early warning station). Lotte Glob *is* v good. One of the huts intriguingly called Laxford Lodge, No.1380 . . . ? Village open Apr-Oct 10am-6pm. Café.

1745
MAP 2
B4
SKYEBATIKS, ARMADALE and PORTREE SKYE: 400m from Mallaig ferry and in centre. V original hippyish 'batiks'- cotton fabrics of ancient Celtic designs in every shape and size. Mainly hand-made, majorly colourful; they're a unique souvenir of Skye. Quite pricey.

1746
MAP 2
C2
ACHIN'S BOOKSHOP, LOCHINVER: At Inverkirkaig 5km from Lochinver on the 'wee mad rd' to Achiltibuie (1309/SCENIC ROUTES). Unexpected selection of books in the back of beyond providing something to read when you've climbed everything. Outdoor wear too and gr hats. The path to Kirkaig Falls and Suilven begins at the gate. 7 days; 9am-6pm. Adj café 10am-5pm.

1747
MAP 2
C2
KNOCKAN GALLERY AND CRAFTS, ELPHIN, nr ULLAPOOL: On the A835 Ullapool-Lairg rd 22km N of Ullapool nr the Knockan Outdoor Centre. Jewellery the main feature here, made with gemstones from the wilderness all around you and inspired by the scenery and wildlife. Mar-Oct; Mon-Sat 9am-6pm. Cl Sun.

1748
MAP 1
A1
IONA ABBEY SHOP: Iona via Calmac ferry from Fionnphort on Mull. Crafts and souvenirs in a room off the Abbey cloisters, the proceeds from which support a worthy, committed organisation. Christian literature, tapes etc, but mostly artefacts from nearby and around Scotland. Celtic crosses much in evidence, but then this is where they came from! Mar-Oct 9.30am-5pm.

1749
MAP 2
B7
CARBOSTCRAFT POTTERY, CARBOST: Judith Nicholl's family business nr the Talisker distillery (1186/WHISKY) produces an array of trad pottery, incl the notable 'torn pots'. Her colourful new shop in Bayfield Rd, Portree (nr TO) sells these and other innovative glassware, soft furnishings, pictures etc. Some inspired designs and ideas (glass fish that float in flower vases), but what to buy, and for whom? Open AYR Mon-Sat; 9am-lateish. Pottery; Apr-Sept 9am-5pm.

BRODIE COUNTRY FARE: By main A96 betw Nairn and Forres, nr Brodie Castle (1408/CASTLES). Not a souvenir shoppie in the trad sense, more a drive-in one-stop shopping experience. Quality deli food, a fairly up-market boutique and every crafty tartanalia of note. The self-serve restau gets as busy as a motorway café. 7 days till 5.30/6pm.

1750
MAP 3
A2

HOUSE OF BRUAR, PITLOCHRY: Another roadside emporium and shopaholic honey pot this time on the A9 N of Blair Atholl esp for those who just missed Pitlochry. General Harrods in the N feel (I'd still recommend McNaughtons (1774/OUTDOOR SHOPS), though the food side is sound (good range of Scottish cheeses, Mackays ice cream etc). Falls nearby for more spiritual sustenance (1278/WATERFALLS). 7 days, till 8pm (6 in winter).

1751
MAP 6
C2

OCTOPUS CRAFTS,nr FAIRLIE, nr LARGS: On main A78 Largs to Ayr rd. Smaller set up than above, but, crafts, wines and cookshop an excellent restau (1077/SEAFOOD RESTAUS) and a seafood deli. An all-round road side experience. Everything here is hand-made and/or hand-picked. Even the wines are well chosen. Good pots. Glass and wood. They also run courses. Cl Mon.

1752
MAP 1
C3

BALBIRNIE CRAFT CENTRE, MARKINCH: Follow signs for Balbirnie Park from Glenrothes road system, but off the A92. Farmyard courtyard of craft workshops and retail in country park nr Balbirnie House Hotel (721/FIFE HOTELS). Jewellery, glasswork, ceramics, leather and embroidery - bit of everything really. Nice that something's made in Glenrothes that isn't made in millions. 7 days (Sun afternoons only).

1753
MAP 5
C3

ALDIE WATER MILL, TAIN: 01862 893786. Off the A9 nr S Tain. Restored picturesque mill with local history in the beams. Adj craft shop houses individual, attractive home furnishings all locally made. The tapestry scenes, made from hand dyed/spun wools and jute, framed with driftwood are done real good. Pippa Lee's sturdy willow basketry is the real McCoy and her jewellery unique. Ware from the nearby pottery, which you can also visit (there's also a guesthouse up the track). 7 days; 10am-5pm in season - phone at other times.

1754
MAP 2
D2

BORGH POTTERY, BORVE, ISLE OF LEWIS: On NW coast of island a wee way from Stornoway, but not much of a detour from the rd to Callanish where you are probably going. Alex and Sue Blair's pleasant gallery of handthrown pots with strong glazes; domestic and grd wear. Some knits. Open AYR 9-6pm. Cl Sun.

1755
MAP 2
B1

BORVEMOR STUDIOS, SCARISTA, ISLE OF HARRIS: All-round arts, crafts and gaelic culture one-stop, with café and accom. Adj the famous beach (1254/BEACHES), so more than one reason to come here. Good work! May-Sept 10am-5pm, Cl Sun (longer hrs July/Aug).

1756
MAP 2
B2

THE STUDIO CRAFT SHOP, PLOCKTON: 8km over hill from Kyle at the corner of the two 'main' streets in this picturesque and much-loved village (1233/COASTAL VILLAGES). Well-chosen knick-knacks, jewellery and good selection of local artist's work. 10am-1pm, 2-6pm. Cl Sun.

1757
MAP 2
C3

SIMPLY SCOTLAND, ST ANDREWS & EDINBURGH: 158 South St and Royal Mile. superior selection of contemporary Scottish ceramics, jewellery and knits. Streets ahead of the streets of Pitlochry, Callander etc for superior souvenirs.

1758
MAP 5
D2

JUST SCOTTISH, STONEHAVEN: Small selective arts/crafts shop in main st adj the sq. Anta and other brand leaders, but other interesting stuff like, Jonathan Eadie's candelabras. 10-5.30pm. Cl Sun.

1759
MAP 3
D6

GALLOWAY LODGE PRESERVES, GATEHOUSE OF FLEET: on main st of compact town. Packed with local jams, marmalades, chutneys and pickles. Scottish pottery by Anta, Highland, Stoneware and Dunoon. Good presents and jam for yourself. 9.30am-5pm Mon-Sat, and Sun afternoons in summer.

1760
MAP 9
C4

E/CRAFTS AND THINGS, nr GLENCOE VILLAGE: On A82 betw Glencoe village and Ballachulish. Eclectic mix of so many baubles that some are literally hanging from the rafters. Mind, body & spirit books (like this one) and reasonably priced knit/outerwear. Good coffee shop, with local artist's work on walls. Dave's an all-round nice guy. Feb-Dec 9am-5.30pm (later in summer).

1761
MAP 2
C5

DRUMLANRIG CASTLE, nr THORNHILL, nr DUMFRIES: A whole day out of things to do (1214/COUNTRY PARKS) including the craft centre in the old stable/courtyard to the side of the house. Studio-type shops with leather work, jewellery, dried flowers and T-shirts. Hire a bike and ride while you decide.

1762
MAP 9
C2

WHERE TO BUY GOOD WOOLLIES

1763   **JUDITH GLUE, EDINBURGH and ORKNEY:** Next to Holiday Inn Crowne Plaza
MAP A   in Royal Mile and opp the cathedral in Kirkwall. Distinctive hand-made
D3   jumpers, the runic designs are a real winner. Also the widespread but individual
Joker stoneware (jewellery and animal clocks v popular), condiments and
preserves. The landscape prints of Orkney are by twin sister, Jane. We liked the
wind-up Baygen radio. Open AYR 7 days 9am-6pm.

1764   **NUMBER TWO, EDINBURGH:** St Stephen Pl. They were here on the corner of St
MAP A   Stephen Pl in the first 1960s flush of alternative culture, long before their
C1   trail-blazing range of Scottish machine and hand-made knitwear could be called
'designer'. Still innovative, still filling the shop with the cardies that Liz Taylor
once admired (not Lana Turner).

1765   **LYNDA USHER, BEAULY:** 01463 783017. Knits and the 100% natural yarns, plus
MAP 2   textiles. V selective and based on the owner's personal choice; Lynda is a big
D3   name in Scottish knitting circles. Open AYR; Mon-Sat 10am-6pm (til 5pm in
winter).

1766   **BELINDA ROBERTSON:** 0131 225 1057. Palmerston Pl, Edin. Queen of the
MAP A   commissioned cashmere creations; you can only choose from the *prêt-à-
porter* collection in her showroom here (or in London). Her team of 7 girls design
and process the stock which is made up in Hawick. **HILARY ROHDE'S** the other
cashmere designer par excellence. She's too big time even to give out a phone-
number (and I promised I wouldn't).

1767   **HUNTER'S OF BRORA, BRORA, SUTHERLAND:** Main rd N (the A9) towards
MAP 2   Helmsdale. Certainly among the best of the larger scale mill-type emporia.
D2   Bales of their own stylish tweeds or choose from the made up clothing selection.
Trad but unstuffy stalwarts, and some gr hats - the bow brim is a must. Open
AYR Mon-Sat.

1768   **RAGAMUFFIN, SKYE:** On Armadale Pier, so one of the first or last things you can
MAP 2   do on Skye is rummage through the Ragamuffin store and get a nice knit. Every
B4   kind of jumper and some crafts in this Aladdin's cave; incl tweedy things and hats.
They're also in Edin in the Royal Mile. **OVER THE RAINBOW:** Quay St, Portree (rd
down to harbour) can be expensive but is individual and generally excellent.

1769   **JOHNSTONS CASHMERE CENTRE, ELGIN:** Large Mill Shop kind of operation and
MAP 3   full-blown visitor attraction nr the Cathedral (1429/RUINS). 'The only British mill
B2   to transform fibre to garment' (yarns spun at their factory in Elgin and made into
garments in the Borders) and though this is more British High St than
Bloomingdales, New York, these jumpers will keep you just as warm. Mon-Sat 9-
5.30pm, summer 9-6 pm and w/ends July/Aug.

1770   **ST ANDREWS WOOLLEN MILL, ST ANDREWS:** At the bottom end of N St nr the Old
MAP 5   Course, a vast emporium/indoor market of every conceivable woolly from heavy
D2   knits to mitts. Some of the big names (you know, Nick Faldo), hand-mades,
cashmere and also tweeds, kilts etc. Mon-Sat 9am-5pm and Sun in season.
AUCHTERLONIES next door has, since 1895, had everything anyone would ever
need on a golf course; more or less a must for the golf-crazed tourist. Same hrs.

1771   **LOCHCARRON VISITOR CENTRE, GALASHIELS:** If you're in Galashiels (or Hawick),
MAP 8   which grew up around woollen mills, you might expect to find a good selection
C3   of woollens you can't get everywhere else; and bargains. Well, tough! There's no
stand-out place, but L Carron (formerly 'Peter Anderson') is a big tourist
attraction with mill tours (Open AYR 4 times a day), exhibits and an okay mill
shop. Hawick did invent the Y-front.

1772   **CHAS N. WHILLANS, HAWICK** (and **GALASHIELS, PEEBLES** and elsewhere): Their
MAP 8   main shop is in Hawick (Teviotdale Mills, over the bridge at S end of main st;
C3   instead of continuing on A7, turn rt and they're on the rt). They stock all the local
big names incl a good range of Pringle, Lyle & Scott and Braemar. Best to stick to
the classic cuts; the 'fashion' versions are not too warm and not too cool.

HARRIS TWEED

1773   **THE REAL HARRIS TWEED, ISLE OF HARRIS:** To be awarded the Harris Tweed Orb
MAP 2   Mark, this distictive wool cloth has to be hand woven from yarn which has been
B2   dyed and spun in the Outer Hebrides. Much is processed industrially and finds
its way into jackets etc in department stores all over the world. The real McCoy

however is still woven and worked in Harris, mainly in the S in places on or off the Golden Road (1307/SCENIC ROUTES).The places to recommend are:

CLO MOR, LICEASTO: 10km S of Tarbert. The true trad passed on from the doyenne of Harris Tweed making, Marion Campbell to Anne Campbell who here dyes her own wool over an open fire using lichens, heather flowers, indigo, ragwort etc, the wool spun by hand on a trad spinning wheel. The tweeds are hand-waulked, treaded in soapy water, pounded on a wooden board and washed in the stream. Authentic this is! Ann receives visitors Mon-Fri 9am-5pm (or phone 01859 530364).

LUSKENTYRE HARRIS TWEED: NO 6, LUSKENTYRE: 2km off W coast on main rd S to Scarista and Rodel. Donald and Maureen Mackay's place is notable for their bright tartan tweed. 9.30am-6pm Cl Sun.

JOAN McCLENNAN: NO 1, DRINISHADDER: Further down the Golden Rd. I don't know, but I've been told, this is where you find the real golden fleece. Go look for it.

THE BEST OUTDOOR SHOPS

Includes outfitters (gentlemen's outfitters) and some mention of kilts.

✚ ✚ **MACNAUGHTON'S, PITLOCHRY:** Station Rd on corner of main st and opp Hunter's (same firm) who sell the outdoor/non-Scottish end of their incredible range. A vast old-fashioned outfitter with acres of tartan attire - incl obligatory tartan pyjamas and dressing gowns! Make their own cloth, and 9m kilts prepared in 10 wks. This really is the real McCoy. 7 days till 5.30pm (5pm Sun).
1774
MAP 4
C2

✚ ✚ **GRAHAM TISO, EDINBURGH:** 0131 225 9486 Rose St; just one of the many outlets of this legendary outdoor suppliers (huge new outlet for 1998 in Commercial St, Leith) also at outposts in - **INVERNESS, ABERDEEN, DUNDEE, GLASGOW, STIRLING, AYR, EAST KILBRIDE** too! Whether you're off to climb a munro or just planning a Sunday stroll they can kit you out and equip you. Probably the biggest range of boots in Scotland.
1775
MAP A
C2

✚ ✚ **KINLOCH ANDERSON, EDINBURGH:** Commercial St, Leith. A bit of a trek from uptown, but firmly on the tourist trail and rightly so. Experts in Highland dress and all things tartan; they've supplied *everybody*. They design their own tartans, have a good range of men's tweed jackets; even rugs. Mon-Sat 9am-5.30pm (5pm winter). E-mail: enquiries@kinlochanderson.com.
1776
MAP A
xE1

STEWART, CHRISTIE & CO, EDINBURGH: 63 Queen St. Est 1792 and still selling breeches! (On request.) Highland outfitter, tailor and saddlery - tartan waistcoats, Harris Tweed jackets, sporrans etc. 9am-5.30pm. Sat till 5pm. Cl Sun.
1777
MAP A
C2

NOTE: Rather than buy an expensive new kilt or have one made, there are a few places in Edin where you can buy second-hand. **ARMSTRONGS:** 83 Grassmarket and 313 Cowgate, Mon-Sat; **ST STEPHENS ST:** second-hand shops with jackets, kilts, tweeds etc when available Mon-Sat. Also believe it or not: **THE ARMY AND NAVY STORES:** Brunswick Pl, Leith Walk.
1778

GREEN WELLY SHOP, TYNDRUM: On main A82 rd W to Oban/Ft William. Adj Clifton coffee shop (1111/TEAROOMS). Outdoorwear emporium in strategic position, with racks of Goretex and other membranes. Berghaus, Barbour and the all-important midge helmet (now, there's a souvenir!). 7 days, till 5.30pm.
1779
MAP 6
A2

MORTIMERS & RITCHIES, GRANTOWN ON SPEY: 3 & 41-45 High St (the main st) respectively of this respectable Speyside holiday town where fishing gear is somewhat in demand (though odd to find 2 similar high quality shops adj). Mortimers more exclusively angling for your custom, but both have a big range of flies. Outdoor clothing with all the big names betw them and every shade of olive. Ritchies also have guns if you want to kill something. Both cl Sun.
1780
MAP 2
E3

NANCY BLACK, OBAN: 3 shops around Argyll Sq in centre of Oban, a 'chandlery', an outdoor shop (all the big names in breathable linings) on the corner and a fashion-for-fogeys shop in the middle. From Scottish knits to Swiss army knives. Cl Sun.
1781
MAP 1
B1

D CROCKART & SON, STIRLING: Outdoor clothing secondary to the serious selection of huntin'-fishin'-shootin' equipment (esp fishing – shop supplies permits). **R.R. HENDERSON'S** and **KIRK'S** adj shops also in Stirling (since 1923) are almost funky.
1782
MAP 6
B3

1783 **NEVIS SPORT, FORT WILLIAM:** 01397 704921; the pyramid shaped building nr the
MAP 2 High St. Extensive ski/outdoor shop; specialising in hill walking and climbing
C4 gear. Snowboards and skis for hire. Self-serve cafe, bar and craft shop. Total outdoor experience and since it might be raining in Ft William, this shop is a good
place to while away some time . . . indoors.

THE BEST GARDEN CENTRES

1784 ✚ **KINLOCHLAICH HOUSE, APPIN:** On main A28 Oban-Ft William rd just N of Pt
MAP 1 Appin t/off, the West Highlands' largest nursery/grd centre. Set in a large
B1 walled grd filled with plants and veg soaking up the climes of the warm Gulf
stream. Donald Hutchison and daughter nurture these acres enabling you to reap
what they sow; with a huge array of plants on offer it's like visiting a friend's grd
and being able to take home your fave bits. Charming cottages for let 01631
730342. 7 days: 9am-5.30pm (10.30am Sun). Cl Sun in winter.

1785 ✚ **DOUGAL PHILIP'S WALLED GARDEN CENTRE, nr S QUEENSFERRY:** 0131 319
MAP 7 1122. 18km from Edin. Perhaps the only plant shop in the world where the
B1 drive in makes you feel like a character from Jane Austen - that's the view of
Hopetoun House for you (a stately home begun by William Bruce in 1699, but
mainly an important work of the Adam family, o/look the Forth, open Easter-
Oct 10am-5.30pm). DP's is in its old walled grd. This is where Edinburgh's
discerning gardeners come for their greens. Vendor of Captain Scarlet roses.
Dougal does know his onions. Open AYR 10am-5.30pm.

1786 ✚ **INSHRIACH, nr KINCRAIG, nr AVIEMORE:** On B970 betw Kincraig and
MAP 2 Inverdruie (which is on the Coylumbridge ski rd out of Aviemore), a grd
D4 centre, nay a nursery, that puts most others in the shade. Specialising in alpines
and bog plants, but with neat beds of all sorts in the grounds of the house by the
Spey and frames full of perfect specimens, this is a potterer's paradise. Mon-Fri
9am-5pm, Sat 9am-4pm. Cl Sun.

1787 ✚ **FINDLAY CLARK, MILNGAVIE, GLASGOW:** In Campsie countryside N of city,
MAP B 20km from centre via A81 or A807 (Milngavie or Kirkintilloch rds) or
xC1 heading for Milngavie (pron 'Mullguy'), turn rt on Boclair Rd. Vast grd complex
and all-round visitor experience; an institution. 'Famous' coffee shop (the famous
waitresses tend to be local babes; this may distract the dads), saddlery with
everything except horses; labels from Crabtree & Evelyn to Fisons, plus books,
clothes and piles of plants; and live pets. 9am-9pm (till 7pm in winter).

1788 **BEN LOMOND NURSERY, BALMAHA, LOCH LOMOND:** Nearer Conic Hill than Ben
MAP 6 Lomond, on the B837 just before Balmaha. Family-run, supplying the trade and
B4 gardeners in the know, as well as passing motorists, particularly with bedding
plants grown in their greenhouses on the side of the loch. 9.30am-6pm, 7 days.

1789 **DOCHFOUR, LOCH NESS:** On A82 Inverness-Ft William rd 12km S of Inverness. 20
MAP 2 acres of terraced Victorian grd in the grounds of Dochfour House. Yew hedges
D3 with not a leaf out of place enclose formal grds for ambling about in. Largish
shrubs are esp cheap. Pick your plants by example. Open 7 days 10am-5pm
(Sat/Sun 2-5pm).

1790 **BRIN SCHOOL FIELDS, FLICHITY, nr INVERNESS:** Off A9 S of Daviot, 12km S of
MAP 2 Inverness, then 10km W along rd to Farr. An old school and playground
D3 dedicated to herbs, plants and all the potions and lotions that come from them.
Tearoom in the school room. Apr-Oct 8.30am-7pm, Sun 2-5pm, Cl Thu.

1791 **FLOORS CASTLE, KELSO:** 3km outside town off B6397 St Boswells rd (grd centre
MAP 8 has separate entrance to main visitors' gate in town). Set amongst lovely old
D3 greenhouses within walled grds some distance from house, it has a showpiece
herbaceous border all round. Newly extended coffee shop and patio. Centre is
open AYR. 10am-5pm. (1472/COUNTRY HOUSES.)

1792 **CHRISTIE'S NURSERY, KIRRIEMUIR:** 01575 572977. On long straight stretch of A926
MAP 4 to Blairgowrie in the village of Westmuir, 4km from Kirriemuir. Looking towards
D3 the Sidlaw Hills, this is a family-run nursery specialising in hardy plants (orchids,
alpines etc) with unique stocks of rare plants. This is where those in the know go
for gentians, (they are world specialists); primulas and advice about the rock grd.
Mar-Oct 10am-6pm; outwith these times, phone first.

1793 **GLENDOICK, GLENCARSE, nr PERTH:** On A85, 10km from Perth, in the fertile Carse of the Tay. A large grd centre notable esp for rhododendrons and azaleas, a riot of which can be viewed in the nursery behind (May only). New popular coffee shop. 7 days till 6pm.

MAP 4 D4

CHRISTIE'S, FOCHABERS: On A98 going into town from Buckie side. Huge grd centre and forest nursery, the centre of a family empire which has florists, hotels and a golf course. Good for shrubs, indoor plants etc and a gr place for keen and not-so-keen gardeners to browse around. Famous floral clock and aviary – an all-round shopping/recreational experience. 9am-5pm, 7 days.

1794 MAP 3 B2

KESKE NURSERIES, CLACHAN, NORTH UIST: In the remote heart of wild and watery N Uist on main rd to Benbecula S of Lochmaddy and just after Clachan Stores and the t/off for Bayhead a cottage nusery and a . . . bus full of plants (tomatoes when we visited). Idiosyncratic app, but certainly the Hebridean choice for trees, shrubs, veg and bedding plants. Go on, make a statement - plant a tree in this treeless tract. Open AYR 1pm-late. Cl Sun.

1795 MAP 2 A3

SMEATON GARDENS, EAST LINTON: 2km from village on N Berwick rd (signed Smeaton). Up a drive in an old estate is this walled grd going back to early 19th century. Wide range; good for fruit (and other) trees, herbaceous etc. Nice to wander round, an additional pleasure is the 'Lake Walk' halfway down drive through small gate in woods. 1km stroll round a secret finger lake in magnificent mature woodland. You're only supposed to go during grd hrs (10-4.30, Sun from 11.30; Cl w/ends Jan/Feb).

1796 MAP 7 D1

THE CLYDE VALLEY: The lush valley of the mighty Clyde is grd centre central. Best reached say from Glas by M74, jnct 7, then A72 for Lanark. Betw Larkhall and Lanark there's a profusion to choose from and many have sprouted coffee/craft shops. Pick your own fruit in summer and your own picnic spot to eat it.

1797 MAP 1 E3

THE BEST MARKETS

✝ ✝ **THE BARROWS, GLASGOW:** A market spread out around the streets and alleys in the E End, app via the Tron at the end of Argyle St and then the Gallowgate. Acres of cheap stuff, old and new, in shops, doorways, stalls, sheds and round the back. As with all gr markets, it's full of character and characters and it's still possible to find bargains and collectibles. Wander and rummage all over, but look esp for the Square Yard and the Cartwheel opp in Stevenson St West (parallel to Gallowgate) and also for the Upstairs Market in Gibson St at the side of Barrowlands (643/GLASGOW NIGHTLIFE) where you'll find the Barras as it always was, plus everything from clairvoyants to the latest scam (e.g. computer games, bootleg tapes). Sat and Sun only, 10am-5pm.

1798 MAP B E3

DENS ROAD, DUNDEE: A kind of mini-Barrowland in the Hilltown i.e. on the hill N of town centre area of Dundee. By car you have to negotiate the bewildering and irritating one-way system. The market, which sells all kinds of junk, cheap essentials and nonsense, is all undercover in sheds and has a particular atmos. Open Tue, Fri, w/ends.

1799 MAP 4

LANARK MARKET: Principally a cattle auction, and apart from the spectacle and sawdust of the ring, of interest to those of us who ain't farmers or butchers, mainly for the café (1103/CAFÉS) but also for the incredible fruit market in one of the big sheds. There's nothing quite like it in Scotland (except on Thu at Stirling Cattle Market where the same McKechnies purvey similar high-quality and vast-quantity stuff). Mon 8am-3 or 4pm.

1800 MAP 1 E3

INGLISTON, outside Edin on A8 nr Airport; **EAST FORTUNE,** off A1 E of Haddington; **KINROSS** jnct 5/6 of the M90. All tacky markets on unattractive sites nr Edin. Possibly declining popularity due to bootsales and just as well. They're all on Sundays. I mention them just in case you wonder what the traffic's all about, but best to avoid.

1801 MAP 7 B1

EDINBURGH MARKETS: The remarkable thing about Edin and all its aspirations to be seen as a major European city is that, unlike all the others, it doesn't have a st market. All attempts to actuate one are met with huge popular support e.g. the Grassmarket Fair (w/ends during the Festival), the Market on the Shore, Leith in early June. But, for various reasons, they just don't happen. Trains to Glas leave every half hour. Leith may happen more permanently in 1998 or 1999 if I've got anything to do with it.

1802

AUCTIONS AND JUNKYARDS

1803
MAP 1
D3
✠ **BURNTHILLS DEMOLITION, QUARRELTON, JOHNSTON, nr GLASGOW:** 01505 329644. M8 to Paisley, town centre then follow signs for Johnstone. Left at 'Iceland' at the top of the rise, left again at the police stn, rt into S William St and it's on your left around the bend. A yard, full of Victorian sinks and a warehouse that's an Alladin's cave of fascinating and useful junk; old bikes, stuffed polar bears, stained glass and lots of stuff whose original purpose has long been forgotten. Quite spooky upstairs; watch out for The Mummy! Mon-Sat 9am-5pm Sun noon-5pm. About 12km from airport.

1804
MAP 2
E3
✠ **AULDEARN ANTIQUES, AULDEARN, nr NAIRN:** Doris Milton's cornucopia of junk, quality antiques and architectural salvage in an old manse 2km from main st (via Lethen Rd) which is 3km from main A96 Nairn-Forres rd. Serene spot for browsing through courtyard of shops and a churchful of furniture. Kids welcome. 7 days from when they get up till when you've gone.

1805
MAP A
C2
✠ **THE LANE SALES, EDINBURGH:** Lyon & Turnbull's sale in Thistle St Lane behind its George St showrooms. At the back they are far from elegant. It's possibly why these Tue, Wed and Fri morning sales are still popular with Edinburgh's army of antique dealers, many of whom got the bug here. All kinds of junk, furniture and bric-à-brac is on view for an hour, then auctioned at 11am. 'Somebody once got an original William Blake' sagas keep the cowboys going. Afterwards, have coffee at the Laigh in Hanover St (168/TEAROOMS). Other furniture/antique sales on Wed/Sat (0131 225 4627). **PHILLIPS**, 65 George St, has a general sale of 'antiques, later furniture and effects' first Tues of every month (0131 225 2266).

1806
MAP 7
C1
SAM BURNS' YARD, PRESTONPANS, nr EDINBURGH: 01875 810600. On the coast rd out of Musselburgh; if you get to Prestonpans you've missed it. By a gate in the wall you'll see cars on the kerb of a long straight stretch. The yard has piles of old bikes, assorted 'stuff' and is full of domestic and office furniture stored both outdoors and in sheds. Popular with Sunday browsers although you wonder who might want a rusted filing cabinet or a second-hand toilet. 7 days until 5pm, Sun from 12.30pm.

1807
MAP A
xD1
EASY(EDINBURGH ARCHITECTURAL SALVAGE YARD): 554 7077. Couper St off Coburg St (at N end of Gr Jnct St nr mini roundabout). Warehouseful of original house fittings and the place to go for baths, sinks, radiators, fireplaces, doors (there are rows of them) and all the other bits of Old Edin that used to be thrown out but which are now worth lots. They also have a branch at 85/87 Colvend St, **GLASGOW** 0141 556 7772. Similar set ups at **Angus Architectural Antiques**, Hill St, Arbroath, in harbour area (01674 674291) and **TAYMOUTH ARCHITECTURAL**, Perth Rd, Dundee (01382 223801).

1808
MAP B
D2
R McTEAR and **J.A. CATHCART, GLASGOW:** Two auctioneers in opp lanes off St Vincent Pl near George Sq. McTear's at 4 N Court has sales every Fri (view Thu) and Cathcart's at 20 Anchor Lane on Wed. Mornings. See the *Herald* on Mon for details.

1809
MAP 5
C3
LADYBANK AUCTION: 01337 830488. Kinloch St along from railway stn in flat village in middle of farming Fife. Weekly sale of all kinds of household stuff from Victoriana through nifty 1950s to 1970s collectibles. Eminently worth a gander. Fri 6pm. Viewing Thu till 9pm, Fri from 10am.

1810
MAP 6
D3
ROBERTSON'S AUCTION, KINBUCK: 01786 822603. 6km N of Dunblane on B8033. Second Sat every month at 10am. Viewing: Thur and Fri 9am-4pm, (and Thur 7.30-9pm). Antiques/furniture-stripping. **COMRIE AUCTION:** 01764 670613. In old church on main st. Occasional Tues at 10.30am. Viewing: Sat 10am-1pm, Mon 9am-6pm. **CRIEFF AUCTION:** 01764 653276. Galvelmore St off rd in from S. Every Wed. Viewing: Tue 10am-8pm, Wed 9-11am: sale starts 11am. These 3 salerooms in Perthshire are like 'country sales'; general goods and antiques. Gr for furniture and bric-à-brac. Much of it finds its way into antique shops. These sales can be addictive.

1811
MAP 4
E2
TAYLOR'S AUCTIONS, MONTROSE: 01674 672775. Panmure Row. Auction Rooms for regular sales of household furniture and effects every second Sat and some Fridays. Some antique and quality stuff but all kinds incl bric-à-brac, jewellery, grd furniture (viewing: Fri 2-5pm and 6-9pm; Sat 9-10.30am). Often fascinating just to wander round; you're bound to see something you want.

SECTION 11

Museums, Galleries, Theatres and Music

THE MOST INTERESTING MUSEUMS

For EDIN galleries, see pp. 44-5; GLAS, see pp. 80-1.

1812
MAP 9
E3

✝ ✝ **THE SECRET BUNKER, nr CRAIL/ANSTRUTHER:** The nuclear bunker and regional seat of government in the event of nuclear war – a twilight labyrinth beneath a hill in rural Fife so vast, well documented and complete, it's utterly fascinating and quite chilling. Few 'museums' are as authentic or as resonant as this, even down to the 1950s records in the jukebox in the claustrophobic canteen. Makes you wonder what 300 people would have felt like incarcerated down there, what the Cold War was all about and what secrets They are cooking up these days. Apr-Oct 10am-5pm.

1813
MAP 7
D1

✝ ✝ **MUSEUM OF FLIGHT, nr HADDINGTON, E LOTHIAN:** 01620 880308. 3km from A1 S of town. In the old complex of hangars and nissen huts at the side of E Fortune, an airfield dating to World War I (there's a tacky open-air market on Sundays), a large collection of planes from gliders to jets and esp wartime memorabilia has been respectfully restored and preserved. Inspired and inspiring displays; not just boys' stuff. Marvel at the bravery back then and sense the unremitting passage of time. From E Fortune the airship R34 made its historic Atlantic crossings. Apr-Oct 7 days; 10.30am-5pm (till 6pm Jul-Aug).

1814
MAP 9
B2

✝ **THE ABBOT HOUSE, DUNFERMLINE:** Maygate in town centre 'historic area'. V fine conversion of ancient house demonstrating the importance of this town as a religious and trading centre from the beginning of this millennium to medieval times. Encapsulates history from Margaret and Bruce to the Beatles. One of the few tourist attractions where 'award-winning' is a reliable indicator of worth. Café and tranquil grd; gate to the graveyard and Abbey. 7 days 10am-5pm.

1815
MAP 1
B2

✝ **EASDALE ISLAND FOLK MUSEUM:** On Easdale, an island/township reached by a 5min (continuous) boat service from Seil 'island' at the end of the B844 (off the A816, 18km S of Oban). Something special about this grassy hamlet of white-washed houses on a rocky outcrop which has a pub, a tearoom and a craft shop, and this museum across the green. The history of the place (a thriving slate industry erased one stormy night in 1881, when the sea drowned the quarry) is brought to life in displays from local contributions. Easter-Sept 11am-5pm.

1816
MAP 2
B1

✝ **THE BLACK HOUSE AT ARNOL, LEWIS:** 01851 710501. The A857 Barvas rd from Stornoway, left at jnct for 7km, then rt through township for 2km. The trad thatched dwelling of the Hebrides, with earth floor, bed boxes and central peat fire (no chimney hole), occupied both by the family and their animals. Remarkably, this house was lived in until the 1960s. Smokists may refect on that peaty fug. Open AYR: Cl Fri and 1-2pm.   HS

1817
MAP 2
D1

✝ **STRATHNAVER MUSEUM, BETTYHILL:** 01641 521330. On N coast 60km W of Thurso in a converted church which is v much part of the whole appalling saga: a graphic account of the Highland clearances told through the history of this fishing village and the Strath that lies behind it from whence its dispossessed population came; 2,500 folk were driven from their homes - it's worth going up the valley (from 2km W along the main A836) to see (esp at Achenlochy) the beautiful land they had to leave in 1812 to make way for sheep. Apr-Oct: 10am-5pm. Cl Sun. Nov-March: Tue/ Thur 10am-4pm; Wed / Fri 2-4pm. Cl for lunch.

1818
MAP 3
D1

✝ **SCOTLAND'S LIGHTHOUSE MUSEUM, FRASERBURGH:** At Kinnaird Head nr Harbour. The N East's newest attraction, so signed from all over. Purpose-built and v well done. Something which may appear to be of marginal interest made vital. In praise of the prism and the engineering innovation and skill that allowed Britain once to rule the seas (and the world). A gr ambition (to light the coastline) spectacularly realised. *At Scotland's Edge* by Allardyce and Hood is well worth taking home. Apr-Oct 10-6pm (Sun afternoons); winter closes at 4pm.

1819
MAP 2
C4

WEST HIGHLAND MUSEUM, FORT WILLIAM: Cameron Sq off main st, listed building next to TO. Now refurb yet retains mood; the setting doesn't overshadow the contents. 7 rms of Jacobite memorabilia, archeology, wildlife, clans, tartans, arms etc all effectively evoke the local history. Gr oil paintings line the walls, incl drawn battle plan of Culloden. The anamorphic painting of Charlie isn't so bonny, but a fascinating snapshot all the same. Cl Sun.

1820
MAP 1
D3

SUMMERLEE, COATBRIDGE: 01236 431261 West Canal St. Follow signs. Here in the Iron Town is this tribute to the industry, ingenuity and graft that powered the

Industrial Revolution and made Glas gr. Anyone with a mechanical bent or an interest in the social history of the working class will like it here; totty kids and bored teens may not. Tearoom. 10am-5pm. Winter (12-5pm w/ends).

DOUNE MOTOR MUSEUM, DOUNE: 01786 841203. Gr example of how a particular personal interest can develop into something to interest everybody – or at least everyone who likes beautiful things. You don't need to be a car nut to drool over these. Not the range of Glasgow's Transport Museum (584/OTHER ATTRACTIONS), but many 20th-century classics incl a Morgan like mine. Apr-Nov, 10am-5pm. Café. Occasional events.
1821
MAP 6
D3

SKYE MUSEUM OF ISLAND LIFE: Kilmuir on Uig-Staffin rd, the A855, 32km N of Portree. The most authentic (or at least official) of several converted cottages on Skye where the poor crofter's life is recreated for the enrichment of ours. The small thatched township includes agricultural implements as well as domestic artefacts, many of which illustrate an improbable fascination with the royal family. Flora Macdonald's grave is nearby (1480/MONUMENTS).
1822
MAP 2
B3

AUCHENDRAIN, INVERARAY: 8km W of town on A83. A whole township reconstructed to give a v fair impression of both the historical and spatial relationship betw the cottages and their various occupants. Longhouses and byre dwellings; their furniture and their ghosts. 7 days. Apr-Sept 10-5pm (not Sat in Apr).
1823
MAP 1
C2

COMBINED OPERATIONS MUSEUM, INVERARAY: Grounds of Inveraray Castle. Old WW II soldiers come from all over to relive the time when they praticed leaping out of boats into freezing L Long, swimming in full kit to shore then hiking, manfully, up the nearest hill. The secret training seemed to work - they did help to turn the tide of the war. Check TO for hrs.
1824
MAP 1
C2

INVERARAY JAIL: 'The story of Scottish crime and punishment' (*sic*) told in 'award-winning' reconstruction of courtroom with cells below, where the waxwork miscreants and their taped voices bring local history to life. Makes you think that guided tours of Peterhead can't be far off. Open AYR, 10am-5pm.
1825
MAP 1
C2

ARCTIC PENGUIN aka MARITIME HERITAGE CENTRE, INVERARAY: 'One of the world's last iron sailing ships' moored so you can't miss it at the loch side in Inveraray. More to it than would seem from the outside; displays on the history of Clydeside (The *Queens M* and *E* memorabilia etc), Highland Clearances, the Vital Spark. Lots for kids to get a handle (or hands) on. 7 days till 6pm; 5pm winter.
1826
MAP 1
C2

BONAWE, IRONWORKS MUSEUM, TAYNUILT. At its zenith, (late 17th - early 18th century), this ironworks was a brutal, fire-breathing monster, as 'black as the Earl of Hell's waiscoat'. But now, all is calm as the gently sloping grassy banks carry you around from warehouse to foundry and down onto the banks of L Etive to the pier, where the finished product was loaded on to ships to be taken away for the purpose of empire-building (with cannonballs). 7 days. April-Sept. 10-5pm.
1827
MAP 1
C1

SCOTTISH FISHERIES MUSEUM, ANSTRUTHER: 0333 310628. In and around a cobbled courtyard o/look the old fishing harbour in this busy East Neuk town. Excellent evocation of trad industry still alive (if not kicking). Impressive collection of models and actual vessels incl those moored at adj quay. Crail harbour 9km up the coast, for the full picture (and fresh crab/lobster). Open AYR 10am-5.30pm, Sun 11am-5pm (Cl 4.30pm in winter).
1828
MAP 5
E3

ROBERT SMAIL'S PRINTING WORKS, INNERLEITHEN: Main st. A trad printing works till 1986 and still in use. Fascinating vignettes/instant history. Have a go at hand setting, then have a go at Caldwell's cone holding (1149/ICE CREAM). May-Sep, Mon-Sat 10am-5pm, Sun 2-5pm. W/ends in Oct.
1829
MAP 8
B2

SHAMBELLIE HOUSE MUSEUM OF COSTUME, NEW ABBEY, nr DUMFRIES: Another obsession that became a museum. On 2 floors of this country house set among spectacular woodlands. Fab frocks etc from every 'period'. Apr-Oct 11am-5pm.
1830
MAP 9
D3

ABERFELDY WATER MILL, ABERFELDY: Mill St off main st. Excellent renovation made all the more authentic because it was restored in 1983 by a 7th-generation millar, Tom Rodger, and once again is producing good healthy (organic) oatmeal that you can buy for your porridge. The weight of the water in the buckets turns the wheel; life goes round. The tearoom serves, amongst other things, a v fine fly cemetery. Apr-Oct 10am-5pm (Sun cl. 5.30pm).
1831
MAP 4
B3

THE MOST INTERESTING
PUBLIC GALLERIES

For EDIN, *see pp. 51;* GLAS, *pp. 86.*

1832 ⚜ **ABERDEEN ART GALLERY:** Schoolhill. Major gallery with temp exhibits and
MAP 3 eclectic permanent collection from Impressionists to Bellany. Large bequest
from local granite merchant Alex Macdonald in 1900 contributes fascinating
collection of his contemporaries: Bloomsburys, Scottish, Pre-Raphaelites. Excellent
watercolour rm. An easy and rewarding gallery to visit. 10am-5pm (Sun 2-5pm).

1833 ⚜ **THE FERGUSSON GALLERY, PERTH:** Marshall Pl on corner of Tay St in distinctive
MAP 4 round tower (former waterworks). The assembled works on two floors of
C4 J D Fergusson 1874-1961. Though he spent much of his life in France, he had an
influence on Scottish art and was pre-eminent amongst those now called the
Colourists. It's a long way from Perth to Antibes 1913 but these pictures are a
draught of the warm S. Mon-Sat 10-5pm.

1834 ⚜ **KIRKCALDY MUSEUM AND ART GALLERY:** Nr railway stn, but uptown Kirkcaldy
MAP 5 isn't easy to find your way around, so ask. One of the best galleries in central
C4 Scotland. Unmentioned in all previous editions of this book; shows you how much
I know. History of 19th/20th-century Scottish art on the walls esp
Colourists/McTaggert/Glasgow Boys. And Sickert to Redpath. Museum ain't bad
also. Kirkcaldy doesn't get a lot of good press, but this and the parks (1227/PARKS)
are worth the journey (plus Valente's - 1084/FISH AND CHIPS). 7 days till 5pm.

1835 ⚜ **HORNEL GALLERY, KIRKCUDBRIGHT:** Broughton House where he lived, now a
MAP 9 fabulous evocation with collection of his work and atelier as was. 'Even the
C4 Queen was amazed'. Beautiful grds to river. April-Oct. 7 Days 1-5.30pm. NTS

1836 ⚜ **DUFF HOUSE, BANFF:** Nice walk and easy to find from town centre. Important
MAP 3 outstation of the National Gallery in meticulously restored Adam house with
C2 interesting history and spacious grounds. Ramsays, Raeburn, portraiture of mixed
appeal and an El Greco. Maybe OTT for some, but major attraction in the area (go
futher up the Deveron, 1629/WOODLAND WALKS).

1837 **THE PIER ART GALLERY, STROMNESS, ORKNEY MAINLAND:** On main st (1234/
COASTAL VILLAGES), a gallery on a small quay which could have come lock, stock
and canvases from Cornwall. Permanent St Ives-style collection of Barbara
Hepworth, Ben Nicholson, Paolozzi and others shown in a *simpatico* environment
with the sea o/side. Temporary exhibs downstairs. A breath of art. Cl Mon.

1838 **PAISLEY ART GALLERY AND MUSEUM:** High St. Permanent collection of the world
MAP 1 famous Paisley shawls and history of weaving techniques. Other exhibs usually
D3 have a local connection and an interactive element. Notable Greek Ionic-style
building. Mon-Sat 10am-5pm.

1839 **MACLAURIN GALLERY, AYR:** In Rozelle Park and the only art in these parts.
MAP 1 Temporary exhibs change every month (incl local artists' work). 5 galleries, and
C4 additional 5 rms of art in Rozelle Hse; craft shop. Apr-Oct: Mon-Sat 10am-5pm,
Sun 2-5pm.

1840 ⚜ **SCULPTURE AT GLENKILN RESERVOIR, nr DUMFRIES:** Take A75 to Castle
MAP 9 Douglas and rt toShawshead; into village, rt at T-jnct, left to Dunscore,
D3 immediate left, signed for reservoir. Follow rd along loch side and park. Not a
gallery at all but sculpture scattered amongst the hills, woods and meadows
around this reservoir in the Galloway Hills 16km SE of Dumfries. One or two
are obvious, the others you just have to find. Epsteins and Moores. I found 3
(there are thought to be 6 in all), but not the King and Queen who had their heads
removed – now, that's vandalism. This is an enchanting place and the artworks
are part of it.

1841 **COLLEONARD SCULPTURE GARDEN, BANFF:** On the A97 Huntly rd, 2km from town
MAP 3 and the big public art collection in the N, Duff House (see above). A more
C1 modest enterprise, the strange environmental artworks of Frank Bruce arranged
around his leafy grounds. Frank and his missus live in the house, but you can
wander undisturbed and wonder at his carving skills (and what he's on about).
Should be in more public collections. Summer 9.30-5.30pm.

WHERE TO SEE AND BUY
INEXPENSIVE ART AND CERAMICS

McEWAN GALLERY nr BALLATER, DEESIDE: A surprising place to come across, but for over 20yrs this cottage gallery has been dealing and educating us in 19th/20th century, mainly Scottish Art. Delightful house. They wrote the book! Summer exhibs, but open AYR 10-6pm (Sun 2-6pm). 300m up A939 Tomintoul rd.
1842
MAP 3
B4

THE LOST GALLERY, MIDDLE OF NOWHERE, ABERDEENSHIR: Best reached off the A944 Strathdon rd at Bellabeg, though don't follow the sign for 'Lost', the one you see in postcards. Fabulous small gallery of work by contemporary Scottish artists incl the owners. Absolutely worth the drive. AYR 11am-5pm. Cl Tues.
1843
MAP 3
B3

STRATHEARN GALLERY, CRIEFF: 32 W St (western extension of Main St). Highly regarded (by Scottish Crafts Council and others) gallery with pottery downstais. Fine and applied arts. Open AYR: Thu-Sat in winter and Cl Sun.
1844
MAP 4
B4

TOLQUHON GALLERY, nr ABERDEEN: 01651 842343. Betw Ellon and Oldmeldrum and nr Haddo House (1466/COUNTRY HOUSES) and Pitmedden (1208/GARDENS) - follow signs for castle, an interesting ruin for kids to clamber. Real art at realistic prices. (Pron 'T'hon'.) 11am-5pm, Sun 2-5pm. Cl Thu.
1845
MAP 3
D3

JUST ART, FOCHABERS: Main st, the A96 through Fochabers E of Elgin. Changing exhibs of serious and selected mainly Scottish artists. Good ceramics. A must stop on this rd along the coast. See GARDEN CENTRES (1794).
1846
MAP 3
D2

ST ANDREWS FINE ART: Crowded walls of Scottish art from 1800-present. Includes some good work from kent contemporaries. Peploe-Redpath and their chums.
1847
MAP 5
D2

COURTYARD GALLERY, CRAIL: 42 Marketgate S (main st). Pictures, prints and sculpture from contemporary Scottish artists. Excellent selection. 11-5pm. Cl Tues.
1848
MAP 5
E3

STABLES GALLERY, FALKLAND: Converted stables in Back Wynd off main st in conservation village. Not major pictures, but nice watercolours, echings and mainly antique ceramics. W/end afts in summer.
1849
MAP 5
C3

McIAN GALLERY, OBAN: 10 Argyll Sq. 19/20th-century work by Scottish artists. Some notable names ('Glasgow School'). Pottery, prints. Mon-Sat 9am-5pm.
1850
MAP 1
B1

ROWAN GALLERY, DRYMEN: Main St opp Salmon Leap Inn. Contemporary Scottish painting, jewellery and ceramics. Mon-Sat 10-5pm, Sun 11-5pm.
1851
MAP 6
B4

BUTH NAN DEALBHAN, LOCHINVER: Centre of Lochinver where the tourists come; paintings, photographs and inticate hand drawn and inked maps of Scotland. Same people: **GAILEIRIDH ASAINTE:** 01571 855238. 9km N of Lochinver on B869 to Drumbeg. In the former Stoer smithy; watercolours, prints and photos.
1852
MAP 2
C2
1853
MAP 2
C2

MORVERN GALLERY, BARVAS, ISLE OF LEWIS: Coast rd just N of Barabhas 5km from Callanish and those stones. Farm steading kind of gallery with exceedingly well-selected work, mainly local. Painting, tapestry, ceramics and original knits that are so good I ordered one and fully intend to wear it at the launch event for this book. Baking. AYR 10am-5pm. Cl Sun.
1854
MAP 2
B1

GALLERY HEINZEL, ABERDEEN: 21 Spa St. Major commercial gallery in city with credibility. A showcase for NE arts with changing exhibs. Frequent attendees of the Glasgow Art Fair Mon-Sat 10-5.30pm.
1855
MAP 3
B3

LOGIE STEADING nr FORRES: Estate courtyard in beautiful countryside 10km S of Forres though not so obvious to find. Nr pleasant woodland walk and picnic spot. For directions, see 1618/WOODLAND WALKS. Well chosen art and ceramics from Highland artists and workshops. Tearoom. Certainly one of the best small galleries in N Scotland and well worth detour from the coast or the A9. May-Oct 11am-5pm (Sat/Sun 12-5pm).
1856
MAP 3
A2

THE DEGREE SHOWS, EDINBURGH/GLASGOW ART SCHOOLS: Work from final-year students. Discover the Bellanys/Howsons of the future. 2-week exhibition after manic first night (mid June).
1857

THE GLASGOW ART FAIR: Recently established market place for contemporary art with mainly Scottish and important London ones with Scottish connections. Held in mid April in pavilions in George Square. I think it's pretty good, but then I would. 0141 552 6027 for details.
1858
MAP B
D2

GAY SCOTLAND THE BEST!
Edinburgh

Edinburgh's gay scene continues to develop though the 'pink triangle' around the Playhouse Theatre is now more of a circuit centred on Broughton St where apart from the proclaimed gay bars etc, there are now many gay-friendly places happy to cater for the 'community' and take the pink pound. As for other tourists, Edin is an easy city for the gay tourist to visit.

1859 BARS AND CLUBS

MAP A
D2 **CAFE KUDOS:** 556 4349. 22 Greenside Pl. Part of frontage of Playhouse Theatre. Civilised rather than overtly cruisy café-bar; epitomises Edin really. Now owned by a city councillor and a local radio stn DJ (where else in the UK would you get that). Contemporary, light ambience with big open windows and tables in the st in summer. Food. You don't have to get drunk. 7 days till 1am.

D2 **NEW TOWN BAR:** 538 7775. 26 Dublin St. Basement and v sub-basement bar in residential New Town. Mixed crowd. Island bar good for eyes across the rm. Downstairs - called **INTENSE** , open Thur-Sun - is , fairly intense; cruisy and gets full-on. That carpet has seen everything. 7 days till 1.30am; w/ends 2.30am.

D2 **ROUTE 66:** 557 3379. Few doors down from the Playhouse nr the next r/bout. Nothing special bar, but that's being picky. Major mid to late evening rendezvous and for those not necessarily . . . up for it. 7 days till 1am. You go there and then you go to:

D2 **CC BLOOMS:** 556 9331. Next to Playhouse. This is more like it (i.e. like every other Gay Bar UK); packed most nights upstairs and down (in the revamped disco). Last port of call for many, so gets Desperately Seeking Susan nr the dancefloor. Always queues nr the witching hour. After this there's only the park and that's dangerous, so get on with it here. 7 days till 3am.

C2 **FRENCH CONNECTION:** 225 7651. Rose St Lane N nr Castle St. Small, intimate bar out on a limb in the drinking zone. But that has its attractions. You will not come and go unnoticed. Oldies and youngies; the twain do meet. 7 days till 1am.

E2 **JOY:** Info Line 467 2551. Scotland's 'most upfront' gay club gets moved about from pillar to post, but maybe that's how it keeps fresh 'n' wet. No point in a book that lasts 2yrs saying where they are now, but look out for flyers.

1860 OTHER PLACES

D2 **BLUE MOON CAFE:** 556 2788. 36 Broughton St. Friendly and always busy neighbourhood café at the heart of quarter with all-day menu and committed agenda. Non-gay friendly. 2/3 rms with food, drink and conversation. If you are arriving in Edin and don't know anybody, come here first. Food 7 days till 11.15pm , 12.15 w/ends (183/GREAT CAFÉS).

D2 **OVER THE RAINBOW:** 478 7130. 32 Broughton St. A café-restau changing hands at time of going to press. Camp and well done decor on the Wizard of Oz theme; proper restau menu and avowedly gay (all the rest around here will merely be taking your shilling). Opening hrs may change.

E1 **NO. 18:** 553 3222. 18 Albert Pl. Sauna for gentlemen. 12-10pm. Sun 2-10pm.

1861 HOTELS

D2 **MANSFIELD HOUSE:** 556 7980. 57 Dublin St. Small New Town guesthouse and ok gay stay. Candelabra in the hall, various other camperie. Breakfast on a tray. No public rms – you'll have to leave your door open. New Town Bar (*see above*) up the st.
5RMS JAN-DEC X/X XPETS XCC XKIDS MED.INX

C2 **LINDEN HOTEL:** 557 4344. 9 Nelson St. Also in New Town. A real hotel; not exclusively gay. Thai restau (good) and bar. Prob the best for all-round facs, but not everyone here is a friend of Dorothy. 20RMS JAN-DEC T/T PETS CC KIDS INX

GARLANDS: 554 4205. 48 Pilrig St. Quiet st of many other guesthouses about 2km from scene (but nr sauna). 5RMS JAN-DEC X/X PETS XCC XKIDS CHP

Glasgow

BARS AND CLUBS

Big improvements of late, the scene developing in the Merchant City around Virginia St/Wilson St nr Bennets. In Glasgow, many bars close at midnight, but may open till 1am at w/ends.

DELMONICA'S: 552 4803. 68 Virginia St. Newly refurb stylish pub with long bar **D3** and open-plan in quiet lane in Merchant City. Food till 7pm. Pally, pre-club crowd later on. Some event nights. 7 days till midnight.

POLO LOUNGE: 553 1221. 84 Wilson St. Classiest Glas gay bar yet by same people **D3** who own Delmonica's and Caffe Latte. Comfortable and clubable by day, cruisier by night. Downstairs disco (Fri-Sun) with 3am licence; otherwise till 1am.

AUSTINS: 332 2707. 183A Hope St. Downstairs bar in busy central st out of zone. **D3** Older chaps and young friends. More mixed in daytime. 7 days till 1am.

WATERLOO BAR: 221 7539. 306 Argyle St. Old-established bar and clientele. Not **D3** really for trendy young things. You might not fancy anybody but they're a friendly down to earth old bunch. 7 days till midnight.

SQUIRE'S LOUNGE: 221 9184. 106 W Campbell St. Below st level; not exactly a dive **C2** bar but small and can be cruisy. This bar has an agreeable anonymity - you could be anywhere in the W. Mixed ages. Trashy music. 7 days till midnight.

SADIE FROSTS: 332 8005. 8 W George St in front of Queen St Stn and underneath **D2** Burger King. Downtown cruisy bar, well placed for the brief encounter. Gets jumpy near closing time (midnight, 7 days). **SAPPHO'S :** Glasgow's all women bar is also here. All types. Pool table (7pm-12, not Mon).

BENNETS: 552 5761. 80 Glassford St. For 20yrs the real disco. Everybody goes in **D3** the beginning – and in the end. Recent facelift, so she's looking good again. Wed-Sun 11pm-3am, Tues is 'traditionally' straight night.

OTHER PLACES

CAFFE LATTE: 553 2553. Corner of Virginia St/Wilson. Recently opened café- **D3** bistro at heart of gay st; antithesis of the cruise-bar. Laid-back atmos; snacks and food all day till midnight.

CLONE ZONE: 552 3103. As in London, shop for mags, videos and things to play with. 7 days till 6pm (Thur-Sat till 10pm, Sun till 7pm).

CENTURION SAUNA: 248 4485. 19 Dixon St above Aer Lingus. Till 10pm or later.

HOTEL

ALBION HOTEL: 339 8620. 405 N Woodside Rd off Gr Western Rd. Currently **B1** Glasgow's only prospect is gay-friendly (i.e. they advertise in Gay Times) rather than gay. It's a start. 16RMS JAN-DEC T/T PETS CC KIDS MED.INX

ABERDEEN

Gay scene in Aberdeen in disarray at time of going to press. Only one bar/club, but more due.

CLUB CASTRO: 01224 624472. Nethergate near Marks and Spencer just behind Union St. Small, friendly pub (and downstairs up-your-kilt disco at w/ends). Less sun-tanned clientele than many. And ladies who never lunch. 7 nights till 2am.

DUNDEE

DEVA'S: 01382 226840. 75 Seagate nr Cannon Cinema. Okay pub, small-city scene, but if you're in Dundee for the night, you might. 7 days till 11pm/midnight.

LIBERTY NIGHTCLUB: 01382 200660. 124 Seagate. Along from the above so follows on. Bar and dancefloor. Everybody knows everybody else, but not you. This may have its advantages. Wed-Sun till 2.30am.

HOTELS ELSEWHERE

Not many to choose from. None of these are exclusively gay, but they are more than 'friendly'.

AUCHENDEAN LODGE, DULNAIN BRIDGE: 01479 851347. A Highland retreat in an area with lots of outdoorsy things to do. Innovative cooking. (Eric and Ian well on the case xxx/HIGH HOTELS). 7RMS JAN-DEC X/T PETS CC KIDS TOS MED.INX

ARDMORY HOUSE HOTEL, ISLE OF BUTE: 01700 502346. Sounds good. Reports please.

THE MOST HAPPENING NIGHTCLUBS

Many of the best clubs come and go and there's little point in mentioning them here. Some are only on once a week with no permanent venue. Consult The List *magazine (Edin and Glas) for up-to-date info, and look for flyers.*

1868 GLASGOW

MAP B *Glas is a club city, but the dreaded curfew remains – check the following for the current 'rules'.*

D3 Clubs at **THE ARCHES: SLAM, COOL LEMON** and occasional others: 221 9736. At the Arches Theatre, Midland St (639/NIGHTLIFE), w/ends only. Glasgow's finest. Slam on Fri, others by rotation. 2/3 vaulted archways, serious sound system and v up-for-it crowd.

D3 **ARCHAOS:** 204 3189. 25 Queen St. Huge dance emporium on 3 floors incl Betty's Mayonnaise. Central dance floor has state-of-the-art lighting. Balconies upstairs for action-checking and chilling. Atmos more rarified the higher you go.

D3 **THE TUNNEL:** 204 1000. 84 Mitchell St. Once defined club culture in Glas. Still high glam quotient and designer ambience with vogue-ish crowd. W/ends (Ark and Triumph, summer 1997) and student nights. On same circuit as Liverpool's Cream, so big name DJs every month.

D2 **THE APARTMENT:** 221 7080. 23 Royal Exchange Sq. Colin and Kelly Barr's stylish drinking club kind of disco for older more discerning types. Exclusivity is part of the deal, but they have been known to let in any old footballer and hairdresser. Usually have their finger on the pulse and the rt guest lists, so whatever they're up to next is probably cool.

D2 **JET:** 337 3777. 15 Benalder St, W End. Constantly under threat from city planners who want to knock it down, it thrives on adversity and in its latest incarnation hosts a different club every night of the week. Cheaper drink.

D2 **TIN PAN ALLEY:** 248 8832. Mitchell St. Spacious clubland over 3 floors and many yrs. Good for new talent (DJs that is) on certain nights, otherwise mainstream.

C3 **THE SUB CLUB:** 248 4600. 22 Jamaica St. Long-running, but revamped and still v much a scene. Eclectic music policy. Fri/Sat (some Thurs and Suns).

C2 **REDS:** Upstairs at Nico's, 379 Sauchiehall St. Safe, studenty. Not so bad. W/ends.

C2 **THE GARAGE:** 332 1120. 490 Sauchiehall Street. The big night out for cheap drinks, chart sounds and copping off. Totally unpretentious. Live bands as advertised.

1869 EDINBURGH

MAP A *Edin club culture has improved a lot in the last 2yrs. Most clubs are still weekly or occasional events, but they tend to use the same venues. These are the ones to look out for:*

D2 **THE VENUE:** 557 3073. Calton Rd behind Waverley Stn. Long-established (in club terms) venue for clubs on w/end nights (mainly live bands during the week). Top nights - **PURE** (considered a major club night in Scotland) **TRIBAL FUNKTION, DISCO INFERNO.**

D3 **LA BELLE ANGELE:** 225 2774. Hastie's Close off Cowgate at Gilded Balloon. W/ends. Occupants vary but esp good fun are **YIP YAP, MANGA and BIG BEAT.**

CAVENDISH: 228 3252. West Tollcross, upstairs it has **THE MAMBO CLUB** Fri and Sat (on 2 floors) African/reggae/generally good vibes music for v mixed crowd - good for oldies who like to dance.

D3 **MERCADO:** 226 4224. 36-39 Market St behind Waverley Stn. Probably Edinburgh's longest-running club venue. Recent revamp and infusion of good club organisers means that it's a go-area again - try **TFIF** for fun or **BURGER QUEEN.**

D3 Two clubs that we hope hang around (but who knows): soul jazz grooves at **LIZZARD LOUNGE** in **CAFE GRAFFITI** on Sat (Mansfield Pl Church) and **CLUB LATINO** which moves around, so look for flyers.

C2 **THE DOME:** 624 8633. George St. Home to **WHY NOT?** a kind of disco-mating venue for over-25s.

GOING PLACES: Edinburgh's trail-blazing easy listening club. Long before it was hip they were playing airport and dinner-dance music here. Styly crowd of all ages. Venue changes, look for fliers or notices in Black Bo's, Blackfriars St (260/BEST FOOD).

JOY: Scotland's best gay club. Has moved around in the last year so check for fliers in the Blue Moon (1860/GAY SCOTLAND) (188/GREAT CAFÉS). *E1*

REST OF SCOTLAND
1870

CLUBS IN ABERDEEN, *see p. 115*

BATHGATE, ROOM AT THE TOP: 01506 635707. Menzies Rd, Bathgate. You can spend half an hr driving round the centre of Bathgate before you twig that the huge thing next to Safeway is a purpose-built nightclub - UK's biggest. (Cream and Ministry of Sound? We spit in your grandmother's milk.) Proprietor doesn't like the word superclub, hyperbole wouldn't do it justice. Opened May 1997, design values to turn Conran green, capacity of 2600, more dance floors, bars, nooks and (snogging) crannies than you can count. We dropped our bacon sandwich. *MAP 7 A2*

DUNDEE, MARDI GRAS: 01382 205551. S Ward St. Capacity crowd of 1,250 most w/ends. 1997 fave with Dundonians enjoying commercial sounds and good lights. Jazz bar, vodka bar, with large seating areas from where you check out who's in and what they're wearing. Security relatively low-key. They have umbrellas if it's raining when you queue. Wed-Sun 10.30pm-2.30am. *MAP 4*

INVERNESS, BLUE: Find Safeways, this relatively recent (well the other club in Inverness, Mr G's though refurb has been here for donkies, clubwise) purpose-built club is opp the supermarket and behind its pub, the Forty-Five (good unpretentious, contemporary bar). Designed by the same team who did the Tunnel (Glasgow's definitive 1980s club) this is a v good groove to find so far N of Manchester. Bars up and down. Good floor. Thur-Sun. *MAP 2 D3*

STIRLING, FUBAR: 01786 472619. Murry Place. Now long-established bar and club in downtown Stirling. Most of its moments probably passed, but mixed crowd with oldies and kids on separate floors. W/ends. *MAP 6 D3*

KIRKCALDY, JACKIE O'S : 01592 264496. On the Esplanade. Unpretentious, non-stressful *palais de danse*. Wed-Sun 9pm-2am. Still going after all these yrs (unlike Jackie). And behind it: **CAESAR'S:** 01592 201389. Second danceria on same esplanade and not much to choose, but similarly packed w/ends. Everyone seems to be wearing River Island (including me) and people sing along to the hits of the moment. Bouncers bounce. Thur-Sun till 2am. Also in Fife, nearby in **DUNFERMLINE** the nitespots are: **LIBERTY** 25 Kirkgate - the newer place to go; 2 storey dance halls, music from every damned decade. 7 days; phone for hrs 01383 621515. **LORENZO MARKS,** St Margarets St; an old fave still packs them in. *MAP 5 C4*

IRVINE, AQUARIUM: 01294 311414. 1 Beach Park, Harbourside. Thur-Sat 11pm-3am. The big discorama on the Ayrshire coast. Theme nights. *MAP 1 C6*

SALTCOATS, METROPOLIS: 01294 602213. Hamilton St in centre of small town N of Ayr, 45km from Glas. Unlikely toon for a nightspot, but clubbers have been converging here for a wee while now. Mainly kids stuff, but check for oldie sessions if you're in the area for the night (ok I know that's unlikely). *MAP 1 C3*

AYR, CLUB DE MAR: 01292 611136. 1 Arthur St. The older of the two clubs in Ayr ain't at all bad. The other **THE TEMPLE:** 01292 885717 off the main (pedestrianised) st behind Burger King run by young Jamie Sutherland whose nice dad bought him a nightclub; ain't bad either. Both are close geographically and spiritually to the High St. And musically - expect Radio One night-time stuff. Both are friendly and safe as House. Oldies will survive; Ayr is (officially) an E free zone. *MAP 1 C4*

THE MOST INTERESTING THEATRES AND CINEMAS

For EDIN, *see p. 52; and* GLASGOW, *see pp. 88-9.*

1871
MAP 1
B1
MULL LITTLE THEATRE, DERVAIG, MULL: 01688 400377. 'The smallest theatre in Britain' is still there after more than 25 years. On edge of dinky Dervaig, 10km from Tobermory. Bar and acceptable restau adj at the Druimard Country-House Hotel. Tiny auditorium, so you're almost on top of the actors. Never predictable. Its incongruity is part of its appeal. A slice of Seigfried Sassoon and a nip of Whisky Galore. Easter-Oct. Curtain up 8.30pm. Cosy seats; cosy intervals.

1872
MAP 1
E3
CUMBERNAULD THEATRE: 01236 732887. Nr old part of this new town on a rise o/look the ubiquitous dual carriageway (to Stirling). Follow signs for Cumbernauld House. Bar/café-restau and 300-seat theatre (in the round) with a mixed programme of one-nighters and short runs of mainly Scottish touring companies. Also concerts, drama workshops and kids' programmes. A community-based and vital theatre, one of the better reasons to 'relocate in Cumbernauld'.

1873
MAP 8
C3
BOWHILL LITTLE THEATRE, BOWHILL HOUSE, nr SELKIRK: 01750 20732. Tiny theatre off the courtyard below Bowhill House with intermittent mixed programme (must phone), but always delightful, esp with supper afterwards (also phone to book).

1874
MAP 4
C3
PITLOCHRY THEATRE: 01796 472680. Modern rep theatre across river from main st performing usually 6 plays on different nights of the week. With a well-chosen programme of classics and popular works, the 500-seat theatre is often full. V mixed Sunday concerts and foyer fringe events. Coffee bar open at all times. Best places to eat before or after show: **PORTNACRAIG** adj, by river (01796 472777), or excellent **EAST HAUGH HOUSE** on rd S, 2km town centre (01796 473121).

1875
MAP 2
D3
EDEN COURT THEATRE, INVERNESS: 01463 234234. An important theatre complex making a vital contribution to the cultural life of the Highlands. Diverse programme of theatre, dance, variety, all kinds of music, opera, trad – the occasional coup. Easy to book by credit card; lots do sell out. Theatre bar and the Ness over there. Cinema programme of selected art-house/first-run movies. What would Inverness watch without it? Good luck, Colin!

1876
MAP 5
D2
BYRE THEATRE, ST ANDREWS: 01334 476288. Abbey St or South St. Serious theatre in receipt of big lottery funding, so total rebuild going on in the lifetime of this book. Watch this space . . . then theirs.

1877
MAP 8
C3
THE WYND, MELROSE: 01896 823854. Hidden behind the Teddy Melrose shop (xxx/KIDS) this 80 seater regularly entertains locals and even Edin folk too. Ibsen, musicals, folk and jazz. Intimate atmos in an intimate town.

1878
MAP 1
B6
CAMPBELTOWN PICTURE HOUSE: 01586 553657. Campbeltown, Argyll. Cinema Paradiso on the Kintyre peninsula. Lovingly preserved art deco gem; a shrine to the movies. Opened 1913, closed 1983, but such was the tide of nostalgic affection that it was refurbished and reopened resplendent in 1989. Shows mainly first-run films. To see a film here and emerge onto the esplanade of Campbeltown L is to experience the lost magic of a night at the pictures.

1880
MAP 3
D3
VICTORIA CINEMA, INVERURIE: 01467 621436. Owned since the last heyday of cinema by the patently non-Mafia Donald family of Aber, the last gr picture palace in the N. Maybe one day it'll be run by H S, but for now it's bingo some nights and movie magic the others. Bar - and sweets.

1881
MAP 1
D2
THE NEW PICTURE HOUSE, ST ANDREWS: 01334 473509. On North St. 'New' means 1931 and, apart from adding another screen (the small Cinema 2), it hasn't changed much, as generations of students will remember with fondness. Mainly first-run flicks and Oct-May, there's a programme of late-night cult/art movies. You can still smoke in the rear balcony. So quaint! So refreshingly non-smokist.

MAP 9
D3
THE ROXY, KELSO: 01573 224609. Horsemarket. A cinema from my youth, still remarkably here and unchanged; still the smell of hot celluloid. Few better places to watch a first-run movie or an art flick and enjoy "real Scottish popcorn". Sun, Tues, Wed, Sat and bingo on Mon, Thur & Fri. Don't ever close y'hear.

WHERE TO FIND GOOD FOLK MUSIC

EDINBURGH *(see also 355/NIGHTLIFE and festivals see below).* 1882

Good bars to frequent, some with regular and some with occasional live music, include: MAP A

THE TRON CEILIDH HOUSE: 220 1550. Hunter Sq. One of Edinburgh's major live venues, up and downstairs. Busy, friendly, folky. **SANDY BELL'S aka THE FORREST HILL BAR:** Famous and forever. Sometimes you could look in and wonder why; other times you know you're in exactly the rt place. Music every night except Tues and Sun. **FIDDLER'S ARMS:** Grassmarket. And fiddle they do on Monday nights. Good crack and blether at all times (237/'UNSPOILT' PUBS). **WEST END HOTEL BAR:** 225 3656. Palmerston Pl. A good place to stay or just to hang out with the Highlanders. Some trad folk live at w/ends and whenever (21/INDIVIDUAL HOTELS). **BANNERMAN'S:** Cowgate. Occasional live bands through the back. Not just folk, but it has a folky atmos (248/REAL ALE; 209/SUN BREAKFAST). Finally **ROYAL OAK** Infirmary St. Late-night sing-along (293/LATE BARS).

GLASGOW *(see also 642/NIGHTLIFE).* 1883

THE CLUTHA VAULTS: 167 Stockwell St. E end nr Clyde. Gr atmos for the drink MAP B and the music. Mixed programme: readings Tues, bluegrass Sat afternoons. **HALT BAR:** Woodlands Rd. Amongst a mixed music programme, always some folk for the kind of folk who inhabit the bar (523/GREAT 'GLASGOW' PUBS). Wednesdays. **RIVERSIDE:** 0141 248 3144. Fox St off Clyde St. Fri and Sat have ceilidh dances with a proper band and the full works. Doors open 8pm, band on 9pm and often full by 10pm. Just as you imagined it. **SCOTIA BAR:** 112 Stockwell St. The folk club and writers' retreat and all things non-high cultural. Club meets Wed night and Sat afternoon. Always the 'right folk' here (519/GREAT 'GLASGOW' PUBS). **VICTORIA BAR:** Bridgegate. Near the Scotia and a similar set-up. Fri and Sat night sessions of Irish/Scottish trad music.

REST OF SCOTLAND 1884

CEILIDH PLACE, ULLAPOOL: (796/INEXP HIGHLAND HOTELS).

DEAN TAVERN, NEWTONGRANGE: Home of the estimable Nitten folk club on Thursdays.

VICTORIA INN, HADDINGTON: Haddington folk Club on Wednesdays.

THE ROAD HOUSE, DUNFERMLINE: Dunfermline Folk Club on Wednesday.

MISHNISH HOTEL, TOBERMORY, MULL: (1009/BLOODY GOOD PUBS).

PICK OF THE FOLK FESTS

GLASGOW CONCERT HALL, CELTIC CONNECTIONS: 0141 332 6633. Major jamboree every Jan. 3 weeks of concerts, ceilidhs and gatherings. Broad appeal.

EDINBURGH: 0131 554 3092. 10 days before Easter. The biggest festival.

INVERNESS: 01738 623274. Easter w/end. 01349 830388. Highland Festival 3 days, end June. 01463 715757. Summer Festival July/Aug, Balnain House.

SHETLAND: 01595 694757. Mid-April long (and they mean long) w/end.

GIRVAN: 01848 200474. Early May long w/end.

ORKNEY: 01856 851331. End of May 3 days.

ISLAY: 01496 302413. End of May over 2 weeks, till June.

ARRAN: 01770 302341. Early June 6 days.

KILLIN, nr STIRLING: 0141 887 9991. End of June. A gr newcomer 3 days.

STONEHAVEN: 0141 887 9991. Mid-July 3 days.

SKYE: 01470 582224. End July/Aug 6 days.

ISLE OF BUTE: 0141 887 9991. End July long weekend, trad.

AUCHTERMUCHTY: 01337 828732. Mid-August w/end.

TARBERT: 01880 820343. End Sept long w/end.

THE BEST OF ROCK AND POP MUSIC

1885   EDINBURGH (dial 0131)

MAP A   **INGLISTON EXHIB CENTRE and MURRAYFIELD STADIUM:** Rarely used, biggies only (U2, REM, Pope). **PLAYHOUSE THEATRE:** 557 2590. Major theatre in Scotland, most regular programme, holds 3,000. More infrequent as concert venue while they get thro the musicals (not many to go). **USHER HALL:** 228 1155. Gr auditorium, but mainly classical. **THE VENUE:** 0131 557 3073 and **LA BELLE ANGELE:** 225 2774. Main small club venues for emerging and local bands. Check the *List* for programmes. **QUEEN'S HALL:** 668 2019. Most diverse (choral, jazz, art pop). Good atmos. Used every night; your best bet if you just want to go somewhere for decent music.

1886   GLASGOW (dial 0141)

MAP B   **SCOTTISH EXHIBITION AND CONFERENCE CENTRE:** 248 3000. Scotland's major venue for arena rock'n'roll (or Pavarotti). Used occasionally. **ROYAL CONCERT HALL:** 332 6633. Full programme of mainly classical music, but also a civilised theatre for more thoughtful pop. **BARROWLANDS:** Doesn't have its own box office. Ticket info 552 4601. The world-famous ballroom; pure rock'n'roll. Must be sampled (643/NIGHTLIFE). **PAVILION THEATRE:** 332 1846. Intimate, tiered music hall with v mixed programme incl hypnotism and hip and hyped pop. **KING TUT'S WAH WAH HUT:** 221 5279. St Vincent St. City's main club venue for live bands; well established on national circuit. Check the *List*. **THE CATHOUSE:** 248 6606. 15 Union St. Club venue for contemporary rock. **THE GARAGE:** 332 1120. 490 Sauchiehall St. Largish club for emerging bands.

1887   ABERDEEN (dial 01224)

MAP 3   **ABERDEEN EXHIBITION HALL:** 824824. Similar to SECC above, but only a few major acts go this distance (tho Oasis did). **THE CAPITOL THEATRE:** 583141. Old theatre/cinema in main st. Occasional concerts. God knows I have been there. **MUSIC HALL:** 632080. Medium-range civic (sit/stand).

CEILIDHS IN THE CITY

One element of Scottish culture enjoying a revival is the ceilidh (though fashionability waning). This is not just an excuse to down large amounts of alcohol, but is a friendly get-together easy to join in. Trad dances like the Gay Gordons and eightsome reels are usually 'called' and most of them are easy to pick up. Ceilidhs in towns and villages likely to be more impromptu affairs.

1888   THE RENFREW FERRY, GLASGOW: Enter by Clyde Pl via Jamaica St Br from N of
MAP D   river or Bridge St. A real ferry moored on the Clyde – brilliant ambience for
B3   ceilidhs and gigs of all kinds. Fri 9pm-2am. Tickets at quay or in adv from Ticket Centre, Candleriggs (0141 227 5511), usually sold out by 10pm. Visitors and locals. Gr bands.

1889   THE RIVERSIDE, GLASGOW: 0141 248 3144. Fox St off Clyde St. The place that
MAP 3   started the ceilidh revival in Glas. Upstairs in quiet st, the joint is jumping. Fri/Sat
B3   from 8pm, fills up quickly. Good band. Good, mixed crowd.

1890   THE ASSEMBLY ROOMS, EDINBURGH: 0131 220 4349. George St. Municipal halls but
MAP A   grand, the venue for all kinds of culture (esp during the Festival), and though a
C2   long way from the draughty village hall kind of jig, they've been positively reeling to the sounds of the Robert Fish Band. Ceilidhs generally last Fri of the month. Watch local press, e.g. the *List* magazine for details and pay at door.

1891   WEST END HOTEL, EDINBURGH: 0131 225 3656. 35 Palmerston Pl. Edinburgh's
MAP A   Heilan' hame hotel has occasional sessions of music/singing and story-telling
A3/B3   (more like a trad ceilidh) but no dancing. This is where to come (or phone) to find out where the others are (occasional ceilidhs held in the church hall nearby).

1892   CALEDONIAN BREWERY, EDINBURGH: Contact: 01698 385251. Slateford Rd. At
MAP A   time of going to press, ceilidhs every Sat in the Festival Hall in the brewery from
A4   8pm-11.45pm. Bands vary but the couple of hundred heuchin' teuchin' punters have a good time regardless.

SECTION 12

The Islands

THE MAGICAL ISLANDS

1893
MAP 2
B3
✝ ✝ **RAASAY:** A small car ferry (car useful, but bikes best) from Sconser betwPortree and Broadford on Skye takes you to this, the best of places. The distinctive flat top of Dun Caan presides over an island whose history and natural history is Highland Scotland in microcosm. The village with MED.INX hotel and bar (and rows of mining-type cottages) is 3km from jetty. The Outdoor Centre (01478 660226) in the big hoose (once the home of the notorious Dr No who, like others before him, allowed Raasay to go to rack and ruin) has courses galore. They'll put you up if they've got rm (mostly bunkrooms). The views from the lawn, or the viewpoint above the house, or better still from Dun Caan with the Cuillins on one side and Torridon on the other, are *sans pareil* (1925/ISLAND WALKS). There's a ruined castle, a secret rhododendron-lined loch for swimming, seals, otters and eagles. Much to explore. Go quietly here. *Calmac ferry from Sconser, 4 or 5 times a day, not Sun. Last return 5.35pm (later in summer).*

1894
MAP 1
B2
✝ ✝ **JURA:** Small regular car ferry from Pt Askaig on Islay takes you into adifferent world. Jura is remote, scarcely populated and has an ineffable grandeur indifferent to the demands of tourism. Ideal for wild camping, alternatively the serviceable hotel and pub (1914/ISLAND HOTELS) in the only village (Craighouse) 15km from ferry at Feolin. Walking guides available at hotel and essential esp for the Paps, the hills that maintain such a powerful hold over the island. Easiest climb is from Three Arch Br; allow 6hrs. In May they run up all of them and back to the distillery in 3hrs. Jura House's walled grd is a hidden jewel set above the S coastline; myriad wildflowers and Australasian trees with scenic walks to the shore. The Corryvreckan whirlpool (1932/ISLAND WALKS) is another lure, but you may need a lift in a 4 wheel drive to get close enough to walk, and its impressiveness depends upon the strength of the tides. Orwell's house (Barnhill; where he wrote *1984*) is not open, but there are many fascinating side tracks: the wild west coast; around L Tarbert; and the long littoral betw Craighouse and Lagg. (Also 1256/BEACHES; 1513/GRAVEYARDS.) With one rd, no st lamps and over 2,000 deer the sound of silence is everything (you came for). *Western Ferries* (01496 840681) *regular 7 days, 5min service from Pt Askaig.*

1895
MAP 1
A1
✝ ✝ **IONA:** Needs little commendation from little me; and many people think there are too many visitors there already. Packed with daytrippers – not so much a pilgrimage, more an invasion – but Iona still enchants, esp if you can get away to the Bay at the Back of the Ocean (1236/BEACHES) from the hill above the Abbey. Or stay: Argyll Hotel best (01681 700334) or B&B. Abbey shop isn't bad (1748/CRAFT SHOPS). Everything about Iona is benign; even the sun shines here when it's raining on Mull. Wonder why that is. *Reg 5min Calmac service from Fionnphort till 6 or 7pm (earlier in winter).*

1896
MAP 2
B4
✝ ✝ **EIGG:** After changing hands, much to-do and *cause célèbre*, the islanders seized the time and Eigg is finally theirs; and of course, ours. A wildlife haven for birds and sealife; otters, eagles and seal colonies. Scot Wildlife Trust warden does weekly walks around the island. July is the 'Month of Music' with lots of ceilidhs. Small tearoom at pier. Bicycle hire 01687 482438. 2 croft houses at Cleadale near Laig bay and the Singing Sands beach; contact Sue Kirk 01687 482405 (knows loads about all aspects of island). She also offers full board accom and caters for vegn and other diets. 2,000 sheep on island. *CalMac (from Mallaig) 01687 462403 or (better, from Arisaig) Arisaig Marine 01687 450224 every day in summer. No car ferry; but motorbikes poss. Day trips to Rum and Muck.*

1897
MAP 2
B4
✝ ✝ **RUM:** The large island in the group S of Skye, off the coast at Mallaig. The Calmac ferry plies betw Canna, Eigg, Muck and Rum but not too conveniently and it's not easy to island-hop and make a decent visit. Rum is the most wild and dramatic. It has an extraordinary time-warp mansion-house in Kinloch Castle which lets out 3 of its incredible rms to guests, but is mainly a museum (guided tours tie in with boat trips), and below stairs a hostel contrasts to the antique opulence above. There is also a bistro, but it must be pre-booked (no lunch). Details: 1915/ISLAND HOTELS. Rum is run by Scottish Natural Heritage and there are fine trails, climbs, bird-watching spots. Coffee-shop at the Community Hall (open for day-trippers). 2 simple walks are marked for the 3hr visitors, but the island reveals its mysteries more slowly. The doric temple mausoleum to George Bullough, the industrialist whose Highland fantasy the castle was, is a 12km walk across the island to Harris Bay. And sighting the sea eagles may be one of the best things that ever happens to you. *Calmac ferry from*

Mallaig via Eigg (3.5hrs) or Canna at an ungodly hr. Also from Arisaig (Murdo Grant 01687 450224) Tues/Thur in summer (3hrs ashore). The civilised journey.

GIGHA: Romantic small island off Kintyre coast; with classic views of its island neighbours. Easy access to mainland (20min ferry trip) contributes to an island atmos that lacks any feeling of isolation. The island remains a whole estate; with grds open at the main house (1704/GARDENS) and the hotel run by the family (1912/ISLAND HOTELS) providing comfortable surroundings, good whisky, Gigha cheeses and seafood. The locals are relaxed (now) and friendly; with bike hire, B&B (CHP) and good home-cooking available courtesy of the estimable McSporran family at the post office on the ferry rd (01583 505251). Best Walk: Left after golf course (9 hole), through gate and follow track (signed Ardailly) past Mill L to Mill and shore; gr views to Jura. (1-B-2) See: Double Beach, where the Queen once swam off the Royal Yacht; two crescents of sand on either side of the N end of the isthmus of Eilean Garbh (seen from rd but path poorly marked). *Calmac ferry from Tayinloan on A83, 27km S of Tarbert (Glas 165km). One an hour in summer, fewer in winter. Cars exp and unnecessary.*

1898
MAP 1
B3

✝ **ULVA:** Off W coast of Mull. A boat leaves Ulva Ferry on the B8073 26km S of Dervaig. Idyllic wee island with 5 well-marked walks incl to the curious basalt columns similar to Staffa, or by causeway to the smaller island of Gometra; plan routes at boathouse 'interpretive centre' and tearoom (with Ulva oysters). No accom. A charming Telford church has services 4 times a yr. Ulva is a perfect day away from the rat race of downtown Mull. *Continuous 5min service during day in summer. Ferryman:* 01688 500226.

1899
MAP 1
A1

✝ **ERISKAY:** Made famous by the sinking nearby of the SS *Politician* in 1941 and the salvaging of its cargo of whisky, immortalised by Compton Mackenzie in *Whisky Galore*, this Hebridean gem has all the 'idyllic island' ingredients: perfect beaches (1543/MARY, CHARLIE AND BOB), a hill to climb, a pub (called the Politician and telling the story round its walls; it sells decent pub food all day in summer), and a small, frequent ferry. There's only limited B & B and no hotel, but camping is ok if you're discreet. Eriskay and Barra together – the pure island experience. (Also 1500/CHURCHES *and see* THE WESTERN ISLES *p.252). Car ferry* (01878 720261) *from Ludaig, S Uist (10km S Lochboisdale)5 per day in summer (3 in winter). Passenger boat* (01878 720238) *twice per day, acc to tides, also serves Barra.*

1900
MAP 2
A4

MINGULAY : Deserted mystical island nr the southern tip of the Outer Hebrides, the subject of one of the definitive island books, *The Road to Mingulay*. Now easily reached in summer by daily trip from Castlebay, Barra with 2hr journey and 3hrs ashore (enquire at TO or Castlebay Hotel, the boat operators 01871 810223). Last inhabitants left 1912. Ruined village has the poignant air of St Kilda; similar spectacular cliffs on W side with fantastic rock formations, stacks and a huge natural arch - best viewed from boat. Only birds and sheep remain here.

1901
MAP 2
A4

✝ **COLONSAY:** Newly accessible to daytrippers (with the ferry round trip); this island haven of wildlife, flowers and beaches (1247/BEACHES) deserves more than a few hrs exploration. V congenial hotel and pub (1911/ISLAND HOTELS), with self-catering units nearby. Some holiday cottages, but camping discouraged. Interesting coffee/craft/bookshop adj to hotel. A wild 18-hole golf course - its £5 membership is cheap if you stay the year. Semi-botanical grds adj to Colonsay House and fine walks, esp to Oronsay (1928/ISLAND WALKS). Lucy McNeill's home cooking and painting (incl t-shirts) activities available. at 'The Barn' (01951 20034). *Calmac from Oban (or Islay) Mon, Wed, Fri. Crossing takes just over 2hrs.*

1902
MAP 1
A2

LISMORE: Sail from Oban (car ferry) or better from Pt Appin 5km off main A828, the Oban-Ft William rd, 32km N Oban and where there's an excellent seafood bar/restau/hotel (1082/SEAFOOD RESTAUS), to sit and wait. A rd goes down the centre of the island, but there are many hill and coastal walks and even the nr end round Pt Ramsay feels away from it all. History, natural history and air. Bike hire on island from Mary McDougal 01631 760213 who will deliver to ferry. Tearoom 3km S of ferry, a pleasant stroll. *Calmac service from Oban, 4 or 5 times a day (not Sun). From Pt Appin (32km N of Oban) several per day. 5mins. Last back 8.15pm (6.15pm winter).*

1903
MAP 1
B1

CALMAC: 0990 650000

THE BEST ISLAND HOTELS

1904
MAP 2
A4

✠ **CASTLEBAY HOTEL, BARRA:** 01871 810223. Prominent position o/look bay and ferry dock. You see where you're staying long before you arrive. Exceptionally good value hotel at the centre of Barra life with nice owners who are always there. They run the boats to Eriskay and Mingulay, so they can sort out your days out. Good restau and bar meals (1936/WESTERN ISLES). Adj bar one of the best bars for crack and car culture in Scotland and with more than a dash of the Irish (1011/BLOODY GOOD PUBS).

12RMS JAN-DEC T/T PETS CC KIDS INX

1905
MAP 2
B4

✠ **EILEAN IARMAIN, SKYE:** 01471 833332. Isleornsay, Sleat. 60km S of Portree. Tucked into the bay this Gaelic inn with its gr pub and good food provides famously comfortable base in S of the island. A Skye must.

12RMS JAN-DEC T/T PETS CC KIDS TOS MED.INX

1906
MAP 2
B2

✠ **ARDVOURLIE CASTLE, HARRIS:** 01859 502307. Just off main rd 45mins S Stornaway (14km N Tarbert). Not so much a castle, but a charming Victorian lodge meticulously restored by Derek Martin, a former professor at Imperial College and his sister Pamela. Huge bathrooms. Dinner by gaslight. Derek is an excellent chef. Everything home-made. Gradually developing grds down to loch. They've planted 7,000 trees. Reporting people and places like this gives the task of this book both a purpose and a pleasure.

4RMS APR-OCT X/X PETS XCC KIDS TOS MED.EX

1907
MAP 2
B2

✠ **SCARISTA HOUSE, SOUTH HARRIS:** 01859 550238. 21km Tarbert, 78km Stornoway. On the W coast famous for its beaches and o/look one of the best (1254/BEACHES). Self-catering rms in separate block, but fixed menu meals in dining room o/look sea are excellent. No TVs, phones, but many books. The golf course over the rd is exquisite. This is the real peace and quiet.

5RMS MAY-SEPT X/X PETS OC KIDS TOS EXP

1908
MAP 1
B1

✠ **WESTERN ISLES HOTEL, TOBERMORY, MULL:** 01688 302012. Victorian edifice more reminiscent of a stn hotel in town – till you see the view from your bed-rm. Great atmos, individual rms and lounges. Refurb conservatory also looks over the harbour and bay. Choice of dining incl eastern variations (Spices Bistro). This hotel is the epitome of grand island hospitality.

26RMS JAN-DEC T/T PETS CC KIDS TOS MED.EXP

1909
MAP 1
C4

✠ **KILMICHAEL, BRODICK, ARRAN:** 01770 302219. On main rd to castle/Corrie, take left at bend by golf course and you're in the country. 3km down track is this delightful small country-house hotel with v individual rms and many ornaments. Best menu around; waiters wear white gloves which is weird. Precious perhaps, but nice.

6RMS JAN-DEC T/T PETS CC KIDS TOS MED.EX

1910
MAP 2
B2

BAILE-NA-CILLE, TIMSGARRY, UIG, LEWIS: 01851 672242. 58km W of Stornoway via Garynahine and Leurbost. A far-away and much-loved refuge which takes you in and restores the battered spirit. O/look sea. Easy-going; you're one of the family and they welcome yours (923/KIDS). Couldn't visit this time round, but things don't change much. No smk.

9RMS MAR-OCT X/X PETS CC KIDS MED.INX

1911
MAP 1
A2

ISLE OF COLONSAY HOTEL: 01951 200316. 400m from ferry (and they will collect you) a convivial, comfortable island spot. If you sit in the bar for long enough you'll meet all the islanders. Adj 'Virago' coffee/craft shop sells and publishes books! Picnic boat trips to seal colony or wildflower places are among many activities arranged. See 1902/MAGICAL ISLANDS.

11RMS MAR-OCT X/X PETS CC KIDS MED.EX

1912
MAP 1
B3

THE GIGHA HOTEL, ISLE OF GIGHA: 01583 505254. A short walk from the ferry (or they will collect you) on an island perfectly proportioned for a short visit; easy walking and cycling. New resident's lounge peaceful with dreamy views to Kintyre. Good menu with local produce in bar or dining-rm. Island life without the remoteness.

13RMS APR-OCT T/T PETS CC KIDS TOS MED.EX

1913
MAP 2
B3

VIEWFIELD HOUSE, PORTREE, SKYE: 01478 612217. One of the first hotels you come to in Portree on the rd from S (driveway opp gas stn) and you need look no further. Individual, grand but comfortable, full of antiques and *objets d'art,* though not at all stuffy; this is also one of the best-value hotels on the island. Log fires, communal dinner; you have the run of a remarkable country house.

11RMS APR-OCT X/X PETS CC KIDS MED.EX

1914 **JURA HOTEL:** 01496 820243. Craighouse, 15km from Islay ferry at Feolin.

Serviceable, basic hotel o/look Small Isles Bay; will oblige with all walking/exploring requirements. Pub is social hub of island. Rms at front may be small, but have the views. 18RMS JAN-DEC X/X PETS CC KIDS INX

MAP 1 B3

KINLOCH CASTLE, RUM: 01687 462037. The fantastic OTT edifice of a Victorian entrepreneur George Bullough now mainly a museum, but 3 opulent rms are available. The bathrooms are from another world. Servant quarters have hostel accom. Bistro dining by arrangement. Island has superb wildlife. Run by Scottish Natural Heritage. 9RMS + HOSTEL MAR-OCT X/X X/PETS XCC XKIDS EXP/CHP

1915 MAP 2 B4

PORT CHARLOTTE HOTEL, ISLAY: 01496 850360. Recently refurb and vastly improved hotel in one of the nicest island villages on Islay which is full of good things not just whisky (1934/ISLAY; 1184/WHISKY). Tasteful rms most o/look bay (and conservatory) and good dining using local produce. 10RMS JAN-DEC T/X PETS CC MEDINX

1916 MAP 1 A3

ISLE OF BARRA HOTEL, BARRA: 01871 810383. The other hotel in Barra once owned by George Macleod who has the Castlebay. Euroblock exterior, but comfortable inside with gr setting and rms o/look fab Tangasdale Beach. Nr Seal Bay (1258/BEACHES) and other quiet places. Bar the locals like. 3km from town (and bike hire, 1936/WESTERN ISLES). 38RMS MAR-SEPT X/T PETS CC KIDS MED.INXP

1917 MAP 2 A4

FLODIGARRY, SKYE: 01470 552203. Staffin, 32km N of Portree. A romantic country house o/look the sea, with Flora Mac's cottage in the grounds. Good food, gr crack in the bar; you'll be reeling. Report: 9917/COUNTRY-HOUSE HOTELS. 19RMS JAN-DEC X/X PETS CC KIDS TOS EXP

1918 MAP 2 B3

THE BEST RESTAURANTS IN THE ISLANDS

✝ **KINLOCH LODGE, SKYE:** 01471 833333. In S on Sleat Peninsula, 55km S of Portree signed off the 'main' Sleat rd, along a long characterful track. Lord and Lady MacDonald's family home/hotel offers a taste of the high life without hauteur; a setting and setup especially appreciated by Americans and other visitors. Lady Claire's stints at the stoves are renowned, as are the cookery books that result. Dinner almost a theatrical event, (the dining-rm: lined with oils, furnished with antiques, glinting with silver). Fixed menu. The dresser groans (with perfect cheeses) as do waist bands. But you simply must leave rm for the puds. EXP

1919 MAP 2 C4

✝ **THE THREE CHIMNEYS, SKYE:** 01470 511258. Colbost. 7km W Dunvegan on B884 to Glendale. Shirley and Eddie Spear consistently win every award going; so easy to see why. Their truly authentic island restau in a converted cottage is a peaceful culinary retreat. Food is prepared using local ingredients; from the creel-caught seafood to the Highland meat, veg and dairy produce. Whether for light lunch or memorable dinner, the standard and attentiveness is equally good. Home-baked breads are as good bread gets and cheeses exemplary Gr wine list. We think Eddie and Shirley are brill. Apr-Nov. Lunch, afternoon tea, dinner LO 9pm. Cl Sun. EXP

1920 MAP 2 B3

HARLOSH HOUSE, SKYE: 01470 521367. Nr Dunvegan (6km S signed off A863). O/look the wide sweep of L Bracadale and those Cuillins. Peter and Lindsey Elford have built a big reputation for their evening meals (they don't do lunch); awarded 2 AA rosettes for no-nonsense menu; emphasis on local seafood. MED

1921 MAP 2 B3

KILMICHAEL HOTEL, ARRAN: 01770 302219. 3km from seafront rd in Brodick, this is the place to go for dinner. Report: 1993/ARRAN. MED

1922 MAP 1

CASTLEBAY HOTEL, CASTLEBAY: 01871 810223. V decent plain cooking in informal dining-rm or bar o/look castle and bay. Scores mainly when fresh from the bay (lobster) or off the beach (cockles in garlic butter), but their sticky toffee pudding is exactly as it ought to be. Inexpensive wines. MED

1923 MAP 2 A4

CALGARY FARMHOUSE AND DOVECOTE RESTAU, MULL: 016884 400256. 7km from Dervaig on B8073 nr Mull's famous beach. Roadside farm setting with inexp light, piney bedrms and a bistro/wine bar restau using local produce. Relaxed, cosmo atmos. Patron also makes grd furniture! Gallery/coffee shop in summer. A quiet spot over the hill from busy wee Tobermory. INX

1924 MAP 1 B2

LOCHBAY INN, SKYE: 01470 592235. 14km N Dunvegan (1935/SKYE). INX

CREELERS, ARRAN: 01770 302810. Edge of Brodick (1933/ARRAN).   MED

BUSTA HOUSE, SHETLAND: 01806 522506. 35km N of Lerwick (1939/SHETLAND).
MED

FANTASTIC WALKS IN THE ISLANDS

For walk codes, see p. 10.

1925 **DUN CAAN, RAASAY:** Probably my favourite island walk, left out last time because
MAP 2 we don't want all you lot up there, but hey! (1322/VIEWS). Take ferry
B1 (1893/MAGICAL ISLANDS), ask for route from Inverarish. Go via old iron mine;
looks steep when you get over the ridge, but it's a dawdle. And amazing.
10KM   XCIRC   XBIKE   2-B-2

1926 **THE LOST GLEN, HARRIS:** Take B887 W from Tarbert almost to the end (where at
MAP 2 Hushinish there's a good beach,maybe a sunset), but go rt before the Big House
B2 (signed Chliostair Power Stn). Park here or further in and walk up to dam (3km
from rd). Take rt track round reservoir and the left around the upper loch. Over
the brim you arrive in a wide, wild glen; an overhang 2km ahead is said to have
the steepest angle in Europe. Go quietly; if you don't see deer and eagles here,
you're making too much noise on the gneiss.   12KM RET   XCIRC   XBIKE   2-B-2

1927 **CARSAIG, MULL:** In S of island, 7km from A849 Fionnphort-Craignure rd nr
MAP 1 Pennyghael. 2 walks start at pier: going left towards Lochbuie for a spectacular
B1 coastal/woodland walk past Adnunan Stack (7km); or rt towards the imposing
headland where, under the cliffs, the Nuns' Cave was a shelter for nuns evicted from
Iona during the Reformation. Nearby is a quarry whose stone was used to build
Iona Abbey and much further on (9km Carsaig), at Malcolm's Pt, the extraordinary
Carsaig Arches carved by wind and sea.   15/20KM   XCIRC   XBIKE   2-B-2

1928 **COLONSAY:** (1902/MAGICAL ISLANDS). From hotel or the quay, walk to Colonsay
MAP 1 House and its lush, overgrown intermingling of native plants and exotics (8km
A2 round trip); or to the priory on Oronsay, the smaller island. 6km to 'the Strand'
(you might get a lift with the postman) then cross at low tide, with enough time
(at least 2hrs) to walk to the ruins. Allow longer if you want to climb the easy
peak of Ben Oronsay. Tide tables at shop or hotel.   12+6KM   XCIRC   BIKE   1-A-2

1929 **THE OLD MAN OF STORR, SKYE:** The enigmatic basalt finger visible from the
MAP 2 Portree-Staffin rd (A855). Start from car park on left, 12km from Portree. There's
B3 a well-defined path through or around the clump of woodland towards the cliffs
and a steep climb up the grassy slope to the pinnacle which towers 165ft tall. Gr
views over Raasay to the mainland. Lots of space and rabbits and birds who make
the most of it.   5KM   XCIRC   XBIKE   2-B-2

1930 **THE QUIRANG, SKYE:** *See* 1320/VIEWS for directions to start pt. The strange
MAP 2 formations have names (e.g. the Table, the Needle, the Prison) and it's possible to
B3 walk round all of them. Start of the path from the car park is easy. At the first
saddle, take the second scree slope to the Table, rather than the first. When you
get to the Needle, the path to the rt betw two giant pinnacles is the easiest of the
3 options. From the top you can see the Hebrides. This place is supernatural;
whole parties of school girls could disappear here. So might you if you're not
careful.   6KM   XCIRC   XBIKE   2-B-2

1931 **HOY, ORKNEY:** There are innumerable walks on the scattered Orkney Islands and
MAP 2 on Hoy itself; on a good day you can get round the north part of the island and
see some of the most dramatic coastal scenery anywhere. A passenger ferry leaves
Stromness 2 or 3 times a day and takes 30mins. Make tracks N or S from jnct nr
pier and use free Hoy brochure from TO so as not to miss the landmarks, the bird
sanctuaries and the Old Man himself.   20/25KM   CIRC   MTBIKE   2-B-2

1932 **CORRYVRECKAN, JURA:** The whirlpool in the Gulf of Corryvreckan is notorious
MAP 1 and classified by the Royal Navy as unnavigable. Betw Jura and Scarba; to see it
B2 go to far N of Jura. From end of the rd at Ardlussa (25km Craighouse, the
village), there's a rough track to Lealt then a walk (a local may drive you) of 12km
to Kinuachdrach, then a further walk of 3km. Phenomenon best seen at certain
states of tide. Consult hotel (1914/ISLAND HOTELS) and get the walk guide.
(1894/MAGICAL ISLANDS). Alternative trip by boat; Craobh Haven boats (01852
500664).   6/24KM   XCIRC   XBIKE   2-C-2

THE BEST OF ARRAN

FERRY: Ardrossan-Brodick, 55mins. 6 per day Mon-Sat, 4 on Sun. Ardrossan-Glas, train or rd via A77/A71 1.5hr. Claonaig-Lochranza, 30mins. 10 per day (summer only). *The best way to see Arran is on a bike. See foot of page.*

WHERE TO STAY

KILMICHAEL HOUSE, Brodick: 01770 302219. 3km from the main rd through town down a lane in real country. Attention to detail and guests. Refined, some may feel, precious atmos. All rms v individual. *The* place to eat on Arran, but book (1909/ISLAND HOTELS).
6RMS   JAN-DEC   T/T   XPETS   CC   KIDS   TOS   MED.EX

AUCHRANNIE HOUSE, Brodick: 01770 302234. Old house enlarged but not altogether enhanced by mod cons. Some rms do look into 'the country'. Good pool, gym. Arran's up-market hotel; conservatory restau and busy with bar meals. Time-share city in grounds. 28RMS   JAN-DEC   T/T   XPETS   CC   KIDS   TOS MED.EX

THE LAGG HOTEL, Kilmory: 01770 870255. Far S coaching inn with terraced grds on river. Small renovated rms.
15RMS   JAN-DEC   T/X   PETS   CC   KIDS   MED.EX

ROSABURN LODGE, Brodick: 01770 302383. 2km Brodick, rd to Corrie and Castle. Welcoming family house. Book!
3RMS   JAN-DEC   X/T   PETS   XCC   KIDS   CHP

CORRIE HOTEL: 01770 810273. Cheap, cheerful sea- and roadside hotel in cosy Corrie. Good crack in bar. Seaview best.
16RMS   JAN-DEC   X/X   CC   PETS   KIDS   CHP

S.Y. HOSTELS: at Lochranza (01770 830631) and Whiting Bay (01770 700339). Both busy Grade 2s in picturesque areas (Mar-Oct), 25 and 15km from Brodick.

CAMPING AND CARAVAN PARKS: at Glen Rosa (302380) 4km Brodick; Lamlash (01770 600251), Lochranza (01770 830273). And Glen Rosa has idyllic river side camping.

WHERE TO EAT

CREELERS, Brodick: 01770 302810. Widely commended seafood restau 2km from Brodick on castle/corrie rd. Cheerful, consistently good. They catch and smoke their own. Apr-Oct, lunch and 7-10pm. (102/SEAFOOD RESTAUS.)   MED

CARRAIG MHOR, Lamlash: 01770 600453. On front, a proper restau amongst the usual seaside fodder, and a real chef (Peter Albrich). Book. Seafood esp. Dinner only, 7-9pm.   MED

BURLINGTON HOTEL, WHITING BAY: 01770 700255. The local choice; bistro (cl Sun) and dining-rm with chef Robin Gray ex-Creelers.   INX

HAROLD'S: 01770 830264. At the Distillery Visitor Centre, Lochranza. Good light menu in light even clinical rm with running water accompaniment. LO 9pm. INX

BRODICK BAR: Best pub food in Brodick? No booking. Cl Sun.   CHP

WHAT TO SEE

BRODICK CASTLE: 5km walk or cycle from Brodick. Impressive museum and grds. Tearoom. Flagship NTS property. (1414/CASTLES.)   NT

GOAT FELL: 6km/5hr gr hill walk starting from the car park at Cladach nr Castle and Brodick or sea start at Corrie. Free route leaflet at TO. (1569/HILLS.)   2-A-2

GLENASHDALE FALLS: 4km, but 2hr forest walk from Glenashdale Br at Whiting Bay. Steady, easy climb, silvan setting. (1279/WATERFALLS.)   I-B-1

CORRIE: The best village 9km N Brodick. Go by bike. Good pub. (1246/COSTAL VILLAGES.)

MACHRIE MOOR STANDING STONES: Off main coast rd 7km N of Blackwater Foot. Various assemblies of Stones, all part of an ancient landscape. We lay down there.

GLEN ROSA, GLEN SANNOX: Fine glens – Rosa nr Brodick, Sannox 11km N. I-B-2

WHAT TO DO

GOLF: Lots of it. Brodick (01770 302513); Lochranza (01770 830273); Lamlash (01770 600296); Whiting Bay (01770 700487). Corrie and Machrie (9 holes).
TENNIS/ SWIM: Enquiries TO. **CYCLE HIRE:** Brodick 3 places along front, but esp Brodick Cycles (302460); also Whiting Bay (700382). 3-speed or mountain bikes.

TOURIST INFO: 01770 302140 **CALMAC:** 0990 650000

THE BEST OF ISLAY AND JURA

FERRY: Kennacraig-Pt Askaig: 2hrs, Kennacraig-Pt Ellen: over 2hrs. Pt Askaig-Feolin, Jura: 5mins, frequent daily Western Ferries 01496 840681.

BY AIR: from Glas to Pt Ellen Airport in S of island. BA 0345 222111.

WHERE TO STAY

PORT CHARLOTTE HOTEL, PORT CHARLOTTE: 01496 850360. Restored Victorian inn and gdns on seafront of conservation village. Restful place, restful views. Good bistro style menu, the best around.   10RMS JAN-DEC T/X PETS CC KIDS MED.EX

HARBOUR INN, BOWMORE: 01496 810330. Recently refurb to highish standard. Lovely conservatory with bay views and gr food by proprietor chef Scott Chance. Lunch and 7-9pm; must book.   4RMS JAN-DEC T/T PETS CC KIDS MED.INX

KILMENY FARMHOUSE, nr BALLYGRANT: 01496 840668. De luxe home from home; antique furniture, hill views. House party atmos: scones and pancakes on arrival, sherry before dinner (shared table). 3RMS JAN-DEC X/X XPETS CC KIDS TOS MED.INX

THE MACHRIE, Port Ellen: 01496 302310. 7km N on A846. Ongoing refurb by new owners. Restau and bar meals in clubhouse atmos. Gr beach and golf.
27RMS JAN-DEC X/T PETS CC KIDS MED.INX

BRIDGEND HOTEL, Bridgend: 01496 810212. On roadside betw Bowmore and Pt Charlotte. Some rms small. Good lounge bar. 10RMS JAN-DEC T/T PETS CC KIDS MED.EX

LOCHSIDE HOTEL, Bowmore: 01496 810244. Probably best selection of Islay malts in the world; Alistair Birse delights in them and his 'whisky weekends'.   MED.INX

JURA HOTEL, Craighouse: 01496 820243. The hotel for the island. Situated in front of the distillery by the bay. Front rms best. 18RMS JAN-DEC X/X PETS CC KIDS INX

CAMPING, CARAVAN SITE, HOSTEL at Kintra Farm. 01496 302051. Off main rd to Pt Ellen; take Oa rd, follow Kintra signs 7km. July-August B&B in farmhouse. Grassy strand, coastal walks. **ISLAY YOUTH HOSTEL** Pt Charlotte 01496 850385.

WHERE TO EAT

HARBOUR INN, BOWMORE and **PORT CHARLOTTE HOTEL:** see above.

KILCHOMAN HOUSE: 01496 850382. 20mins Bruichladdich off A847 towards Machir and behind church. Local produce; v personal. Must book.   MED

CROFT KITCHEN: Pt Charlotte. 01496 850230.   Joy and Douglas Law have combined this coffee (latte, macchiato) and gift shop by day, with restau by night (BYOB, but licence 1998). March-October 10am-8.30pm. Book in season.   INX

THE OLD GRANARY: Kintra Farm (as Camping, above). Good basic menu in 'barn' setting. Walk on beach after. May-Sept 5.30-11pm, July-August noon-11pm. CHP

BALLYGRANT INN: 01496 840277. S of Pt Askaig. Pub grub, curry a speciality. INX

WHAT TO SEE

ISLAY: THE DISTILLERIES esp Laphroaig and Lagavulin (classic settings) by Pt Ellen; tours by appointment. Bowmore has regular glossy tour (1184/WHISKY); **MUSEUM OF ISLAY, THE CREAMERY, WILDLIFE INFO AND FIELD CENTRE** (1404/WILDLIFE): all at Pt Charlotte; **AMERICAN MONUMENT** (1478/MONUMENTS); **OA** and **LOCH GRUINART** (1388/BIRDS); **PORT CHARLOTTE** (1238/COASTAL VILLAGES); **KINTRA** (1635/COASTAL WALKS); **FIN-LAGGAN:** The romantic, sparse ruin on 'island' in L Finlaggan: last home of the Lords of the Isles. Off A846 5km S of Pt Askaig. Cross the fen by br or boat.

JURA: (1894/MAGICAL ISLANDS); **THE PAPS OF JURA; CORRYVRECKAN, BARNHILL** (1932/ ISLAND WALKS); **KILLCHIANAIG, KEILS** (1513/GRAVEYARDS); **LOWLANDMAN'S BAY** (1256/BEACHES); **JURA HOUSE WALLED GARDEN**.

WHAT TO DO

GOLF at Machrie (1666/GOLF IN GREAT PLACES); **PONY-TREKKING** at Rockside Farm (01496 850231), Ballyvicar (01496 302251); **SWIMMING** at Bowmore (01496 810767); **BIKE HIRE:** Polly Taylor (01496 850488), Brian Palmer (01496 810653); **MARINE CHARTERS:** 01496 850436.

TOURIST INFO: 01496 810254. **CALMAC:** 0990 650000.

THE BRIDGE: the hump (which is all it has given to a lot of the locals); unromantic but convenient; from Kyle. **THE FERRIES:** Mallaig-Armadale, 30mins. Tarbert (Harris)-Uig, 1hr 45mins (Calmac, as Mallaig). **THE BEST WAY TO SKYE** is Glenelg-Kylerhea, 10mins. Continuous Apr-Oct (not Suns in April) 01599 511302.

WHERE TO STAY
(*See also* ISLAND HOTELS, *p. 246*).

EILEAN IARMAIN: 01471 833332. 15km S of Broadford on A851. V Gaelic inn on bay with dreamy views, good food and gr pub (1905/ISLAND HOTELS).
12RMS JAN-DEC T/X PETS CC KIDS MED.INX

FLODIGARRY: 01470 552203. 30km N Portree on A855. Far-flung N of the island; the views exceptional. Relaxed country-house ambience; local liveliness in the bar. (917/COUNTRY-HOUSE HOTELS.)
19RMS JAN-DEC X/X PETS CC KIDS TOS EXP

VIEWFIELD HOUSE, PORTREE: 01478 612217. One of the oldest island houses; it's been in the MacDonald family over 200yrs. Unique and antique atmos. (1913/ISLAND HOTELS.)
11RMS APR-OCT X/X PETS CC KIDS MED.EX

ROSEDALE, PORTREE: 01478 613131. Snug harbour location; some rms small but well appointed and central.
23RMS MAY-SEPT T/T PETS CC KIDS MED.EX

SKEABOST: 01470 532202. 11km W of Portree on A850. Tranquil country house in lovely grds with 9-hole golf and salmon fishing on R Snizort. Chef Angus McNab continues to produce gr food.
26RMS MAR-DEC T/T PETS CC KIDS TOS MED.EX

UIG HOTEL, UIG: 01470 542205. N of island nr ferry to Hebrides; on hill side with sweeping views and a friendly welcome. 17RMS APR-OCT T/T PETS CC KIDS MED.EX

DUNTULM CASTLE HOTEL, TROTTERNISH: 01470 552213. Adj Flodigarry (see above) and same owners. O/look Tulm island and Outer Hebrides this is an idyllic place at a real good price.
29RMS APR-OCT X/T PETS CC KIDS CHP

TALISKER HOUSE, TALISKER: 01478 640245. Not really a hotel and they'll perhaps not welcome this inclusion, but too good to leave out. Situated nr Talisker bay, this lovely family home is a retreat from Skye tourism. Good hill walking and fishing in nearby lochs.
3RMS MAR-NOV X/X XPETS XCC KIDS MED.I MED.INX

S.Y. HOSTELS: At Kyleakin (biggest, nearest mainland), Armadale (interesting area in S), Broadford, Glen Brittle (v Cuillin), Uig (for N Skye, ferry to Hebrides). **INDEPENDENT HOSTELS** at Kyleakin and Staffin (942/941/HOSTELS).

CAMP/CARAVAN PARKS: Glen Brittle (01478 640404). L Greshernish at Edinbane; 18km Portree (01470 582230) – gr site and facs. Uig and Staffin - ask at TO.

WHERE TO EAT
THREE CHIMNEYS: 01470 511258. 7km W of Dunvegan on B884. Superb home cooking day and night. Best this far N in UK (1920/ISLAND RESTAUS). MED

KINLOCH LODGE: 01471 833333. 13km S Broadford off A851. Classy food in almost theatrical atmos at Lady Claire's table(s) (1919/ISLAND RESTAUS). EXP

HARLOSH HOTEL: 01470 521367. Nr Dunvegan, off A863 (5km). Peter Elford's unpretentious but highly regarded (fixed) menu. 2 AA whatsits. Apr-Oct. (1921/ISLAND RESTAUS.) MED

LOCHBAY SEAFOOD: 01470 592235. 12km N Dunvegan off A850. Small; simple fresh seafood in loch side setting. We love (1073/SEAFOOD RESTAUS). INX

AN TUIREANN CAFE: 01478 613306. Nr Portree. Coffee shop/gallery. Wholefood and chat in a cultural caff. Also **BEN TIANAVAIG** (1061/ VEGN RESTAUS).

ARDVASAR HOTEL: 01471 844223. Sleat in far S near Mallaig ferry. Local seafood a speciality. Perhaps a more informal alternative to Lady Claire. MED

SEAGULL RESTAURANT, nr BROADFORD: 01471 822001. S of village on main rd, 10km Kyleakin. Best straight restau in S; local ingredients mixed with a European spoon. Skye folk fave. Apr-Oct 7 days 5-10pm (Sun lunch 12.30-2.30pm). INX

THE LOWER DECK, PORTREE: 01478 613611. On harbour where Dan and Joan Corrigall buy the fish they sell locally and serve here. Taste the sea. Takeaway next door has seafood sandwiches. Apr-Oct 7 days 11am-10pm. INX

SLIGACHAN HOTEL: Surprisingly good seafood in hotel (not pub). *See also* 1186/WHISKY.

WHAT TO SEE
THE CUILLINS (1956/BIG ATTRACTIONS); **RAASAY** (1893/MAGICAL ISLANDS); (1925/ISLAND WALKS); **THE QUIRANG** (1920/VIEWS); (1930/ISLAND WALKS); **OLD MAN OF STORR** (1929/ISLAND WALKS); **DUNVEGAN** (1417/CASTLES); **EAS MOR** (1781/WATERFALLS); **ELGOL** (1324/VIEWS); **SKYEBATIKS** (1324/CRAFT SHOPS); **SKYE MUSEUM OF ISLAND LIFE** (1822/MUSEUMS); **FLORA MACDONALD'S GRAVE** (1480/MONUMENTS); **EDINBANE POTTERY and CARBOSTCRAFT** (1742/1749/CRAFT SHOPS); **FAIRY POOLS** (1335/PICNICS); **SKYE BREWERY**(1032/REAL ALES); **SLIGACHAN HOTEL:** (1186/WHISKY).

WHAT TO DO
GOLF at Skeabost (*previous page*) and Sconsor (01478 612277); **FISHING:** ask at hotels; Skeabost, Eilean Iarmain (*previous page*) and Greshhornish House (01470 582266); **SWIMMING** at Portree Pool (01478 612655); **BIKE HIRE:** Island Cycles (01478 613121); Broadford Bikes (01471 822270); **RIDING:** (01470 532439); **CEILIDHS:** In this most Highland of islands 3 hoolies are worth mentioning, all welcoming to visitors, usually a grand *mêlée* if not a riot: **EDINBANE LODGE HOTEL:** 22km from Portree, 12km Dunvegan just off A850. Wed/Sat, June-Sept and New Year's Eve. Gets hot but don't chill out without midge cream. **FLODIGARRY COUNTRY-HOUSE HOTEL:** 32km N Portree. V north, v Staffin and the stuff of a damned good shindig. Every Sat, plus other nights. Backpackers from adj hostel (941/HOSTELS), locals and hotel guests happily get down. Till 11.30pm officially. **COMMUNITY CENTRE, PORTREE:** Not a ceilidh, but the full-on Friday-night-on-Skye experience. Don't go if you don't drink or don't like natives. Pay at door.

TOURIST INFO: 01478 612137.   **CALMAC:** 0990 650000

THE BEST OF THE WESTERN ISLES

FERRIES: Ullapool-Stornoway, 2hrs 30mins, (not Sun). Oban/ Mallaig-Lochbois dale, S Uist and Castlebay, Barra; 5hrs. Uig on Skye-Tarbert, Harris (not Sun) or Lochmaddy, N Uist 1hr 45mins. Also Leverburgh, Harris-Otternish, S Uist Check Calmac. Local ferry: Ludag, S Uist-Eoligarry, Barra. check local TOs.

BY AIR: BA 3 times daily (2 Sat; not Sun). Inverness/Glas. Local 01851 702340. BA Otter to Barra/ Benbecula from Glas (1 a day). Linkline 0345 222111.

WHERE TO STAY
ARDVOURLIE CASTLE, N HARRIS: 01859 502307. 14km N of Tarbert on shore of L Seaforth in hills of N Harris. Victorian hunting lodge. Fab (1906/ISLAND HOTELS).

SCARISTA HOUSE, S HARRIS: 01859 550238. 20km S of Tarbert. Nr famous but often deserted beach; celebrated   retreat. Also Self-catering accom (1907/ISLAND HOTELS).

BAILE-NA-CILLE: 01859 672242. Nr Uig 50km W of Stornoway off A858. Welcomong old manse in far W. Report: 1910/ISLAND HOTELS.

CASTLEBAY HOTEL, CASTLEBAY, BARRA: 01871 810223. O/looks ferry terminal in main town. Excellent value. Good food. Brilliant bar (1904/ISLAND HOTELS; 1011/BLOODY GOOD PUBS).

ISLE OF BARRA HOTEL, BARRA: 01871 810383. Modern purpose-built hotel on gr beach 3km W of Castlebay. Seaviews are see views (1917/ISLAND HOTELS).

ROYAL HOTEL, STORNOWAY, LEWIS: 01851 702109. The best value and most central of the 3 main hotels in town. All usual comforts. Barnacle bistro and Boatshed (probably 'best' hotel dining).   26RMS   JAN-DEC   T/T   PETS   CC   KIDS   MED.INX

PARK GUEST HOUSE, STORNOWAY: 01851 702485. James St. Refurbished town house with surprisingly good menu and comfy rms. Superior guesthouse and a place to eat even if not staying.   9RMS   JAN-DEC   X/T   XPETS   XCC   XKIDS   TOS   CHP

LEACHIN HOUSE, TARBERT, N HARRIS: 01859 502157. 2km N on A859. Small, Victorian family house. Personal touch in furnishings, food and your excursions. Shared dinner. A Wolsely Lodge.   2RMS   JAN-DEC   X/T   XPETS   XCC   KIDS   INX

LOCHBOISDALE HOTEL, LOCHBOISDALE, S UIST: 01878 700322. In last town nr tip of Uists at ferry terminal o/look bay. Mainly fishing hotel with all rods catered for. Gr local bar. Rms vary. 18RMS JAN-DEC X/T PETS CC KIDS MED.EX

HOSTELS: Simple hostels within hiking distance. 2 in Lewis, 2 in Harris, 1 each in N and S Uist (Barra pending). Excellent hostelling holiday prospect (xxxx/HOSTELS).

WHERE TO EAT

PARK GUEST HOUSE and THE BOATSHED, the ROYAL HOTEL, STORNOWAY: (*see above*). The top two in town. Park is a restau so don't be put off by guesthouse tag. V TOS (Tues-Sat). Latter a bit up-market with seafood emphasis. High teas then LO 9pm.

TIGH MEALROS, GARYNAHINE, LEWIS: 01851 621333. On A858 22km SW Stornoway. 2km S of Callanish. Unpretentious surf 'n' turf. Scallops (dived) a special. BYOB (but watch the narrow entrance when you leave). Open AYR. LO 9pm.

COPPER KETTLE, DALBEG, LEWIS: 01851 710592. 6km N of Carloway W of Stornoway. Signed off main rd down track to lily-filled lochan. Tables on terrace in summer for tea and tiny restau with excellent plain cooking. Must book dinner.

COFFEE SHOPS at AN LANNTAIR GALLERY, STORNOWAY, and CALLANISH VISITOR CENTRE, LEWIS. The latter esp good. Daytime hrs (1447/PREHISTORIC SITES).

ARDVOURLIE and SCARISTA HOUSE, HARRIS: (*see above*). Dinner possible for nonresidents. Both a drive from Stornoway. Fixed menus. Book well in advance.

FIRST FRUITS TEAROOM, TARBERT, HARRIS: Nr TO and ferry to Uig. Home-cooking that hits the spot if a bit stodgy (you may have walked or come far for this). Good atmos. 10.30am-early evening (8pm July/Aug). Lunch only, in winter.

THE BEST OF MULL

1937
MAP 1

FERRY: Oban-Craignure, 40mins. Main route; 5-8 a day. Lochaline-Fishnish, 15mins. 9-15 a day. Kilchoan-Tobermory, 35mins. 7 a day (not Sun in winter).

WHERE TO STAY
See also ISLAND HOTELS AND RESTAUS, *pp. 246-7.*

WESTERN ISLES, TOBERMORY: 01688 302012. High above town, classic views over bay; real individuality, fire in foyer, gr conservatory. Good suites and restaus.

26RMS JAN-DEC T/T PETS CC KIDS TOS MED.EX

TOBERMORY HOTEL: 01688 302091. On waterfront, cheapish/cheerful. Gr location.

17RMS JAN-DEC X/X PETS CC KIDS MED.INX

CALGARY FARMHOUSE, CALGARY: 01688 400256. Nr Dervaig On B8073 nr Mull's famous beach. Gallery/coffee shop and good bistro/restau.

9RMS APR-OCT X/T PETS CC KIDS MED. INX

DRUIMARD COUNTRY HOUSE, DERVAIG: 01688 400345. Small, country place beside Mull Little Theatre and heart of Mull village; conservatory bar, books. Bistro style dining; see the show first. 5RMS JAN-DEC T/T PETS CC KIDS MED.EX

KILLIECHRONAN HOUSE: 01680 300403. Set in its own 5,000 acre estate in the wooded bay in the W of the narrowest part of the island. Spacious old lodge house, designed for comfort. 6RMS APRIL-OCT X/X PETS CC X/KIDS TOS EXP

S.Y. HOSTEL: In Tobermory main st on bay (938/HOSTELS).

CARAVAN PARKS: At Fishnish (all facs, nr Ferry) Craignure and Fionnphort.

CAMPING: Calgary Beach, Fishnish and at Loch Na Keal shore.

WHERE TO EAT

WESTERN ISLES: 01688 302012. (*See above.*) Good dining-rm, *cuisine marché;* bar meals in refurbished conservatory undoubtedly the nicest rm in town; and eastern cuisine (Bangkok to Beijing) in Spices Bistro. (1908/ISLAND HOTELS). MED

CALGARY FARMHOUSE: 01688 400256. Dovecote Restaurant. Local produce in v atmospheric wine-bar setting, run by mellow people (1924/ISLAND RESTAUS). INX

OLD MILL COTTAGE: 01680 812442. Lochdonhead. Guest house and restau. Only 4 tables, so expect personal service. Good rep. on the island. *The* B&B for motorheads come rally week in October.

THE PUFFER AGROUND, SALEN: 01680 300389. Roadside café/restau. Cl Sun/Mon.

THE GREEN BARN: 2km Tobermory centre. Highly recommended (114/TEAROOMS).

WHAT TO SEE
TOROSAY CASTLE: Walk or train (!) from Craignure. Fabulous grds and fascinating insight into an endearing family's life. Teashop. (1416/CASTLES.) **DUART CASTLE:** 5km Craignure. Seat of Clan Maclean. Impressive from a distance, good view of clan history and from battlements. Teashop. (1415/CASTLES.) **EAS FORS:** Waterfall on Dervaig to Fionnphort rd. V accessible series of cataracts tumbling into the sea (1280/WATERFALLS). **THE MISHNISH:** No mission to Mull complete without a night at the Mish (1009/BLOODY GOOD PUBS).

WHAT TO DO
EXCURSIONS TO IONA (from Fionnphort) and **ULVA** (from Ulva Ferry) (1895/ 1899/MAGICAL ISLANDS); **STAFFA** (from Fionnphort or Iona) and **THE TRESHNISH ISLES** (Ulva Ferry or Fionnphort). Marvellous trips in summer (1382/BIRDS); walks from **CARSAIG PIER** (1927/ISLAND WALKS); or up **BEN MORE** (1592/MUNROS); **CROIG** and **QUINISH** in N, nr Dervaig and **LOCHBUIE** off the A849 at Strathcoil 9km S of Craignure: these are all serene shorelines to explore. **AROS PARK** forest walk, from Tobermory, about 7km round trip. **GOLF:** Tobermory (01688 302020). Craignure (01688 302372). Both 9 holes. **FISHING:** Info: 'Tackle and Books' (01688 302336). **BIKE HIRE** (01688 302226).

TOURIST INFORMATION: 01688 302182. **CALMAC:** 0990 650000.

THE BEST OF ORKNEY

FERRY: P&O (01224 572615) Stromness: from Aber - Tue and Sat, takes 8hrs; from Scrabster - 2/3 per day and 1 on Sun (winter: 1 daily, no Sun) takes 2hrs. From John O'Groats to Burwick (01955 611353), 40mins, up to 5 a day in summer.

BY AIR: BA (0345 222111) to Kirkwall: from Aber - 3 daily; from Edin - 1 daily; from Glas - 1 daily. No flights on Sun.

WHERE TO STAY
FOVERAN HOTEL, ST OLA: 01856 872389. A964 Orphir rd; 4km from Kirkwall. Bobby and Ivy Corsie's Scandanavian style hotel is a friendly informal place serves trad food using best local ingredients; separate vegn menu. offering gr value. Comfortable light rms; grdn o/look Scapa Flow. Good restau.
8RMS JAN-DEC T/T PETS CC KIDS TOS MED.INX

AYRE HOTEL, KIRKWALL: 01856 873001. Roy and Moira Dennison have spent the last 6 yrs refurb their family hotel in line with TO standards; which has resulted in them having the highest grading on the island. Situated on the harbour front, the whole place is well tidy and well established. It's where to stay in Kirkwall.
33RMS JAN-DEC T/T PETS CC KIDS MED.EX

BARONY, BIRSAY: 01856 721327. 40km from Kirkwall. Basic accom in wild corner by loch. Brown trout fishing, walks, sea air. Cabin style 'HMS Hampshire' bar.
10RMS APR-OCT T/T PETS CC KIDS INX

MERKISTER, HARRAY: 01856 771366. A fave with fishers and twitchers; also handy for archaeological sites. Bedrms now all *en suite*. À la carte or table d'hôte in the conservatory o/look the loch.
14RMS MAR-NOV T/T PETS CC KIDS MED.EX

STROMNESS HOTEL: 01856 850298. New owners from Edin are refurb this Victorian hotel so it will be functional and not just funky. Inexp bar meals o/look harbour; beer gdn and bistro soon.
42RMS MAR-NOV T/T PETS CC KIDS MED.INX

OAKLEIGH HOTEL, STROMNESS: 01856 850447. Basic accom (kids free if sharing) in family hotel on cobbled st in old town. Cellar restau; good vegn dishes. Harbour out back and Charley . . . wood turning.
6RMS JAN-DEC X/T PETS XCC KIDS CHP

WOODWICK HOUSE, EVIE: 01856 751330. Comfy country house and gdn, nr shore with views of islets. Managed by the Dandelion Trust charity, it's a gr retreat. Home cooking, local produce. Good value.
5RMS JAN-DEC X/X XCC KIDS INX

S.Y. HOSTELS: 01856 850589. At Stromness (excellent location, Grade 2), Kirkwall (the largest), Hoy, Rackwick, Eday and the wonderful Papa Westray. **PEEDIE HOSTEL, KIRKWALL:** 01856 874500. Ayre Rd; by the sea. Private bedrm, own keys.

CAMPING/CARAVAN: At Kirkwall and Stromness (both 01856 873535).

WHERE TO EAT

THE CREEL, ST MARGARET'S HOPE: 01856 831311. On S Ronaldsay, 20km S of Kirkwall. In the wild area where seals vie with the fishermen. Decent food (AA rosette) though fairly exp - all main courses are £15. Many sauces over meat or fish. Clootie for pud or Orkney cheeses. Popular with the islanders. Dinner only. Seal Rescue Centre nearby.

MED

FOVERAN HOTEL, ST OLA: 01856 872389. 4km Kirkwall. *As above.*

MED

HAMNAVOE, STROMNESS: 01856 850606. Leslie's Close off main st. Seafood is their speciality, or haggis, neeps and tatties. Mar-Oct; Tue-Sun 7pm-late.

INX

THE STRYND, KIRKWALL: 01856 871552. Up lane beside TO. New, bright sunflower tearoom; snacks, home made cakes. Mon-Sat 10am-5pm, Sun in season.

CHP

THE COFFEE SHOP, STROMNESS: Nr the harbour office. Good toasties, blackboard specials. Gets busy - fill yourself up before the ferry journey! Apr-Oct; Mon-Sat 9am-6.30pm, Sun 9am-5pm. Winter; Mon-Sat 9am-5pm.

CHP

WHAT TO SEE

SKARA BRAE: 25km W Kirkwall. Amazingly well-preserved underground labyrinth, a 5,000-year-old village (1445/PREHISTORIC SITES).

THE OLD MAN OF HOY: on Hoy; 30min ferry 2 or 3 times a day from Stromness. 3hr walk along spectacular coast (1931/ISLAND WALKS).

STANDING STONES OF STENNESS, THE RING OF BRODGAR, MAES HOWE: Around 18km W of Kirkwall on A965. Strong vibrations (1446/PREHISTORIC SITES).

YESNABY SEA STACKS: 24km W of Kirkwall. A precarious cliff top at the end of the world (1560/SPOOKY – or spiritual – PLACES).

ITALIAN CHAPEL: 8km S of Kirkwall at first causeway. A special act of faith. (1495/CHURCHES).

SKAILL HOUSE: at Skara Brae. 17th century 'mansion' built on Pictish cemetery. Set up as it was in the 1950s; with Captain Cook's crockery in the dining-rm looking remarkably unused. Apr-Sep; 7 days 9.30am-6.30pm (11.30am on Sundays) or by appointment - 01856 841501. Tearoom and visitor centre due soon and HS link with Skara.

ST MAGNUS CATHEDRAL (1495/CHURCHES); **STROMNESS** itself (1234/COASTAL VILLAGES); **PIER ART GALLERY** 1837/INTERESTING GALLERIES); **TOMB OF THE EAGLES** (1450/PREHISTORIC SITES); **MARWICK HEAD** and many of the smaller islands (1389/BIRDS); **SCAPA FLOW** (1534/BATTLEGROUNDS; 1728/DIVING); **HIGHLAND PARK** (1190/WHISKY); **PUFFINS:** (1390/BIRDS)

WHAT TO DO

GOLF: Golf courses open to public at Kirkwall and Stromness. **SWIMMING:** Pools at Kirkwall, Stromness and Hoy. **FISHING:** Permits not required, though permission needed to fish at L of Skile. **SCUBA DIVE:** PADI training, trips, guesthouse, shop at Burray (01856 731269). **BIKE HIRE:** Helga's Cycles (01856 821293).

TOURIST INFO: 01856 872856 or 01856 850716.

THE BEST OF SHETLAND

1939

FERRY: P&O (01224 572615) Aber-Lerwick 14hrs (leaves 6pm arrives 8am) Mon-Fri (not Tue). Also via Orkney (leaves Aber on Sat at noon and Stromness at noon on Sun; also Tue Jun-Aug).

BY AIR: BA (linkline 0345 222111, Shetland 01950 460345) from Aber (4 a day, 2 Sat, 3 Sun). From Inverness (1 a day, not w/ends). From Glas (1 a day). From Edin (1 a day, not Sun). From Wick (1 a day, not Sun).

WHERE TO STAY

BUSTA HOUSE: 01806 522506. Historic country house at Brae just over 30mins from Lerwick. High standards, excl restau, gr malt selection. Most guides agree it's where to stay on Shetland. 20RMS JAN-DEC T/T PETS CC KIDS MED.EX

BURRASTOW HOUSE: 01595 809307. But this is the other place to go (40mins

Lerwick) and the setting and the dining are as good (some say better - TO say 'highly' commended). Peaceful Georgian house with views to Island of Vaila. Wonderful home-made/produced food. 5RMS MAR-DEC X/X PETS CC KIDS MED.EX

SUMBURGH HOTEL, SUMBURGH: 01950 460201. Recently refurb manor house in v S of mainland 42km from Lerwick. Next to airport and Jarlshof excavations. Sea views as far as Fair Isle (50km S). Beaches and birds!
32RMS JAN-DEC T/T PETS CC KIDS MED.INX

KVELDRO HOTEL, LERWICK: 01595 692195. Pron 'Kel-ro'. Probably best proposition in Lerwick; o/look harbour. Reasonable standard at a price. Locals do eat here. 17RMS JAN-DEC T/T PETS CC KIDS LOTS

SCALLAWAY HOTEL, LERWICK: 01595 880444. Main St. Recent refurb after a distant fire. More economic option than above, but we have no reports except that it's good. 24RMS JAN-DEC T/T PETS CC KIDS MED.INX

S.Y. HOSTEL in Lerwick, Isleburgh House: 01595 692114. Recently upgraded and v central. The **SAIL LOFT** at Voe (25km N of Lerwick). And bods (fisherman's barns - cheap sleep in wonderful sea-shore settings. Check TO for details. Bods at Grieve Hse, **WHALSAY**; Betty Mott's cottage, **SCAPNESS**; Wind Hse Lodge, **MID YELL.**

CAMPING/CARAVAN: CLICKIMIN, LERWICK 01595 694555. **LEVENWICK** 01950 422207.

WHERE TO EAT

BUSTA HOUSE, BRAE & BURRASTOW HOUSE, WALLS: (*see above*). The best meal in the islands.

MONTY'S BISTRO and DELI, LERWICK: 01595 696555. Mounthooley St nr TO. Deli with takeaway and upstairs bistro. Renovated building in light Med decor. Raymond Smith left for the world and came back to open here. Best bet in town. Italian menu on Thur nights. Bistro: Cl Sun/Mon. Lunch and LO 9pm. MED

LERWICK HOTEL: 01595 692166 and the **KVELDSRO HOTEL:** (pron 'Kelro') 01595 692195 all have pub food and fairly reliable dining-rms (the Kveldsro is 'up-market' and exp).

Pub food also recommended at the following:

THE WESTINGS, WHITENESS: 01595 840242. 15km Lerwick for lunch. **THE MID BRAE INN, BRAE:** 32km N of Lerwick, 01806 522634. Lunch and supper till 9pm, 7 days. All home-made, superb fish 'n' chips. Bar till 1am.

HERRISLEA HOUSE, TINGWALL: 01595 840208. 7km NW of Lerwick. Lunch and supper till 9pm, 7 days. Basic, good home cooking. New folk.

WHAT TO SEE

MOUSA BROCH and **JARLSHOF** (1449/PREHISTORIC SITES), also **CLICKIMIN** broch.

ST NINIAN'S ISLE, BIGTON: 8km N of Sumburgh on W Coast. An island linked by exquisite shell-sand. Hoard of Pictish silver found in 1958 (now in Edin). Beautiful, serene spot.

SCALLOWAY: 7km W of Lerwick, a township once the ancient capital of Shetland, dominated by the atmospheric ruins of Scalloway Castle. **SHETLAND WOOLLEN COMPANY** is worth a rummage.

NOUP OF NOSS, ISLE OF NOSS, off BRESSAY: 8km W of Lerwick by frequent ferry and then boat (also direct from Lerwick 01595 692577), May-Aug only. Excellent.

UP HELLY AA: Festival Lerwick on the last Tuseday in Jan. Ritual with hundreds of torchbearers and much fire and firewater. Norse, northern and pagan. A wild time.

SEA RACES: the impressive Viking Convoy each summer and the Boat Race when yachts sail from Norway. Tall ships due 1999. **BONHOGA GALLERY:** and mill cafe. 01595 830400. **GO -KARTING:** new for the island 01950 477509, and **GOLF RANGE:** at Moor Park, Gulberwick 01595 694959.

TOURIST INFORMATION: 01595 693434.

SECTION 13

Local Centres
Where to eat and stay, what to do and see

THE BEST OF AYR

WHERE TO STAY

FAIRFIELD HOUSE: 01292 267461. Fairfield rd. 1km centre on the front. Rarely that the 'best' hotel in town *is* the best - this is! De luxe facs incl pool/sauna/steam, conservatory brasserie and breakfast and notable (2 AA rosettes) Fleur de Lys restau (Fri/Sat). 33RMS JAN-DEC T/T PETS CC KID EXP

NORTHPARK HOUSE: 01292 442336. 3km from centre on rd to Alloway and Burns Country Trail. Comfy Ayrshire mansion in park setting nr Belleisle (1651/GREAT GOLF). Some weddings. Good restau. 5RMS JAN-DEC T/T PETS CC KIDS MED.EX

LOCHGREEN HOUSE: 01292 313343. Monktonhall Rd, Troon 12km N on way in from Ayr. White seaside mansion nr famous golf courses of Troon (1648/GREAT GOLF). Elegant setting and decor; civilised wining and dining. 14RMS (7 IN COURTYARD) JAN-DEC T/T PETS CC KIDS EXP

SAVOY PARK: 01292 266112. 16 Racecourse Rd. Period mansion house with fab public rms. Family-run for 30yrs. 16RMS JAN-DEC T/T PETS CC KIDS MED.INX

PIERSLAND, TROON: 01292 314747. 12km N of Ayr (659/AYRSHIRE HOTELS).

BURNS MONUMENT, ALLOWAY: 01292 442466. 5km S of Ayr (660/AYRSHIRE HOTELS)

KYLESTROME: 01292 262474. 11 Miller Rd. Recent refurb *à la mode*. Nr centre. Not a lot of character, but adequate. 12RMS JAN-DEC T/T PETS CC KIDS TOS MED.EX

OLD RACECOURSE: 01292 262873. 2 Victoria Park. On corner of Old Racecourse (arterial) Rd, 2km from centre. 'Modernised', good value. Locally rated for food incl afternoon/high teas. 10RMS JAN-DEC T/T PETS CC KIDS INX

THE RICHMOND: 01292 265153. 38 Park Circus. Best of bunch in sedate terrace nr centre. Nice folk. 6RMS JAN-DEC X/T XPETS XCC KIDS CHP

S.Y. HOSTEL: 01292 262322. Craigwiel Rd, off Racecourse Rd close to seafront, 10min walk to centre. Sleeps 86. Book ahead service (essential June, July, Aug).

CARAVAN SITES: **Cragie Park** nr centre. 01292 264909. 90 pitches, no tents. Good location is **Heads of Ayr**, 9km S on A719 rd to Dunure/Culzean 442269. Most facs at **Sundrum Castle**, 10km E off A70; 'holiday camp atmos', 570057. But BEST is **Skeldon** nr Dalrymple, 14km S by A713 on the banks of Doon. 560502.

WHERE TO EAT

Ayr is well served by 4 places below which cover the range from seriously good food to trad Scottish caff cuisine. Look no further than:

FOUTERS: 01292 261391. 2 Academy St (661/AYRSHIRE HOTELS). Still the best!

THE HUNNY POT: 37 Beresford Terr off centre but nr TO, Popular cafe/restau with exemplary home-baking and light meals. Mon-Sat 10am-10pm, Sun 11am-5pm.

THE STABLES: 41 Sandgate, downtown location in courtyard of shops. Coffee shop/bistro with wine bar ambience and enlightened attitude. Imaginative Scottish menu. No smk rm. Till 5pm. Cl Sun. INX

THE TUDOR RESTAURANT: 8 Beresford St (1007/TEAROOMS). Superb caff. Till 8pm.

Also running: **PIERRE VICTOIRE:** 01292 282087. Auld Brig. Gr address, gr setting. Pierre again but bistro formula perhaps beginning to wear thin. INX
PIERRINO'S: 01292 269087. Alloway Pl. The credible Italian. LO 10pm. INX

WHAT TO SEE

CULZEAN (1409/CASTLES); **DUNURE VILLAGE** (1244/COASTAL VILLAGES) and nr (3km S on the A719) the **ELECTRIC BRAE**; **BURNS HERITAGE TRAIL** (1551/LITERARY PLACES); **GAILES/TROON/PRESTWICK/TURNBERRY/BELLEISLE** (*see* GREAT GOLF, *p.* 212); **MAGNUM, IRVINE** (1694/LEISURE CENTRES); **GO BANANAS** (1363/KIDS); **CLUBS** (1870/NIGHTCLUBS).

WHAT TO DO

SWIMMING: V good pool complex at S Beach Rd (01292 269793), and at Prestwick, off the road in from Ayr (01292 474015). **RIDING:** Ayrshire Equitation Centre, all standards, country setting. Book! 01292 266267. **TENNIS:** Good all-weather courts at Citadel Pl and Craigie Av near Craigie Park. Just turn up.

TOURIST OFFICE: Burn's Statue Sq. 01292 288688. Jan-Dec.

THE BEST OF DUMFRIES

WHERE TO STAY

COMLONGON CASTLE, CLARENCEFIELD: 01387 870283. 14km S via A75 t/off at Collin on B724. Turn rt at Clarencefield, signed for hotel and up 2km avenue of trees to privately owned castle with hotel in adj manor house. Ownership handed-on down the family, so refreshing breeze has blown through the old place. Ghost however, still in residence. Romantic spot; popular for weddings.

11RMS MAR-DEC T/T XPETS CC KIDS EXP

CAIRNDALE: 01387 250555. Surprising spa concealed within this corporate friendly old faithful; conference centre now being added. Visiting somebodies stay here. Café is popular lunch venue for all sorts.

30RMS JAN-DEC T/T PETS CC KIDS EXP

STATION HOTEL: 01387 254316. 49 Lovers' Walk. The best all-round business/ tourist hotel in town with decent upgrading of the trad stn-hotel elegance and ambience (from 1896); central and often full. 'Bistro' as well as dining-rm.

32RMS JAN-DEC T/T PETS CC KIDS TOS MED.EX

ABBEY ARMS 01387 850489 (676/SW HOTELS). **CRIFFEL INN** 01387 850305 both in **NEW ABBEY** 12km S of Dumfries A710. 2 gr pubs.

4/5RMS JAN-DEC X/T PETS CC KIDS INX

EDENBANK/LAURELBANK: 2 reasonably-priced places on Laurieknowe, a main rd leading S from centre. Edenbank (01387 252759) is a small town house hotel with bar. Lauriebank (269388) more a guesthouse, privately owned, more intimate.

10/4RMS JAN-DEC/FEB-NOV T/T /X/T PETS CC/XCC KIDS INX/CHP

No SYH, Dumfries College accom: ask at TO. No camping and caravan parks recommended in immediate area. Nearest: **SANDYHILLS:** 01387 780257. 34km S by A710. Well-managed and equipped site in prominent beach location. Apr-Oct.

WHERE TO EAT

PIZZERIA IL FIUME: 01387 265154. Hidden inside Dock Park by St Michael's Br, underneath Riverside pub. Usual Italian menu but gr pizzas and cosy tratt atmos. 6-10pm (lunch in Summer) 7 days.   INX

OPUS: 01387 255752. 95 Queensbury St. Innovative vegn restau on the alternative st in town. Eclectic menu; owner will do requests. A breath of air. (1069/VEGN-FRIENDLY). Mon-Sat 9am-4.30pm. Cl 2.15pm Thurs.   INX

BENVENUTO: 01387 259890. 42 Eastfield Rd, off Brooms Rd – follow signs for Cresswell Maternity Hospital. Sort of surreal wooden hut setting next to owner's chippy. 5pm-late. 7 days.   INX

BRUNO'S: 01387 255757. 3 Balmoral Rd, off Annan Rd. Well-established Italian eaterie beside **BALMORAL** chippy (1096/FISH AND CHIP SHOPS). 6-10pm, Cl Tue.

INX

PIERRE VICTOIRE: 01387 265888. 117 Queensbury St above Tam O' Shanter Inn. Safest bet for bistro food in town. 7 days. Lunch and 6.30pm-whenever.   INX

THE OLD BANK: 01387 253499. Snacks in converted bank.

WHAT TO SEE

ROCKCLIFFE (1239/COASTAL VILLAGES); **ROCKCLIFFE TO KIPPFORD** (1640/COASTAL WALKS); **SOUTHERNESS** (1668/GOLF IN GREAT PLACES); **SWEETHEART ABBEY** (1528/ABBEYS); **CRIFFEL** (1575/HILLS); **CAERLAVEROCK** (1381/BIRDS); **CAERLAVEROCK CASTLE** (1426/RUINS); **DUMFRIES MARKET; ELLISLAND FARM** (1552/LITERARY PLACES). And **GARDENS** all off A75: **CASTLE KENNEDY GARDENS** 75 acres laid out around 2 acre lily pond, 2 lochs; rare species. Apr-Sep 10am-5pm. **GLENWHAN GARDENS, DUNRAGIT** enchanting 12 acre hill side, tamed and lovingly hewn into lush overflowing haven. Gr views and walks. Mar-Oct 10am-5pm. **THREAVE GARDEN, nr CASTLE DOUGLAS** for all seasons. AYR 9.30am-sunset.

WHAT TO DO

SWIMMING: Modern pool on river side nr Buccleuch St Br (01387 252908); **GOLF:** Southerness 25km S on A710 or Powfoot, 20km SW on B724 (01461 700327); **RIDING:** Barend at Sandyhills on 34km S on A710 (01387 780663).

TOURIST OFFICE: Whitesands. 01387 253862. Jan-Dec.

THE BEST OF DUNFERMLINE AND KIRKCALDY

WHERE TO STAY

KEAVIL HOUSE HOTEL, CROSSFORD, DUNFERMLINE: 01383 736258. 3km W of Dunfermline on A994 towards Culross (1236/COASTAL VILLAGES) and Kincardine. Rambling mansion house in grounds within a suburban area of town, converted into modern business-type hotel with all facs incl separate leisure club (not bad pool). Best Western.   33RMS JAN-DEC T/T PETS CC KIDS TOS MED.EX

DAVAAR HOUSE HOTEL, DUNFERMLINE: 01383 736463. Grieve St which is a bugger to find; you'll have to ask. Georgian mansion in suburban st. Serviceable accom. Local reputation for food.   8RMS JAN-DEC T/T PETS CC KIDS TOS MEDINX

STRATHEARN HOTEL, KIRKCALDY: 01592 652210. Frankly there's nowhere in Kirkaldy you'd even recommend to your mother-in-law, the 2 'business' hotels, the Dean Park and the Parkway included. This hotel on Wishart Pl opp Ravenscraig Park on coast rd and main rd E from town, about 3km from centre may suffice. Ravenscraig is a beautiful coastal park for respite.   18RMS JAN-DEC T/T PETS CC KIDS INX

THE BELVEDERE, W WEMYSS, nr KIRKCALDY: 01592 654167. However, this is worth the 8km trek E of town via A955 coast rd. At beginning of neat village, a curious mixture of dereliction and conservation. Views of bay and Kirkcaldy from comfortable rms in cottages and on the seafront, all white and with red-tiled roofs. Nice pictures, decent menu.   21RMS JAN-DEC T/T PETS CC KIDS MED.INX

No **HOSTELS** (SYH at Falkland is miles away, good) or campsites to recommend. Along coast from Kirkcaldy starting at Lundin Links (15km E), there are many.

WHERE TO EAT IN AND AROUND DUNFERMLINE

IL PESCATORE, LIMEKILNS: 01383 872999. 7km from town via B9156 or to Rosyth, then Charlestown. Recently refurbished favourite and the best pasta etc around. Now has 6 inexp rms above. Once we came from Edin and had my birthday do here. It's esp good for that kind of thing. 7 days, LO 11pm.   INX

CAFE RENE: 01383 623798. 19 Carnegie Dr opp Fire Stn. Popular, jolly eaterie with food from everywhere and we do mean everywhere. 7 days LO 10pm. Next door:

NOBLE CUISINE: 620555. Up-market-ish Cantonese. 7 days, LO 11pm.   INX

THE NEW VICTORIA: 724175. The 'Vic' upstairs opp City Chambers at end of the High St since 1923. 50 main courses; an institution. 7 days till 7pm (later w/ends).

WHERE TO EAT IN AND AROUND KIRKCALDY

THE OLD RECTORY, DYSART: 01592 651221. 5km E (733/FIFE RESTAUS).

HOFFMAN'S: 204584. **LA GONDOLA:** 640085. Both nr Harbour. One is good pub-style food (book w/ends). Other is the best Italian with live Enzo on Suns a must.

FEUARS ARMS: 205025. 66 Commercial St. Seems good. Lunch and dinner w/ends.

MAXIN: 01592 263406. 5 High St at the W end. The best Chinese. 7days.   INX

VALENTE'S: 01592 205774. Not sit-in, but *absolutely the best* fish (1084/FISH AND CHIPS).

WHAT TO SEE

ABBOT HOUSE, DUNFERMLINE (1814/MUSEUMS); **PITTENCRIEFF & RAVENSCRAIG PARKS, DUNFERMLINE** (1226/TOWNPARKS) and **BEVERIDGE PARK, KIRKCALDY** (1227/TOWN PARKS); **CARNEGIE CENTRE, DUNFERMLINE** (1705/SWIMMING POOLS); **DUNFERMLINE ABBEY** (1549/MARY, CHARLIE AND BOB); **KIRKALDY ART GALLERY** (1834/PUBLIC GALLERIES); **PILLANS, KIRKCALDY** (1140/BAKERS); **BETTY NICOL'S** (1030/REAL ALES); **JACKIE O'S & CAESAR'S, KIRKCALDY** (1870/NIGHTCLUBS).

WHAT TO DO

SWIMMING/INDOOR SPORTS: *As above.* **GOLF:** Kirkcaldy is nr some of the best (*see* GOLF, *p. 213*). **TENNIS:** Both towns have municipal and private courts. Check TO. **DUNFERMLINE:** Abbot House, Maygate. 01383 720999. Easter-Sept.

TOURIST OFFICES

DUNFERMLINE: Abbot House, Maygate. 01383 720999. Easter-Sept.

KIRKCALDY: 19 White's Causeway. 01592 267775. Jan-Dec.

THE BEST OF FORT WILLIAM

WHERE TO STAY

INVERLOCHY CASTLE: 01397 702177. 5km out on A82 Inverness rd. One of Scotland's gr hotels. Victorian elegance recently refurb and impeccable service. (779/HIGHLANDS HOTELS).   16RMS JAN-DEC T/T XPETS CC KIDS LOTS

THE MOORINGS: 01397 772797. Banavie (follow signs), 5km out on A830 Corpach/Mallaig rd. O/look the Caledonian canal by 'Neptune's Staircase'. Refurb nautical theme, piped music, good dining-rm (2 AA rosettes). Mariner's 'Wine bar' more fried.   24RMS JAN-DEC T/T PETS CC KIDS TOS MED.INX

HIGHLAND HOTEL: 01397 702291. Union Rd. High above town (best place to be), with gr views esp when you walk out the front door to the terraced lawns. Rms basic but foyer has character. Conveyor belt to the Highlands, but maybe untrendy tackiness is charming.   112RMS MAR-NOV X/T PETS CC KIDS MED.INX

ONICH HOTEL: 01855 821214. At Onich 16km S on A82. Loch side; good value.

LODGE ON THE LOCH: 01855 821237. Onich as above (790/HIGHLANDS HOTELS).

GLENLOY LODGE: 01397 712700. 1920s compact groud-level house beside R Loy. Tucked away in scenic location.   9RMS MAR-OCT X/X PETS XCC KIDS INX

S.Y. HOSTEL at GLEN NEVIS: 01397 702336. 5km from town by picturesque but busy Glen Nevis rd. The Ben is above. Grade 1. Fax poss. Many other hostels in area (ask at TO for list) but esp **FW BACKPACKERS:** 01397 700711, Alma Rd.

CAMPING/CARAVAN SITE, GLEN NEVIS: 01397 702191. Nr hostel. Well-run site, mainly caravans (also for rent). Many facs incl restaus and much going on.

WHERE TO EAT

CRANNOG: 01397 705589. On loch front. Seafood (1080/SEAFOOD RESTAUS).

THE MOORINGS: 01397 772797. 5km by A830. (*See above.*)

AN CRANN, BANAVIE: 01397 772077. 7km centre via Mallaig rd, then signed at Banavie. A local favourite, this stone barn nestles in the countryside and offers ecelectic mix of curries and snacks at lunch, then evening meals with exotic sauces and home-made puds. V Scottish, v friendly. Easter-Oct: 12-4pm and 6-9pm. INX

CAFÉ CHARDON: 01397 772077. Coffee shop upstairs at Peter Maclennan's well-kent emporium in the main st (or access via side lane). The auld alliance continues here with pastry delicacies and every kind of filled roll. Mon-Sat 9-5pm.   CHP

CAFÉ BEAG, GLEN NEVIS: 01397 703601. 5km along Glen Nevis rd; past 'Braveheart' car park (!) and visitor centre. Log cabin, cosy atmos; open fires, books, games - retreat here from the rain. Wholefood and good veggie. 8am-9pm.   INX

WHAT TO SEE

Most of the good things about Ft William are outside the town, but these incl some v big items esp the Ben and the Glens (Glens Nevis as well as Coe):

GLENCOE: 30km S (1304/SCENIC ROUTES; 1603/SERIOUS WALKS; 1533/BATTLE-GROUNDS); **GLEN NEVIS** (1267/GLENS); **BEN NEVIS:** 6km E on Glen Nevis rd (1604/SERIOUS WALKS); **WEST HIGHLAND WAY** (1598/LONG WALKS); **STEALL FALLS**, Glen Nevis (1283/WATERFALLS); **GLENCOE SKIING** (1689/SKIING); **AONACH MOR SKIING** (1688/SKIING); **THE GROG AND GRUEL** (1028/REAL ALE); **MUSEUM** (1819/MUSEUMS). **NEVIS RANGE GONDOLA:** Aonach Mor (*see below*), open AYR, is a big attraction. Go up for the incredible view and the air and the Ben over there.

WHAT TO DO

GOLF: Ft William Golf Club (01397 704644). 5km towards Inverness on A82; **SWIMMING/SPORTS:** Lochaber Centre (01397 704 359). Beyond main st and Alexandra Hotel. Squash, sauna, 2 gyms, climbing wall, swimming (with flume). **TENNIS:** One court at Lochaber Centre, free of charge. **SKIING:** Aonach Mor. (01397 705825). 12km via A82. Scotland's most modern ski resort (1688/SKIING). Gondola goes up in summer for the view. **BIKE HIRE:** Off-Beat Bikes (01397 704008). Main St and ski base stn.

TOURIST OFFICE: Cameron Square. 01397 703781. Jan-Dec.

THE BEST OF HAWICK AND GALASHIELS

HAWICK *and* GALASHIELS *are the largest centres in the region, but distances betw towns aren't gr. This page includes* SELKIRK, MELROSE *and* JEDBURGH, *all within 20km. See also* THE BEST HOTELS AND RESTAUS IN THE BORDERS, *pp. 99-100.*

WHERE TO STAY

SUNLAWS HOUSE HOTEL, KELSO: 01573 450331 (697/BORDERS HOTELS).   LOTS

BURTS, MELROSE: 01896 822285 (699/BORDERS HOTELS).   MED.EX

WOODLANDS, GALA: 01896 754722. Windyknowe Rd off A7 in Edin direction, A72 to Peebles. Substantial mansion above town centre with elegant hall, spacious public rms and local reputation for food and service.
9RMS JAN-DEC T/T PETS CC KID MED.EX

HUNDALEE HOUSE, JEDBURGH: 01835 863011. 1km S. Jedburgh off A68. Lovely 1700 manor house in 10 acre gdn. Brilliant value, gr base, views of Cheviot hills. Nr the famously old Capon Tree.   5RMS MAR-OCT X/T XPETS XCC KIDS CHP

WHITCHESTER, HAWICK: 01450 377477. On Roberton Rd off A7, 4km S of Hawick. They call it a 'Christian guesthouse' and this may be a tad Jesus-sandal for some, but it is the best-value accom in the area and the house is tastefully done. Dinner has vegn option. Non-alcoholic wines (*sic*), but you can BYOB (thank God).   8RMS FEB-DEC X/X PETS CC KIDS TOS MED.INX

GLEN HOTEL and **HEATHERLIE HOTEL, SELKIRK:** 01750 20259/21200. Both family-run hotels in manor houses with views over town. Well-run, dependable. Selkirk makes a good touring centre.   9/7RMS JAN-DEC T/T X/T PETS/XPETS CC KIDS INX

CROSS KEYS, KELSO: 01573 223303. Recently refurb, we haven't stayed but it's a cheaper alternative to Sunlaws; it dominates the impressive square.
25RMS JAN-DEC T/T PETS KIDS MED.INX

S.Y. HOSTELS: V good in this area (934/HOSTELS).

CAMP/CARAVAN PARK: at Jedwater, Camptown, 11km S Jedburgh. 01835 840 219.

WHERE TO EAT

MARMIONS, MELROSE: 01896 822245 (704/BORDERS HOTELS).

MELROSE STATION, MELROSE: 01896 822546 (705/BORDERS HOTELS).

BURTS HOTEL, MELROSE: Local faves (699/BORDERS HOTELS).

LE PROVENCALE, NEWTOWN ST BOSWELLS: 01835 823284. Monksford Rd signed as you come off the A68 Edin Rd from N. Rene & Elizabeth Duzelier have worked in the hotel trade across Europe and offer euro know-how for local enjoyment. Authentic French food and wine. Lunch and 7-9pm. Cl Sun/Mon. INX

GREEN'S DINER, GALASHIELS: 01896 757667. 4 Green Street. Latino eaterie proclaiming to be, "exactly like nowhere else" which it certainly is in Gala. 3 separate menus: all day, coffee, dinner offer eclectic mix and buzzing atmos. Mon, Tue 10am-5pm, Wed-Sat 10am-10pm. Cl Sun.   CHP

SHISH TANDOORI, GALASHIELS: 01896 758735. 82-86 High St. Haven't tried but comes highly recommended locally. Food cooked fresh to order.   INX

WHAT TO SEE

THIRLESTANE CASTLE, LAUDER (1475/COUNTRY HOUSES); **TWEED FISHING** (*see below*); **PENIEL HEUGH** (1483/MONUMENTS); **MARY QUEEN OF SCOTS' HOUSE** (1539/ MARY, CHARLIE AND BOB); **ANCRUM** (1517/GRAVEYARDS; 1347/PICNICS); **ABBEYS** (1525/JEDBURGH; 1526/DRYBURGH; 1529/MELROSE); **PRIORWOOD** (1206/ GARDENS); **ABBOTSFORD** (1556/LITERARY PLACES); **EILDON HILLS** (1585/HILL WALKS); **RUBERSLAW** (1578/HILLS); **SCOTT'S VIEW/IRVINE'S VIEW** (1328/1329/VIEWS); **LILLIARD'S EDGE** (1535/BATTLEGROUNDS); **LOCHCARRON** and **CHAS WHILLANS** (1771/1772/WOOLLIES); **TEDDY MELROSE** (1367/KIDS).

WHAT TO DO

SWIMMING: V good leisure facs both in and around Hawick and Galashiels. Galashiels Pool (01896 752154) at Livingston Pl up the hill from the one-way main st is excellent (1708/SWIMMING POOLS). Hawick's Teviotdale Leisure Centre (01450 374440) has squash courts, a gym (Universal) and a pool with fun stuff as well as length swimming. Jedburgh and Selkirk also have pools. **GOLF:** Good courses at Minto, nr Denholm (01450 870220) (18); Selkirk (01750 20621) (9);

Melrose (01896 822855) (9); Hawick (01450 372293) (18); Jedburgh (01835 864175) (9). All picturesque, in fair condition, available to visitors. **RIDING:** Cowdenknowes, Earlston (01896 848020). Kailzie Stables nr Peebles (01721 723703). **TENNIS:** Galshiels, Abbotsford Terr; Hawick, Wilton Lodge Park; also Melrose. **CYCLE HIRE:** Galashiels, 58 High St (01896 57587); Hawick, 45 N Br St (01450 373352); Peebles, 3 High St (01721 720844). **FISHING:** There can be last-minute vacancies even on the famous Tweed. Tweed Foundation (01898 666 412); J Leeming's independent agency (01573 470280). Tackle: Angler's Choice, Melrose (01896 823070); Tweedside Tackle, Kelso (01573 225306).

TOURIST INFORMATION:

HAWICK: Common Ground. 01450 372547. Apr-Oct.

GALASHIELS: 01896 755551. Apr-Oct.

JEDBURGH: Murray's Green. 01835 863435. Jan-Dec.

THE BEST OF INVERNESS

WHERE TO STAY
THE BEST
CULLODEN HOUSE: 01463 790461 (781/HIGHLANDS HOTELS).   LOTS

DUNAIN PARK HOTEL: 01463 230512 (787/HIGHLANDS HOTELS).   EXP

BUNCHREW HOUSE: 01463 234917 (787/HIGHLANDS HOTELS).   LOTS

KINGSMILLS HOTEL: 01463 237166. Culcabock Rd. In suburban area S of centre nr A9. Modern, v well-appointed hotel with high standards; excellent bedrms.

84RMS JAN-DEC T/T PETS CC KIDS EXP

BEST OF THE REST
STATION HOTEL: 01463 231926. Academy St. Works as a v central, bit old-fashioned hotel/meeting place. Midst of one-way system; train is best arrival. Good foyer; grand staircase leading to variable rms. Gloomy dining-rm. The trad Highlander hotel.

70RMS JAN-DEC T/T PETS CC KIDS EXP

GLENDRUIDH HOUSE: 01463 226499. Old Edinburgh Rd, the edge of town (centre 3km - phone for directions); gr outlook and welcome. Fresh food, fine malts, comfy with service. No smk.

7RMS JAN-DEC T/T XPETS CC KIDS MED.INX

COLUMBA: 01463 231391. Ness Walk nr main br, o/looks river and castle – central, convenient (though parking tricky). Reasonable facs. 'Scottish Entertainment' most nights. Takes bus parties.

86RMS JAN-DEC T/T PETS CC KIDS MED.INX

ARDMUIR/BRAENESS/FELSTEAD: 01463 231151/712266/231634. 3 hotels on Ness Bank, along the river opp Eden Court and v central. Felstead more a guesthouse and cheaper. All family-run, basic. Many other hotels in this st. These ones are decent value.

10/11/7RMS VARIES X/T PETS CC KIDS CHP

3 GOOD HOSTELS nr THE CASTLE. S Y HOSTEL: 01463 231771. 1 Edinburgh Rd; Large official hostel. More funky are the **STUDENT HOSTEL:** 236556. 8 Culduthel Rd, opp SYH above (935/HOSTELS) and 3 doors down **BAZPACKERS** 717663.

CAMPING AND CARAVAN PARKS: Most central (2km) at **BUGHT PARK,** 01463 236920. Well-equipped and large-scale municipal site on flat river meadow. Many facs. App via A82 Ft William rd. More picturesque at **SCANIPORT,** 01463 751351. 8km SW on B862, the scenic route to Ft Augustus. Rural.

WHERE TO EAT
DUNAIN PARK HOTEL: As above. 3 adj elegant dining-rms; drawing rm for *avant/après*. The country-house hotel on the L Ness edge of town where the good burghers come for Ann Nicholl's honest-to-goodness cookery and wish they'd left more rm for the sideboard of traditional puds. Excellent wines; and malt list.

MED

CAFE ONE: 01463 226200. 10 Castle St nr the Castle. On site of many previous attempts incl 2 different Pierre Victoires, at last a restau that really works. Contemporary decor and cuisine in hands of good team. Reasonably priced for this standard of food and service.

MED

LA RIVIERA at the **GLEN MORISTON HOTEL:** 01463 223777. Ness Bank. On rd along river. Comfortable elegant dining-rm with effective Italian menu well known as a place to eat in this town (MED). Hotel not listed above, but major refurb afoot that may lift it and restau into the 'best in town' position. Same owners run:

RIVA: 01463 237377. 4 Ness Walk by the main br. Central, immediately popular (opened 1997) Italian café/restau open all day, every day (Suns from 2pm) for coffee and ice cream (Capaldi's 1159/ICE CREAM) and full pasta/pizza range. INX

RIVER CAFÉ: 01463 714884. 10 Bank St on busy river side st. Small airy café/restau no relation to London version, but similar Med kind of menu (and meatier Scottish variants). Owner even looks like Rose Gray. LO 9pm. INX

BOAT HOUSE, AULDEARN: 01667 455469. Just off A96 3km E of Nairn. Sympathetically converted building about 30mins from Inverness. Chef Charlie Lockely who impressed at Café One (*above*) installed here summer 1997 and his presence enough to make it a place to watch. I hadn't tried by press-time. MED

SHAPLA: 01463 241919. 2 Castle rd on town side of br from Riva above. Recent (1997) Indian restau with Tandoori and Balti menu. Roadside rm and better upstairs lounge with river views. Open late (LO 11.30pm). Locals have always rated **RAJA:** 237190, behind the post office in town. INX

THE LEMON TREE: 18 Ingle St, pedestrianised town centre st and other entrance from behind M&S. Unlikely high st location for recently opened unpretentious family-run café with home-bakes, own burgers, stovies etc. 7days 10-5/6pm. CHP

CASTLE RESTAURANT: Castle St. Excellent greasy spoon (xxx/CAFÉS).

WHAT TO SEE
THE NESS ISLANDS: Islands in the stream of R Ness joined by iron br and to both banks. A fine place to stroll of an evening. App via Bught Park or Ness Walk (by Eden Court) and from Dores Rd. **BALNAIN HOUSE:** Centre for the Study and Appreciation of Scottish Trad Music on Huntly St, the riverside. Café and shop, library and chat (Gaelic, if you want). 10am-5pm. (8pm summer).Cl Mon. **CULLODEN** (1531/BATTLEGROUNDS); **CLAVA CAIRNS** (1448/PREHISTORIC SITES); **LOCH NESS** (1598/BIG ATTRACTIONS); **THE PHOENIX** (1012/BLOODY GOOD PUBS); **EDEN COURT THEATRE** (1875/THEATRES); **SOUTH BANK, LOCH NESS** (1314/SCENIC ROUTES); **GLEN AFFRIC** (1265/GLENS); **AQUADOME** (1692/LEISURE CENTRES).

WHAT TO DO
GOLF: Inverness Golf Club (01463 239882); Torvean (on A82) (01463 711434) Championship course at Nairn (01667 452787), 25km E (1658/GREAT GOLF). **SWIMMING:** Aquadome (01463 667500) (1692/LEISURE CENTRES). **RIDING:** Highland Riding Centre (01456 450220), Drumnadrochit along L Ness. **TENNIS:** Inverness Tennis and Squash Club. Bishop's Rd (01463 230751). Also Municipal Courts at Bellfield Park (just turn up, 7 days). **CYCLE HIRE:** Gt Glen Cycle Hire 01463 627414. Also at Bazpackers Hostel (above) 717663.

TOURIST OFFICE: Castle Wynd. 01463 234353. Jan-Dec.

THE BEST OF OBAN

WHERE TO STAY
MANOR HOUSE: 01631 562087. Gallanach Rd. On S coast rd out of town towards Kerrera ferry, o/look bay. Quiet elegance in contemp style, and a restau that serves (in an intimate dining-rm) probably the best meal in town. If your timing's rt, you might catch the local lighthouse engineers taking off on a sortie in their tiny chopper from the pad o/side. 11RMS JAN-DEC T/T PETS CC KIDS TOS EXP

BARRIEMORE HOTEL: 01631 566356. Corran Esplanade. The last in a long sweep of hotels to N of centre and, though I'd have to admit that I haven't tried all of them, I'd say this was streets above the rest. Nice people in residence, gr view of the sea. B&B only (651/ARGYLL HOTELS). 11RMS MAR-JAN X/T PETS CC KIDS INX

GLENBURNIE HOTEL: 01631 62089. Corran Esplanade. And this one is also good. Family run B&B. Full of family stuff, family photos and familiar furnishings. Could make you feel homesick. 14 RMS JAN-DEC X/T PETS CC KIDS MED/EX

CALEDONIAN HOTEL: 01631 563133. Station Sq. There are several Victorian/ municipal gothic edifices in Oban from the days when, as now, there were many visitors. Hard to know what to recommend: rms vary enormously, as does service etc. Here at least you are definitely at the centre of things – the pt. Try to get a rm at the front; and eat out. 70RMS JAN-DEC T/T PETS CC KIDS MED.EX

S.Y. HOSTEL: 01631 562025. On Esplanade (i.e. on the front). Grade 1.

CAMPING/CARAVAN SITES: Ganavan Sands, along coast rd (3km); grassy site adj to beach/leisure area (not quiet, plenty to do). 80 pitches, no tents. 016315 66479.

WHERE TO EAT

AIRDS HOTEL: 01631 730236. Pt Appin. 40km N by A828. A long way to go for dinner, but if you're in the area you just might want to eat at one of the best restaus in Scotland (644/ARGYLL HOTELS).   EXP

THE MANOR HOUSE: (*see above*). The best hotel dining-rm in town. Creative sauces on fresh seafood and other good things. Booking essential.   EXP

JULIE'S COFFEE HOUSE: 01631 565952. 33 Stafford St. Only 6 tables, so it's worth booking for dinner. Just three or four choices for each course, but what there is comes freshly prepared.   INX

THE BOXTREE: 01631 563542. 108 George St. Friendly little bistro in the middle of town. Better than you'd expect on this or any other main st. All day.   INX

THE STUDIO: 01631 562030. Craigard Rd off main st at Balmoral Hotel. Up the hill to find this candle-lit restau. Interesting menu that contains one or two mesquite dishes and for the real Desperate Dans, a Catalonian-style mixed grill. Often have to book. Apr-Oct, 5-10pm.   IXP

SALMON CENTRE: 01852 316202. 12km S at Kilninver on L Feochan. Worth the trip for the view alone. Seafood and salmon. See the life of salmon exhib, then eat them. 7 days, 10am-10pm. Dinner menu from 6 pm.   MED

THE BARN BAR: 01631 564618. 6km S at Lerags nr Foxholes Hotel. Popular out-of-town run for good pub food in bistro atmos. Kids welcome. Attached to chalet park but not unpleasant situation. 7 days, 11am-9pm (Closed Jan).   INX

WHAT TO SEE

DUNOLLIE CASTLE: On rd to Ganavan (1435/RUINS); **GLEN LONAN:** Gr wee glen starting 8km out of town (1272/GLENS); **SEALIFE CENTRE:** 16km N on A28 (1376/KIDS); **RARE BREEDS FARM:** 4km S from Argyll Sq (1377/KIDS); **McIAN GALLERY**; **OBAN INN:** (*see* WHISKY, *p.* 151); **McCAIG'S TOWER or FOLLY:** You can't miss it, dominating the skyline. A circular granite coliseum. Superb views of the bay. Many ways up, but a good place to start is via Stevenson St, opp Cally Hotel. Free, Open AYR (1487/ MONUMENTS). **KERRERA:** The island in the Sound reached by regular ferry from coast rd to Gallanach (4km town). Ferries at set times, but several per day – check TO. A fine wee island for walking, but pack your lunch. **LISMORE:** The other, larger island (1903/MAGICAL ISLANDS). Ferry from Oban (Calmac) or Pt Appin (passengers only). **DUNSTAFFNAGE CASTLE:** Signed and visible off A85 betw Oban and Connel (7km). 13th-century. V early type of castle, more of a ft, really. Unoccupied, except for the odd Clan McDougall spectre rattling around in the dungeons. Impressive setting and in good repair. Chapel in the woods **ARDCHATTAN:** 20km N via Connel. Along N shore of L Etive, a place to wander amongst ruins and grds. Tearoom. If you're along that way, go to the end of the rd at Bonawe where the famous granite that cobbled the world was (and still is) quarried. Bonawe Ironworks is open as a museum. **MINIATURES EXHIBITION:** Pier Front. You would imagine that Her Majesty the Queen must have seen just about everything by now, but apparently not. She spent 45mins. out of a hectic royal day peering at tiny 1/12 scale saxophones and miniscule French writing desks with working secret compartments and other assorted masterpieces in miniature. She must have had her reading specs with her.

WHAT TO DO

GOLF: Glencruitten (01631 562868) (1670/GOLF IN GREAT PLACES); **SWIMMING:** Oban swimming pool at Dalriach Rd (01631 566800); **PONY-TREKKING:** Achnalarig Farm, Glencruitten (01631 562745); **WINDSURFING:** Oban Windsurfing, Ganavan (01631 564380). Also at Linnhe Marine (01631 730227), 32km N via A828. Incl waterski and sailing (1713/WATER SPORTS); **FISHING:** Plenty on lochs and R Awe and Avich – check TO; **BIKE HIRE:** Oban Cycles (01631 566996).

TOURIST INFORMATION: Argyll Sq. 01631 563122. Jan-Dec.

THE BEST OF PERTH

WHERE TO STAY

BALLATHIE HOUSE, KINCLAVEN: 01250 883268. 20km N of Perth via Blairgowrie rd A93/left follow signs after 16km just before the famous beech hedge; or A9 and 4km N, take B9000 through Stanley. Former baronial hunting lodge beside the R Tay. Relaxed and informal atmos in definitive country house. Kevin MacGillivray's award-winning food. Fishing by arrangement with Estate office. Separate lodge at good rate. Nice people above and below stairs.

38RMS JAN-DEC T/T PETS CC KIDS TOS LOTS

HUNTINGTOWER HOTEL: 01738 583771. Crieff rd (1km off A85, 3km W of ring route A9 signed). Elegant, modernised mansion house o/side town. Good grds with spectacular copper beech. Subdued, panelled restau with decent menu (esp lunch) and wine list. Good service. 28RMS JAN-DEC T/T PETS CC KIDS TOS MED.EX

ROYAL GEORGE: 01738 624455. Tay St by the Perth Br over the Tay to the A93 rd to Blairgowrie and relatively close to Dundee rd and motorway system. Br is illuminated at night. Georgian proportions and elegance. Queen Victoria came by in 1842 now popular with farmers. 42RMS JAN-DEC T/T PETS CC KIDS MED.EX

SUNBANK HOUSE: 01738 624882. 50 Dundee Rd. On main rd out of town over river but removed from traffic and with good views of town and Tay. Gordon and Florence Laing retiring after 14yrs. See what happens to the 'inexp de luxe'. Nr Branklyn Gdns/Kinnoul Hill. 11RMS JAN-DEC T/T XPETS CC KIDS INX

S.Y. HOSTEL: 01738 623658. 107 Glasgow Rd in suburban area off main rd 1km centre. Grade 1 hostel, mostly larger dorms. No café.

CAMPING AND CARAVAN PARKS: SCONE RACECOURSE, 01738 552323. 4km NE of centre via A93 to Blairgowrie and left after Scone Palace. Grassy, flat site set amongst whispering pines. 150 pitches. Also **CLEEVE**, 01738 639521, off Glasgow Rd near ring route (2km) and 3km from centre. Narrow tree-ringed site nr rd. Sheltered, but some traffic noise. 100 pitches.

WHERE TO EAT

LET'S EAT: 01738 643377. 77 Kinnoull St. *The* place to eat (750/PERTHSHIRE HOTELS).

NO. 33: 01738 633771. George St. Bar with bar meals and à la carte restau serving credible and v edible seafood (1083/SEAFOOD RESTAUS). Gravadlax a speciality. Complementary puds like elderflower ice cream and the best selection of white wine in town. LO 9pm. INX(BAR)/MED

PIERRE VICTOIRE: 01738 444222. 38 South St. Airy, woody rm. Cheapish and cheerful bistro à la mode. 7 days. INX

KRUNGTHAI: 01738 633090. 161 South St. Another of the Thai places that have bobbed up everywhere like a prawn in a tom yum soup. Authentic fare offered by Thai owner/chef has earned good local rep. Lunch and till 11pm, 7 days (11.30pm w/ends). INX

PACO'S: 01738 444888. Café on corner of High St and S Methven St. Surprisingly cosmo feel to airy café in the centre of one of Scotland's most conservative towns. Restau nearby, both are rated. CHP/MED

BEPPE VITTORIO: 01738 628555. 181 South St. Little Italian brother of Pierre Victoire; the first franchise o/side Edin. Large busy rm not cramped like many Pierre's. I think it's better. Sound on Italian staples, perfectly good pesto. INX

HIGH PORT: 01738 444049. 47 South St. Bistro on main st with Turkish twist courtesy of Danny De Vito lookalike owner. Many kebabs, some veggie, goodish Turkish wines. Lunch, 6-11pm. Cl Sun. INX

ALMONDBANK INN: 01738 583242. Main St, Almondbank. Old pub looking down to R Almond in village 4km along Crieff rd W of ring route and A9. Pub lunches/suppers (6.30-8.30pm). Popular with locals. Book w/ends. INX

MARCELLO'S: 143 South St. Pizza pasta pitstop. Takeaway only. Noon-11pm (midnight Fri/Sat). Good looking guys knead the dough. INX

BETTY'S: 67 George St. Old-world parlour tearoom with gr home-baking, dish of the day and delicate soups. Opp art gallery. Licensed. 10am-5.30pm. Cl Sun.

LEMON TREE: Mill St. next to Ellery's deli. Innovative veggie restau. INX

WHAT TO SEE
KINNOUL HILL (1581/HILLS); **FERGUSSON GALLERY** (1833/PUBLIC GALLERIES); **GLENDOICK** (1793/GARDEN CENTRES); **ellery's** (1168/DELIS).

CHERRYBANK GARDENS/BRANKLYN GARDENS: Cherrybank is off Glasgow Rd, 18 acres of formal grds around the offices of United Distillers, notable esp for heathers. Open May-Oct 9am-5pm. Branklyn is signed off Dundee Rd beyond Queen's Br; park and walk 100m. A tightly packed cornucopia of typical grd flowers and shrubs. Open 7 days 9.30am-dusk.

PERTH THEATRE: 01738 621031. Established 1935 and Scotland's most successful repertory theatre (Ewan MacGregor got his first break here). Bar/coffee bar and restau. Essential all-round centre even for non-theatregoers.

WHAT TO DO
SWIMMING: Excellent large leisure centre with flumes pool and 'training' pool for lengths. Part of it is outdoors. Best app via Glasgow Rd (01738 630535). **SPORTS CENTRE:** The Gannochy or 'Bells' Complex for multigym (Universal), squash (5 courts), badminton etc. Hay St off Barrack St (01738 622301). **GOLF:** Interesting course on Moncreiffe Island in the middle of the Tay (01738 625170). Good course at Murrayshall, New Scone. Excellent course at Blairgowrie (01250 872622) (1669/GOLF IN GREAT PLACES).

TOURIST INFORMATION: 45 High St. 01783 638353. Jan-Dec.

THE BEST OF STIRLING 1948
MAP 6

WHERE TO STAY
THE GEAN HOUSE, ALLOA: 01259 219275. 12km E (683/CENTRAL HOTELS).

STIRLING HIGHLAND: 01786 475444 (684/CENTRAL HOTELS).

BLAIRLOGIE HOUSE: 01259 761441. 7km E on A91 (685/CENTRAL HOTELS).

PARK LODGE: 01786 474862. 32 Park Terrace off main Kings Park Rd, 500m from centre. Rather posh hotel in town house nr the park and golf course. Objets and lawns. Dinner taken (and recommended) at the Heritage, below. Mrs Pillinger's B&B at number 35 also looks good. 4RMS JAN-DEC T/T PETS CC KIDS MED.EX

THE HERITAGE: 01786 473660. 16 Allen Park, a quiet suburban st v close to centre, TO and main Bannockburn Rd. Owned by same folk as above; cheery French chef. Georgian town house. 4RMS JAN-DEC T/T PETS CC KIDS MED.INX

PORTCULLIS HOTEL: 01786 472290. Castle Wynd, which is no more than a cannonball's throw from the castle itself and one of the best locations in town. Pub and pub food place below; upstairs only 4 rms, but 3 have brilliant views of Castle/graveyard/town and plain. 4RMS JAN-DEC X/T PETS CC KIDS MED.INX

STIRLING MANAGEMENT CENTRE: 01786 451666. Not strictly speaking a hotel, but is as good as. Fully serviced rms on the univ campus (7km from centre in Br of Allan). Usually not full. Sports/entertainment facs nearby. Not so cheap anymore for distant location. 74RMS JAN-DEC T/T XPETS CC KIDS MED.INX

THE GOLDEN LION: 01786 475351. 8 King St. V central, large, functional with not so gr 'Gr Food Stop', but handy for shops/stn/Stirling stuff. 71RMS JAN-DEC T/T PETS CC KIDS MED.EX

S.Y. HOSTEL: 01786 473442. On rd up to castle in recently renovated jail is this new-style hostel, more like a budget hotel (932/HOSTELS).

CAMPING AND CARAVAN PARK: WITCHES CRAIG at BLAIRLOGIE, 01786 474947. 5km E on A91, St Andrews rd. Small park conveniently located and in meadow below the wonderful Ochils. Wallace Monument shows you the way home. Apr-Oct.

WHERE TO EAT
HERMANN'S: 01786 450632. At the 'Tolbooth' entering from either Broad St or St John's St on rd up to Castle. Hermann Aschaber's corner of Austria where schnitzels and strudels figure along with Cullin Skink and other good Scottish produce. 2 level, ambient well run rms with cheery aproned staff. MED

STIRLING MERCHANT: 01786 473929. 39 Broad St. Also on rd up to Castle. Long standing restau site, but this version gr improvement. Scottish theme to food and decor with pikestaffs upstairs, softer tartans in the bistro. INX

SCHOLARS at the STIRLING HIGHLAND HOTEL: 01786 473052. The up-market, up-by-the-Castle eaterie in town, the Stirling Highland a good conversion of an old school hence the name (684/CENTRAL HOTELS). Tries to live up to reputation. EXP

PACOS: 01786 446414. Nr TO in town centre. Tex-mex restau as the one in Perth. We didn't try, but good feel and LO 10.30pm. INX

PIERRE VICTOIRE: 01786 448171. Friars St, a pedestrian precinct off the main through rd for traffic and opp the Royal Bank. The national bistro chain in Stirling - natch! Usual individuality, cheap lunches, but fading appeal? INX

THE EAST INDIA COMPANY: 01786 471330. 7 Viewfield Pl. Still proclaim to be the best Indian in town. Maybe so. Good atmos in woody basement rm. Pakora bar for snacks upstairs. Open 7 days till 11pm. INX

KAM'S GARDEN: 01786 446 445. 4 Viewfield Pl nr E India (above) so best Chinese and best Indian adj. Calm; and Kam cuisine. LO 11pm 7 days. INX

ITALIA NOSTRA: 01786 473208. 25 Baker St. Gr name. The tratt to try (Bar Italia, Br of Allan at the Walmer Hotel also recommended). The fetching neckerchiefs have long gone, but fetching waiters remain. Busy atmos. 7 days. 11/12pm. CHP

CAFÉ ALBERT at the ALBERT HALL: 01786 448171. Unusual success story for a café/bistro created in a municipal hall, Hot dishes, baguettes, imaginative snacks. Newspapers and a relaxed atmos. Mon-Sat 9-5pm. CHP

THE BARNTON BAR AND BISTRO: 01786 461698. Barnton St opp main post office. Perenially popular. Jukebox. All-day breakfast, baked potatoes, hefty sandwiches. Newspapers. 7 days. Food till 8pm, then bar takes over. CHP

DUFFIN'S: 17 Friar St. Daytime coffee shop with gr snacks and esp round the world muffins. It's the shop stop. CHP

ALLAN WATER CAFE, BRIDGE OF ALLAN: 8km up the rd in Br of Allan main st nr br itself. Great café, the best fish 'n' chips 'n' ice cream (1099/CAFÉS). CHP

WHAT TO SEE
STIRLING CASTLE (1406/CASTLES); **WALLACE MONUMENT/THE PINEAPPLE** (1479/1485/MONUMENTS); **BANNOCKBURN/SHERIFFMUIR** (1537/BATTLEGROUNDS); **THE OCHILS** (1586/HILL WALKS; 1609/GLEN AND RIVER WALKS); **LOGIE OLD KIRK** (1519/GRAVEYARDS); **PARADISE** (1350/PICNICS); **DUNBLANE CATHEDRAL** (1503/CHURCHES).

STIRLING OLD TOWN JAIL: St John's St on rd up to Castle. Guided tour and put-up job, but rather well done. Live actors. Kids will be quiet or simply tortured. Open AYR (4pm winter).

THE GHOST WALK: A stroll through old part of the town nr the castle: 'a world of restless spirits and lost souls' (sound familiar?). Info: TO or 01786 450945.

RAINBOW SLIDES: Nr Railway Stn. A leisure centre with good 25m pool and gym (Pulsestar) and for kids 3 water slides of varying thrill factors. Open 7 days (Sat and Sun till 4pm). Check times: 01786 462521.

WHAT TO DO
SWIMMING/SPORTS: (*see above*). There's also a pool at the University Sports Centre and at the Stirling Highland Hotel (with squash). **GOLF:** Stirling Golf Course v central at Queens Rd. Quite testing and one of best in area (01786 464098). **BIKE HIRE:** Stewart Wilson Cycles, 49 Barnton St (01786 450809).

TOURIST INFORMATION: Dumbarton Rd. 01786 475019. Jan-Dec.

1949
MAP 2

THE BEST OF ULLAPOOL

WHERE TO STAY
ALTNAHARRIE INN: 01854 633230. 2km Ullapool other side of L Broom (by private boat). One of the v best (907/COUNTRY-HOUSE HOTELS).

8RMS   APR-OCT   X/X   PETS   CC   KIDS   LOTS

THE CEILIDH PLACE: 01854 612103. 14 W Argyle St. Eclectic individualism; something to celebrate (796/INEXP HIGHLAND HOTELS). Also cheap 'bunkhouse' accom.

24RMS   JAN-DEC   T/X   PETS   CC   KIDS   EXP/CHP

268   LOCAL CENTRES

MOREFIELD HOTEL: 01854 612161. Edge of town A835 heading N. Surreal location in midst of housing estate. Small motel cabins and gr seafood amongst big varied menu (1079/SEAFOOD RESTAUS). 10RMS JAN-DEC T/T PETS CC KIDS INX

TAIGH-NA-MARA: 01854 655282. 15km S then 5km up opp side of L Broom. 3 bed cottage on loch side; seclusion and sustenance (1059/VEGN RESTAUS). INX

TIR ALUINN: 01854 612074. Leckmelm 5km S on A835. Rambling country house in large grounds beside the loch with gr views. Basic accom and tariff. 14RMS MAY-SEPT X/T PETS XCC KIDS INX

S.Y. HOSTEL: 01854 612254. On Shore St (the front) converted from cottages. Grade 2. Can book by fax. Also at Achiltibuie (same number) 40km by rd, 22km by footpath. A good base for this scenic area; book in summer.

CAMPING/CARAVAN SITE: 01854 612054. Ardmair Pt. 6km N on A835.

WHERE TO EAT
THE CEILIDH PLACE: *as above.*

THE MOREFIELD HOTEL: *as above.*

SCOTTISH LARDER: 01854 612185. Ladysmith St. Lauri Chilton's new restau serves hearty Scottish fare; pies, veggie, salads, local seafood. 5.30-9pm. Adj guesthouse. INX

WHAT TO SEE
CORRIESHALLOCH GORGE: 20km S (1284/WATERFALLS); **AN TEALLACH** 40km S by rd (1321/VIEWS); **ACHILTIBUIE:** 40km NW (1309/SCENIC ROUTES); **STAC POLLAIDH** (pron 'Polly', 1568/HILLS); **HIGHLAND STONEWARE** and **KNOCKAN GALLERY** 1741/1747/CRAFT SHOPS); **HIGHLAND RARE BREEDS FARM** (1374/KIDS). **LOCH BROOM** pool/leisure centre 01854 612884.

TOURIST INFORMATION: Argyle St. 01854 612135. Easter-Nov.

THE BEST OF WICK AND THURSO

WHERE TO STAY
FORSS HOUSE HOTEL, nr THURSO: 01847 861201. 8km W on A836. The MacGregor's family home set in 20 woodland acres by the sea is the best quality hotel for miles. Popular restau (you should book), comfortable spacious rms and 5 chalets in the grounds too. Breakfast in the conservatory then birds, walks, old mill and waterfall. Fishing. 10RMS JAN-DEC T/T PETS CC KIDS TOS MED.EX

PORTLAND ARMS, LYBSTER: 01593 721208. On main A9 20km S of Wick and 45km S of Thurso by A895. A coaching inn since 1851; still hospitable. Large comfy rms sprawl across the Georgian house filled with family photos, antique chairs and tapestries. Teas thoroughout the day are followed by the popular evening meals in bright dining-rm. 20RMS JAN-DEC T/T PETS CC KIDS TOS MED.INX

BORGIE LODGE HOTEL, nr BETTYHILL: 01641 521332. A836 12km W of Tongue. Secluded trad huntin', shootin', fishin' sort of a place: 20 hill lochs and 2 rivers with salmon and trout. Shooting on the adj 12,000 acre estate and Jacqui's acclaimed cooking to come home to. 7RMS FEB-DEC X/X PETS CC KIDS TOS MED.INX

ROYAL HOTEL, THURSO: 01847 893191. Trail St in town centre. Sprawling stone inn upgraded to comfortable commercialism. All mod cons and pool/leisure complex planned shortly. Some say it can be cold here in Thurso - so take your vest. 105RMS JAN-DEC T/T PETS CC KIDS MED.INX

BREADALBANE HOUSE HOTEL, WICK: 01955 603911. Family hotel close to harbour and town centre. Victorian house with cosy dining-rm, adj bar and large bedrms. 10RMS JAN-DEC X/T PETS CC KIDS INX

ACKERGILL TOWER, nr WICK: 01955 603556. A rare treat (964/GET-AWAY-FROM-IT-ALL)

S.Y. HOSTEL: 01955 611424. At Canisbay, John O'Groats (7km). Wick 25km. Regular bus service. The furthest flung youth hostel on the mainland.

CAMPING AND CARAVAN PARK, DUNNET BAY: 01847 821319. On grassy strand nr wonderful crescent of beach; a nature reserve. 14km N of Thurso. **THURSO, Scrabster Rd:** 01955 603761. Exposed cliff top site to W of town.

WHERE TO EAT
FORSS HOUSE HOTEL, PORTLAND ARMS, BORGIE LODGE HOTEL: *(all as above)*

LA MIRAGE, HELMSDALE: 60km S. Viva Las Vegas! (822/INEXP HIGHLAND RESTAUS). INX

THE BOWER INN: 01955 661292. In the middle of the nowhere betw Wick and Thurso; off coast rd at Castletown on B876 (1km Bowermadden crossrds, signed Gillock). An old fav with the locals; now under new management. Coaching inn with 2 dining-rms and fairly extensive menu. Peat tools on the timbers; farmers at the bar could tell you how to use them. LO 9.30pm. Good Sunday lunch. INX

THE UPPER DECK, SCRABSTER: 01847 892814. 3km W of Thurso in busy pt area o/look BP and ferry terminal for Orkney. New owners, so 1950s kitsch interior we like, due to be revamped. 'Turf' (meat) on upper deck and 'surf' (fish) on top deck. Adj bar. Lunch and 7-11pm, 7 days. INX

DUNNET TEA-ROOM by DUNNET HEAD: 01847 851774. 15km N of Thurso by coast rd. Extensive menu. Apr-Oct 3-8pm (831/INEXP HIGHLAND RESTAUS). CHP

OLD SMIDDY INN, THRUMSTER: 01955 651256. 7km S of Wick on A9. New bar/restau/café full of smiddyish stuff. Snacks, meals and blackboard specials. 7 days; Sun-Thur 12-2pm, 5.30-8.30pm; Fri and Sat all day. LO 9pm. CHP

QUEENS HOTEL and CENTRAL HOTEL: both in Wick town centre. Haven't tried, but both popular with locals for bar food. INX

WHAT TO SEE
DUNBEATH: 32km S of Wick (1554/LITERARY PLACES; 1612/GLEN AND RIVER WALKS); **CAIRNS OF CAMSTER:** 15km S of Wick (1457/PREHISTORIC SITES); **BETTYHILL MUSEUM:** 50km W of Thurso (1817/MUSEUMS); **NORTH COAST BEACHES** (1261/BEACHES).

WICK HERITAGE CENTRE: 01955 605393. In town centre; June-Sept. **CAITHNESS GLASS CENTRE, WICK:** 01955 602286. Home of popular gift ware; factory and visitor centre; by the airport.

THE TRINKIE: A walk along the rocky coast E of Wick or drive through housing schemes until cliff rd appears (ask locals). Flat rocks, an open-air pool; a good spot. 2km further for the 'Brig O' Trams'.

WHALIGOE STEPS: On A9 N of Lybster; down track nr cottages and pond, by Cairn O' Get sign. Infamy regained after Big Yin's visit; 365 stone cliff steps to sea where herrings used to be landed and cured. Unsignposted so ask locally for directions if lost, and go carefully.

WILDLIFE CRUISE, JOHN O' GROATS: 01955 611353. June-Aug; 90min trips to sea stacks, birds and **JOHN O' GROATS - ORKNEY:** May-Sept day trips.

WHAT TO DO
SWIMMING: Wick (01955 603711), Thurso (01847 893260). Both central. **GOLF:** Wick (01955 602726), Thurso (01847 893807), Reay (01847 811288). **SURFING AND WINDSURFING:** Esp round Thurso. TO have leaflet about beaches. **RIDING:** Dunnet Trekking. Glorious trekking on Dunnet Beach (01847 851689). **BIKE HIRE:** From Wheels (01955 603636). **VIKING BOWL:** built using old US naval bowling lanes; cinema soon (01847 895050).

TOURIST INFORMATION

WICK: Whitechapel Rd. 01955 602596. Jan-Dec.

THURSO: Riverside. 01847 892371. Apr-Oct.

HOLIDAY CENTRES
Pitlochry

WHERE TO STAY
KILLIECRANKIE HOTEL: 01796 473220 (744/PERTHSHIRE HOTELS). MED.EX

PINE TREES: 01796 472121. Off Main St (743/PERTHSHIRE HOTELS). MED.EX

DUNFALLANDY HOUSE: 01796 472648. Just out of town (2km), but away from all that. Dinner a treat. V good value country-house hotel. 9 rms. MED.INX

WHERE TO EAT

KILLIECRANKIE HOTEL: Go those miles (5) to dinner; or bar meals! *(above).* INX
EAST HAUGH HOTEL: 01796 473121. 3km S off A9. Gr bar meals/restau. MED

PORTNACRAIG: 01796 472777. By theatre, on river. An insider choice. INX
OLD SMITHY: 01796 472356. Main St. Coffees/restau. 7 days. LO 8.30pm. INX
MILL POND BISTRO: Burnside Apartments, 500m up Braemar rd. A good find. MED
PRINCE OF INDIA: 01796 472275. Off main st by McNaughtons. Unusually good Indian. MED
MOULIN INN: 01796 472196. Notable for pub food and atmos (1019/REAL ALE). 6km uphill. LO 9.30pm. CHP

WHAT TO SEE

THE SALMON LADDER: From Main St and across dam to see 34-pool fish ladder (salmon leaping May-Oct, if you're lucky) and Hydro Board displays *(sic)*; **BEN Y VRACKIE:** Local fave with fab Trossachs views climbed from Moulin (2km from town). Rd behind Moulin Inn. Car park. 734m. Scree at top; and goats; **FASKALLY WOODS/LINN OF TUMMEL WALKS:** Well-marked woodland walks around L Faskally and Garry R. Can incl the Linn (rapids) and Pass of Killiecrankie (1536/BATTLEGROUNDS). START: town/Garry bridge/visitor centre; **WOOLLEN SHOPS:** Many major chains and local shops in one small area/the main st. **PITLOCHRY THEATRE** (1874/THEATRES); **QUEEN'S VIEW** (1331/VIEWS); **EDRADOUR DISTILLERY** (1188/WHISKY); **MACNAUGHTON'S** (1774/OUTDOOR SHOPS); **MOULIN INN** (1019/REAL ALE).

Inveraray

WHERE TO STAY

GEORGE HOTEL: 01499 302111. On main st and in the Clark family for centuries (no, really – 1790). A gr value hotel – ales, good pub food, real fires. CHP
LOCH FYNE HOTEL: 01499 302148. On A83 rd out of town towards W, o/look loch. Personally run. Good bar meals. MED.INX

WHERE TO EAT

THE GEORGE/LOCH FYNE HOTELS: Bar meals esp. *(See above.)* CHP
LOCH FYNE OYSTER BAR: 01499 306217. 14km E on A83. INX
CREGGANS INN: 01369 860279. 32km E and S via A83/A815. On opp bank of L Fyne, but 35mins by rd. Bar meals/restau. MED

WHAT TO SEE

INVERARAY CASTLE: Home of the Duke of Argyll and clan seat of the Campbells. Spectacular entrance hall; chronicle of Highland shenanigans unfurls in the gilded apartments. Fine walks in grounds esp to the prominent hill and folly (45mins up). Apr-Oct. **COMBINED OPERATIONS MUSEUM:** Inverary Castle grounds (1824/MUSEUMS); **CRARAE:** 15km S on A83; **ARDKINGLAS WOODLAND:** 17km E on A83 (1211/GARDENS). **AUCHINDRAIN:** 8km S on A83; **INVERARAY JAIL** (1825/MUSEUMS); **ARGYLL WILDLIFE PARK:** 4km S on A83 (1378/KIDS).

St Andrews

WHERE TO STAY

OLD COURSE HOTEL: 01334 474371 (720/FIFE HOTELS). LOTS
RUFFLETS: 01334 472594 (722/FIFE HOTELS). EXP
RUSACKS: 01334 474321. A Forte hotel, rather exp (but most hotels in St Andrews are overpriced). Near all courses and overlooking the 18th of the Old. Nice sun-lounge, but dining-room is v indoors. LOTS
ASHLEIGH HOUSE: 01334 475429. 37 St Mary's St. On Crail rd (A917) towards E Sands Leisure Centre 1km centre. Golfy, on a budget. INX
ARGYLE HOUSE: 01334 473387. 127 North St. On corner of Murray Park with numerous guest-house alternatives. This one is central and adequate. INX
NUMBER TEN: 01334 474601. 10 Hope St. Bit of Edinburgh Newtown in calm st nr centre. Georgian elegance etc. 10 rms. INX
GLENDERRON: 01334 477951. 9 Murray Park. A guest house with only 5 rms, but tasteful and good value. The one to choose on this street of a myriad. INX
MORTON OF PITMILLY and **KILCONQUHAR**

WHERE TO EAT

THE PEAT INN: 01334 840 206. 15km SW (729/FIFE HOTELS). EXP

THE VINE LEAF: 0134 477497. 131 South St. Excl new contemporary restau thro' passageway behind the baked potato place looking out to 'herb gdn'. Light, inventive menu not so meaty. Good vegn. MED

THE DOLL'S HOUSE: 01334 477422. Church Sq. V central cafe/restau that caters well for kids (and teenagers). Eclectic range, Smillie people and tables outside in summer. INX

GRANGE INN: 01334 472670. 4km E off Anstruther rd A917. In new hands at time of going to press, but this country pub has always had good local rep.

CIAO ROMA: 01334 472090. 89 South St. Branch of Edinburgh Italian, here to good effect. Bustling atmos. Relatively exp, but good pasta and open late. MED

NEW BALAKA: 01334 474825. 'Best Curry in Scotland' winner. Certainly as good as many in the city top ten. MED

MERCHANT'S HOUSE and **BRAMBLES** (1127/TEAROOMS). Both excellent. Daytime.

WHAT TO SEE

THE TOWN ITSELF: The lanes, cloisters, gardens and the University halls and colleges; the harbour and the botanic gardens. Perfect lawns; **THE CASTLE RUINS:** Founded in 13th cent on promontory; good for clambering over. 'Escape tunnel' to explore (if not tall). Spooky by night along this shore; **BRITISH GOLF MUSEUM:** Sophisticated audio-visual exhibition illustrating history and allure of the game. Even non-players will enjoy. **THE HIMALAYAS:** the most brilliant putting green; piles of fun, near the beach. Apr-Oct till 8pm, 7 days. Many **GOLF COURSES** (1660/GREAT GOLF); **WEST SANDS/KINSHALDY BEACH** (1259/ BEACHES); **LEUCHARS CHURCH:** 9km by A91 N (1501/CHURCHES); **TENTSMUIR:** 20km by A91/A919 N (1402/WILDLIFE); **NEW PICTURE HOUSE** (1880/THEATRES); **JANETTA'S** (1148/ICE CREAM); **ST ANDREWS FINE ART**; **CATHEDRAL** (1438/RUINS); **SEALIFE CENTRE**; **EAST SANDS** (1699/LEISURE CENTRES).

Royal Deeside: Ballater and Banchory

WHERE TO STAY

DARROCH LEARG, BALLATER: 01339 755443. Town mansion above/off (at tight bend) A93 on way in from Braemar. Reasonably priced/friendly. MED.

BANCHORY LODGE, BANCHORY: 01330 822625 (765/NE HOTELS). EXP

RAEMOIR, BANCHORY: 01330 824884. Large mansion in secluded grounds 3km town by Raemoir Rd off A93. Relaxed and discreet. 9-hole golf and tennis. LOTS

TOR-NA-COILLE, BANCHORY: 01330 822242. Town mansion above/just off main A93 on way in from Ballater. Nr golf. Antiques in tasteful/individual rms. EXP

BALLATER GUEST HOUSE, BALLATER: 01339 755346. INX

WHERE TO EAT

DARROCH LEARG, BALLATER: 01339 755443. Growing reputation (*see above*).

THE OAK ROOM, BALLATER: 01339 755858. EXP

THE GREEN INN, BALLATER: 01339 755701. With 3 inexpensive rms above. Scottish fresh prod, home cooking. (774/ NE HOTELS.) MED

THE BLACK-FACED SHEEP, ABOYNE: 01339 887311. Near main rd. Coffee shop/gift shop with excellent home-baking. Daytime hrs (1112/TEAROOMS).

MILTON RESTAURANT: 01330 844566 (777/ NE HOTELS). MED

THE WHITE COTTAGE, nr ABOYNE: 01339 886265. On main A93 4km towards Banchory. Cottage dining and conservatory. Good home-cooking/atmos. MED

WHAT TO SEE

CRAIGIEVAR/DRUM (1421/1422CASTLES); **FASQUE** (1468/COUNTRY HOUSES); **CRATHES** 1199/1477 GARDENS/COUNTRY HOUSES; **BALMORAL** 1423/CASTLES; **LOCHNAGAR** (1594/MUNROS); **ALBERT MEMORIAL** (1488/MONUMENTS); **GLEN MUICK** (1297/LOCHS); **CAMBUS O'MAY** (1351/PICNICS); **GOLF:** Well-managed/picturesque courses, open to visitors at both Ballater (01339 855567), and Banchory (01339 752447). Both 18 holes; **FISHING:** Difficult, not impossible, on Dee (try 01339 886891 or 01738 821121) or on R Feugh (N bank only) – permits from Feughside Inn (01330 850225); **WALKS:** Walks down both sides of the Dee, esp Ballater to Cambus O'May, 7km; **VIEWPOINTS:** Up Craigendarroch, the Hill of the Oaks, Ballater, from Braemar Rd (45mins). Scolty Hill and Monument, Banchory. Ask for directions.

SECTION 14

The Likes of You and Me

THE BIG ATTRACTIONS

Amongst the 'top ten' (paid admn) and the 'top ten' (free admn) visitor attractions, the following are really worth seeing:

KELVINGROVE ART GALLERY; THE BURRELL COLLECTION: 578/579 MAIN ATTRACTIONS.

THE MUSEUM OF TRANSPORT; THE GLASGOW BOTANICS; THE GALLERY OF MODERN ART: 584/585/586/OTHER ATTRACTIONS.

THE PEOPLE'S PALACE, GLASGOW: 581/MAIN ATTRACTIONS.

EDINBURGH CASTLE; HOLYROOD PALACE; EDINBURGH ZOO; THE NATIONAL gallery: 304/305/309/308/MAIN ATTRACTIONS.

THE EDINBURGH BOTANICS: 312/OTHER ATTRACTIONS.

CULZEAN CASTLE; STIRLING CASTLE: 1409/1406 CASTLES.

ABERDEEN ART GALLERY: 1832/PUBLIC GALLERIES.

THE OTHER MAJOR ATTRACTIONS ARE:

1955 **LOCH LOMOND:** App via Stirling and A811 to Drymen or from Glas, the A82
MAP 6 Dumbarton rd to Balloch. Britain's largest inland waterway and a trad
B3 playground, especially for Glaswegians; jet-skis, show-off boats.

W bank Balloch-Tarbert is most developed: marinas, cruises, ferry to Inchmurrin Island. Luss is tweeville, like a movie set (it was used in the Scottish TV soap *Take the High Road)* and a good place to buy that souvenir tea towel. Rd more picturesque beyond Tarbert to Ardlui (933/HOSTELS); *see* 1003/BLOODY GOOD PUBS for the non-tourist/real Scots experience of the Drover's Inn at Inverarnan.

E bank more natural, wooded; good lochside and hill walks (1584/HILL WALKS; 1589/MUNROS). Rd winding but picturesque beyond Balmaha towards Ben Lomond (936/HOSTELS).

1956 **THE CUILLINS, SKYE:** This hugely impressive mt range in the S of Skye, often
MAP 2 shrouded in cloud or rain, is the romantic heartland of the Islands. The Red
B3 Cuillins are smoother and nearer the Portree-Broadford rd; the Black Cuillins gather behind and are best approached from Glen Brittle (1602/SERIOUS WALKS; 1781/WATERFALLS). This classic, untameable mt scenery has attracted walkers, climbers and artists for centuries. It still claims lives regularly. For best views apart from Glen Brittle, *see* 1308/SCENIC ROUTES; 1324/VIEWS. Vast range of walks and scrambles (*see also* 1335/PICNICS).

1957 **THE DISCOVERY, DUNDEE:** The main attraction in Dundee. Central river side
MAP 4 location at Discovery Point and state-of-the-art visitor centre. This tall-masted
D3 ship, built in Dundee for the 1901 Antarctica expedition with Scott and Shackleton, lies permanently at anchor. A research vessel designed to withstand the ice, it was built using local shipbuilders' long experience from whaling (for whale craft history, see the Broughty Ferry Museum in the Castle on the Esplanade). Go below decks to see a surprisingly comfortable abode. 'Marvel' at the officers' mess, the penguin in the oven (!), the thickness of the hull. 10am-5pm (till 4pm Nov-Mar), opens 11am on Sun. But don't miss the frigate **UNICORN** further along in dockland, the oldest British warship afloat. ADMN

1958 **LOCH NESS:** Most visits start from Inverness (1945/INVERNESS) at the N end via
MAP 2 the R Ness. Ft Augustus is at the other end, 56km S. L Ness is part of the still-
D3 navigable Caledonian Canal linking the E and W coast at Ft William. Many small boats line the shores of the R Ness, and one of the best ways to see the loch is on a cruise from Inverness (Jacobite Cruises 01463 233999) or Drumnadrochit (L Ness Cruises 01456 450395). Most tourist traffic uses the main A82 N bank rd converging on Drumnadrochit where the L Ness Monster industry gobbles up your money. If you must, the 'Official' L Ness Monster Exhibition is the one to choose. On the A82 you can't miss Urquhart Castle (1442/RUINS); see also Dochfour (1789/GARDEN CENTRES). But the two best things about L Ness are: the S rd (B862) from Ft Augustus back to Inverness (1314/SCENIC ROUTES; 1314/WATERFALLS); and the detour from Drumnadrochit to Cannich to Glen Affric (20-30km) (1265/GLENS; 1608/ GLEN AND RIVER WALKS; 1277/WATERFALLS).

FAVOURITE SCOTTISH JOURNEYS

A miscellany of memorable journeys by trains, boats and planes.

WEMYSS BAY-ROTHESAY FERRY: Calmac 01475 650100. The glass-roofed stn at Wemyss Bay is the railhead from Glas (60km by rd on the A78), and has the atmos and vitality of an age-old terminus. The frequent ferry (Calmac) has all the Scottish traits and sausage rolls you can handle, and Rothesay (with its winter grd and castle and period seaside mansions) appears out of blood-smeared sunsets and rain-sodden mornings alike, a gentle watercolour from summer holidays past. Go to the (Victorian) toilet when you get there.
1959 MAP 1 C3

LOCH ETIVE CRUISES: 01866 822430, though booking not essential. From Taynuilt (Oban 20km) through the long narrow waters of one of Scotland's most atmospheric lochs, a 3hr journey in a small cruiser with indoor and outdoor seating. Pier is 2km from main Taynuilt crossroads on A85. Leaves 2pm (and 10.30am in summer). Travel into the heart of the Highlands, the loch sides inaccessible by car; deer and golden eagles may attend your journey.
1960 MAP 1 C1

GLENELG-KYLERHEA: The shorter of the 2 remaining ferry journeys to Skye now the br has come, and definitely the best way to get there if you're not pushed for time. The drive to Glenelg from the A87 is spectacular (1305/SCENIC ROUTES) and so is this 5min crossing of the deep Narrows of Kylerhea. Apr-Oct (frequent) 9-6pm and Sun in summer (10-6pm). 01599 511302.
1961 MAP 2 C4

CORRAN FERRY: From Ardgour on A861-Nether Lochaber on the A82 across the narrows of L Linnhe. A convenient 5min crossing which can save time to pts S of Mallaig and takes you to the wilderness of Moidart and Ardnamurchan and which is a charming and fondly regarded journey in its own rt. Runs continuously until 8.50pm summer, 6.20pm winter.
1962 MAP 1/2 C4

THE *MAID OF THE FORTH* CRUISE TO INCHCOLM ISLAND: 0131 331 4857. The wee boat (though they say it holds 200 people) which leaves every day at different times (phone for details) from Hawes Pier in S Queensferry (15km Central Edin via A90) opp the Hawes Inn, just under the famous railway br (311/MAIN ATTRACTIONS) and also from the pier at N Queensferry. 45min trips under the br and on to Inchcolm, an attractive island with walks and an impressive ruined abbey. Much birdlife and also many seals. 1hr 30mins ashore. Tickets at pier.
1963 MAP 7 B1

THE WEST HIGHLAND LINE: Info: 0345 484950. One of the most picturesque railway journeys in Europe and quite the best way to get to Skye from the S. Travel to Ft William from Glas, then relax and watch the stunning scenery, the Bonnie Prince Charlie country (MARY, CHARLIE AND BOB, *pp.193-4*) and much that is close to a railwayman's heart go past the window. Viaducts and tunnels over loch and down dale. Also possible to make the same journey (from Ft William to Mallaig and/or return) by steam train on certain days. Journey time 1hr 45mins. Check on 01397 703791. For anyone interested in trains, there's a museum in the restored stn at Glenfinnan. Trains for Mallaig leave from Glas Queen St about 3 times a day and takes about 5hrs.
1964 MAP 2

FROM INVERNESS: Info on 0345 484950. Two less-celebrated but mesmerising rail journeys start from Inverness. The journey **to Kyle of Lochalsh** no longer has an observation car in the summer months, so get a window seat and take an atlas; the last section through Glen Carron and around the coast at Loch Carron is especially fine. There are 4 trains a day and it takes 2hrs 30mins. Inverness **to Wick** is a 3hr 30min journey. The section skirting the E coast from Lairg-Helmsdale is full of drama and is then followed by the transfixing monotony of the Flow Country (it's the best way to see it). There are 4 trains a day in summer.
1965 MAP 2

THE PLANE TO BARRA: Most of the island plane journeys pass over many smaller islands (e.g. Glas-Tiree, Glas-Stornoway, Wick-Orkney) and are fascinating on a clear day, but BA's daily flight to Barra is doubly special because the island doesn't have an airport and you land on Cockleshell Beach in the N of the island (11 km from Castlebay) after a splendid app. The Otter holds only 15 passengers and leaves and lands according to the tide. 0345 222111.
1966 MAP 2

THE ESSENTIAL SCOTTISH BOOKS

FICTION

Iain Banks, *The Wasp Factory; The Bridge*
George Douglas Brown, *The House with the Green Shutters*
George Mackay Brown, *Greenvoe; The Masked Fisherman*
John Buchan, *The 39 Steps/Short Stories*
Lewis Grassic Gibbon, *Sunset Song*
Neil Gunn, *Highland River; The Silver Darlings*
Alasdair Gray, *Lanark*
Archie Hind, *The Dear Green Place*
James Hogg, *Confessions of a Justified Sinner*
Robin Jenkins, *The Cone Gatherers*
A L Kennedy, *Night Geometry and the Garscadden Trains*
William McIlvanney, *Docherty*
Bess Ross, *A Bit of Crack and Car Culture*
Sir Walter Scott, *The Heart of Midlothian; The Two Drovers and Other Stories; Old Mortality*
Robert Louis Stevenson, *Kidnapped; Master of Ballantrae; Catriona; Short Stories*
Muriel Spark, *The Prime of Miss Jean Brodie*
Alexander Trocchi, *Cain's Book; Young Adam*
Alan Warner, *Morvern Callar*
Irvine Welsh, *Trainspotting*

NON-FICTION

Boswell and Johnson, *Journey to the Western Islands*
Jim Crumley, *A High And Lonely Place*
Raymond Eagle, *Seton Gordon: A Highland Gentleman*
Antonia Fraser, *Mary Queen of Scots*
George MacDonald Fraser, *The Steel Bonnets*
Elizabeth Grant of Rothiemurchus, *Memoirs of a Highland Lady*
Muriel Gray, *The First Fifty: Munro-Bagging without a Beard*
Osgood Mackenzie, *100 Years in the Highlands* (out of print but still available at Inverewe Grds)
Gavin Maxwell, *Ring of Bright Water*
William Poucher, *The Magic of Skye*
John Preble, *1000 Years of Scotland's History; The Lion in the North; The Highland Clearances; Culloden; Glencoe*
TC Smout, *A History of the Scottish People*
Nigel Tranter, *The Story of Scotland*

POETRY

Robert Burns, *Collected Songs and Poems*
Norman McCaig, *Collected Poems*

A FEW THINGS THE SCOTS GAVE THE WORLD

The population of Scotland has never exceeded 5 million.

The decimal point
The Bank of England
The overdraft
Documentary films
Colour photographs
Encyclopaedia Britannica
Postcards
The gas mask
The advertising film
The bus
The steam engine
The fax machine
The photocopier
Video
The telephone
Television
Radar
The telegraph
The lawnmower
Continuous electric light
The alpha chip
The Thermos flask
The Hypodermic syringe

Anaesthesia
Antiseptics
Golf clubs
The 18-hole golf course
Tennis courts
The bowling green
The thermometer
The gravitating compass
The threshing machine
Insulin
Penicillin
Interferon
The pneumatic tyre
The modern road surface
The kaleidoscope
Marmalade
The self-acting fountain pen
The Mackintosh
Gardenias
Dolly, the cloned sheep

THE BEST EVENTS

UP HELLY AA: Info: 01595 693434. Traditionally on the 24th day after Christmas, but now always the last Tues in Jan. A mid-winter fire festival based on Viking lore where 'the Guizers' haul a galley thro the streets of Lerwick and burn it in the park; and the night goes on.   **1967**   **JAN**

CELTIC CONNECTIONS, GLASGOW: Tickets and info: 0141 227 5511. A huge festival of Celtic music from round the world held in the Royal Concert Hall and other city venues over 2/3 weeks. Concerts and ceilidhs.   **1968**   **MAP B**   **JAN**

BURNS NIGHT: The National Bard celebrated with supper. No single major event.   **1969**   **JAN 25TH**

GLASGOW ART FAIR, GLASGOW: Info: 0141 552 6027 (as long as my lot are still organising it). Britain's most significant commercial art fair o/side London held in mid-April in tented pavilions in George Sq with selected galleries from Scotland and UK.   **1970**   **MAP B**   **APRIL**

MELROSE SEVENS: Info TO 01896 822555. Border town of Melrose completely taken over by tournament in their small is beautiful rugby ground. 7-a-side teams from all over incl international. It's just a good place to go, fanatical or not. *See p. 262* for accom and eats.   **1971**   **MAP 8**   **C3**   **APRIL**

FIFE POINT TO POINT, LEVEN, FIFE: 01333 360229. Major 'society' i.e. county set, get-together at Balcormo Mains Farm. Sort of Scottish equivalent of Henley with horses organised by Fife Fox and Hounds. Range Rovers, hampers and Hermes with Julia Scott-Barrett and her chums.   **1972**   **MAP 5**   **D3**   **APRIL**

PAPS OF JURA HILL RACE, ISLE OF JURA: Details from the hotel 01496 820243. The amazing hill race up and down the 3 Paps or distinctive peaks (total of 7 hills altogether) on this large remote island (1894/MAGICAL ISLANDS). About 150 runners take part on the 14 mile challenge from the distillery in Craighouse, the village.   **1973**   **MAP 2**   **B2/**   **B3**   **MAY**

FLOWER SHOWS, STRATHCLYDE PARK & AYR: Info 01292 612000. Many Scottish towns hold flower shows, mainly in autumn, but the newly created (1997) National Gardening Show run by the Royal Horticultural Society is now a major event in the gardening calendar. Info 01698 252565 and for Park see (1218/COUNTRY PARKS). The show in Ayr run by the local authority is the biggest flower and vegetable show.   **1974**   **MAP 1**   **E3/**   **D4**   **MAY/JUNE & AUGUST**

COMMON RIDINGS, BORDER TOWNS: Info Jedburgh TO 01835 863435. The Border town festivals. Similar formats over different weeks with 'ride-outs' (on horseback to outlying villages etc) , 'shows', dances and games, culminating on the Fri/Sat. Total local invovement. Hawick is first, then Selkirk,Peebles/Melrose, Gala, Jedburgh, Kelso and Lauder end of July.   **1975**   **MAP 8**   **D3**   **MAY-JULY**

ROYAL HIGHLAND SHOW, INGLISTON SHOWGROUND, EDINBURGH: 0131 333 2444. The premiere agricultural show in Scotland and for the farming world, the event of the year. Animals, machinery, food and shopping. Compulsive for some, big day out for the masses.   **1976**   **MAP 7**   **B1**   **JUNE**

SEAFOOD FESTIVAL, EYEMOUTH: Eyemouth TO 018907 50678 for details. A festival of seafood: from its landing and preparation through to eating. Accompanied by non-stop music, st theatre and that awful Morris dancing! Over 2 w/end days.   **1977**   **MAP 8**   **D1**   **JUNE**

BARRA LIVE, BARRA: Contact Hector MacInnes 01871 810270. A massive ceilidh with strong Irish flavour, the high point of the summer on this fabulous island. Everybody comes. Held in a marquee on Tangusdale Machair by the beach.   **1978**   **MAP 2**   **A4**   **JULY**

GAME FAIR, PERTH: Held in the rural and historical setting of Scone Palace, this is a major Perthshire day out and a gathering for the hunting, shooting, fishing and of course, shopping brigade. Details: 01738 552300.   **1979**   **MAP 4**   **C4**   **JULY**

SCOTTISH TRADITIONAL BOAT FESTIVAL, PORTSOY: Perfect little festival in perfect little Moray coast town nr Banff over a w/end in late June. Old boats in old and new harbours, open-air ceilidhs, great atmos. 01261 842951.   **1980**   **MAP 3**   **C1**   **JULY**

T IN THE PARK, BALADO AIRFIELD, KINROSS: Scotland's highly succesful pop   **1981**

festival with all that is current in Britpop and beyond. The T stands for Tennants, the sponsors who are much in evidence. Not as life style affirming as Glastonbury, but among the best fests in the UK. Info AYR from Kinross TO: 01577 863680.   **JULY**

1982
MAP A
EDINBURGH FESTIVAL, EDINBURGH: 0131 557 1700. The 3 week 'biggest arts festival in the world' with the Military Tatoo and major opera/music/drama. The big fireworks are on the last Thursday. Incorporates The Fringe Festival with hundreds of events every night; Fringe Sunday on the second w/end. Also the International Film Festival. A jazz Festival and (mainly for delegates on a bit of a jolly) the TV festival. Edin is full.   **AUGUST**

1983
MAP 8
B2
TRAQUAIR FAIR, INNERLEITHEN: Info: 01896 830323. Craft and music fair in the grounds of Traquair House (xxxx/COUNTRY HOUSES) S of Edin and during the Festival so a welcome and laid-back respite. Not on in 1997 because it got too big, likely in 1998.   **AUGUST**

1984
MAP 5
D2
LEUCHARS AIR SHOW, LEUCHARS nr ST ANDREWS: Info: 01334 839000. Major air-show held over one day in RAF airfield with flying displays, exhibitions, classic cars etc.   **SEPT**

1985
INTERNATIONAL SCOTCH WHISKY FESTIVAL, SPEYSIDE AND EDINBURGH: Starting 1997 over Hallow'een, the festival that's been waiting to happen. Beautiful countryside in all its autumn gold and the festival city over a w/end. I must declare an interest; the industry, doubtless will wait and see.   **OCTOBER**

1986
MAP 1
B1
TOUR OF MULL RALLY, ISLE OF MULL: Info Tobermory TO 01688 302182. The highlight of the national rally calendar is this raging around Mull w/end. Though drivers enter from all over the world, the overall winner for the last few yrs has been a local man. There's usually a waiting list for accom, but camping ok and locals put you up.   **OCTOBER**

1987
MAP 3
ABERDEEN ALTERNATIVE FESTIVAL, ABERDEEN: Arts festival with bias towards music. Also drama, comedy etc. Usually interesting programmes. Tickets 01224 641122.   **OCTOBER**

1988
MAP 5
ST ANDREWS NIGHT: Not such a big deal, but dinners etc and cultural ID.
                                                                    NOV 30TH

1989
MAP A
EDINBURGH HOGMANAY, EDINBURGH: Everywhere gets booked up, but accom 557 1700; info 473 2001. Still in its infancy though already one of the world's major winter events. Launched on the 29th with a Torchlight Procession through the city centre and a Fire Festival on Calton Hill and with a full 4 day largely populist programme. Main event is the Street Party on 31st, ticketed for the first time in 1997/1998. You have to hope that everyone will be good as well as happy. I like to think I do my bit.   **DEC/JAN**

GET ON THE MOBILE MOMENTS

ROBERT THE BRUCE'S CAVE nr GRETNA GREEN:. Cove Estate, Kirkpatrick Fleming, Off A74, through village, down rd by London House Inn, over railway crossing. 6km Gretna - Emma goes one June day. When half of Scotland (and a few more down S) were hunting him after one betrayal too many, the Irvings hid Rab in the cave used to store family valuables. Carved into the hillside it must have been a damp and desolate redoubt. Other reported sites for his hide-outs include Arran and Jedburgh - but the stillness and sense of history here made it the real McCoy for Emma who got on the mobile blower to rave. An ancient monk carved a stone inscription above the cave commemorating the important visitor - so of the many Bruce caves, this must be the one . . . Entrance fee only 35p. Mr Ritchie's additional history is free. Emma couldn't believe that spider. `1990 MAP 9 D3`

ROOM AT THE TOP, A NIGHTCLUB IN BATHGATE: "For most people who live in Edin (New Town), W Lothian is regarded as a bit downmarket - slag heaps, dull wee towns and Livingston where you can get lost in a car park, let alone the rd system", Keith writes. "Huge shock then, to dither around the centre of Bathgate for half an hr before realising that the big thing next to Safeway is a nightclub. A v serious club, that in design terms, gives anything similar in Edin a good slap and sends it home for an early night". It opened May 1997, has a capacity of 2,600 and is more or less, stunning. There are loads of bars and dance spaces, and although it plays some retro sounds in its 1970s/1980s room, big-name DJs have made the trek from down S, and from Edin/Glas. So impressive Keith dropped his Greggs cheese pastie, the Biro and his dog-eared notebook. But not the phone. Room at the Top: Menzies Rd, Bathgate 01506 635707. `1991 MAP 7 A2`

POMPADOUR RESTAURANT, EDINBURGH: Keith writes: "There is no way to describe the feeling you have when you've written 85 per cent of the Edin section to this book and your Mac crashes. The QuarkXPress file has corrupted and it slowly dawns that there's no back-up" *(Keith, you must be joking!)* "Instead of spending the evening bawling my eyes out, like a true pro I went to review a(nother) big restaurant instead - the Pompadour at the Caley. It was raining and the joint was quiet - just an elderly American couple, a family out for a treat and me. Staff outnumbered diners and it was one of those dark Edin evenings when the rain just teems. There was a pianist. He played 'Moon River' and 'Nightingales Sang in Berkely Square'. The asparagus Hollandaise was perfect and I finished with fresh strawberries and cream. Another meal in a restaurant I couldn't normally afford! As I wandered off into Lothian Rd, the overall weirdness of the day suggested a stiff drink for some perspective. The Subway W End still had its elastic happy hour going, while a solitary couple on the dance floor shrugged around to 'Lust for Life'. I had to phone somebody". *(Keith later rewrote the lot. You have the result. Lesson: always back-up.)* `1992 MAP A`

KILLER WHALES OFF THE COAST OF LEWIS: Graeme writes: "Having braved the CalMac crossing from Uig to Tarbet, in decidedly inclement weather, the skies suddenly parted to reveal a watery sun hanging over the Isle of Lewis. Experienced skipper, Hamish Somebody was waiting to take me, and a small party of intrepid whale watchers, round the wind swept coast of Harris and into the Atlantic in the hope of spotting some migrating Minkes. After about an hr of gannets, storm petrels and the odd curious dolphin we noticed that the local seal population was abandoning the ocean, for the safety of the rocks, as if their lives depended upon it. Suddenly, the massive, sleek snout of a killer whale breached the water betw our boat and the fleeing seals, which scattered in terror and straight into the trap set by the other half of this deadly pair. Slightly shaken, having witnessed the premature end of a seal's short life, we turned back, without indecent haste, towards the safety of dry land". Graeme woke up in his comfortable Glas W End flat. Fantasy or reality? He'd been working hard on the book. He had to tell somebody. `1993 MAP 2 B2`

PETERHEAD POWER STATION AT NIGHT: I'm driving to Peterhead at night from Cruden Bay, the spectre of this this twentieth-century industrial complex appears all illuminated on the right. It is not the prison. Weirder even than Grangemouth and with steam rising. Then a blob of light shimmers in the sky. I climb the hillock that o/look the power station and watch the blob disappear. It's not Rosewell (or Bonnybridge, but very X-Files nevertheless). From somewhere in the N of Scotland, somewhere in the summer of 1997, I have to phone home. `1994 MAP 3 E2`

SEVEN THINGS TO DO
BEFORE YOU DIE

1995 **LOCHNAGAR ON THE LONGEST DAY:** Nr Ballater via L Muick. Leave evening before
MAP 3 and camp/keep your vigil kind of thing. 4hrs to get up. Take map, good boots,
B4 food, dram etc. From first light across the Cairngorm Plateau, the Dee Valley,
Morvern, Bennachie appear; and God, if you're lucky. Later, in Aug the Royal
Family are beneath you (1594/MUNROS).

1996 **SANDWOOD BAY, KINLOCHBERVIE:** Another place to go in the long light of summer
MAP 2 days. It's a fair trek from the N (Cape Wrath) or even (more usually) the southern
C1 app via Balchrick and Kinlochbervie (1249/BEACHES). Take a tent, some beers and
wine; a few friends. Sit in the long sunset and/or the dawn. The summer will pass;
and the winter.

1997 **A WEEKEND AWAY WITH GOOD FRIENDS OR SOMEONE YOU LOVE:** As long as it's
sympatico, does it really matter where? There are plenty suggestions in preceding
pages (*see esp pp. 131-2, and pp. 126-7*, GET-AWAY-FROM-IT-ALL). But for that
special pampering **KINNAIRD, CROMLIX, ISLE OF ERISKA** are among the v best
country hotels in Britain. The food, the service; the grounds are yours (*p. 120*
COUNTRY HOUSE HOTELS).

1998 **THE TRESHNISH ISLANDS:** Go especially when the puffins are there too. The trip
MAP 1 to the Treshnish (from Ulva Ferry on Mull) on a summer's day is a voyage of
A1 discovery (incl Staffa). Go in July, walk amongst these enchanting creatures
before they disappear back into the cold Atlantic. Purify the soul. (1382/BIRDS.)

1999 **ST KILDA:** The most westerly islands in the UK, 110 miles into the Atlantic.
MAP 2 Remote, symbolic, superlative in every way, ingrained deep in the spiritual heart
A3 of the Scots. The community evacuated in 1930 represented the last in an age of
innocence and freedom now gone forever; life was hard but perfectly attuned to
this dramatically beautiful place. Highest sea cliffs in UK, premier sea bird
breeding stn. Village of Hirta conserved. NTS (0131 226 5922) arrange 'working
parties' (May-Aug, 14-day trips from Oban) or boat charter from Oban 3 times
a yr (01254 826591). 10-day cruises.

2000 **THE AONACH EAGACH or THE CLUANIE RIDGE:** Two awe-inspiring ridges; in good
MAP 2 weather among the most exhilarating walks in the world. The first is definitely
C5/ not for the faint-hearted, but most of us could do them once in a lifetime. So do
C3 them before you're too doddery. And go with someone who's done them before
or knows hill-walking. Just go with somebody good (1603/1605/SERIOUS WALKS).

2001 **THE JED and THE CARTER BAR, nr JEDBURGH:** A personal odyssey that I haven't
MAP 8 done yet. I was born and lived all my childhood nr the banks of the R Jed in
D4 Jedburgh. I've long had the notion to follow the river much further than we often
did as lads, into the Cheviots to find its source. It's close to the Carter Bar, the
southern border with England on the A68. But crossing here, can be done any
day - it's the high place where the Borders of Scotland are spread out before you
with hardly a house in sight. There are a couple of hamburger vans and the
occasional piper, but otherwise it's a stirring place and quite the best way to arrive
in Scotland. Jedburgh is 18km down the rd. There's Robert the Bruce's cave high
up in cliff side on your left at the first br, 2km from town. And the ancient Capon
Tree, 500m further on. I came here on the day I finished this edition of *Scotland
the Best!* for a final perspective. I hope this book will see you rt. The Carter Bar
is a good place to come in; a good place to leave. Enjoy our country; there's
nowhere else like it.

LIST OF MAPS

THE HIGHLAN
Map 2

CENT
Map

ARG
AYRS
CLYDE
Ma

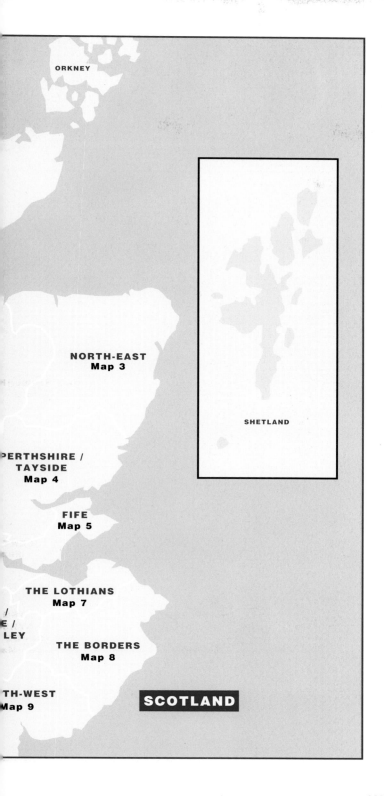

ORKNEY

NORTH-EAST
Map 3

PERTHSHIRE /
TAYSIDE
Map 4

FIFE
Map 5

THE LOTHIANS
Map 7

/
E /
LEY

THE BORDERS
Map 8

TH-WEST
Map 9

SHETLAND

SCOTLAND

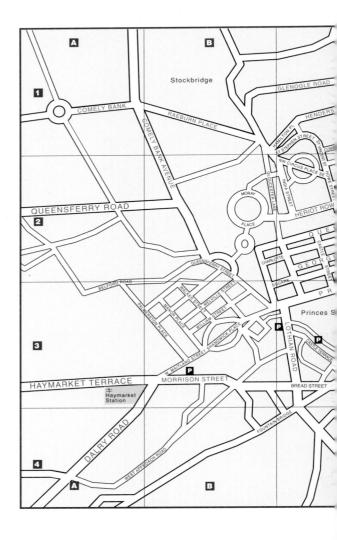

Stockbridge

GLENOGLE ROAD

HENDERS

COMELY BANK

RAEBURN PLACE

COMELY BANK AVENUE

HAMILTON PL
ST STEPHEN STREET
ST VINCENT ST
CUMB

NW CIRCUS PLACE BE
HOWE STREET
GLOUCESTER LANE
INDIA STREET

MORAY
PLACE

HERIOT ROW

QUEENSFERRY ROAD

QUE
HERIOT GDN STREET
GEO

QUEENSFERRY STREET

CHARLOTTE
SQUARE

GE O R G E

P R

BELFORD ROAD

WALKER STREET
MELVILLE STREET
WILLIAM STREET

PALMERSTON PLACE

LANE PLACE

SHANDWICK PLACE

Princes S

P

LOTHIAN ROAD

CASTLE TERRACE

P

N MAITLAND STREET

P

MORRISON STREET

BREAD STREET

HAYMARKET TERRACE

✚ Haymarket
Station

DALRY ROAD

WEST APPROACH ROAD

FOUNTAINBRIDGE

A

B

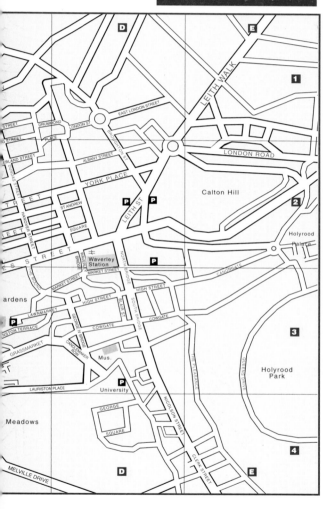

MAP A: Edinburgh City Centre

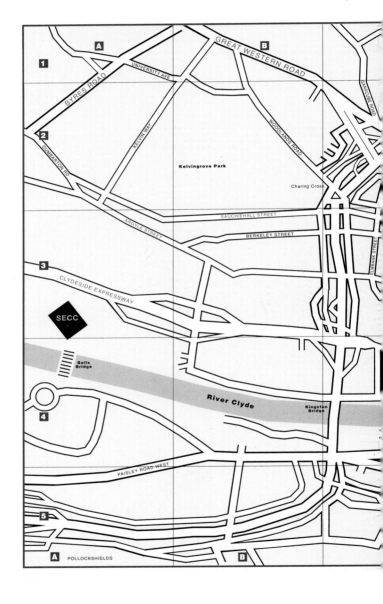

A   GREAT WESTERN ROAD   B

1

BYRES ROAD

UNIVERSITY AVE

DUMBARTON RD

2

KELVIN WAY

WOODLANDS ROAD

Kelvingrove Park

Charing Cross

GARSCUBE ROAD

SAUCHIEHALL STREET

ARGYLE STREET

BERKELEY STREET

ELMBANK STREET

3

CLYDESIDE EXPRESSWAY

SECC

Bells
Bridge

River Clyde

Kingston
Bridge

4

PAISLEY ROAD WEST

5

A   POLLOCKSHIELDS   B

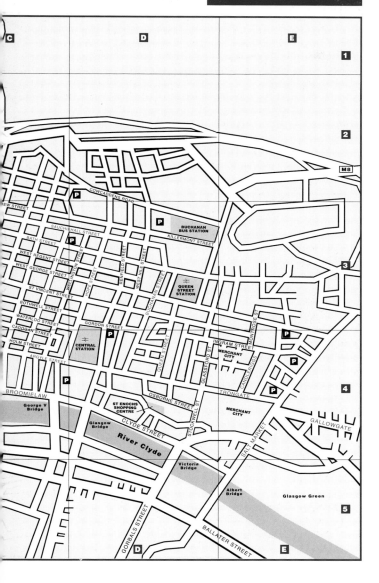

MAP B: Glasgow City Centre

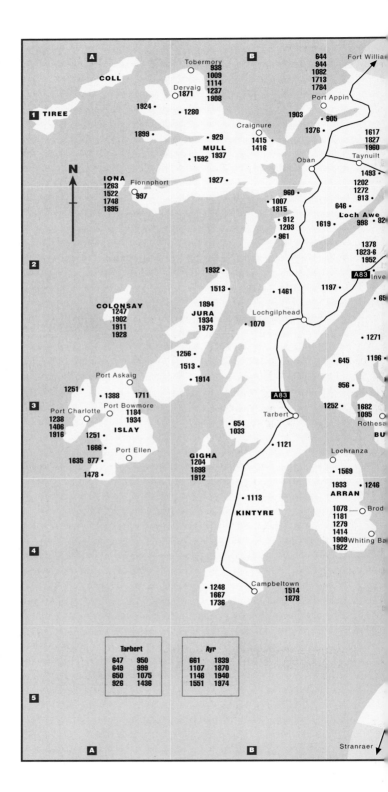

A

COLL

1 TIREE

1924 •
Dervaig
○1871

1899 •

• 1280

Tobermory
○
938
1009
1114
1237
1908

Craignure
○
1415 •
1416

• 929
MULL
• 1592 1937

• 1927

IONA
1263
1522
1748
1895

Fionnphort
○
997

N

B

Port Appin
○

1903

1376 •

644
944
1082
1713
1784

Fort Willia

• 905

Oban
○

960 •
• 1007
1815
• 912
1203
• 961

1617
1827
1960
Taynuilt
○
1493 •
1202
1272
913 •

646 •
Loch Awe
1619 •
998 • 82

2

COLONSAY
1247
1902
1911
1928

1932 •

1513 •

1894
JURA
1934
1973

1256 •

1513 •

• 1914

Port Askaig
○

1251 •

• 1388 1711
Port Bowmore
○ 1184
1934

3
Port Charlotte
○
1238
1406
1916

ISLAY

1251 •

1666 •

1635 977 •

1478 •

Port Ellen
○

• 1461

Lochgilphead
○
• 1070

A83

Tarbert
○

• 654
1033

• 1121

GIGHA
1204
1898
1912

• 1113

KINTYRE

• 1248
1667
1736

Campbeltown
○
1514
1878

1378
1823-6
1952

A83 Inve

• 65

1197 •

• 1271

• 645

1196 •

956 •

1252 •

1682
1095 ○
Rothesa
BU

Lochranza
○
• 1569

1933 • 1246
ARRAN
1078 ○ Brod
1181
1279
1414
1909 Whiting Ba
1922

Tarbert	
647	950
649	999
650	1075
926	1436

Ayr	
661	1839
1107	1870
1146	1940
1551	1974

4

5

A

B

Stranraer ↓

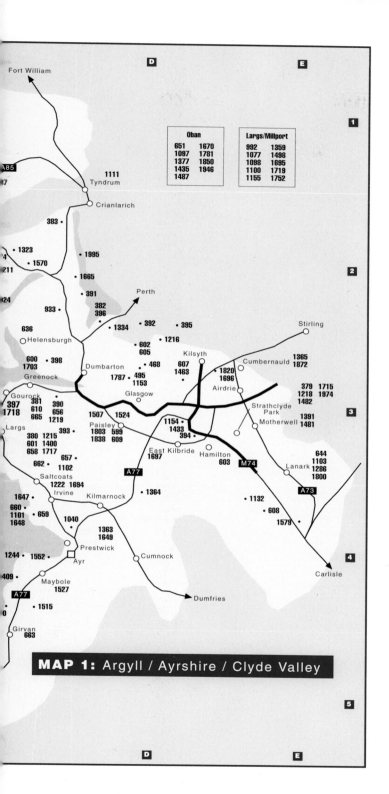

MAP 1: Argyll / Ayrshire / Clyde Valley

Oban	
651	1670
1097	1781
1377	1850
1435	1946
1487	

Largs/Millport	
992	1359
1077	1498
1098	1695
1100	1719
1155	1752

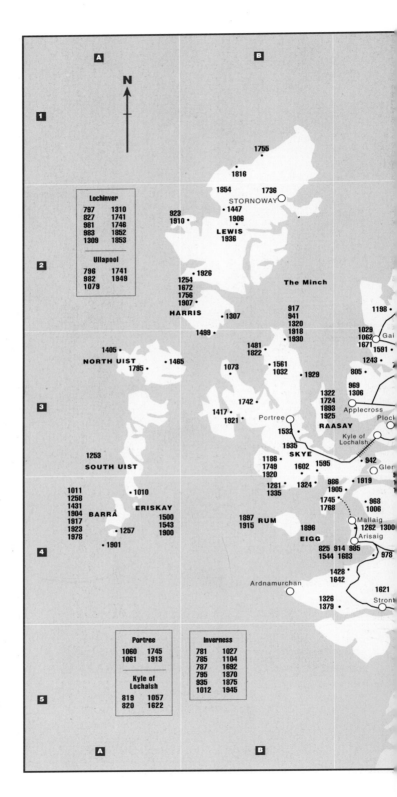

N

1755

1816

1854   1736

STORNOWAY○

923 •
1910 •

• 1447
1906

LEWIS
1936

1198 •

Lochinver

797	1310
827	1741
981	1746
983	1852
1309	1853

Ullapool

796	1741
982	1949
1079	

• 1926
1254
1672
1756
1907 •

HARRIS   • 1307

1499 •

The Minch

917
941
1320
1918
• 1930

1029
1062 Gai
1671
1591 •

1405 •

NORTH UIST • 1465
1795 •

1481
1822 •

1073
•

• 1561
1032

• 1929

1243 •

805 •

969
1306

1742 •

1417 •
1921 •

Portree ○

1322
1724
1893
1925

RAASAY

Applecross

Ploc

1253

SOUTH UIST

1532 •

1935 •

SKYE

Kyle of
Lochalsh ○

1186 •
1749 •
1920 •

1602 • 1595

• 942
Glen

1011
1258
1431
1904
1917
1923
1978

• 1010

BARRA **ERISKAY**

• 1257

• 1901

1500
1543
1900

1281 •
1335

1324 •

986 •
1905

1919 •

1745
1768

• 968
1006

1897
1915

RUM

1896

EIGG

• 1262 1300
Mallaig ○
Arisaig ○

825 914 985
1544 1683

• 978

1428 •
1642

Ardnamurchan

1621

1326
1379 •

Stron ○

Portree

1060	1745
1061	1913

**Kyle of
Lochalsh**

819	1057
820	1622

Inverness

781	1027
785	1104
787	1692
795	1870
935	1875
1012	1945

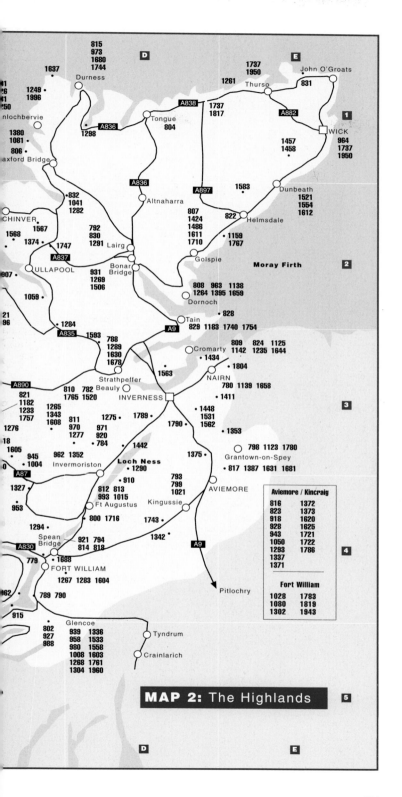

MAP 2: The Highlands

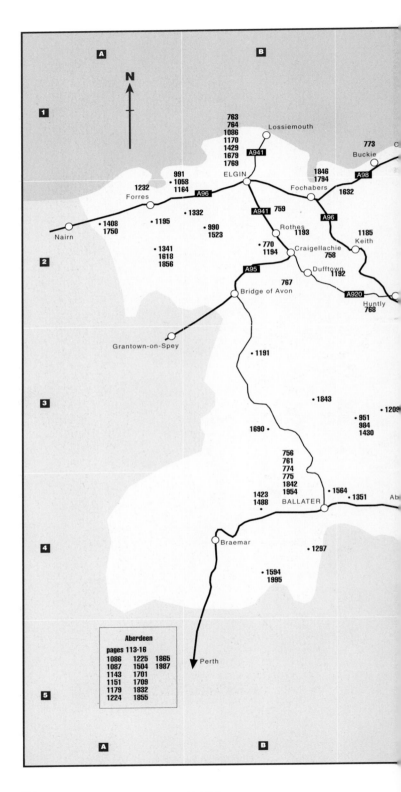

N

763
764
1086
1170
1429
1679
1769
A941

Lossiemouth

773
Buckie

991
• 1058
1164
A96
ELGIN

1846
1794
A98

1232
Forres

Fochabers

1632

• 1408
1750
Nairn

• 1195

• 1332

A941 759

• 990
1523

Rothes
1193

A96

1185
Keith

• 770
1194

Craigellachie
758

• 1341
1618
1856

Dufftown 1192

A95

767

Bridge of Avon

A920

Huntly
768

Grantown-on-Spey

• 1191

• 1843

• 1209

• 951
984
1430

1690 •

756
761
774
775
1842
1954

• 1564

1351

1423
1488
•

BALLATER

Ab

• 1297

Braemar

• 1594
1995

Perth

Aberdeen		
pages 113-16		
1086	1225	1865
1087	1504	1987
1143	1701	
1151	1709	
1179	1832	
1224	1855	

A

B

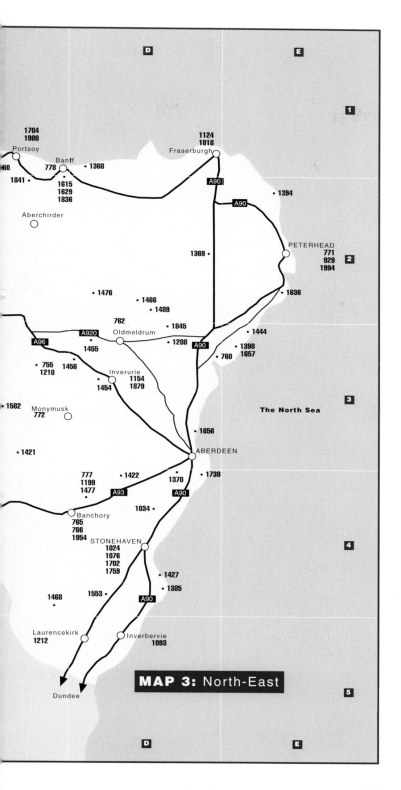

MAP 3: North-East

Portsoy
1704
1980

Banff
778

1368

60

1841

1615
1629
1836

Aberchirder

Fraserburgh
1124
1818

A90

1394

A90

PETERHEAD
771
929
1994

1369

1636

1476

1466
1489

762

1845

A920
Oldmeldrum

1208

A90

1444

A96

1455

1398
1657

760

755
1210

1456

Inverurie
1154
1879

1454

1582

Monymusk
772

1421

1656

ABERDEEN

777
1199
1477

1422

1370

1738

A93

A90

1034

Banchory
765
766
1954

STONEHAVEN
1024
1076
1702
1759

1427

1385

1468

1553

A90

Laurencekirk
1212

Inverbervie
1093

Dundee

The North Sea

D

E

1

2

3

4

5

MAPS   293

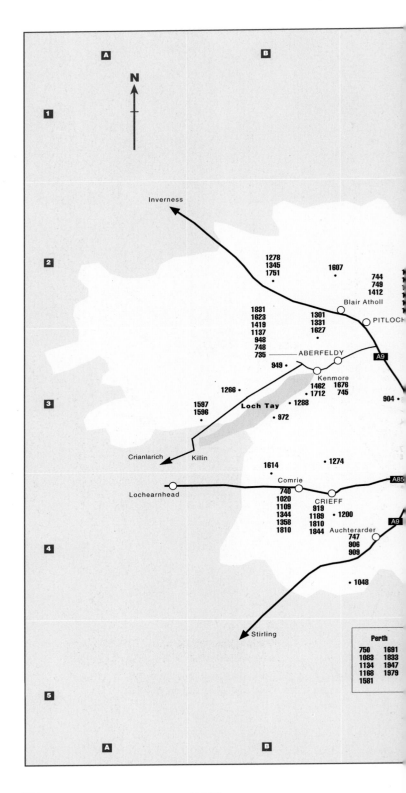

Inverness

1278
1345
1751

1607

744
749
1412

Blair Atholl

PITLOCH

1831
1623
1419
1137
948
748
735

1301
1331
1627

ABERFELDY

A9

949

Kenmore

1266

1462 1676
1712 745

904

1597
1596

Loch Tay

1288

972

Crianlarich   Killin

1614   1274

Comrie

A85

Lochearnhead

740
1020
1109
1344
1358
1810

919
1189
1810
1844

CRIEFF

1200

Auchterarder
747
906
909

A9

1048

Stirling

Perth	
750	1691
1083	1833
1134	1947
1168	1979
1581	

294   M A P S

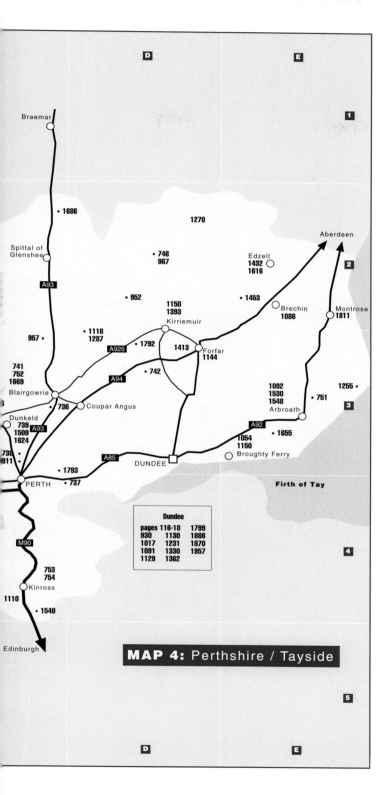

MAP 4: Perthshire / Tayside

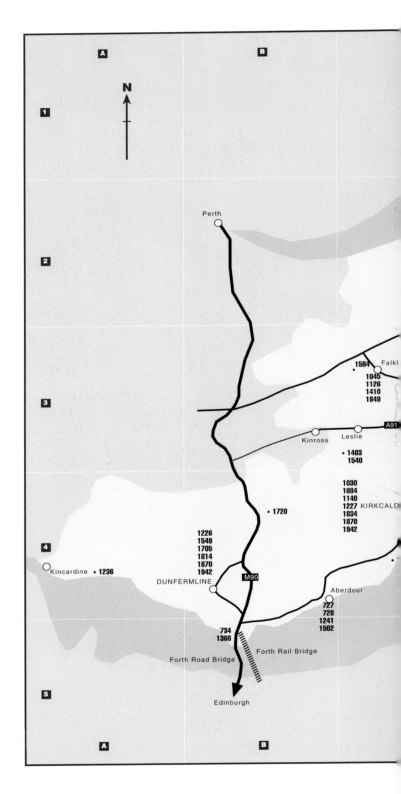

Perth

1584 Falkl
1045
1126
1410
1849

A91

Kinross Leslie

• 1403
1540

1030
1084
1140
1227 KIRKCALD
1834
1870
1942

• 1720

1226
1549
1705
1814
1870
1942

Kincardine • 1236

DUNFERMLINE M90

Aberdour

727
728
1241
1502

734
1360

Forth Rail Bridge

Forth Road Bridge

Edinburgh

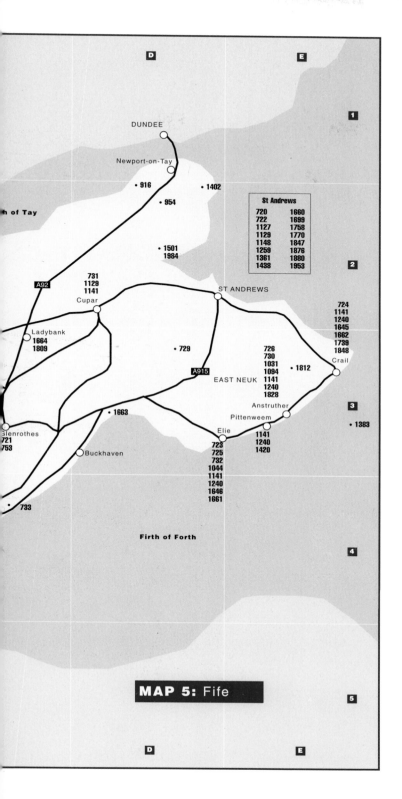

MAP 5: Fife

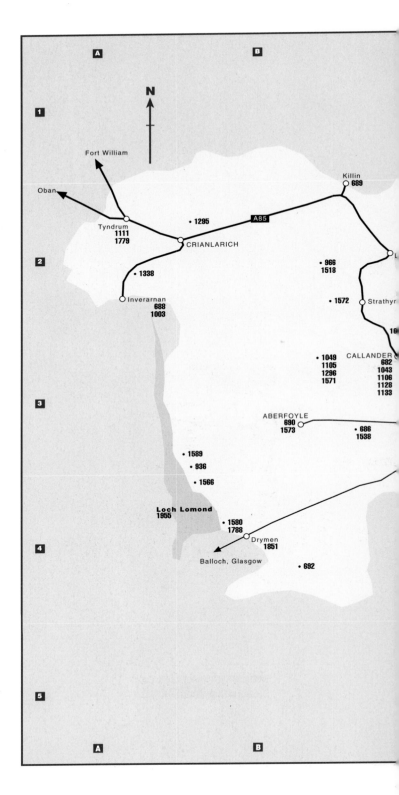

N

Fort William

Oban

Killin
689

Tyndrum
1111
1779

• **1295**

A85

CRIANLARICH

• **966**
1518

L

• **1338**

• **1572**

Strathyr

Inverarnan
688
1003

18

• **1049**
1105
1296
1571

CALLANDER
682
1043
1106
1128
1133

ABERFOYLE
690
1573

• **686**
1538

• **1589**

• **936**

• **1566**

Loch Lomond
1955

• **1580**
1788

Drymen
1851

Balloch, Glasgow

• **692**

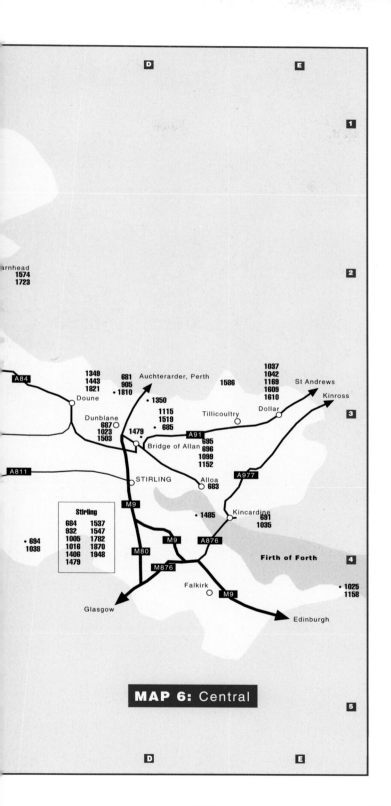

arnhead
1574
1723

A84
Doune

1349
1443
1821

681
905
• **1810**

Auchterarder, Perth

1586

1037
1042
1169
1609
1610

St Andrews

Kinross

Dunblane
687 ○
1023
1503

• **1350**

1115
1519
• **685**

Tillicoultry ○

Dollar ○

1479
•

Bridge of Allan

A91

695
696
1099
1152

A811

STIRLING ○

Alloa ○
683

A977

Stirling

684	**1537**
932	**1547**
1005	**1782**
1016	**1870**
1406	**1948**
1479	

M9

• **1485**

Kincardine ○
891
1035

M9
M80

M9

A876

Firth of Forth

• **694**
1038

M876

Falkirk ○

M9

• **1025**
1158

Glasgow

Edinburgh

MAP 6: Central

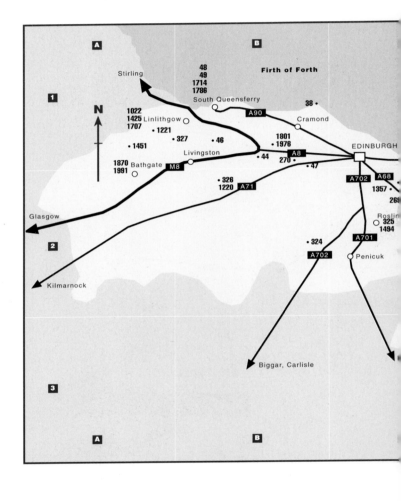

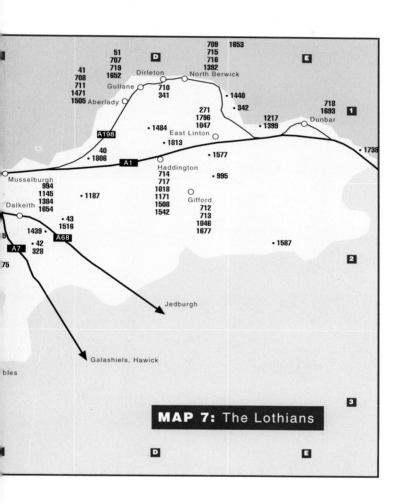

MAP 7: The Lothians

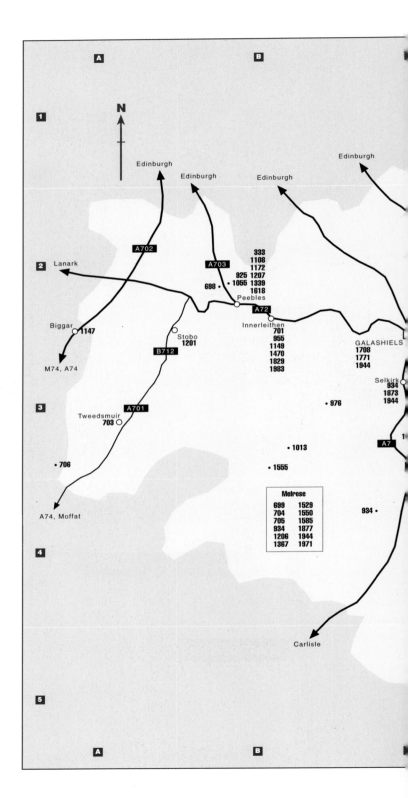

N

Edinburgh

Edinburgh

Edinburgh

Edinburgh

A702

Lanark

A703

333
1108
1172
925 1207
698 • 1055 1339
1618
Peebles

A72

Innerleithen

Biggar ○ 1147

M74, A74

Stobo
1201

B712

701
955
1149
1470
1829
1983

GALASHIELS
1708
1771
1944

Selkirk ○
934
1873
1944

A701

Tweedsmuir
703 ○

• 976

A7

• 1013

• 706

• 1555

A74, Moffat

Melrose	
699	1529
704	1550
705	1585
934	1877
1206	1944
1367	1971

934 •

Carlisle

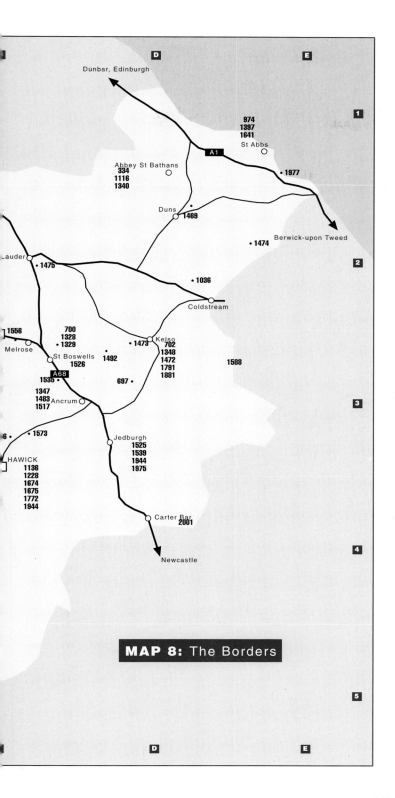

Dunbar, Edinburgh

974
1397
1641
St Abbs

A1

• 1977

Abbey St Bathans
334
1116
1340

Duns
1469

• 1474

Berwick-upon Tweed

Lauder

• 1475

• 1036

Coldstream

1556

700
1328
• 1329

Melrose

• 1473 Kelso
702
1348
1472
1791
1881

St Boswells
1526

1492

1588

A68

1535 •

697 •

1347
1483 Ancrum
1517

6 •

• 1573

Jedburgh
1525
1539
1944
1975

HAWICK
1136
1228
1674
1675
1772
1944

Carter Bar
2001

Newcastle

MAP 8: The Borders

D

E

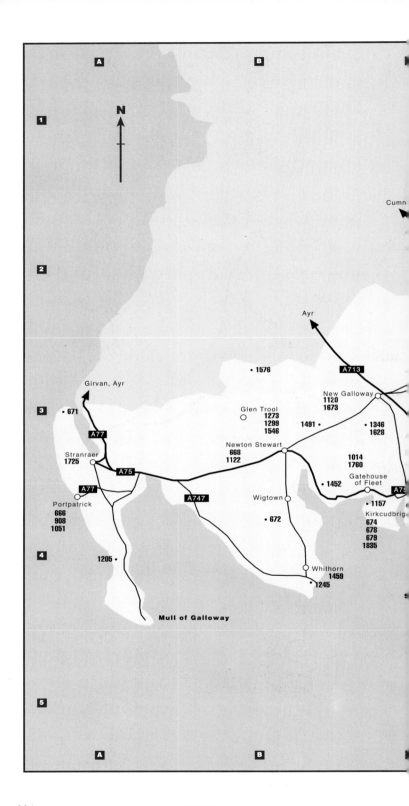

Cumn

Ayr

A713

· 1576

New Galloway
1120
1673

Girvan, Ayr

Glen Trool
○ 1273
1299
1546

1491 ·

· 1346
1628

· 671

Newton Stewart
668
1122

1014
1760

A77

Gatehouse
of Fleet

A7

Stranraer
1725

A75

· 1452

· 1157

A77

A747

Wigtown

Kirkcudbrig
674
678
679
1835

Portpatrick
666
908
1051

· 672

1205 ·

Whithorn
1459
· 1245

Mull of Galloway

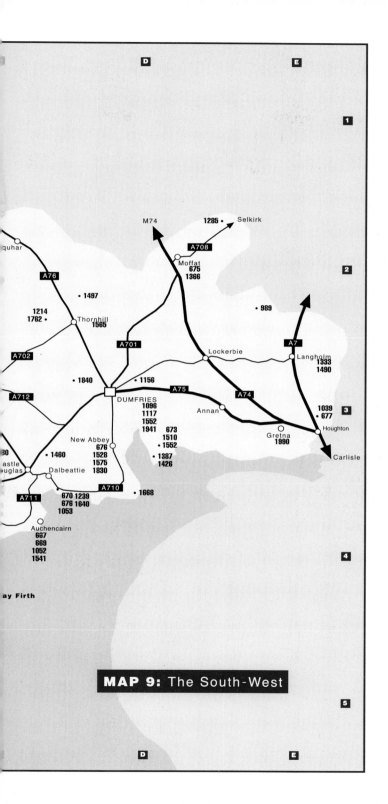

M74

1285 • Selkirk

A708

Moffat
675
1366

quhar

A76

• **1497**

1214
1762 • Thornhill
1565

• **989**

A702

A701

Lockerbie

A7 Langholm
1333
1490

A712

• **1840**

• **1156**

A75

DUMFRIES
1096
1117
1552
1941 **673**
1510
• **1552**

A74

Annan

1039
• **677**

Gretna
1990

Houghton

Carlisle

New Abbey
676
1528
1575
1830

• **1460**

• **1387**
1426

astle
uglas

Dalbeattie

A711

A710

670 1239
676 1640
1053

• **1668**

Auchencairn
637
669
1052
1541

ay Firth

MAP 9: The South-West

INDEX

Note: The numbers given are page numbers. Names of towns are in bold type. Bold page numbers indicate that a page or more is devoted to a place.